Advance Praise for *Memory Warp*

"Must Paul Revere ride twice? Mark Pendergrast was heroic in opposing the recovered memory craze twenty years ago. It's back—but so is he, with an urgent and eloquent plea for adherence to scientific truth about the mind."

—Frederick Crews, author *The Memory Wars*
and Freud: The Making of an Illusion

"In *Memory Warp***,** Mark Pendergrast has captured not only the personalities of all those involved, but the science (or lack thereof) underlying the repressed memory debate. His compassionate, even feminist, account makes for compelling reading that explains how the repressed memory epidemic arose and (unfortunately) continues."

—Elizabeth F. Loftus, Ph.D., UC Irvine Distinguished Professor of Social
Ecology, and Professor of Law, and Cognitive Science,
author, *The Myth of Repressed Memory*

"Reading *Memory Warp* could save your finances, your sanity, your family, and even your life. If you seek mental health treatment in the US health care system, you are at serious risk of being harmed by reckless methods based on dangerous junk science theories and practices. Mark Pendergrast has written a compelling, well-researched book about the epidemic of false memories of abuse that occurred in the final part of the 20th century and continues in a reduced—though still dangerous—form to this day, negatively impacting the lives of millions of people."

—R. Christopher Barden, Ph.D., J.D., scientist-clinician-attorney-legislation
and public policy expert specializing in multi-disciplinary analysis and reform

"Science writer Mark Pendergrast makes a strong case that the repressed memory controversy is far from over and offers a clear warning about the worst pseudo-science in psychology in the modern era. *Memory Warp* is brilliantly written, with jaw-dropping details, stories, and insights that are novel, fascinating, and engrossing."

—Lawrence Patihis, Ph.D., Director of the Cognition and
Memory Laboratory. University of Southern Mississippi

D1615677

"A brilliantly written, powerful, and meticulously documented exposé of the contemporary recovered memory movement. Pendergrast demolishes the widespread myth that suggestive techniques designed to recover supposedly repressed memories – and the often devastating effects of these techniques on psychotherapy clients and their families — are a thing of the past. This extremely important book is a reminder that, in the words of William Faulkner, 'The past is never dead. It's not even past.'"

—Scott O. Lilienfeld, Ph.D., Professor of Psychology, Emory University, co-author, *Facts and Fictions in Mental Health* and other books

"*Memory Warp* is a thorough, calm, and devastating look at how memory works and doesn't work, and how pseudo-scientific claims about 'repressed memories' have ruined lives."

—Edward Dolnick, author, *Madness on the Couch*

"In the 1990s, as families were shattered by wide-spread belief in repressed memories (especially through psychotherapy), Mark Pendergrast stepped up to become a leading figure in the vanguard of truth and reason with his groundbreaking book, *Victims of Memory*. Now, over 20 years later, he again sounds the alarm that the dangerous embers of repressed memory belief still burn underneath our cultural surface and threaten to burst once again into flame. With precision, thorough documentation, and scientific insight, *Memory Warp* brings to light the shared cultural mythology that the public and so many 'professionals' still believe, promote, and practice. Compelling and reasoned, *Memory Warp* is a must-read."

—Paul Simpson, Ed.D., forensic psychologist, author, *Second Thoughts*

Memory Warp

Other books by Mark Pendergrast

Beyond Fair Trade

City on the Verge

For God, Country and Coca-Cola

Inside the Outbreaks

Japan's Tipping Point

Mirror Mirror

The Most Hated Man in America

The Repressed Memory Epidemic

Uncommon Grounds

Victims of Memory

Children's books

The Godfool

Jack and the Bean Soup

Silly Sadie

Upper Access titles are available at special discounts for bulk purchases. Please contact the publisher to inquire. For such inquiries, contact Steve Carlson, *steve@upperaccess.com*.

Memory Warp

How the Myth of Repressed Memory Arose
and Refuses to Die

Mark Pendergrast

Upper Access Books
Hinesburg, Vermont
www.upperaccess.com

Published by Upper Access Books
87 Upper Access Road, Hinesburg, Vermont 05461
802-482-2988 – *www.upperaccess.com*

ISBN 978-0-942679-41-0

Library of Congress Cataloging-in-Publication Data

Names: Pendergrast, Mark, author.
Title: Memory warp : how the myth of repressed memory arose and refuses to die / Mark Pendergrast.
Description: Hinesburg, Vermont : Upper Access Books, [2017] | Includes bibliographical references. |
Identifiers: LCCN 2017013233 (print) | LCCN 2017024907 (ebook) | ISBN 9780942679427 () | ISBN 9780942679410 (alk. paper)
Subjects: LCSH: False memory syndrome. | Recovered memory. | Adult child sexual abuse victims. | Repression (Psychology)
Classification: LCC RC455.2.F35 (ebook) | LCC RC455.2.F35 P45 2017 (print) | DDC 616.85/822390651--dc23
LC record available athttps://lccn.loc.gov/2017013233

Printed on acid-free paper in the United States of America

17 / 10 9 8 7 6 5 4 3 2 1

Acknowledgments

THANKS TO STEVE CARLSON, MY publisher and editor at Upper Access Books, not only for making the text read well, but for his thoughtful comments and suggestions, and to graphic artist Kitty Werner for making the book look so good.

I used to be a librarian, but now I use the services of reference librarians all the time. Kudos to all who helped to render this book as scholarly and complete as I could make it.

I wish I could list all of the people affected by the repressed memory epidemic with whom I corresponded. I interviewed many of you for hours. You may remain anonymous, but you know who you are, and thanks for sharing your experience with me. Among those I could not cite by name are all the desperate people who have written to the National Center for Reason and Justice, which was begun by activists Bob Chatelle and Jim D'Entremont to call attention to the sex abuse hysteria that has imprisoned far too many innocent people.

To all those who have helped to debunk the pseudoscience of repressed memories, multiple personalities, and Satanic ritual abuse cults, my eternal gratitude. Check the "Note on Sources" for those who have written in depth on these issues. I won't name you all here, but experimental psychologist Elizabeth Loftus, psychologist Richard McNally, psychiatrist Paul McHugh, and psychologist-lawyer R. Christopher Barden top the list. You are my heroes.

And a final shout-out to psychology professor Lawrence Patihis, who conducted the first extensive survey, with my participation, to determine the alarming extent of the on-going repressed memory epidemic.

Dedicated to the millions of families
and individuals whose lives have been
impacted by the repressed memory epidemic

Contents

Introduction: The Return of the Repressed 11

1   How to Become a Survivor 25

2   The Memory Maze 65

3   How to Believe the Unbelievable 125

4   Multiple Personalities and Satanic Cults... 155

5   And a Little Child Shall Lead Them (and Be Led)............................ 202

6   A Brief History: The Witch Craze, Reflex Arcs, and Freud's Legacy.....236

7   Cultural Contexts 274

8   Survivorship as Religion 306

9   Conclusions and Recommendations 336

Note on Sources 430

Index.. 436

Introduction: The Return of the Repressed

As our medical schools and graduate programs fill with students who were born after 1989, we meet young mental health professionals-in-training who have no knowledge or living memory of the Satanic ritual abuse (SRA) moral panic of the 1980s and early 1990s. But perhaps they should. Cautionary tales may prevent the recurrence of pyrogenic cultural fantasies and the devastating clinical mistakes they inspire. —Richard Noll, *Psychiatric Times*, 2014

IT HAS BEEN OVER TWO decades since I wrote *Victims of Memory*, an exploration of the debate over the accuracy of so-called repressed or recovered memories of sexual abuse. In his book review in *Scientific American,* Daniel Schacter, the Harvard psychology professor whose work on memory helped to inform my own, called *Victims of Memory* "an impressive display of scholarship…a comprehensive treatment of the recovered-memories controversy." Now it is time to revisit and update this extraordinary phenomenon. Although "repressed memories" have been widely discredited among those who study the science of memory, there appears to be a resurgence of belief in this dangerous theory. Consequently, I have updated my research on the subject. The book you hold in your hands is partly a social and cultural history of our recent past, documenting how this incredible juggernaut of pseudoscience and malpractice, which caused so much harm, came to be. But it also shows how these misguided theories continue to fester. They will inevitably cause another major outbreak and damage the lives of additional millions of people if we do not learn from the past. Rather than calling it a new edition, I have given it a title to indicate the drama and urgency of the subject: *Memory Warp: How the Myth of Repressed Memory Arose and Refuses to Die.**

The first edition of *Victims of Memory* was published in 1995 at the height of the epidemic of false memories of childhood sexual abuse, fomented by a misguided, pseudoscientific form of psychotherapy. The theory behind this fad stemmed from Sigmund Freud's work a century beforehand, in the 1890s. He called it his "seduction theory," which he himself soon abandoned. (*See detailed*

---

* For a longer, more academically oriented textbook on the subject, see my book, *The Repressed Memory Epidemic: How It Happened and What We Need to Learn from It*, by Mark Pendergrast (Springer, 2017).

coverage in Chapter 6.) But the idea—that people can "repress" or "dissociate" years of traumatic childhood memories and then recall them as adults—refused to die, in part because it provides an appealing plot device for novels, movies, and sensational media coverage, and because many psychologists have imbibed the theory somewhat like mother's milk. It has become an underlying professional assumption that people really can and do banish traumatic memories from their consciousness. And Freud himself promulgated his modified theory as "the return of the repressed"—the pseudoscientific notion that buried desires or fears return in symbolic dreams or actions.

Freud's theory was resurrected in the 1980s by a group of self-described feminist therapists who were concerned about sexual abuse and who believed that women with "symptoms" such as depression, eating disorders, or sexual issues must have been molested as children and repressed the memories so that they had no current knowledge of a horrific childhood. Only by remembering the abuse—often incest—would they be healed. These therapists believed that they could help their clients unearth these repressed memories through methods such as hypnosis, dream analysis, interpretation of bodily pangs, induced panic attacks, or group experiences. In 1988, with the publication of *The Courage to Heal,* by Ellen Bass and Laura Davis, this movement exploded into a full-fledged epidemic in which women in therapy became convinced that they should accuse their fathers of having raped them for years during their childhood and, with the encouragement of their therapists, they cut off all contact with their families.

"Before" and "after" therapy letters such as these became all too common.

May 1987

Dear Dad,

Just a note to thank you for taking such good care of me and my friend during our much-too-short stay. My friend is impressed and a bit envious of the loving relationship and open lines of communication which you and I share....I love you and I'm glad you're my dad!

Love "D"

November 1989

I am writing this letter for two reasons: (i) to attain closure for myself regarding my relationship with you and (ii) in the hope that you will seek help before you hurt anyone else the way you hurt me. I have spent 37 years of my life denying and minimizing the torture that was my childhood and adolescence...I genuinely hope this letter causes you to seek help—you are a very sick man. I do not wish to hear from you unless you are willing to admit the things you did to me and to seek help for your sickness.

"D"

It was ironic that "feminist" therapists were the avatars of this destructive phenomenon. One retractor (someone who later realized she had developed false memories due to misguided therapy) wrote poignantly about her own recovered-memory experience, in which she became convinced that she had so-called multiple personality disorder. "It robs women of all power and control over themselves. If I really hated women and wanted to keep them in a completely powerless and childlike state, the best way to do that would be to remove their faith and trust in their own minds and make them dependent." That is precisely what happened in this form of "therapy," which frequently managed, quite literally, to turn women into helpless, suicidal children clutching their teddy bears and shrieking in imagined pain and horror. The repressed-memory hunt breathed new life into one of the most damaging and sexist traditions in our culture—the subtle message to women that they can gain power and attention primarily through the "victim" role.

It is difficult to convey how saturated our culture became with the repressed memory phenomenon. In her 2010 memoir, *My Lie*, retractor Meredith Maran described her quest to recall how her father must have abused her. "I drove back across San Francisco Bay [in 1989], back to Planet Incest, where the question was always incest and the answer was always incest and the explanation was always incest, and no one ever asked, 'Are you sure?'"

Many hundreds of lawsuits were filed by therapy patients with brand new abuse "memories." Thousands of stunned parents became the first innocent people targeted by the repressed memory epidemic. In 1992 the National Organization for Women published *The Legal Resource Kit on Incest and Child Sexual Abuse*, noting that many adult victims had no idea what had happened to them until they entered therapy. "Civil legal remedies are crucial to deter these acts." In the 1990s, over 500 reported cases were filed in which the only evidence stemmed from recovered memories—15 percent were criminal, 85 percent civil cases. Hundreds of additional cases were quietly settled without formal filings, as many parents were embarrassed, devastated, and terrified, or they wished to avoid a lawsuit against an obviously mentally ill daughter.

In their landmark 2015 book, *Mistakes Were Made (But Not by Me)*, social psychologists Carol Tavris and Elliot Aronson offered a succinct summary of the absurdities of the repressed memory epidemic:

> Under hypnosis, they said, their therapists enabled them to remember the horrifying experiences they had suffered as toddlers, as infants in the crib, and sometimes even in previous lives. One woman recalled that her mother put spiders in her vagina. Another said her father had molested her from the ages of five to twenty-three, and even raped her just days before her wedding—memories she repressed until therapy. Others said they had been burned, although

their bodies bore no scars. Some said they had been impregnated and forced to have abortions, although their bodies showed no evidence. Those who went to court to sue their alleged perpetrators were able to call on expert witnesses, many with impressive credentials in clinical psychology and psychiatry, who testified that these recovered memories were valid evidence of abuse.

As families were torn asunder by such recovered memory allegations, in 1992 Pamela and Peter Freyd founded the False Memory Syndrome Foundation, recruiting a stellar board of scientific advisers such as Elizabeth Loftus, Martin Orne, and Paul McHugh. The FMS Foundation began to educate psychologists, the media, and the general public about the hazards of suggestive therapy based on the unproven theory of massive repression. In return, the true believers in repressed memory called the FMS Foundation a group of perpetrators in denial, rather than anguished parents who had lost their children to a delusion.

Members of the British False Memory Society, founded in 1993, were equally vilified. American psychiatric fads and social concerns spread with astonishing rapidity throughout the English-speaking world. There is a paradoxical historic symmetry involved here. Near the end of the two-century-long European witch craze, the Puritans imported witch-hunting to North America. As a result, in 1692, twenty innocent people were put to death in Salem, Massachusetts. Three hundred years later, Americans returned the favor by exporting the paranoid search for mythical Satanic ritual abuse cults, repressed incest memories, and child sex rings.

As this book documents, the American virus was carried by "experts" who ventured across the Atlantic to share their views with British colleagues. More than that, however, the ground was prepared by the printed word. Not since *The Malleus Maleficarum* was published a few years after Gutenberg's invention have we seen such evidence of the power of books to affect lives. In particular, *The Courage to Heal* spread the gospel of recovered memory and spawned many imitators.

As the epidemic of illusory abuse memories was more widely recognized in the mid-1990s, many professional associations issued cautionary statements, such as this 1994 conclusion from the American Medical Association: "The AMA considers recovered memories of childhood sexual abuse to be of uncertain authenticity, which should be subject to external verification." As a consequence of scientific books and articles by psychologists, sociologists, and critical thinkers such as Elizabeth Loftus, Richard Ofshe, Carol Tavris, Richard McNally, Paul McHugh, Harrison Pope Jr, Frederick Crews, John Kihlstrom, Paul Simpson, Elaine Showalter, and others, the public began to realize there were serious, controversial issues involved with recovered memory therapy and diagnoses of multiple personality disorder (MPD).

Given the powerful ideological and political movement pushing the epidemic, and the enormous financial rewards involved in turning a depressed housewife into an MPD patient needing years of expensive hospitalizations, scientific information and academic debates were insufficient to halt the burgeoning international epidemic of false memories. Instead, in the late 1990s, million-dollar lawsuits against therapists, brought by women whose lives and families had been nearly destroyed by the misguided therapy, caused a decline in the overt practice of repressed memory therapy and resulted in the closing of most dissociative disorder clinics in which alleged MPD patients had been held in a modern version of mental health snake pits. These lawsuits were mounted by lawyer-psychologist R. Christopher Barden, who used a multidisciplinary approach of litigation, prosecution, regulation (licensing revocations), education of the public through the media, and proposed legislation. Barden hammered home the point that such controversial, potentially harmful forms of psychotherapy were egregious examples of consumer fraud and the lack of informed consent. As a result, the epidemic was widely criticized and publicized by the turn of the century, and repressed memories were no longer admissible (when so identified) in most courtrooms.*

As Harvard psychology professor Richard McNally observed in 2005, "The notion that traumatic events can be repressed and later recovered is the most pernicious bit of folklore ever to infect psychology and psychiatry. It has provided the theoretical basis for 'recovered memory therapy'—the worst catastrophe to befall the mental health field since the lobotomy era."

Most reputable memory scientists agree with that assessment. "There is no good scientific evidence that these unconscious forces exist," wrote psychologist Charles Fernyhough in *Pieces of Light*, his 2012 book on memory. "Traumas are remembered, and they are remembered only too painfully. They may not be thought about for a long time…but they are not forgotten."

In *Victims of Memory*, I included four chapters of verbatim interviews—with therapists, "Survivors," the accused, and retractors—conducted in the early 1990s at the height of the repressed memory epidemic. These interviews, available in the book, *The Repressed Memory Epidemic* (Springer, 2017), and on my website, www.markpendergrast.com, offer compelling evidence that many psychotherapists were invested in a belief in repressed memories of sexual abuse, and that they helped clients (mostly women) to recall mythical abuse. The interviews document the human devastation that resulted.

It was a terrible phenomenon, and I am proud that my book, along with many

---

* In his article in *Psychiatric Times* quoted at the beginning of this introduction, Richard Noll wrote that the epidemic "ended as suddenly and incomprehensibly as it started." That is inaccurate. Repressed memory therapy was widely discredited through lawsuits and scientific and investigative publications. For a good legal summary, see R. Christopher Barden, "Memory and Reliability: Developments and Controversial Issues," in *Witness Testimony in Sexual Cases: Evidential, Investigative and Scientific Perspectives,* NY: Oxford U. Pr., 2016. Unfortunately the epidemic did not end, but continues. Most psychiatric treatment units for multiple personality disorder were, however, abruptly shut down by the lawsuits.

other books, articles, and lawsuits, helped to alert the public, professionals, and the courts to the perils of the repressed memory epidemic. I have written many other books about an array of topics—the histories of coffee, Coca-Cola, disease detectives, and mirrors, among others—that have taken me all over the world. But *Victims of Memory* has been my most important work. I certainly don't want this to come off as braggadocio, but when someone tells you, "Reading your book saved my life. I was going to kill myself," it means so much. Or emails out of the blue such as this one: "After realizing my 'recovered memories' acquired during my 'therapy' were delusions, your book gave me the confidence to pursue my lawsuit and psychology board complaint."

It was also in writing about this issue that I became a science writer. I realized that the scientific enterprise was not simply a dry intellectual pursuit. It demands hypotheses that can be proved or disproved, encourages the use of control groups, requires studies that replicate results. Scientists are not immune to error, by any means, but when they have overreached and drawn wrong or fraudulent conclusions—as with cold fusion, perpetual motion machines, phrenology, or thalidomide—further exploration and experimentation eventually provided correctives. But repressed memory theory is pure pseudoscience, a matter of faith rather than anything that can be proved or disproved. I came to realize that science and accompanying informed consent can save sanity and lives.

Nonetheless, despite the furor over false memories produced by pseudoscientific theories, those who believed in recovered-memory therapy did not give up their dogma or belief system—and that includes not only those in the United States, but in Canada, the United Kingdom and other English-speaking countries, the Netherlands, and elsewhere. The repressed memory epidemic spread like a pandemic wave. Thus, in 2002, when I spent two months working in Bradford-on-Avon for the British False Memory Society, I found that the belief in repressed memories, multiple personalities, and Satanic ritual abuse cults was thriving there. I concluded that the UK lagged the USA by a few years but had learned from Americans all too well.

Kevin Felstead, the communications director of the British False Memory Society, wrote on March 30, 2017, "We have taken eight new cases in March alone, including another tragic case yesterday. We were involved in two separate Crown Court trials in January." Far from winding down, the BFMS is, unfortunately, busier than ever.

Indeed, the sex abuse hysteria virus cross-pollinated from multiple directions, not just from the United States. For instance, New Zealand therapist James Bennett ventured to England in 1986 to indoctrinate disciples in his disturbing version of recovered memory therapy called "primary activation." Rosemary Crossley's "facilitated communication," a kind of human Ouija board using severely handicapped children, was exported from Australia to the United States in 1989, resulting in many false accusations of sexual abuse. *(See Chapter 3.)* Swiss psychologist Alice Miller was a formative influence in the recovered memory movement. And Czech Stanislav Grof took his "holotropic breathwork"—a form of hyperventilation often leading to "memories," along with violent shaking, gagging, vomiting, and speaking in tongues—to the USA in 1967, but it also found its way, along with other alarming techniques, to the Findhorn Foundation in Scotland.

In other words, no one should get too smug about "those crazy Americans." Instead, we should examine how human beings—wherever they may live—can come to believe in destructive untruths. How can well-intentioned people cause such grievous harm? How can the past be rewritten with such ease? These are questions that transcend national borders.

During the summer of 1995, I ventured to England to conduct interviews with British recovered memory therapists, Survivors, accused parents, and retractors. The stories I heard were, unfortunately, all too familiar to me. When I took taxis in London, I learned that the cabbies had to pass a stringent series of tests before they were certified as possessing "The Knowledge." It struck me as ironic that British taxi drivers were better trained than British psychotherapists. If you wanted to get from Victoria to the Strand, you were in capable hands. But *caveat emptor* to anyone who opened his or her vulnerable mind to a psychotherapist untutored in the science of human memory.

Rather than facing the overwhelming evidence that a sizable number of their profession violated the Hippocratic oath—"First, do no harm"—the professional associations reacted to the controversy mostly by looking the other way, while trying decorously to cover their behinds. They preferred to sweep this embarrassing epidemic under the rug, dismissing it as the work of a few fringe therapists, while still maintaining that the theory of repressed memory has validity. As psychologist Richard Noll observed, they would rather "move on silently and feign forgetfulness."

Thus, repressed memories did not disappear. Indeed, the idea that people could completely forget years of childhood sexual abuse and then remember the abuse later has become enshrined in the popular imagination, despite its widespread, scientific debunking.

Once an idea enters the cultural mainstream, it has a way of resurfacing like a bloated corpse every few years. The corpse has risen again, if it ever truly sank. As the 21st century dawned, repressed memories began to come back into style with the mounting hysteria over accusations of sexual abuse by priests. While most of the priest cases involved always-remembered abuse that was all too real, a subset, such as the case that sent Paul Shanley to prison in 2002, were encouraged through repressed memory therapy. In 2015, sociologists Carol Tavris and Elliot Aronson observed, "while the [repressed memory and day-care sex abuse hysteria] epidemics have subsided, the assumptions that ignited them remain embedded in popular culture." They were correct that the underlying assumptions remain. Unfortunately, the repressed memory epidemic has not really "subsided." While it was slowed by scientific analysis and retractor lawsuits, the epidemic continues to this day.

Since the height of the repressed memory epidemic, media coverage has swung wildly between solid scientific reports on the malleability of memory to uncritical regurgitation of recovered memory claims. Most young journalists don't know what happened during the "Memory Wars" decade that followed the 1988 publication of *The Courage to Heal* and similar books. Add to that the impact of the Internet and acceptance of fake news and conspiracy theory as reality, and you have a recipe for disaster.

It is an indication of our culture's continuing credulity and fascination with allegedly hidden sexual abuse that a fake news story in late 2016 alleged that Comet Ping Pong, a pizza restaurant in northwest Washington, was harboring young children as sex slaves as part of a child-abuse ring led by Hillary Clinton. A 28-year-old father went to the restaurant and opened fire with his assault rifle. Luckily, no one was hurt. We have not learned sufficiently from the past, and we could be condemning ourselves to repeat it. But we may call it by another name, undoubtedly a more pleasant-sounding one.

Or maybe our culture won't even need to rename it. Just as this book was about to go to press in 2017, Netflix aired *The Keepers*, a seven-part series that heavily promoted the theory of repressed memories by resurrecting and validating a previously dismissed Baltimore case from the early 1990s. The series purveys all the old stereotypes, including a psychologist who explains confidently: "Some things we experience are so unbearable and so painful that we shut them out." This popular series could undo years of good memory science in the public arena. See Chapter 9 for a detailed critique.

I have called this book *Memory Warp* principally because repressed memory therapy really does warp the brain, re-enforcing a synaptic network of false memories that can come to seem as true as events that really occurred. "Warp" is a strong term for an amazing process. Who would believe that it was even possible to persuade otherwise normal people that they were raped for years in their childhood and completely forgot it? And that they would "remember" such prolonged abuse at the hands of their parents or other trusted caregivers?

Warp can also refer to the lengthwise threads on a loom, around which other threads (the weft of the woof) weave to create a fabric. In Chapter 7, I explore the cultural context that spawned this late-20th-century witch hunt and that continues to foster it and other forms of sex panic. This was not an isolated phenomenon, but part of a cultural, on-going *zeitgeist* that anthropologist Roger Lancaster identified in his 2011 book, *Sex Panic and the Punitive State*, where he explored not only the repressed memory and Satanic ritual abuse craze, but paranoia over child kidnapping, the ill-advised war on drugs, mass incarceration, children "playing doctor" prosecuted as sex offenders, and many other issues. "The never-ending parade of sex panics provides an important model—part metaphor and part blueprint—for the pervasive politics of fear," wrote Lancaster.

Although the overt practice of recovered memory therapy lessened, the mind-set behind it never disappeared. The majority of therapists still believe in this pseudoscience; they are just hesitant to espouse it openly. And the general public has accepted the myth. A 2014 survey by psychology professor Lawrence Patihis and colleagues found that 81% of college students agreed that "traumatic memories are often repressed," and 86% thought that if someone had emotional problems and needed therapy, that they might very well have suffered from childhood sexual abuse, even if they had no memory of the abuse; 83.9% of the general public thought that traumatic memories are often repressed. The majority of practicing psychotherapists thought so, too—60.3% of clinical psychologists, 69.1% of psychoanalysts, and, for "alternative" therapists who practiced hypnotherapy or believed in internal personalities, the consensus on repressed memory validity went up to 84%. "The disconnect between psychological science and clinical practice is an unconscionable embarrassment [to the profession]," Walter Mischel, then president of the Association for Psychological Science, observed in 2009, and this disturbing data offer proof that he was correct.

So the theory of repressed memory did not go away. It just went underground. Most therapists who specialize in trauma continue to believe in the theory of repression, and many continue to encourage clients to recall mythical abuse memories in order to get better. But in general they don't write about it or brag about it, and lawyers who call witnesses who have recalled such "memories" in court do not advertise their origins. While repressed memory excavation practices were banned from credible medical schools and hospitals, the practice continues in the offices of independent counselors, social workers and even massage therapists.

In the process of writing this book, I contacted Professor Patihis at the University of Southern Mississippi and asked if he might conduct a survey to show how many people had come to believe they had repressed memories of abuse. He agreed, and together we worked on the first-ever such survey, conducted through Amazon Mechanical Turk, an on-line method. Over 2,000 people completed the questions, and we will publish a detailed report in a professional journal in the near future. But I can report that the preliminary data are astonishing and alarming. I will go into more detail in the final chapter of this book, but we found that over 5 percent of those surveyed (ranging from age 20 to 98) had recovered abuse memories in therapy. Adjusting the data for gender, ethnicity, and race reduces that to 4 percent. If that is representative of the adult U.S. population, that means that over 9 million people in this country have come to believe that they suffered childhood abuse but completely forgot it until they sought psychotherapy.

What shocked me most about the survey results was the indication that the repressed memory epidemic still continues in an underground but robust manner. As expected, it seems to have peaked in the early 1990s, when 18 percent of those entering therapy retrieved abuse memories, and declined in a tsunami of lawsuits and licensing revocations from 1994–1997. But in the current decade, starting in 2010, 8 percent of those seeking therapy came to believe they were abused as children, without any previous memories.

Many of the anonymous comments were equally disturbing. A 26-year-old woman who took the survey wrote, for instance: "I believe I have repressed memories from trauma! I am highly suspicious of something that may have happened, but I am not sure and have no memory." If this young woman seeks out a "trauma therapist," she is likely to find her sought-after abuse memories.

In 2014, investigative journalist Ed Cara wrote about the Castlewood Treatment Center in Missouri, which specialized in eating disorders but ended up convincing a number of patients, well into the 21st century, that they harbored repressed memories and multiple personalities and that they had been in Satanic cults. "The belief that hidden memories can be 'recovered' in therapy should have been exorcised years ago," Cara wrote. "But the mental health establishment does not always learn from its mistakes—and families are still paying the price."

A woman in a Ph.D. program in clinical psychology at a well-known university wrote to me long after the repressed memory epidemic had subsided. She preferred to remain anonymous, so I will call her Barbara. "I have been shaken by the lack of awareness of this problem [recovered memory therapy/false memories] at the centers where I have been trained. Most of the therapists I know claim to maintain neutrality regarding memories, but they also believe that massive repression exists in some or many cases. In addition, there are still so many young women and men who continue to come to therapy looking for reasons for their pain, and my experience is that some of them will go the way of abuse memories, even if the therapist does not. In my short time as a student therapist at this university's student health center, I was asked by clients more times than I would have ever expected if forgotten abuse might be a cause of their unhappiness. I still see copies of *The Courage to Heal* on my colleagues' bookcases."

Barbara didn't learn much about this issue in grad school. "Honestly, I don't remember much instruction about recovered memories at all, except for a brief mention during a psychopathology class that the diagnosis of DID [dissociative identity disorder, the new name for multiple personality disorder] is controversial." A belief in multiple personalities, allegedly created to forget horrendous memories, represented a kind of lunatic fringe during the repressed memory epidemic—yet it remains enshrined in the *Diagnostic and Statistical Manual of Mental Disorders*, the psychiatric bible.

One of the social workers with whom Barbara worked still believed in recovered memories and "stressed to me that she feels it is important to remain open to what the client brings." At another walk-in clinic, there was a social work student who "spoke openly about the memories her clients were uncovering, and spoke proudly about having helped a client realize that what she'd interpreted as a physical problem was actually a body memory." Indeed, in 2014 Bessel van der Kolk, the chief proponent of the idea of a "body memory," published the book, *The Body Keeps the Score,* which continued to promote the dangerous idea that "the body remembers what the mind forgets." The book received rave reviews, even in journals such as *Nature* and *New Scientist,* despite the fact that it contains two chapters espousing a pseudoscientific belief in massive repression/dissociation.

Linda Ross, whom I called "Robin Newsome" in the second edition of *Victims of Memory,* is one of the few therapists who once believed in repressed memories and has had the courage to go public to try to undo the harm, on National Public Radio's *This American Life* program. She told me about the first time she met parents who had lost all contact with their children because of alleged unrepressed abuse memories:

> In the fall of 1993, I attended my first local FMSF meeting. I wasn't sure what to expect. These were the accused, after all. I remembered all that I had learned about how all perpetrators are in denial. I expected a room full of defensive parents. What I found instead was a group of sad and shocked parents who asked the same question their daughters asked: "How could she do this to me?" I had been so supportive of women and their repressed memories, but I had never once considered what that experience was like for the parents. Now I heard how absolutely ludicrous it sounded. One elderly couple introduced themselves, and the wife told me that their daughter had accused her husband of murdering three people. Another woman had been accused of being in a Satanic cult that had used babies for sacrifices. This woman in a pink polyester suit was supposed to be a high priestess. The pain in these parents' faces was so obvious. And the unique thread was that their daughters had gone to therapy. I didn't feel very proud of myself or my profession that day.

Once Ross realized what harm she had done, she went back to find her former clients to try to undo the damage. She believes that most therapists and ministers are still afraid to cast doubt on recovered memories. "If someone came to their pastor saying that they thought they had been a horse thief in a former life," she says, "the pastor would say, 'As Christians, we don't believe in reincarnation.' And the same thing would happen if they remembered being abducted by aliens. But if they said they went to a therapist and had begun to recover abuse memories, the pastor will say, 'Really? Can we pray for you?' They would completely believe it."

There is a high-profile case that provides alarming (and surprising) evidence that repressed memory therapy is alive and well and continuing to do damage in our legal system. It turns out that many of the allegations against Jerry Sandusky, the ex-Penn State football defensive coach, were based on repressed memories. "That doorway that I had closed has since been reopening more," an alleged victim testified at the trial in 2012. "Through counseling and different things, I can remember a lot more detail that I had pushed aside than I did at that point." When I contacted him after the trial, he told me: "Actually both of my therapists have suggested that I have repressed memories. My therapist has suggested that I may still have more repressed memories that have yet to be revealed, and this could be a big cause of the depression that I still carry today."

There is compelling evidence that repressed memories were responsible for many of the Sandusky allegations, including Aaron Fisher, "Victim Number One." It is a complex case that involves not only repressed memories but a media blitz, police and civil lawyers scouting for alleged victims, and millions of dollars awarded to troubled young men. It requires its own book, which I have recently finished—*The Most Hated Man in America: Jerry Sandusky and the Rush to Judgment* (Sunbury Press, 2017).

With *this* book, I am sounding an alarm and re-educating professionals and the general public about how memory actually works. *Memory Warp* provides a much-needed history lesson about how, in the late 20th century, several million families—my educated estimate, though no one can establish firm statistics (*see Chapter 9*)—were destroyed by an epidemic of false memories of sexual abuse.

Some accusing adult children retracted their repressed memory allegations, while others established uneasy contact but never apologized. In all too many cases, however, elderly parents have died without ever seeing their children again. "I am now 93 years old and having a very hard time," wrote one man in 2015. "The reason is that my wonderful wife passed away recently. Her last words were 'Where are my daughters?' Then she looked at me and said 'I love you.' Then she closed her eyes. She was 85 years old. We have not seen or heard from our daughters for 23 years."

For years, the False Memory Syndrome Foundation, founded by Pamela and Peter Freyd in 1992, provided a well-researched newsletter and support system for families shattered by repressed memory allegations. The *FMSF Newsletter* offered updates and information on the latest scientific papers on memory and suggestibility, and back issues remain available online. But the Foundation is winding down, shifting primarily to a Facebook page, the False Memory Syndrome Action Network. In November 2016 Freyd wrote that she expected her organization to continue for only a few more years. "We continue to receive a small but steady stream of calls for help from families and questioning patients, and occasional calls from the media, students or attorneys." But the massive attention to the repressed memory disaster of the late 1980s and early 1990s has clearly passed. Still, Freyd continued, "We wish we could say that the constellation of beliefs that were the foundation of the recovered-memory phenomenon had disappeared, but the reality is that those beliefs linger in some segments of the population."

Freyd's wording implied that only a small minority still believe in repressed memories. But, as I've pointed out here, it is not just a fringe group that continues to support this discredited theory. It is the majority of the population. In other words, critical thinkers and multi-million-dollar lawsuits may have won the scientific and legal battle over false memories, but they appear to be losing the long-term "memory wars," as Frederick Crews called them. This book is a much-needed corrective.

And it is not only a matter of repressed memory therapy. We have been in the throes of a kind of sex abuse hysteria since 1983, when the McMartin Preschool case erupted into public consciousness, followed by over a hundred day-care cases in which young children were subjected to grossly leading interviews, resulting in false accusations of sexual abuse against caregivers, which I document in a chapter in this book as well. This kind of memory manipulation of children predated the massive search for repressed memories in adults, but it is related, and it too has continued to occur, although not in the most obviously leading manner.

As bad as the recovered-memory mess was, its close relative—the false allegations dragged out of young children—was even worse, as I document here in Chapter 5. These two phenomena—recovered-memory therapy and the coercive questioning of young children—are the result of the same therapeutic mindset that simply assumes guilt and then presses toward a foregone conclusion. All of the children's denials were disregarded until many finally "disclosed" under enormous pressure. Just as adults' memories were rewritten, so were young children's recollections molded by therapists, social workers, and police, sometimes including bribes, threats, and hours without food or water. Just as adults' memories were rewritten, so were young children's recollections molded. In such cases, the children were indeed abused—by the reckless interviewers, invasive pediatricians, and investigators.

In all too many cases, the two phenomena were directly linked, as in the

Massachusetts case of Ray and Shirley Souza, documented in Chapter 5. While in recovered-memory therapy, the Souzas' daughter had a dream about them abusing her, which she considered proof. She then warned her sister and sister-in-law that Mom and Dad were evil sex offenders. Thus started the intensive questioning of the grandchildren.

For years, I served on the board of the National Center for Reason and Justice (NCRJ, www.ncrj.org), an organization that supports people who are falsely accused or convicted of crimes against children. The vast majority of those who contact the NCRJ were accused of child sexual abuse. I helped to start a group of NCRJ volunteers (I am still one of them) to respond to the avalanche of email submissions that the tiny, underfunded NCRJ could not investigate. While I cannot vouch for their innocence, these desperate people—the accused or supportive family members or friends—have told stories that are all too similar. They usually have few resources and little education. The accusations often arise in custody or divorce disputes, from students wanting to get back at a teacher, or consensual sex between those close in age where one was a minor.

In such cases, the accused are usually assumed to be guilty until proven innocent. Their overworked and often incompetent public defenders pressure them into taking a plea bargain, making it virtually impossible to appeal, and they end up on sex offender registries that make it difficult to find a job or a place to live. As U. S. District Judge Jed Rakoff wrote in 2014, "our criminal justice system is almost exclusively a system of plea bargaining, negotiated behind closed doors and with no judicial oversight. The outcome is largely determined by the prosecutor alone." Because of draconian mandatory sentencing laws, "a significant number of defendants plead guilty to crimes they never actually committed."

And those accused of child sexual abuse are under particularly intense pressure to take a plea. In the United States today, the new virtual scarlet letters S. O. might as well be branded on foreheads, for "Sex Offender." Labeled sex offenders are, as Roger Lancaster put it, "the last pariahs."

In short, we have learned little from the day care sex abuse hysteria, either. "Believe the Children" (but only when they say they were abused) was the mantra in those bad old days, and it continues to echo well into the 21st century.

So—let us rewind back to the 1980s and 1990s, a time that spawned both the repressed memory epidemic and the day-care sex abuse hysteria, and see how they came about and what impact they had. In the process, we will learn how memory actually works and how malleable it can be, especially when figures of authority exert influence on vulnerable people seeking help for the most urgent problems in their lives. It is important that we learn from the past, and not "repress" the memories of what amounted to a modern witch hunt in the late 20th century.

1

How to Become a Survivor

Two postings on a computer bulletin board:

Jan. 1, 1993. Hi everybody, my name is Gretchen. I am from Germany and in the States for about 16 months now. I am 30 years old, married and after 4 miscarriages in 18 months we went to marriage counseling. I also have a sexual problem, no desire at all. The counselor and a therapist are both convinced that I was sexually abused as a kid, but I don't remember anything. They said it is probably so bad, that I had to block it out or it would have killed me. Now I am running around and try to remember .... I know I was hit every day, I was the only child. But sexual abuse never occurred to me at all.... God, I have so many questions and hope somebody will answer me and share their experience with me.*

Jan. 1, 1993. Dear Gretchen, You're not alone in this! I had no memories of being sexually abused until about one and a half years ago. About 3 years ago, I started reading books on the subject and every "effects" list described me to a T. I didn't have any memories, but I just had a really strong feeling that something happened.... When I stopped thinking of memories in visual terms, I started to realize that I was remembering things all the time. Reactions, feelings, panic attacks, fears & phobias are all memories.... Reading books on sexual abuse is a really good way to retrieve memories. Pay attention to what you react to. For example, I was reading The Obsidian Mirror *and she was talking about how her abuser had stuck monopoly pieces inside of her. I had a panic attack when I read that and then had flashbacks of a similar incident happening to me. Books that I would recommend are #1* The Courage to Heal *(this is the BEST book—very validating if you have no memories)....*

THE WIDESPREAD SEARCH FOR REPRESSED memories of sexual abuse began to mushroom in 1988 with the publication of *The Courage to Heal,* by Ellen Bass and Laura Davis, which informs readers: "*Forgetting* is one of the most effective ways children deal with sexual abuse. The human mind has tremendous powers of repression. Many children are able to forget about the abuse, *even as it is happening to them.*"** They continue: "You may think you don't have memories, but often as

---

*   The grammatical errors in this quotation were in the original. Readers may assume that all misspellings or other errors within direct quotations, throughout this book, are from the original source. I make this note here, rather than interrupting the text with the standard "sic." Also, throughout this book, when words are italicized within direct quotations, they were italicized in the original source, unless otherwise noted.

**   Citations to *The Courage to Heal* refer to the 1992 second edition. A fourth edition came out in 2008. The essential message remains the same.

you begin to talk about what you do remember, there emerges a constellation of feelings, reactions, and recollections that add up.... To say, 'I was abused,' you don't need the kind of recall that would stand up in a court of law."

In this chapter, we will examine how *The Courage to Heal* and other books popular in the late 1980s and 1990s encouraged illusory memories of sexual abuse—mostly in women, though men also recover "memories." At first blush, false accusations of incest seem hard to imagine. How, outside of a brainwashing prisoner-of-war torture compound, could people be convinced of such a horrendous delusion, particularly if their relationships with their accused parents were once warm and loving? How could perfectly normal women come to have vivid memories of fondling and oral sex at the age of three, or frequent sexual intercourse with their fathers as teenagers, or prolonged immersion in Satanic sex cults, if these events never took place?

The Horror of Real Incest and Child Sex Abuse

Before reviewing *The Courage to Heal* in detail, it is necessary to understand how and why Ellen Bass and Laura Davis came to write it. In the 1970s, during the early days of the women's movement, the horrifying extent of sexual abuse and incest first began to surface, although children had been subjected to such abuse for all of recorded history. Up until then, official statistics claimed a tiny incidence in the general population. In one "definitive" 1955 study, researchers estimated that there were only 1.1 cases of incest per million persons. Even when incest was recognized, it was often minimized or even sanctioned by male psychologists. Some victims were told that they were only fantasizing, based on Freud's presumptions about Electra and Oedipus complexes. Freud thought that all children between ages three and six go through a stage of sexual desire for the opposite-gender parent (*see Chapter 6*).

During Freud's Victorian era, child prostitution was widespread, with virgins bringing top dollar because of the fear of syphilis. In England, a 14-year-old was worth 100 pounds, but parents could sell a beautiful preadolescent for 400 pounds. In his 1885 newspaper exposé, journalist W. T. Stead reported being sickened by the sight of children, three to five years old, being chloroformed before serving as sex partners for adult men. Around that time, the anonymous author of *My Secret Life* complained of the difficulties of penetrating prepubescent girls, though he had no moral compunctions about it. "It is the fate of such girls to be fucked young," he asserted, "neither laws social or legal can prevent it."

Sex historian Vern Bullough points out that the Industrial Revolution brought a sharp increase in the sexual abuse of prepubescent children. Until then, such activity seems to have been relatively rare, although sexual relations between adults and adolescents have always been permitted in some cultures.. In modern times, however, there are more documented cases of adult males assaulting younger children. As a newspaper reporter in 1949, Bullough observed a two-and-a-half-year-old girl who was "taken to surgery with a mangled vagina and a damaged urethra." She had been raped by her father. His editor refused to publish the story, saying he ran a "family newspaper" unfit for such items.[*] Four years later, the famed Kinsey report, *Sexual Behavior in the Human Female* (1953), revealed that 24 percent of respondents "had been approached while they were preadolescent [13 or younger] by adult males who appeared to be making sexual advances, or who had made sexual contacts with the child." Despite this alarming statistic, the authors implied that the victims were responsible: "Repetition [of preadolescent contacts with adults] had most frequently occurred... with relatives who lived in the same household. In many instances, the experiences were repeated because the children had become interested in the sexual activity and had more or less actively sought repetitions."

They concluded that there was really nothing to worry about: "We have only one clear-cut case of serious injury done to the child, and a very few instances of vaginal bleeding which, however, did not appear to do any appreciable damage." Wardell Pomeroy, one of the Kinsey report authors, went even further in 1976, telling a *Penthouse* interviewer: "Incest between adults and younger children can also prove to be a satisfying and enriching experience, although difficulties can certainly arise."

With some male psychologists expressing such opinions, it is little wonder that women and many men were finally becoming vocally outraged by the 1970s. In 1975, Susan Brownmiller published *Against Our Will: Men, Women and Rape*. Although her book was primarily a blistering attack on male attitudes toward rape, Brownmiller also made the connection with incest: "The unholy silence that shrouds the inter-family sexual abuse of children and prevents a realistic appraisal of its true incidence and meaning is rooted in the same patriarchal philosophy of sexual private property that shaped and determined historic male attitudes toward rape."

Incest victims began to speak out in women's groups and in books. In 1974, Ellen Bass, a young feminist creative writing instructor, received a crumpled half-sheet of paper from a shy student. "Her writing was so vague, so tentative," Bass recalls, "that I wasn't sure what she was trying to say, but I sensed that it was important." Slowly, with encouragement, the student wrote about the pain of her father's sexual assaults. Shortly afterward, probably because their teacher shared

---

* For further histories of child sexual abuse, see Rush, *The Best-Kept Secret;* Wasserman and Rosenfeld, "An Overview of the History of Child Sexual Abuse"; and Breiner, *Slaughter of the Innocents: Child Abuse Through the Ages and Today.*

similar stories, one woman after the other wrote horror stories for Bass. "I was stunned by the number of women who had been sexually abused," she says. "I was deeply moved by the anguish they had endured."

In 1978, Bass and five women from her Boston writing workshops began collecting stories for an anthology. Their timing was perfect. That same year, Louise Armstrong published *Kiss Daddy Goodnight,* which included many incest accounts, and therapist Sandra Butler's *Conspiracy of Silence: The Trauma of Incest* came out. Other books and articles quickly followed, authored by David Finkelhor, Christine Courtois, Florence Rush, Judith Herman, and others. Swiss psychologist Alice Miller exerted a tremendous influence when her work about traumatized children was translated into English. By the time Bass published her 1983 anthology, incest was a subject of great interest among the general public.

Very little of this early material about incest mentioned repressed memories, though Freud had made the concept of repression a theoretical given. Most of the women who were finally speaking out had never had any trouble remembering that they had been abused. It was all too real for them. Their problem was being *unable to forget it.* Even the title of the 1983 Bass anthology, *I Never Told Anyone,* implied that although the victims of incest had remained silent all these years, they had never forgotten. Often, they revealed confused, mixed feelings about their experience. Jean Monroe, whose father fondled her breasts from the time she was nine until her teens, spoke of the "terrible betrayal" of her trust, but she also said, "As an adult I've always been very happy sexually. Somehow I got an affirmative sense of my own personal sexual power from my father."

The notion of repressed incest memories had been quietly growing during the 1970s, however. In 1975, for instance, the director of a Philadelphia sex offender program told an audience of psychotherapists: "If the sexual attack is dealt with improperly or repressed it may cause serious psychological problems." Louise Armstrong's *Kiss Daddy Goodnight,* published in 1978, contained the story of Jenny, who told her: "Until about a year ago I had no awareness that any of it had happened. I had completely removed it from any form of consciousness." Indeed, Armstrong herself "recovered" a memory of oral sex that purportedly occurred when she was 14. And Sandra Butler's *Conspiracy of Silence (1978)* contained the story of Evelyn, who was "flooded with [incest] memories which had been repressed. . . . Even now, the memory has an unreal feeling to it."

Consequently, it is not surprising that a few of the women in the 1983 Bass anthology also talked about having repressed all memory of their abuse. "My healing began with my simultaneous decision to accept myself as a lesbian and to enter therapy," wrote Yarrow Morgan. In therapy, she recovered forgotten memories of abuse by her mother and father while she was still in her crib. Similarly,

"R.C." dreamed and recovered memories of how her father forced oral sex upon her from the time she was four until she was 11. "I have met and loved my rage," she said. She too had recently "come out" as a lesbian and was completing a master's degree in counseling.

Morgan's and R.C.'s stories—and their attitudes—signaled a fundamentally different kind of incest memory, wrapped in mystery, horror, rage, and gender politics. They contrasted sharply with the stories of always-remembered incest, which described the molestation within the context of daily life.[*] For example, in describing her always-remembered abuse, Jean Monroe remembered: "Suddenly the bedroom door bangs open and the children come running down the hallway. Daddy hastily closes my top and slides back in his chair." Relieved, she escaped his fondling to join a game of hide-and-seek.

By comparison, repressed-memory stories such as Yarrow Morgan's often described the abuse scenarios in some detail—Yarrow recalled "a pink and purple worm-like thing—but they did not mesh with everyday life circumstances. Rather, they involved unremittingly negative and violent violations. Often, such "recovered memories" asserted that the abuse began in early infancy, while the always-remembered accounts usually began around age nine or later.

The Search for Lost Memories

Something odd had happened between the late 1970s and the early 1980s. The appalling extent of real abuse, and the reluctance of many women to disclose it, had led some therapists to conclude that many women had *repressed* all memory of their abuse. After all, as Florence Rush had pointed out, Freud had initially helped to uncover incest memories through hypnosis in the mid-1890s, only to reverse himself and declare his findings invalid. What if Freud had been right in the first place? The hunt for buried memories was on, particularly in Massachusetts.

Judith Herman, a Harvard-affiliated psychiatrist and feminist, actively encouraged women to recall abuse. In 1981, she published *Father–Daughter Incest,* which, like the 1983 Bass anthology, primarily told stories of women who had always recalled their abuse. Its index did not contain references to memory, repression, or dissociation. Herman had already come to believe in the existence of massive repression, however, citing the case of a 25-year-old who came to an emergency room with anxiety attacks and a vivid fantasy of being pursued by a man with a knife. "It later emerged in psychotherapy," Herman wrote, that a

---

[*]   As sex-abuse researcher David Finkelhor has pointed out, "Almost all studies report statistics showing that children are more vulnerable to sexual abuse starting in the preadolescent period between ages 8 and 12." In addition, almost all molesters are male. In contrast to these well-documented facts, "recovered memories" often deal with violent and repeated abuse of much younger children, and *mothers* are frequently accused of the offenses.

sexually harassing boss had "reawakened previously repressed memories of sexual assaults by her father." From ages 6 to 14, she now recalled, she had been forced to masturbate him, but she had managed to forget all about it until that moment.

In her 1981 book, Herman referred to "an informal network of therapists in private practice in the Boston area," all of them staunch feminists who now began to hunt for repressed memories.* Throughout the early 1980s, in Herman's individual and group therapy, women used hypnotic age regression, dream analysis, and induced "flashbacks" to retrieve their repressed memories. Ellen Bass, who had served as a mental health counselor in Boston, was probably part of the informal network trading stories of lost memories, and she took them with her to California.

Clinical psychologist Denise Gelinas, who co-founded the Incest Treatment Program at a hospital in Springfield, Massachusetts, was also part of the network. In 1983, Gelinas published "The Persisting Negative Effects of Incest," a very influential article, in the journal *Psychiatry*. In it, she described the "subtle and varied" repercussions of incest, including depression, low self-esteem, alcohol or drug abuse, anxiety, and marital difficulties. The effects of incest, Gelinas stated, "are so persistent they can emerge many years after cessation of abuse, and so pervasive they can blight the victim's past, present and future." Once therapists identified potential victims, "previously repressed memories begin to emerge and become available for work," the psychologist wrote. "Recognition of the patient as an incest victim allows the therapist to see the affect and memories as the potentially curative, cathartic emergence of a long-buried traumatic neurosis."

The following year, Judith Herman and Emily Schatzow published an article entitled "Time-Limited Group Therapy for Women with a History of Incest." It was a curious paper. At first, it appeared that Herman and Schatzow had chosen 30 *bona fide* incest victims for group therapy. It soon became apparent, however, that many participants did not actually recall abuse, but had been referred by other therapists as likely candidates for memory retrieval. "We may have been overzealous in encouraging ambivalent women to join a group," the authors opined. In fact, the first goal proposed by group members was "recovery of memories," while other women described their goal differently: "I just want to be in the group and feel I belong." During the third or fourth session, "the leaders introduced the idea of telling the incest story in more detail," which resulted in "discharge of a great deal of feeling." Finally, after rehearsal of their memories set off a "chain reaction," another session was devoted to "shared fantasies of revenge."

---

* Herman almost certainly included Ann Burgess, a Boston psychiatric nurse, in her "informal network." Burgess, who in the late 1970s had studied men convicted of having sex with groups of adolescent boys, coined the term "sex rings," which led to the myth of widespread ritual abuse cults ferrying children about for their nefarious pleasure. Burgess also helped promote the use of children's drawings to diagnose sexual abuse.

Also in 1984, Jeffrey Masson published *The Assault on Truth: Freud's Suppression of the Seduction Theory,* in which he popularized the idea that Freud had been right when he hypnotized his patients (or applied his "pressure method") and encouraged them to recall repressed memories of incest. Freud coined the term "abreaction" to describe what he considered an emotional reliving of forgotten trauma, and for a while he believed he had found the key to his patients' problems in life. Masson vilified Freud for a failure in moral courage by abandoning the theory. Masson's work provided an important scholarly cornerstone for the nascent Incest Survivor Movement and its renewed search for repressed memories. Soon modern therapists would once again encourage "abreaction." *(See Chapter 6 for a critique of Freud's "seduction theory.")*

That same year, 60 million viewers tuned in to an ABC made-for-TV movie called *Something About Amelia,* in which the "something" bothering the teenage girl turned out to be incest. Her wealthy, well-respected, good-looking father was forcing his daughter into sexual relations. The national attention was riveted on this obscene, hidden problem.

Meanwhile, Judith Herman's "informal network" had extended well beyond the Boston area. It snaked its way across the United States, up into Canada, jumped the ocean to Great Britain, and reached halfway around the world. In 1978, New Zealand therapist Elizabeth Ward visited the United States, where she formed close ties with colleagues in an incest clinic. Back in Australia, she began working in the Canberra Women's Refuge, forming an incest group in 1979. "The American experience," she wrote, "had 'taken the scales from my eyes.'" In 1984, the London-based Women's Press published Ward's book, *Father-Daughter Rape,* in which she called for "an end to the patriarchal nuclear family," suggesting it be replaced by "matriarchal skills and values." Though most of Ward's informants had always recalled their abuse, there were hints that recovered memory cases were just around the corner. "Just recently I've remembered this part," said Sonia. "I find it hard to remember a lot of detail—I'm sure that's because I've blocked it out," asserted Virginia. In her book, Ward referred to an "international network of feminist caring" and to "women's movement "speak-outs" in many countries.

That same year, a Welsh press published feminist Angie Ash's *Father-Daughter Sexual Abuse: The Abuse of Paternal Authority,* a slim radical feminist broadside based on her masters dissertation, which relied heavily on U.S. sources. It identified incest as the inevitable result of the "patriarchy."

Particularly in England, the emotionally-charged word "incest" came to be used for virtually any sexual contact with children. In 1981, Incest Survivor Campaign literature redefined incest as "the sexual molestation of a child by any older person perceived as a figure of trust or authority," explaining that "blood relationship and taboo are red herrings." Incest was simply "the abuse of power." By 1983, the organization was claiming that 20 per cent of the British female population were incest survivors.

In the meantime, the idea that someone could completely forget horrendous abuse, then suddenly recall it years later, had been popularized in *Michelle Remembers*, a 1980 account of how Michelle Smith, a depressed young woman of 27, sought therapy with psychiatrist Lawrence Pazder in the wake of three miscarriages. A psychology major in college, she had a long history of nervous complaints, stemming in part from a childhood spent with an alcoholic father. Her mother had died when Michelle was 14, and her father gave her to her grandparents to raise.

Under the charismatic care of Dr. Pazder, Michelle began to "remember" lurid scenes from her childhood under a kind of auto-hypnosis. Although he did not consciously invite her fantasies, it is clear from the book (written by therapist and patient, who have subsequently divorced their respective spouses and married one another) that Pazder encouraged a dependent relationship based on his believing everything he heard. "The only way people were really helped," Pazder thought, "was to allow them to go into their feelings." Not only that, "he had the strongest sense that he and Michelle were about to embark on something significant."

Indeed they were. Michelle eventually convinced herself and Pazder that she had repressed memories of grotesque abuse at the hands of a Satanic cult, led by the devil himself, when she was five years old. Her mother had actively participated in the cult.[*]

Throughout her months of "remembering," Michelle disclosed that she had been held naked in a cage full of snakes, that the sadists had burned and butchered stillborn babies and fetuses in her presence, killed kittens, and forced her to perform lurid sexual acts. At one point, she claimed they surgically attached horns to her head and a tail to her spine. Finally, Michelle supposedly was allowed to go home with her mother and promptly repressed the memory of her trauma until she felt safe enough to recall it with the sympathetic Dr. Pazder.

By the mid-'80s, the disturbing evidence of actual incest was increasingly publicized. Back in 1978, Diana Russell had conducted a survey of 930 randomly selected women in the San Francisco area. Her researchers conducted lengthy interviews. None of them fished for repressed memories. Russell published the results in 1986 as *The Secret Trauma: Incest in the Lives of Girls and Women*. Her

---

[*]   *Michelle Remembers* fails to mention Michelle's two sisters, neither of whom recalled any abuse. A family friend described the mother as a woman "whose whole life was for her children. You couldn't have a nicer, more charming person." Other claims fell apart when examined. For instance, a neighbor and former teacher recalled Michelle attending first grade regularly in 1955 just when she was supposedly locked in a basement for months at a time.

findings were shocking. Using a fairly moderate definition of incest (unwanted actual or attempted sexual contact between relatives), she found that 12 percent of the women had been incest victims before the age of 14. The mean age at which incest occurred was just over 11 years old. The prevalence rate for *all* sexual abuse, including extra-familial, was 28 percent for those under 14. Using somewhat broader definitions (including experiences with exhibitionists as well as other unwanted non-contact sexual experiences), the figure rose to 48 percent before 14. A similar study of 248 random women, conducted by Gail Wyatt in Los Angeles, confirmed Russell's findings.*

Since that time, many figures about sex abuse have been thrown around—some much lower, others higher. Much depends on the definition of incest. Step-fathers are far more likely to molest their step-daughters, for instance. The U.S. incidence of incest in which biological fathers have intercourse with their children appears to be one percent or less, according to several independent studies. Regardless of the particular figure one chooses to believe, it is clear that the incidence of sexual abuse is alarmingly high. As Russell asserted, it appears to have profound consequences for many victims, affecting, to one degree or another, their ability to trust, to form relationships, to hold jobs. It is almost impossible for a man to conceive of how often a woman feels threatened in our society. Walking down the street, women are constantly aware, at some level, that they are vulnerable to attack.

While Diana Russell's book helped to alert the public to the extent of sex abuse, it also, unfortunately, helped promote the idea that many memories of abuse might have been relegated to the subconscious. "Repression is a common protective mechanism employed by victims of all ages," Russell asserted, "but particularly victims of childhood traumas …. Deliberate silence on the part of the victim and all who know about this trauma is more common. This silence makes repression all the more likely to occur." She referred to a 1985 speech Judith Herman made to the American Psychiatric Association, claiming that those who were abused in very early childhood or who had endured violent abuse were most likely to resort to "massive repression."

The following year, Cathy Ann Matthews, an Australian clergyman's wife in her fifties, published her first-person account of recovered memories, providing a model for many other such books in years to come. Clearly influenced by Elizabeth Ward's work at the Canberra Women's Refuge, Matthews's book began unequivocally: "Repression has burst its bonds." Though she had previously remem-

---

* Russell's and Wyatt's studies have been criticized, however, on several grounds, among them: (1) Russell instructed interviewers to ask, "How upset were you by this experience – extremely upset, somewhat upset, or not very upset?" There was no allowance for the possibility that the episodes were experienced as positive in any way. (2) Incest was defined too broadly, as including *any attempted* sexual contact between relatives, *no matter how distant the relationship.*

bered "a fairly normal childhood, externally happy [in] an ordinary everyday suburban home," she now believed that she had endured years of incest. "Now, as though doors have been flung open, those first fifteen years of my life are bursting forth with an agony almost beyond endurance."* By the mid-'80s, the idea that incest victims routinely repressed their memories appears to have filtered inland from Massachusetts and California and found purchase in the American heartland. In 1985, for instance, Mary Ann Donaldson, a therapist in Fargo, North Dakota, published her report on women in group therapy, many of whom had recovered "memories" in the process of therapy. "The therapist should provide a safe environment," Donaldson wrote. "To break through the powerful denial, a process of memory recollections is a starting point." She quoted one client, who reported her experience as "very, very intense—the day that it first surfaced in the office I felt that it was happening to me right then." Donaldson cautioned that after the initial revelation of abuse, "the memories, perceptions about memories, and feeling reactions must be experienced in doses." She recommended group therapy for its "quickly developing intensity."

In 1987, Judith Herman published "Recovery and Verification of Memories of Childhood Sexual Trauma" in *Psychoanalytic Psychology*, a widely cited professional paper that emphasized the extent and validity of repressed incest memories. *(For a critique of Herman's paper, see Chapter 2.)*

By that time, the idea of recovered memories had spread to England as well, where social workers were warned that sessions with children using anatomically correct dolls might trigger "reliving of suppressed sexual abuse in the interviewer's own childhood." The following year, in 1988, a British television documentary, *The Nightingale Roars*, told the story of middle-aged Constance Nightingale, who had, for most of her life, according to one credulous critic, "blocked from her memory a childhood of terrible abuse."**

The time was ripe for a major popular book on repressed memories. Indeed, many other threads came together to prompt Ellen Bass and Laura Davis to write *The Courage to Heal* in 1988. There was, for instance, the mass hysteria over sex abuse in day-care centers. In 1983, frightened, suspicious parents of children attending the McMartin Preschool had taken their offspring to therapists.

The preschoolers, after repeated questioning and prodding, came to believe that their teachers were monsters who had violated them in fantastic ways, and soon many other day-care centers were closed down and their employees jailed. *(See Chapter 5, "And a Little Child Shall Lead Them")* Other factors included the

---

*   Matthews expanded her original 1986 book and published it in 1990 as *Breaking Through*. The same year, an Australian docudrama of the same name riveted television viewers.

**   Constance Nightingale subsequently died, but Nightingale Books, a Shrewsbury publisher named in her honor, distributed American recovered memory and ritual abuse books in the U. K.

victimology movement, the fragmentation of the modern family, and other so-cial pressures.

Ellen Bass, creative writer and feminist, was the perfect person to synthesize and popularize the Incest Survivor Movement, along with her student Laura Davis. Their critics complained that Bass and Davis have no training in psychology, but that hardly mattered. Plenty of psychologists and social workers believed precisely the same things, though they might have used fancier terminology and published in academic journals. What Bass and Davis wrote was not so much a psychological primer, however, as it was a religious creed.

The Courage to Accuse

It is impossible to exaggerate the influence that *The Courage to Heal* exerted. Most of the women I interviewed in the 1990s told me that they had read the book not just once, but obsessively, over and over again. "I keep it on my bedside table. Like the Bible." That comes from a "Survivor" quoted in the frontispiece of the 1992 edition.* Another wrote, "In the moments when I am most alone, I pick up your book and know that there is understanding." For those who always recalled sexual abuse but who were afraid to talk about it, *The Courage to Heal* may well provide the support and encouragement to seek help. Unfortunately, it has also served as reinforcement for questionable recovered memory theories and techniques. It is worthwhile, therefore, to understand exactly what Bass and Davis wrote in this book, which has sold over a million copies in several editions.

The main trouble with the book is that the primary intended audience consisted not of women who were abused, but rather women who *thought* they might have been abused, but who didn't remember it. In the introduction, Bass and Davis wrote, "Often the knowledge that you were abused starts with a tiny feeling, an intuition. It's important to trust that inner voice and work from there. Assume your feelings are valid." They asserted that this is the beginning of an inevitable progression. "So far, no one we've talked to thought she might have been abused, and then later discovered that she hadn't been.

The authors promised that reading their book would be a "cathartic healing experience," but they warned that in the process, many women "have also reported feeling terrified, furious and anguished." Others experienced nightmares and flashbacks. But that's only to be expected. No pain, no gain. In fact, "if you breeze through these chapters, you probably aren't feeling safe enough to confront these issues." Eventually, however, women who suffer through all this would be whole and healed—and that is the *only* way they could become whole and healed.

---

* Throughout this book, I have capitalized the term "Survivor" to identify those who have recovered "re-pressed memories" of sexual abuse and labeled themselves incest survivors.

In the first chapter Bass and Davis wrote, "The long-term effects of child sexual abuse can be so pervasive that it's sometimes hard to pinpoint exactly how the abuse affected you. It permeates everything: your sense of self, your intimate relationships, your sexuality, your parenting, your work life, even your sanity. Everywhere you look, you see its effects." By addressing female readers as "you," the authors automatically drew them in, presuming that they had indeed been abused. Then Bass and Davis asked a number of questions which, if answered in the affirmative, presumably indicated that someone was a victim of sexual abuse.

Do you feel powerless, like a victim?... Do you feel different from other people?... Do you have trouble feeling motivated? ... Are you afraid to succeed? ... Do you feel you have to be perfect? ... Do you use work or achievements to compensate for inadequate feelings in other parts of your life? ... Do you have trouble expressing your feelings? ... Do you feel confused much of the time? ... Are you prone to depression? ... Do you ever use alcohol, drugs, or food in a way that concerns you? ... Do you feel alienated or lonely?... Do you find that your relationships just don't work out? ... Do you find yourself clinging to the people you care about?... Do you expect the people in your family to change?

The list of questions went on at some length. But other than the most well-adjusted and boring person on earth, who *wouldn't* answer some of these questions affirmatively? Sure, I sometimes feel powerless. I seem to be different from other people, and I often feel awkward and confused. Yes, I work hard. Sometimes I'm lonely and depressed. *Of course* I cling to the people I care about. It is an easy leap from there—if you are vulnerable, which is a good bet if you picked up *The Courage to Heal*—to think "Oh, my gosh! I must be an incest victim!" Bass and Davis reinforced this belief. "If you feel overwhelmed reading this chapter, remember that you have already lived through the hardest part—the abuse itself. You have survived against formidable odds." It's hard not to admire the way the authors subtly transformed the reader. Not only are you a secret incest victim, but a Survivor, a hero.

Their next chapter, "Coping," reinforced this first lesson in victimhood and Survivorship. "Coping is what you did to survive the trauma of being sexually abused," Bass and Davis assured the reader. Such management skills could include just about anything. "You may have become a superachiever, excelling in school and taking care of your brothers and sisters at home. You may have forgotten what happened to you." Other coping skills include minimizing and rationalizing the abuse, or denying that it happened. Although the authors didn't use the word "dissociation," they described how abused children sometimes "actually leave their bodies and watch the abuse as if from a great distance." Other coping devices include mental illness, suicide attempts, or addictions.

Bass and Davis identified another more widely hailed coping mechanism: eating disorders. If you are overweight, it's because you were sexually abused and you're protecting yourself, rendering yourself unattractive. The same logic applies to anorexia: "If [incest survivors] don't grow breasts, develop full hips, become curvy, they won't be attractive." On the other hand, bulimia was interpreted quite literally as a way of throwing up the past. "As children, many survivors had fingers, penises, and objects shoved into their body openings. You may have had a penis shoved into your mouth. You may have gagged or vomited."

In short, there was hardly a human characteristic or problem that would not suffice to prove that you were abused or that you are coping. Even denying abuse was proof that it happened.

Having thus prepared the reader, convincing her that she was probably abused, Bass and Davis described "The Decision to Heal" and "The Emergency Stage." It is evident from an introductory quotation that "healing" is pretty scary stuff. "If you enter into healing, be prepared to lose everything," this Survivor advised. "Healing is a ravaging force.... It rips to shreds the structures and foundations I built in weakness and ignorance." If this is healing, then some people might prefer to remain ill.

Yet the warning was necessary, because the authors quite clearly wanted their readers to embark on a very painful journey. Only when all their fundamental assumptions were destroyed, when their family relationships lay in ruins, would they develop their new identity as Survivors.

The quotes from women going through this process are revealing, horrifying, and sad:

- It was hard to make that leap .... I was giving up a person [myself] who was really a very viable, powerful, self-reliant human being.... Into what void would I be thrown if I let go of this stuff? I felt like a raw muscle walking around for a long time.

- For a long time, I felt like a victim of the process.... The whole thing felt out of my control, like being swept up in a hurricane.

- Breaking through my own denial, and trying to fit the new reality into the shattered framework of the old, was enough to catapult me into total crisis. I felt my whole foundation had been stolen from me. If this could have happened and I could have forgotten it, then every assumption I had about life and my place in it was thrown up for question.

- I just lost it completely. I wasn't eating. I wasn't sleeping.... I had terrible nightmares about my father. I was having all kinds of fantasies.... Physically, I was a mess. I had crabs. I hadn't bathed in a month. I was afraid of the shower.

Bass and Davis admitted that the process they recommend as necessary *often* destroys marriages and intimate relationships. "It can even be hard to sleep, to eat, or simply to stop crying." They quoted another Survivor with approval: "You can't go back. You can't unremember," she said, then added wistfully, "I spent so many years not hurting at all." In other words, "healing" such as this was likely to turn a basically happy life into a painful one. The authors justified this by asserting that "deciding to actively heal is terrifying because it means opening up to hope."

During this "emergency state," which Bass and Davis said could last for years, Survivors often experience "a profound sense of disorientation." They cut off relations with everyone except other Survivors, who understand what they are going through, and their therapists. "I dropped everything else in my life," wrote one woman. "It was like there were large six-foot-high letters in my living room every day when I woke up: INCEST!" Another explained why she dropped all of her old friends: "I had no energy to deal with other people or their problems.... The people I used to call up and say, 'Hi. Let's go roller skating,' I didn't bother to call any more." Instead, the all-wise therapist became the center of their lives, a replacement for the lost father and mother: "The only thing that saved me when I felt totally cut off from everything was that I had my therapist's phone number written many places, all over my house," wrote one Survivor.

Bass and Davis got to the heart of the matter in "Remembering," a chapter in which they described what repressed memories feel and look like. "Often the memories are vague and dreamlike," they explained. They will appear disjointed, in fragments. "You may not know exactly when the abuse began, how old you were, or when and why it stopped." They described flashbacks as very brief moments of reliving the abuse, like a slide show in which you get only the briefest glimpse and must guess the progression of what comes before and after.

Bass and Davis recommended "regression," carefully avoiding the term *hypnosis,* which might scare some people. They quoted a Survivor who began to talk in "a five-year-old's voice, using words and concepts that a five-year-old might use." Various stimuli can "trigger" a memory, according to the authors—a touch, smell or sound. Your nightmares can provide clues to the abuse. Or, they said, "The body remembers what the mind chooses to forget," adding that "memories are stored in our bodies, and it is possible to physically re-experience the terror of the abuse." Consequently, if you have pelvic pains, feel that you are suffocating and can't breathe, or manifest other bodily complaints, they may be memories.

Reading books such as *The Courage to Heal,* or watching television talk shows in which Survivors recount their stories, helped to produce memories, according to Bass and Davis. "As the media focus on sexual abuse has increased, more and more women have had their memories triggered." A strong reaction to someone else's story was a give-away. "Often women become very uncomfortable (nauseated, dizzy, unable to concentrate, emotional) when they hear another survivor's story and realize that what's being described happened to them too."

Life situations could affect the timing of recovered memories, according to the authors. The birth of a child, a divorce, a father's death, or other transitions could help bring the material to consciousness. Sometimes when your child reached the same age that you were at the time of the abuse, the memories would be triggered.

Regardless of how the memories surfaced, though, Bass and Davis wrote that it was important to "feel the feelings." Unless you really got into your pain, unless you screamed and yelled and hurt and cried, it wasn't good enough. You weren't really experiencing it all, and it wouldn't get out of your system. "You must feel, even if it sends you reeling." One Survivor put it this way: "These memories are literally stored in my body, and they've got to get out. Otherwise, I'm going to carry them forever."

Even though you must experience all this feeling, however, Bass and Davis explained that the process of reassembling the disparate memory fragments could be intellectually stimulating, "a lot like putting together a jigsaw puzzle or being a detective." They quoted a Survivor: "Part of me felt like I was on the trail of a murder mystery, and I was going to solve it. I really enjoyed following all the clues."

These clues could often, over time, lead to multiple perpetrators. "The more I worked on the abuse," one Survivor explained earnestly, "the more I remembered. First I remembered my brother, and then my grandfather. About six months after that I remembered my father. And then about a year later, I remembered my mother." Eventually, she managed to implicate her entire family "Even though it was traumatic for me to realize that everyone in my family abused me, there was something reassuring about it." But what could possibly be reassuring about this? "My life suddenly made sense," she said. Now she could find a simple explanation for every unhappy feeling she had ever had.

Despite every effort to find these elusive memories—obsessing over every bodily pain, every dream, every emotional twinge—some women, Bass and Davis lament, still couldn't quite dredge up memories of abuse. "If you don't remember your abuse," they consoled readers, "you are not alone. Many women don't have memories, and some never get memories. This doesn't mean they weren't abused." At this point in the book, Bass and Davis had convinced readers that if they had any problems at all, then they were, of course, sexually abused. Just because they didn't remember it—that should be no obstacle. "If you don't have any memory of it," the authors continued, "it can be hard to believe the abuse really happened. You may feel insecure about trusting your intuition and want 'proof' of your abuse." If that happens, just give it some time. "The unconscious has its own way of unfolding that does not always meet your demands or your timetable."

Bass and Davis quoted a woman—"her story is a good model"—who had never retrieved her abuse memories but managed to rationalize that failure. "I obsessed for about a year on trying to remember," this Survivor related. Tired of trying, she thought to herself, "All right, let's act *as if*." So she simply decided to act *as if* she had memories and not worry about it. After all, "I had the symptoms. Every incest group I went to I completely empathized. It rang bells all the time." When she occasionally worried that perhaps she was accusing her father unjustly, she prompted herself, "Why would I be feeling all this anxiety if something didn't happen?" So, she concluded confidently, "I'm going with the circumstantial evidence, and I'm working on healing myself." She went to incest groups where, when she admitted shamefacedly that she had retrieved no specific scenes, people were still sympathetic.

Having hopefully convinced their readers that they really were sexually abused, Bass and Davis attempted to prevent any backsliding in the chapter, "Believing It Happened." It is inevitable, they wrote, that you will question your memories at first. "Often in the beginning stages, belief in your memories comes and goes." Don't worry, though. "One practical way to validate your abuse is to look at your life. If you see the effects of abuse.... you can trust that your belief is sound." In order to maintain this belief system, the authors recommended attending support groups with other Survivors who will "validate" the memories and reinforce them.

They then related the story of Emily. "When confronted with the abuse, her parents denied everything and her father offered to see a counselor, take a lie detector test, anything, to prove his innocence." What's wrong with that? Plenty. Whenever Emily talked with her parents, she became ill. "The conflict between what she knew inside and what they presented was too great." The solution? Try to sort all of this out with her parents with a good counselor? Try to understand the pain and confusion her father was experiencing, and appreciate his efforts to reconcile? No. "It was only when Emily broke off all communication with her family and established a consistent relationship with a skilled therapist who believed her that she stopped doubting herself and got on with her recovery." Bass and Davis concluded with words worthy of theologians: "Believing doesn't usually happen all at once—it's a gradual awakening."

The next few chapters simply reinforces these familiar lessons. Join a Survivor's group. Rehearse your memories, repeating them, writing them down, making them more real. Cherish those people who support your new belief system, but jettison those who express even the slightest doubt. "There is a weeding out that goes on in relationships," Bass and Davis wrote. "Some people may be threatened. Some will go blank or be shocked. These people may be reminded of their own abuse. . . . Some people will be horrified. Some may not even believe you initially. Some may be incredibly rude." For many relatives who did not react in the precisely prescribed manner, reading this passage explained why they were cut off even though they were not accused themselves, and even though they reacted with horror and empathy. They were simply "weeded out."

Following pop guru John Bradshaw, Bass and Davis spent another chapter encouraging women to contact their wounded, innocent "child within," to reconnect with "her softness, her *sense* of trust and wonder." Essentially, this entailed a literal regression to childhood in which adult women decorated whole rooms as though for a five-year-old. "I'm going to build a tent out of bed sheets and we'll [*referring to herself and her inner child*] sit inside and read stories by flashlight," one Survivor wrote. "There will be glow-in-the-dark stars on the tent ceiling too. Oh, I love being little!" In its most extreme form, the search for "inner children" sometimes led to a belief in multiple personalities, as we shall see later.

After a brief chapter on mourning the loss of "the fantasy that your childhood was happy," Bass and Davis cut to the heart of the therapy. In the chapter "Anger—The Backbone of Healing," they whipped women into a towering rage against their supposed perpetrators. "Anger doesn't have to be suppressed or destructive," they wrote. "It can be both a healthy response to violation and a transformative, powerful energy." If women couldn't "get in touch" with their anger, Bass and Davis suggested working themselves into it. "A little like priming the pump, you can do things that will get your anger started. Then, once you get the hang of it, it'll begin to flow on its own." To get going, women should imagine an innocent child being raped, or read Survivor anthologies. Listen to other people's stories. "You can hear their fury and be incited." Sometimes, just "physically taking an angry stance, making menacing gestures and facial expressions" will prompt the proper mood. "Therapy and support groups can be ideal places for stirring up anger." Similarly, you could break old dishes, pound on your bed with a tennis racket, or just scream a lot.

Bass and Davis considered it therapeutic to fantasize castrating or murdering the perpetrator, but they warned that carrying out such acts could land you in jail. Better to sue the bastard. "Another woman," they added helpfully, "abused by her grandfather, went to his deathbed and, in front of all the other relatives, angrily confronted him right there in the hospital."

Mothers were not exempted from this flood of rage. Only if they were lucky enough to have been divorced early on, or if they completely believed the accusing daughter and separated then, were they likely to escape blame. "You do have a right to be angry at your mother," Bass and Davis wrote. "Mothers of abused children are often fearful, self-protective and denying." Consequently, "if your mother didn't protect you, looked the other way, set you up, or blamed you, you are inevitably carrying some feelings of anger." Unless your mother *also* abused you, the authors urged some moderation. "You must not direct your anger toward her. The abuser deserves his share." Parceling out rage shouldn't be the problem, though. "As you allow yourself to know the genuine depth and range of your anger, you will find there's enough to go around."□

Once their Survivors were properly enraged, Bass and Davis encouraged them to confront their abusers, though they added a disclaimer that no one should feel unduly pressured into a confrontation. There were numerous reasons for confronting—to make the perpetrator suffer, to extract revenge, to break the silence, or to demand money. "When you confront the abuser or disclose your abuse, you are deciding to give up the illusions. . . . You must be willing to relinquish the idea that your family has your best interests at heart."

They encouraged thorough preparation before such a confrontation, starting with friends and siblings who were "most likely to be allies." Then, "you set the boundaries, you pick the timing, you pick the turf. . . . You can role-play possible scenarios in therapy or with supportive friends. Practice saying the things you want to say and responding to different reactions. You can write out the things you want to get across and memorize the essential points." The confrontation could take place in person, at a therapy session, or through a letter or phone call. One Survivor stood in the receiving line at her older brother's wedding and passed out sealed envelopes containing her accusations against him. Whatever method you choose, Bass and Davis said, make it a surgical strike. "Go in, say what you need to say, and get out. Make it quick."

It wasn't necessary to wait until you had really clear memories. "If your memories of the abuse are still fuzzy," however, "it is important to realize that you may be grilled for details." One Survivor's aunt, for instance, had the audacity to suggest in a letter: "These are very serious charges and you had better present some factual evidence to back it up." Do not be dismayed by such unreasonable demands. "You are not responsible for proving that you were abused."

If you decided not to confront ("Your parents may be paying your tuition at school, and you can't yet afford to be economically self-sufficient"), you could

---

*   As Carol Tavris convincingly documented in her book, *Anger: The Misunderstood Emotion* (1982), "getting in touch with your anger" and releasing it is not necessarily a constructive or therapeutic activity. Despite the conventional psychological wisdom that regards anger as some sort of internal object in need of venting, Tavris pointed out that the emotion "is as much a political matter as a biological one." Often, ventilating our rage does not provide a catharsis. It simply makes us more angry. Tavris suggested an alternative remedy: developing a sense of humor.

still satisfy your hatred in other ways. Write a nasty letter but don't mail it unless you decide to. "Do not be reasonable .... Be as angry and hurt and blunt as you want." Draw a picture of your abuse and publish it in a Survivor newsletter. Burn a photo of your father. Get a friend to act out the perpetrator role in a psychodrama, while you confront him.

Finally, Bass and Davis dealt with the delicate topic of forgiveness, of which they clearly disapproved. "You may never reach an attitude of forgiveness, and that's perfectly all right.... Why should you? First they steal everything else from you and then they want forgiveness too? Let them get their own. You've given them enough." Some Christian Survivors may have been brainwashed by church sermons, but they shouldn't worry. "If there is such a thing as divine forgiveness, it's God's job, not yours."

Bass and Davis also counseled counselors. "Believe the survivor," they admonished. "You must believe that your client was sexually abused, even if she sometimes doubts it herself. Doubting is part of the process of coming to terms with abuse. Your client needs you to stay steady in the belief that she was abused." This was part of the necessary validation. "If a client is unsure that she was abused but thinks she might have been, work as though she was." Remember, "no one fantasizes abuse." The therapist must act as a "witness." "Validate anger as a sane, healthy response." If the Survivor wished to confront her abuser, "help her to prepare thoroughly. And if possible, be available to facilitate confrontations." Above all, Bass and Davis stressed one important commandment: "Be willing to believe the unbelievable."

The Courage to Heal continued for over 500 pages, finally winding down with case studies of "Courageous Women" and, in the 1992 edition, a lengthy "Resource Guide" with over 600 books, support groups, organizations, newsletters and audiovisuals on incest, ritual abuse cults, meditation, outdoor programs for Survivors, multiple personalities, male survivors, abuse by siblings. There's even a board game, "Survivor's Journey." Only in America could an entire Incest Survivor industry have sprung up so quickly to relieve frightened, angry women—and their insurance companies—of their money.

There was even a section telling women how to order vibrators and other sex toys. Throughout *The Courage to Heal* were selections that border on pornography—all of it lesbian or masturbatory. "Slowly I spread my legs, opening myself up, positioning myself under the stream of water which falls down, caressing my vulva. I feel the heat, the fire of life, creep into my solar plexus, spreading warmly into my thighs and buttocks." Or, "My palms engulf your breasts, your fingernails cruise across my belly. We rock until you lie on top of me. You press your knee against my cunt, whisper I want you Baby."[*]

The Courage to Heal strongly encouraged women to become lesbians as part of the politically correct expression of Survivorship. With very few exceptions, the examples of relationships given in the text involved only women. References to healthy sex with men were few and far between. "If you were abused by a man, you may find male genitals scary or repulsive," wrote Bass and Davis, both lesbians themselves. Later, the authors used the same kind of suggestive approach to lesbianism as they did with repressed memories. "If you think you might be a lesbian but the idea scares or disturbs you, what you're feeling is natural. It's common to have doubts and questions in the coming-out process. Try reading about lesbians who are comfortable with themselves. Read coming-out stories." Besides, the authors explained, there's a lot more to being a lesbian than mere sex. It's a way of life. "There's music, art, politics. There's a culture, a supportive community. There's an emotional, philosophical, and spiritual connection to women."

Of course, there's nothing wrong with masturbation or sex between women. Nonetheless, the message conveyed by *The Courage to Heal* was, at best, confusing. Lesbian poet Adrienne Rich once wrote an essay complaining about "compulsory heterosexuality." That was certainly a valid grievance. But by the late 1980s many women must have felt that it was virtually compulsory to become a lesbian in order to become a true Survivor. Not only that, but there was an implication that a history of sexual abuse *produces* this sexual orientation, thereby stigmatizing it as somehow not a free choice or genetic predisposition, but one more coping mechanism, a reaction to trauma. It was precisely this sort of thinking that gay men and women had fought for years. Lesbianism as a sexual orientation, or even as a choice, is fine—but as a creed that encourages a generalized hatred of men and a search for repressed memories of abuse, it is disturbing.

Other Survivor Literature

The Courage to Heal spawned a seemingly endless stream of books, articles, newsletters, organizations, and TV movies about repressed memories of sexual abuse—how to extract them, how to cope with them, how to get back at the perpetrators. They repeat the same injunctions to contact inner children, vent rage, squelch doubts, and terminate family relationships. The titles themselves told quite a story—*Toxic Parents* by Susan Forward (1989) or *Divorcing a Parent* by Beverly Engel (1990). I will only skim some of the more important and widely quoted Survivor books here.

Secret Survivors, by E. Sue Blume (1990), was famed primarily for its "Incest

---

* In another surprising passage, Bass and Davis revealed that "many [Survivors] masturbate while reading incest literature."

Survivors' Aftereffects Checklist," which included 34 items, many quite common, such as a "pattern of ambivalent or intensely conflictive relationships," depression, phobias, anger issues, "feeling crazy, feeling different," low self-esteem, eating disorders, fear of the dark, swallowing or gagging sensitivity, or even wearing too many baggy clothes. Some "aftereffects," such as "desire to change one's name" or "humorlessness or extreme solemnity," seemed to be *products* of therapy or reading too many Incest Survivor books rather than symptoms. Others appeared to include the entire population, such as number 17: "High risk taking ('daring the fates'); inability to take risks." That pretty much covered every contingency. And, of course, there's number 26, the one sure symptom of repressed memories: "Denial, no awareness at all."

It was hardly surprising, then, that Blume wrote, "At any given time, *more than three quarters of my clients* are women who were molested in childhood by someone they knew." Of course, most of them didn't realize they were Survivors until Blume convinced them. "Many, if not most, incest survivors *do not know* that the abuse has even occurred!" She added that "most survivors need many years, and often many therapists, before they can face the truths of their past." Blume then began to rope in her reader. "The incest survivor may appear to be ... successful, talented, appealing, even happy. Yet underneath, she may feel as if she were rotting.... If you are reading this and looking at your own life, you may be experiencing uneasiness, even sudden fear. You may suddenly begin to cry. The intensity of your reaction may confuse you, especially if it is accompanied by a strong denial—'No! This couldn't have happened to *me!*'" Naturally, Blume asserted that such a reaction proved that the reader was, indeed, abused.

According to Blume, almost any woman could qualify as an incest victim, even without dragging up memories of fondling, forced oral sex, or intercourse. "Must incest involve intercourse?" she asked. "Must incest be overtly genital? Must it involve touch at all? The answer was no." She elaborated: "There are many other ways that the child's space or senses can be sexually violated. Incest can occur through words, sounds, or even exposure of the child to sights or acts that are sexual but do not involve her."

In 1989, the year before *The Courage to Heal* became widely available in the U.K., Scottish rape crisis counselors Liz Hall and Siobhan Lloyd published the British equivalent, *Surviving Child Sexual Abuse: A Handbook for Helping Women Challenge Their Past*. Their influential book repeated all of the stereotypical beliefs about repressed memories and how to unearth them. Their list of symptoms included "headaches, stomach problems, chronic backache, psychosomatic pains and illness, cystitis, asthma and eczema," as well as epilepsy, insomnia, nightmares, eating disorders, and "over-positive descriptions of childhood." Many children who were sexually abused learned to deal with the abuse "by denying its reality," they asserted, "by dissociating themselves from it or by repressing it partially or completely." Nor is this uncommon. "Such total amnesia frequently occurs though there are often clues that something unpleasant has happened in a woman's childhood."

Hall and Lloyd warned that emerging abuse memories might be "vague and without much detail" at first, but that counselors must encourage them and must themselves *believe the memories.* They should ask potential Survivors questions such as, "You have been describing a number of difficulties that are often found in women who report that they were sexually abused as children. I wonder if this has ever happened to you?" Then, memories should be elicited using journals, artwork, or oral disclosure. It helps to tell the woman that "everyone has a child within her. A woman should be reassured that 'her' child was abused and needs to tell a safe and trusted adult." When the client expresses doubts about the reality of such memories, she should be reassured that "the main issue is that this memory/thought is bothering her" and that "only by breaking the silence about her memories will they lose some of their pain." The authors recommend incest survivor groups as good places to discover and process new memories.

Other important Commonwealth Survivor books included:

Rescuing the "Inner Child": Therapy for Adults Sexually Abused as Children, by Penny Parks (U.K., 1990). Parks was an American incest Survivor who played a key role in importing recovered memories and inner child work into the United Kingdom.

Breaking Through: No Longer a Victim of Child Abuse, by Cathy Ann Matthews (Australia, 1990). This was an expanded version of the 1986 book, *No Longer a Victim,* an Australian account of recovered memory.

Dance With the Devil, by Audrey Harper, with Harry Pugh (U.K., 1990). A born-again evangelical Christian, Harper related her recovered memories of serving as a "brood mare" in a Satanic cult. The first British book on Satanic Survivorship, this had enormous influence.

Seven for a Secret: Healing the Wounds of Sexual Abuse in Childhood, by Tracy Hansen (U.K., 1991). This was a "Christian" book about how to retrieve sex abuse memories.

Children for the Devil: Ritual Abuse and Satanic Crime, by Tim Tate (UK, 1991). This controversial book was withdrawn by the publisher following legal action but continued to influence social workers looking for supposed ritual abuse cases. Tim Tate was largely responsible for an influential 1989 television program on Satanic abuse.

The Filthy Lie: Discovering and Recovering from Childhood Abuse, by Hellmut Karle

(UK, 1992). A British case history by a respected psychologist, this book gave a boost to recovered memories and multiple personality disorder (MPD).

Surviving Secrets, by Moira Walker (UK, 1992). Walker was a Leicester psychologist and a leading trainer among health professionals. This book espoused belief in recovered memories and ritual abuse.

Emotional Incest

That broad definition of incest became part of the Survivor dogma. If your father ever walked around naked, if he ever discussed his own sex life with you, if he walked into your bedroom without knocking, if he looked at you in what you considered a lustful manner, if he commented on your growing breasts, if he hugged you a little too long, if you overheard him making love—that was incest. In fact, even if he did none of those things, he may simply have loved you too much, for the wrong reasons. "To the casual observer," wrote Patricia Love in *The Emotional Incest Syndrome* (1990), "the parents may appear loving and devoted. They may spend a great deal of time with their children and lavish them with praise and material gifts. But in the final analysis, their love is not a nurturing, giving love—it's an unconscious ploy to satisfy their own unmet needs."

When Love wrote about "emotional incest," she was not simply employing a metaphor. She believed that she was identifying another form of real incest, which Kenneth Adams called "covert incest" in his similar book, *Silently Seduced* (1991). "These are strong words, I know," wrote Love, "but I use them advisedly. Just as children are powerless against a parent's sexual advances, they are powerless against an emotionally invasive parent." She described Gwen, a well-educated client who at first saw no problem with her father. "All she saw was what she had gained from the relationship—praise and affection, extra privileges, patient tutoring, and shared confidences."

Systematically, therapist Love destroyed that love, twisting it into confusion and then hatred. "The difficult task I faced in the coming weeks was to help Gwen see the negative consequences of this excessive devotion. It would be unsettling for her to see how she had been harmed by her relationship with her father, but confronting this fact would give her insight into her puzzling emotional problems."

Like so many of these books, Love's began with a checklist to see whether you were a "Chosen Child," a victim of emotional incest. If you answered "yes" to three or more, that means you qualified:

1. I was the source of emotional support for one of my parents.

2. I felt closer to one parent than the other.

3. I got the impression a parent did not want me to marry or move far away from home.

4. Any potential boyfriend or girlfriend was never "good enough" for one of my parents.

5. I felt I had to hold back my own needs to protect a parent.

6. I felt responsible for my parents' happiness.

7. I sometimes felt invaded by a parent.

8. One of my parents had unrealistic expectations of me.

9. One of my parents was preoccupied with drugs/alcohol, work, outside interest, or another sibling.

10. One of my parents was like my best friend.

Almost anyone would identify with three or more of those statements. Being human, most parents are sometimes unhappy and let their children know it, seeking emotional support from them.* It is almost inevitable that a child will, at times, feel closer to one parent than another. Most parents aren't ecstatic at the thought of their offspring moving far away, just as they may be critical of the potential mate a child brings home. In the crucible of the nuclear family, every child sometimes feel invaded. I don't know of any parent in the world who doesn't have "unrealistic expectations." The list of preoccupations—drugs, alcohol, work, outside interest, another sibling—would qualify almost anybody. And is it *bad* for a parent to be a best friend as well?

There was, of course, much that was true in these books. In many marriages or divorces, a father or mother may rely much too heavily on children for emotional support. In such situations, children can feel acute responsibility beyond their years. While this phenomenon is unfortunate, however, it is fairly normal and widespread, and it is *not* incest, emotional or otherwise.

These books were as insidious as *The Courage to Heal* and its ilk. To be a victim of "emotional incest," you didn't have to drag up any new memories. As recovered-memory therapist Renee Fredrickson noted, one moment a client thought of her extended family as "a hardworking, family-oriented group of people that she grew up admiring, loving, and laughing with." But then "the kaleidoscope shifted, and she suddenly saw an incest family, complete with abusers, alcoholics, and emotionally damaged people."

In other words, you simply had to shift your perception of always-remembered

---

* Many parents face particular difficulties along these lines in the wake of a divorce, as Judith Wallerstein pointed out in her landmark 1989 book, *Second Chances: Men, Women, and Children a Decade After Divorce.* "When a marriage breaks down," she wrote, "most men and women experience a diminished capacity to parent. They give less time, provide less discipline, and are less sensitive to their children, being caught up in the personal maelstrom of divorce and its aftermath. Many parents are temporarily unable to separate their children's needs from their own." Wallerstein also noted that "many children assume responsibilities well beyond their years as they undertake to psychologically advise and physically nurture a troubled parent."

childhood events such as back rubs, games of chase, or ghost stories, turning them into evidence of long-lasting abuse. Even the positive aspects of parenting—love, devotion, praise, pride, honesty, emotional support, treating children as real individuals instead of minor dependents—were taken as evidence of abuse by Patricia Love. At least Love didn't encourage readers to cut off all relationship with their parents. "You don't have to like your parents; you don't have to agree with them on important issues; you don't have to have similar tastes or values. All you need to do is see them and accept them for who they are." That's the sort of common sense that children have to re-learn every generation. Parents are not perfect.

Unfortunately, Kenneth Adams, in *Silently Seduced*, was more blaming.[*] He encouraged the same sort of rage, augmented by support groups, as did Ellen Bass and Laura Davis. "Let go of your idealized image of the seductive parent," he urged. "Acknowledge that the attention you received was violating and abandoning." He wanted clients to "set boundaries and separate" from parents. "If you feel guilty, which is likely, remind yourself it is not your job to be your parent's spouse. Expecting it to be your job is a violation and abusive. You also may need to have no contact at all with this parent for a while." At least Adams saw reconciliation as a possibility. "In time as you work through these feelings and set appropriate boundaries, your feelings of love and compassion for your parent may return." Forgiveness might be in order, he said, but "it is important that you not forgive too soon."

Liberal parents of the Baby Boom generation may have been particularly susceptible to charges of emotional or sexual abuse of their children. In 1983, Ellen Bass herself wrote the following about the parenting of her daughter Sara:

> When she was a toddler and her father or I were undressed, drying off from a shower or putting our clothes on in the morning, she would sometimes comment on our genitals, saying "vagina" and patting my vagina, or "penis" and touching her father's penis. We would say, "Yes, that's my vagina," or "Yes, that's my penis," let her pat for a moment, and continue drying or dressing. I consider this healthy. She is curious about the world, and genitals are part of it.

Most people would find that scenario somewhat disturbing. In interactions between adults and children, touching, let alone "patting," of genitals is inappropriate, at least in our culture.[**] But the larger view that Bass expressed at that time

---

[*]   Adams' book offered a grab-bag of Recovery Movement clichés. "Covert incest" led to addictions, and one could become addicted to anything." It involved "the murder of their souls." One of his clients made the triumphant progression from covert incest to recovering repressed memories that were "validated through her dreams."

[**]   In some cultures, it is considered normal for children to touch their parents' genitals or *vice versa.* In various cultures in the past (Peru, Egypt, Persia), outright incest was even sanctioned. According to a 1992 article by

was reasonable—that the human body was natural and wonderful, that children should be comfortable with their bodies, and that occasional nudity was not a big deal. By the late 1980s, however, such attitudes were interpreted in retrospect by Bass's followers as incest, emotional or otherwise.

Men Can Be Survivors, Too

"Emotional incest" was more of an equal-opportunity accusation than the physical variety. Men could complain about how their mothers smothered them with invasive affection just as often as women could identify breached boundaries.

One of the constructive results of the Survivor Movement was the recognition that boys, too, have been subjected to widespread sexual abuse for centuries. Because of cultural influences in our society, boys and men are less likely to come forward with their stories. While the true incidence of abuse of boys was unquestionably higher than anyone conceived until recent years, however, the search for repressed memories was just as hazardous for men as for women.

In *Victims No Longer* (1988), Mike Lew provided the male equivalent to *The Courage to Heal*, with Ellen Bass writing the foreword. "When clients tell me they have no recollection of whole pieces of their childhood," therapist Lew commented, "I assume the likelihood of some sort of abuse." Many of his clients arrived at his doorstep already intent on recovering memories. "If only I knew for certain," they told him, "then I could deal with it. It's the uncertainty that's so hard." Although Lew cautioned them that simply retrieving the memories might not make them completely well, he gladly helped clients along, suggesting "hypnosis, psychodrama, guided imagery, psychoanalysis, meditation, massage, or any other combination of mind and body work."

Like their female counterparts, male Survivors had to give up the myth of a happy childhood. "The adult survivor may remember his childhood as having been perfect," Lew wrote. "He may paint over the grim details with softer colors. When a client presents 'too perfect' a picture of childhood, I find that it is usually a good idea to look further." Lew gave examples of how various men's memories were first triggered. "I was having a massage," one Survivor wrote, "and when he had me turn over onto my stomach I began to shake uncontrollably." Such catalysts might result in clear memories or simply "the feeling that something happened."

The rest is all quite familiar to anyone who read *The Courage to Heal*. Lew encouraged confrontation after much rehearsal. "If you choose to provide advance notice, you will need to consider how much information you are going

---

anthropologist Claudia Konker, "In a variety of contemporary cultures it appears that adults may affectionately sniff, kiss, blow upon, fondle, and praise the genitals of young male and female children." But not one has documented what effect such ministrations have upon the children's development or attitude toward sex.

to supply about the subject of the meeting. Remember, this confrontation is *for your benefit alone.*" Therefore, you need to manipulate the situation in your favor. "This isn't a debate or a jury trial. There is no need to argue."

Lew even provided a model accusatory letter from Ivan, complete with memories "from my birth to age four-and-a-half," in which the sadistic mother cut the child with a knife This was so scary that Ivan forgot it completely for decades. "You may have done the same," he confidently informed his mother. "Whatever you've chosen to do with your memories, I can't stand mine anymore. This really happened. To me. So, if you draw a blank, reach back and try to see it." Ivan sent copies of the letter to his uncle, brother, father, therapist, minister, and selected friends.

Like Ellen Bass and Laura Davis, Mike Lew spawned imitators. In 1990, for instance, Mic Hunter published *Abused Boys: The Neglected Victims of Sexual Abuse,* in which he described the familiar process of repression, dissociation, and recovery. The most compelling portions of the book, however, were the personal testimonials at the end. "My name is Greg, and I am a recovering incest victim," one began, in imitation of an Alcoholics Anonymous meeting. "I am writing my story to say that what happened to me was real, my feelings are valid." He sought counseling when he was depressed because of a job demotion. "My memories of the incest only started to surface after I had been in therapy for a while. Even now my memories are few and sketchy."

Sonny Hall had been in therapy for 14 years, but "it is only in the last year that I have known that I am recovering from incest." Allen, another Survivor, lay on his bed one night trying to find his memories. "I laid there trying to listen to my body, my spirit." He worked himself up into a panicky state until he began gagging. "It was then I knew the awful truth: I was getting in touch with recalling the abuse I had suffered at my father's hands." His father, he thought, had stuck his finger in his rectum while choking him. "So many questions answered: why I hated turtleneck sweaters, neckties; anything on my throat brought me back at some level to my father choking me."

Some of the stories in *Abused Boys* revealed more about the therapeutic climate than about abuse. "All my girlfriends eventually told me about how they had been sexually abused as children," Jim revealed. When he himself went to therapy, his counselor pounced on an apparently normal family story, saying, "That sounds like sexual abuse to me." In subsequent sessions, the therapist would identify yet another example of sexual abuse that had somehow eluded Jim.

Another self-described Survivor, Kent, first found a male therapist who seduced him sexually, then one who convinced him that his father had anally raped him.

One story, however, did not mention repressed memories and was probably a true account. Unlike the others, it did not involve mystical, fragmentary memories from early childhood. When he was 16, Daniel's new stepmother seduced him. "I was ecstatic, guilty, frightened, and ashamed. I fell in love with her."

A Textbook for Memory Invention

While *The Courage to Heal* may have been the bible of the Incest Survivor movement, *Repressed Memories: A Journey to Recovery from Sexual Abuse* (1992), by clinical psychologist Renee Fredrickson, was its lethal textbook. If you wanted to produce grotesque memories of abuse that never occurred—and you had a strong stomach—this was the book for you.

"Denial is overcome only by patient growth in the opposite direction," Fredrickson stated. "In reading this book, whenever you find yourself worrying—'What if I'm wrong?'—try to always ask yourself the opposite question—'What if I'm right?"

Fredrickson related the story of Carolyn, who gradually came to believe that her father had molested her. "Her anger and grief were enormous. For months she suffered emotionally, physically, and spiritually. She had crying jags, eating binges, suicidal feelings, and bouts of depression." Fredrickson unquestioningly assumed that all of these were symptoms of abuse rather than results of therapy. "I never felt like my problems were connected to my past," Carolyn told her. "To be honest, they still don't seem related."

Another patient exclaimed during a session: "But I feel like I'm just making this up!" Fredrickson ignored her concern. "I urged her to continue, explaining that truth or fantasy is not of concern at the beginning of memory retrieval work."

Fredrickson provided the now familiar "symptoms" of abuse—"failed relationships, depression, anxiety, addictions, career struggles, and eating disorders," adding that "the list is as varied as the human spirit"—or imagination. "Let yourself know what the most hopeless or shameful problem in your life is," she advised. "Try saying to yourself three or four times a day for one week, 'I believe this problem is about my repressed memories of abuse.' After a week, write down or talk over with a friend how you see the problem now. Speculate on how it may relate to how you were abused." You didn't have to be mentally ill or overtly disturbed to have been sexually abused. "Most people who have repressed memories are not odd or weird. As a matter of fact, most are models of normalcy. This form of amnesia lurks in the background of millions of ordinary, high-functioning Americans."

Members of the family system all fit neatly into three categories, according to Fredrickson: offender, denier, or victim. "Sexual abuse is always intergenerational," she flatly stated, "and everyone in a sexually abusive system takes one of these roles." Noting that "even the most apparently healthy family can have depths of sickness that astound outsiders," she urged the reader to make a list of nuclear and extended family members. "List any problem or dysfunction you know of or suspect.... Err on the side of overstating problems, rather than on the side of denial.... Signify their role and yours using 0 for offender, D for denier, and V for victim."

Fredrickson encouraged women to believe that they were abused as infants by several perpetrators. "How old do you think you were when you were first abused? Write down the very first number that pops into your head, no matter how improbable it seems to you.... Does it seem too young to be true? I assure you it is not." She asserted that "dissociation always occurs during abuse," and that, further, "abusers are usually dissociated during the abuse, too." In other words, not only would the victim forget the abuse, so would the perpetrator — or perpetrators, as the case may be. "Multiple abusers increase the likelihood of memory repression. The sheer number of abusers becomes overwhelming."

Fredrickson primed potential Survivors to become suspicious of any stray feelings they might have. "Bedrooms, bathrooms, basements, and closets are common places where sexual abuse occurs, so be alert to reactions to those places or to objects in them. Ordinary household items that can be vaginally or anally inserted are often used during abuse, like bottles, sticks, or penis-shaped foods or objects." Once such paranoid visions were implanted, almost anything could become evidence or a "trigger" for memories of abuse. Buying a cucumber at the grocery store could engender panic. "Extraordinary fear of dental visits is quite often a signal of oral sexual abuse."

The heart of *Repressed Memories* described specific methods for retrieving abuse memories, including guided imagery, dream work, journal writing, body work, hypnosis, art therapy, and rage work. The author's description of "imagistic memory work"—actually a form of hypnosis—was detailed and revealing. First, under the guidance of a therapist or friend, you seat yourself, close your eyes, and relax, breathing deeply. Try to picture some kind of abuse. "If nothing surfaces, wait a bit, and then give your best guess in answer to the questions [of your guide]. If you feel resistance or skepticism, try to go past it." Afterward, your guide should follow up with questions to "fill in any blanks." You should consider any scene you envisioned as a "freeze-frame photograph" out of sequence. "You want to develop a sequenced slide show, showing the action from beginning to end." At first, "you may be hesitant because you are in a new situation and do not understand what is being asked of you." But don't worry, it will come. It's important to understand that this is an exercise in imagination. "You are not trying to stimulate your recall memories. Instead, you need to let yourself imagine or picture what might have happened to you."

Some dull subjects had a hard time with this process. "Occasionally, you may need a small verbal push to get started. Your guide may suggest some action that seems to arise naturally from the image you are picturing." The guide should always remember to use the present tense, to increase the feeling that this visualization was actually happening right then. As a helpful example, Fredrickson quoted one suggestible subject: "Vera was remembering being tied spread-eagled on a table with her grandfather looming over her, holding a knife in one hand and a live rat in another." Vera picked up the story: "He cuts the rope from around my neck and starts to shove the rat in my mouth. I am squirming, trying to get away, and he says, 'Do you want the rat or me?' Then he puts his penis in my mouth."

After getting the hang of it, visualizing abuse should be a breeze, according to Fredrickson. "Once through the initial pitfalls, sequencing proceeds smoothly for a time. You will be able to freely share your images and awarenesses. Action builds, and you become deeply engaged in the process, curious to find out what your mind will picture." In other words, at this point, the supposed Survivor should become the heroine of her own internal movie. She was fulfilling her therapist's expectations, and she would be praised for reporting abuse—the more gruesome, the better. "The most traumatic act of the abuse," Fredrickson explained, "is usually the act that culminates in the orgasm of the offender. At this point, you are completely dissociated ... and you may say such things as, 'I must be making this up,' or 'I'm just saying what you want me to say.' Repressed memories rarely seem real when they first emerge."

I will not inflict much more of this kind of thing on the reader. Fredrickson interpreted dreams, body memories, hypnosis, and art therapy in the same inimitable fashion. Everything confirmed abuse. If her patients wanted to seek some sort of confirmation, such as pediatric records, they were discouraged: "You can ... become too caught up in seeking external proof rather than internal relief. External proof of repressed memories is elusive, buried under the massive weight of the family's denial system." Like Bass and Davis, Fredrickson said that "you cannot wait until you are doubt-free to disclose to your family.... Once you make the decision to go ahead, the actual disclosure is an empowering experience.... Avoid being tentative about your repressed memories. Do not just tell them; express them as truth. If months or years down the road, you find you are mistaken about details, you can always apologize and set the record straight."

Finally, if your parents steadfastly denied everything, perhaps it's just that they didn't remember it either. "Do not retreat. You may want to suggest that the abuser has repressed all memory of the abuse.... A suggested response might be to look him or her in the eye and say, 'You and I both know that what I am saying is true.'"

Not all self-help authors took such an extreme position. For instance, Wendy Maltz, author of *The Sexual Healing Journey: Guide for Survivors of Sexual Abuse* (1991), didn't think that *forcing* repressed memories was a good idea. "Don't try to force recall," she advised. "Memories will emerge when you are ready to handle them." Unfortunately, such a "moderate" position was in some ways more persuasive than the forceps method advocated by Fredrickson. Simply telling a client that she *may* have memories, and that they *would* come up on their own, was enough to set the obsessive mind-search in gear. Maltz helped it along. "If you feel ready to investigate your memories of sexual abuse, the following exercises may help you."

After telling women to think about their earliest sexual experiences and to pay close attention to sexual dreams and fantasies, Maltz came to the clincher: "Spend time imagining that you were sexually abused, without worrying about accuracy, proving anything, or having your ideas make sense. As you give rein to your imagination, let your intuition guide your thoughts." As they visualize the hypothetical abuse, women should ask themselves what time of day it is, who is there, what sort of touch is happening, what emotions are raised, and the like. "Who would have been likely perpetrators?" she added.

Psychoanalyst Charlotte Krause Prozan explained how she used dream analysis to help her patients recall assumed sexual abuse in her 1993 book, *The Technique of Feminist Psychoanalytic Psychotherapy*. She revealed that she herself was sure she had been abused, even though she couldn't recall it: "I have the utmost confidence in the knowledge of what happened, even without the actual memory, and this personal experience was a great help to me in my work with my own patients who struggled with memories of sexual abuse. The work is like putting together a huge jigsaw puzzle."

The Academics

Thus far, I have primarily cited popular authors. What about the more serious studies by Ph.D. types, with footnotes and four-dollar words? Surely, they did not accept this same oversimplified dogma, did they? Unfortunately, many did, conveying the same concepts as Bass and Fredrickson (herself a Ph.D., actually). Well-known "experts" such as Lenore Terr, Roland Summit, John Briere, Karen Olio, Christine Courtois and many others published almost identical material, though their writing styles were less sensational. The most influential of the academics was Judith Lewis Herman, who helped to promote the concept of repressed memories in the first place. Her magnum opus, *Trauma and Recovery* (1992), garnered glowing reviews. Laura Davis, co-author of *The Courage to Heal*, called Herman's book "a triumph."

Much of *Trauma and Recovery was* an accurate description of post-traumatic stress disorder (PTSD) and a review of literature about trauma in general, from war to the Holocaust to rape. Unfortunately, Herman's book was also polemical and slanted by ideological zeal from the outset. In her introduction, Herman equated repressed individual memories with societal problems: "Denial, repression, and dissociation operate on a social as well as an individual level." Her logic allowed her to equate "vast concentration camps created by tyrants who rule nations" to "small, hidden concentration camps created by tyrants who rule their homes." In some cases, this equivalency may hold true, but there is a fundamental distinction. No one completely forgot the Holocaust, though some neo-Nazi revisionists attempted to write it out of history. Yet Herman assumed that millions of women had managed to erase all conscious memory of abuse from their minds.

There was a stock answer to this observation. The context, Herman said, was all important. Because prisoners lived in Dachau or Auschwitz continuously, the experience was impossible to forget. But a child, terrorized by Daddy every night, had to get up every morning to a make-believe world of a smiling father presiding over the middle-class breakfast table. She could not handle this enormous disparity, so she repressed the memories of abuse.

In her ninth chapter, "Remembrance and Mourning," Herman repeated some by-now familiar concepts. Traumatic memories would return in fragments, like "a series of still snapshots or a silent movie." The task in therapy was to "provide the music and words," with the therapist playing the role of "witness and ally, in whose presence the survivor could speak of the unspeakable." Unlike our usual concept of a neutral counselor, Herman emphasized that "the moral stance of the therapist is … of enormous importance. It is not enough for the therapist to be 'neutral' or 'nonjudgmental'." Instead, the professional must "affirm a position of moral solidarity with the survivor."

Even though the initial memories may seem unreal, the therapist must help to "reconstruct the traumatic event as a recitation of fact. Out of the fragmented components of frozen imagery and sensation, patient and therapist slowly reassembled an organized, detailed, verbal account, oriented in time and historical context." Herman approvingly quoted a fellow counselor: "We have them reel it off in great detail, as though they were watching a movie, and with all the senses included. We ask them what they are seeing, what they are hearing, what they are smelling." At the same time, Herman encouraged her clients to *feel* their violation and rage. "The recitation of facts without the accompanying emotions is a sterile exercise." She recommended "flooding" sessions in which "the patient narrates a script aloud to the therapist, in the present tense, while the therapist encourages him to express his feelings as fully as possible."

The therapist also "facilitates naming and the use of language." In other words, if you *called* something abuse, if you learned the proper jargon—repression, dissociation—you were halfway there on the journey to a new worldview. Herman quoted a Survivor's advice: "Keep encouraging people to talk even if it's very painful to watch them. It takes a long time to believe. The more I talk about it, the more I have confidence that it happened, the more I can integrate it."

Even with such rehearsal, "both patient and therapist must develop tolerance for some degree of uncertainty, even regarding the basic facts of the story. In the course of reconstruction, the story may change as missing pieces are recovered." Everyone must learn to "live with ambiguity." Herman gave the example of Paul, a 23-year-old who described his abuse in a pedophilic sex ring to an excited female therapist. "Paul suddenly announced that he had fabricated the entire story." He threatened to quit therapy unless she believed him, but the wily therapist managed to bring Paul around. "I can't pretend to know what happened," she told him. "I do know that it is important to understand your story fully, and we don't understand it yet. I think we should keep an open mind until we do." Eventually, Paul came to believe that "his recantation was a last-ditch attempt to maintain his loyalty to his abusers."

Several people believed that Judith Herman was really quite reasonable, since she warned in one brief paragraph that "therapists have been known to tell patients, merely on the basis of a suggestive history or 'symptom profile,' that they definitely have had a traumatic experienc…. In some cases patients with only vague, nonspecific symptoms have been informed after a single consultation that they have undoubtedly been the victims of a Satanic cult." While such cautionary words were laudable, the rest of Herman's advice clearly urged therapists to search for repressed memories—just wait until the third or fourth session before validating the abuse.

Even in this one cautionary paragraph, Herman went on to say, "The therapist has to remember that she is not a fact-finder and that the reconstruction of the trauma story is not a criminal investigation. Her role is to be an open-minded, compassionate witness, not a detective." Yet lawsuits were in fact built on such cases. Families, lives, careers were destroyed because of what happened in these "open-minded" therapy sessions.

Later, Herman recommended the judicious use of hypnotic age regression, sodium Amytal, psychodrama, group therapy, and dream analysis. Like Bass and Davis, she discouraged forgiveness and encouraged rage, quoting a dialogue from a group therapy session:

Melissa: I'd like to break his knees with a bat.

Laura: He deserves it. I've had fantasies like that.

Margot: Go on. Don't stop now!

Melissa: I'd like to start methodically on one knee and then move on to the next. I chose that because it would make him feel really helpless. Then he'd know how I felt.

In short, one shouldn't worry about whether one's memories are truthful or not, but it is good to react violently to them.

Ritual Abuse and Multiple Personalities

The most extreme claims of repressed memories involved supposed ritual abuse, and they almost invariably led to a diagnosis of multiple personality disorder, otherwise known as MPD, now renamed dissociative identity disorder (DID). First "diagnosed" around the turn of the century *(see Chapter 6)*, multiple personalities were considered rare until the publication of *The Three Faces of Eve* by Thigpen and Cleckley in 1957. Their book told the story of "Eve," in reality Christine Costner Sizemore, who ultimately graduated from 3 to 22 different internal personalities. But it was *Sybil,* published in 1973 and made into a popular movie in 1977, that really spawned the modern crop of multiples and provided the cornerstone for an assumed background of sexual abuse. Sybil came to Dr. Cornelia Wilbur as a severe anorexic and soon revealed a second side of herself named Peggy. Over time, 16 different entities emerged, all having "split" from the original, allegedly because of horrendous sexual and physical abuse.

With the publication in 1980 of *Michelle Remembers,* already mentioned, the element of Satanic ritual abuse was added, along with the possibility of demonic possession. Also in 1980, psychiatrist Ralph Allison published *Minds in Many Pieces,* in which he described an exorcism of one of his multiple personality patients. The same year, the third edition of the *Diagnostic and Statistical Manual of Mental Disorders (DSM-II1)* first recognized multiple personality disorder as a *bona fide* psychiatric disorder. Because insurance companies will pay only for mental illnesses sanctioned by the *DSM,* multiple personalities suddenly became lucrative and acceptable. The 1980s witnessed a veritable explosion of MPD cases, though many of them were diagnosed by a small cadre of "specialists" including Richard Kluft, Robert Mayer, Bennett Braun, Philip Coons, Eugene Bliss, Colin Ross, Cornelia Wilbur, and Frank Putnam. Curiously, while the majority of therapists are women, most of the MPD specialists were men. Before 1980, there were only 200 or so references to multiple personalities in the professional literature. Since then, over 25,000 people have been diagnosed with the disorder.

While theorists such as Bass and Herman spoke primarily about repression, the MPD specialists preferred to identify "dissociation" as the primary method of forgetting abuse. In their model, the memories never reach normal conscious-

ness and, therefore, are never forcibly pushed down into the subconscious. Instead, the abuse is so awful that the victim's mind cannot survive if it remains
aware. Therefore, the mind splits off, or dissociates, forming alternate personalities to "take" the abuse. Usually, these "alters," as the internal identities were
called, are not aware of the "core personality" or of one another, and the core is
equally amnesic toward its alters.

Surprisingly, many MPD clients appeared to be "high-functioning," seemingly normal individuals who were themselves completely unaware that they harbored multiple alters. Only under hypnosis or through suggestive interviewing
did they reveal themselves to the savvy therapist, who could then question each
personality, calling them forward in turn. The therapists were usually alerted to
the possibility of MPD when their patients reported an inability to remember
whole chunks of their childhood. These cases often progressed in stages. First,
the patient revealed simple repressed memories of abuse, often by a father or
grandfather. Then, hints of far-worse horrors surfaced. Eventually, these patients
remembered ritual group abuse, often involving worship of Satan. In a group
setting, they were subjected to hideous sexual and physical abuse. As part of the
ritual, babies were hacked to death and eaten, blood and urine drunk, feces consumed, and every other conceivable horror experienced. As a flier from Survivors
of Incest Anonymous put it, "the physical component usually includes torture,
at times maiming and disfigurement, and even death. The sexual component of
Ritual Abuse is often violent, purposefully painful, intended to degrade and de-
humanize, and to orient the victim toward sadism."

These ritual abusers routinely turned out to be some of the parents' best
friends—bowling buddies, fellow Elks, or the local bridge club. In other words,
some of the worst abusers were pillars of the community. Often, the doctors in
the group helped to dispose of the telltale remains, erasing all hospital records
of the birth. These Satanic cults would go to any length to confuse their victims.
Often they dressed up in bizarre fashion, so that if the children reported what had
occurred, no one would believe them. "Mind control" methods such as strobe
lights, electrical shocks and hypnotic spells were used to make the victims forget
or dissociate. Finally, they were told repeatedly, "This never happened. You will
never remember this."

The Survivors of SRA (Satanic ritual abuse) consequently regarded themselves
as a sort of elite inside the Incest Survivor community. They had seen it all. They
had suffered monstrously, beyond belief. Their interior beings included not only
the standard wounded inner children, but an entire host of strange alters, often
including animals, the opposite sex, and spiritually uplifting "inner self helpers"
who served as gatekeepers and guides. An MPD Survivor had the opportunity

to speak in different voices, to discover layers and layers of personalities, and to garner hushed respect and sympathy.

Many such Survivors had no desire to "integrate" their personalities. They preferred to speak not of a "disorder," but of a multiple-personality "dignity." They reveled in their own internal community, a kind of self-contained 12-step group. They wrote poetry, sang songs, and painted exotic portraits of their abuse. Like William Adams, one MPD songwriter and singer, they may have used a singular name on the album cover or poetry collection, but they referred to themselves in the plural. "A concert of my music," Adams said, "is a concert of many hearts and minds, for I am actually we. Our songs are a testimony to both the incredible agony that we all lived through in our childhood, to the amazingly creative way we coped with abuse."

For the sensation-hungry media, stories of ritual abuse were a godsend, beginning with a 1985 20/20 TV program, "The Devil Worshippers." A 1988 Geraldo Rivera TV special on ritual abuse really got the ball rolling, as did the publication of *Satan's Underground in the* same year, a first-person account by Lauren Stratford, a Survivor who had retrieved previously forgotten memories. By 1993, the horrifying, titillating tales of unspeakable ritual abuse hit the front covers of *Ms. Magazine* and *Vanity Fair*. The *Ms.* cover depicted an innocent infant in a devil serpent's coils, admonishing the reader to "BELIEVE IT! Cult Ritual Abuse Exists." The story, "Surviving the Unbelievable," was written by the pseudonymous Elizabeth Rose. The reader had to search very carefully to deduce that the author did not remember all of this horror until quite recently. She believed that she was abused by her mother and aunt in an intergenerational cult when she was four and five years old. "My mother became pregnant a few months after I was inducted into the cult," Rose wrote. Seven months later, her labor was induced by a cult doctor. "Two days later, I was forced to watch as they killed my baby sister by decapitation in a ritual sacrifice ... followed by a communion ritual, during which human flesh and blood were consumed." She went on to assert that her mother and best friend were both gang-raped repeatedly. "Other sexual abuse includes the raping of young girls or infants. Both girls and boys may be sodomized or penetrated with symbolic objects, such as a crucifix, or with weapons."

Although the *Vanity Fair* piece purported to present a more "balanced" viewpoint, author Leslie Bennetts clearly believed the stories. In "Nightmares on Main Street," she uncritically accepted 34-year-old Aubrey's "memories of secret Satanic rituals practiced by Aubrey's family on the dark nights when her parents, grandparents, and neighbors wore robes and carried torches." Aubrey's memories included repeated impregnations and early induced labors, after which her babies were sacrificed and consumed. Bennetts also wrote of Tiffany, another Survivor whose "body alone provides some form of corroboration," since it exhibited "a baffling array of unexplained scars and other injuries." Tiffany calmly asserted: "The first rape was when I was two; my father had molested me before that, but this was the first actual penetration, and he cut my vagina with a knife in order to achieve that. I have the scars."

While MPD did not yet flourish outside North America, the Satanic ritual abuse scare did, largely through training seminars offered in 1988 in England by U. S. "experts" such as Pamala Klein and Chicago police detective Jerry Simandl. In July of 1989, a British television program, "Cook Report: The Devil's Work," appeared to substantiate alarming claims that Satanic cults were abusing children all over England. Soon, British therapists such as Valerie Sinason and Phil Mollon were hearing tales of grotesque ritual sexual abuse and murder from female clients. Sinason edited a professional book, *Treating Survivors of Satanist Abuse*, which was published in 1994. Similar horror stories and therapeutic interest spread to New Zealand and Australia.

Entering the Mainstream: "The Terrible Truth"

By the early 1990s, belief in an epidemic of repressed memories had become what academic sociologists term an "urban legend," a piece of folklore that is commonly accepted as true. Because that phraseology implies that such rumors persist only in cities, I prefer the term "contemporary legend."

Many such legends were debunked during this period, once they were proven, indisputably, to be untrue. The actor who had played "Mikey" in the Life Cereal commercials went on TV to assure people that he had not been killed by "Pop Rocks" candy exploding in his stomach. New York City sewer workers explained that baby alligators flushed down toilets had not turned the sewer system into the Everglades. Pepsi drinkers could rest assured that they would not find hypodermic needles in their soft drinks. But acceptance of repressed memories and Satanic cults remained, with few coming forward to challenge the evidence, or lack thereof.

Nursing journals featured articles about how to spot possible repressed memories. Police departments and psychological associations offered seminars on ritual abuse. Joan Baez, who came to believe she had multiple personalities, sang a song about Satanic cults. Gloria Steinem embraced her inner child and the concept of repression, attending a 1990 conference of the International Society for the Study of Multiple Personality & Dissociation to espouse the reality of Satanic ritual abuse cults. Actress Roseanne Barr Arnold discovered in therapy that she had been abused in her cradle, trumpeting her new status as a Survivor on talk shows, then wrote a book declaring that she housed twenty multiple personalities named, among others, Piggy, Fucker, and Bambi. Heidi Vanderbilt published a lengthy diatribe on incest and repressed memories in *Lear's*. Weekend retreats promised to help women retrieve their memories. Made-for-TV movies such as *Ultimate Betrayal* sympathetically portrayed "real life" cases of recovered incest memories.

Perhaps most frightening, the dogma had flowed from popular self-help books to well-honed fiction that presented engaging, believable characters suddenly remembering abuse. *A Thousand Acres* (1991), Jane Smiley's story of a constricted Midwestern farm family, won the Pulitzer Prize and the National Book Critics Circle Award. Ginny, the protagonist, has repressed all memory of her father's abuse, while her sister Rose has always remembered it. Finally, on page 228, Ginny experiences a "flashback" to her teenage years, while lying on her childhood bed: "Lying there, I knew that he had been in there to me, that my father had lain with me on that bed, that I had looked at the top of his head, at his balding spot in the brown grizzled hair, while feeling him suck my breasts." She jumps up, but she knows that there are more memories to come. "Behind that one image bulked others, mysterious bulging items in a dark sack, unseen as yet, but felt."

Smiley enshrined all the familiar stereotypes. "I remembered that he carried a lot of smells—whiskey, cigarette smoke, the sweeter and sourer smells of the farm work." Ginny always assumed a "desperate limp inertia" during these sex scenes, which she miraculously banished from her consciousness until years later.

Good fiction can be more convincing than truth. One critic praised Smiley for her "persuasive and powerful voice," and he was right. The *Boston Globe* called her characters "hauntingly real." *Publishers Weekly* stated that the plot remained "always within the limits of credibility." One friend told me I ought to read the book because it had repressed memories in it. "But these are real," she assured me, "because her sister always remembered it." I had to remind her that this was a work of fiction.

Finally, popular magazines ran articles such as "The Terrible Truth," which appeared in an October 1992 issue of *Self,* written by A. G. Britton, a beauty editor for the magazine. I will end this chapter with a summary of this article, since it provides a telling case study to which I will refer in future chapters.

In 1989, the 33-year-old Britton lost her job, had a miscarriage, and sank into a "heavyhearted depression I couldn't shake." She sought therapy, as she had at several other times in her life since her late teens. "During one session," she wrote, "it popped out of my mouth that I may have been sexually molested when I was young." She had a disturbing dream, but no real memories. "It was all very vague, but my therapist said that whenever a person suspects abuse, it most likely did occur."

Britton may not have read *The Courage to Heal* at this point, but she almost certainly had absorbed the dogma—whether consciously or not—including the idea that dreams can reveal abuse. Her therapist further encouraged the idea that she had probably been abused. Consequently, the progression of the story from here on is all too predictable. Once the suspicion was planted, it grew.

Britton began to experience mysterious ailments—her left leg and arm grew numb. "I saw doctors and physio-therapists and chiropractors, but no one could find anything physically wrong with me." She experienced anxiety attacks, more depression, and a "free-floating rage." She sought out yet another counselor. "During the very first visit to my new therapist, she told me it sounded as if I were suffering from Post-Traumatic Stress Disorder." After seeing this therapist for six months, "the episodes of distress had come to dominate my life. If I didn't remember the trauma that was feeding them, I was afraid I would be consumed by them."

Like the woman on the computer bulletin board quoted at the beginning of this chapter, Britton decided that she had been having "memories" all along "in symbols, body problems, emotions that seemed to come from nowhere ..., in the automatic closing of my throat when eating a pleasant food." Then one day, exhausted, she lay down for an afternoon nap. "Suddenly, my body went numb, and I felt a tremendous pressure on my chest. I couldn't breathe. I tried to relax, but the feeling got worse. Then I had a vision of what looked like a huge, hairy burned potato close to my face." When she reported this experience to her therapist, "she confirmed what I already knew: I had experienced my first [real] memory. 'It sounds like fellatio,' she said. I felt something crumble within me."

After this, a "siege" commenced. "It was as if an earthquake were ravaging my very being, leaving my subconscious open to the world.... I had only the foggiest sense of what was real and what were my memories." Her symptoms and anxiety attacks grew worse. She began to lose weight. "Terror would shoot through my body, making me feel as if I were being lifted off the ground." Britton decided to change therapists yet again, since she wasn't getting any better. She sought out Dr. Straker, a psychiatrist she had seen years before. "He explained how repressed memory emerges: first in the body, then in the emotions and finally as actual memory." Straker medicated Britton, but she continued to experience what she interpreted as flashbacks.

"I would lose the ability to speak. My tongue would get all gummed up as if I were an infant. I wouldn't be able to read or spell. My body would become listless, and my motor control felt askew.... I would have an incredible urge to bite through things." She and Straker concluded that she was reliving her infancy between the ages of six months and two years, including the pain of teething. She experienced "strange and uncontrollable fears." She dreamed of ripping apart a bulbous fish with her teeth. In another dream, she tasted something salty.

Finally, after all this preparation, Britton had her first "fully realized, intellectual memory" in which she saw herself, barely over a year old, at the beach. "My father was pinning my arms up over my head so that they were pushed against my ears in a painful way. He was relentlessly shoving his penis in my mouth. In a rage, I was trying to bite it off." She could now explain everything. "There it was: the answer to 30 years of pain and anguish and confusion." Her father had molested her from the time she was six to eighteen months old, she decided. Following this breakthrough, the memories began to come back more easily. "I remembered sitting in my crib, watching my father come at me with instruments in his hand, his fingers smelling of antiseptic."

Britton's parents had separated when she was not yet two, and her father died when she was 16. Her mother appeared to corroborate her memories. "She said my father had been a very troubled man and seemed to have an addict's sex drive." And, in fact, he *had* taken care of his infant daughter much of the time. "He had convinced her he was a better father than she was a mother."

Now, Britton bravely proclaimed herself a Survivor. "I'm still reclaiming parts of my life that had been lost in the fog," she explained. "My tragedy will always be there. I was raped of my childhood."

2

The Memory Maze

Great is this power of memory, exceedingly great. 0 my God, a spreading limit-less room within me. Who can reach its uttermost depth? Yet it is a faculty of soul and belongs to my nature. In fact I cannot totally grasp all that I am.

—St. Augustine, 399 A.D.

WE'VE ALL EXPERIENCED SUDDEN, SEEMINGLY involuntary recall of incidents, faces, and emotions from the past. Triggered by a particular perfume, a snatch of melody, a photograph, or a voice on the telephone, our pasts can sometimes rush back with surprising intensity and vividness. "Why, I hadn't thought of Mrs. Carnes in years," you might say. "I remember that teacher so clearly now, it's just as if she were in the room with me." Recalling that second-grade class, you might also flash on Steve Barber, the creep who always chased you and called you names, and the hot flush of fear and anger can be sudden and fresh.

It is, therefore, not beyond the realm of possibility that someone might either forget or actively "repress" an unpleasant memory, a traumatic event that would pop back into consciousness years later with the proper stimulus. Memory researchers have long recognized that people tend to rewrite their pasts to some degree, making themselves into heroes or transforming their family trips from bickering sojourns into golden moments, or *vice versa*. So isn't it intuitively reasonable to think that the sex abuse Survivor accusations may all be true? How many of us are living with versions of our pasts that are essentially myths of happy childhoods, or fabrications to defend our fragile egos?

In the following pages, I'll summarize what researchers have found regarding repression and dissociation. From the standpoint of pure science, these concepts have been neither proven nor disproven. No hypothesis is ever immune from modification—a black swan may appear, or the Earth could flatten—but it is certainly possible to look carefully at the evidence and draw probable conclusions.

But the repressed memory debate presents challenges. It is usually impossible to corroborate either Survivors' memories of sexual abuse or their accuseds' anguished denials. The alleged events purportedly took place years ago, and, except for the group abuse envisioned in ritual-abuse scenarios, there would usually have been no witnesses other than parent (or uncle, grandparent, babysitter, teacher) and child. Few pedophiles seduce their victims in public. By its very nature, sex abuse is a private, hidden act. Therefore, determining guilt or innocence is usually a matter of emotion, character, and conviction.

Similarly, belief in the concept of repression comes down to—well, just that: *belief.* Because there is no way to verify or refute it, and because the stakes are so high, both sides of the debate over repressed memories have tended to become polarized, angry, vociferous, and dogmatic. Considering literature such as *The Courage to Heal* and the other disturbing material presented in the previous chapter, however, it is easy to see how induced memories of abuse could come to seem quite real. And from what memory researchers have told us, it is unlikely that people would forget years of traumatic events. Still, we must look at all sides, particularly because of the prevalence of *real sexual abuse.*

Reconstructing the Past

One thing should be made clear at the outset. Most of those who make accusations based on "recovered memories" are not consciously lying, even if their version of the past may be incorrect. For them, the imagined memories are real, sometimes even more compelling than memories of actual events from childhood. Given that, how can anybody argue that *all,* or at least *most,* of these "memories" are inaccurate? Any explanation of how delusional memories can occur must include an examination of how our minds recall the past.

Without our memories, how would we define ourselves? Memories *are* who we are. Arguably, it is our capacity to remember, reflect, and verbalize on the past that separates us from other animals. Because we can recall the past and project it into the future, we understand cause-and-effect, we can create hypotheses. Memory allows us to be scientists, poets, storytellers, and creators.

But there is also a darker side to this capacity to remember and interpret past events, smells, and sounds. We nurture the inevitable pain and suffering we encounter, seeking explanations, and incorporating them into our self-concepts. We know that something similar might happen again. Because we see ourselves as active agents in the world, creating our own environments and destinies, we think that we must prevent some future disaster. In short, we worry. We have known pain, disappointment and abuse, and we nurse and rehearse their effects. We are historians.

Dream and nightmare, creative joy and paranoia, nostalgia and terror—all seem central to the human experience, and all rely on thoughts and interpretations of the past. This would probably be true even if our memories served as absolutely accurate recording devices and we all agreed on shared events. In fact, however, our minds, mini-lightning storms of tiny electrical currents snapping over billions of synapses awash in a sea of hormones, still defy our understanding. Little won-der, given this compelling description by science writer Philip J. Hilts:

> The neurons, then, are like minute sea creatures, packed side to side like tiny bristles, several hundred billion of them in the whole cranial vault, and each in a frenetic state of decision or indecision. Each bristle has thousands of fine fila-ments to connect to others, and with the billions of cells, times the thousands of filaments, times the different signals which may pass between each reaching tentacle and another, there are, all told, tens to hundreds of trillions of tender signaling junctions formed among neurons.

We reassemble memories from all over our brains—a bit from the visual cortex near the back, a snippet from the audio cortex on either side of the brain near the ears, more from the olfactory bulb near the cortex's bottom front, and so on —and every time we recall a memory, we change it a little and then reconsolidate it through synaptic re-enforcement.

We do not record the past in neat computer-like bits and bytes. It is almost impossible to discuss the mechanisms of memory without employing misleading metaphors. Plato compared the mind to a wax writing tablet, the advanced tech-nology of his era. For Freud, the brain functioned something like a giant plumb-ing system or steam engine, with uncomfortable material stashed away in the cesspool of the subconscious and leaking out when the pressure reached a critical point. Modern researchers have used other metaphors: the mind as a giant filing cabinet, library, or computer.

The trouble with all such comparisons is the implication that we remember ev-erything that has ever happened to us—that every smell, sound, sensation, joy or trauma has been encoded somewhere in the brain, and, if only the proper com-mand or button is pushed, it will all come flooding back.* Pop psychologists have repeatedly promulgated this notion, as in this passage from *Unlocking the Secrets of Your Childhood Memories* (1989): "Every experience we've had since birth has been recorded and tucked away safely in our brains. Like the most sophisticated computer in the world, the brain retrieves [memories] we need when we need them."

In similar fashion, neurosurgeon Ben Carson, the newly appointed Secretary of Housing and Urban Development in the Trump Administration, claimed in 2017 that the human brain "remembers everything you've ever seen, everything you've ever heard. I could take the oldest person here, make a little hole right here on the side of the head, and put some depth electrodes into their hippocampus and stim-

---

*   The concept of permanent memory traces isn't particularly new. In 1777, German philosopher Johann Nico-las Tetens wrote: "Each idea does not only leave a trace … somewhere in the body, but each of them can be stimulated—even if it is not possible to demonstrate this in a given situation."

ulate and they would be able to recite back to you verbatim a book they read 60 years ago. It's all there, it doesn't go away, [you] just have to learn how to recall it."

But the brain does not function that way, as every modern memory researcher knows. "One of the most widely held, but wrong, beliefs that people have about memory is that 'memories' exist, somewhere in the brain, like books exist in a library, or packages of soap on the supermarket shelves," psychologist Endel Tulving observed, "and that remembering is equivalent to somehow retrieving them. The whole concept of repression is built on this misconception."

British experimental psychologist Frederic Bartlett first made this point in his classic 1932 text, *Remembering: A Study in Experimental and Social Psychology*. "Some widely held views have to be completely discarded," he asserted, "and none more completely than that which treats recall as the re-excitement in some way of fixed and changeless 'traces.'" To the contrary, he held that remembering is "an imaginative reconstruction, or construction, built out of the relation of our attitude toward a whole active mass of organized past reactions or experience."

Based on his experiments, Bartlett concluded that our memories generally serve us well, not by offering photographic recall, but by selectively sampling experience and molding it so that our lives have purpose and meaning. "In a world of constantly changing environment, literal recall is extraordinarily unimportant." In other words, the human species has evolved a brain that is adaptable, nimble, versatile and imaginative, but not always accurate. We literally "re-member," patching together the puzzle bits of our past. Biological memory researchers sometimes call this process the "reconsolidation" of memory, though it should not be taken to mean that memories are created from scratch every time we recall something. They are, however, subject to distortion and amendment. "Because retrieval makes memory labile and subject to change," wrote Joe LeDoux in *Anxious* (2015), "reconsolidation is taking place constantly—in fact, potentially every time we remember something."

Because of this tendency toward "best guesses," many of us display "source amnesia" (or "source confusion"), the misattribution of where we got a particular memory, even of a recent event. For instance, I am often quite sure I've told a friend something, when in fact it was someone else I told. Source amnesia is far more common with events from the distant past, however. Thus, it is fairly common to construct a memory that encompasses details from several sources, including, perhaps, family photos, real memories of a bedroom, stories we have heard, or movies we have seen. Then the memories can seem quite accurate. A reconstructed incest abuse memory may, for instance, contain the always-remembered feel of a father's stubble against a child's tender face during a goodnight kiss, or the smell of his after-shave. That may be combined with a grotesque, stereotyped scene from a book or movie to form a coherent but misleading narrative.

In addition, we forget a good deal more than we remember. That's why one common method employed by recovered-memory therapists works so well. They ask clients to recall their childhoods in detail, looking particularly for "missing chunks of time." If a client cannot recall anything about third and fourth grade, for instance, that supposedly indicates that massive abuse took place during that time, so terrible that the memory had to be repressed, or an alternate personality had to be created. This explanation is quite convincing until one examines how normal memory works. We recall the highs and lows of our lives, with very little in between. It isn't surprising, then, that people don't remember much from their childhoods. Most of us don't, unless cued with a particular name, smell, or event. At that point, someone who didn't recall third grade at all might suddenly realize that he or she remembers quite a bit from that time, such as a pet dying, a particular vacation, or a change in bedrooms.

Not only do we simply forget a good deal, our versions of the personal past are highly colored by our own emotions and family myths. Most of us recognize that our siblings tend to recall the same events from quite different perspectives. I may remember those touch football games with great fondness, for instance, whereas for my brother they were pure torture.

After recounting a salient memory of her childhood, the narrator in Sue Miller's 1990 novel, *Family Pictures*, admits that her memory is faulty:

> My sister Liddie says it's her memory, her story, one she told me much later. . . .
> And yet it seems as clear to me as a picture I might have taken. I could swear
> this was exactly what happened. But that's the way it is in a family, isn't it? The
> stories get passed around, polished, embellished. . . . And, of course, there's also
> the factor of time. Of how your perspective, your way of telling the story—of
> seeing it—changes as time passes. As you change.

The classic Japanese film *Rashomon* makes the same point, allowing four characters who witnessed a violent episode to recall different versions, filtered through their own biases and perspectives.

We are also quite capable of projecting emotions and reinterpretations backward through time, and of creating absolutely clear memories of events that never occurred. This comes as shocking news to everyone, because it threatens our cherished sense of self. Who should know better than *we* what *we* have experienced?

Yet our memories are infinitely more suggestible and malleable than we would like to believe. A 1952 study dramatically illustrates the point. Twelve subjects in group therapy were asked to recall childhood memories involving parents, siblings, and sexual experiences. The Freudian therapist conducting the study was particularly interested in stories about rejecting fathers and flirtatious little girls.

The memories were transcribed onto a pack of cards, shuffled, and presented to the subjects from three months to four years later. *None of the patients could identify all of their previously reported memories.* On average, they correctly recalled *half* of them.

Given the proper stimulus and the awful surmise that our parents might have done something really reprehensible to us—buried in the mists of our murky childhood memories—*many of us could come to believe in the reality of grotesque events that never took place.* That, in fact, is what appears to have happened to millions of frightened, confused, angry adults in the United States in the final years of the 20th century.

As long ago as 1923, German psychiatrist Karl Jaspers noted that "nearly all memories are slightly falsified and become a mixture of truth and fantasy." Jaspers specifically addressed the creation of illusory memories. "With the phenomena of false memories, the patient gets a sudden image of a previous experience that has all the vivid feeling of a memory, but in actual fact nothing, not even a slender basis for it, is really remembered. Everything is *freshly created.*" His work was published in an English translation in 1963, but it appeared that few American psychologists learned much from it.

Because of what Frederic Bartlett called an "effort after meaning," we tend to rewrite our pasts to make them match our current attitudes and opinions. Our memories, Bartlett noted, "live with our interests and with them they change." Thus it isn't surprising that memories "display invention, condensation, elaboration, simplification and all the other alterations which my experiments constantly illustrated." Bartlett did not, of course, assert that memories bore no relationship to real events of the past. He posited that we can indeed recall specific details, particularly through words and visual images, but we weave those bits into a reconstructed narrative.

Our unique language capacity allows us to communicate, not only with one another, but with ourselves. In one sense, *we use words to tell ourselves the constantly reinvented story of our lives.* We are, preeminently, a species of internal novelists. That explains our insatiable desire to write and read imagined stories, which distill and interpret experience and render it meaningful. It is, as Bartlett put it, "the struggle to get somewhere, the varying play of doubt, hesitation, satisfaction and the like, and the eventual building up of the complete story accompanied by the more and more confident advance in a certain direction."

When we struggle to remember events from our lives, we begin with a general attitude or framework, then fill in the gaps with probable dialogue and detail. Or, as psychologist Stephen Crites put it: "To the extent that a coherent identity is achievable at all, the thing must be made, a story-like production with many pitfalls, and it is constantly being revised, sometimes from beginning to end."

Similarly, we can summon up fragmentary visual images and edit them into an internal movie of our lives. "The immediate return of certain details is common enough," Bartlett wrote, "and it certainly looks very much like the direct re-excitation of certain traces." Once these images pop up, "the need to remember becomes active, an attitude is set up." From these beginnings, a visual scenario develops, the psychic camera rolls, and the imagination—whose root word, after all, is "image"—takes over.

Indeed, brain-scan research indicates that our brains treat visualized fantasies quite similarly to sights we actually witnessed, and the primary olfactory cortex lights up when people contemplate the words *perfume* or *coffee*. "The brain, it seems, does not make much of a distinction between reading about an experience and encountering it in real life," a science writer summarized in an article aptly entitled "Your Brain on Fiction."

In a way, we become expert actors in the internal drama of our own lives. At first, these memories may seem tentative, but with repeated visualization, or the verbal repetition of the stories, they become more real. *Memory, then, is largely a product of rehearsal.*

Given this background, much of the advice in *The Courage to Heal* and other Survivor literature becomes more understandable and frightening. Again and again, Survivors were urged to visualize the abuse scenarios as slide shows, videos, or movies in their heads, running them mentally until they become real. Similarly, they were encouraged to repeat their abuse stories, giving them concrete language, making them real. Writing a story down gives it more of an objective reality. Ellen Bass and Laura Davis specifically recommended following the lead of Irena Kelpfisz, who, as they noted, "developed an exercise that enables you to piece together things you can't possibly know about your history or the history of your family. This form of 'remembering,' which [Kelpfisz] calls 'imaginative reconstruction,' can be a valuable tool .... Although you write about things you couldn't realistically know, the result often seems chillingly real."

In a classic example of circular thinking, Bessel van der Kolk, a Harvard psychiatrist who defends the reality of repressed memories, explained that he believes a story if it *sounds* good. "If you read a great book and the characters are true to life, that's how people really feel and interact with each other." Van der Kolk compared true recovered memories to a good novel; he relied on "the internal coherence of the story, how it all hangs together," to determine its believability. In 1895 Sigmund Freud made the same kind of observation. "It still strikes me as strange that the case histories I write should read like short stories." He even admitted that they "lack the serious stamp of science," though Freud usually claimed that his stories and hypotheses were based on the purest science.

In *Dancing With Daddy* (1991), Betsy Petersen recounted how she utilized the Kelpfisz process to "remember" her abuse. Like Van der Kolk, she came to believe the memories because they made a good story. During therapy, she became obsessed with the idea, *"I'm afraid my father did something to me."* She had a "sense of urgency," wanting to *know* for sure. Consequently, she decided to make it up. "I had no memory of what my father had done to me, so I tried to reconstruct it. I put all my skill—as reporter, novelist, scholar—to work making that reconstruction as accurate and vivid as possible. I used the memories I had to get to the memories I didn't have." Using what she already knew about her father—a calm, didactic physician who wore steel-rimmed glasses—she wrote a short story called "Surgeon's Hands," set in 1945, in which she imagined him abusing her in her crib when she was three years old:

> I lie there with his fingers crawling over me. I keep jerking, I can't help it, jerking under his fingers. I think it hurts, but I'm not sure. My flesh is so soft down there, so different from the firm skin all over the rest of me. He rubs against the bars of the crib and his eyes cross and roll up behind his glasses. Suddenly he groans and slumps over the bars. His finger stops moving. Is he dead?

Re-reading what she had written, Petersen "began to scream and curse and cry. I cried so hard I wet my pants." She took this self-generated horror to be evidence that her imagined scenario was true. "The feelings that came up for me were so intense I felt they must be grounded in some reality." Her therapist encouraged her. "I wanted to believe it: I wanted not to be crazy," Petersen explains. Subsequently, "wanted or not, memories came" in the form of daydreams as she lay in the sun on a couch. "I sink into the welter of images, and there is a moment when one of them sharpens, and I can see it clearly. Then it drifts out of focus again and disappears."

Bartlett would have understood Petersen's description, because he observed that visual images tend to appear as isolated fragments. "The course of description, when images abound, is apt to be more exciting, more varied, more rich, more jerky," he noted. "There is an image, and meaning has to be tacked on to that, or, perhaps more accurately, has to flow out of it, or emerge from it, before words can carry the process further." This method of reconstruction has the evolutionary advantage of surmounting mere chronological logic. It permits intuition, inspiration, and poetry. "A man can take out of its setting something that happened a year ago, reinstate it with much if not all of its individuality unimpaired, combine it with something that happened yesterday, and use them both to help him to solve a problem with which he is confronted today." Unfortunately, when that "problem" involves a suspicion of sexual abuse, its "solution" can be devastating. As Bartlett explained, "The device of images has several defects that are the price of its peculiar excellences."

Psychological Turf Wars

Ever since Freud, the psychology profession has split itself into two camps—the experimental and the clinical—each viewing the other with suspicion, condescension, and, quite often, contempt.

The experimental psychologists conduct research in controlled conditions, attempting to prove or disprove particular hypotheses regarding mental phenomena. By changing one variable at a time, they try to isolate particular cause-and-effect sequences. In trying to explore the human psyche, however, they are largely hampered by ethical constraints. No one, for instance, would look with favor upon a scientist who raised a human child without any touch or affection, just to see how it fared. Therefore, when Harry Harlow conducted his famed experiments to determine the importance of early nurturing touch, he studied monkeys instead. Similarly, experimental psychologists often use rats, frogs, guinea pigs, or other animals, studying how their brains work, hoping to arrive at conclusions that might be legitimately applied to humans.

Memory and mind researchers have, however, been able to use human subjects, as long as they did not abuse them. Until the last few decades—with the exception of Frederic Bartlett's work—most experiments involving memory concentrated on rote learning of meaningless material. The human subjects risked only the abuse of boredom. Few of the experiments applied to the real world of conflicted emotions and difficult decisions. As Ulric Neisser commented in a 1978 speech, "If X is an interesting or socially significant aspect of memory, then psychologists have hardly ever studied X." Endel Tulving agreed. "There is exceedingly little in the first hundred years' worth of mainstream memory research that is relevant to the repressed memories controversy." In the 1990s, however, memory researchers such as Neisser, Elizabeth Loftus, and Nicholas Spanos conducted intriguing experiments with human subjects, trying to cast light on how we recall and interpret events from our lives.

The experimentalists tend to distrust the clinicians, who generalize from their anecdotal experience with clients and make assertions without controlled scientific proof. This split within the field became pronounced in the early part of the 20th century when Sigmund Freud, the ultimate clinician and systematizer, posited the existence of various mental drives and defense mechanisms, all based on his experience with a limited patient pool. As psychologist J. Victor Haberman wrote in 1914, "These mechanisms have in no way as yet been shown to exist," adding that "the method employed by Freud to prove their existence is scientifically false."

Haberman complained that American clinicians had uncritically accepted Freudian theories, publishing scores of questionable articles. "In most, absolutely no attempt is made at more than the mere statement of cases," he asserted. "Were a man to make a bold statement as to a new method of cure in carcinoma, sharp criticism would be applied to his work and his announcement; but the American Freudist may publish the very quintessence of inanity and it is accepted without challenge or comment." Not much has changed since 1914. Freud's fundamental tenets, the experimental psychologists note, have never withstood scientific scrutiny. They are simply intriguing myths until proven otherwise. As one critic asserted in 1975, "Psychoanalytic theory is the most stupendous intellectual confidence trick of the 20th century."

The clinicians, on the other hand, complain about their experimental colleagues, hiding in their sterile labs, trying to draw conclusions from timid, limited experiments on college students. What do they know about real life? The clinicians pride themselves on their active involvement with individual clients whose life stories pour out during therapy sessions. Sure, the therapists sometimes read about experimental evidence, but it seems worlds away from their practice, from the real needs of their patients. The experimental psychologists may dismiss a case study as mere "anecdotal" evidence, but that one person's history is unique, indubitable. And when clinicians saw hundreds of such patients, many of whose cases seemed to verify Freud's theories about transference, denial, and repression, who was to tell them that they could not draw valid conclusions, just because they didn't wear white coats and carry on double-blind experiments?

Until the last few decades, this turf war between psychologists didn't mean much to the average layperson. After the publication of *The Courage to Heal*, however, the battle over esoteric theories and evidence for and against repression became a life-or-death issue for millions of people—the patients and therapists who believed in recovered memories, and the devastated parents and others accused of sexual abuse that they claimed never occurred. In court, "expert" psychological witnesses such as Lenore Terr or Elizabeth Loftus swayed juries toward crucial decisions. Because of such testimony, innocent people may have been jailed or fined, or the guilty may have gone free. Consequently, these convoluted arguments over obscure psychological mechanisms have had dramatic real-life consequences.

Repression: For and Against

In a 1989 speech to his peers, experimental psychologist David Holmes reviewed numerous laboratory attempts to prove the existence of repression. "Despite over 60 years of research involving numerous approaches by thoughtful and clever investigators," he concluded, "at the present time there is no controlled laboratory evidence supporting the concept of repression." He could not say with certainty that people did not repress memories, because it is impossible to prove a negative; similarly, no one can disprove the existence of ghosts. But he suggested that it might be appropriate to abandon the theory, filing it under "interesting but unsupported." Holmes suggested, somewhat facetiously, that a cautionary truth-in-packaging label should be inscribed in therapists' waiting rooms: "Warning. The concept of repression has not been validated with experimental research and its use may be hazardous to the accurate interpretation of clinical behavior."

In fact, as Robert Youngson pointed out in his 1998 book, *Scientific Blunders* (which includes a chapter on repressed memory therapy), "The history of science is littered with remarkable errors," most of which were committed by those who allowed confirmatory bias to slew their conclusions, so that they found what they were expecting. Good scientific results are *falsifiable*—that is, they can be proven to be untrue. As with ghosts, however, there is no way to disprove the elusive theory of repressed memory.

In his 1997 book, *Why People Believe Weird Things*, Michael Shermer listed 25 fallacies that can lead to misguided certainty, almost all of which apply to those who espouse a belief in repressed memories. "Theory Influences Observations...The Observer Changes the Observed...Anecdotes Do Not Make a Science...Scientific Language Does Not Make a Science...Bold Statements Do Not Make Claims True...Rumors Do Not Equal Reality...Emotive Words and False Analogies...Overreliance on Authorities...The Need for Certainty, Control, and Simplicity." Shermer called one category *Ad Ignorantiam*, "where someone argues that if you cannot disprove a claim it must be true." Instead, the burden of proof should go in the other direction; extraordinary claims require extraordinary evidence, as Carl Sagan observed.

David Holmes knew that his conclusions about the concept of repression would be dismissed by the clinicians, who, he noted, would argue that the laboratory research was "contrived, artificial, sterile, and irrelevant to the 'dynamic processes' that occur in the 'real world.'" He also noted, however, that when some experimental results initially appeared to validate repression, the clinicians were eager to embrace it.* Only when further experiments cast doubt on the concept did they disregard the laboratory. Holmes then went on the offensive. "The clinicians retreat to their consulting rooms for evidence for repression, but what evidence have they produced there?" Only "impressionistic case studies ... unconfirmed clinical speculations."** Finally, he referred to a videotape shown

---

* For instance, believers in repression might cite experiments in "directed forgetting," in which people were asked to forget words from a previously presented list. Compared to words they were told to remember, they had lower recall for these. Yet trauma-related words weren't so easily forgotten, especially by those who had suffered from traumatic events.

** Holmes would undoubtedly agree with one 1910 cynic who, commenting on various psychological theories, noted "a curious similarity in their appeal to their own clinical experience.... The exponents of the sexual theory, the suggestion theory, the sleep theory ... alike appeal to experience for confirmation of their opinion, *and find it.*"

during the conference that was supposed to demonstrate repression in a client. "But there was no agreement between the conferees concerning when, or even if, repression had occurred" in the video.

The experiments described by Holmes involved college students remembering various words. In one such experiment, subjects were first tested for recall of a group of nouns. Then one-third of them were told that most of their responses were signs of "serious pathology." Another third were told that their answers indicated high creativity and leadership potential. The final third received neutral feedback. The first two groups displayed poorer recall than the final control group. Once the deception was explained, all three groups showed comparable levels of recall. "From these results," Holmes said, "it was concluded that decreased recall following stress was due to interference rather than to repression."

From the clinicians' viewpoint, however, this experiment proved nothing of the sort. Any number of other factors could be at play, including repression, which has also been defined as "motivated forgetting." And regardless of what the experiment showed, it was difficult to see how it applied to incest memories. Some of Holmes's adult subjects were mildly "traumatized," but certainly the test situation was not comparable to the violent sexual abuse of a child. On the other hand, how could one ethically replicate such trauma in an experimental setting?

"Proof" for Repression

On the other side of the debate, three studies and one other case have been widely cited to "prove" the prevalence of repressed memories of sexual abuse. The first two relied on self-identified Survivors and consequently did not contribute much to the debate, but they deserve mention because they have been quoted prominently elsewhere.

In 1987, Herman and Schatzow published a study of 53 women attending their therapy groups ("Recovery and Verification of Memories of Childhood Sexual Trauma," in *Psychoanalytic Psychology*). Of those, 64 percent reported that they had forgotten at least some of their abuse before recalling it years later in therapy; 28 percent had "severe memory deficits." Most of their "memories" were recovered in the highly emotional hothouse atmosphere of the group process. "Participation in group proved to be a powerful stimulus for recovery of memory," Herman wrote, adding that it was sometimes necessary for her to intervene to "slow the process" when it got out of hand.

Herman and Schatzow claimed that the majority of these stories were confirmed in some manner. "Twenty-one women (40 percent) obtained corroborating evidence either from the perpetrator himself, from other family members, or from physical evidence such as diaries or photographs. Another 18 women (34 percent) discovered that another child, usually a sibling, had been abused by the same perpetrator. An additional five women (9 percent) reported statements from other family members indicating a strong likelihood that they had also been abused." That sounds impressive until closely examined. Unfortunately, we are dealing with apples and oranges here. Yes, in one case, Andrea's stepfather admitted to "fooling around" with her, but she had *always* remembered that abuse. More typical is the case of Doris, who "regressed" during group sessions and was "flooded with memories which included being raped by her father and being forced to service a group of her father's friends while he watched." Doris reported that her younger sister had once asked her, "Did Daddy ever try anything funny with you?" She took this as corroboration, though the discussion went no further.

The trouble with confirmations such as these is that they are unverified and second-hand. We have only the word of the accusers, eagerly and uncritically accepted by their therapists. In group, Claudia had recalled "being handcuffed, burned with cigarettes, forced to perform fellatio, and having objects introduced into her rectum and vagina" between the ages of four and seven. Claudia supposedly searched her brother's room and found handcuffs and a diary "in which he planned and recorded his sexual 'experiments' with his sister in minute detail." It is impossible to know whether this is an accurate account or not, because the case reports are "composites," according to the authors. Certainly, if Claudia had produced this diary, it would serve as horrifying evidence of the alleged crimes. But we have only Claudia's word for this, and she was under pressure to please Herman and Schatzow by coming up with some confirmation.

Given what we know about Judith Herman and her belief system *(see Chapter 1)*, it is not difficult to imagine that she would accept virtually anything as validating the memories.* A woman could tell her mother that she recalled incest by her uncle, and the mother might say, "I always knew there was something funny about him." A sibling, upset and alarmed by her sister's allegations, might enter therapy intent on "remembering" similar incidents. When she, too, found buried memories, this would be taken as corroboration rather than an extension of the suggestion process.

Similarly, Briere and Conte's 1993 study ("Self-Reported Amnesia for Abuse in Adults Molested As Children," in *Journal of Traumatic Stress*) of 450 male and female Survivors relied on a "clinical sample" recruited by therapists. Of these, 59.3 percent reported amnesia regarding the abuse at some time before the age of

---

* I wrote to Judith Herman, asking her to set up an interview with any clients who might provide confirmed stories involving repressed memories. She declined. Outright fabrications in such cases may be more frequent than one would think. During the witch craze, for instance, many subjects surreptitiously loaded their mouths with pins so that they could vomit them on cue. Similarly, in one repressed memory case, an accusing daughter forged a threatening letter from her father.

18. Compared to those who had always remembered their abuse, the patients who had recovered repressed memories generally reported molestation at an earlier age and over a longer time span. They were victimized by multiple perpetrators who used more violent techniques. These findings fit neatly with Survivor dogma. The more horrible, the more gut-wrenching the abuse, the more likely that it would be forgotten.

However, to an outside observer, an alternative explanation seems more plausible. Briere and Conte's findings may indicate that nearly 60 percent of their sample were never abused at all. Under the influence of their therapists and books such as *The Courage to Heal*, they may have come to believe in imagined memories which, not surprisingly, were more violent and included more perpetrators than the memories that real sex abuse victims had never forgotten. As we have seen, patients are actively urged to imagine brutal scenes, multiple offenders, and years of repressed abuse. With therapists such as Renee Fredrickson encouraging women to visualize abuse at extremely early ages, it is natural that this sample would "remember" back to the crib.

The third study ("Recall of Childhood Trauma: A Prospective Study of Women's Memories of Child Sexual Abuse," in *Journal of Consulting and Clinical Psychology*), conducted by sociologist Linda Meyer Williams at the Family Research Laboratory of the University of New Hampshire, is far more interesting. From 1973 to 1975, the National Institute of Mental Health funded a study of sexual assault victims who had been brought to a city hospital emergency room in a major northeastern city. Nearly two decades later, Williams and her researchers located and interviewed 129 women from the study—without telling them exactly why. Instead, the subjects were simply told that this was a follow-up study on women who, as children, had received medical care at the city hospital.

During the extensive interviews, which averaged three hours, the women were questioned about their childhoods and adult lives. After "sufficient rapport" was established, the interviewers asked the women to report any instances of sexual abuse that they could recall. The questions were posed several times in different ways, following the methodology first used by Diana Russell in the study already described in Chapter 1. Of the 129 women in the study, *38 percent failed to report* the specific incidents documented by their hospital visits. Williams, who called her findings "quite astonishing," clearly thought that she had found evidence of repression. She believed that "women who were abused in early childhood—and who are now more likely to have forgotten the abuse—will recall the abuse in the next several years."

There are, however, other ways to interpret her data. Sixty-eight percent of those who did not report the specific target incident *did* report other instances of sexual molestation. It seems safe to assume that anyone who was *routinely* subjected to abuse might not remember every single time it occurred. In other words, we may not be dealing with "repression" so much as a particular incident lost in a flood of repeated abuse. Eliminating those cases brings the sample down to 12 percent who did not report the incident and failed to report any other abuse either. It would be interesting to examine the ages of that smaller sample, which Williams did not analyze separately. Eleven victims out of the total sample were three years old or younger at the time of the abuse, while another 31 were between four and six. Because few people remember specific events that occurred prior to the age of four, it seems plausible that many of those who did not recall the abuse were simply not old enough.

There are other possible reasons for non-reporting. For some, the abuse may not have been traumatic enough to report in the context of this particular interview. Sexually abused children, perhaps fondled by an otherwise nurturing family member, do not always experience the incident as abusive.*

Alternatively, some may have recalled the abuse and chosen not to report it. Others may simply have forgotten it. We do not remember everything—even every bad thing—that has ever happened to us. It is not necessary to assume that such forgetting involves psychological defense mechanisms. In one U.S. government study, for instance, 14 percent of those involved in a car accident did not recall it a year later. Similarly, over 25 percent of those in another study did not remember a hospitalization after a year. Are these surprising statistics the result of mental avoidance, conscious non-reporting, repression, or simply bad memory?

Late in 1995, Linda Williams published an ancillary paper ("Recovered Memories of Abuse in Women with Documented Child Sexual Victimization Histories," *Journal of Traumatic Stress*) based on the same survey of 129 women. This one involved 75 women who *did* recall the "index" event. Of these, 12 reported that there was a time when they did not recall the sexual abuse. None of these cases were examples of "massive repression." Five of them involved women who were only two or three years old at the time of the abuse, making their "memory" of the event extremely doubtful, since the abuse came during the period of infantile amnesia *(see the end of this chapter)*. It is likely, in these cases, that they were told about the abuse later and then incorporated these stories as their own "memories." Two of the cases involve four-year-olds who were supposedly raped—yet doctors failed at the time to find medical evidence of abuse. Since penile penetration of a four-year-old not only leaves scars, but is often life-threatening, we have to question the veracity of these events. Other cases may

---

* The fact that some children are not traumatized by an adult's sexual attentions is acknowledged even by feminist researchers such as Diana Russell and Allie Kilpatrick. This fact does *not* mean that sexual abuse of children is ever "all right."

not involve actual amnesia so much as not thinking about the memories. One woman, for instance, reported that "when she is happy, she forgets."

One of the problems with self-reported periods of amnesia involves a kind of chase-your-tail logic. Williams' research assistants asked these women, "What was your age at the time you forgot and the time you remembered?" How do you remember when you forgot something? By definition, you can't. How can you recall how long you didn't remember? All you can logically say is, "I suddenly remembered this incident. I had not thought about it for years." In the case of limited events that were not perceived as particularly traumatic at the time, it isn't surprising that they would be forgotten and then recalled later. Such may have been the case with Kim, a seven-year-old whose teenage step-brother snuck into her bed and masturbated against her. She recalled the incident at 22 when she was reminded by her cousin that she had been abused.

Of the studies that purport to indicate the reality of repression, then, the Williams studies are definitely the most credible, but they fall far short of proof. It is instructive to compare her first published study to a 1990 report entitled "Child Abuse: Adolescent Records *vs.* Adult Recall," by Donna Della Femina *et al.,* published in *Child Abuse & Neglect,* which bears a striking similarity. Femina and her co-authors interviewed 69 subjects who had reported abuse nine years earlier while jailed. Of these, 26 failed to mention their traumas. In other words, 37.7 percent did not report abuse that was known to have occurred—almost exactly the same percentage as in the Williams study. But Femina and her colleagues went one step further and *re-interviewed* those who failed to report, trying to find out why. The answers had nothing to do with repressed memories. The commonest explanations were "a sense of embarrassment, a wish to protect parents, and a desire to forget."

Another study, published in 1994 ("Memories of Childhood Sexual Abuse," in *Psychology of Women Quarterly*), deserves mention, because one of the three investigators was Elizabeth Loftus, one of the most prominent repressed-memory skeptics. She and two colleagues questioned 105 New York City female graduates of a drug abuse program. Fifty-seven, or 54 percent, reported some form of childhood sexual abuse. Of those who were abused, 52 completed a further questionnaire about their memories. Ten of this group claimed to have forgotten the abuse for a time prior to recalling it. In other words, 19 percent of the women could be interpreted as having repressed their memories.

Again we are left with inconclusive evidence, however. We are not told whether the abuse was violent or mild, one-time or ongoing, or at what age it occurred. As Loftus noted, "It would be fruitful to probe further to find out how and when that [memory] recovery came about. According to the study report, all of these women had been involved in 12-step programs as well as individual and group counseling, at the height of the repressed memory epidemic. It would be surprising if some of them had not retrieved "memories"—whether true or confabulated—during that suggestive process.*

In 2004, psychologist Michael Anderson and colleagues published an article entitled "Neural Systems Underlying the Suppression of Unwanted Memories" in the prestigious journal *Science*. In typical sensationalistic style, the media trumpeted the study as "Proof of Brain's Ability to Suppress Memories" and "A Freudian Theory Proved." But close examination of Anderson's study prompts no such conclusion. He presented word pairs such as "steam-train" and "jaw-gum" to subjects, then asked some of them, when shown only the first word, to try to forget the second word. He scanned their brains with functional MRI during the process. Those subjects who were told to forget the second word dutifully recalled it less frequently. Perhaps this is proof that "directed forgetting" can work, although it may also indicate compliant subjects who were trying to do the right thing.

Anderson's conclusions regarding the brain scans were questionable, since it is not a simple matter to say what's going on in the brain from such evidence. But more important, the ability to recall word lists has no relevance to the debate over whether people can "repress" traumatic memories of years of childhood abuse. As psychologist Harrison Pope Jr observed, the study provided "no evidence that you can involuntarily develop amnesia for an entire traumatic experience." As psychologist Richard McNally observed in his book, *Remembering Trauma*, "deliberate attempts to suppress emotionally disturbing thoughts tend to backfire," since people seem to have more difficulty forgetting them

Dr. Corwin's Videotapes

One more case, reported by psychiatrist David Corwin in a 1997 article in *Child Maltreatment* ("Videotaped Discovery of a Reportedly Unrecallable Memory of Child Sexual Abuse: Comparison with a Childhood Interview Videotaped 11 Years Before"), was widely hailed as proof for repressed or dissociated memories. In 1984, Corwin was hired to evaluate abuse claims in a bitter, five-year custody dispute over a six-year-old daughter he called Jane Doe, who later identified herself in public as Nicole Taus. The father had been granted custody after a hospital identified burn scars on the child's feet that the mother had allegedly inflicted. Subsequently, the child "disclosed" sexual abuse by the mother as well. Corwin videotaped his three interview sessions with the child, which spanned

---

* I asked Elizabeth Loftus whether she felt this study indicated the reality of repressed memories, and she responded that she wrote the questions for the study back in 1991. "In retrospect, I don't think asking people whether they forgot for awhile tells you much. Roseanne Ban Arnold claims to remember her mother molesting her when she was six months old. If she were in our sample, she would probably answer 'Yes' to the question. How would we interpret that?"

four months. During the sessions, the child alleged that the mother had burned her feet and had put her finger inside the child's vagina during baths, starting at the age of three, "probably 99 times." Corwin verified that in his opinion the abuse had occurred, and the mother consequently lost all visitation rights. Oddly, she was not prosecuted for child abuse.

In 1995, when Taus was seventeen, Corwin got back in touch with her and again videotaped her reaction as he asked her about the alleged child abuse. At that point, her father had died and she was living with a foster mother, but she had recently resumed contact with her real mother, who emphatically denied having abused her. "It felt so good to have her hug me," Taus said. "I could tell that was my mom." She began to rebuild a relationship with her, inviting her to share Thanksgiving with her, going shopping together, and inviting her to her swim meets. Taus was "very, very happy with that," according to her stepmother.

Nicole Taus was confused about what to think, so she wanted to see the videos of herself at six. "I don't know what happened to me as a little girl," she had told her stepmother. "I've got this memory, and I've got that memory, and I've been told this, and I've been told that."

Before showing the old videos to her, Corwin asked what Taus recalled about them. She remembered the allegations about the burnt feet and that sexual abuse was also part of it. Then she closed her eyes and said, "Oh, my gosh. That's really weird. I accused her of taking pictures of me and my brother and selling them and I accused her of—when she was bathing me or whatever, hurting me." She thought she could actually recall the pain in the bathtub. "It's like I took a picture, like a few seconds long, a picture of the pain."

Then Corwin let the 17-year-old view all 2.5 hours of his videotaped interviews of her when she was six. As she watched, she held her head and screamed, "Oh God! She did it! She did it. I can see it. I can see it." Afterwards, she told Corwin: "The little girl I see in those videotapes I don't see as [how she] made up those things, and it doesn't make sense to me that knowing the truth I would out-and-out lie like that. And I have to believe that to some extent my mom did hurt me." She concluded that perhaps her mother sincerely denied the abuse because she herself didn't remember it, perhaps because she had multiple personalities, as her father had once told her. "She did it and she never remembered," Taus concluded. "She did it and later on, you know, if the memory was erased, she was in a different part of herself and she doesn't remember any more."

Subsequently, Nicole Taus called her mother and screamed at her, "I know that you molested me." She cut off contact with her, became angry and depressed, and soon left her fostermother's home as well.

David Corwin not only wrote up this story but showed excerpts from the videotapes at meetings. The case of "Jane Doe" was hailed as proof for the accurate recovery of repressed or dissociated traumatic memories, convincing even experimental psychologists Stephen Lindsay and Jonathan Schooler. Lawyers presented the case at conferences, expert witnesses cited it in court as concrete proof of the validity of repressed memories, and professors began teaching the case in their university courses.

But psychologists Elizabeth Loftus and Melvin Guyer, acting like good journalists, dug into the case and cast doubt on it in two articles published in the *Skeptical Inquirer* in 2002. As they pointed out, the 1984 videotapes may have followed years of poorly conducted, leading interviews with little Nicole. "In those days, few experts were aware of the way children's memories can be tainted by interviewers who are on a mission to find evidence of sexual abuse. Few knew how to interview children in nonsuggestive, noncoercive ways." (*See Chapter 5.*)

Corwin had neglected to quote from the Febuary 1984 report of a clinical psychologist, who had interviewed everyone involved in the case and had reviewed the police and court records. He thought that perhaps the abuse allegations "exist only in the mind and fantasy of [the father] and are communicated to [Nicole] as [the mother] contends." He observed that Nicole's narration did not seem spontaneous: "She has told her story numerous times to a number of different people and she now sounds mechanical." As for the burned feet, he said: "It was never determined if her feet and hand were indeed burned, since Nicole has a fungus condition that causes her skin to blister and peel."

Loftus and Guyer also discovered that the father had been physically abusive to Nicole's older brother, drank to excess, and had committed insurance fraud. He was not the sympathetic figure Corwin had depicted in his article.

Most crucially, the investigative psychologists did not accept that the videotapes provided evidence of recovered memories. Rather, the first thing Taus recalled was inaccurate, that she had accused her mother of taking pornographic pictures of her and her brother—something she had never said during her 1984 taped interviews. That story apparently originated with her stepmother, who did make such unsubstantiated claims. Nor had Taus entirely forgotten the sex abuse allegations. "There was ample evidence that [Nicole] talked about the abuse allegations on innumerable occasions with several people between the two sessions during which she was videotaped, undermining claims of massive repression or dissociation," concluded Loftus and Guyer.

Thus, the real lesson of the Nicole Taus case appears to be that the child had been indoctrinated by her father and stepmother, resulting in the 1984 taped allegations. Then, upon watching those tapes as a young adult, Taus came to believe that the allegations must have been true. They did indeed trigger traumatic memories of being abused in the bathtub, but those memories were probably false in the first place.

Lenore Terr: Story-Time

In her 1994 book, *Unchained Memories: True Stories of Traumatic Memories, Lost and Found*, psychiatrist Lenore Terr purported to prove the existence of repressed memories. She did not. Instead, she offered a few anecdotal cases, served up with a tantalizing mix of irrelevant biological studies, presented as if they provide valid experimental underpinnings for her assertions. In her prologue, Terr explained that she decided to write the book "in short-story style because that format is enjoyable and relatively uncomplicated." Her stories do make compelling, simple reading, but the unwary reader is likely to swallow Terr's pet theories as though they were proven facts.

Terr made her name by studying the Chowchilla, California, children who were kidnapped and buried alive for two days in 1976. "I found that every one of the kidnapped children retained detailed, precise memories of what had happened, even in [a] later study," Terr wrote. That should surprise no one. But Terr then concluded, based on a 1988 report on 20 children who were repeatedly abused before the age of five, that *repetition* will *diminish* recall. She termed a single traumatic event "Type I," and numerous such assaults "Type II." She asserted that a child "well rehearsed in terror" by Type II trauma would probably repress all of the memories.

Her evidence for this theory is questionable. While the Chowchilla children ranged from 5 to 14 years of age, all of Terr's "Type II" subjects were under 5 years old at the time of their abuse. Over half of them were below the age of three. Because almost no one remembers *anything* from that time of life, it is not necessary to theorize about repression to explain the lack of recall.

Terr said that she could spot "behavioral memories" of very early trauma, even without verbal reports, but her interpretations of children's play were subjective—and biased by what she already expected to find. In one case where she failed to spot telltale signs, she did not already know that the child had supposedly been abused. She explained: "I probably did not see any behavioral memories in her case because I was not yet looking."*

Most behavioral psychologists would disagree with the Type I/Type II theory, citing the concept of classical conditioning. The more often the same terrible thing happens to people, the more likely that they will remember it and react with dread and fear. Rather than continuing to believe that Daddy is a wonderful man, in other words, abused children would exhibit automatic fear because of the association between Daddy and unpleasant events. The children might

---

* Terr's 1988 study became even more suspect when she revealed that one subject was abused as a seven-month-old "Satanic worship victim"—almost certainly a false allegation, since there has never been any evidence to validate such widely rumored "Satanic" cults (*see Chapter 4.*)

not remember each precise event, but they would certainly know that they had been repeatedly traumatized. Memory researcher Larry Squire, who was quoted in Terr's book as though he agreed with her conclusions, told me that "she twisted my data for her own ends" and that her Type II theory "doesn't make any sense to me at all. She says you would remember one event but forget multiple incidents. I would think it would be the other way around."

Indeed, if we were to believe Terr's theory, then many of the same Chowchilla children who vividly recalled being buried alive for two days would forget all about it if they were entombed on a monthly basis. Every time, they would march down into the sunken vehicle blithely unaware, protected by the marvelous defense mechanism of Type II massive repression.

A representative example of the case studies in Terr's book is that of one Gary Baker (a pseudonym), who came to believe that his mother had thrown him into an irrigation ditch, nearly let a train run over him, locked him in a refrigerator, held his head in a toilet, masturbated with a white dildo in front of him, and stuck a red baseball bat up his rectum. Terr accepted all of these recovered memories as accurate, without question. One hot, humid day at the end of a five-hour drive, soon after his girl-friend dumped him, Gary saw three sudden images, including the red baseball bat. Then he blacked out. He soon entered therapy and retrieved the rest, running the images like color videos in his head. His brother Barry eventually located his own repressed memories of being locked in a freezer chest, which constituted sufficient confirmation, although no one else in his family believed Gary.

Also, "as a kid, Gary could hold a note on his saxophone longer than anybody else at school," so that proved that he was thrown into an irrigation ditch, where he learned to hold his breath.

In the same chapter, Terr cited a shock-aversion study conducted on fruit fly larvae. Five days following their aversive shocks, after their metamorphosis into flies, they still remembered their training. What, one may inquire, does this have to do with repressed memories? "Eight electroshock cycles to a fruit fly larva suffice to alter the behavior of the adult fly," Terr wrote. "One drowning attempt can change a child's life."

That strikes me as quite a leap. I don't think that most of us need a fruit fly experiment to prove to us that attempting to drown an infant is a truly horrible thing to do. Because the adult flies weren't hypnotized to determine whether they could recall their abuse as larvae, the study says nothing about repressed memories of human beings.

In 1996, psychology professor Jennifer Freyd, who had come to believe that her father molested her after she retrieved abuse memories, published *Betrayal Trauma*, in which she espoused theories similar to Lenore Terr, whose work she cited favorably. Freyd theorized that children were more likely to forget all about repeated sexual abuse if trusted caretakers, such as parents, were the perpetrators. "The more the victim is dependent on the perpetrator—the more power the perpetrator has over the victim in a trusted and intimate relationship—the more the crime is one of betrayal. This betrayal by a trusted caregiver is the core factor in determining amnesia for a trauma." In other words, if you were repeatedly raped by your father, you were likely to repress the memory because you couldn't tolerate the idea that such an important figure in your life would do such a thing to you.

Miss America and Other Famous Victims

Three well-publicized cases are often cited as anecdotal evidence of massive repression, so they deserve at least brief examination.

The 1958 Miss America, Marilyn Van Derbur Atler, reported in 1991, when she was 53, that her father had routinely sexually violated her from the age of five until she left for college. She said that she had repressed all knowledge of the abuse for a few years, remembering it at age 24.

Brown University public policy professor Ross Cheit said that he woke from a 1992 dream feeling a "powerful presence" in the room, which he identified as William Farmer, an administrator of the San Francisco Boys' Chorus summer camp, which Cheit had attended in the late 1960s. Later that day, he recalled repeated molestation by Farmer. After some investigation, Cheit confronted Farmer by telephone, taping the conversation, and the former camp administrator admitted molesting him. Farmer was later convicted of child sexual abuse.

In a similar case, Frank Fitzpatrick, a Rhode Island insurance adjuster, recalled sexual abuse by James Porter, a former Catholic priest, who had been his confessor in 1962 when Fitzpatrick was 12 years old. When Fitzpatrick contacted other altar boys, they, too, recalled abuse. Over 100 Father Porter victims came forward. He was tried and convicted of sexual abuse.

As convincing as these cases may sound, they do not prove the existence of massively repressed memories. Marilyn Van Derbur Atler's case is of great interest, because her oldest sister, Gwen Mitchell, said that she was sexually abused by her father and never forgot it. I interviewed Gwen, and her story rang true to me, though there is no physical proof. When she was seven, she alleged, she woke to find her father masturbating her. Until she left home at 18, he continued periodically to fondle her while he masturbated to climax. Gwen learned to turn her body off. She did not respond sexually during the abuse. She never told anyone about it, but she always recalled it vividly. "I used to plot his murder in egregious ways in the dark."

Until Marilyn told her that she, too, had recalled being abused, Gwen told me,

"I thought I was the only one. Mother used to say that he liked me the best. He called me the Countess, so I believed I was special and the only one." Gwen believed that Marilyn did indeed repress her memories. She thought that perhaps she, too, repressed memories of actual intercourse, which she did not recall.

Nonetheless, Gwen's experience does not prove that Marilyn was raped for years and forgot it. Marilyn claimed that her father was raping her from age 5 until age 18 and that she had absolutely no conscious memory of the abuse. She would kiss her boyfriend (later her husband) Larry chastely good night, from the time she was 15 until 18, then go into her bedroom to be raped by her father, and forget it all by the next morning.

While Marilyn Atler says that she initially recalled her abuse at age 24, after years of gentle prodding by DeDe Harvey, a family friend and counselor, her saga appears a bit more complicated. According to her own testimony, she *really* began recovering memories when she turned 40 in 1984 and experienced a debilitating form of psychosomatic paralysis. "My memories and feelings surfaced and overwhelmed me with anguish from 1984 through 1988." For several years, she did what she terms her "work," which included over 100 deep massages and rolfing sessions, at least 60 acupuncture sessions, 50 sessions of hypnosis, neurolinguistic programming, dance therapy, bioenergetics, self-defense therapy, small group meetings of incest survivors, inner-child work, and frequent sessions with her therapist. She also read "hundreds of articles and 72 books" on incest. Her night terrors finally stopped in 1988 when she was put on anti-depressant medication.

One could certainly surmise that as a young adult, Atler may have pushed painful childhood memories to the background in order to concentrate on her busy role as college student and beauty queen. But that's very different from the massive memory repression required by Alter's later beliefs about her past. There are several possibilities. (1) Marilyn Atler may not have been sexually abused by her father, but after somehow learning about, or sensing, her sister's experience, she developed a belief in her own memories. (2) Atler may have been fondled in the same manner as Gwen and attempted to "forget" about it while she pursued fame as Miss America. Though she did not forget, she denied it to herself until she was 24. Then, when she was 40, she actively pursued more violent "repressed memories" of events that never occurred. (3) Atler's recovered memories may all be accurate.

From my discussions with Ross Cheit, I was convinced that he did indeed recall incidents of sexual abuse after the passage of many years, but it is unclear to me how frequently he was molested. Cheit believes the incidents occurred nightly during the month of August in 1968, when Bill Farmer was the camp administrator. He also thinks that another incident occurred the previous year, when Farmer visited the camp briefly.

Cheit's memories were not particularly traumatic when they came back to him. "They were like remembering the time I stole something from the variety store and got caught." Mostly, he was embarrassed and experienced a "visceral uneasiness."* He had genuinely liked Farmer, and their sexual encounters were not altogether unpleasant for him. "There were no threats. I never sensed danger. I didn't fear him. He was nice to me."

It was only months later, when his therapist suggested that he purchase a book about male survivors, that Cheit reframed his experience. "It was such a stark title, *Abused Boys*, and here I was holding it in this public place. I felt like a kid with *Playboy*, ashamed to be holding it, and everyone would know why I was going to buy it." For the first time, he said to himself, "This book is about me. I was an abused boy. I couldn't say words like 'molest' without cringing."

Curiously, Cheit had always recalled another sexual incident at the camp in which a black counselor kissed him on the lips. He was repulsed and got away quickly. Cheit did not know why he forgot about his experience with Farmer and always remembered this kiss. "I find it puzzling, that's for sure," he told me.

I would guess that Cheit always remembered the kiss because he found it revolting and therefore memorable. His sexual initiation with Farmer, on the other hand, was not particularly upsetting. "I didn't dread it," he told me. "I wasn't thinking, 'Oh, my God, he's going to come in again.' There was some feeling of apprehension about it, but it was more tied up with guilt and confusion about sex."

Despite recalling his sexual abuse years after it occurred, when I spoke to him in 1994 Ross Cheit did not know whether to call his memory "repressed" or not, nor did he necessarily believe the kind of massive repression reported by other Survivors in which years of abuse were supposedly siphoned off from consciousness. As the years went by, however, Cheit became a dogmatic voice asserting the reality of repressed memories and in 2014 published *The Witch-Hunt Narrative*, disputing that the modern sex abuse hysteria is comparable to the witch craze of the 16th and 17th centuries.

As with Cheit, it appeared that Frank Fitzpatrick was indeed molested by a trusted adult figure, Father James Porter. But, as with Cheit, it is questionable whether this memory was truly "repressed." In a 1993 speech, Fitzpatrick said that he "didn't really forget" his rape, but pushed it out of his consciousness for many years. In other words, although he played an important role in making public serious abuse, his case may add little to the repressed-memory dispute.**

---

*   Cheit clearly believes that the long-forgotten molestation was at least partly responsible for his life problems. He had entered therapy a few months before recalling the abuse, although he insisted that his therapist never suggested the possibility of sexual abuse. "I was very unsettled, more than ever before in my life. I felt somehow adrift, as if some anchor in my life had been raised. I had doubts about my marriage, my job, everything."

**   Since the "Father Porter case" was so widely hailed as proof of recovered memory, I made a concerted effort to interview Porter victims. According to Massachusetts psychiatrist Stuart Grassian, who conducted a survey

Psychiatrist Elizabeth Feigon suggested three possible reasons that people might have claimed to have recovered memories of abuse, when in fact they had always remembered their experience. (1) They must claim repressed memories to collect money in a lawsuit; otherwise, the statute of limitations would have run out. (2) When repressed memories were popular, some people were ashamed to admit having known all along and not told. (3) Those who have always remembered may have yearned for the attention, drama, and sympathy available to those claiming recovered memories.

Cases of Real Denial

Whenever falsely accused parents protested their innocence, they were inevitably labeled "in denial," implying that they really did commit incest and were simply incapable of admitting it. This unfair characterization made many critics of repressed memory automatically reject the entire concept of denial. Yet there is indeed a human tendency to deny unpleasant reality, and at times the power of denial can be truly astonishing.

In 1938, psychologist Milton Erickson wrote of two cases in which women whose traumatic experience was well-documented subsequently denied that reality. Although we have here second-hand testimony from 80 years ago, it is nonetheless worth examining, since Erickson's observations were compelling.

In Case 1, Erickson described two girls, ages 9 and 11, who were arrested in a raid on a whorehouse, along with 12 male patrons and the girls' parents, who prostituted their own children. Full confessions were obtained from the parents, patrons, and children. "In addition," Erickson wrote, "medical examination of the girls disclosed numerous bruises and injuries [and] that they had been subjected to vaginal and rectal coitus and infected with syphilis and gonorrhea, both rectal and vaginal."

Erickson interviewed the girls four times, with two months between each interview. During the first interview, conducted during the first week of their institutionalization, "both told their story readily, easily and completely, manifesting much unhappiness over and repugnance to their experiences." They expressed "great satisfaction" over the punishments given to the adults, including their parents. At the same time, they recalled "pleasurable, though guilty, feelings" about their sexual experiences.

By the third interview, four months later, the girls did not want to talk about the

---

of 43 Porter victims, 18 percent reported "no thoughts" of the abuse until triggered by media reports or calls in 1992. That may mean that eight of the subjects had completely forgotten the abuse, though the questionnaire's wording was not altogether clear on this point. According to Grassian, most of those were molested in only a single instance, and he could not say whether they involved traumatic penetration. Despite my repeated requests, however, neither Fitzpatrick nor Grassian would put me in contact with Porter victims, and Fitzpatrick would not talk to me about his experience.

sexual abuse, but "seemed to be interested only in immediate matters. Question-ing about their past experience elicited an utterly inadequate account, in which even major details were denied or greatly minimized. Rectal coitus was emphati-cally and resentfully denied by both." Now there was no pleasurable recollection, only repugnance. "Ma wouldn't let anybody do those things," one of the girls said.

By the time of the final interview, six months later, "strong resentment was ex-pressed over my interest in the story," Erickson observed. No information was giv-en spontaneously other than the declaration that it was "all a lot of nasty lies." The girls defended their parents. They stated that "some bad men came to the house, but nothing bad happened." Erickson concluded that "they seemed to have no real recollection of the whole experience as an actual happening in their own lives. At no time could their sincerity or their full belief in their statements be doubted."

Case 2 also involved denial, though not of sexual abuse. A young man on pa-role was driving his girl friend to a motel when, because of his reckless driving, the car overturned and burst into flames, pinning the young woman underneath. "The man freed himself but made no effort to rescue his companion," Erickson wrote. Passing motorists rescued the girl, but she was severely burned. At the trial, the girl testified against her boyfriend with "much bitterness and hatred."

Eight months later, however, she changed her mind and tried to secure a retrial, saying that she had given misleading testimony. "She's nuts!" the man told Erickson. "She told the truth the first time." He didn't want a retrial, since he feared a longer sentence. When Erickson interviewed the girl, he found her "obviously sincere." She now believed that "the man had exerted every effort possible to rescue her" and gave a detailed account which Erickson considered "a process of retrospective falsification and misconstruction." She explained that her long period of hospitalization had given her time to realize how mistaken she had been. "No human being would do such a thing nor could anybody endure being so treated," she said. She emphasized that to be deserted under such circumstances would be "intolerable."

What are we to make of these cases? In Case 2, it appears that we do indeed have testimony to the malleability and suggestibility of memory. In this case, the woman has reconstructed her past, reinventing her boy friend's behavior after the accident, rehearsing it in her mind until it became real to her. She could not bear to think that he would abandon her.

In Case 1, it is not quite as clear that the two girls had literally rewritten their past. It appears likely that they were sick of talking about it and resented Erick-son's repeated visits and insistence that they again recount the unpleasant events. Nonetheless, it is clear that they were "in denial" about their parents' behavior and the extent of their abuse. Quite probably, the two girls contributed to one an-other's new version of reality by discussing it and reshaping their past collectively.

Do these cases provide proof for the concept of repression? No, but they do speak to the human capacity to rewrite the past and to deny reality.

Elizabeth Loftus: "That Woman"

Frederic Bartlett's work on memory spawned other research, though much of it was ignored in the United States until Elizabeth Loftus and Ulric Neisser reclaimed it.* (Donald Broadbent, Alan Baddeley, R. Conrad, Graham Hitch, Endel Tulving, Larry Weiskrantz, and others had sustained and enlarged on the Bartlett tradition.) Loftus, a University of Washington psychology professor, became fascinated with the malleability of memory early in her academic career. Her conclusions sound remarkably similar to Bartlett's: "Every time we recall an event, we must reconstruct the memory, and with each recollection the memory may be changed— colored by succeeding events, other people's recollections or suggestions, increased understanding, or a new context." Memory, she asserts, is "an amoeba-like creature with powers to make us laugh, and cry, and clench our fists. Enormous powers—powers even to make us believe in something that never happened."

In 1974, Loftus published an article entitled "Reconstructing Memory: The Incredible Eyewitness" in *Psychology Today,* mentioning how testimony on her research had helped acquit a defendant. Within days, defense lawyers were clamoring for her services. Consequently, for the next four decades, Loftus became a fixture in courtrooms as well as psychology labs. On the stand, she routinely annoys prosecutors, explaining how easy it is to bias a line-up by showing the witness a photograph of the suspect beforehand; how "unconscious transference"—confusing a person seen in one situation with someone in an entirely different context—can lead to false identifications; how our memory fills in gaps according to our expectations."

In the classic Loftus experiment, subjects (usually college students) were shown a series of slides depicting a car that turned right at an intersection with a yield sign, then hit a pedestrian on the crosswalk. Half of the subjects were given misleading information embedded in questions asked immediately after the viewing. "Did another car pass the red Datsun while it was stopped at the stop sign?" As a result, over 80 percent of the test subjects later asserted that they had seen a stop sign rather than a yield sign. Over the years, Loftus conducted hundreds of increasingly sophisticated experiments on memory distortion on more than 20,000 subjects. During the course of her work, she has created quite a few men-

---

* Neisser is famous, among other things, for debunking "flashbulb" memories, which purport to preserve important moments in nearly photographic form. While most people think they remember exactly where they were and what they were doing when Kennedy was assassinated or when the *Challenger* exploded, Neisser showed that they are in fact wrong most of the time.

tal artifacts, as she wrote in a 1992 article: "People have recalled seeing nonexistent items, such as broken glass, tape recorders, and even something as large and conspicuous as a barn [in a bucolic scene that contained no buildings at all], and have recalled incorrect traits for items they did see, such that a clean-shaven man developed a mustache, straight hair became curly, a stop sign became a yield sign, and a hammer became a screwdriver."

Loftus concluded that "misleading information can turn a lie into memory's truth. It can make people confident about these false memories and also, apparently, impair earlier recollections. Once adopted, the newly created memories can be believed as strongly as genuine memories." Loftus asserts that such mental distortion does not rely on particularly unusual traits or circumstances. In fact, she and a co-author once boasted that they could create a "brave new world" of manufactured images: "Give us a dozen healthy memories [and] we'll guarantee to take any one at random and train it to become any type of memory that we might select...regardless of its origin or the brain that holds it."

Never one to flee from controversy, in 1990 Loftus wound up testifying in a landmark court battle based on Eileen Franklin Lipsker's "recovered memories" of how her father, George Franklin, had raped and murdered her friend Susan Nason in 1969 when both girls were eight years old. The case was meticulously reported by Harry MacLean in his book, *Once Upon a Time*. On the stand, Loftus explained that memory is not like a videotape recorder; that stressful events can cause fewer details to be recalled; that witnesses often incorporate new facts into old memories. She pointed out that the more frequently erroneous memories are repeated, the more confident the reporters become. During cross-examination, however, Loftus had to admit that none of her experiments dealt with repressed memories of traumatic events. Sure, someone might mistake a peripheral detail such as a yield sign rather than a stop sign, but none of her subjects failed to remember the main events. No one forgot that a car had hit a pedestrian.

At the same trial, psychiatrist Lenore Terr's folksy style won over the jury. Terr recounted her theory of Type I and Type II memories and asserted that a mind holding repressed memories of trauma was like an abscess waiting to burst. Once it pops out, it will be as clear as the event itself. Terr stated with great confidence that she could tell whether someone's memory was true or false, based on the level of detail, emotional involvement, and presenting symptoms.[*] The jury found George Franklin guilty, and the case was widely hailed as "proof" of repressed memories.

Loftus remained unconvinced. George Franklin had unquestionably been a terrible father who had physically, emotionally, and perhaps sexually abused his

---

[*]   Terr presented her own highly colored version of the Eileen Lipsker Franklin case in *Unchained Memories,* including the misinformation that Susan Nason's autopsy revealed semen in her vagina.

wife and children. But whether Eileen's memories were accurate or not remained a question. For one thing, as Harry MacLean documented in his book, Eileen's story kept shifting, changing. First she said that the memory had appeared in a dream, then that she visualized the scene during therapy sessions while hypnotized. When she found that such testimony would be inadmissible, she asserted that she had never been hypnotized and had instead remembered the murder spontaneously when her five-year-old daughter looked up at her.* That had supposedly triggered the hidden memory of Susan Nason's immobilized gaze just before George Franklin crushed her head with a rock.

Many other details of Eileen's memory metamorphosed as time went by, including a clearly visualized black molester with an afro whom Eileen then magically transformed into a white friend of her father's. MacLean also described how Eileen bathed in the sympathy and attention which the trial brought her. (On this point, at least, MacLean and Terr agree. In her book, Terr describes Eileen "glowing like the moon" in the company of sympathizers.)

What MacLean did not understand at the time he covered the trial, however, was how therapists in the late 1980s were actively encouraging their clients—especially those with relationship troubles—to believe that repressed memories of sexual abuse were the true cause of their problems. Seeking help for her troubled marriage and depression over a miscarriage, Eileen saw two counselors who helped her retrieve such incest memories: clinical psychologist Katherine Rieder and marriage and child counselor Kirk Barrett. Over the course of a year, beginning in the summer of 1988, Rieder, who specialized in "codependency issues," helped Eileen recover her first sexual abuse memories relating to her father (she visualized him inserting his finger into her vagina when she was six or seven). Later, when Eileen switched to Barrett, who held a masters in psychology, she remembered the murder scene as well as actual incestuous intercourse.

Barrett's testimony takes up less than a page of *Once Upon a Time*. MacLean described him as "soft-looking, a mellow Teddy bear, with a tanned, pillowy face." The therapist explained in a low, soothing voice how, during five sessions in June and July of 1989, Eileen had recovered her memories of the murder. During his testimony, a juror, reporter, and research assistant fell asleep. While his monotone made for a boring witness, it undoubtedly served him well as a hypnotist.

MacLean himself later realized that he missed this crucial point. "Quite frankly," he wrote in a letter to me, "I didn't know enough to suspect that memories of childhood sexual abuse could be therapeutically induced. That information

---

* MacLean suggested that Eileen may have gotten the idea for this final version from Lenore Terr, who had appeared with her on a *Today Show* segment. Terr had stated that repressed memories could be triggered when "one's own child is the age one was at the time of the event in the first place."

didn't hit the public arena until the False Memory Syndrome Foundation came into existence, and I certainly never encountered it in my research or interviews."* MacLean was not alone. Leaving the courtroom, Elizabeth Loftus didn't know anything about *The Courage to Heal*, but she was determined to pursue the suspect area of recovered memories.

But how could she show experimentally that memories of sexual abuse or other traumas could be implanted? If she succeeded, the experiment itself would constitute a form of mental abuse, convincing the innocent subject that something horrible had happened to him or her. Aside from her own ethical concerns, the Human Subjects Committee at the University of Washington would never allow such an experiment. The problem appeared insurmountable, but Loftus devised a clever analogue. She suggested that her research assistants, such as Jim, tell a younger sibling, such as 14-year-old Chris, that he had been lost in a shopping mall (a mythical event) when he was 5 years old, but that a nice man wearing a flannel shirt had found him and brought him back to their parents.

Two days later, Chris remembered how he had felt that day. "I was so scared that I would never see my family again. I knew that I was in trouble." Two weeks later, Chris had rehearsed the memory in some detail, filling in the gaps. He recalled, with some emotion, how he had been frightened and cried. He had created an image of his rescuer, who was bald and wore glasses. Even after he was "debriefed" and told that the story wasn't true, Chris clung to it "Really? I thought I remembered being lost ... and looking around for you guys. I do remember that, and then crying, and Mom coming up and saying, 'Where were you? Don't you ever do that again.'" Six subjects, 25 percent of the pilot sample, ranging in age from 18 to 53, developed memories of being lost in a mall at the age of five. In 1994, Loftus published the book, *The Myth of Repressed Memory*.

Therapists such as Judith Herman and Karen Olio scoffed at Loftus's experiments. "The notion that therapists can implant scenarios of horror in the minds of their patients is easily accepted because it appeals to common prejudices," Herman said. Olio dismissed the false mall memories as irrelevant. Anyone could believe in such a common, mild trauma. That's very different from repressed memories of sadistic sexual abuse. The two events aren't comparable. Although "suggestions can affect us—perhaps influence our choices at the supermarket, maybe even our vote for president—to claim that such suggestions have fundamentally and falsely altered an entire client population's understanding of themselves and their histories seems grossly exaggerated," Olio concluded.

As a result of her experiments and her outspoken criticism of therapists who lead their patients to believe in sexual that may never have occurred, Loftus be-

---

* Since MacLean wrote those words, the decision against George Franklin was overturned, and he was released in 1996.

came the lightning rod for the controversy over the "backlash" against the Recovery Movement. One prosecutor called her a "whore," and an accuser's mother told her she was joining hands with the murderers and rapists of the world. Returning from a conference, Loftus found herself seated next to a therapist who, when she discovered her seat-mate's identity, swatted Loftus while shrieking, "You're that *woman!* You're that *woman!*"

Yet Loftus is, herself, a victim of childhood sexual abuse. When she was six years old, her babysitter used to rub her arm gently, which was comforting and pleasant. One night, though, "he took his pants off, pulled my dress off over my head, and removed my underpants. He lay down on the bed and pulled me on top of him, positioning me so that our pelvises touched. His arms circled around me. I felt him pushing against me, and I knew something was wrong. Embarrassed and confused, I squirmed off him and ran out of the room. After that, there is only blackness …. My memory took him and destroyed him." Clearly, Loftus recognizes the horror of sexual abuse and how it can indeed distort the memory. On the other hand, she never forgot this incident.

Loftus understands how insidious personal memories can be, particularly when a trusted authority figure such as a family member or therapist validates them. At a family reunion, one of Loftus' uncles told her that when she was 14, she had been the one to find her mother's drowned body. Although she was initially sure that the story was untrue, "I actually started to think maybe I did," she recounted. Over the next few days, she began to visualize the scene: her mother floating face down in the pool, young Beth's approach and horror. Perhaps this explained why she was so upset whenever she thought about her mother. Maybe it even accounted for her compulsive workaholic nature, trying to avoid this primal scene. Soon afterwards, however, her brother called to tell her that her uncle had been mistaken.

Because of her principled support for those falsely accused on the basis of repressed memories, and her debunking of the case that David Corwin touted as proof for massive repression, Loftus was sued in 2003 by Nicole Taus, who claimed defamation, invasion of privacy, infliction of emotional distress, and fraud, even though Loftus and her co-author had never revealed her name—Taus herself did so by filing the lawsuit. In response, Loftus's long-time employer, the University of Washington, started an investigation against her for "scientific misconduct," impounding her files for nearly two years, and not allowing her to discuss or write about the case. In 2007, the California Supreme Court finally ruled in Loftus's favor, and the protracted lawsuit ended.

Loftus took a new position at the University of California at Irvine, where she has continued her research on memory distortion, for which she has received multiple awards, including the 2010 Scientific Freedom and Responsibility Award from the American Association for the Advancement of Science. In her acceptance speech, she said she had never imagined she would become "the target of organized, relentless vitriol and harassment." To preserve their freedom, she urged fellow scientists to speak out "against even the most cherished beliefs that reflect unsubstantiated myths."

Although vilified by the Survivor Movement, Loftus tried to take a moderate stand. She did not deny the possibility that repressed memories may exist. In fact, she expressed a belief in them, employing her own definition. "If repression is the avoidance in your conscious awareness of unpleasant experiences that come back to you, yes, I believe in repression." That is not the same mechanism hypothesized in most of these cases, however, as she pointed out. "If it [repression] is a blocking out of an endless stream of traumas that occur over and over that leave a person with absolutely no awareness that these things happened, that make them behave in destructive ways and re-emerge decades later in some reliable form—I don't see any evidence for it. It flies in the face of everything we know about memory."[*]

In the 21st century, a new generation of experimental psychologists followed Loftus's lead, demonstrating how easy it is to create false memories. In 2016, Julia Shaw published *The Memory Illusion*, a summary of her own and other's work. "I have convinced people they have committed crimes that never occurred, suffering from a physical injury they never had, or were attacked by a dog when no such attack ever took place," she wrote. *The Memory Hackers* (2016), a Nova program on public television, featured one of Shaw's subjects recalling an illusory crime in three sessions. In that study, over 70 percent of her subjects developed false memories. "What could have been turns into what would have been turns into what was," the experiment psychologist explained. Her conclusion? "Any event, no matter how important, emotional or traumatic it may seem, can be forgotten, misremembered, or even be entirely fictitious. . . . All of us can come to confidently and vividly remember entire events that never actually took place."

Wilder Penfield, Karl Lashley, and the Search for the Engram

One of the fallacies that Elizabeth Loftus fought against is the notion that memories reside in specific places in the brain, ready to pop out under the proper stimuli. In the 1930s—and continuing through the 1950s—Wilder Penfield, a Montreal neurosurgeon, stumbled onto "proof" of such localization while operating on epileptics. To help locate the damaged area of the brain, Penfield would stimulate various points of the temporal lobe with a weak electric current. He found that

---

[*]   Social psychologist Richard Ofshe agreed with Loftus, going even further in denying the existence of what he termed "robust repression."

when he electrified a particular point in the brain, some of his patients spontaneously recalled what he took to be specific memories. In 1969, he wrote that "neuronal connections . . . can be followed again by an electric current many years later with no loss of detail, as though a tape recorder had been receiving it all."

Penfield's assertions were gobbled up by the popular press, and they have continued to influence many psychologists and laymen, who believe that his findings proved his contentions. Yet the "memories" Penfield evoked were problematic for a number of reasons. First, they were reported by epileptic patients whose brains were not working normally. Second, during Penfield's long career, only 40 patients out of 520—7.7 percent—whose temporal lobes were stimulated reported having such memories. Third, the "flashbacks" reported by the patients were not necessarily replications of real events that had occurred in their pasts. One patient, for example, visualized her own birth. Another said she "seemed to be at the lumberyard," even though she had never been near one in real life. As Ulric Neisser pointed out, these were probably "synthetic constructions and not literal recalls." Fourth, stimulation of precisely the same spot produced the same memory *only* if the probes were conducted in rapid succession. Otherwise, different responses arose.

Loftus suggested that "these so-called memories, then, appear to consist merely of the thoughts and ideas that happened to exist just prior to and during the stimulation."

Another problem with Penfield's reports was his own attitude about them. They excited him, and he let his patients know this. This could easily have led to distortions in reporting, because the patients knew the expectations he had that they would "remember" something. "I think I saw the river," one patient offered hopefully. "I had a little memory—a scene in a play," another said.

The eager surgeon took all such reports as proof that he was probing the mysteries of the mind. "I was more astonished, each time my electrode brought forth such a response." While acknowledging that another neurologist interpreted such episodes as "dreamy states" or "psychical seizures," Penfield asserted, "It was evident at once that these were not dreams. They were electrical activations of the sequential record of consciousness, a record that had been laid down during the patient's earlier experience. The patient 'relived' all that he had been aware of in that earlier period of time as in a moving-picture 'flashback.'" Nearing the end of his career, Penfield expressed a somewhat mystical attitude about the human brain, asserting that "the mind may be a distinct and *different essence.*"

Penfield believed that he had discovered the elusive "engram," a word popularized by Harvard psychologist Karl Lashley in the 1920s. During the same decades when Penfield was zapping his patients' gray matter, Lashley was training rats to run in a maze, then cutting out different portions of their brains and turning them loose in the maze again. As expected, the rats didn't perform as well the second time. But what vexed Lashley was his inability to find any particular portion of the brain that contained the full memory or ability to remember the maze. He kept hoping that when he snipped the crucial area, the rat would just stumble randomly around the maze, completely at a loss. But that didn't happen. Regardless of which cortical section he removed, the results were the same. In 1929, he wrote that "the maze habit, when formed, is not localized in any single area of the cerebrum." Another 20 years of maze running and rat mutilation failed to alter his findings. In 1950, Lashley concluded that "somehow, equivalent traces are established throughout the functional area," adding that "all of the cells of the brain must be in almost constant activity, either firing or actively inhibited."

Lashley died in 1959, but he would be pleased to know that subsequent testing indicates that synapses fire like fireflies all over the brain when it is learning or trying to recall something. Or, as biological memory expert Larry Squire put it, "*all* cortical regions are involved in both processing and memory storage, though always within functionally specified domains."* Not only that, but each mini-ensemble of neurons can encode more than one piece of information, each with its own electrical or chemical activity pattern. There appears to be great potential for biological interference with memory. "Memory for whole events is stored widely," Squire wrote, "not in a single location; literal or biologic forgetting can occur, so that recollection of past events is a reconstruction from fragments, not a veridical playback of past events." Although other tests indicate that some skills and emotions are somewhat localized, it appears that a specific "memory" simply does not exist at one particular point in the brain.

Bartlett was right when he talked about a "schema" to which the mind refers. Whenever we remember something, we literally reconstruct it, grabbing tiny bits of imagery and information from millions of neurons that interconnect in a vast and complex web. Until that moment, the memory cannot be said to "exist" at all. As one science writer put it, "it is only potential, latent, a wraith implicit.... It is a ghost in the machine."

Implicit and State-Dependent Memory

Thus far, I have been speaking of memory in its commonly understood form,

---

*   Studies of "split-brain" subjects—epileptics whose corpus callosum was surgically severed—indicate that the right and left sides of the brain can act independently. The right side specializes in nonverbal, spatial, intuitive thought, while the left side offers language expertise. But that does not mean that all language, for instance, resides in one brain hemisphere. Instead, several anatomical regions contribute to every thought in dynamic interplay. As science writer Jeremy Campbell noted, "a simple concept like 'grandmother' may be spread out across a region of the [neural] network."

what the specialists call *episodic* or *declarative* memory—our ability to recall the personal past and tell someone what happened. Recovered memory therapists have, however, latched onto another type of memory which, because it cannot be articulated in words, is termed *non-declarative* or *implicit* memory. Like much research on the unseen, scientists have deduced the existence of implicit memory and how it works primarily by observing the behavior of organically damaged patients such as Henry Molaison, long known to memory students only as H. M., a Connecticut man who, at the age of 27 in 1953, underwent radical brain surgery to cure his severe epileptic seizures. Most of his hippocampus and amygdala and part of his temporal lobe were removed. His tragic story was movingly and thoroughly recounted by Philip J. Hilts in his book, *Memory's Ghost*.

As a result of the surgery, Molaison displayed severe but specific memory deficits. He could remember his birthday, the names of his teenage girl friends and other events of his youth, but he failed to recognize his current doctor, whom he saw every day. It turns out that the hippocampus is a kind of way-station where short-term declarative memory is processed, then farmed out to other parts of the brain. Without it, Molaison could not construct long-term memories, though his pre-operational experience remained safely in neuronal connections elsewhere in the cerebral lobes.

There *is* one kind of subtle long-term memory that Molaison could master, however. When presented with the same puzzle day after day, he could not consciously recall having seen it before—yet his performance steadily improved. Here was evidence that a form of implicit memory was at work, and that it relies on a separate brain area. Researchers have named this *procedural* memory, the ability to perform a particular act without consciously remembering it. Another form of implicit memory involves the emotions. In 1889, for instance, Sergei Korsakoff, who first identified organic amnesia, noticed that while one of his patients had no explicit memory of an electrical shock, he subsequently sought to avoid the black box that administered it.

Harvard psychologist Daniel Schacter, who studied implicit memory, concluded that "mood effects on implicit memory may be greater than those on explicit memory" and that "information on which [people] operate could affect performance and behavior implicitly, without any corresponding phenomenal awareness." Moreover, in normal subjects without organic brain damage, implicit and explicit memory probably work in tandem. In the case of "state-dependent" or "mood-dependent" memories, the implicit, unconscious awareness may be triggered when a person gets into the same emotional or physical state. Reinstating the context in which an event took place has indeed been shown to improve memory in many cases. Some research psychologists and biologists believe that such research *might* apply to the retrieval of repressed or dissociated trauma memories, though Schacter emphasized that the findings are "no more than suggestive." The hypothesis holds that while the conscious mind may not recall the trauma, the hidden, implicit memory of the abuse could remain.

Therapists and researchers eager for scientific underpinnings for their belief in massive repression embraced implicit memory. Thus Lenore Terr wrote in *Unchained Memories:* "One wonders if many of the mute night child's memories were laid down as nondeclarative, or implicit, memories. Such memories could not have been retrieved in words." Yet such an explanation requires a huge leap of intellectual faith, jumping from brain-damaged patients and studies of word-association to forgotten sexual abuse memories. The evidence—derived from hypnosis, multiple-personality cases, and psychogenic amnesia—is highly suspect, as documented in Chapters 3 and 4, and probably stems more from suggestibility and expectation than from any form of real memory, implicit or otherwise. Yes, implicit and state-dependent memories exist, but that does not mean that a woman who hates bananas is necessarily reacting subconsciously to a memory of her father's erect penis, as many trauma therapists believed.

Schacter, who has conducted studies on two "multiple personality disorder" (MPD) subjects, became far more skeptical of the phenomenon. "It has only become apparent in the past few years, largely through the repressed memories controversy, just how powerful the iatrogenic [doctor-induced] influences on memory can be," he wrote to me. "I would be much less likely now to consider studying an MPD patient.... It is abundantly clear now that some of the recovery therapists have created enormous problems for patients and society. Indeed, implicit memory, rather than reflecting the existence of repressed memory, may sometimes be the basis for constructing false memory." Schacter was quoted in *The New York Times* in May of 1994, warning how "the confabulator picks out a bit or piece of an actual memory, but confuses its true context, and draws on other bits of experience to construct a story."

Psychologist John Kihlstrom, who co-authored articles on amnesia and memory with Schacter, agreed. "The evidence is just not there [for the validity of recovered memories]. There is, to my knowledge, not a single published study that [has] attempted to verify the memories recovered by hypnosis and drugs." He added that "in the final analysis, memory isn't like reading a book; it's like *writing a book from fragmentary notes.*" In the cultural atmosphere that produced *The Courage to Heal,* therapists grasped at implicit memory as the "scientific" justification for what Kihlstrom called a "peculiarly perverse logic." Context can indeed affect memory, not only by cuing a forgotten item, but by creating an expectation. As one researcher on state-dependent memory recently wrote, "The role of context on false recognition has been largely neglected."

Neuroscience and Repressed Memories

In the last few decades, scientists concerned with the mysterious inner workings of the brain have produced many interesting studies. None could either prove nor disprove the existence of repressed memories, though work on the chemistry of highly emotional memories tends to verify the 1891 observation of philosopher and psychologist William James: "What interests us most vividly at the time iswhat we remember best. An experience may be so exciting emotionally as almost to leave a scar on the cerebral tissues." In other words, strong emotions (whether positive or negative) produce strong memories, less subject to distortion and decay than normal memory. The research of James McGaugh, Larry Cahill, Joseph LeDoux and others all confirm this finding. Epinephrine (more commonly known as adrenaline) and cortisol are released by the brain when we are stressed. These hormone apparently cause a chain reaction in which other hormones called "endogenous opiates" (natural opium-like substances produced by the brain) go to work in the thalamus and amygdala, parts of the limbic system situated near the hippocampus. The amygdala, a brain region critically involved with emotional arousal, reinforces the work of the hippocampus, which transfers short-term into long-term memory. It appears that emotional memories are recorded on two simultaneous and somewhat independent tracks—implicit and declarative—that mutually reinforce one another.

"Emotional arousal enhances the storage of memories," James McGaugh concluded in a 2013 article, "thus serving to create, selectively, lasting memories of our more important experiences. The neurobiological systems mediating emotional arousal and memory are very closely linked." Thus both animal and human studies have provided "compelling evidence that stress-induced activation of the amygdala and its interactions with other brain regions involved in processing memory play a critical role in ensuring that emotionally significant experiences are well-remembered."

From an evolutionary standpoint, this finding makes perfect sense. Humans need to be able to respond appropriately to future situations. By reinforcing a biological mechanism for recalling highly emotional events better than others, evolution guarantees that we will be able to seek out pleasurable situations in the future and avoid unpleasant, dangerous ones. It also helps explain the survival mechanisms that produce post-traumatic stress disorder (PTSD) in which those who have undergone profound trauma sometimes suffer from involuntary, intrusive memories. Indeed, as several researchers have noted, "the hallmark symptom of PTSD is the reliving or recollection of the traumatic event in the form of intrusive thoughts." That is certainly what Holocaust historian Lawrence Langer concluded in his book, *Holocaust Testimonies: The Ruins of Memory.* Indeed, in

1999 I asked three giants of Holocaust studies—Lawrence Langer, Elie Wiesel, and Raul Hilberg—if they were aware of any cases of massive repression of traumatic Holocaust memories. None knew of such cases.*

"People who have survived concentration camps, systematic torture by despotic political regimes, and repeated rapes—from the victims of Serbian 'ethnic cleansing' to the Korean 'comfort women' of World War II—do not forget," observed Elizabeth Loftus in 2002. "They remember, painfully, to this day."

"The current evidence from systematic and methodologically sound studies strongly suggests that memories of traumatic events are more resistant to forgetting than memories of mundane events," a 2012 article summarized, after the authors reviewed the professional literature.

In the 1990s, research seemed to indicate that massive doses of stress hormones such as cortisol might actually *impair* memories, since Vietnam veterans suffering from PTSD were found to have smaller hippocampi than nonveteran control subjects. But a landmark 2002 study cleverly disproved that theory. Researchers found identical twins in which one had developed PTSD after being in combat, while the other had not fought. Yet in all such cases, both twins had small hippocampi. It thus appears that having a small hippocampus may be "a predisposing factor for PTSD (or maybe just a meaningless correlate)," as memory researcher Joe LeDoux observed.

Those who experience an intensely stressful event may not recall every detail of it accurately. When threatened with a gun during a bank holdup, for instance, people tend to focus primarily in frozen terror on the gun itself and cannot recall many other details, including the identity of the person holding the gun. This "weapon focus" is well-documented. But they don't forget the main gist of what happened.

Thus, it is hypothetically possible, though unlikely, that stress from sexual abuse would indirectly lead to incomplete memories. Such conclusions are, as Daniel Schacter put it, "intriguing speculations." Even if stress did contribute to a smaller hippocampus, such damage to memory would be universal rather than particular, according to psychologist Larry Weiskrantz. "There is no evidence that any such hormonal secretion would block or weaken a *specific* memory. In other words, having a slightly shrunken hippocampus would be bad across the board."

In addition, a smaller hippocampus would not explain how missing memories could be retrieved later. As neuroscientist James McGaugh put it, "Even if we could release these high doses that impaired memory, that would provide no explanation for recovered memories—they are, like Clementine, lost and gone forever."

---

* Binjamin Wilkomirksi's *Fragments* (1996), recounting his recovered memories of horrific Holocaust childhood experiences, won numerous awards before it was debunked. He was born Bruno Grosjean, was not Jewish, and had confabulated his Holocaust memories in therapy.

One promising biological approach to memory may help to prevent post-traumatic stress disorder. If patients are given the beta blocker propranolol (used to treat high blood pressure) soon after a traumatic event, it appears to block the action of stress hormones and could perhaps be used to treat PTSD. Protein formation blockers may work in the amygdala as people recall stress and the memory is re-consolidated. Thus, the scientific documentary, *The Memory Hackers* (2016) showed how neurobiologist Karim Nader's rat experiments first demonstrated in 2000 that fear memories could be "erased." As the narrator explained: "The act of remembering must make memories vulnerable to change," which Frederic Bartlett demonstrated in the 1930s. The documentary then demonstrated how Dutch experimental psychologist Merel Kindt has used propranolol to treat people with a spider phobia. First she had them approach a tarantula so that their fear was fresh, then had them take the pill. Her hypothesis is that the drug prevents the "reconsolidation" of the fear memory, and a man who was once terrified of spiders could now stroke the tarantula like a pet. But the theory of reconsolidation of memory may not be the best way to view the results. It is not that Kindt's patients forgot that they were dealing with spiders. As James McGaugh pointed out: "The treatments may decrease the emotionality without eliminating the memory of the event."

The Memory Hackers also featured neurobiologist and psychiatrist Eric Kandel, with fascinating footage showing how he filmed new dendrites and synapses growing in a Petri dish. Kandel's work earned him the Nobel Prize in Physiology or Medicine in 2000. Yet Kandel has also endorsed the pseudoscience of repressed memory.

In a 1994 article in *Discover Magazine*, Kandel—who has an alarming respect for Sigmund Freud and who once wanted to be a psychoanalyst—suggested a biological, scientific foundation for a belief in massive repression. His coauthor was his daughter, Minouche Kandel, a lawyer who worked with battered women and was understandably concerned with the impact of abuse. But she also espoused a belief in repressed memories. The Kandels began their article with the case of Jennifer H. (Hoult) as an example of true recovered memories. Hoult's "memories," however, arose in therapy with an unlicensed psychotherapist whom she saw for relationship problems. During guided imagery sessions, she pictured her father molesting her. "It was like … on TV if there is all static," she explained. "I slowly opened my eyes in the session and I said, 'I never knew that happened to me.'" It appeared to be a classic case of bad therapy leading to illusory memories.

The Kandels reviewed the theory of implicit memory, then discussed rat studies indicating that large doses of endogenous opiates may weaken memory storage. "Such studies give us a biological context for considering how traumatic memories might be suppressed in humans," the Kandels wrote.

The Kandels finished the article—daughter Minouche perhaps writing the conclusion—by complaining about "media and academic critics ... using the wedge of doubt to publicly discredit the very existence of delayed memories," criticizing them as part of a "backlash," and ending with a rousing quote from Judith Herman.

Eric Kandel spent his career studying the behavior of the sea slug *Aplysia*. He chose the slug because of its extremely simple nervous system and has systematically sought to discover what he calls the "cellular alphabet" of learning. His pioneering work demonstrated that neurons establish new connection between synapses in response to new experiences. I won't go into his experiments in detail but will merely point out that some other memory researchers, such as Steven Rose in *The Making of Memory* (1992), have criticized Kandel for his reductionist approach. Kandel once gave a talk, for instance, on the theme, "Psychotherapy and the Single Synapse."

Although Eric Kandel is a giant in the field of memory research, in this case he wrote outside his expertise within that field. Indeed, it is ironic that he appeared to rely in part on the rat studies of James McGaugh, who is himself extremely critical of the notion of repressed memory. "I know of no credible scientist (excluding Kandel) who thinks that Freudian ideas have any credibility," McGaugh wrote to me in 2017. "Certainly they do not influence any current psychological or neuroscience thinking or research." He also questioned the suggestion that experimental studies somehow indicate that opiates may "suppress" traumatic memories in humans. "That makes no sense. The studies of opiate effects (many from my laboratory) on memory do not indicate that the drugs suppress memories. They simply impair the consolidation of memories."

Bessel van Der Kolk and Body Memories

Unfortunately, McGaugh underestimated the extent of continuing belief in repressed memories. Boston University psychiatrist Bessel van der Kolk, founder and director of the Trauma Center in Brookline, Massachusetts, has gone much further than Eric Kandel in asserting the scientific validity of recovered memories. Van der Kolk even professes a belief in the widely discredited notion of "body memories," which he christened with the more scientific-sounding label "somatic memory" in a 1994 article, "The Body Keeps the Score." Van der Kolk reviewed an impressive array of studies on the biological and neurological effects of trauma, most of which support the fact that traumatic memories are difficult to forget. Indeed, van der Kolk wrote that PTSD patients often "get mired in a continuous reliving of the past." He quoted Pierre Janet, who noted that "certain happenings ... leave indelible and distressing memories—memories to which the sufferer continually returns, and by which he is tormented by day and by night."*

---

* The extent to which such pseudoscientific notions permeated therapeutic thought is alarming, as one survey

Yet van der Kolk grasped at studies of implicit memory to conjecture that many traumatic memories are completely forgotten at the conscious level, only to be recalled indelibly at the "somatosensory level" as "visual images or physical sensations." Unlike the fragile conscious memory, he posited, these implicit memories are "impervious to change." Throughout his hypothetical constructions, van der Kolk slipped in tell-tale conditional words—"catecholamines *could* stimulate active coping mechanisms"; "state-dependent memory retrieval *may* also be involved in dissociative phenomena in which traumatized persons *may be* wholly or partially amnestic"; "intense affect *may* inhibit proper evaluation and categorization of experience." [*Italics added.*]

As Harvard psychologist Richard McNally observed, "van der Kolk's theory is plagued by conceptual and empirical problems.... Measures of implicit memory are subject to change and distortion just like measures of explicit memory." Not only that, but there is no logical way to trace a bodily sensation back to some particular hypothetical, unremembered narrative event. "Memories are not stored 'in the body' [that is, in muscle tissue], and the notion of 'body memories' is foreign to the cognitive neuroscience of memory," McNally concluded. Besides, as psychologist Charles Fernybough observed in 2012, "Implicit memories for a traumatic event can persist, but they cannot be converted back into explicit memories unless those memories are already there."

In 2014 van der Kolk published *The Body Keeps the Score*, a book with the title taken from his 1994 article. In it, he wrote compellingly about PTSD and his therapy with people who really have suffered horrendous experiences. Yet he continued to promote the theory of massive repression/dissociation, spending an entire chapter on the case of "Julian" (real name, Paul Busa), whose testimony sent Catholic priest Paul Shanley to prison.

Busa met Shanley at age six but had no memory of abuse until 2001, when he was twenty-five years old and learned that others were accusing Shanley. Busa eventually came to recall games of strip poker, bending over so Shanley could stick his finger up his rectum, oral sex, and sitting in a church pew while the priest fondled him. These abuse memories were "quite incoherent and fragmentary," van der Kolk noted, as well as acknowledging that for "those who had been traumatized and subsequently developed PTSD...their memories were reserved essentially intact forty-five years after the war ended."

Yet van der Kolk believed Busa. "In Julian's case, the sensations, thoughts and emotions of the trauma were stored separately as frozen, barely comprehensible fragments." Four of Shanley's accusers had recovered memories of abuse. The

---

of 38 counselors' beliefs in "body memories" revealed. One therapist, for instance, asserted that "within each cell there's a mitochondria that has the capacity for recording events."

other three were apparently too unbelievable to take the stand, so Busa was the only witness in the 2002 Massachusetts trial. Nonetheless, Shanley was convicted.

In 2007, Shanley's lawyer sought a new trial on the basis of ineffective counsel and the fact that repressed memories were not generally accepted in the scientific community. Nearly a hundred of the world's leading psychiatrist and psychologists signed an amicus curieae brief explaining that so-called "repressed memories" had never been shown to exist. Yet the court upheld Shanley's conviction, which van der Kolk gleefully recounted. Once again, he wrote, he had triumphed in court. "In a 1996 case I had [also] convinced a federal circuit court judge in Boston that it was common for traumatized people to lose all memories of the event in question only to regain access to them in bits and pieces at a much later date."*

In *Whores of the Court: The Fraud of Psychiatric Testimony and the Rape of American Justice*, psychologist Margaret Hagen detailed the flaws in the 1996 case, in which van der Kolk cited the Judith Herman and Linda Williams studies as "proof" for repression and told the judge: "There is no scientific basis to believe that…victims could fake such memories and fool psychiatric tests." As Hagen observed, "What on earth can Dr. van der Kolk have meant by that?"

In December 1996, van der Kolk was asked whether he had read any literature on the perils of false memories through hypnosis. No. How did van der Kolk tell the difference between true and false memories? "There is such a thing as internal consistency, and if people tell you something with internal consistency and with appropriate affect, you tend to believe that the stories are true." Yet people who believed they were abducted by aliens also told highly emotional, detailed stories. For van der Kolk, *belief* trumped science.

Like many other psychotherapists who encouraged people to believe that they had been subjected to years of childhood sexual abuse and had repressed it, van der Kolk asserted that it really didn't matter whether the memories were true or not. "As a therapist treating people with a legacy of trauma, my primary concern is not to determine exactly what happened to them but to help them tolerate the sensations, emotions, and reactions they experience without being constantly hijacked by them." Yet van der Kolk's testimony was crucial to putting innocent people in prison. "During this period [of the Catholic pedophile scandal] I examined more than fifty adults who, like Julian, remembered having been abused by priests. Their claims were denied in about half the cases." That meant that it is likely that some two dozen falsely accused priests were found guilty.

---

* Van der Kolk neglected to mention the court cases in which lawyer/psychologist Christopher Barden prevailed after deposing van der Kolk and getting him to admit using faulty or missing data in some of his studies. "Van der Kolk fled from the process server and dropped out of multiple cases rather than turn over his claimed data," Barden asserted.

The ultimate problem with van der Kolk's attempts to provide a scientific basis for massive repression/dissociation is that they are self-contradictory. Even if we ignore the overwhelming evidence that extreme trauma is remembered consciously all too well, it is difficult to understand how conscious memories would ever be retrieved in his scenario. According to van der Kolk, such explicit memories would be destroyed by an overabundance of glucocorticoids and other stress hormones. Then how are they to be "triggered," if they are not there? In other words, van der Kolk cannot both destroy his cake and eat it too.

Candace Pert is another brain biochemist whose work has been cited as "proving" the existence of "body memories." In 1986, she wrote an article examining how "neuropeptides," opiate-like hormones used in the brain, were also found elsewhere. "We discovered," she wrote, "that the receptors [for neuropeptides] were scattered throughout not only the brain but also the body." Her conclusion? "In the beginning of my work, I matter-of-factly presumed that emotions were in the head or the brain. Now I would say they are really in the body as well," though she admitted that "some scientists might describe this idea as outrageous." At the end of her article, Pert joined the ranks of scientists-turned-mystics, espousing her belief in immortality because "mind and consciousness would appear to be independent of brain and body."

While it is true that there are receptors for various hormones scattered throughout the body, that does not mean they hold emotions *per se,* and certainly not memories. As James McGaugh pointed out, "No one can seriously doubt that fear, love, joy, horror, etc., are expressions of brain activity." While hormones such as adrenaline "have important actions in the periphery," he added, "they do not create memories there. The concept of 'body memories' is nonsense, if by that you mean that memories are stored outside of the central nervous system. The notion that because there are receptors for neuropeptides located outside of the brain, there is also memory at those receptors, is at best a very strange hypothesis for which there is no evidence."

In short, although some scientists believe in the concepts of massive repression, dissociation to forget trauma, and body memories, there is no good evidence for these concepts. *No one really knows* how the mind works. We have the merest hints and guesses, based primarily on studies with monkeys, rats, chickens, and other simpler life forms such as sea slugs, and on brain scans that suggest the location of active synaptical activity. We must be very cautious in drawing conclusions from such studies and scans. As psychiatrist Sally Satel and psychologist Scott Lilienfeld pointed out in *Brainwashed: The Seductive Appeal of Mindless Neuroscience* (2015), "many of the real-world applications of human neuroscience gloss over its limitations and intricacies, at times obscuring—rather than clarifying—the myriad factors that shape our behavior and identities."

Unfortunately, scientists are human beings, too, and they sometimes jump to seductive conclusions, especially if the conclusions fit their hypotheses and place them on the cutting edge, as Michael Anderson and his colleagues apparently did with their brain scans of people directed to forget particular words, covered earlier in this chapter. "The history of many scientific subjects is virtually freed from … constraints of fact," Stephen Jay Gould wrote in *The Mismeasure of Man*. "Some topics are invested with enormous social importance but blessed with very little reliable information. When the ratio of data to social impact is so low, a history of scientific attitudes may be little more than an oblique record of social change."

In Peter Huber's book, *Galileo's Revenge,* he described the hallmarks of what he terms "junk" or "pathological" science:

> Pathological science often depends on experiments at the threshold of detect-ability, or at the lowest margins of statistical significance. The claims frequently emerge from a body of data that is selectively incomplete; wishful researchers unconsciously discard enough "bad" data to make the remaining "good" points look important. That the measurements are at the very threshold of sensitiv-ity is an advantage, not an obstacle: data that don't fit the theory are explained away; those they fit are lovingly retained. Professional statisticians call this "data dredging." Dredging is easiest in loose and formless mud. Thus, pathological science does best when recording swings in mood, disruption of brain-wave patterns, and things of that sort.

Society and culture have influenced scientists throughout history. The phrenol-ogists of the early 19th century were convinced that they could determine human character by studying the shape of the head, for instance. Much more recently, in the 1940s and 1950s, reputable scientists and physicians sanctioned prefrontal lobotomies to attack the problem at its source, thereby turning thousands of pa-tients—mostly women—into placid mental zombies.

In the 1960s, memory researchers thought they had discovered the "molecules of memory" and could simply inject RNA from rats or worms into their peers and "teach" them previously learned skills. As memory researcher Steven Rose noted, these experiments could "all be explained by inadequate statistics, faulty experimental design, [and] overenthusiastic interpretation of ambiguous results."

Contrary to popular belief, scientists may be *more* prone to stubborn, dogmatic beliefs than other humans, because they often devote their entire professional lives to a single hypothesis. In addition, scientists are clearly influenced by their social milieu Some establish credibility through real discoveries and then veer into quackery. As Freud-critic Richard Webster observed, "many 'great' scientists have gone on to create significant pseudo-sciences," adding that "sometimes the prestige and authority which they have earned through their genuine contributions to science has both encouraged them along the path of folly at the same time that it has silenced or eclipsed their critics." We must therefore be wary of accepting the latest "scientific" hypothesis "proving" the reality of repressed memory.

William James got it right over a century ago when he quoted Charles Richet, another psychologist: "Who of us, alas! has not experienced a bitter and profound grief, [an] immense laceration? In these great griefs, the present endures neither for a minute, for an hour, nor for a day, but for weeks and months. The memory of the cruel moment will not efface itself from consciousness."

The Connectionist Computer Model

During the 1960s and '70s, computer scientists believed that they could replicate the brain's functioning, producing "artificial intelligence" equal to the ability of humans. After all, a computer's switching element responds much more quickly than does the relatively slow brain synapse. But the programmers failed miserably, largely because they assumed that computers, with their central processing units and specific memory sites, worked like the brain. In the 1980s, however, programmers began to imitate the "connectionist" brain model, hooking up their computers in "massively parallel" fashion. Rather than attempting to program one computer memory with the "right" answer, they challenged their computers to think. By hooking up 300 "artificial neurons," each a mini-computer, one programmer produced "NETtalk," which gradually taught itself to read aloud.

In his thought-provoking book, *The Improbable Machine* (1989), Jeremy Campbell discussed how the connectionist model revolutionized not only computer programming, but our notion of how and why the mind works. "We are systematically illogical and biased," he wrote. "The world in which the brain evolved is a great deal more untidy and less circumscribed [than a serial computer], full of ambiguity, deceit, problems that sprawl in ungainly fashion ... information that is incomplete or contradictory." As a result, one's mind readily accepts "imperfect information, generalizing, filling in the missing parts from its large reserves of worldly knowledge."

As Campbell repeated in a variety of ways, we don't think logically, and we rely largely on stereotyped generalizations, fitting experience into preordained categories. Human memory is "much less reliable than a computer, but it is vast, and associative by its very nature. Human memory cannot help but connect one thing it knows with another thing it knows. It puts the world together in such a way that, given just a small fragment of information, it can amplify that fragment instantly." Consequently, "the mind is a bundle of paradoxes. It has insight, but at the cost of more-or-less frequent errors. It harnesses the `vice' of prejudice in order to make new discoveries about the world."

We have, in other words, come full circle, back to Frederic Bartlett. Campbell concluded that "the mind thrives and flourishes on gaps; it tolerates great gaping holes in what it hears and reads, because it is so adept at filling in the holes with what it knows." As an example, Campbell asked us to consider the following two sentences: "A man wearing a ski mask walked into the bank. One of the tellers screamed." While a computer would not understand why the teller screamed, most of us would immediately apply a "bank-robber schema," and we would probably be correct. Of course, as Campbell pointed out, "the bank in question could have been in Aspen, Colorado, and the teller might have screamed because she saw a mouse run across the floor."

In most conditions, the brain works pretty well, even though it relies not so much on logic as on interpretations of generalized experience. And it turns out that the language we use is fundamental to the thinking and remembering process. Words serve as mini-schemata, calling up different connotations and memories. Thus, in one of Elizabeth Loftus's experiments, subjects who were asked to describe two cars "smashing" together reported fictitious broken glass, while cars that just "hit" didn't evoke this error. "Language is the mirror of the mind," Campbell asserted, and it explains much of our "associative" thinking. "The mind seems to be metaphorical to its foundations."

But how does all of this apply to the millions of "Survivors" who retrieved what they believed to be memories of sexual abuse? For better or worse, our society produced a "sex abuse schema" that leaps to assumptions based on incomplete information. Consider these two sentences: "The father sat on his daughter's bed. He said, 'I love you so much, Princess,' and kissed her goodnight." In the 1950s, that would have called up a Father-Knows-Best schema. In the 1990s and thereafter, it might call up potential incest. Metaphors such as "emotional incest" became literally accepted truth. Once the mind's normal schemata of "loving family" or "happy childhood" were systematically destroyed through reading and therapy, an alternative connection was made. "My therapist thinks I came from a dysfunctional family. I am very unhappy. I have all of these symptoms they talk about. All these books can't be wrong. I think maybe I was abused. Therefore, I probably was abused. It's only a matter of finding the memories."

As Campbell concluded, "Memory becomes interpretation. It is not a filing cabinet, nor a set of index cards, but a hermeneutical system. A cue that triggers a memory is a sort of puzzle that has to be solved, a riddle with multiple possible answers that must be disentangled so that the right answer pops out." Unfortunately, when the "puzzle" is pre-defined—"I think maybe I was sexually abused but repressed the memory"—the right answer *doesn't* pop out. "In remembering," wrote Campbell, "people not only distort and interpret information from the past so as to make it fit what they know or believe in the present; they seem to add new information. The more distant the event, the more material the mind adds."

Memory Palaces, Haunted Houses, and Memory Savants

Before the invention of the printing press, humans honed the art of mass memorization to pass on oral traditions—an art that has lasted to this day in one form or another, and which yields intriguing parallels with the guided imagery technique of recovering traumatic memories. The ancient methodology relies on the associative nature of the brain, as Frances Yates documented in *The Art of Memory*. Around 500 B.C., Simonides left a feast just before the roof caved in, crushing his fellow revelers. He discovered that he could identify the roomful of mangled corpses on the basis of where each banqueter had been sitting at the table before the roof caved in. Similarly, 16th century Jesuit Matteo Ricci could build a "memory palace" in his mind and store different bits of information in different rooms. By "hiding" a different fact or memory image behind a sofa here or a gargoyle there, Ricci could then walk through the room and "retrieve" them in the desired order.

Perhaps significant to our understanding of the repressed memory phenomenon, bizarre sexual imagery seemed to provide helpful associations for Christian philosophers such as Albertus Magnus, who suggested that "we should imagine some ram, with huge horns and testicles, coming towards us in the dark." During the Renaissance, the memorists turned mystical, focusing their systems on the memory of a pre-existent Divine Source. The new art of memory made common cause with magic, alchemy, numerology, astrology, radical symbolism, and piety. Memory became associated with vivid imagination. The guided-imagery search for repressed memories, in which people search through mental rooms until they find frightening molestation, followed in this tradition.

It takes practice with such mnemonic associative tricks for most people to achieve extraordinary feats of accurate memory recall, but there are also autistic savants such as the character played by Dustin Hoffman in the 1988 movie *Rain Man*, who can make complex mathematical calculations in their head or recall factual information with uncanny accuracy, even though their brains are clearly damaged in other ways. No one understands what causes autism or this unusual isolated ability.

There is yet another type of extraordinary memory that can occur in otherwise normal individuals, however. In 2000, a 34-year-old woman named Jill Price emailed memory researcher James McGaugh, claiming an "unbelievable ability to recall my past" in considerable detail since she was eleven years old. "It is nonstop, uncontrollable and totally exhausting," she complained. "Most have called it a gift but I call it a burden. I run my entire life through my head every day and it drives me crazy!"

McGaugh was skeptical, but when he tested Price, he found that she could indeed recall daily events of her life with extraordinary accuracy, as verified by her past journals, without resort to mnemonic tricks. He subseqently located and tested a total of 55 similar people whom he called "highly superior autobiographical memory individuals, " or HSAMs, some of whom were featured in a 2016 Nova program, *The Memory Hackers*, on public television. Their brain scans indicated that areas such as the putamen and caudate in the basal ganglia near the bottom of the brain were larger than normal, and the white matter tract, the uncinate fasciculus, which connects the hippocampus and amygdala to the frontal cortex, is more active.

Unlike Jill Price, most of the HSAMs appear to appreciate their special skills. Most have successful careers. A disproportionate number are left-handed and many have obsessive-compulsive tendencies. Only two were married when I interviewed McGaugh in early 2017. "It's difficult to live with someone who is constantly correcting you," he hypothesized. McGaugh hopes, through his research on HSAMs, to "learn something truly new and important about the functioning of the most complicated and interesting known structure in the universe, our brain—and the most important thing it does is learn and remember."

But what do such memory savants tell us about the the supposed return of repressed memories? Not much. They do not prove that some people really do have computer-like brains that record every moment of their lives. As McGaugh wrote, Jill Price "does not recall the minutest details of daily experience. She has trouble remembering which of her keys go into which lock. She makes lists of things she needs to do." Nor do other HSAMs remember all of their experiences in precise detail. In now-standard false memory tests, HSAMs performed as badly as normal subjects, proving susceptible to false recognition from an associative word-list and mistaken remembrance of a nonexistent plane crash. They were *worse* than controls in recalling details of a photographic slide show. As Lawrence Patihis, James McGaugh, Elizabeth Loftus, and fellow authors of that study observed, "Finding false memories in a superior-memory group suggests that malleable reconstructive mechanisms may be fundamental to episodic remembering."

Infantile Amnesia and Preverbal Abuse

Jean Piaget, the famous child psychologist, had a vivid memory of a traumatic event that took place when he was two years old. "I was sitting in my pram, which my nurse was pushing in the Champs Elysees, when a man tried to kidnap me. I was held in by the strap fastened around me while my nurse bravely tried to stand between me and the thief. She received various scratches." Piaget recalled what her face looked like, how a crowd gathered, how a policeman with a white baton appeared, how the would-be kidnapper fled. But the entire episode turned out to be a fabrication. When Piaget was 15, his former nurse, newly converted to the Salvation Army, wrote to the family confessing that she had faked the scratches. There had been no kidnapper. Piaget concluded that he must have heard detailed accounts of the story as a child and created his own "visual memory" of an entirely fictitious event.

This anecdote illustrates how we can create vivid memories of events that never occurred. In fact, a 2017 Google search for "I remember being born" came up with 9.1 million hits. It is amazing how many people hold cherished memories that could not be real. When I give speeches about memory, cautioning against the dangers of repressed memory therapy, I invariably raise the most hackles when I say that no one remembers anything before the age of three. I try to tell people gently that whatever "memories" they have from that period have been rehearsed and visualized, based on family stories or pictures, but they are most certainly not true memories.

In one clever study, researchers told participants that they had extraordinarily well-coordinated eye movements because they were born in hospitals that hung colored mobiles over their cribs. Over half of those in the study later claimed to remember the mythical mobiles.

Most experimental psychologists would not have believed in Piaget's "memory" in the first place, because of the well-known if little-understood phenomenon of infantile amnesia. Very few people remember much before the age of five. And hardly anyone—except people who, like Piaget, visualize a possible scenario—remembers anything at all before the age of three.* Freud offered a dubious psychological explanation. He believed that intense infantile sexual conflicts must be repressed, though he offered only his own idiosyncratic self-analysis as evidence for his opinion.

However, Freud also referred to an interesting survey conducted by V. and C. Henri, published in 1897. The Henris obtained the self-reported earliest memories of 123 respondents. The majority (88) recalled an event between the ages of two and four. As Freud noted, "the most frequent content of the first memories of childhood [in the Henri study] are on the one hand occasions of fear, shame, physical pain, etc., and on the other hand important events such as illnesses, deaths, fires, births of brothers and sisters." In rare instances, simple images apparently devoid of emotional content were reported, such as a bowl of ice set on

---

* Ulric Neisser and Elizabeth Loftus, the two prominent memory researchers, crossed swords over the issue of infantile amnesia. Neisser and a cohort published a study in which they claimed that childhood memories might begin as early as two. Loftus questioned the Neisser study, asserting that "these apparent memories are the result of educated guesses ... or external information acquired after the age of two."

a table. Despite the infrequency of these blander images, Freud focused on them, asserting that they were "screen memories" for disturbing events too difficult for the child to face.

Because my family moved to a new home when I was five, I can roughly date my earliest memories to when I was three or four. My experience appears to validate the Henris rather than Freud. One day I walked up the hill to our home and bent over to pick up a particularly smooth black stick. It surprised me by wriggling away; it was a long black snake sunning itself, not a stick. When I told my mother, she explained that in Georgia, black snakes aren't poisonous, and I shouldn't worry about it. I also remember the neighbor's boxer, who barked at me through a chain-link fence. And I recall being at a friend's house and running around his dining room table as he chased me with a hatchet. Although Freud would no doubt have had a wonderful time interpreting the phallic snake, it was really only a snake, albeit a startling one. Nonetheless, it appears that early memories tend to be unusual, threatening events that made a big impression.

Others have interpreted infantile amnesia without Freud's recourse to far-fetched theories. Some scientists hypothesize that the infant's nervous system and brain have not developed sufficiently to encode memories. As we have seen, memories are lodged throughout the brain, but the hippocampus and prefrontal cortex appear to play crucial roles. Because those structures mature several years after birth, it is reasonable to assume that early memories simply fail to find a physical purchase. Others believe that the narrative or cognitive self, with its time sense and focus on life's milestones, doesn't develop until three or so, which matches Piaget's concept of a "preoperational period."*

According to linguist Noam Chomsky and neuropsychologist Eric Lenneberg, children are born with the structures necessary for language acquisition, but the brain must develop the skill within a critical early period, or it never will. Cases such as Genie, a girl kept a prisoner in a speechless household until she was 12, appear to confirm this theory. Although Genie subsequently mastered isolated words and phrases, she never learned syntax and could not express herself meaningfully. This finding suggests that fairly sophisticated language may be necessary for the formation of permanent memories. "Language is a logic system so organically tuned to the mechanism of the human brain that it actually triggers the brain's growth," Russ Rymer, author of the book *Genie*, concluded. "What are human beings? Beings whose brain development is uniquely responsive to and

---

* Humans are one of the few species who are self-conscious enough to recognize themselves in a mirror, along with chimpanzees, bonobos, and probably gorillas, dolphins and elephants, as I wrote in my book, *Mirror Mirror*. Human infants generally know that they are the ones in the mirror by age two, clearly a stepping stone toward a sense of narrative self.

dependent on the receipt at the proper time of even a small sample of language." Similarly, visual memory seems to develop slowly.

Regardless of the reasons, the reality of infantile amnesia would appear to be beyond dispute. In the 1990s, however, many therapists and their patients firmly believed that they could remember back to the crib—and what ghastly memories they were! Because the baby possessed no language to describe what was being done to it, therapists informed their patients that they must interpret "body memories" and vague images. Thus, in "The Terrible Truth" *(see Chapter 1),* A. G. Britton came to believe that her constricted throat, feeling of weight on her chest, and visions of hairy potatoes were "memories" of her father forcing sex on her between the ages of 6 and 18 months. Similarly, actress Roseanne Barr Arnold believed that she was abused, beginning at six months, though she semi-retracted her allegations in 2008..

It is difficult to give much credence to such stories, although there is no way to disprove them. The image of an innocent baby being molested is powerful and disgusting, and it is certainly true that the infant could not tell anyone.

In the compelling 1995 *Frontline* documentary "Divided Memories," about the debate over repressed memories, a mother described how she discovered that her husband was forcing oral sex on her five-year-old daughter. When confronted, he admitted it and vowed to stop. The mother never mentioned it again to the daughter, who forgot it. Years later, when the young adult daughter was having difficulties, the mother decided to tell her about the sexual abuse. The daughter then became convinced that she had remembered it and that it explained many of her troubles.

It is not altogether surprising that a five-year-old would forget sexual abuse of limited duration, since it occurred on the cusp of infantile amnesia. It is questionable, however, whether the young adult actually recalled the abuse years later. Given the information that it had occurred, it is natural that she would struggle to picture it and convince herself that she had indeed remembered it.

Infantile amnesia is a troubling subject. It is natural to *want* to believe that if somebody does something horrible to a baby, there will be a way to find out about it later and hold the perpetrator accountable. If such memories could be reliably recovered, justice could be served. Sadly, the opposite seems to be true: the only "memories" of infancy are later constructions that can lead to unjust accusations against innocent people.

As much as I have come to distrust Freud, one of his conclusions appears justified: "It may indeed be questioned whether we have any memories at all *from* our childhood: memories *relating to* our childhood may be all that we possess."

The Verdict on Repressed Memories

During my research, I kept an open mind about the possible validity of "massive repression/dissociation," in which years of abuse may have been forgotten. Actively seeking *just one case* in which such a mechanism clearly occurred, I wrote to over 50 professional psychological associations, including the American Psychological Association, the American Psychiatric Association, the American Association for Marriage and Family Therapy, and others, asking for any verified cases. I received no useful responses.

In some cases, such as that of Ross Cheit, for instance, I believe that sexual abuse can be forgotten, only to be recalled later in life. But in such cases, the abuse covered (1) only a single incident or a very limited period of time and (2) was not perceived as particularly traumatic at the time. In other words, I believe that we are dealing here with simple forgetting, not repression.

As an example, I interviewed a woman I called Melinda Couture in *Victims of Memory*:

> It was my 22-year-old brother-in-law who molested me when I was twelve. He had been drinking, and my sister had left the house briefly. It was a Saturday afternoon, and I was washing dishes at the sink. He sidled up to me and started asking if I knew what breasts were for.... He continued this suggestive, inappropriate questioning. I was dumbfounded. If I could have gotten angry and swatted him with a dishrag, it would have been okay. But I froze into a kind of compliance. He was saying, "Boys want to pet, but don't let them do *this*," as he gave me a free home demonstration, reaching up underneath my shirt to touch my breast. It probably lasted only a few minutes at the most. I heard a door slam, and everything stopped. I was so thankful. It never happened again. For another 15 years, until I was 27, I forgot about it until that night when it suddenly came back to me. I thought, "How the hell could I have forgotten that?"

Although this is an unconfirmed memory, it seems plausible to me. Couture may have wondered how she could have forgotten it, but that is not so unusual. As she explained, "It wasn't all that traumatic. He didn't reach between my legs or anything. That one incident happened, and I forgot it, but I never forgot the verbal harassment from the same person that went on constantly. He was a real boor and later turned out to be an alcoholic. It was like he was always trying to get a rise out of everybody."

Couture's returned memory is similar to several of seven allegedly corroborated cases presented by psychologist Jonathan Schooler and colleagues, while others may have recalled non-traumatizing short-term abuse and then confabulated more prolonged, violent abuse. Two of the cases were far more surprising, although neither involved years of alleged abuse. In one, WB, a 37-year-old woman, recalled having sex with a man who picked her up hitchhiking when she was sixteen. The other, ND, supposedly forgot, until she was 35, that she had been raped in an elevator in the hospital where she was a nurse, and that she had successfully sued her attacker when she was 22 years old.

When WB remembered what happened when she was sixteen, she thought, *My God...I had been raped! I was 16, just a kid! I couldn't defend myself!* Yet she did not recall that she had told her ex-husband about it the day after it occurred. He said she reported it as a "bad experience" in which she had sex "involuntarily" but had not protested. A few days later, she had told him it was "something like rape." She forgot that she had also mentioned the incident to her husband several other times over the years. "In a way," she said, "I have managed to repress the *meaning* of what happened all of these years." So it would appear that WB did not encode the memories as horribly traumatic until years later, when she recalled them again.

It is almost beyond belief that ND could have completely forgotten being raped as a young adult and as well as testifying at the resulting trial. She did, in fact, always recall being sexually abused as a child. ND felt that she had remembered the rape for two years or so after the event, but that when she moved to work at a different hospital, she completely forgot about it.

The cases of WB and ND raise an interesting conundrum. How do people know that they forgot something completely for years? In fact, they could have recalled it several times in the intervening period. "One can forget about a period in which a memory had been remembered," Schooler and his coauthors concluded. Research had already demonstrated that "hindsight bias" could make people over-estimate their prior knowledge in what was called the "knew-it-all-along effect." Now, Schooler christened these inaccurate claims of complete repression as the "*forgot-it-all-along-effect.*"

Harvard psychology professor Richard McNally concluded in 2005, "There is no convincing evidence for the claim that victims *repress* and recover memories of *traumatic* events. To be sure, some victims may not think about disturbing events for many years, *if* the events were not experienced as traumatic — terrifying and life-threatening — at the time of their occurrence. But not thinking about something for a long time is *not* the same thing as being *unable* to remember it, and it is inability to remember that lies at the heart of repression theory."

Other cases of actual forgetting (and possibly remembering) involve children on the cusp of the infantile amnesia period. As we have seen, in the television documentary, "Divided Memories," Ofra Bikel interviewed a mother whose five-year-old daughter really had been subjected to oral sex by her father, who confessed when confronted. No one talked about it again. Years later, when her mother told her about it, the girl, approaching young adulthood, was horrified to learn of it. She didn't remember it, but she naturally obsessed over trying to recall it. Eventually, she was successful in summoning details of what her father had done to her. She visualized it until it seemed horrifying real, just as Jean Piaget envisioned how his nurse had saved him from mythical kidnappers.

I question whether she really recalled the sexual abuse. It is not terribly surprising that she would have forgotten something that happened when she was five, but it is likely that it really was just forgotten. Told that she had been abused, and desperate for an answer to her current problems, the daughter would naturally strive mightily to remember. What she then pictured in her mind could well have been fantasized, however.

I asked Ellen Bass, author of *The Courage to Heal,* for cases of massive repression that had firm corroboration, and she referred me to three women I will call Nancy, Pat, and Laura. None of them, in fact, could provide firm corroboration. Laura subsequently changed her mind about having her story told, so I will not include it here. Since the other two were referred directly by Ellen Bass, whose book played such a central role in encouraging "memory" recovery, I will briefly summarize them.

Nancy was 60 years old and did, indeed, experience severe abuse and neglect as a child, by anyone's standards. She spent her early years with her disturbed mother, who was diagnosed as a paranoid schizophrenic; her alcoholic father; and her mother's various boyfriends. When she was nine, she was taken from her mother and placed in an institution. Nancy always remembered her mother leaving her on a window ledge when she was four years old. She recalled the starvation, living in sleazy hotels, the constant parade of strange men, her father's abusive rages at her mother. She always remembered the "nameless men" who fondled her. She vividly recalled a female social worker trying to seduce her when she was 13.

It was only in the late 1980s, however, that Nancy retrieved memories of sexual abuse by her father and mother. Her corroboration came second-hand, when her sister-in-law told her that her husband, Nancy's twin brother, was also abused and confirmed that Nancy had been, too. Her brother wouldn't talk about it, though. Similarly, Nancy's aunt, now deceased, supposedly confirmed that she had known about the abuse perpetrated by her sister, 13 years her junior. Since the aunt is dead, there was no way to ask her about this, but it is quite possible she was only referring to the truly awful childhood she knew Nancy had endured. That is one reason I never accept second-hand, hearsay testimony in these cases. It is very easy for those who have recovered "memories" to grab onto a relative's halting reaction as clear corroboration. A relative may say, "I always knew your mother was abusive to you," but that does not constitute corroboration.

Pat, then 28, recalled being sexually abused by her cousin Tom, seven years her senior. The memories began to come back in 1994, when she was reading *The Courage to Heal* and writing in her journal. Then she had a dream in which Tom abused her and told her threateningly, "I had fun this weekend. I lit a cat with gasoline." Eventually, she recalled him molesting her for years, then raping her when she was in the sixth grade. As with Nancy, there may be at least some truth to these allegations. When she was five or six, Pat told her mother that Tom had touched her in places he wasn't supposed to. "We figured it was maybe just curiosity with him," Pat's mother told me when I interviewed her. They spoke to Tom's parents and thought nothing more about it.

Ironically, Pat did not remember this initial incident, but she thought she had recalled the others. She was sure they were true, because from her dreams and journals she could identify the different rooms—the bathroom, the basement, the bedroom—where the alleged abuse occurred. Also, Tom's mother wrote to her, "No, he is not denying it. He said every time the family got together for a gathering he would wonder about things." She appeared to be writing only about the initial, acknowledged incident, however. "Tom at that time was only 13 or 14," she wrote in the letter. Therefore, it was not clear what he was not denying or what he meant by wondering about "things." I called Tom, but he would not discuss the allegations with me. It would appear that Tom may not remember these incidents either but fears that perhaps he repressed them, too. In summary, this was a confusing case, in which some sexual abuse apparently took place, but again, the new "memories" were questionable and not firmly corroborated.

When I contacted Judith Herman to ask for confirmed cases of recovered memories, she referred me to Roger Pitman at the VA hospital in Manchester, NH. In his turn, Pitman referred me to his associate, Danya Vardi, who told me that completely repressed memories were extremely rare in her experience. Finally, however, she referred me to Lisa, a 43-year-old Massachusetts woman who supposedly had corroboration for her returned memories.

After a year in Adult Children of Alcoholics, "trying to figure out why my life was screwed up," Lisa joined Overeaters Anonymous, then sought therapy. She eventually "remembered" being abused by eight different people, including her mother and older sister, a grandfather and grandmother, an uncle, two neighbors, and a priest. As her "proof," she cited her younger sisters who were two and three at the time of the abuse. "As I would be telling my sisters about a memory, they would remember a piece of it."

It should be clear by now that many people claim that their memories were "corroborated," when in fact they were not. There is a kind of self-confirmation bias that kicks into gear once a belief system is in place. I spoke to one woman who retrieved memories of abuse by her junior high swimming coach. As "proof" that the memories must be true, she says, "When I heard his wife was pregnant, I got really upset. Why would I have reacted that way otherwise?" Of course, there could be any number of reasons, but once the recovered memory hypothesis is in place, every intuition or reaction is taken as confirmation.

Similarly, many women told me that their memories must be true because they retrieved them outside of therapy, or because their therapists never led them in any way. I am quite skeptical of such claims, particularly if the "memories" came back after *The Courage to Heal* was published in 1988. By that time, particularly for women, the idea that repressed memories of sexual abuse might account for any life problems had become all-pervasive. By 1990, most women must have at least briefly considered the idea that they harbored repressed memories. They might not recall precisely where they heard about this phenomenon—a friend, a talk show, a short story, a book—but the odds are very good that the idea was indeed planted.

And I most assuredly do not believe those cases in which the therapist was supposedly neutral and did not lead the client at all. In all such cases, the therapist conveyed the idea that massive repression was a *possible* explanation. "It could be anything, including repression, but let's not jump to conclusions," the therapist would warn. "I don't want to lead you into anything. These memories will come on their own if they're there." And by that very statement, the therapist was indeed leading the client down repressed memory lane.

These supposedly corroborated, unforced stories led many otherwise responsible journalists to write that cases of massive repression had been confirmed, even though they never explored any specific cases in detail. In her otherwise excellent 1995 piece in the *New York Times Magazine* on the infamous day care case of Kelly Michaels (*see Chapter 5*), for instance, Nancy Hass wrote: "While some of the thousands of people who, aided by therapists, have recalled long-ago instances of sexual abuse have had their claims substantiated, many others are thought to have been grossly manipulated by suggestions." I wrote to Hass, questioning this statement. "If you have any cases in which massively repressed memories have been firmly corroborated, *please* let me know about them," I wrote. She never answered me.

One final case deserves attention. I was initially excited when one of the therapists I interviewed put me in touch with Betsy, a 43-year-old Texan whose father had confessed to her incest allegations. Not only that, but Betsy had retrieved her memories on her own, outside therapy, using Christian recovery books as her guide. She told me that she had always remembered an incident when she was learning to drive at 16. Her father had touched breast, and she had become very upset and told him never to do that again. Now, she had recalled how he fondled and raped her from the age of four until that last attempt at molestation when she was 16—and he had confessed to it.

Then I interviewed George, her 70-year-old father. "Praise the Lord, hello," his wife Rose answered the phone. It turned out that George, Rose, and Betsy all attended a charismatic born-again church. George told me that he, too, had always remembered the incident when Betsy was 16. He did not, however, actually recall any other abuse. A blue-collar factory employee, he had routinely worked from 5 A.M. until the evening, often arriving home as late as 11 P.M. He would then drink straight shots of whiskey to put himself to sleep, and start the routine again the next morning. "I don't remember anything about what Betsy says I did," he told me. "I used to be an alcoholic, so I probably had black-outs. I told her that if she says that I did something, I did. Because I brought my children up to be truthful. So she wouldn't lie. I've tried many a time to get a picture of it. How could I do such a thing? It isn't easy to believe, but when an innocent child tells you what you've done, you've got to know it's true."

In other words, George—like Paul Ingram in Lawrence Wright's *Remembering Satan*—was a devout father who thought he might have a "dark side" and loved his daughter enough to confess to anything she accused him of doing. Unlike Ingram, George had not been able to visualize virtuoso ritual abuse performances, but he seemed equally willing to accept blame for incest, whether or not it ever occurred.

I have been unable to find any corroborated cases of "massive repression/dissociation," in which *years* of terrible abuse were completely forgotten, only to be recalled later, and I have concluded that chasing such claims is a waste of time. They are like Hydra's heads, where two more grow every time you cut one off. For instance, Ross Cheit has created a website that he calls "The Recovered Memory Project" with cases claiming corroborated repressed memories. It is indeed a valuable resource indicating how many people were put in prison or fined for such questionable claims, most of which arose in the 1990s, but it would require years to chase down and investigate each citation, if that were even possible.

In some cases, "corroboration" came from siblings who also recovered memories or claimed always-remembered abuse. In others, the alleged perpetrator "confessed" after coming to believe in repressed memories themselves, or they took a plea bargain rather than face the rest of their lives in prison. Or the accused really had sexually abused someone else, so the recovered memories were assumed to be true. Or the accused had made "inappropriate advances" to another minor. Or relatives remembered the father giving massages to the child. Or somone recalled a single true incident of fondling and then retrieved many more questionable abuse memories.

As Harrison Pope Jr. observed, there are three requirements for proving a case of repressed memory. 1) There must be evidence that a traumatic event actually occurred, which would mean contemporaneous medical evidence of the abuse, reports from reliable and unbiased witnesses (i.e., witnessing actual abuse, although retrospective bias and faulty memory are possible); or confirmation by the perpetrator (excluding those who don't actually recall the abuse but think they must have done it). 2) There must be evidence for psychogenic amnesia, excluding cases in which victims simply tried not to think about the events, pretended that the events never occurred, or appeared to derive secondary gain by merely claiming to have amnesia (i.e. to avoid embarrassment or to extend a legal statute of limitations). 3) You must exclude cases in which amnesia developed for some biological reason, such as head trauma, seizures, or drug/alcohol blackouts. It is up to Cheit or anyone else to produce cases that meet all three criteria.

Thus, I concluded that, although people can forget a single traumatic incident and then recall it years later, it is extremely unlikely that years of abuse could be repressed or dissociated, only to pop back to consciousness with the proper trigger. If such massive repression routinely occurred, why is it only in the late 1980s and 1990s that recalling years of abuse became a wholesale American pastime? Some might answer that uncovering such memories required a skilled therapist to elicit the proper abreaction. Yet consider Arthur Janov's primal screamers of the early 1970s, all of whom were encouraged to relive buried trauma memories (*see Chapter 7*). Of all of Janov's cases related in his first book, only *one* involved incest memories. Why? Clearly, Janov didn't *expect* or *need* sexual abuse as an etiology. Any old trauma would do, so that's what his patients produced. If indeed there were truly so many repressed incest memories, they most certainly would have swamped primal scream sessions."

Although the human mind is capable of many things, "massive repression" is probably not one of them. Having examined cogent experimental and anecdotal evidence, my conclusions are similar to those reached by Harvard psychology professor Richard McNally in his 2003 book, *Remembering Trauma*:

> Events that trigger overwhelming terror are memorable, unless they occur in the first year or two of life or the victim suffers brain damage. The notion that the mind protects itself by repressing or dissociating memories of trauma, rendering them inaccessible to awareness, is a piece of psychiatric folklore devoid of convincing empirical support.

The notion that human beings could be *repeatedly* abused and then completely forget about it defies common sense. I do not believe that a woman could reach the age of 25, 35, or even 55, thinking that she had a relatively normal childhood, only to "discover" through recovered memories that her father had fondled her at 2, forced her into oral sex at 7, intercourse at 11, and taken her for an abortion at 14. Even if such massive repression *were* possible, the victims would surely be psychotic—not the relatively normal women who unearthed these "memories."*

Paul McHugh, long-time head of the Department of Psychiatry at Johns Hopkins, agreed. "Repression on this scale calls for an astonishing power of mind," he observed. "It is implausible on its face, lacks confirmation by research, and

---

* Even Freud, the father of repressed-memory theory, believed that large-scale repression used up so much of a person's limited store of energy that it preempted normal functioning as a human being.

... is usually proposed to patients during therapy without any effort to check any facts." McHugh further debunked the repressed memory phenomenon in his 2008 book, *Try to Remember*.

Some form of forgetting may occur for one-time traumatic events. There are cases of alleged temporary amnesia following a severe shock to the psychic system in which people sometimes wander about in a "fugue state," not even knowing who they are. I am considering only "psychogenic amnesia" here, not "organic amnesia," a loss of memory due to brain damage. Some cases of organic amnesia—particularly those resulting in wartime—have been mistakenly attributed to pure psychological causes, however. In cases of psychogenic amnesia, the memory loss is usually temporary, lasting only a few days, and it is clear that something is wrong with the sufferer.

Even in these instances, it is unclear how many cases are genuine. "It is well known," psychologist Daniel Schacter observed, "that a non-trivial proportion of cases that present with functional retrograde amnesia turn out to be deliberately simulated." British psychiatrist Charles Symonds went so far as to state, "I suspect that all so-called hysterical fugues [i.e., amnesia] are examples of malingering." Symonds delivered a stock speech to his amnesic patients: "I know from experience that your pretended loss of memory is the result of some intolerable emotional situation. If you will tell me the whole story, I promise absolutely to respect your confidence, will give you all the help I can, and will say to your doctor and relatives that I have cured you by hypnotism." This approach, he asserted, never failed.

Not only that, but "fugue state" amnesia appears to be a "culturally bound idiom of distress," having been popular in late nineteenth century France and ending shortly after World War I—and many of these cases did not involved triggering traumatic events. Such instances of psychogenic amnesia may not be conscious deceptions. Rather, they are unconscious role playing, acting out a socially accepted method of avoiding an unpleasant reality.

It is thus possible that single sexual abuse encounters—or those of limited duration—may be forgotten, only to be recalled later in life. If the event in question was truly traumatic, however, experimental evidence indicates that it would probably be remembered. Thus, children who witnessed a parent being murdered recall it vividly, as one would expect. Rather than forgetting it, the children suffer intrusive memories, just as war veterans often suffer from unwanted memories. So, to repeat: if sexual abuse is truly forgotten and then recalled years later, it is likely to happen only for a limited number of incidents, which were not perceived at the time as being particularly traumatic. While such normal forgetting may occur once, however, it would not apply to repeated abuse. Far from blocking out all memories, the abused daughter would think, "Oh, no, here comes Daddy again." She would not forget all such incidents.

Yet every argument for the theory of massive repression assumes some variant of Lenore Terr's Type I/Type II theory—that repeated and horrific abuse is likely to be forgotten, while more minor, isolated incidents are likely to be remembered.* In other words, day after day, a teenager will happily welcome her abuser, not remembering the terrible things he did the day before, or the day before that, but years or decades later, on a therapist's couch, the horrible truth will come pouring out in minute detail.

Because it is impossible to prove a negative, science can never prove, absolutely, that this theory is false in every instance. Science can simply find that there is no convincing and reliable evidence supporting this notion. But it is contrary to both common sense and to whatever objective evidence we have about how human memory works.

---

* Most recovered memory theorists appear to believe that sexual abuse is a special form of trauma, more susceptible to massive repression than other stressors. One amusing cartoon points up the absurdity of this logic. A masked burglar holds a gun on his male victim, who looks shocked. The legend beneath reads, "And now, to make sure you don't remember this robbery, I'm going to have to sexually abuse you."

3 How to Believe the Unbelievable

"I can't believe that!" said Alice. "Can't you?" the Queen said in a pitying tone. "Try again: draw a long breath, and shut your eyes." Alice laughed. "There's no use trying," she said. "One can't believe impossible things."

"I daresay you haven't had much practice," said the Queen. "When I was your age, I always did it for half-an-hour a day. Why, sometimes I've believed as many as six impossible things before breakfast."

—Lewis Carroll, *Through the Looking-Glass*

GIVEN THAT OUR MEMORIES CAN fool us sometimes, it is still hard to understand why or how people would *want* to believe that their parents or other trusted caregivers committed such awful acts upon them.

But it clearly isn't a matter of *wanting* to believe. I have come to regard the initial sexual abuse repressed memory suspicion as being a kind of mental kudzu seed—perhaps a perverse analogue to Jesus' parable of the sower and the seed. In the 1930s, some bright agronomist imported this nifty Japanese vine to my native Georgia, hoping to halt erosion and provide cheap cow fodder. The insidious kudzu, with its broad, shiny green leaves, now covers entire forests, swallowing trees whole. While cows may indeed eat the stuff, I suspect a few of them have been enveloped, too, along the way. Repressed memories seem to grow in the same way. It doesn't take much—just a small seed, planted in your fertile brain by a television program, a book, a friend, or a therapist. Maybe, just maybe, all of your problems stem from childhood incest. Maybe you've forgotten it. Maybe that's why you are uncomfortable at family reunions. Maybe. No, no, that's insane! Forget it, not Dad, not Mom! You try to dismiss the idea. But it won't go away. It takes root, sends out creepers, and grows. Soon the mental kudzu is twining out of your ears, sending roots down to your gut, taking over your life. It's true! Your worst fears were justified!

Numerous types of "evidence" are used to provoke and "prove" the reality of repressed memories. These include hypnotic regression, sodium Amytal, dreams, visualizations, bodily pangs or marks, panic attacks, or just general unhappiness. I will review each of them in turn, but it is important to understand that debunking one method or symptom really isn't the point, because another can easily take its place. Once the seed is planted, once the idea takes hold, it doesn't matter what method is employed. The results are almost foreordained.

Hypnosis: Memory Prod or Production?

Like most people, I once thought that when you sank into a deep hypnotic trance, you could magically tap into your dormant subconscious, unlocking long-forgotten memories. But it turns out that memories "uncovered" in hypnosis are highly questionable.

From its inception—covered in Chapter 10—hypnosis has caused considerable controversy and spawned innumerable myths. One thing that experts agree on, however, is that memories retrieved under hypnosis are often contaminated mixtures of fantasy and truth. In many cases, outright "confabulations"—the psychologists' term for illusory memories—result. Here is an unequivocal passage from the 1989 fifth edition of the *Comprehensive Textbook of Psychiatry*:

> An overwhelming body of research indicates that hypnosis does not increase accurate memory, but does increase the person's willingness to report previously uncertain memories with strong conviction. Furthermore, the hypnotized individual has a pronounced tendency to confabulate in those areas where there is little or no recollection; to distort memory to become more congruent with beliefs ... and fantasies; and to incorporate cues from leading questions as factual memories. Finally there is a high likelihood that the beliefs of the hypnotist will somehow be communicated to the patient in hypnosis and incorporated into what the patient believes to be memories, often with strong conviction.

Psychologist Robert Baker observed that "confabulation shows up without fail in nearly every context in which hypnosis is employed." No experimental study has ever provided evidence that hypnosis helps unlock real memories, although, as one researcher put it, "It is difficult to disregard totally the wealth of anecdotal reports extolling the virtues of hypnotic memory enhancement." Perhaps, then, hypnosis can enhance both real memories and fantasies. Baker did not agree. "I carried out a number of laboratory studies over a period of three and a half years," he wrote "My results in all cases showed no improvement in either memory or incidental memory as a result of hypnosis." On the contrary, Baker concluded that "the hypnotist may unwittingly suggest memories and create pseudomemories, i.e., vivid recollections of events that never happened."

The reason that memories retrieved under hypnosis are suspect goes to the very definition of the process, which invariably includes the concept of suggestion. Clark Hull and A. M. Weitzenhoffer defined hypnosis simply as "a state of enhanced suggestibility." When a subject agrees to be hypnotized, he or she tacitly agrees to abide by the suggestions of the hypnotist. This state of heightened suggestibility can work quite well if the goal is to stop smoking, lose weight, enhance self-esteem, reduce perceived pain, or improve one's sex life. But it is *not* an appropriate method for retrieving supposedly repressed memories, as psychiatrist Martin Orne and psychologist Elizabeth Loftus repeatedly stressed in courtroom settings.

Orne asserted that hypnosis is a technique that "greatly facilitates the reconstruction of history, that allows an individual to be influenced unwittingly, and that may catalyze beliefs into 'memories.'" He emphasized that "we cannot distinguish between veridical [true] recall and pseudomemories elicited during hypnosis without prior knowledge or truly independent proof." Loftus has said virtually the same thing. "There's no way even the most sophisticated hypnotist can tell the difference between a memory that is real and one that's created. If you've got a person who is hypnotized and highly suggestible and false information is implanted in his mind, it may get imbedded even more strongly. One psychologist tried to use a polygraph to distinguish between real and phony memory but it didn't work. Once someone has constructed a memory, he comes to believe it himself."

Consequently, numerous psychologists have recognized that reality is routinely distorted under hypnosis. Theodore R. Sarbin and William C. Coe referred to hypnotism as "believed-in imaginings," while Ernest R. Hilgard called the process "imaginative involvement." J. P. Sutcliffe characterized the hypnotic subject as "deluded" in a purely descriptive sense. Jean-Roch Laurence and Campbell Perry asserted: "Hypnosis is a situation in which an individual is asked to set aside critical judgment, without abandoning it completely, and is asked also to indulge in make-believe and fantasy."

The hypnotized subject is not the only one who is deluded. The hypnotist who believes that he or she is delving for hidden memories takes an active part in the shared belief system. Both hypnotist and subject are engaged in a tacitly accepted mini-drama in which they act out prescribed roles. Psychiatrist Harold Merskey defined hypnosis as "a maneuver in which the subject and hypnotist have an implicit agreement that certain events (e.g. paralyses, hallucinations, amnesias) will occur, either during the special procedure or later, in accordance with the hypnotist's instructions. Both try hard to put this agreement into effect." He noted that "there is no trance state, no detectable cerebral physiological change, and only such peripheral physiological responses as may be produced equally by non-hypnotic suggestion or other emotional changes." Laurence and Perry concurred, explaining that "the EEG [brain wave] of a hypnotized person is formally indistinguishable from that of a person who is relaxed, alert, with eyes closed."*

Eric Greenleaf observed that "the pretense of hypnotist-operator is a sort of

---

* Experts disagree about whether hypnotism involves a "trance state" or not. Ernest Hilgard and Herbert Spiegel were leading proponents of the "state" theory. All agree, however, that whether hypnotic subjects enter trance or not, they are liable to create pseudomemories.

shared delusion which both patient and therapist participate in." He stated that the methods of hypnotic induction are "more like following the rules of social procedure than ... chemical analysis." Robert Baker put it more bluntly: *There is no such thing as hypnosis.*" Numerous experiments have demonstrated that all of the mysterious hypnotic phenomena, such as pain reduction, posthypnotic amnesia, blindness, paralysis, and the like, are simply part of a subject's belief system and, with the sanction of the authority—the hypnotist—they can all magically reverse themselves.

I am not trying to imply that "hypnosis," whether a real state or not, does not have a profound effect, however. The human imagination is capable of incredible feats. And it does not have to be called "hypnosis" to have the same effect. Guided imagery, visualization, sodium Amytal interviews, relaxation exercises, breathing exercises, and prayers to God to reveal abuse are all actually forms of hypnosis. When someone is relaxed, willing to suspend critical judgment, engage in fantasy, and place ultimate faith in an authority figure using ritualistic methods, deceptive scenes from the past can easily be induced.

Hypnotism entails a powerful social mythology. Just as those "possessed" by demons believed in the process of exorcism, most modern Americans believe that in a hypnotic state, they are granted magical access to the subconscious, where repressed memories lie ready to spring forward at the proper command. Hollywood movies have reinforced this mythology, beginning with a spate of amnesia-retrieval dramas, such as Hitchcock's *Spellbound,* in the 1940s. A good hypnotic subject therefore responds to what psychologists call "social demand characteristics." As Baker put it, there is a "strong desire of the subject to supply the information demanded of him by the hypnotist." Psychiatrist Herbert Spiegel said it more directly: "A good hypnotic subject will vomit up just what the therapist wants to hear."

The hypnotist is often completely unaware that he is influencing the inductee, but what psychologists term "inadvertent cuing" can easily occur, often through tone of voice. "It is incredible," wrote French psychologist Hippolyte Bernheim in 1888, "with what acumen certain hypnotized subjects detect, as it were, the idea which they ought to carry into execution. One word, one gesture, one intonation puts them on the track." Simply urging "Go on" at a crucial point, or asking "How does that feel to you?" can cue the desired response. A person who *agrees* to play the role of the hypnotized subject is obviously motivated to believe in that role and act it properly. As hypnotist G. H. Estabrooks wrote in 1946, "the subject is very quick to cooperate with the operator and at times almost uncanny in his ability to figure out what the operator wishes." This goes double for clients in psychotherapy who are desperately seeking to locate the source of their unhappiness.

If the therapist has let them know, either subtly or directly, that they can expect to find scenes of sexual abuse while under hypnosis or through guided imagery, they are likely to do so.

In the introduction to *Theories of Hypnosis: Current Models and Perspectives* (1991), editors Steven Jay Lynn and Judith W. Rhue summarized the views expressed by the majority of the contributors: "Hypnotic behavior is interpersonal in nature .... Subjects' sensitivity to the hypnotist, subtle cues, and the tacit implications of hypnotic communications have a bearing on how they respond." Further, they noted that "subjects may engage in self-deception, may be unaware of the intrapsychic and contextual determinants of their actions, and may engage in behaviors that fulfill suggested demands with little awareness that they are doing so."

Experimental psychologists have long understood that false memories can be implanted during hypnosis. In 1891, Bernheim suggested to a hypnotized subject that his sleep had been disturbed the night before by a neighbor who "coughed, sang, and then opened the window." After the session, the patient elaborated on this illusory event, even adding how someone else had told his neighbor to close the window. Bernheim then told him that the scene had never happened, that he had dreamed it. "I didn't dream it," the patient protested indignantly. "I was wide awake!"

Laurence and Perry performed a similar experiment in 1983. Under hypnosis, subjects were asked to relive a night from the week before. During this experience, they were asked whether they had been awakened by loud noises. The majority took the hint and described the sleep interruption in some detail. After the hypnotic session, most of them continued to express a belief in the sounds. Even after they were told that the hypnotist had suggested the incident to them, they insisted on their reality. "I'm pretty certain I heard them," one subject stated. "As a matter of fact, I'm pretty damned certain. I'm positive I heard these noises." The sequence of these comments is revealing. In three sentences, we hear the subject rehearsing his convictions, progressing from "pretty certain" to "positive." Similarly, those intent on recovering memories of sexual abuse are usually unsure of their newly envisioned scenes at first. It is only with rehearsal and reinforcement that the memories gradually come to seem real and convincing.

Canadian psychologist Nicholas Spanos performed an interesting extension of the above experiment, trying to show that the implanted memories weren't "real," but were instead the result of role playing. As the authoritative hypnotist, he first got his subjects to agree to the memories, then reverse themselves, then agree again, then reverse themselves. By doing so, Spanos asserted that the pseudo-memories were never truly believed, but were simply reported in compliance with role expectations. Yet by the end of the confusing process, four of his eleven subjects still insisted that they had really heard the phantom noises. Here, Spanos appeared to have missed the vital importance of rehearsal and reinforcement in the production of false memories. If 36 percent of his subjects still believed in the "memories" without a therapist insisting on their truth, what kind of results would you get when any doubts are dismissed as attempts to deny the awful truth?

One of the characteristics of well-rehearsed hypnotic confabulations, in fact, is the utter confidence with which they are eventually reported. Such memories tend to become extraordinarily detailed and believable with repetition. "The more frequently the subject reports the event," Martin Orne observed, "the more firmly established the pseudomemory will tend to become." As a final caution, he warned that "psychologists and psychiatrists are not particularly adept at recognizing deception," adding that, as a rule, the average hotel credit manager is a far better detective.

Unfortunately, clinical psychologists and other therapists appear to have little interest in playing detective, even when they realize that hypnotism often produces false memories.* It is easy to see how the disastrous situation evolved, given the attitude of psychologists such as Roy Udolf, who wrote the *Handbook of Hypnosis for Professionals* in 1981. "There is little support in the experimental literature," he wrote, "for many of the clinical claims made for the power of hypnosis to provide a subject with total eidetic [accurate] imagery-like recall of past events." Nonetheless, he went on to assert that "the kind of memory that hypnosis could logically be expected to enhance would be ... affect-laden material that the subject has repressed ... [i.e.,] traumatic early experiences." Moreover, Udolf concluded that it didn't matter whether such elicited memories were accurate or not. "A memory retrieved under hypnotic age regression in therapy may be quite useful to the therapeutic process even if it is distorted, inaccurate, or a total fantasy as opposed to a real memory."

Age Regression: Let's Pretend

One of the most convincing forms of hypnosis, to the observer and the subject, is age regression, in which a client is taken back in time to a sixth birthday or a traumatic sex abuse incident at age four. During such regressions, to all appearances, the adult disappears, replaced by an innocent waif. The subject often speaks in a childish, high-pitched lisp. Handwriting becomes large and primitive.

---

* Most therapists, whether trauma specialists or not, object strenuously to the notion that they should "play detective" or encourage their patients to do so, seeking external corroboration for the "narrative truth" revealed in therapy sessions. The trouble is, some therapists already *are* playing detective by unearthing these supposed trauma memories. They encourage a belief system that has dramatic effects in the real world and *then* invoke their intuitive, subjective therapy stance.

Pictures appear stick-like and lack perspective. During the reliving of a child-hood trauma, a client might scream just as a toddler would and, if frightened enough, might wet her pants.

Yet there is overwhelming evidence that "age regression" is simply role playing in which an adult performs as she or he thinks a child would. As Robert Baker put it, "instead of behaving like real children, [they] behave the way they *believe* children behave." Psychologist Michael Nash reviewed the empirical literature on age regression and concluded that "there is no evidence for the idea that hypnosis enables subjects to accurately re-experience the events of childhood or to return to developmentally previous modes of functioning. If there is anything regressed about hypnosis, it does not seem to involve the literal return of a past psychologi-cal or physiological state." As memory researcher Julia Shaw wrote in 2016, age regression "has been discredited by numerous empirical studies—it just doesn't work reliably as a memory aid."

Even when hypnotically regressed subjects perform credibly, normal control subjects do just as well. As final evidence that hypnotic regression involves simple role enactment, Nash pointed out that "equally dramatic and subjectively com-pelling portrayals are given by hypnotized subjects who are told to progress to an age of 70 or 80 years." Most people would agree that such age progression involves more fantasy than accurate pre-living.*

The ultimate age regression is, of course, to the womb. In 1981, psychiatrist Thomas Verny wrote *The Secret Life of the Unborn Child,* offering examples of just such a feat. Under hypnotic regression, one of his patients reported the following placental message: "I am a sphere, a ball, a balloon, I am hollow, I have no arms, no legs, no teeth.... I float, I fly, I spin." Similarly, one Survivor claimed in a 1993 lawsuit that her therapist had helped her remember prenatal memories. Another therapist helped her patient access a memory of being stuck in the Fallopian tube, which explained her "stuckness" in adult life.

Past Lives and Unidentified Flying Fantasies

Hypnotism has similarly proven indispensable in the search for past lives and in "remembering" UFO abductions. Although nothing is impossible—maybe we really can remember former incarnations, and perhaps aliens actually do snatch us out of our beds—most readers will probably be more skeptical of such claims

---

* In 1954, psychiatrists Robert Rubenstein and Richard Newman came to the same conclusion when they suc-cessfully "progressed" five subjects into the future under hypnosis. "We believe that each of our subjects," they wrote, "to please the hypnotist, fantasied a future as actually here and now. We suggest that many descriptions of hypnotic regression also consist of confabulations and simulated behavior." Incredibly, however, *they exempted repressed memories* from this logic: "We suspect, however, that our doubts do not apply to the reenactment of traumatic past experiences."

than of recovered traumatic abuse memories. Yet the similarities are startling, including the reliving of sexual abuse while under hypnosis. Past-life therapists take people back before their births to previous centuries in which they were raped, tortured, or maimed. Only by recalling and re-experiencing these terrible traumas can they be mentally healed in this life.

"It is extremely common," Jungian therapist Roger Woolger wrote in *Other Lives, Other Selves* (1987), "for childhood sexual traumas also to have past-life underlays. I have frequently found that the therapeutic exploration of a scene of childhood sexual abuse in this life will suddenly open up to some wretched past-life scenario such as child prostitution, ritual deflowering, brother-sister or father-daughter incest, or else child rape in any number of settings ranging from the home to the battlefield." As an example, Woolger quoted one his clients who recalled a scene in a Russian barn during a previous life in which she was an 11-year-old peasant girl: "They're raping me. They're raping me. Help! Help! HELP! There are six or seven of them. They're soldiers."

Hypnotic regression to past lives has a venerable history, reaching back to 1906. Under hypnosis, Miss C, a British 26-year-old, relived the life of Blanche Poynings, a friend of Maud, Countess of Salisbury in the late 14th century. She gave verifiable names and details. When closely analyzed, a previous source for the information was finally revealed. Miss C. had read *Countess Maud*, by Emily Holt, when she was 12. She had unwittingly taken virtually all of the information for her "past life" from the novel.

For quite a while, the search for previous existences died down, but it received a boost in 1956 with the publication of *The Search for Bridey Murphy*. As with every well-documented case, it turned out that Virginia Tighe, the American woman who convincingly relived the life of the Irish Bridey—even reproducing her brogue—had indeed delved into her subconscious. However, what she pulled up was not a previous lifetime, but conversations with a Bridie Murphy Corkell, who had once lived across the street.

Theodore Flournoy, who debunked the earliest past-life regressions, coined the term *cryptomnesia* for this inadvertent mixing of prior knowledge with past lives. Elizabeth Loftus calls the same process "unconscious transference," while other psychologists use the term "source amnesia."*

Regardless of what we call the phenomenon, it offers intriguing evidence that the mind is indeed capable of storing subconscious memories that can be

---

* When he was president, Ronald Reagan proved to be a master of cryptomnesia. The movies in which he had acted appeared to be irretrievably mixed in his mind with reality, so that he frequently repeated fictional stories as if they had actually occurred. At one point, he even asserted he had personally taken documentary concentration camp footage at Dachau following World War II, even though Reagan did not venture outside the United States at that time. As biographer Garry Wills noted, however, "Reagan's war stories are real to him."

dredged up during hypnosis, though Virginia Tighe's memories of her neighbor presumably weren't "repressed," because they weren't traumatic. Those who are recounting tales of their previous lives invariably have read a book, seen a movie, or heard a story about that era or personality. Given the expectation that they will relive another life, their fertile imaginations combine this knowledge with other mental tidbits to create a feasible story. Those who are told to expect some trauma in a previous life add an appropriate rape, suffocation, or burning at the stake to the stew. This is probably not, in most cases, a conscious process of confabulation, because the subjects insist that they have no knowledge of the particular historical period. Similarly, people who are retrieving repressed memories of abuse routinely combine reality with fantasy. They mix their own childhood photographs, stories they have heard, real memories, and stereotyped scenes from *Sybil, The Courage to Heal* or some other source into a satisfactory scene.

As a further indication of human credulity, among the earliest practitioners of past-life regression was Colonel Albert de Rochas, who hypnotized clients during the 1890s. Rochas thought he could literally *progress* his clients into the future. Perhaps if we can *pre-live* the traumas that will be forthcoming in our lives, we might heal ourselves properly now—and confront the evil perpetrator before he has a chance to act!

Similarly, although I consider UFO abduction memories to be far-fetched products of hypnosis, many well-educated, otherwise rational professionals, including David Jacobs, retired Temple University history professor, and Harvard psychiatrist John Mack, who died in 2004, believed in such events. They had proof. They heard their clients recall the abductions while hypnotized. In his 1992 book, *Secret Life: Firsthand Documented Accounts of UFO Abductions,* Jacobs described his clients in terms that should sound familiar by now:

> They were all people who had experienced great pain. They seemed to be suffering from... a combination of Post-Traumatic Stress Disorder and the terror that comes from being raped. Nearly all of them felt as if they had been victimized. As I listened to them, I found myself sharing in their emotionally wrenching experiences. I heard people sob with fear and anguish, and seethe with hatred of their tormentors. They had endured enormous psychological [and sometimes physical] pain and suffering. I was profoundly touched by the depth of emotion that they showed during the regressions.

Similarly, in *Abduction: Human Encounters with Aliens* (1994), John Mack was impressed by "the intensity of the energies and emotions involved as abductees relive their experiences," in which they reported being grabbed against their will and "subjected to elaborate intrusive procedures which appeared to have a reproductive purpose." Mack acknowledged the similarity to repressed memories of sexual abuse. In one case, he said, a woman went to a therapist "for presumed sexual abuse and incest-related problems. Several hypnosis sessions failed to reveal evidence of such events." Instead, however, she recalled being abducted by aliens when she was six. Mack stressed that the UFO therapist must have "warmth and empathy, a belief in the ability of the individual to integrate these confusing experiences and make meaning of them ..., and a willingness to enter into the co-investigative process."

For abductee therapists, that willingness led to a memory-retrieval process that sounds awfully familiar to those who have listened to recovered-memory Survivors. Here is one alien abductee's description of the experience:

> It was ... common for us to seek [memories] out where they were—buried in a form of amnesia. Often we did this through hypnosis.... And what mixed feelings we had as we faced those memories! Almost without exception we felt terrified as we relived these traumatic events, a sense of being overwhelmed by their impact. But there was also disbelief. This can't be real. I must be dreaming. This isn't happening. Thus began the vacillation and self-doubt, the alternating periods of skepticism and belief as we tried to incorporate our memories into our sense of who we are and what we know.

After I published *Victims of Memory*, I heard from a woman who had been one of David Jacobs' abductees but thought better of it. She said he was "a terribly nice man, and he once had a big gathering at his house where I met others who were also 'fellow abductees,' including a seminary classmate of mine. They were lovely people, and quite sane and rational." But she felt uncomfortable with how obsessed they all seemed and how eager Jacobs was for confirmation. "It was hard to let go of my conviction that I had been abducted by aliens—mostly because I felt invested in it—embarrassment, too—and also because David was so invested in it, and my story was so much like that of others."

I am sure that David Jacobs and John Mack felt real empathy for these people who truly believed that they had been taken to UFOs and forcibly subjected to bizarre sexual experimentation.* But their findings seem only to confirm what is already known about hypnotism—that subjects tend to "remember" whatever the hypnotist is looking for. The pain is real—regardless of whether the memories are of past lives, UFO abductions, or incest by parents—but it was probably prompted and encouraged through the dubious means of hypnotic "regression."

---

* John Mack's *Abduction* follows the same basic pattern as that described by Jacobs. His hypnotized subjects revealed that the aliens took sperm and egg samples and inserted probes into their vaginas, anuses, and noses. Mack's aliens, however, were ultimately benign, trying to save humans from ecological disaster. The expectancy effect appears to be at work here: Mack had long been an activist for environmental causes. It appears that his expectations were sometimes quite overt. One reporter invented an abduction story that Mack eagerly accepted. Prior to her hypnotic sessions, he "made it obvious what he wanted to hear."

Investigators such as Jacobs and Mack duped themselves and others because they genuinely wanted to *help* people, especially if, in the process, they could feel that they were also exploring uncharted territory.

In *Victims of Memory*, I interviewed "Katherine Hylander," a past-life therapist who also helped clients recall UFO abductions, spirit possessions, and repressed memories of sexual abuse in *this* life.* "Repressed memories are a major cause of suffering for my clients," she told me. "I see it every day, in about 90 percent of the people who come to see me." She believed that all illness was psychosomatic. "For instance, asthma may be the result of smoke inhalation in another life. An allergy to wheat may stem from a rape in a wheat field, or arthritis from being stretched on a rack during the Inquisition." In one of her morbidly amusing cases, she found that one client's troubled marriage stemmed from having been married to the same man in a former life, in which he strangled her. Then, still under hypnosis, she regressed her to yet another life. "Dear God!" she cried. "I've done it again! I'm married to the same son-of-a-bitch! He's blinded me!"

Facilitated Communication and the Human Ouija Board

That same combination—yearning to save the helpless victim while venturing near the cutting edge of an exciting new discipline—resulted in the questionable practice of "facilitated communication," known familiarly as "FC," which purports to allow those afflicted with autism and cerebral palsy to write their thoughts.

In 1989, Syracuse University education professor Douglas Biklen brought the technique back from Australia, where it had been invented by Rosemary Crossley. Not surprisingly, millions of parents latched onto the hope provided by FC. In a few years, it became a near-religion.

In this technique, a "facilitator," usually a special education teacher, helps support the hand or arm of the autistic child. By sensing where the hand wants to go, the facilitator can help guide the finger to the appropriate letter on a keyboard. According to its advocates, this method has, miraculously, allowed those formerly locked in a silent world to communicate. Students who appeared to have IQs hovering around retarded levels could suddenly write essays on Shakespeare and learn calculus.

But carefully conducted, controlled experiments have shown conclusively that FC is a fraud, even though it was advanced with honorable intentions. It works only when the facilitator knows the answer and can see the keyboard. When an autistic child and a facilitator are shown different objects, the facilitator invariably types what he or she has seen. If only the child is shown an object, the correct

---

* For the full interview with Katherine Hylander and other interviews, see www.markpendergrast.com.

answer is never forthcoming.* These results shocked and saddened many facilitators, who genuinely believed in the process. Others, including Biklen, refuse to give up on it, convinced that FC works only in non-stressful, non-experimental conditions, with the proper established rapport, so it can never be tested.

The flap over FC might simply be an alarming example of a human Ouija board if false allegations of sexual abuse had not sprung from the process. In over 70 cases across North America, Europe, and Australia, autistic children typed out messages that are an exact verbal analogue of the role enactments we've just seen in hypnotic age regression. "Dad suk my prik," a typical example read. "He give luv to my butt." Douglas Biklen warned his trainees to be on the lookout for abuse. In his 1993 book, *Communication Unbound,* he wrote that 10 out of his initial 75 students—i.e., 13 percent—alleged sexual abuse through FC.

Biklen was mild, however, compared to some FC proponents, who wrote that "there is a better than 100 percent likelihood that a disabled child will be molested before he or she is eighteen. Facilitated Communication is confirming those statistics." Primed with such expectations, the facilitators suspected that the helpless, non-communicative autistic child—a perfect victim for abuse—was being molested at home. And so the facilitated accusations poured out. In some cases, autistic girls with intact hymens had supposedly been subjected to hundreds of parental rapes.

I interviewed parents whose lives were upended when their autistic teenage son's school facilitator typed: "Poppa stiks his prik up my butt. He make me mouth cock." They found out later that the facilitator, a young woman, had also typed that the boy wanted to live with her. Subsequent testing proved that the messages were coming from the facilitator, not the teenager, and the judge dismissed the case. But it was devastating to the child as well as the parents. The father had to move out of the home for six months. He never got to testify. "To this day, no one has asked me if I was innocent or guilty. I'd be the first one to go to bat for a sexually abused kid, but to use someone holding someone else's wrist over a keyboard to automatically find me guilty, that doesn't make sense. The attorney for the Child Protection Agency had me guilty from day one."

The allegations generated by facilitated communication serve as a metaphor for the repressed memory search. Although the facilitator may not have been consciously creating the accusations, the words were in fact coming directly from the facilitator's mind, not the child's. In similar fashion, therapists may have no idea that they are implanting memories of abuse.

In introductory psychology textbooks, college freshmen can read the story of Clever Hans, the ingenious horse. Using flash cards and counting frames, his

---

*   In the rare cases in which FC produces a correct word or phrase, subjects could already read and write independent of facilitation.

owner, one Herr von Osten, had taught Hans to read, add, and subtract. By 1904, after four years of intensive tutorials, the horse could answer questions put to him about geography, history, science, literature, math, or current events. Hans tapped his hoof a certain number of times for each letter, and he tossed his head up and down for "yes" and from side to side for "no."

Herr von Osten was thoroughly convinced that his horse was a genius. So were many eminent psychologists and zoologists, who walked away from demonstrations as believers. After all, Hans answered questions correctly even when his owner was nowhere near. The equable equine even got the right answers when questions were asked in languages other than his (presumably) native German. Only psychologist Oskar Pfungst remained skeptical. Like researchers on facilitated communication, he found that Hans could only answer correctly if the questioner knew the answer. He eventually discovered that Hans could not answer any questions when he wore a blindfold. It turned out that the horse was picking up subtle, inadvertent cues from his audience—a raised eyebrow or glance upward when the proper number of hoof-taps had been reached, a slight nod or shake of the head to indicate "yes" or "no." Hans was indeed a gifted horse, but not in the way Herr von Osten thought. So, too, are hypnotic subjects gifted— with vivid imaginations and the capacity to pick up on subtle, inadvertent cues.

Dream Work

Ever since Joseph saved Egypt by properly interpreting the Pharaoh's dreams— and probably long before that—humans have sought deep meaning from the strange stories they picture in their sleep. In our dreams, anything is possible. We can fly, jump through time, read other people's thoughts. Animals can talk, objects appear and disappear quickly, one thing metamorphoses quickly into something else. Sometimes our dreams are exciting, sexy, or soothing. Often, they are bizarre and frightening. What are we to make of them?

No one really knows, not even the most renowned dream researchers who shake people awake to ask what they're experiencing when their REMs (rapid eye movements) indicate that they are in an active dreaming state. Allan Hobson, a Harvard psychiatrist and dream expert, believes that dreams represent "creative confabulations." In his books, *The Dreaming Brain* and *The Chemistry of Conscious States,* Hobson explored how molecules such as amines control our waking consciousness, while acetylcholine appears to dominate our dream state. We do not remember our dreams (other than those we rehearse immediately upon awakening) because the necessary amines aren't available. Our dreams do not represent real-life events. Rather, the chemicals in our brains apparently throw us into a dreaming state automatically every 90 minutes or so. "Every mental product (including dreams) is in some way meaningful," Hobson wrote to me in 1995, "but meanings cannot be confidently determined by either face-value reading or by complex decoding."

Such cautions have not prevented various dream interpreters, including Freud, from asserting with great authority that dream ingredients symbolize certain objects, emotions or events. For example, for Freud a skyscraper might represent a penis. In the second century, Artemidorus used the same kind of logic. For him, a foot meant a slave, while a head indicated a father. The kinky ancient Egyptians apparently dreamed frequently of sexual congress with various animals. One papyrus explained, "If an ass couples with her [in her dream], she will be punished for a great fault. If a he-goat couples with her, she will die promptly."

Modern trauma therapists also used sexual dreams as a form of interpretation. They told their clients to be particularly aware of any night visions that could be interpreted as sexual abuse. This was called "dream work." Not too surprisingly, such dreams were often forthcoming. "Oh, my God!" the woman would report in therapy. "It's all true! In my dream last night, my Dad and uncle were taking turns having sex with me. And I was just a little kid!" Such dreams were taken as recovered memories and presumed to represent literal truth, even though some events seemed unlikely—in one well-publicized case, for instance, a daughter recalled being raped by her mother, who was equipped with a penis.

But if these dreams don't necessarily stem from repressed memories of actual events, where do they come from? From the same place that spawns hypnotically guided fantasies—the fertile and overwhelmed imagination. Here is someone feverishly working on her memory recovery, reading books describing horrible abuse, her life consumed with the possibility that her father did something to her. As Calvin Hall noted in *The Meaning of Dreams,* "It has been fairly well established that some aspects of the dream are usually connected with events of the previous day or immediate past." It is not surprising that someone with an obsession about incest would dream about it. Hall also warned that "dreams should never be read for the purpose of constructing a picture of objective reality," but therapists and patients eager for repressed memories ignored such advice.

The role of *expectation* in all aspects of memory recovery is crucial.* What we expect to see, we see, as Joseph Jastrow observed in his 1935 classic, *Wish and Wisdom:* "Everywhere, once committed by whatever route, the *prepossessed* mind finds what it looks for." Elizabeth Loftus told the true story of two bear hunters at dusk, walking along a trail in the woods. Tired and frustrated, they had seen no bear. As they rounded a bend in the trail, they spotted a large object about 25 yards away, shaking and grunting. Simultaneously, they raised their rifles

---

* Expectancy theory also explains so-called "automatic writing" about sex abuse. Women were told to keep journals and just write whatever came to mind. Repressed memories were then supposed to pour out from the subconscious. Indeed, when dreadful scenes scribble themselves onto the page, they seem to come out of nowhere, but they are, in fact, products of suggestion.

and fired. But the "bear" turned out to be a yellow tent with a man and woman making love inside. The woman was killed. As psychologist Irving Kirsch noted, "response expectancy theory" explains how "when we expect to feel anxious, relaxed, joyful, or depressed, our expectations tend to produce those feelings." At its extreme, such a mindset can even lead to self-induced death, as has been well-documented among tribes in which those under a powerful curse fulfill it by wasting away and dying, unless some way to reverse the curse can be found.

Similarly, when we expect to have a particular type of dream, we tend to perform accordingly. As Jerome Frank noted in *Persuasion and Healing*, patients routinely give their therapists the dreams they want. "The dream the therapist hears is, of course, not necessarily the one the patient dreamed," Frank explained, "since considerable time has usually elapsed between the dream and its report. One study compared dreams reported immediately upon awakening with the versions unfolded before a psychiatrist in a subsequent interview. Any material the patient anticipated would not be approved was not recalled." In his classic 1957 text, *Battle for the Mind*, psychiatrist William Sargant described an acquaintance who had entered first Freudian, then Jungian therapy. "His contemporary notes show that dreams he had under Freudian treatment varied greatly from those he had under Jungian treatment; and he denies having experienced the same dreams before or since." Sargant concluded: "The increased suggestibility of the patient may help the therapist not only to change his conscious thinking, but even to direct his dream life."

Therapist Renee Fredrickson certainly believed in such directives. "You can also prime your dream pump, so to speak," she wrote in *Repressed Memories*. "Before you go to sleep at night, visualize yourself as a little child.... Then suggest that your inner child show you in a dream what you need to know about the abuse." Nor did the dream abuse have to be obvious. Fredrickson described how Diane reported a dream in which "she was on her hands and knees in a kitchen, washing the floor. Floating in the air were green U-shaped neon objects. Her father was standing next to a large mirror over the sink, watching her." Eventually, Diane interpreted her dream as follows: "My father raped me in the evenings when I was cleaning the kitchen.... He would make me crawl around naked while he watched in the mirror. I also believe the green neon things are about a time he put a cucumber in me."

Sleep Paralysis

Another fascinating form of semi-dream, which typically occurs in the twilight state between waking and sleeping, may account for many "repressed memories." The psychological term is either a "hypnogogic" or "hypnopompic" state, respectively referring to the time just before sleep or prior to waking, but more commonly it is just called "sleep paralysis." During this curious in-between semi-conscious state, people often report chilling visions.* Robert Baker described the phenomenon: "First, the hallucinations always occur [just] before or after falling asleep. Second, the hallucinator is paralyzed or has difficulty moving.... Third, the hallucination is usually bizarre.... Finally, the hallucinator is unalterably convinced of the reality of the entire event." The vision's content is often related to the dreamer's current concerns. In one study, as many as 67 percent of a normal sample population reported at least one experience of sleep paralysis, with its attendant hallucinations. Many people experience sleep paralysis during the day, particularly if they take afternoon naps. Those with narcolepsy—a relatively common disorder characterized by brief involuntary periods of sleep during the day, with difficulties resting at night—are particularly prone to these frightening hallucinations.

The word "nightmare" actually stems from sleep paralysis. A "mare," or demon, was supposed to terrorize people—mostly women— by sitting on their breasts, making it difficult to breathe. Often, the mare was an incubus or succubus who also forced the frightened sleeper into sexual intercourse. The following is a 1763 description of the phenomenon:

> The nightmare generally seizes people sleeping on their backs, and often be-gins with frightful dreams, which are soon succeeded by a difficult respiration, a violent oppression on the breast, and a total privation of voluntary motion. In this agony they sigh, groan, utter indistinct sounds [until] they escape out of that dreadful torpid state. As soon as they shake off that vast oppression, and are able to move the body, they are affected by strong palpitation, great anxiety, languor, and uneasiness.

David Hufford wrote an entire book about sleep paralysis, *The Terror That Comes in the Night.* His 1973 interview with Caroline, a young graduate student, sounds quite similar to the reports of many Survivors. When Caroline woke up one day, she reported, "I felt like there was a man next to me with his arm un-derneath my back, and holding my left arm." His smell was quite distinct, "all sweaty and kind of dusty." When she tried to move, he gripped her arm tighter. "Now if I move again, he's going to rape me," she thought. She tried to scream, but she could make no sound. "Then he was on top of me, and I tried to look up to see who it was or something.... I could just see this—it looked like a white mask. Like a big white mask." After several minutes of this horrible experience, Caroline "felt sort of released, you know. And I—I could sit up, and I got the

---

* Two of the interviews in Victims of Memory—of "Frieda Maybry" and "Leslie Hannegan"—provided classic examples of sleep paralysis, as did the experience of A. G. Britton related at the end of Chapter 1.

feeling there was nobody there." In the 1990s, such experiences were frequently interpreted as "flashbacks" or "body memories," and women were encouraged to visualize a face to fill in the blank mask.

Other "evidence" of repressed memories also relates to sleep—or its lack. In *The Courage to Heal,* Ellen Bass and Laura Davis quoted one typical woman's experience as she obsessed over possible repressed memories: "I just lost it completely. I wasn't eating. I wasn't sleeping." Sleep deprivation is a well-established technique used in brain-washing. As sleep expert Alexander Borbely wrote, chronic lack of sleep blurs the borderline between sleeping and waking, "so that the kind of hallucinations that often occur at the moment of falling asleep now begin to invade the waking state as well ... the floor appears to be covered with spider webs; faces appear and disappear. Auditory illusions also occur." In addition, "when sleep deprivation experiments last more than four days, delusions can manifest themselves, in addition to the disturbances of perception. The participants grow increasingly suspicious and begin to believe that things are going on behind their backs."

Flashbacks or Visions?

It is likely, then, that many of the so-called "flashbacks" reported as repressed memories were the result of sleep deprivation, combined with expectancy. Flashbacks themselves have been widely misunderstood. Even in the case of war veterans, these very real terrors, often triggered by the sound of an explosion, are not the reliving of actual events. Rather, they are *worst fear* scenarios, as John MacCurdy pointed out in his classic 1918 book, *War Neuroses.* MacCurdy called such moments "visions," arguably a more accurate term than flashback. Similarly, psychiatrists treating World War II veterans found that leading patients to dramatically "relive" fictional events seemed to help them as much as recalling a real trauma. One man who had been in a tank regiment vividly visualized being trapped in a burning tank. "This had never actually happened, though it must have been a persistent fear of his throughout the campaign," his doctor noted. Similarly, under the influence of sodium Amytal, a 35-year-old Vietnam combat veteran "lived out" a feared fantasy of having been captured and tortured by the Viet Cong, though nothing like that had actually happened to him.

An even more interesting war-related case occurred in a Vietnam veteran's support group. Ed recounted how he had watched a buddy's head explode during a firefight. He had relived this and other harrowing memories in therapy. But when one of his group members called Ed's parents for help in staging a surprise birthday party, his mother said, "What? He's in a veterans' recovery group? But he was rated 4-F. He never was allowed to go to Vietnam!" Even when confronted in the group, however, Ed maintained that his story was true. He had fantasized his "flashbacks" so successfully that they had become real.*

Body Memories and Panic Attacks

People who are trying to recover repressed memories were often told that "the body remembers what the mind forgets," particularly in cases of abuse suffered as a pre-verbal infant. These "body memories" could take the form of virtually any form of physical ailment, from stomach aches to stiff joints. As I document in Chapter 6, psychosomatic complaints such as these have always been common in Western culture and almost invariably accompany general unhappiness and anxiety. Add to this the "expectancy effect," and it isn't surprising that during the "abreaction" or reliving of an event, a woman might feel terrible pelvic pain, or a man might experience a burning anus.

Those in search of memories often submitted to massages by experienced "body workers," who could trigger feelings either by light touch or deeper muscle manipulation. "An area of your body may get hot or feel numb," Renee Fredrickson assured readers in *Repressed Memories*. "Powerful emotions may sweep over you, causing you to weep or even cry out." It is certainly true that people can experience profound, inexplicable emotions while they are being massaged, particularly if they are tense and unhappy in general. When they let down their guards and relax, allowing intimate touch by a stranger, they may weep. Given the admonition to be on the lookout for any stray sensation, many subjects had no difficulty locating and interpreting various body memories. Fredrickson gave two examples: "She [Sarah] was undergoing a passive form of body work involving laying on of hands when she had a slowly burgeoning sense of rage at her father for abusing her." Later on, Sarah discovered that the "exquisite sensitivity" of her toes was caused by her grandfather having shoved wood chip under her toenail.

Some "body memories" took the form of rashes or welts that fit particular memory scenarios. The mind can apparently produce remarkable and sometimes quite specific effects on the body. Some people can consciously control their pulse rates, respiration, or blood flow.

One intriguing case involved Elizabeth K., who entered therapy with psychiatrist Alfred Lechler in 1928 when she was 26. Since her early teens, she had suffered from headaches, nausea, paralyses, blackouts, and bowel disorders. By the time she came to see Dr. Lechler, Elizabeth suffered from insomnia and

---

* Psychologist Michael Yapko reported a similar case in which a man convinced his wife, therapist, and apparently himself that he was experiencing excruciating flashbacks to his imprisonment in a Vietcong bamboo cage. After he committed suicide, his widow tried to locate his official military record and discovered that he had never been in Vietnam.

had attempted suicide. She proved to be highly suggestible, with a tendency to take on any medical symptoms she heard about. Lechler hypnotized her, getting her to produce the classic stigmata of Christ. Later, after she had returned to normal consciousness, the psychiatrist asked her to picture bloodstained tears. Within a few hours, blood welled up inside Elizabeth's eyelids and poured down her cheeks.* In *Michelle Remembers,* Michelle Smith evidently possessed similar powers, producing a red rash on her neck that her psychiatrist interpreted as a welt left by the devil's tail.

Nothing so dramatic need account for most "body memories," however. One of the most common was recounted by A. G. Britton in her article, "The Terrible Truth." She experienced a choking sensation and interpreted that as evidence that her father had forced his penis into her mouth when she was a baby. It turns out, though, that a constricted throat is one nearly universal human reaction to fear and anxiety. In fact, the word "anxious" derives from the Latin word meaning "to strangle." This classic symptom—an inability to swallow and the feeling of being choked—is now one of the diagnostic symptoms for panic disorders. For hundreds of years it was called, among other things, *globus hystericus,* because it felt as though a ball were rising from the abdomen and lodging in the throat.

Many people who feared that they may have been abused suffered repeated panic attacks at unexpected moments and, with their therapists' encouragement, interpreted them as repressed memories surging forth from the subconscious. Yet these little-understood episodes are extremely common As psychologist David Barlow pointed out in his comprehensive text, *Anxiety and Its Disorders,* "Anxiety disorders represent the single largest mental health problem in the country, far outstripping depression." In Western cultures, reports of this affliction are much more common among women than among men, although that is not so in Eastern countries. Surveys indicate that 35 percent of Americans report having experienced panic attacks. Unfortunately, those seeking help for severe anxiety disorders are frequently misdiagnosed, seeing an average of ten doctors or therapists before receiving appropriate help.

As listed in the fifth edition of the *Diagnostic and Statistical Manual of Mental Disorders,* familiarly known as the *DSM-V (2013),* the symptoms experienced during panic attacks (four or more being sufficient by the official definition) sound like a checklist for what trauma therapists interpreted as body memories:

(1) palpitations, pounding heart, or accelerated heart rate, (2) sweating, (3)

---

* It is possible, however, that Elizabeth somehow faked these phenomena. As a psychologist pointed out in 1946, one hypnotic subject, eager to show his abilities, "proved" that he could raise blisters under suggestion. Secret observation through a peep-hole, however, showed him "deliberately rub the bandage with all his strength so as to irritate the skin beneath. Worse still, some subjects were seen to take a needle [and] thrust it under the bandage."

trembling or shaking, (4) sensations of shortness of breath or smothering, (5) feeling of choking, (6) chest pain or discomfort, (7) nausea or abdominal distress, (8) feeling dizzy, unsteady lightheaded, or faint, (9) chills or heat sensations, (10) paresthesias (numbness or tingling sensations), (11) derealization (feelings of unreality) or depersonalization (being detached from oneself), (12) fear of losing control or going crazy, (13) fear of dying.

Surprisingly, Barlow reported that "the overwhelming evidence is that many phobias and the majority of fears are not learned through a traumatic experience." Instead, panic attacks appear to stem from contemporarily stressful life situations and a fearful mindset—though biological factors and early childhood trauma may contribute to a predisposition to anxiety disorders. Psychologists Aaron Beck and Gary Emery gave an example of a typical episode involving a 40-year-old man who, while on the ski slopes, began to feel shortness of breath, profuse perspiration, and faintness. He thought he was having a heart attack. In the midst of this, he had a vivid image of himself lying in a hospital bed with an oxygen mask. It transpired that this man's brother had just died of a heart attack, and he feared the same might happen to him. Similarly, people who thought they may have repressed memories feared that they might be like others they knew (or had read about or seen on television). They, too, could be unknowing incest victims who would have flashbacks. For such people, panic attacks were often triggered when they became over-tired or over-stressed and spontaneously envisioned images of their worst fears, which, in turn, provoked even more anxiety. "Once the fear reaction has started," Beck and Emery wrote, "it tends to build on itself." These "autonomous" images then "persist without the patient's being able to stop them," and they seem utterly real, "as though the traumatic episode were actually occurring *in the present.*"

After the first attack of this inexplicable fear, a vicious cycle can commence in which the very fear of another episode provokes it. This would be particularly likely for a woman who is extremely stressed by the idea that she might have been sexually abused and is minutely aware of every bodily and emotional twinge. As David Barlow noted, "self-focused attention greatly increases sensitivity to bodily sensations and other aspects of internal experience. Furthermore, this sensitivity … quickly spreads to other aspects of the self, such as self-evaluative concerns." Barlow called this process a "negative feedback cycle" which leads to a chronic feeling of helplessness, dependence, and self-absorption. As Ann Seagrave and Faison Covington—two women who overcame their panic attacks—wrote in *Free from Fears,* "We can become frightened to such a degree that we learn to monitor every twitch, every ache, and it is in that way that we often scare ourselves needlessly."

One final point related to panic attacks seems quite puzzling. Attacks are often triggered by deep relaxation exercises such as those which induce hypnosis or guided imagery sessions. In one study, 67 percent of a group of panic-disorder patients experienced three or more symptoms while listening to a relaxation tape. As David Barlow noted, "relaxation is surely the strangest of panic provocation procedures." He hypothesized that it may be caused by a fear of losing control. Whatever the reason, this finding certainly relates to therapy clients led to a "safe place" during deep relaxation exercises. It contributes to our understanding of why they might experience panic attacks during the process.

The scope of what recovered memory therapists sometimes labeled "body memories" is staggering, encompassing virtually every illness or somatic complaint. If you had cancer, asthma, multiple sclerosis, or even AIDS, you may have contracted it because of your undiagnosed repressed memories of sexual abuse. The same applies to tight muscles, stuttering, facial tics, chronic headaches, or diarrhea. Some women recovered memories (and sued for same) after being jarred in an auto accident. Or "body memories" could be extraordinarily vague, including the awkward way one moves. One woman's dance instructor diagnosed her as having repressed memories from observing her in practice.

Symptoms: Pickle Aversion and Eating Disorders

For many potential "Survivors," neither hypnotism nor panic attacks were necessary to believe the unbelievable. *Belief* that they *must* have been molested as children was sometimes enough, without specific "memories." In fact, as we have seen in Chapter 1, Ellen Bass and Laura Davis informed their readers that *symptoms* are sufficient to diagnose repressed memories, regardless of whether they are ever visualized. And herein lies an important point: *belief* always precedes *memory,* and is often sufficient unto itself. The therapeutic or self-help process is largely a matter of re-education.

In a 2001 Harvard study of those who believed they had repressed memories, for instance, many of the subjects were sure that they had been sexually abused as children, but they had no memory of the abuse. Of those, two-thirds had come to that conclusion without the aid of psychotherapy. In other words, they had read self-help books or simply absorbed cultural messages and concluded that there must have been abused and repressed the memory.

Recovered-memory therapist Charles Whitfield would often spend over an hour carefully reviewing the criteria for post-traumatic stress disorder with his clients, encouraging them to identify with the symptoms. Not only did this give him a ready-made diagnosis that an insurance company would pay for, but it labeled the client a victim of PTSD who *must* seek memories as an explanation. "Oh, my God, is *this* what it is?" they exclaimed. "Oh, does this explain a lot of things to me now!" From there, it was a small, almost inevitable step to some form of abuse-memory retrieval. *The Science of False Memory* (2005), by Brainerd and Reyna, for instance, chronicles how therapists assigned "memory work" to clients as homework between therapy sessions.

As a species, human beings seem to have a natural desire for explanations. As soon as they can speak, children begin pestering their parents with "Why? Why? Why?" Often, there is no simple answer, but patients seeking therapy are highly motivated to find specific reasons for their unhappiness so that they can "fix" it. When therapists told them that they had all the "symptoms" of a sex abuse survivor, they could easily believe it. *So that's why my marriage is so difficult, why I yell at my children, why I can't hold a job, why I have low self-esteem, why I feel uncomfortable at family reunions! Now everything falls into place.*

It's an answer that could be adapted to fit almost any question. Holly Ramona, a young California woman whose father successfully sued her therapists, didn't like pickles, whole bananas, mayonnaise, cream soups, melted cheese, or white sauce. According to Lenore Terr and Holly's therapists, her eating habits were compelling evidence that her father forced oral sex on her as a child, because pickles and bananas are penis-shaped, and mayonnaise, creamy soups, and white sauce resemble semen. Of course, this logic could be used to label most of the children in the United States as sex abuse survivors. I don't like bananas, either, and I don't like cooked okra by itself because it's so slimy, but I do not regard these personal aversions as evidence of childhood molestation.

In addition to her distaste for pickles and bananas, Holly Ramona entered therapy with a full-blown eating disorder. She was bulimic, eating large amounts of food and then vomiting in a terrible binge/purge cycle. Both bulimia and anorexia—self-starvation—became epidemic ailments, particularly among young women, in late-20thcentury America. The reasons for such eating disorders are complicated, but they clearly have a great deal to do with societal pressure on women to remain abnormally thin. For quite a while, the conventional wisdom held that women with eating disorders had over-protective, over-involved mothers. But then the blame shifted from mothers to fathers. Many therapists considered eating disorders a nearly fool-proof symptom of childhood incest. Holly Ramona's therapist told her that 80 percent of all eating-disorder patients had been sexually abused.

Psychiatrist William C. Rader, a self-styled expert, wrote that "approximately 85% of eating disordered patients have been sexually or physically abused." He derived this statistic by surveying patients attending his own "Rader Institute," thirteen eating-disorder units located in Alabama, California, Texas, Illinois, Michigan, Missouri, Oklahoma, Washington, and Massachusetts. When I spoke to a psychiatric nurse at a Florida unit, she told me that 90 to 95 percent of their clients found repressed memories of sexual abuse during their stay. Rader was clearly relying on a self-perpetuating set of statistics, created by his own belief system.*

Indeed, many of the inpatient eating disorder units throughout the United States—well over 200 in the 1990s—were virtual memory mills, with Survivor groups meeting daily. The ads for such institutions made their assumptions clear. "Shades of Hope is an all addiction treatment center, specializing in the treatment of Eating Disorders, Co-Dependency, and Survivors of Childhood Abuse," read one. Another promised: "At The Meadows our 'family of origin' therapy uncovers original childhood traumas which often are at the root of eating disorders."

Yet there is no scientific evidence that eating disorders stem from childhood molestation, as Harvard psychiatrists Harrison Pope and James Hudson, specialists in the field, repeatedly stressed. "Current evidence does not support the hypothesis that childhood sexual abuse is a risk factor for bulimia nervosa," they wrote in a 1992 article in the *American Journal of Psychiatry*. There are "no differences in the prevalence of childhood sexual abuse between bulimic patients and the general population." Despite such findings, thousands of vulnerable women desperate for help with their eating disorders continued to search for repressed memories.

This search was particularly unfortunate, since many patients with eating disorders respond to conventional medical treatment with anti-depressant drugs such as Prozac. In a 1995 article, Susan McElroy and Paul Keck described three case studies of women with eating or obsessive-compulsive disorders, all of whom initially believed that they harbored repressed memories. All three responded quickly to medical treatment.

I will end with a cautionary tale recounted by psychologist Kay Thompson. A female client sought therapy for help with a dental gag reflex which prevented dentists from working on her. Under hypnosis, she revealed that the gagging started soon after she received a tonsillectomy when she was seven years old. Having located the psychic root of the problem, the hypnotist suggested that it would no longer bother her and, indeed, the symptoms disappeared. When she told her family doctor about this miraculous cure, however, he told her she had never had her tonsils removed. Similarly, several young women with intact hymens "remembered" multiple childhood rapes. The moral: it is all too easy to identify *the* root cause for a current symptom, even though it may be incorrect. There is no way to determine simple causality for human behavior.

---

* Rader's explanations for why Survivors developed eating disorders were illuminating. "For compulsive overeaters, fatty tissue becomes a protective layer." On the other hand, "anorexics may appear more like adolescent males than mature, sexually desirable women," thus avoiding their sexuality. "For bulimics, vomiting can become the mechanism of release for anger and pain. At times, they will actually shout out the name of their perpetrator as they vomit." Rader went on to open off-shore clinics to inject human stem cells into desperately ill clients. His medical license was revoked in 2014.

Drugs

In conjunction with suggestive therapy, drugs can significantly increase the likelihood of illusory sex abuse memories. Even without overt suggestion, physicians and therapists have long recognized that strong sedative compounds can lead to false accusations. "When my father went to medical school in the early 1930s," psychiatrist Harrison Pope noted, "he was admonished never to administer nitrous oxide or other anesthetic agent without a chaperone in the room because of the risk a female patient might wake up and claim that she had been sexually abused." A number of British doctors were accused of abuse by women given midazolam (Versed), even though there were several witnesses in the room who saw no such behavior. Considering the substantial doses of mind- and mood-altering drugs that many depressed people take, it is not surprising that they may be more suggestible. Many women I interviewed in the 1990s reported that they were "walking zombies" because of the multiple drugs they were taking while in therapy or on a psychiatric ward.

The most widely used "memory aid" drugs intentionally used by recovered memory therapists were barbiturates, notably sodium Amytal. American psychiatrist Eric Lindemann introduced sodium pentothal and other barbiturates into psychology in the 1930s. Because Lindemann considered his patients *unable* to refuse to answer questions while drugged, he believed they could not lie. Hence, the drugs became known as "truth serum," and the popular press spread this misinformation quickly. "Narco-synthesis" and "narco-analysis" were the new pseudoscientific buzzwords for abreactive sessions using the drugs.

In fact, Amytal interviews are even *more* likely than simple hypnosis to produce confabulations. The barbiturates do not magically enhance memory. Like hypnosis, they simply render the subject more relaxed and suggestible. According to psychiatrist August Piper, Jr., Amytal produces "slurred speech, drowsiness, a feeling of warmth, distorted memory, and an altered time-sense." In other words, it creates a state "similar to alcohol intoxication." Many therapists told their clients that the drugs actually do promote only true memories, however. As a consequence, a 1991 Ohio jury convicted a psychiatrist of malpractice for injecting a patient over 140 times with "truth serum" to help uncover her repressed memories.

Cognitive Dissonance and Group Contagion

All of the methods discussed thus far can contribute to false belief in sexual abuse, but all of them are reinforced and amplified by the general social context. As Jerome Frank wrote in the introduction to *Persuasion and Healing*, "man is a domestic creature, with infinite social and cultural involvements. He is continually and crucially influencing others and being influenced by others." A full understanding of the memory manipulation process requires examination of such interpersonal pressures.

In 1957, Leon Festinger published *A Theory of Cognitive Dissonance,* which offered an intriguing explanation of how and why people can radically change their opinions. Normally, we maintain an internally consistent world-view. When we experience some kind of disequilibrium—when one of our central beliefs is somehow challenged—it results in an internal conflict that Festinger termed "cognitive dissonance." The more important and dramatic the conflict, the greater the magnitude of the dissonance. When we suffer such massive internal tension, we must come down on one side or the other, or go insane.

Certainly, there could be no greater cognitive dissonance than that produced by the Survivor Movement. A woman was suddenly asked to believe that her father, previously regarded as someone who loved and protected her, raped her throughout her childhood. In *The Courage to Heal,* Ellen Bass and Laura Davis documented the intolerable confusion and upheaval this caused. "The hardest thing was accepting the fact that someone I loved and cherished—my father—could have violated me so deeply," one woman told them. Another said, "It's like you're dissolving and there's nothing to hold on to." A third confessed that "trying to fit the new reality into the shattered framework of the old was enough to catapult me into total crisis. I felt my whole foundation had been stolen from me." Recall the story of Emily, already recounted in Chapter 1. "Every time Emily spoke to her parents she became ill—the conflict between what she knew inside and what they presented was too great." Her solution was to cut off all contact with her parents and seek reassurance from her therapist.

It was this dissonance that kept many people in a belief state that, in retrospect, seems unbelievable. One retractor told me that her therapist had led her to "remember" being in a Satanic ritual abuse cult in which she had murdered babies. "The whole time I kept wondering if it was true or not true, thousands of times a day. If it's not true I must be crazy, but I'm not crazy so it must be true. But how can it be true? But if it is true I'm a murderer and I just want to die."

In order to produce the initial dissonance, of course, one has to accept the idea that has been seeded in one's mind. Festinger pointed out that if the seed-bearer is "seen as expert or very knowledgeable about such matters, the dissonance between knowledge of his contrary opinion and one's own opinion will be greater." Once a situation of intolerable internal conflict exists, the sufferer is under intense pressure to choose one side or the other. Something has to give.

"When dissonance is present," Festinger added, "in addition to trying to reduce it, the person will actively avoid situations and information which would likely increase the dissonance." Simultaneously, she will seek out those who reinforce her new belief system. This insight helps to explain why people with newly found abuse memories cut off all old friends who expressed even the mildest doubts. Festinger pointed out a paradoxical truth—the greater the underlying dissonance, the more confidence a person must feel in the decision to opt for a new world view, and the less likely she will be to reverse that decision. Once you become a Survivor, in other words, it becomes unbearable to consider that you might be wrong. You are stuck with your new identity. To turn back would renew the confusion.

In his classic 1984 text, *Influence*, social psychologist Robert Cialdini made a similar point. "Once we have made a choice or taken a stand, we will encounter personal and interpersonal pressures to behave consistently with that commitment. Those pressures will cause us to respond in ways that justify our earlier decision." One retractor's revealing comment in a letter to her father illustrates this principle. "Right after I brought the lie [the accusation] into the open, I began to doubt its truth. But I couldn't believe that I would do such a thing. I couldn't believe I was capable of making up such a lie, believing it, and then taking it to the lengths I did."

"The social group is at once a major source of cognitive dissonance for the individual," Festinger wrote, "and a major vehicle for eliminating and reducing the dissonance." Bass and Davis repeatedly emphasized how important such groups can be. "Being in a group with other survivors can be a powerful way to vanquish shame. When you hear other women talk about their abuse and are not disgusted, and when you see those same women listen to your story with respect, you begin to see yourself as a proud survivor." This social reinforcement was key to the Survivor Movement. "Social support is particularly easy to obtain when a rather large number of persons who associate together are all in the same situation," Festinger noted. "If everyone believes it, it most certainly must be true."

In *Motel Nirvana*, her 1995 exploration of American New Age beliefs, British author Melanie McGrath made an incisive observation about how *anyone* could be swayed within a restricted group setting:

> I don't think anyone is immune to implausible beliefs, however rational and willful they think themselves to be. It is an easy matter to deny everything you thought you knew and to believe its contradiction rather than to live out your days in bottomless isolation. Only the most rare of individuals will stand up for a belief when all around are declaring its opposite, for most of us feel more anxious to be at ease with each other than we do with ourselves.

It is truly remarkable how suggestible people become in groups, as Solomon

Asch demonstrated in a series of 1956 experiments. Eight college students, assembled in a group, were shown a simple line, then asked to specify which of three alternative lines were the same length. Although the answer was obvious, seven of the students, who were coached ahead of time, answered incorrectly. The real subject of the experiment always reported next to last. Seventy-five percent of these subjects gave an incorrect answer at least once, although when they performed the test alone, they *always* chose the correct response. "At first I thought I had the wrong instructions," one student said, "then that something was wrong with my eyes and my head."

Near the end of his rather dry book, Festinger related a fascinating story about a small sect of people who believed that alien "Guardians" from outer space would arrive at a specific time to whisk them off to another planet just before a huge flood. Prior to this predicted cataclysm, the sect members avoided publicity while quietly preparing for their departure. After the flying saucer and flood repeatedly failed to appear, they reacted in an unexpected manner.

"A message arrived from God which, in effect, said that He had saved the world and stayed the flood because of this group and the light and strength they had spread throughout the world that night." As a result, they now became avid publicity seekers, announcing their epiphany. Festinger explained this illogical behavior as a predictable reaction to increased cognitive dissonance. To preserve their threatened belief system, the sect members became even more dogmatic and sought to proselytize.

This insight may help to explain why women who had recovered repressed "memories" felt compelled to tell the world about them, while real incest victims, who have always remembered their abuse, generally do not. It also predicted that, in the face of increased skepticism, the Survivor Movement would become more vocal and strident, at least for a while.

Frederic Bartlett made similar observations in 1932. "The organized group functions in a unique and unitary manner in determining and directing the lives of its individual members," he wrote, then quoted a bemused British statesman: "I may seem to know a man through and through, and still I would not dare to say the first thing about what he will do in a group." Moreover, Bartlett observed that when a social movement feels itself threatened, "social remembering is very apt to take on a constructive and inventive character, either wittingly or unwittingly. Its manner then tends to become assertive, rather dogmatic and confident, and recall will probably be accompanied by excitement and emotion."

Not surprisingly, many people had their first flashbacks and abreactions in the stimulating atmosphere of the group. When one woman suddenly cried out, fell to the floor, and acted as if she were being attacked, she provided not only a role model, but a powerful stimulus to others. In many groups, members either consciously or unconsciously strove to outdo one another. The emotion was contagious, something like the atmosphere of an old-time revival meeting. Rather than crying out "Praise the Lord!", however, these women were more likely to scream "Keep away from me! I hate you! I hate you!"

The Contexts of Insanity

In conclusion: A vicious cycle of social influence, combined with a widespread belief in massive repression of sexual abuse memories, produced an epidemic of Survivors. In that situation, it was sometimes difficult to ascertain *who* is fulfilling *whose* expectations. A woman entered therapy, already afraid that her problems may stem from repressed memories. Her therapist played into those fears, and between the two of them, they found "evidence" in the form of dreams, flashbacks, body memories, or eating disorders. They saw dysfunction everywhere, and when the client sank into a hypnotic trance, she pictured horrifying events from her childhood.

Once even the smallest image was visualized, the process of *memory rehearsal* commenced, piecing the puzzle bits into a coherent narrative. As Robert Cialdini pointed out in *Influence*, getting someone to commit new beliefs to writing can be powerful reinforcement. "As a commitment device, a written declaration has some great advantages." After all, "there it was in his own handwriting, an irrevocably documented act driving him to make his beliefs and his self-image consistent with what he had undeniably done." Thus, when therapists told clients to write graphically descriptive cut-off letters to accused parents, it helped to solidify their belief in the recovered memories.

As we have seen, some therapists encouraged clients to run mental video tapes of their new-found "memories" until they seemed real. Sometimes this process could become quite literal. In one remarkable article that appeared in *Child Abuse & Neglect* in 1992, several therapists explained how, in 27 cases, they had made a "videotaped disclosure" of their clients who had recovered memories, to act as a reinforcement. "Several viewings of the tape may be required before the patient is able to accept the tape as accurate," they explain.

Recovered-memory therapists usually cited two reasons for their belief in the process: overwhelming affect and convincingly detailed accounts. Unfortunately, powerful emotions are not a guarantee of accurate memories. Anyone who has ever become engrossed in a thriller or dramatic movie knows how easily our emotions can be aroused, even when we *know* intellectually that it is fiction. Similarly, detailed narratives do not necessarily translate to verity. Indeed, some memory experts doubt the accuracy of 20-year-old memories that are recalled in such detail, since they are *more* likely to be confabulations.

The extent to which *expectation* and *context* can determine how professionals view someone was made manifest in a classic experiment conducted by Stanford psychology and law professor D. L. Rosenhan, published in 1973 in *Science* with the compelling title, "On Being Sane in Insane Places." Rosenhan sent eight subjects to 12 in-patient psychiatric wards around the United States, where, during admission, they complained of hearing voices that said "empty," "hollow," and "thud." In reality, the subjects were a graduate student in psychology, a pediatrician, a psychiatrist, a painter, a housewife, and three psychologists. Aside from making up their voices and giving false names and occupations, the subjects did not change their actual personal histories or circumstances. As soon as they were admitted, they ceased simulating any symptoms whatsoever.

"The pseudopatient spoke to patients and staff as he might ordinarily," Rosenhan noted. "Because there is uncommonly little to do on a psychiatric ward, he attempted to engage others in conversation. When asked by staff how he was feeling, he indicated that he was fine." All the subjects also wrote down their observations of the ward, patients, and staff.

None of the pseudopatients was detected. Eventually, each was released with a diagnosis of "schizophrenia in remission," having been kept anywhere from a week to nearly two months. Many of their fellow patients detected the ruse. "You're not crazy," they would say. "You're a journalist or a professor. You're checking up on the hospital." The staff, however, was not so astute. "Patient engages in writing behavior" was the repeated comment on one patient's chart. Another subject accurately recounted his life history, in which, during early childhood, he had a close relationship with his mother, but felt remote from his father. As a teenager, he had become good friends with his father, while his relationship with his mother cooled somewhat. The hospital case summary for him read, "This white 39-year-old male ... manifests a long history of considerable ambivalence in close relationships."

As Rosenhan observed, "having once been labeled schizophrenic, there is nothing the pseudopatient can do to overcome the tag. The tag profoundly colors others' perceptions of him and his behavior.... A psychiatric label has a life and an influence of its own." As readers will see in the following chapter, Rosenhan's subjects were lucky they did not enter a dissociative disorders unit at a private psychiatric hospital 20 years later. They would have been diagnosed as possessing multiple personalities and kept on the ward indefinitely, not just for two months.

Even in the milder cases of "recovered memory," however, Rosenhan's experiment offers an instructive example. A CNN television reporter—presumably free of childhood sexual abuse—took a hidden camera into a 1993 counseling session with a therapist known to have convinced at least six other women that they were Survivors. The reporter said that she had been "kind of depressed" for a few months, and that her marital sex life had worsened. At the end of the *first session*, the therapist suggested that she might have been sexually abused as a child. When the reporter said she had no such memories, the therapist stated that *many* women completely forget incest. *"They have no idea, in fact. I mean, what you've presented to me, Lee-Anne, is so classic that I'm just sitting here blown away, actually."*

Once a therapist labeled someone a Survivor, everything the client said or did was perceived as evidence to validate the diagnosis. And the client, having accepted the possibility that the label might be accurate, quickly fell into the trap of seeing the same life problems as symptoms of a childhood full of sexual abuse.

Urged to go back and examine childhood pictures for evidence of abuse, many clients found it. "It seems that photos can quite severely mislead our memories," observed experimental psychologist Julia Shaw in 2016, "especially when coupled with deliberate misinformation.... When we see a photo we create a new memory of that occasion.... Possibly even entirely replacing a real visual memory with another." So what may have been a happy trip to the beach might get reshaped into a forerunner of molestation.

Nor was it necessary for many newly self-identified Survivors to retrieve *any* memories of childhood abuse. A substantial number came to believe that they were sexual abuse victims without any memories whatsoever, because it gave them an explanation for their life problems, group solidarity, and a great deal of sympathy. In short, the mechanism to produce false memories—hypnosis, dreams, body memories, or other modalities—is not nearly as important as the expectation that they must harbor repressed memories. Once that belief system is in place, "memories" are usually not far behind.

---

* One concerned younger sister hired a private investigator to make an appointment with her accusing sister's therapist. Though Ruth, the investigator, told the therapist that she had been rear-ended in an auto accident, the therapist led her through guided imagery to believe she had been sexually abused and repressed the memories. At one point, Ruth asked, "How do we know, when the memories come ... that it's not our imagination or something?" The therapist answered, "Why would you image this, of all things? If it were your imagination, you'd be imaging how warm and loving he was.... I have a therapist friend who says that the only proof she needs to know that something happened is if you think it might have."

4 Multiple Personalities and Satanic Cults

Jesus said to him, "Come out of the man, you unclean spirit!" And Jesus asked him, "What is your name?" He replied, "My name is Legion; for we are many." And he begged him not to send them out.

—Gospel of St. Mark 5:8-10

I felt a Cleavage in my Mind— As if my Brain had split— I tried to match it— Seam by Seam— But could not make them fit.

—Emily Dickinson

ONE OF THE MOST INTRIGUING and controversial products of hypnotic suggestion is a belief that some people harbor multiple internal personalities—an idea that first became popular around the turn of the 20th century. *(For the early history of this phenomenon, see Chapter 6.)*

Just as past-life regressions yield "secondary role enactments," a person with multiple personality disorder (MPD) can perform as an entire ensemble in *this* life. Yet many critics have persuasively argued that *the phenomenon of multiple personality is almost invariably an artifact of therapy, produced by the therapist's expectations and the suggestible, vulnerable, attention-seeking client.**

This does not mean that the therapist intentionally creates the condition, nor does it mean that the client suffering from MPD is consciously acting fraudulently. Because the proliferation of multiples is so intimately connected with the hunt for repressed memories of sexual abuse, a brief review of its modern rise is in order. The diagnosis of multiple personality disorder was extremely infrequent until the cases of Eve White (a pseudonym for Christine Sizemore) and Sybil (a pseudonym for Shirley Mason), both of which spawned best-selling books and movies. These two cases have exerted enormous influence, providing models for thousands of others that have come in their wake.

Psychiatrist Corbett Thigpen, co-author of *The Three Faces of Eve* (1957) at first found Eve White to be rather boring—a "neat, colorless young woman." She came to him because of terrible headaches, apparently caused by intolerable tension related to her failing marriage, exacerbated by her unwillingness to raise her daughter Bonnie in her husband's Catholic faith because she herself was a

---

* This alleged condition has been renamed "dissociative identity disorder" (DID) to attempt to avoid the controversial designation, but I will use MPD, which is more familiar and descriptive.

Baptist. Mrs. White's therapy was clearly important to her, as she had to drive 100 miles to meet with Thigpen. Her husband Ralph characterized her as "too good" but possessing a "little erratic streak."

After several sessions, Thigpen suggested hypnosis in order to help analyze a dream. Soon thereafter, Mrs. White apparently experienced amnesia following a huge fight with her husband. Thigpen suggested to her that "unacceptable events are sometimes unconsciously repressed from memory or involuntarily dissociated from awareness," and this seemed to make her feel better. Soon afterward, during a session, Mrs. White appeared "momentarily dazed," looked blank, then transformed her entire appearance. "There was a quick reckless smile. In a bright unfamiliar voice that sparkled, the woman said, 'Hi, there, Doc!'" After some confusing conversation, Thigpen asked "Who *are* you?" and she answered "Eve Black," her maiden name.

Eve Black was everything Eve White was not. She was irrepressible, naughty, sensual, spontaneous. In many ways, she was a duplicate of Morton Prince's "Sally Beauchamp," the lively alternate personality (known as an "alter") in that famous 1906 case.* Dr. Thigpen was clearly taken with Eve Black, noting "how attractive those legs were." Suddenly this boring patient was a lot more interesting. The idea that several entirely separate personalities could co-exist inside one brain or body has always intrigued not only psychiatrists, but the general public. Soon afterward, a third alter, "Jane," appeared as a balanced, intelligent mid-point between the two Eves.

The theory behind MPD posits that the alternative personalities appear due to a severe childhood trauma for which the "core" original personality is amnestic. Eve's parents seemed to be fairly normal, and her major childhood traumas—seeing a drowned man at two and touching her dead grandmother's face at five—weren't sexual.

By the end of the therapy, the three personalities appeared to have integrated, and all was well.

Sybil and Her Traumatized Alters

In September of 1954, a few months after Thigpen and Cleckley published "A Case of Multiple Personality" in the *Journal of Abnormal and Social Psychology,* Shirley Mason moved to New York City and commenced psychotherapy with Dr. Cornelia Wilbur. After three months, Wilbur met Peggy Baldwin, a disturbed child alter, and diagnosed Mason as a multiple personality. Over the next 11 years, in over 2,300 sessions, Wilbur identified 16 different alters before triumphantly integrating them all.

---

* See Chapter 6 for MPD's origins in the late 19th and early 20th centuries, including this Morton Prince case.

In 1973, Flora Rheta Schreiber, a literature professor, actress, and freelance writer, published *Sybil* in a dramatic novelized form, giving Mason the pseudonym of Sybil Dorsett. That book, along with a the subsequent movie, provided a template for the modern epidemic of MPD diagnoses, including the idea that grotesque childhood sexual and physical abuse causes "dissociation" of various alters. Sybil's tortures primarily featured enemas that she was forced to hold while her mother played piano concertos, but the sadistic parent also enjoyed pushing spoons and other items up her child's vagina, making Sybil watch sexual intercourse, and hoisting her up to hang helplessly from a pulley.

Yet investigative journalist Debbie Nathan thoroughly debunked the case in her 2012 book, *Sybil Exposed*:

> Sybil's sixteen personalities had not popped up spontaneously but were provoked over many years of rogue treatment that violated practically every ethical standard of practice for mental health practitioners. Dr. Wilbur had approached Sybil's health problems with a predetermined diagnosis that brooked no alternative explanations. In her therapy she had made extravagant, sadistic use of habit-forming, mind-bending drugs.... After years of this behavior...the two women developed a slavish mutual dependency upon each other. Toward the end of their lives they ended up living together.

Herbert Spiegel, a psychiatrist intimately familiar with Sybil's case, had also come forward to question Shirley Mason's MPD diagnosis. Spiegel first identified highly hypnotizable people and specialized in dissociative disorders. Schreiber thanked Spiegel in her acknowledgments, noting tersely that he called the patient "a brilliant hysteric." Spiegel told me that Cornelia Wilbur had brought Sybil to him for consultation early in her therapy. He had diagnosed her as highly hypnotizable. Whenever Wilbur had to leave town, Spiegel served as Sybil's temporary therapist. In addition, Sybil visited his Columbia University classes annually for a hypnosis demonstration, and she participated in his study of age regression.

"When Sybil came to therapy with me," Spiegel said, "and we were discussing some phase of her life, she asked me, 'Do you want me to be Peggy, or can I just tell you?' That took me aback, and I asked her what she meant 'Well, when I'm with Dr. Wilbur, she wants me to be Peggy.' I told her that if it made her more comfortable to be Peggy, that was fine, but otherwise it wasn't necessary. She seemed relieved and chose not to assume different personalities when she was with me."

Later, Flora Schreiber approached Spiegel to ask if he would coauthor the book, which initially intrigued him. But when he found that they were planning to call her a multiple personality, he objected. Schreiber explained that the publisher was interested only in this sensational approach. When Spiegel told her he wanted no part of such a venture, "she got in a huff and walked out." At subsequent psychiatric conferences, Wilbur refused to speak to him.

Cornelia Wilbur was also instrumental in diagnosing Jonah, another well-known multiple. In 1970, Jonah, a 27-year-old black man, entered the University of Kentucky Medical Center after beating his wife and attacking her with a butcher knife. As he did so, he claimed to be "Usoffa Abdulla, Son of Omega." Under hypnosis with Wilbur, Jonah soon revealed that he had two other alter personalities aside from the violent Usoffa: "Sammy," a rational lawyer/mediator, and "King Young," a seductive lover. Although Jonah was characterized as a "relatively unsophisticated person from a lower socioeconomic group," he was highly imaginative and understood how to keep the attention of five psychiatrists.* He apparently enjoyed frightening them as well, since he announced that he felt another alter brewing that would be "five times worse than Usoffa" and "would probably be somewhere in between dynamite, electricity, and nitroglycerin." This fourth alter failed to materialize, much to the relief of the psychiatrists.

The fascinated doctors administered several batteries of personality tests, EEGs, and the like, claiming that these constituted a "controlled comparison" of the alters, even though their study consisted of one person. They discovered that Jonah's various alters performed differently on emotional material, but that the responses were quite similar for neutral material. This outcome should surprise no one, since role playing would produce just such a result. It should also not come as a shock that the tests identified Jonah as a paranoid schizophrenic. Nonetheless, the five psychiatrists asserted that "the internal consistency of the individual profiles is remarkable and argues against the possibility of faking."

At least, however, they recognized that the MPD role allowed Jonah to "express taboo feelings without having to assume responsibility for them." Indeed, such was the alters' appeal that they were loath to be "integrated" and agreed to join forces only on a trial basis, provided they got "equal representation" alongside Jonah, the core personality. Consequently, they compromised on a new name, "Jusky," an acronym for Jonah-Usoffa-Sammy-King-Young. The psychiatrists gave the newly constituted Jusky their battery of tests. "Unfortunately," they concluded, "some of the results indicate that this new identity may be psychiatrically 'sicker' than any of the others."

Ralph Allison's New Frontier

Throughout the 1970s, Cornelia Wilbur was the acknowledged authority on

---

* The principal author of the Jonah study, Dr. Arnold Ludwig, had long been fascinated by "altered states of consciousness." In 1966, Ludwig wrote an article on the subject in which he revealed that, while taking LSD "for experimental purposes," he had needed to relieve himself. Standing at the urinal, he read a sign, "Please Flush After Using," and realized that the words conveyed "profound meaning."

MPD because of her professional publications as well as the popular novel about Sybil. During the decade, a growing number of other psychotherapists became interested in multiple personalities. California psychiatrist Ralph Allison provided an early networking tool through his newsletter, *Memos in Multiplicity.*

In 1980, Allison published *Minds in Many Pieces,* the first popular professional book on multiple personalities. His account of how he first "discovered" that a patient named Janette suffered from MPD is extremely revealing.

A 29-year-old housewife, Janette was chronically depressed and unhappily married. Her mother had been "a bossy hypochondriac, always whining about imagined ailments." Following a suicide attempt by Janette, Allison had her committed to a psychiatric ward, where he asked Katherine, a resident psychologist, to evaluate her. That night, Katherine called Allison and informed him that Janette was a "classic case" of MPD, "another *Three Faces of Eve.*"

The following day, after a sleepless night, the nervous Dr. Allison informed Janette that "the psychologist who saw you yesterday says there's someone else here with you." Janette looked puzzled. "What I mean is, there's someone inside your head—someone else sharing your body." Still no response. "I want to meet the other person. I think I can if you'll give me a little cooperation." He asked her to close her eyes and relax. Then, in a "commanding, forceful voice," Allison intoned: "Now I want to talk to whoever or whatever spoke to the psychologist last night. Come out by the time I count to three. One ... Two ... Three!" And with that, Janette opened her eyes and, in a loud, grating voice, said, "Okay, doc, what do you want? And God, it's good to get rid of that piss-ass Janette."

Thrilled, Allison observed that "it was like something out of a movie. It was Joanne Woodward changing from Eve White to Eve Black in *The Three Faces of Eve.*" Exactly. Although it is likely that Janette, too, had seen the movie, it did not occur to Allison that he had *cued* his patient into multiplicity. From that humble beginning, he was off and running. Later, through hypnosis, he had Janette "remember" a rape by a schoolyard bully. But that was just the beginning. "We identified traumas through the use of hypnosis and other techniques. Often one memory led to another and we delved deeper and deeper into her past."

Once Allison learned how to look for multiplicity, he began to find it in more patients, including Carrie—a beautiful, tall redhead with a history of severe depression and mood disorders. "I had an odd feeling that this young woman was going to play a unique role in my life. She would influence my work," he noted.

Allison introduced Carrie to Janette, and soon his first MPD patient was counseling his second. "Debra," Carrie's first alter, called Allison her "Daddy" and Janette "Mommy."

Dr. Allison discussed the matter with a parapsychology instructor, who sensed that the spirit of an evil deceased drug addict named Bonnie had invaded Carrie's body. Allison apparently believed this assertion and subsequently carried out a formal exorcism, which he claimed was a success. This didn't prevent Carrie from developing other alters, however, and it didn't stop her from committing suicide the day after he visited her in the hospital—she had been brought there in restraints after a new "alter" violently attacked Allison, screaming "GoddamnmotherfuckingbastardIhateyou." Even her death did not keep Allison from proclaiming his treatment to be successful. "I don't always like being a loner," he wrote in his chapter about Carrie. "It hurts to know that I am ridiculed as a 'fool' by people who don't dispute my successes, but only my methods."*

In *Minds in Many Pieces,* Allison asserted that he had discovered a new, exciting form of therapy. He likened his probing of the mind's inner mysteries to the space program and referred to himself as "an explorer of this second 'frontier.'" Despite appearances that he was creating the very disorder he was supposed to cure, his book exerted an enormous influence, providing models for the "inner-self helper," a kind of guardian angel alter, and the "dark alters" or demons who need to be exorcised.**

The idea of demonic possession, widely believed until the end of the 17th century, appears to have maintained a fairly strong hold even in modern times. With the publication of *The Exorcist* (1971) and its inevitable movie (1973), popular interest in the occult burgeoned. Before that, in the mid-'50s, Thigpen and Cleckley received several suggestions that Eve White might have been possessed by "discarnate spirits." Other correspondents, claiming personal experience with demonic possession, volunteered to "cast out the indwelling fiend they were sure resided in the body of our patient."

Although Thigpen made fun of such notions, many post-Allison therapists took them seriously. *Michelle Remembers,* the recovered memories book about Satanic abuse *(see Chapter 1)* appeared in 1980, and in its wake Satan was given his share of blame for the phenomenon of multiplicity. To lend an air of science, however, demons were often called "introjects." Psychiatrist M. Scott Peck, who charmed those in search of pop spirituality with *The Road Less Traveled* (1978), followed it with *People of the Lie* in 1983, in which he espoused a belief in pure evil and the efficacy of exorcism.***

---

* Carrie's husband sued Allison for malpractice following his wife's suicide, claiming the psychiatrist had prescribed the pills that killed her. Allison not only denied supplying the pills, but said that she was no longer officially his patient at that point. She did, however, come to visit him in his office on the day she killed herself. The lawsuit was unsuccessful.

** Nonetheless, Ralph Allison never became part of the MPD "establishment" and later took a firm stand against the hunt for Satanic ritual abuse. He did not, however, change his mind about MPD.

*** Peck came to believe in evil patients after 400 sessions with a patient named Charlene. The therapist was frustrated because "she totally failed to be affected by it." Rather than blaming himself, Peck concluded that

"The diagnosis of possession is not an easy one to make," Peck asserted, because "the demonic hides within and behind the person. For the exorcism to occur, ... the demonic must be uncovered and brought into the open." To accomplish this, an exorcist must make direct contact with the demons. "When the demonic finally spoke clearly in one case," Peck wrote, "an expression appeared on the patient's face that could be described only as Satanic." That proved that the patient was possessed, even to Peck, who considered himself "a hardheaded scientist."

James Friesen's Multiple Demons

The influences of Ralph Allison and Scott Peck came together in 1991 in James Friesen's *Uncovering the Mystery of MPD,* a popular book about MPD written for a Christian audience. Friesen, a Ph.D. psychologist and minister, was already engaged in "spiritual warfare" against the invisible powers of evil when he discovered multiple personality disorder. He trained himself primarily by listening to a tape about MPD and by reading the works of Allison and Peck.

Friesen's book made it quite clear how he came to believe that most of his clients hid unrecognized alters, and why he insisted that his diagnosis was correct, even in the face of considerable resistance. "Every life experience must be stored and filed somewhere," he wrote, "and no event can be erased. The closest a brain can come to erasing a memory is to become amnesic to what just happened. That involves creating an alternate personality for the occasion." Because it is the alter who remembers the abuse, the memories seemed doubtful to most clients at first. "When dissociated memories start to surface during treatment, they *always* seem unreal. The clients have a hard time accepting the reality of the memory, because it does not seem like it happened to them."

One of Friesen's clients, whom he called Helen, told one of her friends proudly that Friesen was "fascinated with me," though she was skeptical of this MPD business. "She had not yet found out about the awful things that must have happened to her as a young child," Friesen explained. "One of the benefits of dissociation is that the dissociator grows up with healthy alters who know nothing about the abuse. Those alters are the ones who come to therapy, believing they have had a simple childhood. They go through a lot of denial when the truth breaks through the amnesia."

Indeed, "Helen's host alter fought very hard to maintain the posture that she had gone through a normal childhood, and that her family was a good one." The insightful Friesen was eventually able to overcome her resistance and convince Helen of her multiplicity, leading to a series of suicide attempts and hospitaliza-

there was a simple reason: she was evil. "Charlene's desire ... to toy with me, to utterly control our relationship, knew no bounds."

tions. Since "practically all MPD clients have periods of suicidality," the therapist observed, "it may be necessary to protect the life of the client with brief hospitalization."

It is little wonder that one of Friesen's patients told him, "I don't know what I'm doing here, Jim. I've been seeing you for more than a year, and my life is not getting easier. I didn't come here to feel worse! I know you keep saying that all feelings are important, but I'm tired of despair." Another said, "You didn't tell me it would be this painful. This pain will never stop! I will never get over it. It would be better if you would just let me die." In the face of such anguished outbursts, Friesen staunchly maintained his belief in MPD and his therapeutic approach.

Part of that approach was to encourage clients to cut off contact with accused family members and to throw away letters from them without opening them. When confused patients ("certain alters") complained that this appeared un-Christian, Friesen quoted scripture to them, noting that Jesus had said, "Anyone who loves his father or mother more than me is not worthy of me." Thus, he explained, "The Christian thing to do is to let go of 'family members' who are unsafe. After all, family is only 'family' in the Christian sense of the word when it adheres to Christian principles."

Jesus proved to be quite an ally for the therapist. In conducting guided imagery sessions, Friesen encouraged clients to create a "safe place where the hurting alters can go for recovery." Generally, he recommended a meadow with a gently flowing brook and a warm breeze. "For Christians, it is good to have Jesus waiting there to help in any way He sees fit." Leaving the meadow, he conducted his client through an imaginary house, "with a room for each of your alters, and a conference room right by the front door." Then they went into the "screening room," a private mental theater where they could watch abuse memories unfold.

Soon, Friesen's MPD patients were seeing bizarre, hooded figures on their mental screens. They began telling Friesen about Satanic ritual abuse. Fran recalled being placed by her mother in a casket, lowered into the ground, and hearing dirt piled on top. "I couldn't breathe," she remembered. "I've had claustrophobia all my life and [now I know] that is why." At various times during her therapy, she had trouble coming up with new stories. "There were times with my therapist that I just knew the enemy was trying to keep a memory from me, but we would pray and it would be broken." Finally, she remembered being raped by a demon during a ritual. "It was an extremely violent instance of incubus," Friesen explained.

Despite the number of babies sacrificed during the cult activities, no one could ever find any remains. Such lack of evidence didn't faze Friesen. "The perfect way to discredit the children's testimony is to exhume the remains later, after the children have watched them buried! Who would believe a child's story when he says he knows exactly where the baby is buried, but no baby is found at the site?" Satanic abuse perpetrators were, he concluded, "masters at cover-up."

Even patients who had progressed to Satanic abuse memories had a hard time believing them, however. "Those memories in the church basement are crazy!" a client named Carla told Friesen. "They couldn't have happened to me…. I am willing to go through whatever it takes to get the different personalities in me to work together, but those things didn't happen to me! My family is not like that— they couldn't possibly have done that. Maybe my mind is just playing tricks on me. Do you think that could happen, Doctor Friesen? Am I making it all up?" Of course, Friesen assured Carla that she could *not* be making it up. It was all true.

Eventually, after reading *People of the Lie* by M. Scott Peck, Friesen realized that some of his worst MPD/SRA clients contained not just alters, but actual demons, and he began to exorcise them.˙ This was a delicate matter, he cautioned, because it wouldn't do to cast out an indigenous alter. You could tell if it's a demon by the guttural tone of the voice, foaming at the mouth, and general nastiness.

As a model, Friesen related his exorcism of a demon named "Fracture" from his client, Rosie. "In the name of Jesus, all spirits are bound, mute and immobile. You cannot influence Rosie in any way. You cannot hurt her on the way out, and you will be able to respond only if spoken to in the name of Jesus." Then, after finding the name of the demon, along with how and why he entered Rosie, he simply said, "In the name of Jesus, you must leave." Just for good measure, he then did some house-cleaning and ordered any other stray demons to depart as well.

Lest anyone be concerned that his approach was a bit radical, Friesen explained that the "scientific method does not automatically deny that there is a spirit world." Following the lead of Scott Peck, he reassured the reader: "I take a 'pure' scientific approach—I want to be open to all the data, without fitting them into a narrow framework."

It isn't surprising that demonic possession should be identified with multiple-personality disorder. They are different faces of the same essential phenomenon, as Nicholas Spanos, Michael Kenny, and several other observers noted. In each case, a person is convinced that he or she possesses indwelling alternate personalities, often unaware of one another, each with a distinct name and birth date. In either case, it takes an expert—a priest or a therapist—to identify the disorder, to call out the demons or alters, and to converse with them. Finally, this same expert must "cure" the disorder, often at great personal risk, by dispensing with the

---

* In 1995, I met Kathleen Knott, who was identified as having MPD with introject demons by her therapist at Prairie View, Inc., in Newton, Kansas. Four exorcisms failed to heal her. She was suing Prairie View and seeking an injunction to prevent the institution from allowing further exorcisms. In another case, California retractor Kimberly Mark was taken to Idaho so that "Entity Extractors" could excise the monsters supposedly inhabiting her body.

demons and restoring the subject to wholeness and health. As one of Scott Peck's patients commented, "All psychotherapy is a kind of exorcism," and the reverse is true as well.*

Diagnosing the Elusive Multiple

At the 1977 annual meeting of the American Psychiatric Association, Cornelia Wilbur chaired the first organized panel on MPD and invited Ralph Allison to present his views. Allison brought along Henry Hawksworth—an MPD patient who later wrote his own book—as a surprise guest. Subsequently, Allison was asked to chair the panel the following year.

Soon, however, the California psychiatrist was eased out of power by younger colleagues, including Bennett Braun and Richard Kluft, who were determined to lend an air of scientific credibility to the diagnosis. Allison, with his shamanistic belief in demons, proved to be an embarrassment and was effectively shut out of the movement.

By the mid-1980s, under the influence of Kluft and company, an entire MPD industry had arisen, with its own societies, authorities, specialized journals and newsletters. Because of the case of Eve and Sybil, along with lobbying from Ralph Allison and other interested therapists, multiple personality was included in 1980 in the third edition of the American Psychiatric Association's *Diagnostic and Statistical Manual of Mental Disorders (DSM)*, which meant that an MPD diagnosis could draw insurance payments. In the early 1980s, a core group of therapists—Bennett Braun, Richard Kluft, Eugene Bliss, George Greaves, David Caul, Colin Ross, and Frank Putnam—cranked out articles on MPD. Several prestigious psychological journals published special issues devoted to the topic. In 1984, the International Society for the Study of Multiple Personality & Dissociation was founded. In the late 1980s, more popular books and professional articles on multiplicity poured forth.

In 1989, psychiatrist Frank Putnam, who worked at the National Institute of Mental Health, published *Diagnosis and Treatment of Multiple Personality Disorder*, intended as a textbook "for therapists unfamiliar with dissociative disorders." (His work followed *The Treatment of Multiple Personality Disorder* (1986), by Bennett Braun.) Putnam asserted that the initial diagnosis is often "difficult and anxiety-provoking for both therapist and patient." Why this should be so soon became clear. Few of those who suffer from MPD realize that they harbor any internal personalities *until* the therapist seeks them out. To complicate things further, the alters are wily creatures. "The personality system may be actively eluding diagnosis," Putnam wrote.

---

* For the historical background on the switch from demonology to hypnotism and MPD, see Chapter 6.

"The trick," he continued, "is to recognize and follow up [any] manifestations of MPD." It is important to "maintain a high index of suspicion regarding the possibility of covert switching occurring during sessions." Any mood changes, momentary silences, physical shifts, facial tics, or inability to remember past events should be taken as clues to multiplicity. "A clinician will not find MPD if he or she is not willing to look for it." But one must also be willing to wait, usually six months or more, before spotting MPD in a particular patient. That way, the therapist establishes trust, rapport and knowledge of the person's background. During this time, patients should keep diaries in which different handwriting or moods might indicate MPD.

Putnam described the crucial initial contact with an alter. "My first approach is one of indirect inquiry. I broach the subject gently, often first asking the patient whether he or she has ever felt like more than one person." He followed up with other inquiries, such as "Do you ever feel as if you are not alone, as if there is someone else or some other part watching you?" Or, "Do you ever feel as if there is some other part of yourself that comes out and does or says things that you would not do or say?" Once the psychiatrist finally got a positive response, he latched onto it. "In particular, I am looking for either a name or an attribute, function, or description that I can use as a label to elicit this other part directly." A proper name such as Helen was preferable, but Putnam would accept "the angry one" or "the little girl."

Regardless of the label, at this point the therapist should inquire, "Can this other part come out and talk with me?" Quite often, Putnam cautioned, "the alter does not pop out the first time the therapist asks. It is often necessary to repeat the request several times." Hypnotism or sodium amytal (now called Amobarbital) are often useful. "Even if the patient is showing evidence of significant distress with this request, I would urge persistence." Some patients, when repeatedly pushed to produce a balky alter, report "feeling smothered, having a sense of terrible internal pressure." These are signs "highly suggestive of dissociative pathology," Putnam asserted. Sometimes, in order to elicit an alter, an extended interview lasting three hours or longer is useful. "It may be necessary to spend a large part of the day with some highly secretive MPD patients," he cautioned. "During this interview, which is exhausting and stressful for both parties, it is important to continue to probe aggressively."*

By this time, I hope that the reader is as appalled as I am. No wonder the

---

* Putnam's approach was mild compared to MPD specialist Richard Kluft, who often would not let patients take breaks or avert their faces during his lengthy interviews. "In one recent case of singular difficulty," he said, "the first sign of dissociation was noted in the sixth hour, and a definitive spontaneous switching of personalities occurred in the eighth hour." Scott Peck's exorcisms sometimes lasted 12 hours. Another therapist pushed his thumb against a client's forehead while demanding that an alter appear, an approach similar to Sigmund Freud's "pressure method" (discussed in Chapter 6).

patients feel smothered! Here is Dr. Putnam—or any zealous therapist like him— acting like an interrogator during the Spanish Inquisition. He will not take "No" for an answer.* Even relatively normal people would probably buckle under such pressure and produce alters. How much more likely that a vulnerable patient, who approached a therapist in hopes of understanding his or her unhappiness, would succumb?

Putnam preferred to elicit alters without resorting to hypnosis, but often he found it necessary. He began by producing a "benign trance experience," which turned out to be the creation of the by-now familiar "safe and pleasant place." From there, he age-regressed patients, hoping to find traumas and the alters they produced. "It is important to identify a 'target' beforehand and to direct the age regression back to that point in time." Once there, "the act of remembering will produce a florid abreaction that can cause considerable distress for both patient and therapist. Revivification, the experience of vividly reliving an event, is in some ways more traumatic than the original experience."

Like Ellen Bass and Renee Fredrickson, Putnam encouraged his hypnotic patients to visualize their past abuse on a mental movie screen. "Events seen on this screen can be slowed down, speeded up, reversed, or frozen by suggestion as needed.... The patient can also be instructed to zoom in on details, or zoom back and pan for a larger perspective." Having gotten the hang of this internal movie-making, most MPD candidates really took to the process. "Once uncovering work has begun to open the closed doors," Putnam wrote, "the patient will have increased difficulty in keeping painful material out of conscious awareness. This process seems to gather a momentum of its own."**

Indeed, with practice, most MPD patients no longer required hypnotic inductions. Therapists could simply say, "I'd like to talk to Sherry now," and she would instantly appear. Specialist Richard Kluft used an economy of style when he wished to make a particularly important announcement "Everybody listen!" he demanded. His audience was likely to include some standard types: a few traumatized inner children, a suicidal depressive, a protector, a prostitute, and

---

* The ego of some MPD specialists appeared to be matched only by their inability to hear their clients. Psychiatrist Eugene Bliss reported that he intentionally induced a new personality and christened it "Dr. Bliss" in hopes that the alter could help in therapy. "Unfortunately, he was not helpful but instead would complain that the region was both overcrowded and unmanageable." The therapist did not get the message.

** To his credit, Frank Putnam later expressed doubts about many MPD diagnoses, criticizing the vague criteria for the condition, stating that inpatient treatment often worsens the condition, and stressing that hypnosis and sodium Amytal can produce confabulations. In a personal 1994 communication to me, he wrote: "Outside corroboration is absolutely necessary before one undertakes any kind of action outside of the therapy based on such memories. When my book was written, people were not suing their parents for alleged abuse." Putnam did not, however, retract any of the material in his 1989 textbook. Putnam's book reflected not only his own theories, but those of other MPD gurus, particularly Richard Kluft, the acknowledged master of the "scientific" presentation of MPD, writing about the "polysymptomatic pleomorphic presentation of MPD"—by which he meant that he interpreted almost any behavior as evidence of possible MPD.

perhaps a demon or two. Indeed, Kluft held the dubious distinction of having identified 4,500 alters within one patient, a world's record.

"The alters are typically stock characters, with bizarre but completely unimaginative character traits, each one a stereotype," wrote philosopher Ian Hacking. "Personality-switching now happens much more suddenly and instantaneously than in the past. There is no need for a trance or sleep period between alters. The model is 'zapping,' of switching channels on television." Another skeptic, psychiatrist Michael Simpson, complained of "flesh-creepingly embarrassing performances" he witnessed that did not appear to be genuine personalities but amounted to mere "amateur theatrics."

To maintain their therapists' attention, some MPDs went overboard with their alters. George Ganaway, among the few psychiatrists specializing in dissociative disorders, wrote that he personally had encountered "demons, angels, sages, lobsters, chickens, tigers, a gorilla, a unicorn, and 'God'," to name only a few. "The inscapes in which they exist," he added, "have ranged from labyrinthine tunnels and mazes to castles in enchanted forests, high-rise office buildings, and even a separate galaxy."

Once diagnosed, most MPD patients were encouraged to attend group sessions with their fellow multiples. At various inpatient units around the country, they had no choice. Here, the group process worked its wonders, with an ever-escalating level of alter-switching, trauma-reliving, attention-seeking one-upmanship. Ganaway facetiously called such dramatic displays *status abreacticus,* as the patient "'relives' for the therapist's fascination and approval an increasingly expansive repertoire of what both grow to believe are factual trauma memories." Paul McHugh, head of psychiatry at Johns Hopkins, believed that getting MPD patients away from contagious group settings is an important part of any cure; he suggested "isolation [and] counter suggestion."

Of course, suggesting to identified patients that they were not multiples would be abhorrent to Frank Putnam. At some point, he warned, patients will "deny that the MPD is active or even that it ever existed. They may seek to disprove that they are or ever were multiples, and even say that they faked it or made it up." The therapist must accept none of these excuses, he stated. This follows the model of Cornelia Wilbur, who ignored Sybil when her patient wrote: "I am not going to tell you there isn't anything wrong. We both know there is. But it is not what I have led you to believe. I do not have any multiple personalities. I don't even have a 'double' to help me out. I am all of them."

Manufacturing MPD

Usually, it doesn't take all the pressure Putnam exerted to produce a multiple personality case, as psychologist Nicholas Spanos showed in a series of experiments. Spanos became intrigued with the case of Kenneth Bianchi, the "Hillside Strangler," who was diagnosed in 1979 as a multiple personality by therapist John Watkins. It wasn't Bianchi who had murdered all those women; it was his vicious alter, Steve Walker, according to Watkins. Ralph Allison, who was called in as a consultant, agreed.* Spanos read a transcript of Watkins' interview with a hypnotized Bianchi. "I've talked a bit to Ken but I think that perhaps there might be another part of Ken that I haven't talked to." He paused. "Part, would you come and lift Ken's hand to indicate to me that you are here." The hand lifted.** "Would you talk to me, Part, by saying, 'I'm here.'" Bianchi obliged him. Having summoned this Part, Watkins then engaged in the following dialogue:

Part, are you the same as Ken or are you different in any way?

I'm not him.

You're not him. Who are you? Do you have a name?

I'm not Ken.

You're not him? Okay. Who are you? Tell me about yourself. Do you have a name I can call you by?

Steve. You can call me Steve.

After the hypnotic session, Bianchi purportedly could not remember anything about Steve.

In 1985, Spanos decided to replicate this conversation as nearly as possible with a test group of college students, each of whom was asked to play the role of an accused murderer under hypnosis. The students were *not* told anything about multiple personalities. Yet 81 percent of the participants adopted different names and referred to their primary identities in the third person, and 63 percent displayed spontaneous amnesia for the hypnotic session after it was finished. Spanos concluded that the amnesia and MPD were an unconscious fraud, a "strategic enactment" to fulfill a role. "The displays of forgetting exhibited by these patients are selective and context dependent." Finally, he concluded, "these findings indicate that the multiple personality role was viewed by subjects as a credible vehicle for negotiating a difficult personal dilemma."

The following year, Spanos replicated his experiment, adding an age-regression component based on the Bianchi interviews. Not surprisingly, those treated like Bianchi "recalled" traumatic early childhoods that caused them to split off their alters. "My parents hate me," one subject reported. "Sometimes they start slapping

---

*   Several years later, Allison changed his mind when new evidence cast doubt on the truth of many of Bianchi's claims.

**   Such hypnotic instruction—to raise a hand or finger to signify "yes" or "no"—was called "ideomotor signaling" and was widely practiced, despite the obvious hazards of leading the patient.

me around." The subjects seemed to realize instinctively that this traumatic background would "explain" why they were multiples. Their psychopathology provided a means of "disavowing responsibility for past difficulties and for anticipated failures." Spanos concluded that "people who adopt this role often become convinced by their own enactments and by the legitimization they receive from significant others. In this manner such individuals come to believe sincerely that they possess secondary identities that periodically 'take over.'"

All MPD may involve role-enactment. After all, multiple personalities are almost entirely a product of a small cadre of North American therapists. The phenomenon does not exist at all in many cultures, although belief in demonic possession is certainly widespread. This observation led British psychologist Ray Aldridge-Morris to call MPD "an exercise in deception" in his comprehensive 1989 book on the subject. "My initial impetus to write this monograph," he noted, "was the dramatic incidence of multiple personality syndrome in the United States relative to its virtual absence elsewhere in the world. An extensive canvass of psychologists and psychiatrists in Great Britain produced not a single, unequivocal case."

The British Invasion

Since Aldridge-Morris wrote those words in 1989, MPD has indeed made inroads with British therapists and patients, thanks to help from American "experts" and the importation of books such as *Suffer the Child,* in which "Jenny developed multiple personalities in order to survive," according to the Nightingale Books catalog.

The 1992 publication of *The Filthy Lie* by Hellmut Karle, a psychologist at Guy's Hospital in London, gave a tremendous boost to recovered memory, hypnosis, and MPD in England. It tells the dramatic story of Meggie Collins, a depressed, obese middle-aged woman. At first, Karle hypnotized her in an attempt to help her lose weight. Then, after the session, she supposedly told him, "When I was a little girl, my father interfered with me." When he asked her about this revelation later, she repeatedly denied that incest had occurred or that she had said such a thing.*

He "persistently pressed her to say more," and eventually she agreed. He explained that "the memories of experiences which were severely frightening to a child can become separated off from the central memory of the adult, but persist within the mind rather like an embedded foreign body—a septic splinter in your psychic finger." Over the next two years, Karle helped Collins to unearth memories of gang orgies and abuse by various perpetrators. He also located two

---

*   It is quite possible, in fact, that Karle misinterpreted what she said. Collins may have said something about her resentment over her father's interference in her life. It is significant that at that point, Karle cut off the conversation.

internal "alters" named Little Meggie, an eight-year-old, and Big Meggie, twenty. To do so, he frequently hypnotized Collins, encouraging a mental video-screen projection of abuse memories.

The book offers a compelling case study of a *folie à deux* in which doctor and patient collude to produce an iatrogenic illness. Karle's approach was, by his own admission, "more like voyeurism than proper inquiry." The resultant process produced in Collins a "state of continual, unremitting and intense inner turmoil," as she became "determined to unearth all the memories that had been blocked or buried." It occurred to Karle that perhaps his approach was "encouraging her to manufacture further horrors in order to engage my continuing interest," but that did not stop the misguided process, nor prevent him from suggesting she enroll as a full-time patient so that she could "be relieved of her daily responsibilities."

The therapist's fascination with his client deepened when he diagnosed her with MPD, and he decided to write a book about her. "I found myself almost pursuing her now, almost indeed courting her." Later, when Collins did not evince sufficient hatred of her mother, Karle became exasperated with her. "The aggressive and invasive manner in which I pressed Mrs. Collins at this time," he wrote, "came very close to being an assault on her." Finally, the patient learned how to please her therapist by giving vent to "her violent and completely unrestrained rage" at her supposed abusers. "I almost hugged myself with delight," he recounted. "She was simply magnificent as she raged around the room."

The Filthy Lie is a remarkably honest book. Karle admitted that his client's dependence upon him was "quite explicit and at times felt really oppressive." He found this dependence both "rewarding and irksome." He gloried in his heroic savior role, but he also lost considerable sleep and endangered his own health. Karle also admitted that his colleagues universally pooh-poohed the MPD diagnosis. "They tended to interpret what was happening between Mrs. Collins and myself as histrionic manipulation by her," he wrote, "and considered that I was at least in part colluding with the maintenance of her condition." Such, indeed, appears to have been the case. Meggie Collins herself observed near the end of her therapy that "I've planned, I've worked, I've tried to be a good mother and wife, but nothing ever worked." The diagnosis by a consultant psychiatrist during one of her hospital stays seemed accurate. He noted that the patient was "depressed, having difficulties in coping with life, and lonely."

Despite these fairly obvious conclusions, the book was hailed as "proof" of repressed memories and multiple personality disorder. "In Britain," noted one reviewer, "where MPD has made slow but predictable progress, *The Filthy Lie* has been recommended as gospel for recovered memory and MPD enthusiasts—not least because it has the imprimatur of being both British and by a respected psychologist."

The year following publication of Karle's book, Ray Aldridge-Morris conducted a survey of British psychotherapists in an attempt to assess the prevalence of MPD diagnoses in the United Kingdom. He sent an anonymous questionnaire to 680 therapists, only 140 of whom responded. Of these, 15(11 per cent) had diagnosed and treated multiple personality disorder, reporting a total of 53 cases. Two respondents had seen the vast majority of the cases—one diagnosing 20 clients, the other 10, with the others seeing between one and three MPDs. Thus it appears that by 1993, a disturbing number of British therapists were diagnosing MPD, with a very small minority providing the majority of the cases.

A year later, in 1994, a chapter of the American-based International Society for the Study of Dissociation was formed in Great Britain. The same year, the British book *Treating Survivors of Satanist Abuse* was filled with credulous information about MPD, including a chapter by Ashley Conway, a psychologist at Charing Cross Hospital who, ironically, warned that hypnosis should be used cautiously, since "secondary or multiple personalities may emerge at this time." The volume also included a chapter by American psychiatrist Sandra Bloom, who found herself "profoundly shocked" when she first discovered a five-year-old alter. Now, however, the phenomenon was old hat to her, since MPD patients comprised 25 per cent of the in-patient population in her Philadelphia hospital, and a quarter of those were supposedly ritually abused. Bloom, whose dissociative disorders unit was known as "The Sanctuary," had a major impact as a consultant in England. At a 1995 conference in Kensington, London, she told a British journalist, "You should have centers like this [The Sanctuary] all over Britain." She repeated stock recovered memory beliefs about body memories and flashbacks. "They relive the original trauma, consciously and shockingly. It is a terrible thing to witness. They scream and struggle and retch. Nobody could doubt the reality of the appalling things these patients are going through."

The hunt for ritual abuse cases involving young children (documented in Chapter 5) also indirectly spawned an interest in multiple personality cases. British evangelical Christian ex-nurse Maureen Davies, prominent in the U.K. ritual abuse scares of the 1980s, visited the United States in 1990, where she discovered the link between MPD and adult ritual abuse Survivors. "Nobody believes the children," she announced upon her return. "[So now] we're going on the adult survivors." She did so through her Beacon Foundation.

Skeptical Inquirers

Despite such spreading belief in MPD, Canadian psychiatrist Harold Merskey, who published an extensive historical review of the syndrome in 1992, concluded: "No case has been found here in which MPD, as now conceived, is proven to have emerged through unconscious processes without any shaping or preparation by external factors such as physicians or the media…. It is likely that MPD never occurs as a spontaneous persistent natural event in adults." Rather, Merskey asserted, "suggestion, social encouragement, preparation by expectation, and the reward of attention can produce and sustain a second personality."

Anthropologist Michael Kenny echoed Merskey in his book on the subject: "Multiple personality is a socially created artifact, not the natural product of some deterministic psychological process." It is rather a useful "idiom of distress" for our times.

South African psychiatrist Michael Simpson agreed. According to Simpson, MPD is invariably produced by input from "the media, enthused therapists, amateur zealots, other marketers and profiteers, and strong cultural priming." He noted that many MPD patients claimed supernatural or psychic powers such as ESP, clairvoyance, reincarnation, astral travel, and poltergeists. "This suggests the possibility of similar origins for all these experiences," he noted dryly, then quoted a patient who explained: "My therapist educated me, so by the time we decided I had MPD, I knew a lot." American psychiatrist August Piper, Jr., took a similarly jaundiced view of MPD diagnosis. "Few limits exist to the number of 'personalities' one may unearth," he observed. "The number is bounded only by the interviewer's energy and zeal in searching, and by the interviewer's subjective sense of what constitutes a 'personality.'"

The World Health Organization also maintained a healthy skepticism regarding the diagnosis, noting in its 1992 classification system that "this disorder is rare, and controversy exists about the extent to which it is iatrogenic or culture-specific."

Finally, Johns Hopkins psychiatrist Paul McHugh stated flatly: "MPD is an iatrogenic [doctor-induced] behavioral syndrome, promoted by suggestion and maintained by clinical attention, social consequences, and group loyalties."*

If that is so, how do we account for a case like Eve (Christine Costner Sizemore)? She appears to have taken Dr. Thigpen completely by surprise, and her "split" occurred before the current vogue. Thigpen probably cued his patient without being aware of it. He had read Morton Prince's description of Christine Beauchamp. Before "Eve Black" appeared, Thigpen had already hypnotized her at least once and had explained the concepts of repression and dissociation. We

---

* Ever since Morton Prince, MPD specialists have attempted to prove that an individual in different "alter" states displays different physiological functions, becoming, in effect, a different person. Alters within the same person are supposed to have different allergies, eyesight, and handwriting—all anecdotal reports. Frank Putnam and others conducted experiments that apparently indicated different brain wave patterns (EEGs or evoked visual potential) among alters. Although interesting, none of the experiments proved the existence of MPD, as psychiatrist Carol North pointed out in her excellent summary of the physiological studies: "No laboratory measurement has been developed that can differentiate MPD from other disorders."

have only his retrospective account, which is highly colored by his assumption that he did *not* cue her. It is quite possible that he loaned her his copy of Prince's *Dissociation of a Personality* or told her about it, or that she was familiar with the concept of multiple personality in some other way.*

Regardless of how Chris Sizemore initially became a multiple, she thrived on the role and made it a life-time occupation, until her death in 2016 at age 89. At the conclusion of *The Three Faces of Eve, we* are led to believe that her alters were well integrated. Far from it. In the ensuing years, at the urging of her new therapist, she developed a total of 22 personalities with names such as Purple Lady, Retrace Lady, and Strawberry Girl. She published two additional books about her dramatic experiences, in which she name-dropped mercilessly, bragged about her accomplishments, and lamented her inability ever to meet Sybil, her main competition. She had experienced, as she wrote in a revealing passage, "a lifetime of *continual expectancy.*"

Dissociative Disorder Units: Terror in the MPD Mills

Why would a trained professional, whose goal is to help afflicted patients regain mental health, instead push them further toward the brink of complete terror and disintegration?

Sheppard Pratt, a large psychiatric hospital in a northern suburb of Baltimore, provided an example of just how this can happen. After psychiatrist Richard Loewenstein, an MPD specialist, appeared there in 1987, the number of MPD diagnoses skyrocketed—not surprising, given Loewenstein's mindset, as revealed in a 1991 paper. "Dissociation and MPD are primarily hidden phenomena," he wrote. "Patients may deny, minimize, or rationalize their presence." Experienced diagnosticians must, he asserted, be alert to "subtle facial or body shifts by the dissociating patient during the interview." He advised clinicians to search for changes from session to session in "style of clothing, hair, makeup, eyeglasses, posture, level of motor activity, jewelry, handedness, taste and habits," all of which can be "very subtle."

Psychiatrist Donald Ross, the training director for new residents at Sheppard Pratt, was disturbed by Loewenstein's influence, which he perceived as producing young "true believers" in the MPD diagnosis. The process began, Ross posited, when patients with "insecure self-identity and permeable ego boundaries" appeared in the hospital ward. "They present us a therapeutic dilemma we find overwhelming. We want to help. We also want to diminish our anxiety." Up until now, no adequate theory or treatment had appeared to make much difference.

---

*   Harold Merskey pointed out another interesting aspect of the case. Rather than "Eve Black," the actual name of the first "alter" was really Chris Costner, her maiden name. Since she was experiencing marital strife and couldn't allow herself to express it, it's quite possible that this role gave her an outlet. "It was an affirmation of a previous [real] single state which the patient regretted leaving," Merskey hypothesized.

"The conceptual framework of trauma theory, with its emphasis on dissociation and the use of ... hypnosis, offers some promise of helping our patients and reducing our anxiety." It seemed to work. "It gives the patients a dramatic language to express their identity diffusion and their massive internal conflicts or 'parts.' Besides, it engages us in a way that is exciting and reinforcing."

With time, this new approach caught fire, as Ross noted. "A group knowledge of MPD begins to circulate among the patients and, like a contagion of sorts, it multiplies. We see dissociative phenomena more readily.... The therapeutic techniques used—hypnosis, regression, and abreaction—give us a sense that we are doing something and that therapy is moving in an understandable direction." Over a hundred years ago, Sigmund Freud succumbed to the same kind of temptation, as he later confessed: "There was something positively seductive in working with hypnotism. For the first time there was a sense of having overcome one's helplessness; and it was highly flattering to enjoy the reputation of being a miracle-worker."

Unfortunately, the results of such "miracles" at Sheppard Pratt were devastating for people such as Donna Smith and her family. She initially sought help for her bulimia. Primed by therapist Cathy Meyers, Smith had already retrieved extensive "repressed memories" of paternal incest by the time she was committed to Sheppard Pratt in February 1992 just short of her 18th birthday. The intake psychologist spotted six alters during the initial interview. During her 19-month hospital stay, Smith was heavily drugged, frequently held in restraints, hypnotized over 60 times, and attempted suicide twice. In the process, she found 65 new personalities along with memories that her mother had inserted various objects into her vagina before she was eight years old. When other alters claimed that Smith's parents had also abused her two younger brothers, the police came to their home and hauled the terrified boys away in handcuffs to "protect" them.*

Another former Sheppard Pratt patient, who preferred to remain anonymous, never completely fell for the MPD diagnosis, although he said that his therapist at Sheppard Pratt certainly tried her best to turn him into a multiple. "I was harangued by her for not having names for emotional aspects that she felt were alters," he told me. "I kept telling her I was uncomfortable with the whole context of 'alters' and naming them, and she stated that in order for us to have a working relationship, we needed alters with names. At times I found myself desperate to have them just to please her."

Part of the problems at Sheppard Pratt, of course, is inherent to any totalistic institution in which people are cut off from any other reality. As sociologist Erv-

---

* Fortunately, the Smith story had a relatively happy ending. After reading the *Esquire* article, Donna Smith began to question her MPD diagnosis and her memories of abuse. She reconciled with her parents, whom she no longer accused of abuse, and sued her former therapists.

ing Goffman observed in his classic 1961 book, *Asylums,* "their encompassing or total character is symbolized by the barrier to social intercourse with the outside." Typically, Goffman wrote, an inmate's indoctrination begins with "a series of abasements, degradations, humiliations, and profanations of self. [The] self is systematically, if often unintentionally, mortified."

It is not surprising, then, that Sheppard Pratt was not an isolated example. Bennett Braun's dissociative disorders unit at Rush Presbyterian-St. Luke's in Skokie, Illinois, was apparently also fertile ground for MPD contagion. Pat Burgus, once Braun's prize patient, along with several other former patients, sued Braun and his colleague Roberta Sachs for abusive therapy. Her life was nearly destroyed by the process. She became convinced that she had been a high priestess in a Satanic cult. Not only that, but her two sons, then four and five, were also diagnosed as MPD cult members and were hospitalized for nearly three years. The children were given stickers as a reward for coming up with grotesque fantasies. The Burgus family tragedy, which cost an insurance company $3 million, is told in detail in "Therapy of a High Priestess," a chapter in Richard Ofshe and Ethan Waters' compelling 1994 book, *Making Monsters,* and in the 1995 *Frontline* documentary, "The Search for Satan."

Braun was clearly fascinated and moved by his clients' bizarre revelations. Sometimes he would cry along with Burgus. Other times, he apparently became sexually aroused during her lurid descriptions of sexual assaults. With the encouragement of Braun and Sachs, Burgus eventually came up with memories of lit torches being pushed inside her, being buried for days on end, and having to eat the body parts of two thousand people a year. While they ate dinner one night in the hospital, Braun asked Burgus if the cottage cheese reminded her of anything, then wondered aloud whether she had ever opened a human brain. He believed that flowers sent to patients in his unit were really dangerous triggers. "Red roses or white baby's breath means bloody suicide. Pink roses mean hanging," he told other therapists in a 1992 presentation.

And Bennett Braun was not just any psychiatrist. He was the acknowledged leader in the diagnosis of multiple personality in the United States, the expert's expert. Typical of the cutting edge MPD gurus, Braun prided himself on his courage and adventurous spirit, testing the frontiers of human experience. He enjoyed skydiving, technical rock climbing, scuba diving, and horseback riding. He once tried fire walking. He appeared to get a kind of paranoid thrill from his belief in widespread Satanic cults. "About 20 patients have told me they were sent to kill me," he told one reporter.

Another alarming example of MPD treatment in Texas was revealed in an article by Sally McDonald in the *Journal of Psychosocial Nursing.* Psychiatric nurse

McDonald discussed how MPD specialist Judith Peterson, called "Dr. M." in the article, came to Houston's Spring Shadows Glen Hospital in 1990 to head the new dissociative disorders unit. McDonald made startling assertions. Completely supported by new medical director Dr. Richard Seward, and by the hospital administration—because her patients brought in $15,600 a day—Peterson instituted a virtual reign of terror on the ward, according to McDonald. Peterson subscribed to Bennett Braun's methodology, hypnotizing patients and convincing them to relive supposedly forgotten traumas. She believed that virtually every patient harbored multiple personalities formed during Satanic cult abuse. "One young patient was placed in nine-point mechanical restraints for three days," McDonald wrote, "not because he was a threat to himself or others … but because those three days coincided with some Satanic event."*

Twelve nurses fled the unit within a year and a half, but no one dared confront Dr. Peterson directly until she diagnosed a "bright, articulate, preadolescent" girl, an honors student, as having been involved in a Satanic cult. Confined to one room, the girl was denied access to her parents. In weekly staff meetings, nurses begged for a less restrictive environment, asking that the child be given "freedom of movement, peer interaction, fresh air, exercise, and a bed to sleep in," but Peterson refused. The girl became pale, thin, and dispirited. "These nurses knew they were the only advocates this girl had," McDonald wrote. "Alone she was unable to object to what her doctor and therapist thought 'best' for her."

When insurance companies began to question why it was only Peterson and Seward who ever recorded "altered states" or "violent behavior" on the patients' charts, the nurses were pressured to write up such behavior, even though they had never observed it. Nurses were intimidated, constantly written up for nonexistent violations. Peterson "threatened lawsuits so frequently that the nurses were afraid to counter her demands; they spoke in whispers in hallways because she taped their conversations." When the nurse manager sat in on "abreactive sessions," McDonald was horrified by the "coercive, leading nature of these therapy sessions."

Mothers who had hypnotic memories of cult involvement were coerced into getting divorced and giving up their children, McDonald wrote. "Nurses advised these distraught couples to seek legal counsel, especially before signing divorce papers, but the patients were too fragile to pursue outside opinions, and too frightened of incurring the wrath of their therapist, Dr. M. They believed [as she told them in sessions under hypnosis] that she was the expert, and only she could

---

* Satanic cult "experts" identified festival days throughout the year. One inventive list from a Survivor organization provided detailed descriptions. A sampling from September: "Sept. 7: Marriage to the Beast Satan, Sacrifice/Dismemberment. Female child under the age of 21. Sept. 20: Midnight Host, Dismemberment. Hands planted. Sept. 22: Feast Day, Fall/Autumn Equinox. Orgies."

successfully cure them."

In a 1993 *Houston Chronicle* article, journalist Mark Smith quoted several former patients who were suing Judith Peterson. Lucy Abney, 45, who sought treatment for depression, spent nearly a year (and over $300,000) at Spring Shadows Glen and came out with more than 100 alters and vivid memories of ritual abuse. Her two daughters were in state custody. As an example of the paranoia rampant on the hospital ward, Abney described how her husband was turned away when he tried to give her a carnation. Patients were warned that items such as flowers could trigger alter personalities.

According to several former patients and nurses, Judith Peterson specialized in convincing mothers that they had abused their children, who were also supposedly cult members. Then the children would also be admitted to the hospital. In an anonymous interview, a former nurse on the dissociative disorders unit told me that five families entered the hospital in this manner. Of those, three mothers ended up divorced and losing all contact with their children.

Kathryn Schwiderski and her three children were all patients of Judith Peterson at another Houston hospital and came to believe that their entire family had taken part in a Satanic cult. Their collective therapy and hospitalization cost over $2 million. In a 1990 presentation at a national MPD conference, Peterson described a family suspiciously similar to the Schwiderskis (without using their names), including details about "human sacrifice, cannibalism, black hole, shock to create alters (other personalities), marriage to Satan, buried alive, birth of Satan's child, internal booby traps, forced impregnation, and sacrifice of own child." While most of the family members no longer believed in these "memories," 22-year-old Kelly Schwiderski remained convinced that she killed three babies in a "fetus factory" in Colorado.

I interviewed one of Judith Peterson's former patients, who verified much of what McDonald and Smith wrote. Because she insisted on anonymity—out of fear that Peterson would sue her—I call her Angela. During her private sessions with Peterson, Angela found her "charming, even bewitching. She had an air about her of insight and caring. In my first session, she was all ears and supportive emotion. It felt good to have someone who was so attentive to every word that I spoke, every movement that I made." Soon Peterson convinced Angela that she should enter the hospital to see her more often.

Once admitted, Angela couldn't get out. Peterson became "a monster—harsh, hostile, interrogating, guilt-imputing, accusatory," according to Angela. The therapist and her staff tried to convince Angela that she harbored multiple personalities and had been in a Satanic cult. She was heavily drugged. "Dr. Peterson told me my anger came from a cult alter trying to come out, and that physical problems I was having were body memories." Peterson's patients weren't allowed to use the telephone unmonitored, Angela told me. Their mail was censored. Only approved visitors were allowed, and those few were closely watched. "If we weren't cooperative—revealing new alters, talking about Satanism—or were resistant to what we were told about ourselves or our families, we weren't considered 'safe' and often were restricted to the central lobby."

Angela likened the treatment to attempts to break prisoners of war. "They had a board with all the patients' names," she told me, "and every one had an 'S' after it for suicide precaution—not because we were really going to kill ourselves, but because that kept our insurance payments flowing." Finally, Angela escaped when her insurance ran out. "At first, Dr. Peterson was like my angel from heaven, but instead she took me to hell, and I've been struggling to get out ever since."

Another former patient, Mary Shanley (her real name), a 39-year-old first-grade teacher, entered an inpatient unit under Bennett Braun's supervision in the Chicago area in early 1990. She disliked Braun intensely. "He thinks he's God," she told me, "and you'd better think so, too." But Shanley admired Roberta Sachs, her psychologist. Under Sachs' tutelage, Shanley came to believe that her mother had been high priestess in a Satanic cult, and that she, Mary, was being groomed for the position. "I remembered going to rituals and witnessing sacrifices. I had a baby at age 13, supposedly, and that child was sacrificed. I totally believed all of this. I would have spontaneous abreactions, partly because I was so heavily medicated. I was on Inderal, Xanax, Prozac, Klonopin, Halcion, and several other drugs, all at once. No wonder I was dissociating."

After eleven months, Shanley finally got out of the hospital for three months. Then Roberta Sachs called her and asked if she would consult with psychologist Corydon Hammond, who was coming to town to give a workshop. After a hypnotic session during which Hammond tried to get Shanley to name Greek letters and identify a Dr. Green, he announced that she was so highly programmed and resistant that she was not treatable. Her nine-year-old son, however, might still be saved if he was treated in time. Otherwise, the cult would kill him. Shanley's husband believed Hammond, and a week or two later Mary Shanley was taken to the airport, not knowing her destination.

She arrived in Houston in May of 1991 to enter Spring Shadows Glen under the care of Judith Peterson. "When I first met Dr. Peterson, I thought she had this beautiful smile, and she spoke so softly and gently. She's tall and thin, sort of like a china doll, with a porcelain complexion and bright red hair. She's very striking." Once inside the hospital, however, Shanley found Peterson to be precisely the opposite of her first impression. "She was known on the ward as the red-headed bitch," Shanley told me. "She did not like me at all and made no bones about it."

After Shanley called a mental health advocacy hotline to complain, she found herself accompanied "one-on-one" for 24 hours a day by a technician. "I was locked out of my room and kept in the central lobby. I wasn't allowed to use the telephone or to go outside. That's when I took up smoking, so that I could at least go outside briefly. I slept on the floor or on a couch. After I hurt my back in abreactive sessions, they let me drag my mattress out."

Part of Shanley's problem was her honesty. Even though she believed that she had been in a cult and possessed internal alters, she would not make them up on cue to please Dr. Peterson. When she would not perform properly during an abreactive session, she would be kept in restraints for up to nine hours until she said what Peterson wanted to hear. "A lot of the times, the tech and I would discuss what answer she might want." Sometimes, the psychodramatist and another psychiatrist would sit on either side of Shanley during sessions. "If Dr. Peterson asked a question and I couldn't answer, they would talk back and forth, representing my alters, literally talking over my head."

Most of Peterson's efforts concentrated on eliciting information regarding Shanley's son, who was going through a similar abreactive process back in Chicago with Roberta Sachs. Peterson would fax new information to her colleague in Illinois. "It would work the other way, too," Shanley says. "Dr. Peterson told me how my son acted out how he could cut a human heart out of a living body. I thought, there's no way he could imagine that. And I thought, he doesn't lie, I know he's not a liar. So I believed it all."

After over two years in Spring Shadows Glen, Mary Shanley finally got out in 1993. She had lost her husband and child, who still believed in the Satanic cults. She had lost her home and her 20-year teaching career. "I have absolutely nothing. I don't even have enough clothes to wear to my work in a department store." She couldn't teach or hold a federal job because she was on a list of suspected child molesters.

There was hope, however. In 1995, Shanley's horror story was featured in a *Frontline* documentary, "The Search for Satan," making it painfully clear that she was a victim of terrible therapy. Two lawyers—Zachary Bravos of Wheaton, Illinois, and Skip Simpson of Dallas, Texas—represented Shanley and several other patients in suits against Judith Peterson, Roberta Sachs, Bennett Braun, and others. Because of their willingness to take her case, Shanley felt some hope for the future.*

---

* Abusive treatment of patients in dissociative disorders units was part of a larger problem documented by journalist Joe Sharkey in his 1994 book, *Bedlam: Greed, Profiteering, and Fraud in a Mental Health System Gone Crazy.* Sharkey described how private psychiatric hospitals had paid clergymen, school counselors, and other "bounty hunters" for referrals, using hard-sell advertising tactics to attract *new* patients. His book included numerous horror stories, including that of one 13-year-old boy whose insurance paid for 41 group therapy sessions in one day. Curiously, Sharkey did not even mention multiple personality disorder, ritual abuse, or repressed memories.

By the end of 1992, nurse Sally McDonald had been shifted from the adolescent unit to another department because she kept calling Peterson unethical, and the head nurse of the dissociative disorders unit had also been forced out of her position for "insubordination." Morale on the dissociative disorders unit had sunk to an all-time low, according to McDonald. Although nurses repeatedly protested to hospital administrators, nothing happened. Then, in the last week of February, 1993, Medicare officials arrived for a routine hospital inspection. Within hours, they brought in Texas health authorities, and on March 19, the dissociative unit was closed. Two patients walked outside for the first time in two years.

After that, former patients began to talk to the media about their experiences, and at least seven sued. Judith Peterson no longer worked at Spring Shadows Glen, but *she* sued the hospital, McDonald, and another nurse for slander and libel, and she planned countersuits against several patients. Richard Seward worked with prisoners, but he remained on call at the hospital.

Peterson and most of her colleagues settled out of court for an undisclosed sum, while former patient Lynn Carl won a $5.8 million judgment in 1997 against psychiatrist Gloria Keraga, her therapist at Spring Shadows Glen. A federal lawsuit sputtered, however, resulting in a 1999 mistrial when a juror was disqualified because he or she had inadvertently had contact with a prospective defense witness, leaving only eleven jurors. The prosecution decided not to pursue a new trial. Peterson was allowed to keep her license to practice as a psychotherapist.

The charismatic Dr. Peterson had her champions, however. I interviewed 23-year-old Christy Steck, an MPD patient who had been seeing Peterson for four years, and who spent most of 1992 in the dissociative disorders unit at Spring Shadows Glen. Steck had always had stomach problems and other vague physical complaints, which she blamed on her biological mother, since recovering memories of her mother and grandfather abusing her in a Satanic cult. Her first flashback to ritual abuse occurred while she was watching the horror movie *Friday the Thirteenth*. With her therapist's help, Steck was able to identify alters named Tyrant, Tricia, Angela, Whore, and Fucking Bitch. The last two were "real deep parts that answer to whistles, clickers, and metronomes," Steck told me. They were the ones programmed to be sex slaves in pornography and prostitution. She had spots on her body that look like "just birthmarks," she said, but in reality she thought they were tattoos and scars from electroshock torture.

"Dr. Peterson is so sincere and genuine, also strong-willed and dedicated," Steck told me. "When she first met me, she shook my hand and looked into my eyes. I saw the most caring, genuine person I've ever met. She kept holding my hand and said she'd always be there for me, no matter what I said." Peterson confirmed that Steck was not only an MPD, but a *special* kind. While in the dissociative disorders unit, Steck voluntarily entered restraints during abreactive sessions. "I have violent seizures from remembering electroshock, and I have violent alters programmed to kill whoever is hearing this. That's why they put me in restraints. Otherwise, I would try to hurt myself or Dr. Peterson."

Steck called Peterson her "savior" and insisted that she had "always given me the freedom to choose my own path." The therapist often asked her, "Okay, do you want to go back to the cult, or do you want to work? If you're not going to talk, why should I bother to work with you?" Steck called Peterson "tough but caring," and said that the therapist never really pressured her. "She gives people a choice of what to believe. She never says, 'I believe that's what happened.' She says, 'It's up to you to figure out what happened.'"

When Steck's insurance had almost run out, Bennett Braun flew in from Rush Presbyterian in Chicago to evaluate her. Braun's 500-page report, which discussed her abuse and suicide attempts in detail, allowed the doctors to declare Steck a "catastrophic case," so that a special rider on her insurance kicked in to continue to pay for treatment. Later, Richard Loewenstein came from Sheppard Pratt to confirm the diagnosis. When I spoke to her in 1994, Christy Steck was seeing Judith Peterson two or three times a week. "I'm doing better than I ever have in my whole life," she told me. "But I can't be left alone yet. I can't really work, but I clean a couple of houses for people I know well. They stay there while I work. It's just a matter of working through this programming to where I'm not accessible to the cult. The more I see that I've been programmed and brainwashed, the more I can work with it. If I don't see it, I won't get well." She predicted that she would need another four years of "intensive therapy," after which she would probably need a weekly check-up. "I hope some day I'll be integrated."

Finally, in 1994 I interviewed Judith Peterson, and I came to understand how all three of her patients were probably telling the truth. Peterson denied McDonald's accusations. "The lady spelled her own name correctly; almost everything else in that article is a lie," she told me.* She denied that any phone calls were monitored, that patients were held against their will, that they were kept until their insurance ran out. She pointed out that McDonald never worked on the dissociative disorders unit, but only on the adolescent unit.

As for the preadolescent girl who concerned McDonald so much, Peterson as-

---

* When I told her that Peterson said she had lied, Sally McDonald laughed. "I was really careful that anything I wrote was the absolute truth and could be verified. There was much, much more that was deleted. What you read was a watered down version." She told me of an abreactive session during which Peterson asked a child questions, and one of Peterson's associates answered for her. The child never said a word. At the end, Peterson praised the child, saying "You really worked well this session." Asked why the patient had not answered for herself, Peterson allegedly said, "Her alters were mute." Another anonymous nurse told me that until a Texas "patients' rights" bill was passed in 1992, dissociative disorder patients could not use the phone, receive mail, or see their families at all. "They were not allowed off the unit. They lived totally in a closed society, dependent on the whim of the therapist and the M.D. overseeing the unit."

serted that she was a "very acute" case of MPD who tried to crash through a plate glass door in order to escape, and who repeatedly attacked Peterson, once with the broken shards of a compact mirror. "Not infrequently, I've been knocked across the room by violent alters," she told me. Yes, some patients had to be restricted to the central lobby near the nursing station, so they could be watched, but that was only to keep them from hurting themselves or others.

Peterson said that she no longer used the term "abreactive sessions," preferring to speak of "memory processing." Before each session, she asked patients to write down their new memories, which may have come through flashbacks, journaling, artwork, dreams, or body memories. Then, after placing them in a "light hypnotic state," she encouraged them to go through each memory to "deal with the feelings" and perform "cognitive restructuring."* These sessions clearly got quite intense, with patients purportedly reliving torture and electric shock treatment. "They have pseudo-grand mal seizures," Peterson told me.

She was no longer so sure that her patients were actually involved in Satanic ritual abuse cults. Rather, the ritual abuse may have been used "as a screen and creator of terror. Underneath it, in terms of complex alter layers, is organized crime." In other words, she believed that criminal gangs intentionally terrified her patients, often making them mistakenly *believe* that murders had taken place. "They have ways of tricking people; they're given drugs, and they're terrified and confused." The crime groups did this in order to produce "synthetic alters" who would act in pornographic films or become prostitutes. Other patients, she thought, were thus treated by the Ku Klux Klan.

Of course, Peterson could not tell for sure whether these memories were accurate. "My patients tell me very bizarre stories." She simply listened. "I'm a guide, asking 'What happened next?' I don't lead them." Yes, she had heard stories of murdered babies. "It doesn't particularly matter if it's true or not. I wasn't there. The dilemma of true or not true is up to them." Of one thing she was certain, though: "These people don't make up the terror; that's pretty hard to do. They also don't make up the electric shocks. They have body memories of them." That accounted for the pseudo-seizures.

Judith Peterson, then 48, seemed genuinely outraged that her integrity had been impugned. She had always considered herself an altruistic, idealistic person trying to help the world. She began her career working with migrant workers and Head Start children and parents. She considered going into the Peace Corps. She had only tried to help those who came to her "depressed, anxious, overwhelmed." In her workshops, she said, she even warned against the dangers of telling pa-

---

* For a full written description, see Sachs and Peterson, *Processing Memories Retrieved by Trauma Victims and Survivors: A Primer for Therapists* (1994).

tients during an initial session that they must have been sexually abused. "Yet here I am so viciously attacked," she lamented. She explained her former patients' dissatisfaction by referring to their mental condition. "Basically, these patients are sociopathic. They have their own reasons for targeting me," she said darkly.

Peterson sent me a revealing article she had published in *Treating Abuse Today*, in which she compared her plight with that of her abused patients, coping with "existential crises at a depth I never thought imaginable." She complained, "Those I tried to help sadistically turned on the very person who reached out to help." This article eloquently expressed Peterson's experiences and beliefs:

> I've spent timeless moments, hours, days and years listening to those with souls that were shattered. I moved from being a therapist who thought incest was the worst thing imaginable, to hearing of abuses so unimaginable that I walked out of therapy sessions stunned.... Sometimes I would just cry over the range and extent of human cruelty. There are no words to express what I have felt as I have heard people describe everything from having a broom handle stuffed up their anus to having their teeth electrically shocked. I have listened to a mother describe how she tied her small child to the bars of a crib before putting something in every orifice of the body—a rag already in the mouth to prevent screaming. I've listened to descriptions of electroshock on a baby and the baby's seizures.

Despite Peterson's willingness to share the pain of mothers' "horror of damaging those they love," however, some of these same mothers had turned on her. "The shame and guilt were then transferred to me, the therapist. Kill the messenger. Lie. This client relived the trauma by victimizing me. Suddenly, the therapist is the victim."

Peterson was stung by allegations that she separated families and encouraged Child Protective Services (CPS) to take her patients' children away. "I've found something new in our field," she told me. "There's a high degree of mothers who have perpetrated their children." When she discovered this during therapy sessions, she was mandated by law to inform social services. "It's almost impossible to persuade CPS to let children stay with their families under such circumstances. The CPS people are, unfortunately, mostly incompetent and overworked."

I came away from my interview with Judith Peterson thinking that she was intelligent, assertive and quite possibly insane. She did not think that she was leading her patients. She completely believed that they were inhabited by violent, dangerous internal personalities, that they were a danger to themselves and their families, and that she was striving to heal the wounds of terrible past trauma. She could not admit the possibility that the terror they were experiencing might be an artifact of her therapy rather than symptoms of past abuse.

The stories about Judith Peterson told in these pages only skim the surface.

As more of her clients began to speak publicly, the incredible paranoia she inspired—and the destruction of families—became clearer. In 1995, Houston journalist Bonnie Gangelhoff wrote a devastating article on Peterson called "Devilish Diagnosis." One former Peterson client told Gangelhoff, "Every day was total chaos…. You could be talking to someone and suddenly they would switch personalities. I started doing it, too. It all started to seem so normal." The husband of a former client revealed that Peterson told him that "people could control my wife by transmitting sequences of phone tones to her over the telephone." Peterson herself wrote to the Texas licensing board, complaining that "an alter was programmed to knife me in my office."

Dissociation and the Absent-Minded Professor

While most therapists told their clients that they held *repressed* memories, MPD specialists relied on the subtler notion of *dissociation*. The concept of dissociation was invented by Pierre Janet, who, in his old age, warned: "Beware, it is only an idea that I express. It is an hypothesis for your research." Yet precious little controlled scientific research would follow. Psychiatrist Fred Frankel objected to the broad, indiscriminate use of the term "dissociation," complaining of the "large number of vague concepts" it appears to cover, and comparing it to the all-inclusive "hysteria" of the last century.

According to one definition of dissociation, it is "a psychophysiological process whereby information—incoming, stored, or outgoing—is actively deflected from integration with its usual or expected associations." That's a windy way of explaining the process of daydreaming, spacing out, and losing track of normal consciousness.

If that's what dissociation is, most of us experience it at times. "Highway hypnosis" is one widespread type of dissociation, in which a driver on a familiar stretch of road or an Interstate suddenly snaps to, arriving at a destination or landmark without remembering much of the drive at all. This is the sort of "lost time" experience that MPDs are supposed to experience frequently. There's no question that the phenomenon exists. I have even been able to time it. I often listen to audio books while taking long trips. My thoughts sometimes drift onto other matters, and I suddenly realize that I've been listening without hearing. I can go back and find the exact point where my mind took off.

But is it necessary to use this concept of "dissociation," with its assumption of a solitary, normal mind from which something splits? I don't think so. We can think consciously about several things at once, but there is a limit. When we concentrate on one particular strand of thought, we aren't necessarily splitting *from* anything. We are simply *paying more attention* to one thing than the other. Rather than dissociation, I would coin the term "kaleidoscope thinking." In our constantly churning minds, different thoughts roll into view, coalesce, then disappear. Some of us are better than others at blocking out everything except what we're thinking about. That's the very definition of the absent-minded professor.

While taking a morning shower, I sometimes become so preoccupied with planning my day that I forget whether I already shampooed or not. I'm sure that I've washed my hair twice plenty of times. But it isn't this normal type of dissociation that concerns trauma therapists. Rather, it is what they believe to be a capacity to "space out," to numb our feelings, to enter a self-induced trance state, to split off one portion of the mind from another in order to endure otherwise unendurable abuse. Again, there is experiential validation for this phenomenon on a limited basis. We *do* tend to go numb or experience a feeling of unreality when we are threatened, frightened, or wounded. In extreme cases, people sometimes go into physical and psychological shock. They wander aimlessly in a "fugue state" and sometimes present themselves as having amnesia immediately afterward.

As I mentioned in Chapter 2, some authorities question whether true psychological amnesia actually exists. But in any event, there is *no* scientific proof of massive "dissociation" in the sense that it has been used by some trauma therapists. It is a hypothesis that has been taken for granted, but, as with repression, we are left in the realm of *belief* rather than *proof.*

Certainly, people have the capacity to "take their minds away" from a horrible event, but that does not mean that they can "dissociate" memory of the event completely. As a child, I hated and dreaded having my teeth drilled on. My dentist must have known something about the value of dissociation, since he had mounted a blown-up color photo of a bucolic summer lakeside scene on the wall. I would concentrate on that picture, placing myself beneath a particular tree by the lake, taking myself away from the pain in my tooth. But I was always perfectly aware that the dentist was at work, and I never stumbled out of his office wondering where I had been.

Similarly, if a father rapes his daughter, she might very well concentrate on a crack in the ceiling, numb her feelings, or try to think about something. It might help her to endure the event. But she would not forget what was happening. And it seems far-fetched to assume that she would invent a cast of internal personalities that rival a Tolstoy novel in their complexity.

"Most memory researchers since the early 2000s argue that while dissociation may be possible, people usually do not dissociate during emotional events, and there is no evidence to support a special fracturing process of memory in trauma situations," wrote memory researcher Julia Shaw in *The Memory Illusion* (2016). "It is also unlikely that there is such a thing as repression, hiding emotional memories from direct access."

How, then, can we account for the fact that many people truly *experience* multiple personalities? In a sense, we are all MPDs. Each of us acts different roles every day, assuming radically different personalities as we do so. With a boss, we are the employee—outwardly respectful, perhaps, but sometimes frustrated. With a spouse, we might be romantic one moment, an exasperated mate the next. With a child, we may be a nurturing or frustrated authority figure. "A person might see herself or himself as *authoritative* in the role of employer, *submissive* in the role of daughter or son, *companionable* in the role of wife or husband," writes psychologist Peter Gray. Through it all, each of us maintains a unique sense of identity, but that is often simply a social construct, an illusion.

At times of crisis in our lives, many of us become uncertain of ourselves and our identities. "There are unavoidable transitions in any life in which the content of selfhood is in flux," writes anthropologist Michael Kenny, such as "becoming an adult, finding a place in the world, marriage, having children, facing death." Most societies offer formal rites of passage to ease these transitions, but in modern America, our roles and identities are more amorphous, and the transitions are more difficult. We suffer "identity crises" during which we are much more vulnerable to manipulation because we don't really know who we are, and we desperately desire a firm identity, an explanation for our predicament. It is just at such a crucial crossroad that the therapist comes along with his MPD diagnosis, calling out "parts" of us and labeling them.

Rather than helping a person to develop a better self-concept, the MPD specialist does the opposite. There can be no "self"esteem without a unitary self. These therapists encouraged—indeed, commanded—their patients to shatter psychically. "When the organization of the self-concept is threatened," one psychologist wrote in 1973, "the individual experiences anxiety, and attempts to defend himself against the threat. If the defense is unsuccessful, stress mounts and is followed ultimately by total disorganization."

Grade Fives, Temporal Lobe Spikes, and Personality

Because of media saturation, the MPD role was as well-known by the late 20th century as the demoniac's behavior was in 1600. "People can learn the components of the multiple personality role from a variety of quite different sources (e.g., movies, books, gossip)," Nicholas Spanos noted in 1986. Since then, the MPD myth spread even more widely. By 1991, MPD specialist Richard Kluft could write that "many MPD patients have informed themselves about their condition from the broadcast media and lay and professional literature." He added that a "significant minority" were such voracious readers and researchers that they developed a "broader knowledge base" than their therapists!

Not only that, but the role became more attractive with time. Those who harbored a hundred or more alters objected to their malady being termed a *disorder*. Rather, it was a distinction, or a miracle. While MPD may have commenced because of overwhelming trauma, it released entertaining alters to cope with it. They were interesting, creative personae who allowed the MPD Survivor to use the royal "we" and to take part in endless internal dramas. "I can't imagine being a singleton," one MPD Survivor told me. "How boring that would be!"*

Perhaps she had read *When Rabbit Howls* (1987), written "by the Troops for Truddi Chase." Chase, a commercial artist, real estate agent and sometime legal secretary in her forties, supposedly "went to sleep" at the age of two, when her stepfather raped her. The "Troops" were her 92 alters, including such personalities as Rabbit, Miss Wonderful, Elvira, Lamb Chop, Ean, Mean Joe Green, Sister Mary Catherine, Nails, the Zombie, and the Interpreter.** Of course, Chase was completely unaware of this menagerie until she entered therapy with Robert A. Phillips, Jr., a Ph.D. clinical psychologist who wrote the introduction and epilogue to her book. Before discovering her multiplicity, Chase "had tried unsuccessfully to discover a medical reason for her temper tantrums, periodic blackouts, and a feeling of continual 'dizziness'," Phillips revealed. By book's end, the Troops and Dr. Phillips came to a mutual decision to "maintain multiplicity." As a result, "communication among the Troop members has been enhanced, and there is evidence of increased ability to cooperate and work together."

The MPD role tended to attract extremely creative, suggestible clients with a craving for attention. Most were highly hypnotizable, among the 10 percent of the population psychiatrist Herbert Spiegel called "Grade Fives," on a scale from one to four. These Fives had an uncanny ability to sense what behavior may intrigue a therapist, and they fulfilled all expectations. That did not mean that they were easy patients, however. Rather, they had to up the ante in order to maintain dramatic attention. As soon as one alter appeared to be integrated, another would pop out. Then, just when a whole system seemed to be settled, another whole layer was uncovered, and more alters would pour forth from the mental shrubbery.

Consequently, MPD patients rarely got better. They entered a cycle of extended abreaction and misery which sometimes ended in suicide. After I wrote *Victims of Memory*, I heard from a psychiatric social worker who knew of a local psy-

---

* Those who believe they have multiple personalities have found all kinds of creative outlets through print, paint, or song. Multiples produced their own newsletter and even wrote an anthology called *Multiple Personality Disorder from the Inside Out* (1991), in which alters took turn addressing the reader. "It's Gregory writing this for everybody inside," a typical entry by Cindy B. commenced. But then Gregory was interrupted. "Somebody else inside wants to add that it is very confusing and scary being a multiple...."

** Some multiples claimed to house hundreds of alters, but that's nothing compared to a 16-year-old girl who, in 1583, was found to contain 12,652 living demons.

chiatrist who was convincing many patients that they had multiple personalities. "Two young women treated and diagnosed by him and the therapists he trained set themselves on fire and burned to death." And they were by no means the only ones with supposed MPD who killed themselves.

This may seem a paradox. Didn't I just say that patients reveled in the attention? And isn't this all just role-playing? Yes and no.

Take the example of Canadian Roma Hart, who, feeling overstressed in 1986, went to apply for unemployment insurance. She needed a psychiatrist to sign the requisite form and went to see psychiatrist Colin Ross, who promptly diagnosed her as having multiple personalities. Hart, whose background included extensive theatrical experience, decided to go along with it so that she could get her unemployment checks. "If I became bored, I would pretend to switch personalities just for the hell of it. No one could put any demands on me any more and sympathy was just a phone call away."

But an odd thing happened. Roma Hart began to believe her own play-acting. She became completely dependent on Ross, who put her on large doses of mind-altering drugs such as Halcion. She attempted suicide. She wound up in a locked hospital unit. When she got out, she joined an MPD support group, where Ross told them all how special they were. "We were more creative, more sensitive, and better able to adjust in difficult situations," Hart recalled. "Being diagnosed as an MPD was practically an honor!"

In the groups, a strange competition commenced. "One thing I can tell you about MPD patients," Hart noted, "is that they're competitive. If one recalls an animal personality, then the rest soon will. If one recalls a baby personality, then you better order a case of baby food."

Eventually, by the summer of 1991, Roma Hart's life had become so chaotic that she left Colin Ross, who informed her that she had "failed therapy," that she would never make it. Indeed, for a long time her life continued to be a struggle. Even though she knew intellectually that all her Satanic abuse memories were false, she could not completely shake them. "My parents came for my one-year-old's birthday," she told me late in 1995, "and that night I had nightmares about them being in a cult and trying to hurt my baby. I woke up and thought, 'Maybe it was true. Maybe I'm just in denial.' But of course I know it isn't." Hart sued Colin Ross.

In the case of Roma Hart—and many other MPD patients—role-playing became reality, and the attention-seeking lurched into self-destructive behavior. The syndrome was no longer a game, and the wounded players, expert dramatists, enacted tragic parts. One Latin-American soap opera star became so absorbed in his role that, in real life, he murdered the actress who had jilted him on TV. The same sort of thing could happen with MPD Survivors, for whom the acting became reality; only in their case, the violence was usually directed against themselves.

That is what happened to Gail Macdonald, a young Canadian mother who entered therapy in her small town in Ontario with a soft-spoken, good-looking American therapist whom she called Joe in her 1999 book, *Making of an Illness: My Experience with Multiple Personality Disorder*. Her father really had been an alcoholic, but that wasn't enough for Joe, who took her in guided imagery (hypnotic) sessions to discover her various alters, some of whom ripped off her toenails. Joe inducted her into a group of his other female MPD patients, who competed with one another for his attention. "There was not a single woman in this group who would not harm herself. Often we looked like casualties from war. It wasn't unusual to show up with burns on our bodies or cuts from knives or razor blades."

When Macdonald and several other clients eventually left therapy, their internal voices diminished and disappeared, along with their alters, panic attacks, nightmares, self-destructive behavior, and sleep deprivation. They sued Joe, who settled out of court in 1996 and moved back to the United States to continue his practice. He had been trained to diagnose MPD by psychiatrist Margo Rivera, who is still a professor at Queen's University in Kingston, Ontario, and head of a Personality Disorders Service. Rivera's website advertises her book, *Fragment by Fragment: Feminist Perspectives on Memory and Child Sexual Abuse*, espousing the theory of massive dissociation.

At the end of her book, Gail Macdonald observed that "the discredited 'multiple personality disorder' was replaced by 'dissociative identity disorder,' and the 'personalities' by 'fragments,' but it is the same thing, regardless how you name it."

Macdonald identified herself as highly hypnotizable but was never tested for an intriguing theory. It is possible, though unproven, that abnormally high electrical activity in the temporal lobe of the brain may have something to do with illusory memories. Experimental psychologist Michael Persinger published an intriguing series of papers on temporal lobe EEGs (electroencephalographs). He believed that there is a continuum of temporal lobe activity within the population, ranging from very low to those diagnosed as having temporal lobe epilepsy. Regardless of whether they experience real seizures, those with high electrical activity display an interesting set of phenomena, according to Persinger: "visual hallucinations, the sense of a presence, mystical (paranormal) experiences, unusual smells, anomalous voices or sounds, vestibular movements, and anxiety." Over time, such people often display "stereotyped thinking, a sense of personal destiny or uniqueness, elaborate delusions, and excessive interests in religious or philosophical topics." Persinger's studies indicated that about a third of the population displays "temporal lobe signs." Because nearly 10 percent of the population experiences a seizure at least once, these findings aren't surprising.

Persinger concluded that abnormal temporal lobe activity may be responsible for many mystical experiences. While these experiences can produce a feeling of euphoria and unity with the universe, however, they can also result in intense anxiety, terror, and delusions. All of this takes us back to Wilder Penfield's surgical probing of the temporal lobe. The "memories" he elicited from his patients were, as we have seen in Chapter 2, probably hallucinations, but the implication of the temporal lobe is nevertheless intriguing. During my research for this book, I ran into several cases in which the accusing offspring had been diagnosed with temporal lobe epilepsy. Similarly, Frank Putnam reported "a higher-than-expected apparent incidence of abnormal EEG findings in MPD patients ... and [a] disproportionately high number of case reports of MPD and concurrent epilepsy."

Case reports of temporal lobe epileptics often bear a striking resemblance to those of repressed memory Survivors:

> TF, a 29-year-old married woman, presented with a chief complaint of uncontrollable depression for which she could see no precipitating event. Her symptoms included difficulty falling asleep ... nightmares ... loss of weight, extreme tenseness, anxiety, and occasional panic attacks. She alternated between global hyposexuality [no interest in sex] and driven promiscuous hypersexuality.

This patient, as well as many others, responded well to carbamazephine (Tegretol), an anti-convulsant drug.

Epilepsy researcher David Bear suggested that a cluster of 18 personality traits identifies temporal lobe epileptics (TLEs); his findings were replicated by several other researchers. Among other things, Bear believed that TLEs are frequently irritable, angry, aggressive, depressed, and paranoid, with sudden mood shifts. They are singularly humorless and often believe they have profound personal destinies. They tend to be dependent and "clingy" upon figures of authority. They often feel compelled to write long autobiographical passages. In addition, they commonly complain of "amnestic gaps" before, during, or after seizures, along with other subtler memory disturbances. Their sex drives are often impaired, but sometimes they become oversexed instead. Just before TLE seizures, they routinely get feelings of *deja vu*, smell something odd, and sense impending doom.

There are, however, positive sides to high temporal lobe electrical activity, including creativity and charisma. An impressive array of famous historical figures were purportedly epileptics of one sort or another, including Alexander the Great, Lord Byron, Buddha, Julius Caesar, Dante, Charles Dickens, Feodor Dostoyevsky, Mohammed, Napoleon Bonaparte, Isaac Newton, Blaise Pascal,

Pythagoras, Socrates, St. Paul, Ludwig von Beethoven, and Vincent van Gogh.

In some cases of supposed multiple personality, it was painfully evident that the eager clinician misdiagnosed a client with real physical ailments. One clinical psychologist, for instance, wrote of a 47-year-old Vietnam veteran who entered his office leaning on a cane. "He had a history of seizure disorders, right hemiparesis, right hemisensory loss, and right visual field defect arising from a suspected arterial venous malformation in the basal ganglia region of his brain." Further, the patient's memory was impaired due to a "closed head injury from ten years previously" and a subsequent fall off a ladder. Despite these clear organic problems, the psychologist proceeded to "discover" various alter personalities and hidden traumas to explain his memory gaps. "Later in therapy, it became clear that he had suffered early childhood sexual, physical, and psychological abuse by his father and siblings. He was repeatedly tortured, thrown out of a second floor window, sodomized, and used as an object for sadistic gratification."

Such cases are disturbing, but not the norm. *People need not be "Grade Fives" or exhibit high temporal lobe activity in order to be convinced that they are sex abuse Survivors or harbor multiple personalities. Such beliefs can be instilled in anyone, given the right circumstances and mindset.*

Satan's Minions

An astonishing number of repressed memories of the 1980s and 1990s involved some form of group ritual abuse, usually with an explicitly Satanic component.[*] A high percentage of such ritual survivors believed that they split off internal alters as a result of this dreadful experience.

The events usually unfolded as follows. First, a young woman entered therapy for depression or some other complaint. Her therapist encouraged her to see her family as dysfunctional, and herself as the victim of "emotional incest." Soon, she read self-help recovery books and retrieved memories of physical incest by one family member. Then, as her memories flowed more easily, she named other perpetrators. Finally, she recalled ritual abuse, was diagnosed with MPD, and might wind up heavily drugged and suicidal in a psychiatric ward.

Other writers have convincingly demolished the notion that such cults actually exist.[**] Still, nothing can ever sway those with an invested belief in them. People

---

[*]   *The Courage to Heal* offered a short course in ritual abuse memory, using "Annette" as a role model. "From infancy, Annette was abused in rituals that included sexual abuse, torture, murder, pornography, and systematic brainwashing through drugs and electric shock." Of course, she forgot all of this until she was 48. "I was what they called a 'breeder,'" Annette explained. "I was less than twelve years old. They overpowered me and got me pregnant and then they took my babies. They killed them right in front of me."

[**]   There are three types of "Satanic" or ritual activities that actually do exist: (1) Harmless organized religions led by flamboyant characters such as Anton La Vey, the former circus musician who headed the Church of Satan. (2) Teenagers and others who, as part of societal rebellion, dabble in the occult, draw pentagrams, and

who can believe that a child's heart was surgically removed and replaced with an animal's ticker during ritual abuse, and who refuse to accept physical evidence disproving such an event, are not likely to accept logical arguments either.

After years spent trying to track down such cases, FBI investigator Kenneth Lanning concluded that "there is little or no evidence [for] large-scaled baby breeding, human sacrifice, and organized Satanic conspiracies. Now it is up to mental health professionals, not law enforcement, to explain why victims are alleging things that don't seem to have happened." At least four well-researched books were published by 1993 on this "contemporary legend," and they all reached the same conclusion: this was a hoax, a fraud, a paranoid delusion fomented by the media, credulous therapists, distraught patients, pressured pre-schoolers, fearful parents, and over-excited policemen.*

Two major studies—one American, one British—came to the same conclusion in 1994. Funded with $750,000 by the federal government, Gail Goodman and her team examined thousands of purported cases of Satanic ritual abuse and failed to find any evidence for stereotypical multi-generational cults that sexually abuse children. All they found were "a few 'borderline' cases, typically involving a lone individual or two people whose abuse of children involved Satanic themes."**

A similar study conducted by Jean La Fontaine in Great Britain took a close look at over 200 claims of Satanic ritual abuse. Again, no evidence emerged to support the notion of widespread intergenerational sex abuse cults. La Fontaine found only three cases with any firm evidence. "The three substantiated cases are not instances of Satanism or witchcraft," she concluded. "They are also significantly different from the other cases in the study. They show a single perpetrator of abuse claiming spiritual powers." She explained the mythical ritual abuse cases as a sociological phenomenon. "A belief in evil cults is convincing because it draws on powerful cultural axioms."

Why did so many well-trained therapists believe in Satanic cults? They would tell you that their clients couldn't make up these gory details or display such terror if the stories weren't true. They would say that their clients knew nothing about ritual abuse, yet they came up with the same breeding strategies, sacrificed

---

perhaps sacrifice a stray cat. (3) Aberrant psychopaths such as the Matamoros murderers, who act out the myths they read about or saw in movies. Folklorists call this copy-cat process "legend ostension." Given the seemingly limitless human capacity for evil, it is not surprising that someone would act out an evil myth.

*   The books are: *Satan Wants You*, by Arthur Lyons (1988); *In Pursuit of Satan*, by Robert D. Hicks (1991); *The Satanism Scare* (1991); and *Satanic Panic* by Jeffrey Victor (1993).]

**   Far more disturbing were the cases of "religion-related abuse" documented in the Goodman study. "My client was a 14-year-old boy whose eyeball had been plucked out of his head in an exorcism ceremony," one therapist wrote. "The father performed an exorcism on his children by dismembering and then boiling them. Evidence? The children were dead," wrote another. One mother who thought her 12-year-old boy was possessed by the devil first had sex with him, then decapitated him. Goodman's conclusion seemed rather mild under the circumstances: "Religious beliefs can at times foster, encourage, and justify abusive behavior."

babies, blood-letting, rape, and murder that others across the country—around the world—had reported. Witch-hunters in 1670 made much the same observation, citing "so much agreement and conformity between the different cases" as proof of witchcraft. Of course, that's the way folklore legends work, as sociologist Jeffrey Victor masterfully documented in his book, *Satanic Panic*. The stories floated on the airwaves and bubbled in the rumor mills. Just as someone transported back to a past life doesn't remember where she originally learned about a particular epoch, many ritual abuse survivors honestly believed that they never saw a movie, read a book, listened to a talk show, or overheard a conversation that provided the details they brought forth in a hypnotic session.

Even if they never *did* see such a movie or hear a talk show, the therapists could cue them inadvertently, particularly using the "ideomotor method" in which a hypnotized subject merely raises a finger to indicate a positive response to a leading question. "Familiarize yourself with signals and symptoms of ritualized abuse," one psychologist advised in a handout. He went on to explain that "survivors of ritualized abuse *have many special needs*" and must be seen beyond the normal hour limit. "If you are uncomfortable with the reality of ritual abuse, then you should not be treating survivors of ritual abuse," he asserted. Following this advice had a mutually reinforcing effect in which both patient and therapist felt *special*.

The moral panic over Satanic cults produced a curious partnership between some left-wing radical feminists and selected right-wing Christian fundamentalists.* Members of both groups believed that there was an international conspiracy of sexual abusers who brutalized children, used them in violent child pornography, then murdered and ate them. Cult members, they assured anyone who would listen, included the pillars of society—doctors, lawyers, bankers, policemen. The perpetrators were cunning beyond belief in hiding their revolting activities. To indoctrinate children, cult leaders routinely used electric shock, isolation in closets, mind-altering drugs, and starvation. In addition, according to a pamphlet from VOICES in Action, a Chicago-based Survivor group, brainwashing included the "Black Hole" experience, in which members were "suspended head first into a dark deep pit, the pit containing human/animal parts, blood, rats, snakes, spiders, for up to 24 hours." Sometimes a child was given a "rebirthing ritual" in which he or she was inserted into a cow's abdominal cavity for a while, then pulled out by the high priest.

---

* In his classic 1972 book, *Folk Devils and Moral Panics*, sociologist Stanley Cohen defined the term "moral panic" as a period in which a group or phenomenon is regarded as "a threat to societal values and interests; its nature is presented in a stylized and stereotypical fashion by the mass media; the moral barricades are manned by editors, bishops, politicians and other right-thinking people; socially accredited experts pronounce their diagnoses and solutions."

In 1988, Lauren Stratford published *Satan's Underground,* which exerted a wide influence, despite Stratford's story having been thoroughly discredited by journalists for the Christian publication, *Cornerstone.** In the foreword to *Satan's Underground,* Christian author Johanna Michaelsen admitted that the story was "beyond belief," but explained "that attitude is precisely what Satanists are counting on." After all, "it was only a few short years ago that we had a problem believing that incest was rampant." Michaelsen was not dismayed by the complete lack of evidence of this widespread cult activity. "If there is one thing that cult Satanists do well, it's cover their tracks." Thus, she reasoned, "animals are indeed killed and buried, but are later dug up and disposed elsewhere." No Satanic child pornography had surfaced because it is "carefully kept in vaults of private collectors." And so on. There's no question: "Satanism is on the rise."

In the book itself, Stratford described how her sadistic mother allowed her to be raped by a group of tramps in the basement. That experience was just training for her teenage and young adult experience in a Satanic cult dominated by the evil Victor. The cult members drank a brew of blood, wine, and urine and then gang-raped her. "With each vulgar act, my will to resist lessened," she wrote. Later, she witnessed many other terrible events. "They ordered acts of sexual perversion that went far beyond the descriptions of lewd, perverse, and vile. They ordered the literal sacrifice of animals and even humans—both willing and unwilling victims." She watched "the ultimate sacrifice of a baby—skinned while still alive."

In order to break her, the cult members put Stratford into a barrel and threw dead babies on top of her. Then she became Victor's personal mistress. Only when the cult tired of her and she had a nervous breakdown did the reader learn, on page 120, that she had *entirely repressed all of these memories,* which came back with the help of guided imagery and Jesus. Eventually, she recalled how she had borne three children—Joey, Carly, and Lindy—all of whom were sacrificed to Satan. "What happened to Joey is even now happening to babies, children, and teenagers across the country," Stratford wrote. "Believe the unbelievable!" In the end, however, she was healed by meeting Johanna Michaelsen—the author of the book's foreword—who told her that while they were praying together, "I saw Jesus standing with His nail-scarred hands outstretched toward you."

Modern rumors of Satanic cults represented nothing new, but followed a long tradition in Western culture, as Norman Cohn documented in his 1975 book, *Europe's Inner Demons.* Beginning in the second century, early Christians were accused of "holding meetings at which babies or small children were ritually

---

* "Lauren Stratford" was in reality Laurel Willson, who, although she was clearly a very troubled individual, was not a victim of Satanic cults. The portrait that emerged from the meticulously researched article is of a sad, manipulative, attention-seeking individual. Similarly, in (1993), investigative reporters demolished the story of Mike Warnke, who claimed for years to have been a high priest in a Satanic cult.

slaughtered, and feasts at which the remains of these victims were ritually devoured; also of holding erotic orgies at which every form of intercourse, including incest between parents and children, was freely practiced; also of worshiping a strange divinity in the form of an animal."

The Christians outlived these defamations, only to use them on the Jews, who were supposed to have drunk Christian children's blood in their synagogues and carried on in other disgusting ways. The Catholic hierarchy and various monarchs spread similar rumors about any splinter sects, such as the Waldensians and the Templars. Belief in organized Satanic orgies flowered in the 16th and 17th centuries during the Great Witch Craze. Throughout the centuries, as Cohn described it, "the essence of the fantasy was that there existed, somewhere in the midst of the great society, another society, small and clandestine, which not only threatened the existence of the great society but was also addicted to practices which were felt to be wholly abominable, in the literal sense of anti-human." It was usually the intelligentsia who fomented these conspiracy theories and led the quest for Satanic abusers.

In our own time, that generalization held true. Ph.D. clinical psychologists and psychiatrists—trained as physicians and then mind-healers—were the primary agents to spread authoritative stories of ritualistic abuse and conspiracy. Psychiatrist Bennett Braun explained that "we are working with a national-international type organization that's got a structure somewhat similar to the communist cell structure." He asserted that cult members were "trained to self-destruct" if they remembered too much.

Corydon Hammond, the former president of the American Society for Clinical Hypnosis, was widely respected by his peers and edited a scholarly 1990 volume entitled *Handbook of Hypnotic Suggestions and Metaphors*. "Dr. Hammond is a master clinician of unusual breadth and talent who has become one of the giants in the field of clinical hypnosis," wrote a colleague in that book's foreword.* Hammond traveled throughout the United States, giving workshops on ritual abuse. He dismissed those who are "such intellectualizers and skeptics that they'll doubt everything." Alternatively, those casting doubt might be cult members themselves, he asserted. He described "very organized groups with interstate communication and who use a very, very systematic brainwashing."

Hammond stated that the cult members learned these brainwashing techniques from sadistic Nazi scientists secretly brought to this country by the CIA to conduct mind-control experiments. Drawing on a long tradition of anti-Semitic

* In the *Handbook*, Hammond recommends asking hypnotized MPD clients to raise their fingers in response to the question, "Is anyone inside afraid of...?" His list includes words that were supposedly indicative of a ritual abuse background, including *stars, fire, knives, blood, being photographed, dying, candles, feces, animals being hurt, robes, a certain color, eating certain things, digging in the dirt, Halloween, the equinox,* and *people in a circle.*

rumors, he also asserted that a Jewish teenager named Greenbaum learned the Nazi secrets and now, as a Dr. Green, was coaching cults in the United States. "I know of cases," Hammond said, "where the Mafia likes to use cult people as hit people because they can have one personality who will come out and ... perform a cult blood-cleaning and have no emotions about it, come back and everybody has amnesia for it." To train children in strict obedience, the cults might apply electrodes to a little girl's head and inside her vagina. "Perhaps a finger might be cut off and hung around their neck on a chain as a symbol to them they had better be obedient. They may be given drugs."

Psychiatrist Colin Ross, who wrote an influential 1989 textbook on MPD, agreed with Hammond. In fact, in his proposal for a book to be titled *CIA Mind Control*, Ross disclosed that the U.S. Central Intelligence Agency had been turning children into Manchurian candidates since the 1940s.* "These individuals were systematically abused in laboratory and experimental settings," he wrote. They used "drugs including hallucinogens, sensory deprivation, flotation tanks, electric shock, enforced memorization and other techniques. The programming involved the deliberate creation of multiple personality disorder with specific letter, number and other access codes for contacting alter personalities." In 1993, Ross reiterated his claims to a television journalist, explaining that the "political strategy" to counter his revelations was to assert that "it's all created in therapy, it's fantasy, it's not real."

The paranoia over "mind control" and Satanic ritual abuse took advantage of the modern fear of impersonal and seemingly all-powerful technology. Ever since the 1950s, when a con artist claimed that he could increase the consumption of popcorn and Coca-Cola by flashing "subliminal messages" on a movie screen, Americans have believed that their minds could be controlled by nefarious authorities without their knowledge. Therapists such as E. Sue Blume seized on "virtual reality" technology as an explanation of alien abduction memories. They were *really* just fooled by Satanic cults, according to Blume:

> These groups often employ sophisticated and elaborate special effects and computer-generated "virtual reality" to make people think that they have experienced things which have not really occurred. For example, a victim will "remember" being abducted by aliens to their ships, where "medical experiments"

---

* During the Cold War era of the 1950s and 1960s, the CIA did, in fact, experiment with hypnosis, Amytal, LSD and other mind-altering drugs in an attempt to create an unconscious killing machine or find a way to extract information from spies. As John Marks documented in his 1979 book, *The Search for the "Manchurian Candidate": The CIA and Mind Control*, the unethical secret experiments were complete failures, characterized by "bumbling and pure craziness." Therapists such as Colin Ross and Corydon Hammond took bits and pieces from Marks' book (such as his discovery that the Nazis tried out similar unsuccessful experiments) and recycled the myth of "mind control." *The Manchurian Candidate* was a popular 1959 book and 1962 film starring Frank Sinatra, popularizing the myth that someone could be "programmed" to become a killing machine when properly "triggered."

were performed.

In 1993, therapist David Calof, who published a newsletter, *Treating Abuse Today*, and co-authored *Multiple Personality and Dissociation: Understanding Incest, Abuse, and MPD*, helped an audience at the prestigious Menninger Institute understand the true meaning of a postcard sent by the sister of a woman who believed she had been ritually abuse by her family:

"Dear Sis, Mom and I have been thinking about you. Can't wait to see you again. In the meantime take care of yourself. Love, Sis." Calof explained that his client got this postcard and began to engage in "horrible self-harming behavior." Why? "Mom and I have been thinking about you" means that they can read her mind. What it really meant was, "No matter where you are, or what you are doing I will know if you tell." Then, "We can't wait to see you again." Calof explained: "Now you have to take this in context. This is a woman, the client is a woman who's on the lam from her family and the perpetrating group....She *knows* that if she goes back something terrible is going to happen to her." But the "most insidious part" was: "In the meantime take care of yourself." That was, of course, "an injunction to kill herself." This was a trigger to a mind control programmed by the cult.

That same year, Calof revealed that "we're finding a lot of undiagnosed, unrecovered multiples in nursing homes." He warned against doing abreactive work with an eighty-six-year-old, however. "I learned the hard way. One of my multiples had a stroke during an abreaction. Fortunately, she recovered."

Despite the lack of any physical evidence that Satanic cults exist, and many well-researched books debunking them, many therapists continued to tell stories about ritual abuse. An entire 1994 issue of the *Journal of Psychohistory* was devoted to the topic, with the overwhelming majority of the articles exhorting us to believe, believe. In this issue, one Albany, New York, psychiatrist explained how cult members "injected blood from a chalice into all her [his patient's] orifices and raped her six times each. A mother cat and her kittens were shot with a pistol and were buried with my patient in a coffin-like box. She was then removed, thrown into a lake, cleaned up and brought home." And, of course, she remembered nothing about all this until she entered therapy.

Also in 1994, in England, Tavistock Clinic consultant psychotherapist Valerie Sinason edited *Treating Survivors of Satanist Abuse,* including accounts from 38 professionals, mostly British. As in the United States, belief in ritual abuse was spread through a network of "experts," most of whom belonged to RAINS, the Ritual Abuse Information and Network Support, founded in 1989 with five members. The hysteria over ritual abuse spread rapidly, particularly after three British books came out: *Dance With the Devil,* by Audrey Harper (1990), *Children for the Devil: Ritual Abuse, and Satanic Crime,* by Tim Tate (1991), and *Blasphe-*

mous Rumours, by Andrew Boyd (1991). In February of 1992, Channel 4 aired *Beyond Belief,* a show featuring adult Survivors who had recovered ritual abuse memories, some through Christian "deliverance ministry." An 0800-number "helpline" available after the show received 191 calls, with thousands more failing to get through. Clearly, by that time, many British men and women had recalled abuse memories or were concerned about them. By the summer of 1993, RAINS claimed 150 members, all professionals working with purported ritual abuse victims.

In *Treating Survivors of Satanist Abuse,* RAINS founder and psychiatrist Joan Coleman related horrific recovered memory stories. "One survivor described being left alone, naked and cold, at the age of 4," she wrote, "for three weeks in an underground room, while her mother went abroad. Her only company was the corpse of a woman she had seen killed." Given water but no food (she was expected to dine on the cadaver), the little girl was "finally taken out by her father, who then sodomized her."

In "The Impact of Evil," another chapter of the 1994 book, British consultant clinical psychologist Phil Mollon told the dreadful tales of two ritual abuse clients. During four years of therapy, Helen, a 40-year-old schoolteacher, recalled (among other things) witnessing a man's throat being slit, after which cult members drank his blood from a ceremonial bowl. Mollon's reaction to her stories was "shock, disbelief, horror, dread and terror—including fear for my own safety." He anticipated skeptics who might think the memories untrue. "To counter such doubts, I can say that subsequent communications have provided a full and coherent picture of the ritual context of Helen's abuse."

For five years, Mollon also saw Mary, an Irish divorcee, during which time she developed multiple personality disorder, discovering "Hazel and her gang" within her, created to "ensure that she did not remember or reveal secrets of her childhood." Numerous traumatized child alters also wailed within. Hazel did not, of course, prevail. With Mollon's help, Mary recalled her father, dressed as Satan, raping her during a ritual abuse ceremony. As a "last resort," he suggested that she undergo a "drug-assisted abreaction" (presumably a sodium Amytal session), during which Mary did indeed spill out more tales of abuse. "Many further scenes of horror, macabre, obscene and criminal in the extreme, have since emerged," the therapist informed his readers. Might not Mary be hallucinating? "She does not feel to me to be paranoid," Mollon noted. "She comes across as a warm and caring person, coherent and rational."

"Neither patient nor therapist want to believe what is being communicated," Mollon emphasized. "Both parties have to overcome their inner resistance in order to recover the lost experiences." In closing, Mollon stressed that therapists must "maintain an open mind about what is real and what is phantasy," but it was quite clear where his beliefs lay. Besides, he wrote grandly, "I would rather risk being deluded by my patients—rather risk appearing a fool—than risk abandoning the terrified traumatized child within." In the United States, specialists such as Bennett Braun, Corydon Hammond, Colin Ross, and David Calof received enormous support from books, articles, and conferences where the myths of Satanic cults were repeated and elaborated. As skeptical Harvard psychologist Richard McNally observed wryly: "Trying to build a case for traumatic amnesia by citing numerous studies, all sharing the same fatal flaws, is a pointless endeavor."

In the final analysis, such therapists believed in the cults because they wanted to believe. The sessions in which menacing, evil alters appeared provided the same thrill which exorcists experienced hundreds of years ago. It was challenging, exciting, frightening work—a far cry from the humdrum existence of the routine mental health professional who listened to a boring litany of drab complaints all day long. Yes, it was difficult work—dangerous, in fact, because the cult members might even try to assassinate the therapist. But for the intrepid mind explorer, savior of souls, healer of splintered selves, it was all worthwhile.*

In 2015, Richard McNally summarized the flawed thinking of dissociative amnesia theorists, even in cases where some traumatic event may have occurred:

> They have confused everyday forgetfulness following trauma for an inability to remember the trauma itself. They have confused reluctance to disclose trauma with an inabililty to recall it. They have confused not thinking about something for a long time with an inability to remember it. They have confused failure to encode aspects of a trauma with inability to remember trauma. They have confused childhood amnesia and organic amnesia with dissociative amnesia. Ironically, the diagnosis of dissociative amnesia remains in the DSM-5 despite the absence of convincing evidence that the phenomenon exists.

Unsurprisingly, those eager to "prove" the reality of multiple personalities have attempted to do so with brain scans, which add an aura of indisputable scientific validity. Simone Reinders and colleagues acknowledged that "fantasy proneness and suggestibility are highly correlated, and dissociative symptoms were found to be correlated with fantasy proneness, heightened suggestibility, and susceptibility to pseudomemories." But they were out to prove that the alters were real, so they compared 11 Dutch women diagnosed with MPD/DID to 18 controls (10 of

---

* It is impossible to exaggerate the level of paranoia exhibited by ritual abuse believers. At the end of 1992, for instance, members of the Los Angeles Ritual Abuse Task Force claimed that Satanists were poisoning them with a toxic pesticide pumped into their offices, homes, and cars. Catherine Gould, a clinical psychologist on the task force, told a reporter that the gas had given her blurred vision and faulty memory. Gould should have gone back and read a 1945 article in the *Journal of Abnormal and Social Psychology* entitled "The 'Phantom Anesthetist' of Mattoon: A Field Study of Mass Hysteria," which revealed how citizens in Mattoon, Illinois, became convinced that a mad gasser was pumping a spray gun into their homes.

whom were "fantasy-prone"), who were asked to pretend that they had alternate personalities. "Brain imaging data, autonomic (systolic and diastolic blood pressure, discrete heart rate and heart rate variability (HRV) and subjective (controls' subjective sensorimotor and emotional experiences) reactions were obtained," Reinders wrote, as the subjects enacted a neutral as well as "trauma-related identity state." Her 2012 article then presented an impressive array of incomprehensible charts, numbers, and brain pictures and concluded that the DID subjects reacted differently from the control simulators. This indicated, they concluded, that "DID does not have a sociocultural origin."

That is an unwarranted conclusion. It is no surprise that someone who truly believes that they endured horrendous abuse, and who has rehearsed these "dissociated memories" repeatedly, with great emotion, should have thoughts and emotions that are different from those who are mere actors. Similarly, people who believe they have been abducted by space aliens respond with the same racing hearts and sweaty palms as combat veterans with PTSD, which "underscores the power of belief to drive a physiology consistent with actual traumatic experience," as Richard McNally put it.

Another 2012 study conducted by Rafaele Huntjens and colleagues compared 9 people with alleged DID to 27 normal controls and 23 controls told the simulate DID. All were asked to perform various memory tests, while the DID subjects "switched" between alters. They demonstrated that the various internal alternate personalities were not in fact amnestic towards one another. "The DID patients exhibited memory transfer across identities even though they did not realize it," they concluded. Richard McNally, one of the coauthors, later observed: "People with trauma histories may enact a DID role and simulate amnesia, but it is doubtful if they ever develop amnesia for their traumatic memories."

As Joan Acocella concluded in 1999 in *Creating Hysteria: Women and Multiple Personality Disorder*, "The study of MPD, then, is not a science but a belief system. And like other belief systems, it has become more entrenched in the face of criticism." Acocella was correct that true believers in MPD became even more entrenched in their convictions. But lawyer-psychologist Christopher Barden won multiple million-dollar judgments and settlements in the late 1990s against psychiatrists and other therapists who encouraged clients to believe that they housed destructive internal alters, had been abused in Satanic cults, and had completely forgotten it until they sought therapy as adults. These lawsuits had a dramatic impact, with most dissociative disorders closing down, insurance companies refusing to pay for such therapy, and many therapists losing their licenses. McNally, who wrote a comprehensive book, *Remembering Trauma* (2003) debunking repressed memories, appropriately inscribed a copy of his book to Barden, "the man who did more than anyone to stop the madness of MPD." *

A Warning from Thigpen and Cleckley

In 1984, just as the great MPD hunt was heating up, Corbett Thigpen and Hervey Cleckley, who started the ball rolling in 1957 with *The Three Faces of Eve*, saw what was coming and tried, in vain, to stop it. "Over the last 25 years we have had sent to us hundreds of patients, many of whom were either referred to us by therapists who had already diagnosed them as having the disorder, or who came to us for treatment based upon their desire or belief that they had the illness." Of these, they concluded that perhaps one was genuine. One woman phoned and "went so far as to have each personality introduce itself and speak in a different voice," while another changed her handwriting from one paragraph to the other.

"It seems that in very recent years," the psychiatrists lamented, "there has been even a further increase in the number of persons seeking to be diagnosed as multiple personalities—some patients move from therapist to therapist until 'achieving' the diagnosis." In addition, the psychiatrists noted "a competition to see who can have the greatest number of alter personalities." They objected to Billy Milligan's feigning MPD to get out of a rape conviction.** Thigpen and Cleckly added that "sexual child abuse ... can hardly be used as the core criterion for diagnosing multiple personality disorder." Finally, they concluded: "Everyone changes nearly all the time, and extreme swings of behavior and feelings are hardly unique to multiple personality disorder."

---

* Yet the MPD madness has continued. In 2016, for instance, an Australian man and wife were found guilty of abusing their young adult daughter, who was diagnosed with MPD and who claimed to have recovered memories of grotesque physical and sexual abuse, including being threatened with a chain saw, urinated on, locked in a storage box overnight, and held underwater, as investigative reporter Richard Guilliatt documented in a July 2017 article, "The Unbelievers," in *Weekend Australian Magazine*.

** In 1977, police arrested 22-year-old Billy Milligan for multiple rape. He turned out to be a marvelous actor and con artist who convinced a jury and author Daniel Keyes that he possessed wonderfully diverse alter personalities, including a diffident Brit and a sinister Slav. Luckily for Keyes, who wrote the best-selling *The Minds of Billy Milligan* (1981), Milligan magically "fused" in order to tell him his story, which included allegations that his sodomizing stepfather buried him alive, leaving a pipe over the boy's face for air, into which the sadist then urinated.

5   And a Little Child Shall Lead Them (and Be Led)

Is it not plain that the people had frightened their children with so many tales that they could not sleep without dreaming of the devil, and then made the poor women of the town confess what the children said of them?
—Francis Hutchinson, *Historical Essay Concerning Witchcraft* (1718), describing the 1669 "seduction" of 300 children in Mora, Sweden, which resulted in the burning of 85 "witches"

WHILE THE SEARCH FOR REPRESSED memories began in earnest only after the publication of *The Courage to Heal* in 1988, it was preceded and augmented by another witch hunt in which little children were led to accuse innocent adults of sexual abuse. Although this book focuses primarily on the adult recovery of supposedly repressed memories, the cases involving preschoolers are equally distressing, often resulting in unnecessarily traumatized children and lengthy jail terms for people who committed no crimes. As we will see, the two phenomena—induced child accusations and adult recovered memories—are not only parallel, but have often interacted with one another within the same family.

As a result of increased awareness of the true horrors of child abuse, Walter Mondale championed the passage of the Child Abuse Prevention and Treatment Act in 1974. This landmark legislation offered matching federal funds to states which passed their own laws mandating that doctors, psychologists, police officers, teachers, nurses, and other professionals report any suspected child abuse to the appropriate child protection agency. The act offered anonymity and immunity from prosecution to anyone reporting child abuse. Those who failed to report suspected abuse faced fines or prison sentences.

The legislation produced a self-sustaining bureaucracy of social workers, mental health experts, and police officers who specialize in rooting out sex abuse. The more cases they find, the more funds they receive, and the more vital their jobs appear. The result? Beyond question, many cases of actual abuse have been brought to light. But tragically, the legislation has also encouraged false accusations that have ruined the lives of innocent people, especially during the day-care sex abuse hysteria that began in the 1980s.

The day-care cases were eventually debunked, but a network of self-righteous child protective service workers blanketed America, eager to find offenses, even in cases where little or no evidence exists. A rumor or malicious allegation is enough to start the wheels rolling. Those seeking an exhaustive investigative report on the classic day-care cases should read *Satan's Silence: Ritual Abuse and the Making of a Modern American Witch Hunt (2001),* by Debbie Nathan and Michael Snedeker, describing how, in the authors' words, "the psychotic delusions of a few individuals were translated into public policy," as well as *We Believe the Children: A Moral Panic in the 1980s* (2015), by Richard Beck.

McMartin: the Day-Care Scandal Prototype

In August of 1983, in Los Angeles, Judy Johnson—diagnosed later as a paranoid schizophrenic—noticed that her two-year-old's bottom was red and decided that he had been sexually abused. She called the police. Although the boy could not speak in complete sentences, uttering only the occasional single word, the police assumed that the mother was correct. They did not question the diagnosis of sexual abuse, but at first, it wasn't clear who had sodomized the boy. Perhaps it had been someone in the park. Soon, however, after repeatedly questioning the child, the mother and police became more certain. It was 25-year-old Ray Buckey, one of his day-care teachers at the McMartin Preschool.*

Without further investigation or observation of the day-care center, on September 9 the local California police sent a letter to 200 McMartin parents, warning of "possible criminal acts" such as "oral sex, fondling of genitals, buttocks or chest area, and sodomy, possibly committed under the pretense of taking the child's temperature." As a result, concerned parents began questioning their children intensely. They also called one another and compared notes. The young children—most of whom were three or four—at first denied that anything bad had happened to them at the day-care center. Under a barrage of parental pressure, however, some began to tell stories of how they had been touched.

It is almost impossible to reconstruct how these rumors spread, but by the beginning of November, there was a full-scale panic among the parents, many of whom had taken their children to the police, who questioned them aggressively. Parents began to take their supposedly traumatized children to the Children's Institute International (CII), where Kee MacFarlane and other experts in child sexual abuse interviewed them, using leading questions, coercive techniques, and

---

* Throughout this chapter, I have used real names, since those involved have become public figures. Thus, Judy Johnson and Ray Buckey are correctly identified. All children's names have been changed, however. A 1995 docudrama, *Indictment: The McMartin Trial,* aired on HBO. Although the McMartin case made national headlines and sparked an epidemic of similar day care cases, it was not the first. That honor, starting in 1982, goes to Kern County, California, where 36 people were convicted of being in an alleged pedophile ring. Two died in prison. The others were eventually freed. The 2008 film, *Witch Hunt,* documents the case.

"anatomically correct" dolls. Eventually, over 350 children submitted to the CII "therapy." In *Satan's Silence,* Nathan and Snedeker offer a devastating description of the interview process at CII:

> To put the children at ease, the women [therapists] dressed, clownlike, in mis-matched clothes and multicolored stockings, and sat on the floor with the young-sters. They talked in gentle, high-pitched voices, and encouraged discussion about genitals and sexual behavior that young children hardly knew words for. And they used a new diagnostic device: "anatomically correct" dolls, which came with breasts, vaginas, penises, anuses, and pubic hair. The children were intro-duced to MacFarlane's collection of hand puppets.... The session became a scene of naked dolls with genitals touching, poking and threatening each other. Cloth penises were being inserted into mouths. "Did that happen? Ooh, that must have been yucky," MacFarlane said. "It didn't happen," corrected Tanya; "I'm just play-ing." There was talk of being spirited from the school to molesters' homes, though whether they were people's houses or doll houses was unclear. After prompting from MacFarlane, Tanya named Peggy Buckey as a witness to abuse.

The allegations expanded beyond Ray Buckey to include his sister Peggy Ann, his mother Peggy, his grandmother Virginia McMartin—a septuagenarian in a wheelchair—and three other day-care providers. MacFarlane and her cohorts soon elicited horrifying tales of how the Buckeys and other teachers had forced children to drink blood and urine and had killed animals in front of them, in what sounded like Satanic ceremonies.

Meanwhile, Judy Johnson's account of what her inarticulate two-year-old son was supposedly telling her became more graphic and bizarre. Ray Buckey had worn a mask and sodomized her son while sticking his head in a toilet. She also stated that he forced the boy to ride naked on a horse and molested him, while Buckey dressed alternatively as a policeman, fireman, clown, and Santa Claus. Her charges soon escalated to involve other McMartin Preschool teachers. They had purportedly jabbed scissors into the boy's eyes and shot staples into his ears, nipples and tongue; they had also killed a baby and made him drink the blood. (Other abusers Judy Johnson identified included male models she saw in maga-zines and strangers following her on the highway. Two years later, she was hos-pitalized for psychosis, and a year after that, she died of an alcohol-related liver disease.)*

Eventually, under intense questioning by therapists, parents, and police, many children came to believe that they had actually been molested, embellishing their

---

* In addition to her other mental problems, Judy Johnson may have suffered from Munchausen's Syndrome by Proxy (MSP), a phenomenon in which parents seek sympathy and attention through their children's fictional illnesses. While MSP occurs in some cases, in others the diagnosis has been used to accuse parents who are innocent and are seeking care for their truly ill children.

stories with wild accusations of having been abused in hot air balloons, on distant farms, in cemeteries, and in tunnels under the school.

Lawrence Pazder, the Canadian psychiatrist who co-authored *Michelle Remembers,* the 1980 book about repressed memories of Satanic cults, flew in to tell the police and parents how to spot ritual abuse. Soon, more and more parents and children were convinced that the McMartin Preschool was part of a Satanic cult ring of child pornographers and ritual abusers. Testifying before Congress in 1984, social worker Kee MacFarlane stated: "We're dealing with an organized operation of child predators," asserting that the preschool served as "a ruse for a larger, unthinkable network of crimes against children." In the McMartin case, as well as its numerous imitators, pornographic films and pictures were supposedly taken. None ever materialized.

The media unquestioningly lapped up the sensational McMartin story. Bumper stickers and placards asserting WE BELIEVE THE CHILDREN became popular, and widely quoted misinformation filtered out of California that "children never lie about such things." While the preliminary hearing dragged on for a year and a half before a trial even commenced, similar cases popped up all over the United States and Canada at other day-care centers, replicating many of the McMartin charges, with local variations. Because of unskeptical media coverage and information disseminated by new organizations such as Believe the Children, the necessary ingredients of ritual abuse—including child pornography, sexual "games," unlikely travel, chanting, cannibalism, drinking "magic" liquids, and animal sacrifice—quickly became a part of American folk culture.

A nationwide witch hunt was on in which parents, police, social workers and therapists refused to hear "No" from children. Convinced that the preschoolers had been terrorized into silence, the interrogators believed that only by encouraging, cajoling, and even threatening the children could the "truth" come out. It is possible that some children, in some of these cases, really had been abused. We will never know, however, because the suggestive questioning clearly contaminated the interviews. Under the barrage of pressure, most three- to five-year-olds eventually succumbed; many undoubtedly actually came to believe that their day-care providers had sexually abused them, even though no abuse had occurred.

Children's Suggestibility

Research by psychologists Stephen Ceci at Cornell and Maggie Bruck at McGill University, as well as others, casts light on how easily young children can come to believe in traumatic events that never occurred. For a comprehensive review of these studies, see Ceci and Bruck's 1995 book, *Jeopardy in the Courtroom: A*

Scientific Analysis of Children's Testimony. With minimal leading, one child in Bruck's study accused a pediatrician of trying to strangle her and of pounding a stick up her vagina with a hammer. Fortunately for the doctor, a video recording of his entire examination showed no such events. Similarly, when Ceci's researchers repeatedly asked a little boy whether his finger had ever been caught in a mousetrap, his initial denials turned into full-blown, convincing accounts of how and where his finger had been caught, how much it hurt, and who had taken him to the hospital. Even after his father told him that the mousetrap memory was a fantasy, the boy insisted to a television interviewer that his finger had really been mangled.

As Ceci observed, however, the relatively neutral questioning used in his Cornell studies pales in comparison to the browbeating many children have received from sex-abuse investigators. Ceci watched innumerable videotapes with dialogue such as the following: "I want to stop, I'm hungry, I want to get out of here," a child says. "I'll let you eat, I'll get you a popsicle," the interviewer responds, "but only after you tell me what I want to hear. I know you know. Don't tell me you don't know. I know you know." When the child insists, "No, I don't know, I never saw her do these things," the interviewer keeps berating the child. "Do you want us to tell your friends that you finked out on them, that you won't help them keep her in jail?"

These are exactly the kinds of coercive approaches used in the McMartin and other day-care cases. In their zeal to unmask perpetrators, the therapists and investigators did not consider that they could be leading the children. They were simply frustrated by the children's stubborn refusal to reveal the horrible things that had been done to them. Yet a subsequent study, using the same techniques, demonstrated that 80 percent of three-year-olds agreed, "Yes, it happened," after ten-minute interviews—not the weeks and months of prodding such preschoolers were subjected to in the day care cases.

Some of the actual interview transcripts are truly amazing. "Well, we can get out of here real quick if you just tell me," one investigator in the Kelly Michaels case said. "Come on, do you want to help us out?" The child refused, saying he hated the investigator. Finally, the child caved in, asserting that "I peed in her penis" and that "we chopped our penises off." Similarly, in the McMartin case, therapist Kee MacFarlane questioned a child who held a Pac-Man puppet. "We'll see how smart you are, Pac-Man. Did you ever see anything come from Mr. Ray's wiener?" The child answered, "He never did that to [me], I don't think." MacFarlane ignored him and kept insisting that he reveal what the emission tasted like. "I think it would taste like yucky ants," he hazarded hopefully. "Do you think it would be sticky, like sticky, yucky ants?" she suggested. "A little," the child conceded.

Often, the parents were recruited to help their children "disclose." In one case, for instance, parents were given a picture book about "Fuzzy the Rabbit," whose teacher started teaching the innocent bunnies "secret songs, secret touches on their tummies and bottoms," and warning them not to tell their parents. A fairy rabbit sprinkled "magic power" on Fuzzy, who then summoned the strength to tell his parents about the evil teacher, who was, in reality, a witch.

At around the same time that the day-care cases were making headlines, mothers in bitter custody or divorce cases began to accuse their husbands of having molested their children. Although some mothers deliberately led and instructed their offspring, more frequently they, too, believed that "something" must have happened, once the notion occurred to them. And in the overheated, paranoid atmosphere of the 1980s and early 1990s, that notion was not hard to come by. Having conceived the idea that their former husbands might have abused the children, the mothers replicated the same process of intensive questioning, then took their children to therapists and pediatricians to search for "validation" of abuse.

Similarly, school personnel, instructing children in good touch/ bad touch, sometimes suspected abuse because of a child's behavior or comments. Intense questioning led to a call to Child Protective Services, and the wheels were set in motion.

Most of the stories summarized in this chapter involve day-care centers, but there are hundreds of thousands of unpublicized cases in which parents have been jailed or had their children taken from them with no concrete evidence. Often, the parents were never even interviewed. In many ways, the cases involving small children are *worse* than those involving adults with recovered memories. Parents accused on the basis of repressed memories were at least able to raise their children and could take solace in the reality of those happier times. If they were sued, such older parents generally faced civil charges and could lose a great deal of money, but not their freedom. And such accused parents tended to be well-educated members of the middle or upper class who knew how to research their problem and seek appropriate help.

Many of the day-care workers accused by small children, on the other hand, were not terribly well educated or affluent. They were tried in criminal courts and sent to jail. And in many subsequent low-profile cases, falsely accused parents, teachers, and others didn't know what hit them. Many overworked public defenders strongly urge them to take plea bargains rather than risk decades in prison. And once they take a plea bargain, they are unable to appeal and put on sex offender registries that make it difficult to find a job or a place to live. In addition, in such cases children are stripped of their parents at a crucial developmental period.

Thomas McEachin, who served as a substitute janitor in a Pennsylvania day-care center when he was 18, wrote to me from jail in 1995. "I'm one of them people who was falsely accused." He wanted to take a lie detector test but was refused permission. "I've went up for parole 3 times since 1992 and each time I was turned down because I didn't finish the sex offender program. Well now that I completed the program the psychologist told me that he could not recommend me for parole because I'm in denial of my crime because I won't admit to it."*

McEachin's plight was typical of an on-going Catch-22 situation. Those who really *are* sex offenders usually play the prison game and say the right things in their counseling sessions. Innocent people, on the other hand, refuse to confess to a crime they did not commit, and they are routinely denied parole. And if they do finally get out of prison, they must pay to attend useless sex offender therapy sessions.

This chapter focuses mostly on the day-care cases, but I want to emphasize that the same process has put innocent people in prison throughout the United States. One of those men is Bruce Perkins of Texas. "It seems we have convinced the media that the day-care witchhunt is exactly that," he wrote from his cell in 1996. "Why can they not see that the same people have just moved their tent to the next location with the techniques learned in the big headline cases? How many of us will have to spend the rest of our lives in these hell holes because it is not politically correct to defend an individual who was very obviously falsely accused?"

Bruce and Carol Perkins, high school sweethearts, had two sons. Before the allegations surfaced, the Perkins' family was particularly close-knit. Then a daughter-in-law entered therapy in 1991 for depression and parenting difficulties. Soon she began to uncover supposedly "repressed memories" of abuse by her grandfather when she was a child, and she began to see signs of sexual abuse everywhere. After observing her children "playing doctor" with friends, she grilled them about possible molesters and soon accused several of their playmates and a cousin of abuse. Then, suspecting an adult perpetrator, she asked her four-year-old daughter whether "Pawpaw," her granddaddy Bruce, had ever touched her. She questioned her daughter repeatedly about what Pawpaw might have done, even though the child insisted that nothing had happened.

Finally, in the fall of 1992, the child gave in and told her mother something about Pawpaw Bruce. She frantically called the other daughter-in-law, who questioned her four-year-old daughter. Soon, Child Protective Services became involved, then the sheriff's department. The police questioned both granddaughters closely.

---

* In 1996 Thomas McEachin was diagnosed with keratoconus, a progressive eye disease that affects the cornea that can lead to blindness. McEachin also suffered from a seizure disorder that made it even more dangerous. He successfully sued the prison over lack of treatment but finally got a cornea transplant in 2009. I could find no trace of him in the prison system in 2016. He may have died while still incarcerated.

Fortunately, we have the tapes of a police detective's interviews with the grand-children. Though the children had already been coached by their mothers, the leading nature of the questions is obvious:

> **Interviewer:** Did he ever put anything wet [on your vagina]?
>
> **Child:** Uhh, no.
>
> **Interviewer:** How about, did he ever use any kind of oil or ketchup?
>
> **Child:** Ketchup.

Although Bruce Perkins may very well have put ketchup on the child's ham-burger, it is very unlikely that he poured the condiment onto the child's private parts. Elsewhere, the policeman asked how the child knew that Pawpaw Bruce had also molested her cousin. "Cause my momma told me," she answered.

Eventually, an elaborate set of horrifying accusations came out of these pro-tracted interviews. In October of 1991, Carol Perkins hosted a birthday party for her husband at their house, attended by over forty friends and relatives. Dur-ing the party, Bruce Perkins supposedly lured seven children, including three grandchildren, up to his bedroom, where he stripped them naked, smeared cake, ice cream, ketchup, and mustard on their privates, licked it all off, pushed Lego blocks inside them, took pictures of them, cleaned them up, and sent them all downstairs, with no one the wiser.

Adding to the improbability of this story are several facts. The bedroom door had no lock. Perkins was supposed to have abused a cat during the birthday mo-lestation, even though Carol Perkins hated cats and wouldn't have them in her house. Four of the seven children were not even at the birthday party. No photo-graphs or any other evidence were ever found.

Other allegations were even more preposterous. Perkins was supposed to have taken one granddaughter out to the chicken house and forced her to have inter-course with their dog, after which he cut off the dog's penis and squirted blood all over the child.

As of 2017, Bruce Perkins remains in a Texas prison. Carol visits him as often as she can.

Investigators for state social service agencies wield enormous and arbitrary power, and they are immune from prosecution for anything they do. In effect, they often operate like a mini-Gestapo. I was horrified by what one pragmatic lawyer wrote to me in 1994: "Social workers tend to be overworked, underpaid, undertrained, come from offices with insufficient budgets, and have to deal with people who won't cooperate with their investigations. If social workers were li-able for any alleged misdeed, they would spend half of their time in court.... It is conceivable that some states would be unable to continue their child protective services departments without the extension of immunity."

Once people begin to search for symptoms, they are usually easy to find. Just ask medical students who suspect they are contracting whatever disease they happen to be studying. When parents are told that any trouble their children may be exhibiting is probably due to sexual abuse, or when a pediatrician is told that the anus or vagina probably exhibits signs, the "symptoms" quickly become convincing. Nightmares, bedwetting, sexual play, or a reluctance to reveal the supposed molestation become evidence. Activities such as mutual masturbation and mock intercourse among children have been labeled deviant, abnormal behavior in our society, although these activities are quite common worldwide and are normally tolerated or ignored.*

Tiny white lines on an anus or a bump on a hymen have been labeled "consistent with abuse," even though research reveals precisely the same marks on many nonabused children. Highly educated and well-trained child abuse "experts" are confident that their clinical intuition and experience allow them to differentiate true from false allegations. Yet several controlled experiments have demonstrated their inability to do so. In one such study, the experts performed significantly *worse* than chance, rating the children who gave the most misinformation as the most credible and accurate.

The prior expectations of child interviewers can exert a major influence. In one Ceci study, preschoolers were shown a game-like event and then interviewed about it a month later. Some interviewers were told exactly what had happened, while others were misinformed. They were then asked to elicit the most factually accurate report from each child. Those with the correct information heard no inaccuracies. The others, however, managed to get 34 percent of the three- and four-year-olds to corroborate false events. Not only that, but the children became more and more sure of themselves as they were encouraged to repeat the stories.

But if the children's stories are untrue, where do they come from? Are children's imaginations really that morbid and lurid? The answer appears to be "Yes," as the Brothers Grimm undoubtedly knew. Most of the details elicited from the children are common motifs in normal children's fantasies. One study, conducted by child psychology researcher Frances Ilg and her colleagues, revealed that preschoolers are typically afraid of clowns, Halloween masks, ambulances, monsters

*   A 1991 study of normal sexual behavior in children revealed that 35.5 percent of the boys aged two through six, and 19 percent of the same-aged girls, touched their sex parts in public. In the same population, 22.6 percent of the boys masturbated with their hands, while 16.3 percent of the girls did. Finally, 43.5 percent of the boys and 48.4 percent of the girls had intentionally felt their mothers' breasts. More aggressive sexual play, such as imitating intercourse or inserting objects in a vagina or anus, were very rare in this study. Given the overt sexual questioning that children are subjected to in these cases, however, such unusual acting out might be expected, even in nonabused children. Related studies have shown that many normal preschoolers bathe with their parents and attempt to touch their parents' genitals. Another study found that, contrary to expectations, there was no difference in the level of sexual knowledge between sexually abused and non-abused children.

in the dark, animals, policemen, and burglars—all of which appeared regularly in the day care allegations. In addition, the preoccupation with eating feces, blood, or urine probably stem from children's concerns with toilet training or anything they perceive as forbidden.

The parallels with repressed-memory cases are clear. Indeed, in some instances, the cases use identical "recovered memory" tactics, such as when one therapist in the McMartin case explained to a child: "And so [for] some of the kids, what we do here is we try to improve their memory and we try to unlock their brain. Sometimes when you're real scared, your brain gets locked up.... You honestly don't remember some stuff. It gets stored right back here in the back of your filing cabinet in your brain under 'Z.'"

Even without such an approach, however, the day-care cases provide parallels with recovered memory in adults. Prior expectations on the part of therapists play a key role. In both cases, laundry lists of symptoms encourage people to look for signs of sexual abuse. For the adults searching for memories, these include common problems such as poor relationships, low self-esteem, or depression. For the children, they feature common disturbances in normal preschoolers such as fear of school, genital irritation, or incontinence. Once the abuse hunt has begun in earnest, a vicious cycle commences in which real "symptoms" of trauma are produced by the very process of uncovering the mythical abuse. For hours, children are repeatedly grilled by intimidating adults, asking about sexual matters the children have never even considered. They are then stripped naked while other white-clad adults poke around their vaginas and anuses. Is it any wonder that the children develop symptoms of post-traumatic stress syndrome, or that they begin to engage in sexualized play?

Consider this advice on examining boys suspected of being abused, given in 1990 by American pediatrician Carolyn Levitt: "To clarify the boy's definition of sexual acts, the physician can perform a rectal examination that includes the penetration of the boy's anus by the physician's gloved and lubricated examining finger.... This allows the boy to compare that sensation with the sensation of abuse." It is somewhat frightening to note that, by her own count, Dr. Levitt had examined over 4,000 children on suspicion of child abuse.

In the same year, a therapist suggested that in interviewing boys, clinicians should "tell the client that you are going to ask a series of questions that you don't want him to answer ... because he will probably be dishonest about them." These questions include: "What did it feel like the first time you put your finger or crayon or pencil inside your butt? Can you describe how your ('cum') seminal fluid tastes? When did you first become familiar with how your butt smells?"

Ironically, the children in these instances were indeed being sexually and emotionally abused by the therapists, officials, and medical personnel who were supposed to be protecting them, and they often developed long-term symptoms as a result, including anxiety, insecurity, insomnia, nightmares, fear of strangers, depression, rages, obsession with death, and suicidal impulses. These, of course, were then taken as proof that the original suspected abuse did, indeed, take place.

Abusing Kids in Outer Space and Other Allegations

Fortunately, the public gradually became aware of the hysteria surrounding the classic day care cases, especially after fine public television documentaries on the Little Rascals Day-care in Edenton, North Carolina, aired in 1991, 1993, and 1997. No one watching Ofra Bikel's *Innocence Lost* series could conclude that the day-care workers were guilty. The children's "disclosures" included tales of being thrown into shark-infested waters, taking trips to outer space, and worshiping the devil. The program included damning interviews with three jurors who, convinced that day-care provider Robert Kelly was innocent, finally yielded to group pressure and found him guilty anyway to avoid a hung jury. One of the jurors, it transpired, had been sexually abused as a child and had not revealed that fact during jury selection.

Despite this devastating, widely viewed documentary, however, Kelly remained imprisoned until 1995, when his case was finally overturned and he was released. Before his release, his wife Betsy pled "no contest"—still maintaining her innocence—rather than risk a trial. So did Willard Scott Privott, who owned a video and shoe-repair store and said he never even went into the day-care center. Dawn Wilson, the day-care cook, was convicted, but her case was overturned along with Robert Kelly's.

Kelly Michaels, once an aspiring young actress and day-care worker, was imprisoned for five years for alleged sexual abuse. She was finally released from prison after an appeals court overturned the conviction, questioning the reliability of the children's testimony.

As in most other day-care affairs, her preschoolers were subjected to leading, coercive questioning before they finally caved in and made bizarre allegations that Michaels had inserted various objects into their anuses, vaginas, and penises, including Lego blocks, forks, spoons, serrated knives, and a sword. Michaels was also supposed to have forced children to drink her urine, then removed their clothes so that she could lick peanut butter off their privates.

As an indication of shifting public awareness, Dale Akiki was exonerated late in 1993, after being held for two-and-a-half years without bail in a San Diego case. Akiki, who suffered from hydrocephalus, had an enlarged head and bug eyes, which probably led to the 1989 rumors that he had molested children while he provided child care during church services. In typical fashion, the children were taken for "therapy," where they revealed that Akiki had sodomized them with curling irons and toy firetruck ladders. They said that he had engaged in animal sacrifice, including the killing of an elephant and giraffe.

While many United States residents think of their neighbors to the north as progressive and enlightened, Canadians, too, fell for recovered memories and day-care hysteria in a big way. By far the most disturbing instance occurred in Martensville, Saskatchewan, where a two-year-old's 1991 diaper rash sparked the relentless grilling of children at a babysitting service. Eventually, the children asserted that they had been forced to drink blood and urine and to eat feces while locked in cages in "the devil's church." One boy said that an axe handle was forced inside his penis, while another said his babysitter had cut off a child's nipple and swallowed it. Two of the nine defendants were found guilty and are serving prison sentences. Many Martensville citizens remained convinced that a Satanic cult was operating in the area.

One day-care case was touted as proof that bizarre, sadistic abuse *does* occur. In 1984, 36-year-old Francisco Fuster-Escalona, a Cuban immigrant, and his 17-year-old Honduran wife, Ileana, were accused of molesting children in their home-based babysitting service in Country Walk, Florida, an affluent Miami suburb. The children were subjected to the usual coercive interviews and produced the familiar allegations—oral copulation and sodomy, mind-altering drugs, child pornography, and systematic terrorism. The Country Walk case was distinguished from others by three apparently damning facts: Fuster had been convicted in 1981 for fondling a nine-year-old girl; his six-year-old son tested positive for gonorrhea of the throat; and his wife confessed to the charges and accused him of abusing her as well.

Fuster vehemently denied the 1981 charge.* The other two pieces of evidence were seriously questioned by investigative reporter Debbie Nathan. First, she pointed out that the Centers for Disease Control and Prevention found that the test used for the son's throat gonorrhea was highly unreliable. More than a third of positive findings sent to the CDC came from children who did *not* have the disease. More disturbing, however, is the manner in which Ileana Fuster came to "confess."

---

* According to Fuster, he had attended a party along with Lydia Rivera, his sister-in-law's cousin. Lydia was babysitting for her daughter Laura's best friend, nine-year-old Ruth, while her mother went on her honeymoon. After discovering that his van had been towed and retrieving it late at night, Fuster ended up driving with Ruth in his van for ten minutes—she was supposed to keep him awake—as his wife followed them in her car. It turned out that Lydia's daughter Laura had been raped when she was five. Now the tipsy Lydia Rivera asked Ruth whether Fuster had molested her in his van. According to Lydia, the child denied it. "Well, men do things like that, you know," Lydia insisted. In the following days, Ruth and Laura discussed rape and molestation, and by the time her mother came to pick her up, Ruth was convinced that Fuster had molested her during their ride together. A year later, Ruth testified that she had complained of molestation that first night. Although Fuster passed two lie detector tests, the jury was never told, and he was found guilty.

Ileana, a frightened teenage immigrant, steadfastly maintained her innocence, as well as that of her husband, for nearly a year, despite being held naked in solitary confinement for much of the time. Her own lawyer, Michael von Zampft, pressured her to "confess" and turn state's evidence. Finally, Miami psychologist Michael Rappaport and his partner, Merry Sue Haber, who ran a business called Behavior Changers, were brought in to help persuade Ileana Fuster. During August and September of 1985, Rappaport visited Ileana in her cell at least 34 times, accompanied almost every time by Dade County State Attorney Janet Reno.

Rappaport led Ileana in guided imagery and visualization sessions. Her account of this process is revealing:

> [The two psychologists] explained to me that I was having problems and that they were there to help me.... They diagnosed that I was having blackout of events ... they came almost every day. And then I started seeing them at nights...I kept saying I was innocent but nobody would listen to me. And they said that I was suffering from a blackout and that those things had happened because the kids said it and the kids don't lie.... And you know, before I know it, I was having nightmares.... And they said that that was a way of my system remembering what had actually happened. And then you know, I argue that a little bit, but I got to a point that I was believing that probably those things happened and I just didn't remember because they were so shocking.

The teenager finally confessed, while Reno held her hand and offered encouragement.* Eventually, Ileana came up with suitably outrageous allegations. Her husband had given her drugs and sodomized her with a cross, she said, while he had forced her to give oral sex to a child.

Having confessed, Ileana Fuster was never tried. She did, however, testify against her husband. Before she took the stand, she met with her psychologists to rehearse her testimony. "They didn't want me to make no mistakes, they said," she explained later. Ileana served three years in prison and was then released and sent back to Honduras. In her speech in court during sentencing, she told the judge, "I am pleading guilty not because I feel guilty, but ... for my own interest.... I am innocent of all those charges.... I am pleading guilty to get all of this over."

Francisco Fuster was found guilty and sentenced to six life terms and 165 years in prison. He remains having survived several attempts on his life. A book, *Unspeakable Acts* (1986), which was made into a 1990 movie, presented the abuse as completely factual. The resulting celebrity helped to cinch Reno's reelection, and her reputation as a child advocate later propelled her to the office of U.S. at-

---

* In 1991, Rappaport told journalist Debbie Nathan that Janet Reno had accompanied him on most of these visits. When Reno was nominated for U.S. attorney general and became a national figure, Rappaport retracted his statement. Reno denied being present during the guided imagery sessions.

torney general.* Soon afterward, in her zeal to prevent child sexual abuse inside the Branch Davidian compound in Waco, she sanctioned an attack that resulted in the death of all those inside, including the children.

For a few weeks in 1994, it appeared that Fuster would be granted a new trial. His lawyer flew to Honduras and took a deposition from Ileana in which she retracted her confession and accusations, making it abundantly clear how she was led into making them. Unfortunately, she subsequently became frightened of repercussions and retracted her retraction. Fuster remained in prison.

The Child Sex Abuse Panic Hits the U.K.

While the McMartin case commenced in 1983, it took four more years before a similar full-blown case exploded in the United Kingdom. By the time it did, however, the atmosphere was ripe. Throughout the early and mid-1980s, British concern with childhood sexual abuse grew dramatically, as Philip Jenkins documented in his 1992 book, *Intimate Enemies: Moral Panics in Contemporary Great Britain.* In the early 1980s, Judianne Densen-Gerber, the American "expert" who believed that there was a vast international child pornography industry that abducted children for "snuff" films, flew to England to fan such unfounded fears. Awareness of *real* childhood abuse and neglect also grew, particularly in 1984, when four-year-old Jasmine Beckford was starved, beaten, and ultimately killed by her stepfather in the London Borough of Brent, rekindling memories of the 1973 death of Brighton's seven-year-old Maria Colwell.

Such cases provided emotional ammunition for British feminists such as Emily Driver, who began the Child Sexual Abuse Prevention Education Project in 1984. The same year, an influential conference on childhood sex abuse was held at Teesside Polytechnic, with speeches by American researchers such as Ann Burgess, who explained how to use children's drawing to diagnose sex abuse and who warned about pedophile sex rings. In the same year, the National Society for the Prevention of Cruelty to Children (NSPCC) celebrated its centennial and revitalized its mission and fund-raising by sounding the alarm about childhood sexual abuse. Also in the early 1980s, consultant child psychiatrist Amon Bentovim became a vocal spokesman about the dangers of child sexual abuse, and he diagnosed hundreds of such cases at the Great Ormond Street Hospital for Sick Children in London. His interpretation of children's "disclosures" is illustrated

---

* As the Dade County State Attorney, Janet Reno also spearheaded another sex abuse case in which a 13-year-old boy, Bobby Fijnje (pronounced FAIN-ya) was accused of molesting children while he babysat them at a church. In a familiar scenario, it all started with one child's vague nightmares, then rapidly escalated when the children were questioned intensively. Reno insisted on trying the adolescent as an adult, meaning his name could be released to the media, and he could be incarcerated. Eventually, after one of the longest criminal trials in Dade County history, Fijnje was found innocent.

by his response to a child who told him, "Daddy hit me with a wet fish." It may sound like a fantasy, the psychiatrist says, but in fact it represents the child's "coping" with his father hitting him with his penis. Bentovim was a member of the CIBA Foundation working party that published *Child Sexual Abuse Within the Family* in 1984 amidst a barrage of publicity. Slogans such as "Believe the children" and "Breaking the silence" became commonplace expressions.

In 1985, Channel Four broadcast three different films about the sexual exploitation of children. The same year, American educational psychologist Michelle Elliott, who was living in Sussex, developed the Child Assault Prevention Program for British schools, and a video (imitating a similar American production) called *Strong Kids, Safe Kids* was distributed by National Children's Homes. The following year, Channel Four aired *A Crime of Violence,* produced by filmmaker Audrey Droisen of the Feminist Coalition Against Child Sexual Abuse. Meanwhile, doctors from the Great Ormond Street Hospital and executives from the NSPCC were planning the Child Sexual Abuse Bexley Experiment, in which police and social workers were taught "disclosure work" with children. They were sensitized to the sex abuse experience through dramatic role playing and hypnotic regression. In October of 1986, popular television personality Esther Rantzen aired a special on child sex abuse, subsequently sponsoring "ChildLine," a telephone hotline for abused children. It received 50,000 calls on opening day, and the media publicity was intense.

Finally, that same year of 1986, two Leeds pediatricians, Chris Hobbs and Jane Wynne, published an influential article in the prestigious British medical journal *Lancet* in which they championed California pediatrician Bruce Woodling"s "anal wink test." Actually, variations on this purported indicator of sodomy had a long history in England stemming back to the 19th century, so in a sense it was "coming home," rechristened the "reflex anal dilatation (RAD) test" to avoid the somewhat off-color notion of the anal sphincter winking at doctors. "Buggery in young children," wrote Hobbs and Wynne, "including infants and toddlers, is a serious, common and under-reported type of child abuse."

It was in this highly charged atmosphere that, in 1987, the first major panic commenced in the British county of Cleveland. In January of that year, Australian physician Marietta Higgs arrived as a consultant pediatrician, bringing with her the RAD test, which she taught to fellow physician Geoffrey Wyatt. Within the next five months, the two of them diagnosed 121 local children from 57 families as victims of sexual abuse. They were reinforced by Sue Richardson, the local "child abuse consultant," and Deborah Glassbrooke, a veteran of the ChildLine organization, who established a sex abuse therapy center at the Middlesbrough General Hospital. Quickly, children were removed from their homes. By the end of June, over 200 children had been referred to social services. Though some actual sexual abuse probably had occurred in Cleveland, the cases became so contaminated by the bogus test and leading interviews that it was impossible to determine the truth.

Eventually, the sex abuse hunt in Cleveland collapsed under its own weight, as numbers grew to crisis proportion. The Cleveland police remained extremely skeptical of the "evidence" of the RAD test. Manchester police surgeon Raine Roberts criticized Higgs and Wyatt, observing that their test itself constituted "outrageous sexual abuse" of the children. Dr. Hamish Cameron, a child psychiatrist, offered insightful testimony during the Cleveland inquiry, chaired by Judge Elizabeth Butler-Sloss. "Whenever a new "illness" or treatment is described, a flurry of excitement develops amongst professionals. This has certainly been the case with child sex abuse. However, in addition to the normal excitement generated by any "new" condition, there is an added voyeuristic component arising from the universality of interest in sexual matters."

The lengthy Butler-Sloss report, published in 1988, determined that the critics were basically correct, though it tried to apportion blame equally to everyone involved, treating the disaster as a matter of professional disagreement rather than a misguided witch hunt. The report scored Raine Roberts, for instance, for failing to take a "balanced" approach. Unfortunately, many of the key recommendations of the report were equivocal. It suggested, for instance, that police and social workers should train and work together rather than fight one another. The ironic result was that uncritical belief in pedophile rings spread to the police.

The British Ritual Abuse Fiasco

With the Cleveland debacle receiving such coverage in the British media, one would think that the sex abuse panic would have ceased in England. Such was not the case. Feminists, social workers, and evangelical Christians bound together in an odd alliance to declare that the Cleveland children had really been abused after all, that the authorities were covering it up, that if a witch hunt was on, it was directed against the poor social workers and pediatricians. That same year of 1987, Glasgow University sponsored a child abuse conference on the theme, "Learning from the American Experience," featuring several American experts on sexual abuse, such as Lucy Berliner of Seattle's Harborview Sexual Assault Center. Arnon Bentovim, of the Great Ormond Street Hospital, defended the use of leading questions under some circumstances. Feminist journalist Beatrix Campbell published *Unofficial Secrets,* a 1988 book defending the Cleveland affair and hailing it as the tip of the iceberg of hidden child sexual abuse.

The harbinger for things to come occurred in Nottingham in 1987, the same year as the Cleveland case. It is unclear how much real sexual abuse took place in Nottingham, but there is no question that the Satanic ritual abuse elements—including animal sacrifices, blood being drunk, and adults in ritual robes raping children—were inadvertently planted by overzealous interviewers. In 1988, Ray Wyre helped out. The head of the Gracewell clinic for sex offenders, ex-probation officer Wyre lectured widely about an international ritual abuse network, educating police, social workers, and NSPCC members. He now gave Nottingham social workers Christine Johnson and Judith Dawson a list of "Satanic indicators" he had in turn received from American sources. As it became clear that something was amiss, an inquiry was held. The damning report, suppressed by the Nottinghamshire social services and the Department of Health, concluded that "witch hunts could develop in this country and grave injustice result."

The ritual abuse hysteria was coming to a head by the end of the 1980s. In 1989, ritual abuse was a major theme at three conferences at Reading, Dundee, and Harrogate. Sponsors included the Association of Christian Psychiatrists, and speakers included Americans such as cult cop Jerry Simandl and therapist Pamala Klein, as well as Marietta Higgs and Maureen Davies, a ritual abuse believer who was part of a Christian anti-cult organization called Reachout. In December of 1989, Nigel Bartlett published "Facing the Unbelievable" in the British social work journal *Community Care*, summarizing all of the major ritual abuse dogma. "One of the most damaging reactions a social worker or any other professional can have is disbelief," he wrote. "Trust is eighty per cent of the treatment." Bartlett asserted that "children are being used in Satanic rituals in towns and areas such as Hull, Surrey, Wolverhampton, Telford, Portsmouth, Manchester and Shrewsbury." In 1990, Beatrix Campbell produced a *Dispatches* documentary dramatizing the purported perils of ritual abuse, and the NSPCC issued a statement that "evidence is mounting of child pornography, ritualistic abuse and sex rings involving children."

The stage was set for a series of ill-advised child-snatches in 1990 and 1991, beginning in Manchester, then Rochdale, Merseyside, Epping Forest, and Ayrshire and the Orkney Islands in Scotland. The Rochdale debacle, typical of these cases, began when a troubled six-year-old boy told frightening stories about ghosts and the living dead. Social workers, convinced that he was the victim of a Satanic cult, began the inevitable round of coercive child interviews. Eventually twenty children from six families were taken from their parents. It turns out the boy had been watching horror videos such as *The Evil Dead.*[*]

The Orkney Islands crisis proved to be so absurd that it prompted a widespread

---

[*] In most cases, the children in these cases actually came to believe in their accusations. In a few American and British cases, however, they later admitted to simply lying under immense pressure.

awareness that social services had run out of control. Without any investigation, social workers and police launched a pre-dawn raid on Feb. 27, 1991, removing nine children from four families. Medical examination of the children revealed no evidence of abuse. The terrified children begged to be returned to their parents. The charges appeared ridiculous—an elderly Church of Scotland minister was supposed to have held large Satanic meetings in a local quarry. In a small island community such as South Ronaldsay, the chances of keeping such abuse secret were virtually nil. Fortunately, the children were returned to their homes in April after a quick judgment by sheriff David Kelbie, to be followed by a scathing report by Lord Clyde. As pediatrician D. H. S. Reid observed in *Suffer the Little Children,* his book on the Orkney case, it repeated a similar witch hunt on the islands four hundred years ago. "How many times have we been here before?" he wrote plaintively.

Yet social workers continued to use the same anatomically correct dolls and the same leading interview techniques, with devastating results. *Poppies on the Rubbish Heap,* a 1991 book by Madge Bray, a British social worker, provided evidence that little had been learned by some professionals. She looked back nostalgically to the 1980s, when "the beginning of a body of knowledge was emerging and we devoured new treatment methods (mostly American) greedily." Since Bray and her associates completely believed in these new "disclosure" methods, and sincerely thought they were only helping children to reveal real abuse, they were bewildered by attacks in the media and courts. "It's the bits about us interrogating children. It's the language I object to. I mean, Kafka-esque ordeals and all that," complained a fellow social worker to Bray. "That's the exact opposite of what we do, what we teach, what we're all about!"

With such blindness and entrenched belief systems, it is not surprising that the Pembroke scandal in West Wales commenced in 1991, resulting in the incarceration of six men in 1994. Ann Done, the social worker for a troubled eight-year-old living with his single mother, decided, with minimal evidence, that the child might have been molested. She commenced "direct work" with him, an imported American technique involving dream interpretation, drawing, and questions about his past. Later, he underwent "disclosure work." In October of 1991, the ubiquitous Ray Wyre organized a three-day workshop at the Gracewell Institute for the Pembroke investigative team. The same month, guidelines for abuse cases were issued by the Department of Health suggesting that police and social workers work more closely together in these cases.

In December of 1992—two years after Ann Done began to question the first boy—the arrests began. Eventually, 18 children were taken from nine families, and 11 men and two women were charged. The case came to trial in January of 1994, with the adults accused of "the most depraved and revolting conduct imaginable," according to the prosecution. They had purportedly conducted ritual sex orgies in various homes, sheds, tunnels, seaside caves, and boats at sea, and pictures and videotapes were made at these events. Yet no photos or videos ever emerged. There was no physical evidence. No child had alleged abuse prior to interviews by social workers. And several accusers recanted on the witness stand, one child revealing that the social workers told him that he could not go home unless he admitted the abuse. Nonetheless, only one man won his appeal; the rest remained in prison.

Another case popped up in Bishop Auckland, built on what was apparently a real case of a 14-year-old molester. By this time, the unfortunate effects of the joint training guidelines were evident. It was not simply the social workers, but the police and Crown Prosecution service, who were sucked into the ritual abuse panic. In contrast to many American cases, British law enforcement officers and prosecutors had previously been quite skeptical of the hysteria, demanding firm evidence. In Pembroke and Bishop Auckland, joint training sessions—ironically, one of the suggestions following the Cleveland and Orkney inquiries—apparently infected the police and lawyers as well, binding them together in a closed circle of belief in ritual abuse. Soon, they were hearing and believing tales of voodoo ceremonies featuring devil-worshiping adults and genital mutilation with fish hooks. Fortunately, by January of 1995, the bizarre case collapsed before reaching trial, when the Crown, represented by David Robson QC, determined that it was unwinnable.

In the wake of the 1994 La Fontaine report that found no evidence of British ritual abuse cults, one would think that belief in such myths would have disappeared in the United Kingdom, but British believers in ritual abuse continued to hold conferences and assure one another of its reality. Journalist Margaret Jervis, who later trained as an attorney, accurately predicted more mass false abuse cases. "Satan appears in many guises," she noted ironically in 1996. "Now they are simply redefining ritual abuse under vague headings such as 'organized abuse.' I think foster carers and institutional 'trusted adults' are next in line." The North Wales care home scandals, thoroughly documented by Richard Webster in *The Secret of Bryn Estyn: The Making of a Modern Witch Hunt* (2009), showed that Jervis was correct.

Searching for Abuse Down Under and Elsewhere

The same pattern of sex abuse panic and unjust prosecutions occurred in New Zealand and Australia. In 1987, for instance, a New Zealand mother in a bitter custody dispute accused her ex-husband of molesting their four-year-old twins. Using anatomically correct dolls, the social worker attempted to elicit disclosures. The taped interview is disturbing:

Social worker: Did Daddy ever put his diddle near your vagina?

Child: (laughing): No.

Social worker: Can you show me how he did that?

Child: But my Dad didn't do it.

Social worker: Your Dad didn't? Who did?

Child: Nobody …

Social worker: Cathy, when you go and see Dad, I wonder if Dad sometimes makes your vagina sore?

Child: No, he doesn't.

Social worker: If he did, it would be okay to tell me.

Child: He doesn't.

Social worker: But Mummy said you had a sore vagina.

Child: Yeah, I used to.

Social worker: We want to help so you don't get any more sore vaginas.

Child: I used to have one, but now it's gone. I used to have one at home at Mum's.

Despite these repeated denials, the social worker persisted, calling the mother into the room to help out. Eventually, the girl relented and said her father had touched her vagina. The mother and social worker praised her for being a "good brave girl."

By that year, a sex abuse therapy center had opened in Christchurch. Its brochure warned parents to expect their children's behavior and mental state to deteriorate as "disclosure" proceeded. Therapy, they explained, would get "all the pain, bad memories, worries, fears and feelings out into the open."

In 1992, Peter Ellis, who worked at the Civic Daycare Centre in Christchurch, was charged with sexual abuse. After the day-care children underwent disclosure interviews, the charges escalated. Ellis had supposedly made them drink his urine and eat his feces. He had raped one girl, violated others with his finger or a stick, and urinated on their faces for good measure. He allegedly stuck a needle into one child's rear end, making it bleed. When Ellis's four female coworkers denied that these events could have occurred, they, too were charged with abuse. Many allegations similar to the McMartin case cropped up. The children had supposedly been taken to a private home, had been molested in tunnels under the house, had been forced to stand naked in a circle of adults, and had been used in producing child pornography.

Eventually, all charges against the women were dropped, but Peter Ellis stood trial, despite a complete lack of physical evidence, and was found guilty in 1993 of 16 out of 25 allegations. He lost his 1994 appeal, despite one of the children, then 11, spontaneously coming forward to say she had lied in court. The Appeal Court observed, "We are by no means satisfied that she did lie at the interviews, although she may now genuinely think she did."

In Australia, the "Mr. Bubbles" case broke in Sydney in 1989, followed by the Mornington Childcare case in Victoria in 1991. In both cases, the day-care providers were supposed to have taken children away from the schools and abused them, though there was never any supportive physical evidence. Also, as in many other day-care cases, the abusers were supposed to have dressed up in bizarre costumes to perform their perversions upon the children. All charges were eventually dropped in the Mr. Bubbles case. The owners of the Mornington Childcare and Nursery School were never formally charged, but their business was destroyed anyway. At a closed administrative hearing of the Office of Preschool and Child Care Community Services of Victoria, their license was revoked. A clinical psychologist testified that she felt abuse had indeed occurred—based solely on her second-hand reading of parents' statements. No children ever testified.

Nor were the day-care hysteria cases limited to English-speaking countries. In the late 1980s and early 1990s, such cases popped up in the Netherlands, Denmark, Sweden, Norway, and Germany as well. In the Bjugn, Norway, case, British influences helped fan the flames. In November of 1992, while visiting Trondheim, near Bjugn, Arnon Bentovim of the Great Ormond Street Hospital first concluded that there was a Norwegian "pedophile ring" at work. The following year, Eileen Vizard of the Tavistock Clinic and Ray Wyre of the Gracewell Institute attended a conference in Bergen, where they, too, reinforced belief in widespread abuse. Eventually, the repeatedly interviewed Bjugn kindergarten children named numerous abusers, including the local chief of police. Some of the children described adults standing in circles masturbating into buckets, dressing up as ghosts or pirates, and having sex with animals in barns. In the final event, only one teacher was tried, and he was acquitted.

The "child abuse industry" had spread throughout the Scandinavian countries, as Swedish psychologist Lena Sjogren observed, with inflated abuse figures and a reversed burden of proof in which the accused had to prove their innocence rather than the prosecution having to prove them guilty. It appeared that the American and British "expert" influence was a ticking time-bomb with a delayed fuse.

The Fells Acres Nightmare

In 1986 three innocent people—Gerald "Tooky" Amirault, his sister Cheryl LaFave, and his mother, Violet Amirault—were found guilty of horrendous sexual abuse and sentenced to prison in Massachusetts. The Amiraults' troubles began one sunny spring day in 1984, when four-and-a-half-year-old Murray Caissie, a newcomer to the long-established Fells Acre Day Care Center in Malden, Massachusetts, wet himself during his nap. Deeply embarrassed, he was happy when Tooky changed his pants, cleaned him up, and provided him with alternate clothing kept on hand for such emergencies. Murray carried his wet underwear and pants home in a plastic bag. Nothing more was said of the incident.

Over the summer, Denise Caissie took Murray out of the day-care, but she wrote a note of thanks to Violet Amirault, asking her to hold a place for her son in the fall. All was not well in the Caissie household, however. Murray's father, an unemployed custodian with a violent temper, moved out in April of 1984, returned in October, then left again. Murray had always had a bed-wetting problem, but it worsened that spring. He began to imitate the baby-talk of his 16-month-old brother and to act up more often. One night when Murray was crying because he had trouble urinating, his mother told him how one of her brothers had been molested at camp and how Murray should tell her if anyone ever did that to him. The events that followed are unclear, because several conflicting versions were presented in court. What is undisputed is that on Sunday, September 2, the eve of Labor Day, Denise Caissie called a Department of Social Services (DSS) hotline to complain that a man named Tooky had taken her son to a "secret room" and molested him. It was almost exactly a year after Judy Johnson had sparked the McMartin case.

The following day, two Malden policemen came to the school to request a list of all the children. Violet Amirault sensed that the school, which had been her life for the last 20 years, was in jeopardy, and she protested angrily. "I'll have you people shut down," one of the policemen told her. And he did.

On Wednesday, September 5, two days before the birth of his third child, Gerald Amirault was arrested on rape charges, without anyone ever questioning him. A week later, the police summoned over a hundred parents to a meeting at the station. There, social workers passed out a laundry list of behavioral symptoms which they said might indicate sexual abuse—bedwetting, nightmares, poor appetite, crying on the way to school—and asked parents to report any such problems. Very quickly, about 40 cases surfaced.* Of the children questioned, 19 eventually corroborated, after many sessions, that Miss Vi, Miss Cheryl, and Tooky had molested them in grotesque ways. (They also named most of the other teachers, as well as a mythical Mr. Gatt, but they were never arraigned.) Only nine of the most believable children testified in the trial.

---

* Frantic parents looking for symptoms also had a financial incentive: a $300,000-per-year-per-child insurance policy covered molested children at the day care. Eventually, 18 families would receive about $20 million collectively, over their lifetimes. Money was a motivating factor in some cases because of Victims Assistance programs, a well-meaning source of funds for crime victims which has, unfortunately, been misused in false accusations of sexual abuse.

The investigators had help. Prosecuting attorney Lawrence Hardoon traveled to California to talk to the McMartin trial team and came back full of information and ideas. Not so coincidentally, the children's allegations took on many of the same ritualistic, bizarre aspects. Like Ray Buckey, Gerald Amirault had supposedly dressed as a clown. Whereas the McMartin molesters had taken the children to tunnels underneath the school, Amirault had performed his sodomy, forced fellatio, and assorted other disgusting acts in a "magic room" hidden somewhere in the day-care center. Pediatric nurse Susan Kelley, who published widely about the horrors of ritual abuse, conducted leading interviews with many of the children.

Like Kee MacFarlane in the McMartin case, Susan Kelley refused to take no for an answer. Here is a slightly edited excerpt from one interview, in which she used Bert and Ernie puppets:

Susan Kelley: Would you tell Ernie?

Child: No.

Kelley: Ah, come on [*pleading tone*]. Please tell Ernie. Please tell me. Please tell me. So we could help you. Please.... You whisper it to Ernie.... Did anybody ever touch you right there [*pointing to the vagina of a girl doll*]?

Child: No.

Kelley: [*pointing to the doll's posterior*] Did anybody touch your bum?

Child: No....

Kelley: Would you tell Bert?

Child: They didn't touch me!

Kelley: Who didn't touch you?

Child: Not my teacher. Nobody.

Kelley: Did any big people, any adult, touch your bum there?

Child: No.

Another exchange with a four-year-old shows how Susan Kelley jumped on any comment that might lead to a stereotyped accusation—in this case, the notion that day-care abusers took pornographic photos of naked children:

Kelley: How about when you went to school at Fells Acres, did anybody look at your vagina?

Child: No.

Kelley: Ohh. Did anybody at Fells Acres ever touch your vagina?

Child: No. They took down our pictures.

Kelley: What pictures?

Child: The pictures hanging on the walls.

Kelley: Ohh. Who took your picture?

Child: Not pictures of us—the pictures we drew!

Kelley: Ohh. Did anybody take pictures of girls with their clothes off?

Child: No.*

In testimony before a grand jury, Denise Caissie asserted that Tooky had taken her son out of his classroom to this magic room every day. The evil Amirault also supposedly forced the boy to drink his own urine in front of his teachers, though none of the teachers witnessed such a thing; nor had they ever heard of a magic room, or remembered Tooky taking the child out of the classroom. Judge Elizabeth Dolan presided over the 1986 trial, pioneering in an attempt to spare the children—who were two to five at the time of the alleged abuse and now a year and a half older—from normal confrontive courtroom procedures. The public was barred from the courtroom. Children were seated in little plastic chairs at a miniature table. To make herself less threatening, Dolan removed her black robes and perched on a small chair next to them. The children were positioned so that they did not have to see the accused, and their parents were allowed to sit just behind them to lend moral support. Rules against leading the witness went out the window for the children. When Hardoon asked the children if they had been abused, they often answered that they had not. With sufficiently pointed questions, however, they usually came around. Defense attorneys had to whisper objections. Judge Dolan routinely disallowed them.

The clear presumption was that the day-care providers were guilty, that these children had been so terrorized and abused that the leading questions were justified, and that to subject them to normal courtroom procedures would be to "retraumatize" them. It did not seem to occur to anyone that the children were being psychologically traumatized by the Department of Social Services, the police, and the court, and that they might sustain life-long psychic scars as a result.

Logic, in fact, had little to do with the trial. Children said that they had told their teachers they were going to a magic room, even though no teacher had heard of such a room. They told stories of attacks by a robot, being forced to eat a frog Miss Vi had killed, and being molested by clowns and lobsters. One boy told how he had been tied naked to a tree in the school yard in front of all the teachers and children. Though the teachers denied the incident, and no other child verified it, Amirault was found guilty of other offenses this child recounted—how Tooky had

---

* Susan Kelley's persistence and obvious belief that abuse had occurred isn't surprising, given her published remarks on the reality of Satanic ritual abuse. In 1989, she wrote that ritualistic abuse was "often characterized by forced ingestion of human excrement, semen or blood; ceremonial killing of animals; threats of harm from supernatural powers; ingestion of drugs or 'magic potions'; and use of Satanic songs, chants or symbols."

raped him with a thick pointed stick which looked like a gun, for instance.* Even the accused man's nickname, which derived from the sound his mother made when she chucked him under the chin as an infant, came to sound sinister and revolting in Hardoon's mouth. "Yes, and what else did *Tooky* do to you?"

At one point during the trial, an explicit link between the theory of repressed memories and the day care case was made, though no one questioned it. Lead therapist Renee Brandt, who assisted with children's interviews, testified that "a child begins to disclose the sexual abuse and there is less repression of this material in their mind."

After a 13-day deliberation, the jury returned a guilty verdict. The following year, in a separate trial, his mother and sister were also convicted. For more than seven years, they languished in jail, losing subsequent appeals and repeatedly being denied parole.

Two days after Gerald Amirault's conviction, his lawyers discovered that Shirley Crawford, a 54-year-old juror, had not told the entire truth about her own background. When she was 14, she had been raped and testified at a trial that sent the rapist to prison for ten years. When confronted with this information, Crawford denied having any memory of the rape. She must have repressed it, she said. Judge Dolan believed her and refused to order a mistrial.

Amirault tried not to hold a grudge. "I don't blame the kids and parents. They were as much victims as we were," he told me from his prison cell. He was still bitter that the media coverage and the judge were so one-sided. "When the kids said 'No,' it meant 'Yes.' It was unbelievable. Talk about the deck being stacked against you. You're almost better off killing somebody, really committing a crime. This sex abuse stuff is like fighting ghosts. I just want people to know what really happened, not what was reported in the scandal sheets or the *Boston Herald American*. I'd sit in the courtroom all day long, and we'd have a real good day in court. Then the paper would come out the next day, and I'd say, 'Wow, I can't believe this is the same trial I sat through.' Now when I read the newspaper, I only believe the sports pages; the scores and standings are probably accurate. I take everything else with a pound of salt."

For years, Violet Amirault and her daughter Cheryl LaFave were denied parole because they insisted on their innocence. The parole report for 71-year-old Violet read: "Parole denied. Vigorously denies the offense(s). Until such time as she is able to take responsibility for her crimes and engages in long term therapy to address the causative factors, she will remain a risk to the community if released."

Fortunately, in 1995, in the wake of a public outcry fomented primarily by articles on Fells Acres by *Wall Street Journal* reporter Dorothy Rabinowitz, the moth-

---

* During Amirault's trial, the boy asserted that he had been hung upside down from the tree and forced to eat white pills; at Vi and Cheryl's trial, however, he claimed to be right-side up and did not recall eating pills.

er and daughter were released from prison. They won an appeal based on their inability to face the accusing children in court. Unfortunately, unlike his mother and sister, Gerald "Tooky" Amirault's appeal on the same issue went before Judge Elizabeth Dolan, who had presided over the original trial. Not surprisingly, she denied his appeal, stating in her decision: "The courtroom seating arrangement at issue reduced the risk of trauma to the child witnesses." In other words, Dolan continued to assume that abuse took place and that Amirault was guilty. He remained in prison until 2004, when he was finally released on parole after serving eighteen years in prison for mythical crimes.

Homophobia in the Day Care Case of Bernard Baran

The Fells Acres case spawned the false conviction of Bernard Baran, who remained in prison for nearly 22 years. For compelling coverage of this case, see the documentary film, *Freeing Bernie Baran*. An openly gay 19-year-old, Baran worked as a teacher's aide at the Early Childhood Development Center in his hometown of Pittsfield, Massachusetts, when the Fells Acres case made headlines in September 1984. The mother of a four-year-old boy complained that she "didn't want no homo" working with her child. She and her boyfriend, who were drug addicts and police informants, took the child out of the day care and told the police that Baran had molested him, and the local rumor mill quickly spread the word.

The Massachusetts Division of Family and Children Services put on a puppet show to encourage other children to "disclose" abuse, while notifying all the parents that a child at the day care had gonorrhea (from a flawed test with a high false-positive rating). Using anatomically correct dolls, the child interviewers set to work, eliciting grotesque abuse allegations. "What happened to your peepee hole? Did someone touch your peepee? Were your pants on or off?" therapist Jane Satullo asked one little boy. "This is hard to talk about. Were you scared? Sometimes when we talk about these things we get scared." In other words, the interviews were incredibly leading. "Tell me a little more about what Bernie did to you?" asked the therapist. "He didn't do nothing," the boy said. Ignoring him, Satullo continued, "Did Bernie touch you while in the bathroom? I know you are scared." And so on.

Dan Ford, the prosecuting attorney, called Baran's partner a "fag" and repeatedly displayed his prejudice against gays. In his closing argument during the trial, he told the jury, "Bernard Baran could have raped and sodomized those children whenever he felt a primitive urge to satiate his sexual appetite."

Baran was convicted and given three concurrent life sentences in January 1985. He lost his appeal, while he continued to assert his innocence. Finally, due in large part to the efforts of activists Jim D'Entremont and Robert Chatelle, who went on to found the National Center for Reason and Justice, Baran's new legal team, headed by John Swomley, won his right to a new trial in 2006. Even then, the Berkshire County District Attorney's office appealed. Only in 2009 did the Massachusetts Appeals Court affirm his right to a new trial, in a strongly worded opinion that amounted to an exoneration. Baran was finally freed. But his years in prison had broken his health, and he died in 2014. He was 49 years old.

The Rape of the Souza Family

Seven years after she ruled on the Amirault case, in 1993 Judge Elizabeth Dolan also decided the fate of Ray and Shirley Souza, accused of molesting their two grandchildren. The Souza case is especially interesting because, as in the Texas case of Bruce Perkins, it combines the two types of sexual abuse allegations—repressed memories recovered by adults, and the repeated questioning of little children. Their story is tragic, but not unique. Throughout the United States, adult daughters went to therapy, were encouraged to find repressed incest memories, and then frantically questioned their own small children about what Grammy and Grampa might have done to them. Usually, these family mini-dramas went unpublicized, but because of the criminal trial, the Souzas lost not only their entire family, but their liberty.

Lifelong residents of Lowell, a classic melting-pot New England mill town, Ray and Shirley Souza raised five children. Products of the Depression, the Souzas were determined to give their children many of the advantages and privileges their parents had lacked. Thus, Ray made sure his kids owned bicycles, because he never had one as a boy. Ray worked as an electrical lineman and Shirley as a part-time nurse. In a way, like many other parents in the 1950s, they reared their children permissively. At the same time, they appeared a bit overprotective. Their children came to rely on them perhaps too much.

Sharon, the oldest daughter, lived only two doors away and ate dinner with her parents frequently. Son Scott lived at home for quite a while, while Tommy also spent a great deal of time there as an adult, playing his drums in the basement. David kept more distance, because his wife Heather didn't get along very well with her mother-in-law. The youngest child, Shirley Ann, had a particularly difficult time breaking away from home when she went to college. After a near date rape and the subsequent trial, Shirley Ann sought counseling with a therapist, who apparently encouraged her to search for repressed incest memories and gave her *The Courage to Heal.*

In a dream she had on Father's Day, 1990, Shirley Ann visualized a horrifying scene in which she was raped by her father, her oldest brother, and her mother. Despite the fact that certain elements in the dream appeared unrealistic—Shirley Ann had no arms or legs, her mother had a penis, while her father inserted a crucifix into her vagina—Shirley Ann immediately called her sister-in-law Heather to inform her that her parents were molesters. "Please, please," she said, "keep your children away from Mom and Dad."

As a result, Heather took her five-year-old, Cindy, to a child psychologist. At two, Josh seemed too young. The counselor failed to find any evidence of sex abuse, concluding that the mother was pressuring the child unduly. Undaunted, Heather sought another counselor, an "expert" in spotting abased children. On the very first visit, she proclaimed that Cindy suffered from post-traumatic stress disorder (PTSD) resulting from likely abuse. (Meanwhile, Heather herself, having read *The Courage to Heal,* sought therapy and recovered "memories" that her grandfather had sexually abused her.)

Eventually, all of the Souzas' children except Scott came to believe the charges, which escalated once the Massachusetts Department of Social Services (DSS) became involved. Although initially skeptical, Shirley Ann's older sister Sharon finally concluded early in 1991 that her four-year-old child Nancy had also been molested by their grandparents, after Sharon herself entered therapy and recovered what she considered previously repressed memories of incest and ritual abuse. In the meantime, as Heather and David's marriage deteriorated, Heather began to suspect that David, too, had abused their children. Under her intense interrogation, Cindy complied, telling her mother how David had molested her. Suffering from a nervous breakdown, he checked himself into a psychiatric hospital. Heather subsequently divorced David and later remarried.

Repeatedly questioned by their mothers, therapists, social workers, and police, Cindy and Nancy eventually "disclosed" how their grandparents sexually abused them.

Because of snowballing allegations and various bureaucratic tangles, the case did not come to trial until January of 1993. Robert George, the Souzas' attorney, advised them to waive their right to a jury trial and to rely solely on the decision of Judge Elizabeth Dolan, who had presided over the Fells Acres case.* By the time Ray and Shirley appeared before Dolan in late January 1993, Cindy and Nancy had not seen their grandparents for nearly two years.

There was no hard evidence against the Souzas other than the word of the children and symptoms reported by their parents. When the children testified, they sat in little chairs at a miniature table, with their backs to their grandparents. Judge Dolan descended from her bench to sit next to them. During her testimony, seven-year-old Cindy revealed that her grandparents routinely locked her and her first cousin Nancy in a basement cage.

---

* Robert George advised waiving their right to a jury trial because he knew that juries are often swayed by emotional testimony by innocent little children. It is inexplicable why he would have wanted Judge Dolan to be the sole arbiter, however, since George had worked in the office of the Fells Acres defense team, and he knew that she tended to accept children's testimony and the reality of repressed memories.

Six-year-old Nancy then told Judge Dolan how her grandparents had stuck their entire hands and heads into her vagina, where they would wiggle them around. They also abused her, she said, with a huge multicolored machine, as big as a room, which was kept in the cellar. She did not remember any cage, just as Cindy did not mention any machine.*

Throughout the trial, Judge Dolan indicated that she considered herself an expert on the subject of child abuse. "You know, I've heard all of this material time after time after time," she lamented, adding, "I'm not trying to be a smart mouth or anything.... I'm not saying I know everything but, you know, I have heard a lot in this field over the years. And I've done a moderate amount of reading in this general subject area." She was overtly hostile to Richard Gardner, the expert witness for the defense. Gardner reviewed videotapes of interviews with five-year-old Cindy during which the little girl commented to investigator Lea Savely, "Mommy told me that Papa [*her term for her grandfather*] tied me up." Instead of picking up on this hint of Cindy's confusion, Savely zeroed in on the allegation itself, ignoring the reference to parental pressure: "Did Papa do that?" Cindy muttered, "Uh huh," and Savely followed up with "And what part of your body?" Cindy mumbled: "I forget."

Gardner also objected to the use of anatomically correct dolls because they "sexualize the interview, they draw the child's fantasies into sexual realms. These dolls have very explicit sexual organs with pubic hair, large breasts, often prominent nipples.... Some of them have open mouths, open anuses, open vaginas, larger than average penises." He said that, in other contexts, the use of such dolls would be considered inappropriate: "If this doll were to be used in a school situation, parents would justifiably complain about the competence of a teacher. If a neighbor were to subject the child to such a doll, there would be complaints and indignation."**

Leslie Campis, staff psychologist and associate director of the Sexual Abuse Team at Boston's Children's Hospital, was the prosecution's expert witness to counter Gardner. "Disclosure is understood to be not a single event, but a process," she told the judge. "Initially when asked, children might say no, that nothing has happened to them, because they may not be ready to tell their experience." The second level, she said, is "tentative disclosure," followed by "active disclosure ... sometimes to the point where they talk about it excessively." Campis asserted that

---

* During videotaped interview sessions, Nancy had also alleged that her grandparents forced her to drink a green potion. By the time she testified in court, however, she apparently didn't remember it.

** Several studies demonstrated that the use of anatomically correct dolls can contaminate interviews. Using the dolls, Maggie Bruck found that 75 percent of preschool girls, who did not receive a genital examination during a pediatric checkup, incorrectly indicated that the doctor had touched their privates. "A child may insert a finger into a doll's genitalia," she noted, "simply because of its novelty." She and other researchers suggested that children point to their own bodies to indicate what may have occurred.

it is normal for some children to recant, because "it's their way of trying to make the anxiety go away," even though the abuse really occurred. She said that it is very rare for children to falsely disclose.

"What might a therapist do in situations where a child is not disclosing?" the prosecutor asked. "One would want to ask more direct questions," Campis answered. "And sometimes, one has to recommend that the child be in an extended therapeutic relationship for them to be able to disclose." Yet Campis insisted that "no one who is doing good practice in this area approaches any case with an agenda."

Andrea Vandeven, a staff pediatrician at Children's Hospital, took the stand to discuss her examination of the children, during which she spread their labia and examined their hymens carefully, taking photographs of their private areas. She found no irregularities. She then turned them onto their stomachs, rear ends presented to her invading finger, covered by a surgical glove. Vandeven told Judge Dolan that Nancy's exam was "consistent with anal penetration," particularly because she felt that her anus "spontaneously dilated" more than most she had seen.* Under cross-examination, the doctor admitted that there was no evidence of penetration. She noted, however, that "normal rectal exams are consistent with penetration, with or without dilation." In other words, *any* exam of a child would be considered "consistent with penetration."

Ray and Shirley Souza testified that they never abused their grandchildren. It was obvious that their attorneys had not prepared them for cross-examination, and they came across as extremely defensive. Various old friends and fellow workers briefly took the stand, recalling the loving, unfearful relationship the grandchildren seemed to have with their grandparents. These character witnesses were dismissed by Dolan as "window dressing."

The trial was also notable for those who did *not* testify. Shirley Ann Souza, whose dream sparked the entire affair, did not appear, nor did her therapist. Carmela Eyal, the therapist who finally concluded that Heather Souza was applying undue pressure on Cindy, did not testify. Jeanine Hemstead, the therapist responsible for getting both Cindy and Nancy to disclose, never took the stand. Aside from Richard Gardner, the defense called no expert witnesses—no scientists who had conducted studies on the suggestibility of children, no pediatricians who had studied normal children who present with the same "fissures" and "tears" that supposedly indicate abuse.

---

* A California general practitioner named Bruce Woodling, a self-proclaimed expert in detecting child sexual abuse, promoted the "anal wink test" in the early 1980s. He claimed that if a child's anus dilated and closed spontaneously, it indicated repeated sodomy. He also pioneered the use of the colposcope, which can take magnified photos of the hymen, making any irregularities appear horrific. Only in 1988, when John McCann's studies revealed that normal children also exhibited hymenal irregularities and anal winks, did Woodling's widely accepted theories fall into disrepute.

After a week and a half of testimony, Judge Dolan took another 14 days before she pronounced the Souzas guilty as charged. In her written opinion, Dolan acknowledged that "children are quite capable of *intentional* falsehoods," but she obviously did not feel that they could easily incorporate false memories into their belief systems. She dismissed any inconsistencies or unbelievable stories because of the children's ages: "Age impacts upon perception, memory and verbal capacity." She was particularly impressed by the children's knowledge of wet vaginas. "As a general premise," she wrote, "most young children do not have knowledge of adult sexual activity to support a convincing, detailed lie about sexual abuse."

On the other hand, Dolan also interpreted *unconvincing* details as proof that abuse occurred. Commenting on Nancy's rather odd testimony about feet and elbows being stuck into her vagina, the judge said: "A child who has been coached, programmed or rehearsed in a fabrication is unlikely to include elbows and feet." In other words, if the story appeared plausible, it proved abuse. If the story was implausible, it also proved abuse. Incredibly, Dolan asserted, "There was no evidence of [Sharon's] malice or bias against her-parents"—ignoring her therapy-induced beliefs that her parents had ritually abused her as a child. (The judge had not allowed this evidence to be presented.)

At the end of the trial, Sharon and Heather read emotional statements calling for lengthy jail terms and quoting from letters purportedly written by Cindy and Nancy. Sharon asked Judge Dolan not to be influenced by her parents' age. "People may say they're so old, why send them to jail? I say, they've not always been 61 years old, and they've been doing this for years."

Before the sentencing, however, a public outcry erupted, largely due to the efforts of Richard Gardner, the outspoken Columbia University psychiatrist who had testified for the Souzas in the trial. After the media picked up the story, Dolan repeatedly delayed sentencing. Eventually, she handed down a judgment of 9 to 15 years, but rather than sending the couple to jail, she confined them to house arrest pending their appeal.

"When those kiddos grow up," Ray Souza said of his grandchildren, "they're going to realize that these things never happened. They're bright children and they have a mind of their own, and when nobody's prompting them, when they grow up, they're going to remember, and we'll embrace." But that never happened. Young children in such cases generally incorporate their new abuse memories as an essential part of their belief systems as they grow older.

The Souzas remained under house arrest with ankle bracelets in their Lowell, Massachusetts, home, until 2002. Ray Souza died in 2007. Shirley now has friendly relations with three of her children—Sharon, David, and Scott—but not with Shirley Ann or Tommy. Sharon's children, Nicole and Melissa, still have "memories" of abuse implanted in them as children and won't have anything to do with their grandmother, but she has three granddaughters with whom she is close.

Believing the Children

Richard Gardner wrote several books, including *Sex Abuse Hysteria* and *True and False Accusations of Child Sex Abuse,* about the problems that can arise when people question children *too* intently about possible sex abuse. No one—certainly not Gardner, who worked extensively with traumatized children—would deny the reality or horror of child sexual abuse. Adults can and do sometimes take advantage of the innocence and helplessness of small children, and the resulting confusion, shame, and long-lasting psychic damage can be devastating. We must be extremely careful, however, not to jump to conclusions or engage in coercive, leading interviews once a suspicion is aroused.

The majority of real child molesters prefer older children, usually beginning with grooming activities around the age of nine or ten. Not only that, but the grotesque, violent abuse of preschoolers, commonly alleged in these cases, would cause obvious, permanent damage, if not death. Why, then, did the children in these cases display no ill effects and disclose no abuse until coerced into doing so?

Such considerations did not occur to California psychiatrist Roland Summit, author of "The Child Sexual Abuse Accommodation Syndrome," a 1983 paper that served as a touchstone for overzealous investigators. In that article, Summit noted that "child sexual abuse has exploded into public awareness during a span of less than five years." His paper blasted "any adult who chooses to remain aloof from the helplessness and pain of the child's dilemma." Few could dispute Summit's sentiments regarding the plight of abused children, or his wrath at adults who refused to listen to them.

Yet his description of children's reluctance to disclose sexual abuse spawned coercive measures and belief in grotesque allegations. Summit encouraged investigators to question children repeatedly and to believe their eventual allegations, regardless of their implausible nature. "The more illogical and incredible the initiation scene might seem to adults," Summit wrote, "the more likely it is that the child's plaintive description is valid." He added, "It has become a maxim among child sexual abuse intervention counselors and investigators that children never fabricate the kinds of explicit sexual manipulations they divulge in complaints or interrogations."

As the final stage of his hypothetical syndrome, Summit asserted, *"Whatever a child says about sexual abuse, she is likely to reverse it."* In other words, once a child has disclosed, she is likely to take back the allegations, even though they are true. While Summit was correct that sexually abused children often "accommodate" themselves to powerful adults, it did not occur to him that they might similarly accommodate themselves to powerful adult interrogators intent on hearing abuse allegations.

Summit's original paper was mild and reasonable, however, compared to his statements in coming years. "When there is some level of suspicion," Summit told a television journalist in 1994, "the investigation has to go way beyond the ability of children to tell us about it." The first interview, he explained, rarely results in disclosure. "There has to be more than one interview, and there are times children will say quite sincerely that nothing happened, only later to begin disclosing their experience." Not only that, but "it's not unusual for children in criminal cases to come back and say, 'It never happened. I only said those things because the prosecutor badgered me.'" These children, he believed, were simply "in denial" of their very real abuse. Summit also defended Kee MacFarlane's coercive interview techniques in the McMartin case, even though he admitted he had never reviewed the tapes.

The parallel mindsets of the repressed memory therapists and child sex abuse specialists were striking. "Children never fabricate the explicit detail," Summit insisted, just as those who believed in massive repressed memories cited detailed accounts as evidence for their validity. Child investigators were determined to get children to reveal abuse that never occurred—just as therapists rooted out repressed memories of events that never happened. In both cases, it didn't seem to disturb them that some of the allegations were, to say the least, improbable. A sword stuck into children's privates, for instance, would certainly leave prominent scars, if it didn't kill them. Both the child and adult therapists brushed aside concerns about improbable or downright impossible stories. These exact events may not have occurred, they argued, but they *symbolically* represented some other actual abuse.

I interviewed Steven Normandin, one of the 1986 jurors from the Fells Acres case. "There's still absolutely no doubt in my mind that Tooky Amirault was guilty," he told me. I asked him how he and the other jurors had reacted to some of the more bizarre allegations, such as the little boy who claimed to have been hung naked upside down from a tree while the entire school watched. "Well," he told me, "some of those things were probably exaggerated. But we knew the kids were telling the truth. Besides, Amirault just didn't seem credible when he testified."

It was ironic that the battle cry of those leading the charge in these cases was, "Believe the children!" In fact, the trouble always began in these cases when adults *did not* believe children who truthfully reported that no one abused them.

The mantra would be more accurate if it went, "Believe the children, but only when or if they say they were abused, no matter how incredible, bizarre, or unrealistic their stories may be."

Peggy Buckey's Post-traumatic Stress

In 1990, after a seven-year trial, the longest, most expensive criminal trial in U. S. history, the McMartin preschool defendants were finally exonerated and set free. Yet how free were they? Even those found innocent in such cases still had to cope with how their lives were altered. They lost their livelihoods, their reputations, their homes, and millions of dollars. I interviewed Peggy Buckey in 1995, when she was 68 years old.[*] A decade before, she had been in jail for two years while awaiting her McMartin trial. "I survived four attempts on my life," she told me, "because other inmates hate anyone accused of child molestation." Once she and her son Ray were finally vindicated, she fell apart. "I was afraid of everything, of everyone. I couldn't leave the house or drive a car. I was heavily sedated. They diagnosed me with post-traumatic stress disorder." It took three years for her to recover.

Peggy Buckey volunteered at a soup kitchen for the homeless and kept up an active correspondence with those who have been jailed in similar molestation cases—Bill and Kathy Swan in Kirkland, Washington; Bob and Betsy Kelly and Dawn Wilson in Raleigh, North Carolina; Kelly Michaels in New Jersey; Brenda Kniffen in Frontera, California; Frank Fuster in Bushnell, Florida; Debbie Runyan and Lynn Malcom in Gig Harbor, Washington, and others. She was 74 when she died in 2000.

---

[*]   Peggy Buckey's mother, wheelchair-bound Virginia McMartin, died in 1995 at the age of 88. "She was the single strongest, most committed, most energetic player in the entire saga," her lawyer, Danny Davis, commented. Before she died, McMartin got to see herself portrayed as a heroine in the 1995 television movie, *Indictment*.

6 A Brief History: The Witch Craze, Reflex Arcs, and Freud's Legacy

Woman! A she hell-cat, a witch! To prove her one, we no sooner set fire on the thatch of her house, but in she came running, as if the devil had sent her in a barrel of gunpowder.

—John Ford, *The Witch of Edmonton (1658)*

What history teaches us is that man has never learned anything from it.

—Georg Wilhelm Hegel

"TODAY, MORE WOMEN ARE SEEKING psychiatric help and being hospitalized than at any other time in history," feminist Phyllis Chesler wrote in her seminal 1972 book, *Women and Madness*. She attributed this intensification of an old trend to the "help-seeking" nature of the learned female role, the oppression of women, and role confusion in the modern age. "While women live longer than ever before," Chesler observed, "there is less and less use, and literally no place, for them in the only place they 'belong'—within the family. Many newly useless women are emerging more publicly into insanity."

The female "career" as a psychiatric patient identified by Chesler has a long history, with women often displaying the symptoms expected of them: depression, frigidity, paranoia, vague aches and pains, suicide attempts, and anxiety. And when women rebelled against their passive state, becoming aggressive and sexually active, they were *also* been labeled mentally ill. Chesler tacitly acknowledged this history with a wry observation: "No longer are women sacrificed as voluntary or involuntary witches. They are, instead, taught to sacrifice themselves for newly named heresies."

In Western cultures, both men and women have suffered from bizarre psychosomatic ailments for centuries, always aided and abetted by the "experts" of the era, whose expectations determined which symptoms they would display. Because of societal bias, females, considered the "weaker vessel," were expected to act out the role of the "hysteric" more often than males. Women—almost universally repressed and abused, and sometimes powerless to do much about it—conformed to the role expectation, which at least allowed them sympathetic attention and an emotional outlet for their suppressed and usually justifiable rage.*

The only thing relatively new about the sex abuse Survivor movement was its particularly awful slant—the virulent accusations against parents and other early caregivers. We will briefly examine several historical periods, looking for insights into the modern crisis.

The Witch Craze

If its duration is any indication, the Witch Craze is frightening evidence that human beings are capable of maintaining sustained societal persecution based upon fantasies for a long, long time. For two centuries, the 16th and 17th, most of Europe engaged in a frantic search for evil witches, a process which bore an alarming resemblance to the modern hunt for pedophiles—except, of course, that there really *are* pedophiles, which makes the search for repressed memories more confusing and unlikely to disappear anytime soon.

To the clerics, philosophers and lawyers of the 1500s, there was also no doubt that witches existed and exerted a malevolent force everywhere. Mostly, witches were older women with extraordinary powers who had formed an underground international organization and practiced hideous rituals involving bestiality, murder, rape, and other atrocities. As historian Hugh Trevor-Roper noted, "some of the most powerful minds of the time" applied themselves to studying the witch phenomenon. "And the details which they discover, and which are continually being confirmed by teams of parallel researchers—field researchers in torture-chamber or confessional, academic researchers in library or cloister—leave the facts more certainly established and the prospect more alarming than ever."

What such experts discovered was that elderly and not-so-elderly women were making pacts with the Devil, at whose command they ate boiled children, engaged in sexual orgies, and generally enjoyed themselves in revolting fashion. In between these witch's sabbats, they rendered bridegrooms impotent, killed off neighbors' pigs, and had sex nightly with the Devil, who aroused them as an invisible *incubus.* Thus, any sexual dreams or nightmares could be easily explained, though it was an unwise woman who was caught having such dreams or who reported them.

---

* Men are equally susceptible to psychosomatic ailments, but in Western culture, as in many other patriarchal cultures, they were socially molded to act them out differently, usually with more overt aggression. During the Middle Ages, for instance, the various "dancing attacks," in which masses of people saw visions and jumped about for prolonged periods, afflicted more men than women. In Malaya, women were subject to "Latah," which usually follows a sudden fright, such as stepping on a snake. During Latah, they act in a compliant manner, often wailing. Malayan men, on the other hand, sometimes suffered from "Amok," in which they suddenly seized a weapon and killed anyone within reach until subdued or killed. Those who survived claimed amnesia regarding the entire episode.

The zealous clerics and judges who ferreted out these evil witches had help from numerous manuals which described the symptoms of witchcraft in great detail. The first and most famous, the *Malleus Maleficarum,* or "Hammer of Witches," written by Heinrich Kramer and James Sprenger, was published in 1486. It is a remarkable document which, like *The Courage to Heal,* offers an internally logical and quite convincing way to identify the root cause of the problem. In this case, however, it was witchcraft rather than repressed memories of sexual abuse that wreaked havoc in people's lives. "The *Malleus* lay on the bench of every judge, on the desk of every magistrate," noted Montague Summers in his introduction to the 1948 reprint. "It was the ultimate, irrefutable, unarguable authority."

The *Malleus* included compelling case studies. In the town of Ratisbon, for instance, "a certain young man who had an intrigue with a girl, wishing to leave her, lost his member." He was not merely impotent. "Some glamour was cast over it so that he could see or touch nothing but his smooth body."* In need of a stiff drink, he entered a tavern, where he described his problem to a woman at the bar, "demonstrating in his body that it was so." She immediately adduced that he had been bewitched and asked if he suspected anyone. He did. That night, he accosted an elderly woman in the neighborhood, who maintained her innocence and said she knew nothing of his missing penis. Thereupon he grabbed her, choking her with a towel wrapped around her neck. "Unless you give me back my health," he exclaimed, "you shall die at my hands." Not surprisingly, she submitted. "The witch touched him with her hand between the thighs, saying, 'Now you have what you desire.'" And he was cured.

Compared to *The Courage to Heal,* however, the *Malleus* was in some ways a moderate, well-reasoned document. Take, for instance, the section entitled "Of One Taken and Convicted, But Denying Everything." True, the accused should be kept "in strong durance fettered and chained," and should regularly be visited by officers to "induce him to discover the truth." But the authors cautioned the authorities not to "be in any haste to pronounce a definitive sentence." Indeed, they should urge witnesses to "examine their consciences well." Perhaps their memories were faulty, or "actuated by malice." If the alleged witch maintained his or her denial for over a year, however, and the witnesses didn't recant, the witch should be reluctantly turned over to the secular judges for sentencing and burning.

As Montague Summers wrote in his heavily ironic 1948 introduction, "What is most surprising is the modernity of the book. There is hardly a problem, a complex, a difficulty, which they have not foreseen, and discussed, and resolved. Here are cases which occur in the law-courts today, set out with the greatest

---

* Masculine paranoid delusions such as this story reveals occur worldwide. In Africa and Asia men sometimes suffer from *koro,* a state in which they are convinced that their penises are shriveling up, soon to disappear completely. In Europe and the United States, the same condition is called "genital retraction syndrome."

clarity, argued with unflinching logic, and judged with scrupulous impartiality." Summers did not know how germane his observations would be in another forty years, when *The Courage to Heal* would be published. In a rather bizarre case, in 1993 Lorena Bobbitt acted out the scenario depicted above, but she used a knife, rather than any "glamour," to remove the offending penis.

Speaking of the hunt for witches, Trevor-Roper observed: "Since a system was presupposed, a system was found. The confessions—those disconnected fragments of truth hardly won from the enemy—were seen as the few visible projections of a vast and complex organization, and so every new confession supplied fresh evidence for deductive minds." He pointed out that this insanity did not take place during the Dark Ages or even the Middle Ages. No, it was during the flowering of intellect of the Renaissance period, during the time of Erasmus, Luther, and Shakespeare, whose works, not so coincidentally, roil with witches.* This fact should serve as a "standing warning to those who would simplify the stages of human progress," Trevor-Roper dryly observed. "Even intellectual history, we now admit, is relative and cannot be dissociated from the wider social context with which it is in constant interaction."

Arguably, what made the almost universal hunt for witches possible was the same new technology that sparked the Renaissance and allowed the Bard's work to live forever: the invention of the printing press by Johannes Gutenberg in the mid-1400s. The *Malleus* followed only 30 years later. We suffer from the same irony today during the era of the Internet, instantaneous information retrieval, and fake news. Without the talk shows and their voracious appetite for sensation, without our own printing presses and nightly news, it is unlikely that the dogma surrounding repressed memories would have spread so quickly and effectively, spawning an epidemic of incest charges in the late 20th century, nor would the modern rumors of Satanic cults have gained such easy credence.

At first, it was mainly the clerics who pressed the charges against witches. Quite soon, however, the lawyers took over. By 1600, noted Trevor-Roper, they were "more savage and pedantic than the clergy," having recognized a good source of income when they saw it. The witch trials also lent an enthralling, appalling moral force to their otherwise mundane practices. As one prosecutor bemoaned: "Was ever age so afflicted as ours? The seats destined for criminals in our courts of justice are blackened with persons accused of this guilt. There are not judges enough to try them." Every day, he and his colleagues "return to our homes discountenanced and terrified at the horrible confessions which we have heard." Similarly, whole law firms specialized in representing young women suing their

---

*   In 1598, all of England was riveted by the prosecution of the "witches of Warbois." Young Joan Throgmorton claimed that Mother Samuel, an elderly neighborhood woman, had afflicted her with spirits with imaginative names such as 'First Smack," "Blue," "Catch," "Hardname" and "Pluck." The same year, Shakespeare's *Midsummer Night's Dream* featured a less harmful cousin spirit named "Puck."

"perpetrators" for sexual abuse, based on recovered memories.

Not all of the confessions during the Witch Craze were extracted by torture. Even in England, which abjured such tactics, many "witches" confessed to the most ridiculous charges. As Charles Mackay wrote in 1841, "When religion and law alike recognized the crime, it is no wonder that … the strong in imagination … fancied themselves endued with the terrible powers of which all the world were speaking." Trevor-Roper estimated that, for every victim whose story popped out under duress, there were two or three who genuinely believed they were witches. They had developed very coherent, detailed memories of the orgies in which they had taken part, the babies they had roasted and eaten. Young girls would describe in gory detail how they had been deflowered by the Devil, though examination proved them to be virgins.*

It seems strange, of course, that women would admit to being witches, knowing that they would be burned. Yet as one historian noted, there were advantages to the role: "Think of the power wielded by Satan's Chosen Bride! She can heal, prophesy, predict, conjure up the spirits of the dead, can spell-bind you … cast a love charm over you; there is no escaping!" For a woman without any real authority in society, a belief in such powers could prove quite attractive, despite its hazards. "Again and again," Trevor-Roper wrote, "when we read the case histories, we find witches freely confessing to esoteric details without any evidence of torture, and it was this spontaneity, rather than the confessions themselves, which convinced rational men that the details were true."

This observation is analogous to what I heard therapists say over and over: "You wouldn't doubt these memories if you had seen what I have seen. These women are in terrible pain, reliving the abuse. It is absolutely real, there's no question." The most famous modern case of a self-confessed "witch" is Paul Ingram, the Washington State policeman who obligingly told his interrogators that he had raped his daughters as a priest in a Satanic cult. Ingram is the subject of Lawrence Wright's book, *Remembering Satan*. Only when Ingram confessed an imaginary event planted by social psychologist Richard Ofshe was it clear that he was not a sex abuser after all. I interviewed an accused father who told a similar story of coming to believe he had been a perpetrator in a Satanic cults. Most people accused of a heinous crime that they did not commit go through self-doubts and guilt that could easily, under the right circumstances, be turned into belief in the charges.

Exactly why social movements such as the Witch Craze occur is a difficult question, but it appears that periods of general social unrest provide a standard backdrop. When life is too confusing, a scapegoat helps, whether it be a witch,

---

* The modern Survivor movement yielded similar cases in which young women "discovered" through recovered memories that their fathers raped them throughout their childhoods, yet their hymens were found to be intact.

a Jew, a Communist, or a pedophile. The Witch Craze seems to have flourished particularly in poverty-stricken rural areas. As Trevor-Roper wrote, "If the Dominicans, by their constant propaganda, created a hatred of witches, they created it in a favorable social context." During the two centuries that Europe hunted witches, there were periods of relative prosperity when the tribunals and tortures almost ceased. But when times got rough, so did the handling of witches. To apply the lesson to our times: Ellen Bass and Laura Davis may have written a deadly book, but they can hardly be blamed for the witch hunt for sex abusers. Our society, for a variety of reasons *(see Chapter 7, "Cultural Contexts"),* was ready and eager for their message.

Eventually, the excesses of the Witch Craze drew criticism. Compassionate souls realized that many of the confessions were merely the result of torture and that many of the supposed "witches" were the victims of political feuds or long-standing family rivalries. Still, none of the critics questioned the underlying assumption that there *were* witches who did evil deeds.˙

It wasn't until René Descartes (1596-1650) came along and changed the entire way we thought, giving us a mechanistic universe—with its own problems and prejudices—that witches gradually receded into mythology. Similarly, few now question the validity of the theory of "repressed memories," our Freudian legacy, though such repression may not exist at all *(see Chapter 2, "The Memory Maze").* As Trevor-Roper wrote, "the absurdity of inquisitorial demonology should be a salutary warning to us never to trust the accounts which a persecuting society has drawn up of any esoteric heresy.... Once the mythology had been established, it acquired, as it were, a reality of its own.... It had become part of the structure of thought, and time had so entwined it with other beliefs, and indeed with social interests, that it seemed impossible to destroy it."

By the end of the 17th century, the furious hunt for witches was sputtering out in Europe, but it briefly flourished in one last bright flash in America, where the Puritans lagged behind the times. In 1692, in Salem, Massachusetts, nine-year-old Betty Parris, the local minister's daughter, began to act very strangely. She entered a kind of trance. Her body contorted. She uttered horrible gargling noises and growls. Soon, her cousin Abigail was crawling around the house barking like a dog. "Their arms, necks and backs were turned this way and that way," a contemporary observer wrote, "so that it was impossible for them to do of themselves, and beyond the power of any epileptic fits or natural disease to effect." Choking, they asserted that the devil himself had stuck invisible balls in their windpipes. They felt thorns piercing their flesh.

˙ When Boguet wrote his treatise on witches in 1602, he warned that "torture is both useless and unnecessary," since extracted confessions were compromised. Instead, he simply said to burn them—but humanity compelled him to suggest they be strangled first. "Never was judge more conscientious, more thorough, more bent on extermination," wrote Jules Michelet in his classic history of witchcraft.

The girls' behavior stemmed largely from what they already knew about be-witchment and demonic possession, but it was augmented by Reverend Parris's West Indian slave, Tituba, who could tell a fortune by floating an egg white in a glass. When it revealed the milky shape of a coffin, and the girls' fits amplified, ministers from miles around gathered and asked, "Who torments you?" When the girls failed to name anyone, the ministers suggested likely older women of the town. Just as modern therapists inadvertently cue their patients into visualizing sexual abuse, these ministers dragged accusations out of the young girls, and the first three witches were charged.

In the courtroom, the girls put on a remarkable show. And they were not pre-tending. They *believed* that they were under the influence of witchcraft, and their tortures seemed quite real to everyone. When Martha Corey, one accused wom-an, protested, "We must not believe these distracted children," no one heeded her. When Dame Corey clenched her fists, the girls screamed as if they had been pinched. When she bit her lip, their faces twisted in agony and their mouths bled, showing tooth marks. In the mad search for witches, almost any evidence would do. A birthmark, mole, or genital irregularity could be interpreted as a "witch's teat," a flap of flesh to suckle the Devil.*

The girls fell into fits from almost anyone who looked at them. Neighbors cor-roborated the accusations—yes, they had seen shapes at night, yes, they had been choked and tormented by this witch, by that witch. Friend turned against friend, brother against sister. No one was safe. One four-year-old girl, whose specter supposedly bit Betty Parris, was kept in chains for nine months. A pet dog was executed for practicing witchcraft. In the end, when the accusations had spread to some of the most prominent families in Salem, the judges finally put a stop to the prosecutions.

Why did the Witch Craze afflict Salem? Were the Puritans living in a particu-larly stressful time? Yes. They scraped out their existence in a strange new land, terrified of the Indians, whom they considered savages and demons (even though Native Americans themselves were quite puzzled by the bizarre behavior and be-liefs of the Puritans.) At the heart of the Salem conflict lay an old feud between the Porter and Putnam families. Added to that, there was really no town govern-ment, and the only established values were those provided by the church, which believed in Satan. It was in this climate of fear that the young girls' antics and accusations were taken seriously, and twenty people died as a result. Fourteen of

---

* In the fourth edition of his *Country Justice,* published in 1630, British jurist Michael Dalton wrote about the scientific search for signs such as "some big or little Teat upon their body, and in some secret place, where he (the Devil) sucketh them. And besides their sucking, the Devil leaveth other marks upon their body, sometimes like a blew spot or red spot, like a flea-biting." Because such teats were "often in their secretest parts," they re-quired "diligent and careful search."

them were women, the common scapegoats of a patriarchal era. Women who did not fit the desired cultural stereotypes were suspect—childless women, spinsters, adulteresses, or outspoken "troublemakers."

In the modern era, the accused tended to be the exact opposite—men, particularly those in some position of authority, were the preferred targets. If their public behavior appeared beyond reproach, so much the better. They must be hiding their abusive behavior, but they couldn't fool the questing therapist or the regressed daughter. Truth will out!

Demons

Demonology, a parallel phenomenon, pre-dated the two centuries of the Witch Craze and lasted well beyond it—to this day, in fact.* The belief in demons is widespread and boasts an ancient lineage. The Jews apparently picked up demonology from the Babylonians and Assyrians during the second and first centuries B.C. The concept was adopted by early Christians; the New Testament records numerous examples of possession and exorcism.

As with witches, most people who were possessed by demons were female. There was a symbiotic relation between the two, because witches were assumed to have the power to inject demons into people. Conversely, demoniacs could then unmask witches who had inflicted this misery upon them. Thus, Betty Parris and her cohorts in Salem were considered to be possessed and able to name the perpetrators. As psychologist Nicholas Spanos pointed out, those who thought they were possessed by demons were acting out a carefully prescribed social role. They were expected to be insensitive to pain, be amnesic for what occurred during attacks, experience various sensory or motor deficits, exhibit heightened intelligence or clairvoyance, and be under involuntary control by their demons. Quotations from primary sources are revealing:

- [During the possession state,] her Apprehension, Understanding, and Memory, was riper than ever in her life; and yet, when she was herself, she ... forgot almost everything that passed in these Ludicrous Intervals. (1693)

- Sometimes also she can hear only, and not everybody, but someone

---

* There is no room here for an extended cross-cultural foray into demonology. Anthropologist Felicitas Goodman offered a sympathetic look at world-wide beliefs in *How About Demons: Possession and Exorcism in the Modern World* (1988). It is unclear whether Goodman actually believed in possession or not, but she clearly recognized the efficacy of exorcism for those with the proper belief systems. She noted that "the respective spirit is 'culture-specific.' Normally, *hekura* spirits can enter only during a Yanomamo ritual. The Holy Spirit comes to worshipers during a ritual in a Pentecostal church." It is obvious that cultural expectations accounted for the possessions. As one informant told Goodman, "You see it happening to others and you wonder, will it ever happen to me too? And then it does happen."

whom she liketh and chooseth out from the rest; sometimes she seeth only ... sometimes both hearing and seeing very well, and yet not able to speak. (1593)

- I cannot help myself at all, for he [the demon] uses my limbs and organs, my neck, my tongue, and my lungs ... I am altogether unable to restrain them. (1489)

- An even more certain sign [of possession] is when a sick man speaks in foreign tongues unknown to him ... or when, being but ignorant, the patients argue about high and difficult questions; or when they discover hidden and long-forgotten matters, or future events, or the secrets of the inner conscience, such as the sins and imaginings of bystanders. (1608)

As Spanos pointed out, "the components of the demoniac role were generally well-known to the average person in medieval and late medieval Europe, and the potential demoniac's exposure to 'experts' (usually clerics) served to define the subtleties of the role in great detail." The greatest source of educational information came from the exorcism procedure itself. "As a preliminary to the Catholic exorcism rite," Spanos wrote, "the priest was required to obtain information from the demoniac concerning the number and names of the possessing demons." In other words, the priests provided a "detailed recipe of expected role enactments." In addition, would-be demoniacs could pick up tips by watching the behavior of those who were possessed, both before and during an exorcism.

Because she shared the same cultural frame of reference as the priest, the demoniac usually truly believed that she was possessed and would involuntarily exhibit all of the expected characteristics. In addition, there were benefits that went along with the role, particularly for women who normally had little societal power. They received a great deal of sympathetic attention, the power to identify other witches or predict the future, a lightened work load, a dramatic self-importance. Even so, some women resisted the label. "Periodic denials of being possessed were expected by authorities," Spanos noted, "and were routinely construed as obvious indications of a wily demon attempting to escape divine punishment. Continued refusal to enact the role properly frequently led to punishment administered in the guise of benevolently motivated attempts to free a helpless victim from demonic control."

The Nerve Doctors and the "Hysterics"

Psychosomatic illness didn't originate with the Witch Craze or widespread belief in demonic possession, nor did it perish with the Enlightenment. The duality promoted by Descartes—subject separate from object, mind independent of body—prompted a world-view in which all phenomena could supposedly be explained rationally and scientifically. Descartes erroneously thought that the tiny midbrain pineal gland was the magic connection between mind and body. Unfortunately, this approach merely transferred the cloak of "expert" from the cleric to the physician and, eventually, the therapist. The symptoms and treatment didn't change much. And the real link between mind and body was often ignored.

Part of what makes human beings unique is the power of our imagination, and while that quality allows us to create great art, it also means that we are capable of inflicting very real psychological and even physical injury upon ourselves, all through the power of the mind. By the late 18th century, the paradigm and the expected social roles had shifted, however. Demons were gradually replaced by more "scientific" explanations, and witches were being relabeled "hysterics," a pejorative term deriving from the Greek word for uterus.

Numerous cases of what might be psychosomatic illnesses were reported in antiquity. The Bible records sudden loss of the power of speech, the inability to open the eyelids, terrible contractions of the elbows, wrists and fingers, and fits in which the subjects' limbs twitched spasmodically and they screamed, cursed, and tried to bite those nearby. One of the classic symptoms, *globus hystericus*, has already been described in Chapter 3. Shakespeare's King Lear referred to this choking sensation as he struggled to master his anger: "O how this mother swells up toward my heart! / Hysterica passio, down, thou climbing sorrow."

After the Witch Craze died down, ailments originating through suggestion took on other forms, always those sanctioned by the particular disease model of the era. In his meticulously researched book, *From Paralysis to Fatigue: A History of Psychosomatic Illness in the Modern Era (1993)*, Edward Shorter described over two centuries of quackery, observing that "patients' notions of disease tend to follow doctors' ideas." His conclusion, based on an extensive survey of psychosomatic sickness over the years, was that "the relationship between doctors and patients is reciprocal: As the ideas of either party about what constitutes legitimate organic disease change, the other member of the duo will respond. Thus the history of psychosomatic illness is one of ever-changing steps in a *pas de deux* between doctor and patient."

That unconscious dance led to the repressed memory craze, which followed a long tradition in which women were victimized by their doctors and therapists. As we review cases from the past, bear in mind that many of the "symptoms" that doctors once diagnosed as "irritable spine" or "hysterical insanity" were later interpreted as proof of repressed memories of sexual abuse. Thus, *globus hystericus was* taken as evidence that your father forced fellatio on you when you were in your crib, and other psychologically induced bodily pains were labeled "body memories" of abuse.

Shorter demonstrated that patients in search of an easy answer—or sympathy and attention—conform to the "symptom pool" of the era. "The surrounding culture," he wrote, "provides our unconscious minds with templates, or models, of illness." When it was considered normal to be paralyzed, lo! they were paralyzed. It is the same with supposed sex abuse Survivors, who convince themselves that their anxiety attacks are flashbacks to memories of abuse.

My only criticism of Shorter is that he tended to assume that *all* diagnosed cases of "irritable spine" and the like were purely psychosomatic. A substantial number may have been misdiagnosed organic ailments, as Richard Webster documented in his 1995 book, *Why Freud Was Wrong*. Similarly, some women who were convinced that they harbored "repressed memories" really did have treatable mental or physical illnesses that were ignored by their therapists. Nonetheless, Shorter's identification of vague symptoms as psychosomatic is usually convincing.

In 1702, a London physician named John Purcell described "vapours, otherwise called hysterick fits." Sufferers exhibited the following symptoms:

> First they feel a heaviness upon their breast, a grumbling in their belly, they belch up, and sometimes vomit…. They have a difficulty in breathing and think they feel something that comes up into their throat which is ready to choke them; they struggle, cry out, make odd and inarticulate sounds or mutterings; they perceive a swimming in their heads, a dimness comes over their eyes; they turn pale, are scarce able to stand; their pulse is weak, they shut their eyes, fall down and remain senseless for some time.

For centuries, physicians had blamed a "floating womb" or uterus for hysterical fits. Somehow, they believed that this was linked to perverted sexual desires, including masturbation. In the 1750s, however, Edinburgh physiologist Robert Whytt demonstrated in animal experiments that the spinal cord formed the center of the body's nervous system. A new pseudoscientific era dawned that we unconsciously echo whenever we call someone neurotic or nervous. It was these mysterious "nerves" rather than the uterus or humors that caused "hysterical" maladies. Whytt wrote that such disorders were caused by "a too great delicacy and sensibility of the whole nervous system." As a cynical commentator wrote in 1786: "Before the publication of [Whytt's] book, people of fashion had not the least idea that they had nerves. But a fashionable apothecary [general practitioner] of my acquaintance, having cast his eye over the book .. . [began telling them], 'Madam, you are nervous.'"

The emphasis on nerves led to a new diagnosis by the 1840s: spinal irritation, a disease that mostly afflicted young women. The symptoms were a combination of sensitive spots along the spine as well as peripheral bodily problems—such as pain beneath the breast or near the sternum—which were assumed to be caused by central nervous disorders. It was simple to plant the idea of spinal irritation in a patient, as Walter Johnson, an 1849 physician, related:

> The examiner stands behind the patient, and, commencing just below the neck, makes firm pressure with his knuckles successively on each projecting ridge, or spinous process as it is called, that stands out from the spinal column. Less usually, he tries the effect of scalding the patient by a sponge dipped in hot water. In the course of his investigations, it frequently happens that as soon as he presses or scalds one particular ridge or vertebra, he perceives his patient [to] wince or give some evidence of pain. "Aha!" says the physician, "there it is!"

Because of the doctor's air of authority and certitude, the young women had no doubt that they suffered from an irritated spine and must lie flat on their backs for months at a time. In similar fashion, a "network chiropractor" of the 1990s convinced his patients (mostly women) that his mere touch at the proper place on their spines would release repressed memories of abuse. "Aha! There it is!"

As Walter Johnson commented back in 1849, "Attracting the patient's chief attention and filling her head with the fear that some disease exists in that situation [the spine], greatly misleads the practitioner." A few years later, London surgeon Frederick Skey lamented the spinal irritation rage which had reduced hundreds of healthy young women to a "horizontal or semirecumbent posture for years" and which "excluded [them] from society, debarred their education, restricted their natural food ... simply because a hot sponge created a sensation of uneasiness."

But why would these women have submitted to such absurd beliefs and treatments? Certainly, the authority of the doctor provided a strong inducement, but another contemporary critic astutely noted in 1851 that the diagnosis "appeases their relentless desire to be able to explain everything. Therewith the entire domain [of life's troubles] is reduced to a region that may be palpated with the tips of one's fingers." In remarkably similar fashion, women of the 1990s sought their "repressed memories" as a simple explanation of any problems they experienced in life.

Men, too, conformed to the expectations of the era, but they were firmly separated from their female counterparts, as explained by an 1846 treatise on hysteria by Landouzy, who offered parallel columns for the genders. Hysteria, he asserted, was "the sole prerogative of women ... between puberty and the menopause." Hypochondriasis, however, he proclaimed "exclusive to Man, affecting both sexes, but especially males, usually between 30th and 50th years of life." These hypersensitive men displayed depression, obsession with hygiene, and the "need to consult medical books or to talk to doctors." Men were not, however, expected to faint or fly into convulsive fits, nor were their spines generally problematic.

When spinal irritation passed out of favor, it was replaced by "reflex theory." According to the new dogma, nervous connections running along the spine regulated *all* bodily organs, including the brain, independent of human will. One organ could therefore affect a far-distant organ. Suddenly, the long-suffering uterus came back to the fore. "As the uterus regained its centrality," Edward Shorter wrote, "many women in turn became riveted by internal sensations from the abdomen and attributed various symptoms to supposed pelvic disease." The organs of generation were implicated in numerous troubles, ranging from paralysis to fits. Doctors often diagnosed women by pressing on their ovaries and inducing convulsions. The awful solution? Remove the offending parts, excise the ovaries!

In the latter half of the 1800s, the "reflex arc" came into full flower. Faced with "paralysis of the tongue," doctors deduced its cause: a constipated colon. Similarly, an entire school of German ophthalmologists diagnosed diseases of the eye as stemming from uterine troubles. In a final flourishing of the theory, both European and American doctors concluded that the mucous lining of the nose was neurologically connected to the genitals. Consequently, a nosebleed might supplant menstruation, while chronic masturbation could be cured by nasal operations. In the 1890s, Sigmund Freud, who believed in nasal reflex arcs, allowed his friend Wilhelm Fliess to operate on one of his patients, as we shall shortly see.

Most of the patients who were diagnosed with these ailments were women, and most of the physicians were men.* Nonetheless, there were women such as Mary Jacobi, a New York physician describing herself as a "staunch feminist," who fervently believed in reflex theory. In the late 1880s, she treated a woman with "transient amblyopia," or dimness of vision, concluding that her troubles were uterine. She recommended the "removal of the ovaries for intractable hysteria." Clitorectomies were frequent "cures." There were also a few male patients, diagnosed with irritated mucosal membranes because of excessive masturbation or coitus interruptus. Some underwent nose operations or castration as a solution. But women by far outnumbered men.

Jeffrey Masson assembled some appalling stories in *A Dark Science: Women, Sexuality and Psychiatry in the Nineteenth Century*, documenting abusive practices. In 1865, Gustav Braun, a German physician, published a paper titled "The Amputation of the Clitoris and Labia Minora: A Contribution to the Treatment of Vaginismus." He stated that "under the influence of a salacious imagination, which is stimulated by obscene conversations or by reading poorly selected novels, the uterus develops a hyperexcitability which leads to masturbation and its dire consequences." Braun then described the case of a single 25-year-old woman who was "cured" of such troubles by his operation.

Nearly 20 years later, in 1884, Paul Flechsig, a respected Leipsig psychiatrist, dispassionately described the case of a 32-year-old woman with a long history of psychosomatic troubles and suicidal tendencies. He considered her "hereditarily tainted." A gynecological examination revealed that "the left ovary seemed displaced downward, and the uterus seemed situated too far toward the left." Otherwise, he could discern no abnormalities. Nonetheless, Flechsig concluded that "the pathology of her sexual organs had caused her nervous anomalies.... On the basis of these considerations, castration was resorted to on July 10."

Hypnotism

In the meantime, a parallel psychological phenomenon was taking place. It, too, later intersected with the early theories of Sigmund Freud. In the late 1700s, Franz Anton Mesmer invented the "science" of animal magnetism, posited on the belief that humans have a "subtle fluid" whose unequal distribution can be realigned by a magnetizer who makes "passes" over patients. Mesmer practiced his theory in Vienna until he attempted to cure 18-year-old Maria-Therese Paradis of blindness by taking her into his household. Although he declared her cured, she still apparently could not see. Eventually, the girl's alarmed parents tried to extricate her. Mesmer refused to yield her up, causing a scandal.

Fleeing sexual allegations, Mesmer moved to Paris in 1778, where he became increasingly convinced that the power of animal magnetism resided within himself. He emphasized the need to establish "rapport" with his patients, eliciting an almost mystical bond between the powerful male magnetizer and his weak female patient. He termed this relationship "magnetic reciprocity." Mesmer's flashy therapy—he wore purple robes and held court in a dimly lit room full of mirrors, stained glass, gentle music, and the scent of orange blossoms, while he waved his magnetizing rod and stared deeply into his patients' eyes—attracted women who had vague abdominal complaints and other troubles. Mesmer believed that only when his patients reached a "crisis," characterized by convulsive contortions, would their fluids properly realign themselves.

Not surprisingly, his young women obliged by performing as expected, after which, emotionally and physically spent, they experienced at least temporary symptom remission. All of this took place in a group setting. The women sat in a circle around the *baguet*, a barrel filled with magnetized water and iron filings, studded with movable iron rods to be applied to the afflicted body parts. The patients held hands to facilitate the passage of the magnetic fluid. Because Mesmer could not personally attend to all needs, he hired assistant magnetizers, handsome young men who rubbed patients' spines and breasts while staring intently into their eyes, until they fell into convulsive fits.

"It is impossible," wrote one contemporary, "to conceive the sensation which Mesmer's experiments created in Paris." Eventually, a distinguished scientific commission, whose members included Benjamin Franklin, Antoine Lavoisier, the chemist, and Jean-Sylvain Bailly, the astronomer, was appointed to study the phenomenon. Bailly's report, which completely debunked the proceedings, is revealing:

> The magnetizer acts by fixing his eyes on them. But above all, they are magnetized by the application of his hands and the pressure of his fingers ... an application often continued for a long time—sometimes for several hours. Meanwhile the patients in their different conditions present a very varied picture. Some are calm, tranquil, and experience no effect. Others cough, spit, feel slight pains, local or general heat, and have sweatings. Others again are agitated and tormented with convulsions....
>
> As soon as one begins to convulse, several others are affected.... These convulsions are characterized by the precipitous, involuntary motion of all the limbs, and of the whole body—by the contraction of the throat—by the dimness and wandering of the eyes—by piercing shrieks, tears, sobbing, and immoderate laughter. They are preceded or followed by a state of languor or reverie, a kind of depression, and sometimes drowsiness....
>
> Nothing is more astonishing than the spectacle of these convulsions. One who has not seen them can form no idea of them. The spectator is as much astonished at the profound repose of one portion of the patients as at the agitation of the rest.... Some of the patients may be seen devoting their attention exclusively to one another, rushing toward each other with open arms, smiling, soothing, and manifesting every symptom of attachment and affection.

This scene is startlingly reminiscent of group therapy for sex abuse Survivors experiencing "flashbacks" and "abreactions." As one cried out in response to a terrifying "memory," others responded in kind. Similarly, groups provided a social support system to reinforce the process. Their emotional catharses bound them together in a common experience that was extremely powerful, similar to the solidarity felt at an evangelical gathering.

After the commission's report, Mesmer fled Paris and died years later in anonymous poverty, but his influence continued. His successors abandoned most of the mumbo-jumbo, with the exception of the Marquis de Puysegur, who renamed the phenomenon "artificial somnambulism" and described the relationship to his clients as "intimate rapport." He encouraged his patients to develop an infantile dependence upon him, a kind of early "reparenting" approach in which he played the loving mother or father. Puysegur also believed that he could magnetize elm trees, which the afflicted could then touch to be healed. "To me," noted a fellow magnetizer, "it is obvious that the effect of the tree was nonexistent, and that which occurred in its shade was entirely the result of the confidence that was placed in its magnetic virtue."

As early as 1819, Portuguese priest Abbe Jose di Faria realized that the trance state had nothing to do with magnets. He described the social "demand characteristics" of the subjects, who performed as expected: "They immediately lend themselves to fulfilling these [implied] demands, and sometimes even in spite of themselves, by the power of conviction." The magnets fell into disrepute in America after surgeon Benjamin Perkins began using metallic "tractors" in 1798 to induce a trance state in his patients prior to operations. Others soon discovered that wooden tractors painted silver worked just as well.

But the trance-like state into which Mesmer's patients fell intrigued his followers. James Braid abandoned the mesmeric passes and magnets and popularized the name "hypnotism" in 1843. Braid eventually came to believe that hypnosis worked through the suggestibility of the client. He thought that by concentrating on one idea—such as "my arm cannot bend"—to the exclusion of all else, it would become true. Other magnetizing physicians believed they could cure a new disease called "catalepsy," in which women froze into weird positions and couldn't move. In fact, these physicians both *created* and *cured* catalepsy by hypnotic suggestion.*

Nicholas Spanos pointed out the remarkable similarities between Mesmerism and demonic possession, which it largely replaced. "In both cases," he wrote, "patients convulsed on cue, appeared to be more intelligent and sometimes clairvoyant, reported spontaneous amnesia, engaged in behaviors that were thought to transcend normal capacities ..., and experienced their role enactment as an involuntary occurrence." During both exorcism and magnetism, symptoms tended to become more pronounced until there was some sort of peak crisis with dramatic convulsions, followed by a cure or alleviation of the symptoms.

John Joseph Gassner, a German Catholic priest of the 18th century, provides a direct link between demonology and hypnotism. Gassner believed that he had cured himself through exorcism, and he successfully threw demons out of the afflicted throughout Europe. Anton Mesmer observed some of Gassner's demonstrations and concluded that he really obtained his results from animal magnetism. Gassner regarded faith "an essential condition" for a cure. He usually touched the affected part. He could reputedly make the pulse of his patients vary by sheer will power.

---

* Mesmer did not invent the notion of healing by means of some form of suggestion. Similar modes were practiced by the ancient Chinese, Egyptians, Hebrews, Indians, Persians, Greeks, Romans and others. "More than 4,000 years ago," wrote one historian, "Wang Tai, the founder of Chinese medicine, taught a therapeutic technique that utilized incantations and manual passes over the body of the patient."

He could paralyze their limbs, make them weep or laugh, soothe or agitate them. It never occurred to either Gassner or Mesmer that such behavior stemmed from the power of suggestion rather than their own overweening egos.

Like the modern crop of "multiple personality disorders," the cataleptics proved to be intriguing patients who often displayed supernatural powers of vision or touch. The condition purportedly heightened these senses. One woman could hear only through her stomach, while many cataleptics claimed that they could see their own insides. French magnetizer Charles Despine created and treated numerous cataleptic patients in the early 1800s through hypnosis. In 1822, one of his 20-year-old patients reported that she could read with her fingers. She saw the walls of her room as "diaphanous as glass," and revealed having "double vision of the Hebrides." But Despine's prize pupil was a 21-year-old seamstress named Micheline Viollet who came under his care in 1823. At first, she did not reveal other expected symptoms such as "ecstasy" (a sort of rapturous trance) and somnambulism. When Despine told her that "they surely will one day appear," Micheline obligingly developed the required symptoms. If anyone she disliked so much as looked at her, she would instantly become immobile.

Like many such patients, Micheline went on to become a "healer" with Despine in her own right. The literature of the age is full of women who converted easily from patient to practitioner, having found a vocation in life. Similarly, many Survivors who recovered their repressed memories went on to become therapists who helped others unearth *their* memories.

Over time, cataleptics obliged in such histrionic ways that no one believed them any more. They would pass from conversing perfectly normally to suddenly throwing their heads back and laughing soundlessly, following by rolling around and jumping in the air while whistling. Responding to a few magnetic passes from a doctor, they would be rendered instantly immobile, then switch to sobs, laughter, and an exhausted, convulsive cough. After a half-hour performance, they might strike a pose reminiscent of a praying saint. "We see cataleptics by the dozen," wrote a Viennese doctor visiting Paris in 1857. "The magnetizers put the limbs of the magnetized in positions and directions that defy all laws of gravity and mechanics." Sometimes the cataleptics' seizures even led to self-induced death.

One early young male hypnotic subject came for treatment in 1803 after a year of having fits. He evinced a repugnance for anything made of metal, but particularly copper. During his hypnotic sessions, he felt a kind of peaceful fog envelop him, which protected him from unwelcome intruders, particularly women and children. Whenever they came within ten paces of him, he went into terrible convulsions and protested this "violation of my fog." If he were around in modern times, he might be complaining about his violated "boundaries" and interpret his aversion to metal as evidence that his mother stuck copper forks up his anus when he was a child.

By the late 1800s, a second wave of hypnotists, following James Braid, came to believe that they could *suggest* whatever they wanted to their patients rather than elicit an underlying problem such as catalepsy. Stage hypnotists such as Carl Hansen got their subjects to become as rigid as boards and lie between two chairs. Amused audiences watched subjects munch on raw potatoes which, they were told, were apples. In 1880, Sigmund Freud watched one of Hansen's performances and "became firmly convinced of the genuineness of hypnotic phenomena."

By the late 19th century, according to one chronicler, "so much was hypnosis in the air that becoming hypnotized required little more than a bit of experience: One learned what was expected and then unconsciously did it." This led to many people asserting that they *lived* in a constant state of hypnosis or somnambulism. An 1892 interview with a 26-year-old woman could as easily be a transcript of an early therapeutic session with a future Survivor with repressed memories. "I tell myself that if I died I wouldn't feel any different than right now. That wouldn't bother me. That's the reason you should just let me die." During a hypnosis session, she said she didn't really know what she was doing. "She doesn't feel any of her internal functions.... Everything around her seems unfamiliar, she has no sense of time, nor things, nor persons.... She has no sense of the reality of things and 'lives as though in a dream.'" Such patients were easily convinced a few years later that they were actually multiple personality disorders, a vogue that accelerated soon after the turn of the century.

In the progression from witches and demons to animal magnetism and diagnoses of hysteria, nothing had materially changed other than the role that the patients were expected to play. Many of the symptoms remained the same, although blaspheming against God, speaking in a demonic voice, or defining oneself as possessed became less popular. In many ways, however, as Spanos pointed out, those labeled as "hysterics" shared many characteristics with demoniacs: "They tended to be unhappy women who were socialized into viewing themselves as weak and passive, dissatisfied with their lives, socially and economically powerless, and without access to means of voicing their dissatisfactions or improving their lot outside of adopting the role of a sick person."

The term *hysteria* has been used to cover so many different symptoms that it is virtually meaningless. At various points, it has referred to spontaneous amnesia, convulsions, sensory or motor disturbances, high suggestibility, hallucinations, or anorexia. It has also been applied to a particular type of personality—one prone to violent mood swings, self-absorbed, suggestible, manipulative, frigid, flirtatious—which is, as Harriet Lerner pointed out in a 1974 article, simply a male caricature of femininity, adding that "a girl's immediate social environment puts enormous pressure on her to develop a style of cognition and personality that will lend itself to this diagnosis."* Spanos noted that the diagnosis "did not identify a unitary disorder, pinpoint a valid etiology, or lead to successful treatment." It did, however, provide a legitimation for the new discipline of psychiatry, which yearned for scientific medical trappings characterized by "diseases of the mind."

Charcot's Circus

No history of psychosomatic ailments would be complete without examining the psychiatric circus created by Jean-Martin Charcot at his Salpêtrière, a combination poorhouse, home for the aged, and asylum for insane women. Charcot was a great neurological systematizer who, in the 1870s and 1880s, became fascinated by what he termed "hysteria." It happened that women with mental disorders were housed alongside epileptics, and some who had no apparent organic problems began to imitate the epileptic fits, so Charcot initially labeled them "hystero-epileptics."

Freud critic Richard Webster argued that many of Charcot's (and, later, Freud's) purportedly psychosomatic patients may have actually suffered from real, undiagnosed neurological disorders such as temporal lobe epilepsy, organic brain damage, tuberculous meningitis, encephalitis, Tourette's syndrome, multiple sclerosis, or syphilis.** By ignoring their real ailments and focusing on "hysteria," Charcot effectively blamed the patients for the disorder. On the other hand, it is probable that many of his cases were indeed psychosomatic. Unfortunately, he himself *induced* and *encouraged* their problematic behavior rather than helping to alleviate it. In other words, many of his "hysterics" were iatrogenically influenced to believe in a mythical disease and to act out its appropriate symptoms.

Eventually, the Parisian neurologist charted an inflexible set of rules which he thought characterized such a disorder. Given their cue, the inmates obligingly performed as he thought they would. By pressing on their ovaries, Charcot could switch various bizarre behaviors on or off. His hysterics went through four phases: (1) an epileptic kind of fit; (2) a "period of contortions and *grands mouvements*" otherwise known as "clownism," during which patients flung themselves about, emitted piercing screams, and often took the position of *arc-de-cercle,* arching backwards so that only the head and heels rested on the ground; (3) a period of impassioned poses in which patients assumed exaggerated postures of prayer,

---

* The term *hysteria* could be satisfactorily applied to women who conformed to the social expectations of the era by succumbing to weakness, paralysis, or convulsions. Those who were too independent, who demanded equality or sexual freedom, were considered to be "morally insane," another pseudomedical diagnosis, and were locked away in institutions.

** It is also possible that some of Charcot's patients were faking in order to secure insurance payments. "Railway brain" and "railway spine" were, at that time, recently-named ailments in claims against train companies.

crucifixion, accusation, or the like; and (4) a "terminal period" in which anything could occur, often characterized by hallucinations such as seeing snakes.

Charcot was convinced that hysteria was an organic, hereditary disease, and he would delve vigorously into a patient's family background until he found "evidence" for his theories. In what Edward Shorter called a "crucible of suggestion," the women at the Salpêtrière received further instruction in bizarre behavior when Charcot invited an old-style magnetizer named Victor-Jean-Marie Burq to demonstrate "metallotherapy" on his wards. Soon, Burq was dragging symptoms from one side of a woman to the other with his metallic rods. Fascinated by hypnotism, Charcot began to induce hysteria. When professional colleagues expressed doubts, he threw his demonstrations open to the public.

It became clear to several of Charcot's young associates that he was deluding himself, creating the conditions he was supposedly discovering. "These stage performances," assistant Alex Munthe later wrote, "were nothing but an absurd farce, a hopeless muddle of truth and cheating." While some patients actually thought they were hypnotized, others were simply play-acting. It was also clear that a certain amount of "contagion" was present. One woman would begin screaming and rhythmically beating her fists, and another nearby would take up the same behavior.

In 1885, Charcot began to admit that psychological mechanisms rather than heredity might have something to do with hysteria. He became interested in hysterical symptoms following psychic shocks or accidents, labeling them "traumatic neurosis," or "hystero-neurosis." During that same year, a young Viennese doctor named Sigmund Freud came to study under Charcot for a few months. The experience catalyzed Freud, diverting him from neuropathology to psychopathology. In a letter to his fiancée, Freud wrote that Charcot was a genius who was "uprooting my aims and opinions," giving him a "new idea of perfection." While some critics complained of Charcot's showmanship, the young Austrian physician clearly loved it. "My brain is sated, as if I had spent an evening at the theatre."

Charcot's circus quickly collapsed after his death in 1893, and his carefully constructed phases of hysteria fell into disrepute. Without the master to induce them, the symptoms simply vanished, and no more unfortunate young women balanced on their heads and heels.* But by that time, Freud and Josef Breuer had taken his lead and were sowing the seeds of modern psychology and the theory of repression.

Freud's Mental Extractions

---

* It should be noted, however, that in 1988 neurologist Colin Binnie described a classic *arc-de-cercle* case in a woman diagnosed as epileptic. Thus, there may be some neurological reality to the posture. It may be that some of Charcot's patients included true epileptics from whom they learned this behavior.

Until the last few decades, Freud's pronouncements were treated almost as holy psychological writ. Now critics understand that Freud was just another human being, very much a man of his time. He made genuine contributions to the understanding of psychology, popularizing many ideas that seem self-evident to us now: People often act irrationally, for reasons they don't admit to themselves. Our childhood experiences shape our self-concepts and methods of dealing with the world. Our dreams reveal many personal concerns, fears, and desires. Much goes on in our minds below the conscious level. If we become infuriated at one person, we sometimes deflect that anger illogically onto someone else. We can also be grateful to subsequent Freudians for helping to fight the eugenics movement (and Nazism); for promoting a healthier attitude toward human sexuality; for more humane treatment of children, mental patients, and prisoners; and for many other beneficial modern attitudes.

But Freud has bequeathed us a mixed heritage. Much that we have simply accepted as revealed Freudian truth has never been proved. Essentially, Freud provided a convincing mythology for our times, one that has permeated every aspect of our culture. Some of our most fundamental modern assumptions are based on Freud's pronouncements, and those assumptions may not necessarily be correct. Too often, as psychologist Garth Wood wrote, Freud "dreamed up what was for him a plausible entity [i.e., the id, ego, superego, death wish, Oedipus complex], and then set about finding mental phenomena which for him, but not for others, tended to support it."

Freud followed in the grand tradition of physicians who identified the precise symptoms they expected to find, then proceeded to induce them. Freud believed in much of the quackery that had preceded him, including the notion that excessive masturbation caused neurosis, that there was such a thing as neurasthenia,* that there was a nasal reflex arc, and that hysteria could be provoked by pressing on the ovaries, which he termed "stimulation of the hysterogenic zone." Freud believed in a variety of hands-on therapies, one of which played a significant role in early recovered memory cases, as we will shortly see.

Writing to his friend Wilhelm Fliess in 1895, Freud said, "I have invented a strange therapy of my own: I search for sensitive areas, press on them, and thus provoke fits of shaking which free her [the patient]." That same year, Freud treated a 27-year-old named Emma Eckstein, who came from a prominent socialist family and was active in the Viennese women's movement. Like many "hysterical" or "neurasthenic" patients of the era, she came to Freud with vague complaints, including stomach aches and menstrual problems. He deduced that she suffered

---

*   "Neurasthenia," a catch-all diagnosis coined by American psychologist George Beard in 1881, is discussed in some detail in Chapter 7.

from excessive masturbation that could be cured by operating on her nose. He prevailed on his best friend, Wilhelm Fliess, to perform the operation.

Fliess was a well-respected Berlin ear-nose-and-throat specialist who complained of the "immense multitude" of women who rushed from spa to spa without success, "falling into the hands of quacks." He, on the other hand, knew the scientific truth that their troubles often stemmed from the nasal reflex. At first, he used cocaine on his patients' noses, which provided temporary relief (and a pleasant buzz, no doubt).* Then he cauterized the noses, but that too didn't do the trick. Finally, he decided that removal of a portion of the left middle turbinate bone would permanently cure female sexual afflictions. Freud concurred, and the unfortunate Emma Eckstein believed them.

Fliess bungled the operation, sewing a large piece of gauze into Eckstein's nose. Before anyone realized that, Freud described her worsening condition in a letter to Fliess: "Eckstein's condition is still unsatisfactory; persistent swelling, going up and down 'like an avalanche'; pain, so that morphine cannot be dispensed with; bad nights." She emitted an awful odor. Then another doctor opened her nose and, as Freud wrote, "suddenly he pulled at something like a thread, kept on pulling and before either one of us had time to think, at least half a meter of gauze had been removed from the cavity. The next moment came a flood of blood. The patient turned white, her eyes bulged, and she had no pulse."

Eckstein survived, though she continued to hemorrhage for some time. Freud managed to rationalize the entire affair, assuring Fliess that it was "one of those accidents that happen to the most fortunate and circumspect of surgeons." In the end, Freud even managed to blame Emma Eckstein. Her bleeding was all caused by hysteria! Incredibly, Eckstein remained true to Freud, even becoming a therapist herself. In 1904, using books from Freud's library as her sources, she wrote a short monograph on the dangers of childhood masturbation, recommending special bandages and restrictive clothing to prevent such mishaps. Soon thereafter, she took permanently to her couch, convinced that her legs were paralyzed. She died in 1924.**

Emma Eckstein was one of the first patients upon whom Freud practiced an-

---

*   Freud may have suggested the cocaine treatment to Fliess. Ten years before, Freud proclaimed cocaine a miracle drug, took it himself, and saw it as his road to fame. He introduced his friend Fleischl to the drug as an alternative to his morphine habit. Unfortunately, his friend died a few years later in a cocaine agony, crying that ants were crawling under his skin. In *Freudian Fallacy* (1984), E. M. Thornton argued that *all* of Freud's theories stemmed from his paranoia and hallucinations as a cocaine addict. Freud's letters to Fliess were filled with obsessive concern over his nose and its secretions, and Freud frequently applied cocaine as a curative.

**   In fact, Freud's vanity probably condemned Eckstein to her fate, through his authority and her suggestibility. Dora Teleky, a well-known Viennese physician, "discovered" an ulcer in Eckstein's abdomen and either operated on it or pretended to do so. Immediately, the invalid miraculously recovered. Freud, indignant at this interference, broke off his analysis, declaring, "Well, that's the end of Emma. That dooms her from now on. Nobody can cure her neurosis." Taking her cue from Freud, Eckstein relapsed, never again to leave her couch.

other form of questionable therapy that became the cornerstone for his psychological theories. He concluded that her problems stemmed not only from masturbation (known as "self-abuse" in those days) but from a repressed memory of sexual abuse when she was eight. He prompted her to recall a visit to a confectioners during which the shopkeeper had grabbed her genitals through her clothing. This memory was mild, however, compared to those he eventually elicited from Eckstein in 1897: "I obtained a scene [i.e., a "memory"] about the circumcision of a girl. The cutting of a piece of the labia minor (which is still shorter today), sucking up the blood, following which the child was given a piece of the skin to eat." Like many modern physicians who are "experts" in child sexual abuse, Freud had found physical "evidence" to corroborate this memory.

Taking his lead from Charcot and Bernheim, Freud had begun hypnotizing patients late in 1887, primarily using direct suggestion in an attempt to ameliorate their symptoms. Before that, he had relied primarily on various forms of ablutions ("hydrotherapy"), mild electrical stimulation, massage, and the "rest cure" popularized by American physician Weir Mitchell *(see Chapter 7).*

Soon, Freud started to use hypnosis to access what he suspected were repressed memories. In 1895, in uneasy collaboration with Joseph Breuer, Freud published *Studies in Hysteria,* in which he elaborated his theory that unconscious repressed memories caused hysteria, obsession, and other neurotic symptoms. "The patient only gets free from the hysterical symptom by reproducing the pathogenic impressions that caused it and by giving utterance to them with an expression of affect, and thus the therapeutic task *consists solely in inducing him to do so,"* Freud wrote. The following year, he elaborated on this theory in three essays, making it clear that he considered *repressed memories of childhood sexual abuse* to be the root cause of all hysterical symptoms. Because Freud's theories and methods provided the template for the modern hunt for repressed memories, and because many modern scholars have argued over this crucial aspect of his early work, I will examine his practice during this period in some detail.

Freud based his theory on a small number of cases. He referred to twelve in *Studies in Hysteria,* admitting that most of them were unsuccessful. "But it is my opinion that the obstacles have lain in the personal circumstances of the patients and have not been due to any question on theory," he asserted. "I am justified in leaving these unsuccessful cases out of account." By February 5, 1896, when Freud sent off his first two papers openly proclaiming sex abuse as hysteria's long-sought "source of the Nile," he had added only one new case, bringing the total to thirteen. Surprisingly, by April 21, less than three months later, when he gave a lecture on the subject (published as his third paper, *The Etiology of Hysteria),* Freud claimed to have treated eighteen hysterical patients with his revolutionary method. This is particularly confusing, because Freud wrote to his friend Fliess on May 4, 1896, complaining that "my consulting room is empty" and that "for weeks on end I see no new faces."

Until the end of 1895, Freud relied at least partially on hypnosis to delve into his patients' unconscious. Frustrated by his inability to hypnotize some subjects—and by the outright unwillingness of others—Freud invented a new "pressure procedure" in which his patients lay down, closed their eyes, and allowed Freud to press on their foreheads or squeeze their heads between his hands. They were then to report whatever images or words popped into their heads.

In his 1892 treatment of Elisabeth von R., he first "made use of the technique of bringing out pictures and ideas by means of pressing on the patient's head." Sometimes this pressure prompted detailed scenarios, "as though she were reading a lengthy book of pictures," but when Elisabeth was in a cheerful mood, she often failed to recall anything while Freud pressed on her cranium. Undeterred, the psychologist "resolved, therefore, to adopt the hypothesis that the procedure never failed; that on every occasion under the pressure of my hand some idea occurred to Elisabeth or some picture came before her eyes," but she was simply unwilling to report it. When he insisted that she report these thoughts, she finally obliged him, though it often took two or three head squeezes. "I derived from this analysis a literally unqualified reliance on my technique," Freud wrote with satisfaction.

Freud realized that he was not *literally* pressing memories out of his patients' unconscious. It simply seemed to be an appropriate metaphor, "the most convenient way of applying suggestion." Without apparent irony, he asserted that he could as easily have made his patients stare into a crystal ball. "As a rule," Freud wrote, "the pressure procedure fails on the first or second occasion." Then, however, the flood gates opened, and the patient cooperated, engaged in a fascinating intellectual pursuit. "By explaining things to him," Freud said, "by giving him information about the marvelous world of psychical processes ..., we make him himself into a collaborator, induce him to regard himself with the objective interest of an investigator."

Freud emphasized that this method worked only if the physician assumed an extraordinary importance to the patient akin to a "father confessor who gives absolution." He described one female patient's "quite special relation to the figure of the physician," and another who wanted to kiss him.* Because this personal relationship was so important, Freud observed that he had to work with attractive, intelligent patients. "I cannot imagine bringing myself to delve into the psychical mechanism of a hysteria in anyone who struck me as low-minded and repellent."

---

* Thirty-five years later, Freud still vividly recalled this incident involving "one of my most acquiescent patients" who, upon awakening from hypnosis, "threw her arms around my neck." Freud was saved from any temptation to respond when a servant unexpectedly entered the room.

It also helped if they manifested complete confidence and dependence upon him, the physician, because "a good number of the patients who would be suitable for this form of treatment abandon the doctor as soon as the suspicion begins to dawn on them of the direction in which the investigation is leading."

Before arriving at the crucial traumatic scene, Freud believed that he had to go slowly, establishing rapport and gaining patients' confidence. Then, through "repeated, indeed continuous, use of this procedure of pressure on the forehead," he delved for memories like an archaeologist digging ever deeper. "We force our way into the internal strata, overcoming resistances all the time; we get to know the themes accumulated in one of these strata and the threads running through it." Finally, after pursuing numerous side paths, he could "penetrate by a main path straight to the nucleus of the pathogenic organization.... Now the patient helps us energetically. His resistance is for the most part broken."

In 1895, though he had been using this method for some time, Freud had not yet concluded that all hysteria stemmed from sexual abuse. Perhaps, however, he was merely remaining circumspect, as he later asserted Breuer wished him to be. Even in 1895, he described two sisters who "shared a secret; they slept in one room and on a particular night they had both been subjected to sexual assaults by a certain man." By February of 1896, Freud explicitly blamed hysteria on *"precocious experience of sexual relations with actual excitement of the genitals, resulting from sexual abuse."* These thirteen cases were "without exception of a severe kind" that could be classed as "grave sexual injuries; some of them were positively revolting." Seven of the perpetrators were other children, usually older brothers, while the others were nursemaids, governesses, domestic servants, or teachers. In late April, Freud provided a similar list, then added that the abuser was "all too often, a close relative." He asserted that disgust at food or habitual choking was caused by repressed memories of oral sex, just as indigestion and intestinal disturbances could be explained by forgotten sodomy. In one case, he believed, a child had been forced to masturbate an adult woman with his foot.

During the rest of 1896, Freud appears to have zeroed in on fathers as the culprits. "It seems to me more and more that the essential point of hysteria is that it results from *perversion* on the part of the seducer," Freud wrote to Fliess on December 6, 1896, "and *more and more* that heredity is seduction by the father." In the same letter, he discussed a patient with a "highly perverse father." On January 4, 1897, he wrote in detail about a patient who balked at his seduction theory. "When I thrust the explanation at her [that her father had sexually abused her], she was at first won over; then she committed the folly of questioning the old man himself." When her father indignantly declared himself innocent, Freud's patient believed him, much to her therapist's disgust. "In order to facilitate the work," he concluded, "I am hoping she will feel miserable again."

Soon afterward, Freud was finding more and more disgusting memories (presumably in other clients), going back to earliest childhood. "The early period before the age of one-and-a-half years is becoming ever more significant," he wrote to Fliess on January 24, 1897. "Thus I was able to trace back, with certainty, a hysteria that developed ... for the first time at eleven months and [I could] hear again the words that were exchanged between two adults at that time! It is as though it comes from a phonograph." By September 21, 1897, in a famous letter expressing doubts about his theory, Freud asserted that "in all cases, the *father*, not excluding my own, had to be accused of being perverse."

Did Freud Lead His Patients?

What are we to make of Freud's briefly held "seduction theory?" Did he indeed uncover horrifying repressed memories of paternal incest, or did he provide a template for the modern brand of memory seekers? We can get a clue from Freud's arrogance. "We must not believe what they say [when they deny having memories], we must always assume, and tell them, too, that they have kept something back.... We must insist on this, we must repeat the pressure and represent ourselves as infallible, till at last we are really told something." Or again: "It is of course of great importance for the progress of the analysis that one should always turn out to be in the right *vis-à-vis* the patient, otherwise one would always be dependent on what he chose to tell one." Freud refused to accept no for an answer. "We must not be led astray by initial denials," he wrote during this period, sounding just like the *Malleus Maleficarum* or *The Courage to Heal.* "If we keep firmly to what we have inferred, we shall in the end conquer every resistance by emphasizing the unshakable nature of our convictions." No wonder he could write that "the pressure technique in fact never fails."

It is instructive to read Freud's 1896 description of how he unearthed repressed memories:

> The fact is that these patients never repeat these stories spontaneously, nor do they ever in the course of a treatment suddenly present the physician with the complete recollection of a scene of this kind. One only succeeds in awakening the psychical trace of a precocious sexual event under the most energetic pressure of the analytic procedure, and against an enormous resistance. Moreover, the memory must be extracted from them piece by piece, and while it is being awakened in their consciousness they become the prey to an emotion which it would be hard to counterfeit. Conviction will follow in the end, if one is not influenced by the patients' behavior.

It is clear that Freud's expectations contributed heavily to what he found in his patients' unconscious. "If the memory which we have uncovered does not answer our expectations," he wrote, "it may be that we ought to pursue the same path a little further; perhaps behind the first traumatic scene there may be concealed the memory of a second, which satisfies our requirements better." It required the "most energetic pressure" to "extract" such memories; they never surfaced spontaneously or as whole, coherent events. "Before they come for analysis the patients know nothing about these scenes," Freud proudly noted. "They are indignant as a rule if we warn them that such scenes are going to emerge. Only the strongest compulsion of the treatment can induce them to embark on a reproduction of them." Once they finally produced a suitable memory, they often tried to deny it. "Something has occurred to me now, but you obviously put it into my head," they would say, or "I know what you expect me to answer," or "Something has occurred to me now, it's true, but it seems to me as if I'd put it up deliberately." To these protestations, Freud turned a deaf ear. "In all such cases, I remain unshakably firm." Often, the doctor was even more blunt. "The principal point is that I should guess the secret and tell it to the patient straight out."*

Even 35 years later, when Freud supposedly realized that he had been mistaken, he wrote, "It was necessary to make efforts on one's own part so as to urge and compel him [the patient] to remember. The amount of effort required ... increased in direct proportion to the difficulty of what had to be remembered." These passages, as revealing as they are, hardly convey the extent to which Freud encouraged his patients' "memories" and enthusiastically validated them. His disciple Sandor Ferenczi later described how the early Freud "involved himself passionately and selflessly in the therapy of neurotics, lying on the floor for hours, if necessary, next to a patient in the throes of a hysterical crisis."

When the patients finally brought forth the fantasies their therapist sought, they displayed profound emotions that Freud (and many therapists after him) took to be proof that the memories were real. "While they are recalling these infantile experiences to consciousness, they suffer under the most violent sensations, of which they are ashamed and which they try to conceal." Sounding precisely like Ellen Bass or Renee Fredrickson, Freud dismissed their subsequent denials: "Even after they have gone through them ... in such a convincing manner, they still attempt to withhold belief from them, by emphasizing the fact that, unlike what

---

* Freud critics Jean Scheme, Malcolm Macmillan, and Allen Esterson believe that Freud's patients never actually produced any memories at all, but that Freud only *inferred* incest. It seems quite clear from several quoted passages, however, that many of his patients did indeed "relive" highly emotional traumas in which they eventually came to believe. 'The behavior of patients while they are reproducing these infantile experiences is in every respect incompatible with the assumption that the scenes are anything else than a reality which is being felt with distress," Freud wrote. There is no question, though, that Freud cajoled and bullied them unmercifully, exhorting them to remember. In 1896, he wrote to Fliess that he was "almost hoarse" from pressuring patients ten to eleven hours a day.

happens in the case of other forgotten material, they have no feeling of remembering the scenes." Compare this statement to therapist Renee Fredrickson's observation that "repressed memories rarely seem real when they first emerge."

Incredibly, Freud dismissed the notion that he might have planted any of the memories. *"We are not in a position to force anything on the patient about the things of which he is ostensibly ignorant or to influence the products of the analysis by arousing an expectation."* How did Freud know this? "I have never once succeeded, by foretelling something, in altering or falsifying the reproduction of memories ... for if I had, it would inevitably have been betrayed in the end by some contradiction in the material." Later, Freud reiterated that "I have never yet succeeded in forcing on a patient a scene I was expecting to find, in such a way that he seemed to be living through it with all the appropriate feelings."

Because the stories appeared self-consistent, he believed them. Later, when the memories floated up from as early as one-and-a-half years old, Freud explained why he believed them. "I should not lend credence to these extraordinary findings myself if their complete reliability were not proved by the development of the subsequent neurosis." In other words, Freud, like Lenore Terr and other modern repressed memory believers, insisted that the *symptoms* of the adult *proved* the validity of the memories.

Freud also believed that the remarkable similarity of the stories proved that they were true, just as those who heard about ritual abuse were positive that similar tales constituted validation. Freud wrote about the "uniformity that they exhibit in certain details, which is a necessary consequence if the preconditions of these experiences are always of the same kind, but which would otherwise lead us to believe that there were secret understandings between the various patients." Of course, it was not necessary for the patients to confer with one another for them to confabulate similar stories. Freud *cued* them without knowing it.

Finally, Freud asserted that he had found external corroboration for two cases. Like Judith Herman, however, he appears to have been eager to accept circumstantial evidence as "proof." One patient's older brother admitted having sexual contacts with her in late childhood, so Freud assumed that he had also done so when she was an infant. In another instance, two patients recalled having been abused by the same man. This fact could indicate nothing more than Freud's success at suggesting abuse to his patients, who probably conferred with one another as well. Similarly, many sisters in consultation with one another recovered similar abuse memories at the hands of their father and took that to be corroboration.

Freud himself saw a parallel to the confessions of "witches," but he apparently concluded that the unfortunate witches had *really* all been victims of incest: "Why did the devil who took possession of the poor things invariably abuse them sexually and in a loathsome manner? Why are their confessions under torture so like the communications made by my patients in psychological treatment?" It did not occur to Freud, at the time, that the reason for the similarity was probably quite simple. In both cases, determined interrogators induced the confession/memory of horrors, whether they ever really happened or not. Freud went even further, foreshadowing the rage to find memories of Satanic cults. "I dream," he wrote, "of a primeval devil religion whose rites are carried on secretly, and I understand the harsh therapy of the witches' judges."

In 1896, Freud summarized his real reason for believing the "scenes" of abuse that his patients revealed. They explained everything. They were necessary for his theory. "It is exactly like putting together a child's picture-puzzle: after many attempts, we become absolutely certain in the end which piece belongs in the empty gap; for only that one piece fills out the picture." As we have seen, this same analogy—finding the missing piece which explains the puzzle of one's life—cropped up repeatedly a century later, during the great repressed-memory hunt of the late 20th century.

By 1897, Freud had become less certain of the validity of such memories. He realized that he may have applied too much pressure. Still, in December, he was encouraged by a report from Emma Eckstein, now acting as a therapist, as he wrote to Fliess: "My confidence in the father-etiology has risen greatly. Eckstein treated her patient deliberately in such a manner as not to give her the slightest hint of what will emerge from the unconscious, and in the process obtained ... the identical scenes with the father."

This passage is somewhat confusing, as it appears that Freud may have already treated the same patient and elicited the identical memory, which surfaced again. Even assuming that Eckstein was dealing with a new patient, however, we have only Freud's second-hand assurance that the therapist didn't give the "slightest hint" of the sort of incest memories she sought. In my own interviews with therapists, I repeatedly heard this same assertion: "I never ask leading questions or make suggestions." Yet in virtually every case, the therapist had informed the patient that memories of abuse are often repressed and may resurface during therapy. They did not consider this to be a strong cue. I suspect that Emma Eckstein—obviously a rather troubled and emotional woman who had just recovered her own "memories"—was not quite so circumspect as she thought.

Later that month, Freud again wrote to Fliess, describing another dreadful repressed memory session in which the patient supposedly recalled a scene from when she was six months old, during which her mother nearly bled to death as a result of an injury inflicted by her father. When she was two, she continued to remember, her father "brutally deflowered her and infected her with gonorrhea, so that her life was in danger as a result of the loss of blood and vaginitis." Finally, she vividly described a scene (complete with dialogue) between her father and mother that Freud interpreted as anal intercourse. Clearly, Freud was both repelled and intrigued by these "filthy stories," as he called them, and he apparently believed them, as implausible as such early recollections were.

Hypothesizing that the patient's mind had blotted out many details, Freud drew an analogy to "Russian censorship" in which "words, entire phrases and sentences [are] obliterated in black, so that the rest becomes unintelligible." Then, quoting Goethe, Freud suggested a new motto, which the modern Survivor advocates inscribed on their hearts: "What have they done to you, poor child?"

Eventually, Freud changed his mind, concluding that most of these incestuous events never occurred, that the "memories" were actually a form of fantasy, even wish fulfillment. He couldn't admit, however, that he had actually *planted* these memories. In 1925, Freud wrote that "these scenes of seduction had never taken place," adding that "they were only phantasies which my patients had made up or which I myself had perhaps forced on them." He still couldn't really bring himself to admit his own role, though. Later in the same paragraph, he asserted: "I do not believe even now that I forced the seduction-phantasies on my patients, that I 'suggested' them. I had in fact stumbled for the first time upon the *Oedipus complex.*"

Instead of admitting his own role in forcing clients to recall mythical abuse, he concluded that his client's stories were innate fantasies. As a result, he concocted the Oedipus and Electra complexes, asserting that young children yearned to displace the parent of the same gender and have sex with the other. Freud's entire elaborate edifice was based on his obsession with childhood sexuality. Indeed, children are sensual beings, but whether an "Oedipus complex" accounts for our psychological problems or whether the way we were toilet trained determines our personality is subject to dispute. Controlled scientific studies have repeatedly failed to corroborate such notions.

Much to his credit, Freud emphasized the reality of incest in a 1916 lecture. "Phantasies of being seduced are of particular interest," he said, "because so often they are not phantasies but real memories," reiterating that "you must not suppose ... that sexual abuse of a child by its nearest male relatives belongs entirely to the realm of phantasy." On the other hand, he confused the issue by asserting that "in the case of girls [for whom] their father figures fairly regularly as the seducer, there can be no doubt ... of the imaginary nature of the accusation."

Finally, Freud muddied the waters by saying that it didn't really matter whether the incest was real or imagined. "The outcome [i.e., neurotic symptoms] is the same, and up to the present, we have not succeeded in pointing to any difference in the consequences, whether fantasy or reality has had the greater share in these childhood events." Such relativistic sophism became a standard line for modern therapists, particularly those hunting for repressed memories. "It doesn't matter whether your memories are literally true or not," they would tell their patients. "The emotional truth is valid." Of course, it *does* matter very much to parents as well as to accusing children whether these events actually took place or not.

Despite his retraction of the "seduction theory," Freud continued to promulgate the notion that patients could banish certain traumatic events from their consciousness, and that only by recalling and reliving these crucial moments could they be whole and healed. In fact, Freud never really repudiated his early work. He did not publicly distance himself from the seduction theory until 1906, and in his 1925 autobiography, he still maintained that sexual experience lay behind all neuroses. Writing of his work on repressed sexual abuse memories, he asserted: "I was not prepared for this conclusion and my expectations played no part in it." He still believed that uncompleted sex acts, sexual abstinence, or excessive masturbation caused anxiety and neurasthenia. And he most certainly still believed in repression, which, in 1914, he called "the foundation stone on which the structure of psychoanalysis rests." In 1925, he repeated that "the theory of repression became the corner-stone of our understanding of the neuroses.... It is possible to take repression as a centre and to bring all the elements of psycho-analytic theory into relation with it."

The "pressure procedure" also provided the prototype for classical psychoanalysis. Although Freud later concluded that he should never touch his patients, he continued to have them lie down and use "free association," as he described in a 1913 essay, "On Beginning the Treatment." He remained out of sight, since "I cannot put up with being stared at by other people for eight hours a day (or more)." Freud still preferred well-educated, wealthy clients with mild neuroses. He insisted on hour-long sessions six days a week (along with prompt payment of a substantial fee). He continued to break through his patients' "resistance" to inform them of their true problems. "It remains the first aim of the treatment to attach [the patient] to it and to the person of the doctor." Freud believed that "the patient's first symptoms or chance actions" often betrayed their problems. Thus, he concluded that a young philosopher who straightened the creases of his trousers must have been "a former coprophilic of the highest refinement," or that a young girl who pulled the hem of her skirt over exposed ankles revealed "her narcissistic pride in her physical beauty and her inclinations to exhibitionism."

By enshrining the concept of repression, Freud planted the seeds for the current epidemic of incest accusations. At the same time, as Jeffrey Masson pointed out, Freud's flip-flop also had a disastrous effect on *real* incest victims.* Even though

---

* In his 1984 book, *The Assault on Truth: Freud's Suppression of the Seduction Theory,* Jeffrey Masson complained about the effect of Freud's flip-flop, as well as documenting other Freudian flaws, including the horrendous nose operation on Emma Eckstein in 1895. But Masson miraculously swallowed the 1896 repressed

Freud himself never denied the reality of some incest memories, until recent decades many psychoanalysts routinely dismissed their patients' all-too-well-remembered stories of sexual abuse. "Ah, yes," they would nod knowingly. "Those are just fantasies. Your father didn't *really* do that to you! Your unconscious only *wishes* that he had."

Multiple Personalities

As the turn of the century approached, another fascinating concept emerged—that people could harbor several distinct personalities within the same body and brain. Robert Louis Stevenson prepared the way with *The Strange Case of Dr. Jekyll and Mr. Hyde* (1886), while Oscar Wilde contributed *The Picture of Dorian Gray* (1891).* The fictional stories reflected the underlying Victorian tension between science and irrationality, between puritanical sexual codes and pornographic imaginations. Freud expressed these feelings in his concept of the submerged and violent id, a turbulent repressed unconscious held down by the beleaguered forces of the conscious ego and the prudish superego.

Philosopher Ian Hacking dated the emergence of intense interest in multiple personalities to 1875, the year in which one Felida X was diagnosed by a French surgeon who had an interest in hypnotism. The surgeon was largely motivated by a philosophical argument in support of "psychological positivism," trying to prove to conservatives and the Church that there was no inherently unitary "soul." Felida's dual personality was held to refute the "dogmatic transcendental unity of apperception that made the self prior to all knowledge." In their struggle to sound lofty and scientific, the experts of the age delighted in pedantic jargon. As Hacking put it, the Victorian age introduced "a particular medico-forensic-political lan-guage.... The sheer proliferation of labels in that domain during the 19th century may have engendered vastly more kinds of people [i.e., diagnoses] than the world had ever known before." After Felida, a multitude of multiples ensued, particularly in France, where Pierre Janet applied himself to its proper identification.

Like Freud, Pierre Janet had studied with Charcot and was fascinated with the mechanisms of the mind.** Janet coined the term *dissociation* to describe a mecha-

---

memory scenario without a qualm, asserting that the incest horrors Freud extracted from his patients were all true. Masson's book, with its illogical conclusion, unfortunately served as one of the cornerstones of the repressed memory Survivor movement.

*   Stevenson wrote his Jekyll/Hyde story after reading a "French scientific journal on subconsciousness." There were a few cases of "double" personality documented earlier in the 19th century, but they weren't full-blown multiples. For a skeptical summary, see Michael G. Kenny, *The Passion of Ansel Bourne*. For a more credulous overview, see Henri Ellenberger, *The Discovery of the Unconscious*, pages 126–170.

**   Also like Freud, Janet had his mystical side. He believed, for instance, that time travel would be possible. "Everything that has existed," he proclaimed, "still exists and endures in a place which we do not understand." While Janet sometimes seemed aware of the dangers of suggestibility ("Most frequently, psychotics are acting"), nism that he assumed to exist, just as Freud presumed the reality of repression. Janet theorized that the mind was capable of splitting off from itself in some form, usually to protect itself from distress. The more sensitive, neurasthenic, or hysterical the patient, and the more pronounced the trauma, the more likely that severe dissociation, or even multiple personality, would occur. Janet emphasized the importance of naming each psychic part: "Once baptized, the unconscious personality is more clear and definite; it shows its psychological traits more clearly." In 1887, he hypnotized Lucie, a young woman with a history of "hysterical" symptoms. The following exchange took place while Lucie was hypnotized and practiced automatic writing:

> *How are you?*
> I don't know.
> *There must be someone there who hears me.*
> Yes.
> *Who is it?*
> Someone other than Lucie.
> *Ah. Another person. Would you like us to give her a name?*
> No.
> *Yes. It would be more convenient.*
> All right. Adrienne.
> *Very well, Adrienne. Do you hear me?*
> Yes.

It is fairly obvious from this dialogue that Janet was creating the multiplicity he expected to find. Lucie, already compliant in her hypnotic inductee role, went along with it. This process replicated the exorcist's methodology. He, too, insisted on speaking directly to internal demons, each of whom needed a name. The similarity of the process was not lost on early proponents of multiple personality. They proclaimed that demoniacs had actually been multiple personalities, misdiagnosed by the ignorant, superstitious clerics. In fact, both exorcist and psychologist practiced the same stratagem, and their clients simply complied by acting out the expected role.

The real blossoming of multiple personality diagnoses took place in America, however, after the publication of *The Dissociation of a Personality* by Morton Prince in 1905. Prince, who founded and edited the *Journal of Abnormal Psychol-*

---

he fell into the familiar trap of validating anything his patients said. One visitor was startled to find "housed together many persecutionist patients who fired one another emotionally with fantastic tales." Janet dismissed his criticism, asserting, "I believe those people, until it is proven to me that what they say is untrue." By 1925, however, Janet had become much more cynical, particularly about Freudians, writing: "The psychoanalysts invariably set to work in order to discover a traumatic memory, with the *a priori* conviction that it is there to be discovered.... Owing to the nature of their methods, they can invariably find what they seek."

ogy, saw the exploration of multiple personalities as his ticket to fame. "Abnormal psychology is fast forging to the front as an important field of research," he wrote in the book's preface. He asserted that the field had "long awaited investigation by modern methods." In his introduction, he explained that Janet had revealed simpler forms of dissociation through hypnosis and automatic writing. Trance mediums displayed a more fully developed form. But he, Morton Prince, had identified a full-blown case of multiplicity for the first time. "Such cases are generally overlooked," he assured the reader, because "such persons often pass before the world as mentally healthy persons." Finally, he revealed that he found these cases to be "fascinating objects of study."

In 1898, Miss Christine Beauchamp (an alias for Clara Fowler), arrived on Prince's doorstep at the age of 23. He described her as "a neurasthenic of an extreme type, [suffering from] headaches, insomnia, bodily pains, persistent fatigue, and poor nutrition." In other words, she displayed all the psychosomatic symptoms expected at the time. Even as a child, she was "impressionable ... given to day dreaming and living in her imagination." She clearly attracted the psychologist, who identified in her "that natural refinement of thought and feeling which is inborn, and which is largely made up of delicacy of sentiment and appreciation of everything that is fine in thought and perceptions.... She is well educated and has marked literary tastes and faculties. She is essentially a bibliophile, and is never so happy as when allowed to delve amongst books." Finally, he noted that she was "very suggestible."

Over the next seven years, Prince encouraged an extremely close and dependent relationship with Beauchamp. "During most of this time," he wrote, "she has been under constant, and often for long periods, daily observation." Even when she went away for summer vacation, "a considerable correspondence with each personality has been kept up." In other words, Prince would write to each of three personalities, and they would respond, using different handwriting, samples of which were reprinted in the book. Prince noted that the multiple parts engaged in "a comedy of errors, which has been sometimes farcical and sometimes tragic." That is quite a good description of the entire book, in which Prince painstakingly and unwittingly conned both the young lady and himself.

Yet Prince was utterly convinced that he had not cued his patient. During an early hypnotic session, he was surprised when she denied remembering something she had previously told him. Then he understood her to refer to herself in the third person as "She." Although he sincerely believed that he had discovered a new personality "against my protests and in spite of my skepticism," it is obvious that he eagerly jumped on what he considered a significant clue. "I hastened to follow up the lead offered and asked, as if in ignorance of her meaning, who 'She' was." Not satisfied, he "pursued her relentlessly in my numerous examinations."

Why are you not "She"?

Because "She" does not know the same things that I do.

But you both have the same arms and legs, haven't you?

Yes, but arms and legs do not make us the same.

Well if you are different persons, what are your names?

Maddeningly, Beauchamp refused to take the bait, remaining "evasive, unable to answer; [she] made every effort not to commit herself." Finally, after quite some time, this newly "discovered" personality was labeled first B II, then Chris, and finally Sally.

It seems obvious that Prince unwittingly cued his patient into multiplicity, as his friend William James suspected: "Where you see occasion for singling out definite phases, there is nothing in Nature but a flux of incoherent memories, emotions, impulses, and delusions." James wasn't terribly concerned, however, assuring Prince that to "define any continuum," arbitrary labels had to be applied. That wasn't all there was to it, however. As social anthropologist Michael Kenny observed, "Morton Prince was scarcely a detached scientific observer; he and Miss Beauchamp mutually, though unconsciously, colluded in the composition of a medical drama based on stereotypic nineteenth-century roles."

In many ways, Christine Beauchamp was the ideal candidate for multiplicity. She had a highly developed imagination, read widely, and craved the attention Prince gave her.* Once she entered into the spirit of the roles she was to play, she obviously relished them. She probably came to believe in them herself, until Prince triumphantly discovered "the Real Miss Beauchamp" (a fourth personality) and reintegrated all of them.** At the end of the book, he wrote, without intended irony, that "these states [now] seem to her very largely differences of moods. She regrets them, but does not attempt to excuse them, because, as she says, 'After all, it is always myself.'"

Emil Kraepelin and His Patient

I will conclude this chapter with a case that serves as a parable and warning to both therapist and patient.

Munich, 1904. Emil Kraepelin, author of an influential psychiatric textbook and creator of the term "manic-depression," introduces a patient to his lecture

---

*   It is entirely possible that the whole business about who "She" was stemmed from a misunderstanding, since Beauchamp had apparently read Rider Haggard's book entitled *She*.

**   Not to be outdone, Morton Prince's namesake and competitor W. F. Prince, a firm believer in psychic phenomena, soon hypnotized Doris Fischer, a medium, and announced that she, too, contained multiple personalities. Not surprisingly, her case developed along precisely parallel lines to that of Miss Beauchamp. W. F. Prince eventually adopted Miss Fischer as his daughter.

hall colleagues in the most humiliating, demeaning way: "Gentlemen—the young lady, aged 30, carefully dressed in black, who comes into the hall with short, shuffling steps, leaning on the nurse, and sinks into a chair as if exhausted, gives you the impression that she is ill." Clearly, the doctor thinks otherwise. When he asks her where she is and what the date, she answers correctly in a low, tired voice, without looking up.

A few minutes later, she apparently falls into a deep sleep. "Her arms have grown quite limp," Kraepelin observes. "If you raise her eyelids, her eyes suddenly rotate upwards. Needle-pricks only produce a slight shudder." He sprinkles her with cold water, and she starts up, opening her eyes. She apologizes for having another one of her sleeping attacks.

The doctor then proceeds to describe her history and treatment while she listens. He never names her, but we will call her Sonia. Both of Sonia's parents died when she was fourteen. Educated thereafter in convent schools, she suffered from headaches that were "relieved by the removal of growths from the nose." (The treatment was presumably designed to cure masturbatory tendencies as well.) "She very readily became delirious in feverish illnesses." At the age of seventeen, she took a job as a governess, but she soon became ill, and for the last seven years, she has been "wandering out of the hands of one doctor into those of another."

Sonia had violent abdominal pains and menstrual difficulties. These were ascribed to "stenosis of the cervical canal and retroflection of the uterus." Consequently, five years ago, "recourse was had ... to the excision of the wedge [in the uterus] supposed to cause the obstruction, and the introduction of a pessary [a device inserted into the vagina]." Later, Sonia lost her voice. Her right forearm contracted, as did her left thigh. Doctors treated her with massage, administered electrical shocks, restricted her movement with bandages, and stretched her limbs under an anesthetic.

Next, Sonia complained of "heart oppression and spasmodic breathing, [followed by] disturbances of urination, diarrhoea, and unpleasant sensations, now in one, and now in another part of the body, but particularly headaches." She was also subject to violent mood swings. Seeking a cure, she underwent a series of ablutions in "brine baths, Russian baths, pine-needle baths," followed by more electric shocks. Blessedly, the next treatment involved breathing country air, living at summer resorts, and a stint on the Riviera.

Two years earlier, Sonia's "sleep attacks" grew worse. They would come on even when she was standing up and could last as long as an hour. Hypnotic suggestion didn't help, but cold water and the Faradic current were "fairly effective."

During her current residence, Sonia has begun to have "great attacks," in addition to her other troubles. "We will try to produce such an attack," Kraepelin says hopefully, "by pressure on the very sensitive left ovarian region." After one or two minutes of increasingly strong prods, Sonia has had enough. She throws herself to and fro with her eyes still shut, screaming, "You must not do anything to me, you hound. Pig! Pig!" She cries for help, pushes him away, and twists "as if she were trying to escape from a sexual assault," the doctor explicates, out of breath, but still master of the situation. "Whenever she is touched, the excitement increases. Her whole body is strongly bent backwards."

Suddenly, she collapses and sobs, begging not to be cursed. Kraepelin sprinkles more cold water. Sonia shudders, appears to come to herself with a deep sigh, and looks around as if she doesn't know what has happened. The doctor explains that "we have to deal here with the disease known as *hysteria*." He notes that in her "great attacks," she often repeats a "dream-like recollection" about a horrible gynecological examination she once endured at the hands of a rough Dutch doctor. She also remembers a traumatic curse pronounced on her by an aunt.

Kraepelin believes that all of Sonia's symptoms are psychosomatic, giving as example how he cured her spasmodically clenched hand by applying a gold coin to her wrist. Her sleep was improved by giving her sugar water. "All the various troubles gave way to measures of the same kind, working on the imagination alone."

Finally, near the end of his lecture, the doctor reveals his hostility toward Sonia. "Her illness gives her a certain satisfaction," he observes, "and she resists involuntarily when steps are taken to cure it.... Invalidism has essentially become a *necessity of life to her.*" He complains that "with her growing expertness in illness, the emotional sympathies of the patient are more and more confined to the selfish furthering of her own wishes. She tries ruthlessly to extort the most careful attention from those around her, obliges the doctor to occupy himself with her by day or by night on the slightest occasion."

Despite such attentions, "she calls herself the abandoned, the outcast, and in mysterious hints makes confession of horrible, delightful experiences and failings, which she will only confide to the discreet bosom of her very best friend, the doctor." Kraepelin ends by dismissing the possibility of recovery. "Hysterical insanity is the expression of a *peculiar, morbid tendency....* In our patient, the beginning of the illness goes back to an early age. We cannot therefore expect that treatment will be successful in altering her personality."

The lecture is over, Sonia dismissed. Kraepelin's associates congratulate him on a fine presentation and commiserate with his lot, having to deal with such difficult patients. A few months later, Sonia dies of tuberculosis. The fatal symptoms are undoubtedly misdiagnosed as more hysteria.

What morals can we draw from this dreadful story? The all-powerful Dr. Kraepelin appears to be a monster who treats his patients as objects. The treatments are often inhumane and abusive. He sprinkles water on her, sticks needles into her, pokes and prods her. He apparently gets some kind of sexual, voyeuristic, sadistic thrill from her reactions. Then he interprets her rage as mental illness. He ignores her traumatic stories about a rough pelvic exam (a rape?) and her hostility toward her aunt. He condemns her to eternal pain, telling her that she is incurable. Then he allows her to die. In many ways, she truly *is* "the abandoned, the outcast," as she agonizingly asserts.

Yet Kraepelin also has a point. Her invalidism has become a way of life. Her symptoms are her only way to obtain attention in the context of the institution and, by extension, her society. She has learned to perform the psychological *pas de deux* with her doctors, to comply with their expectations. In the unreal world of the hospital, she has become completely self-absorbed.

Fortunately, society changed dramatically since this 1904 scene. But were Sonia living nine decades later, her expert therapist, her modern-day Kraepelin, would have immediately interpreted her behavior and her symptoms as evidence of sexual abuse—and not just by a Dutch gynecologist. Her cries of "Pig! Pig!" would automatically be perceived as the reliving of a repressed memory of sexual assault, even if no such assault had taken place. This expert, like Kraepelin, would be a voyeur, titillated by his patient's troubles. He, too, would tell her that her problems stem from childhood, that unearthing all the memories may take years, that she may never truly recover.

Perhaps the therapist would hypnotize Sonia and ask, "Can you see your aunt's face? What is she touching you with? How old are you now, Sonia?" From there, the memories might expand to include her mother and father, conveniently deceased and unable to deny anything. And the 30-year-old, in search of sympathy and attention, would be only too eager to confide her "horrible, delightful experiences," regardless of whether they occurred in reality or were produced by dreams, trance states, or massages to unleash "body memories."

I began this chapter by quoting Phyllis Chesler's 1972 book, *Women and Madness,* so let me end with her prophetic warning. "In what ways can therapy 'help' women?" she asked. "Can female therapists 'help' female patients more differently than male therapists? Can feminist or 'radical' therapists 'help' female patients in some special or rapid way?" Her answer was that "people and social structures change slowly if at all," and that "most people simply obey new myths, as inevitably as they did old myths." Consequently, she was both excited and disturbed by the possibilities she saw in feminist psychotherapy. It could, she feared, simply turn into "authoritarianism with a new party line."

Cultural Contexts

I don't know a soul who's not been battered,
I don't have a friend who feels at ease.
I don't know a dream that's not been shattered
Or driven to its knees.

But it's all right, it's all right,
For we've lived so well, so long.
Still, when I think of the road we're traveling on,
I wonder what's gone wrong.
I can't help it, I wonder what's gone wrong.

—Paul Simon, *"American Tune"*

THE REPRESSED-MEMORY CRAZE REPRESENTED THE continuation of a long-standing historical trend in which authorities encouraged troubled women to act out the "symptom pool" of the era and accept an inappropriate diagnosis. But that does not explain why this particularly virulent form of delusion became so popular near the end of the 20th century in the United States, as well as Canada, the United Kingdom, and some countries in continental Europe. In this chapter, I will concentrate on the United States, where the repressed memory epidemic originated. The inevitable questions arise: Why then? Why there?

Revelations about *real* incest initially led to the search for repressed memories, as I documented in Chapter 1. But how could a theory like massive repression, with such shallow scientific grounding, receive such ready and widespread acceptance? And why does it continue to resonate, so that the majority of people and psychologists still believe it?

There are no simple answers. Rather, several historical and cultural threads seem to have woven together to produce a social fabric that was receptive to the sex abuse witch hunt. These threads include victimology, the codependency movement, and a general trend in our society to seek specific causes for a multitude of problems. Permeating all of these factors was a high level of generalized societal stress.

As we saw in the last chapter, a frantic search for scapegoats invariably surfaces during times of cultural upheaval. As Frederic Bartlett observed in 1932, "times of social stress, threat from outside, insurrection from within, any state of high social tension" tend to exacerbate such "persistent tendencies" within a society.

By almost any standard, Americans felt disjointed, pressured, and confused as they approached the turn of the twenty-first century. They faced an insurmountable national debt, a shortage of decent jobs, the spread of AIDS, gratuitous random violence, the breakup of families, newly discovered dangers to their health and environment, an unwieldy health-care system ... the list goes on. Is it any wonder that they wanted to lay the blame somewhere? Who allowed things to get this way, anyway? It must have been the previous generation. They messed everything up, including their children.

But there have been other times of generalized, free-floating anxiety. Why, this time, did a cultural malaise take the bizarre form of unwarranted accusations of sexual abuse? Why weren't Americans searching for witches or branding political subversives instead? Perhaps clues can be found in historical trends involving our national character and attitudes toward psychology, religion, women, and sex.

A Nation in Search of a Disease

In 1881, Dr. George Beard published *American Nervousness: Its Causes and Consequences*, in which he asserted that the stress of modern life, with its telegraph, steam engine, and frantic pace, was causing more and more people to come down with "neurasthenia," a disease that he both invented and treated. Its symptoms, which he himself described as "slippery, fleeting, and vague," included sick headache, exhaustion, ringing in the ears, nightmares, insomnia, flushing and fidgetiness, palpitations, dyspepsia, vague pains and flying neuralgia, spinal irritation, uterine troubles, hopelessness, claustrophobia, lack of sexual interest, and several more pages filled with other options. Beard hypothesized that people inherited a certain finite amount of "nervous force," and that when it was overstrained, neurasthenia resulted.

Beard proclaimed that neurasthenia was a disease of the upper class, whose refined, sensitive nervous systems were overwhelmed by the pace of modern life. While delicate women came down with the ailment most frequently, hard-pressed businessmen could also be afflicted. Overwork, the volatility of economic booms and busts, repression of turbulent emotions, and too much thinking—particularly by women, unaccustomed to such brain strain—supposedly contributed to this high state of nerves. "The rapidity with which new truths are discovered, accepted and popularized in modern times," Beard wrote, "is a proof and result of the extravagance of our civilization."

While we may laugh at Beard's naïveté, his diagnosis clearly struck a chord with the public in his time, a period remarkably similar to its equivalent a hundred years later.

In the '60s (1860s, that is), the United States was torn apart by a controversial war that sometimes pitted family members against one another. In the post-war period, physicians developed an interest in war-induced stress and soon identified similar syndromes in the normal population. The pace of scientific and technological change seemed overwhelming. Religious faith lost ground to materialism and greed in the nation's value system. A flood of immigrants entered the country. Reformers attempted to stem the tides of alcoholism, child abuse, and sexual deviance. Homelessness in the midst of affluence became common. Interest in alternative healing methods using herbs and traditional native American remedies blossomed, along with belief in psychic phenomena. Psychological self-help books proliferated. Some women rebelled against their traditional subservient roles, and many men reacted defensively. In this turbulent society, which stressed individualism over community, the psychologist replaced the priest, as people sought respite from their confusion and unhappiness.

Sound familiar? The above commentary could apply equally to the late 20th century.[*] "Americans are the most nervous people in the world," pharmacist-physician John Pemberton wrote in 1885, the year before he invented Coca-Cola as a "nerve tonic" for neurasthenics. For Pemberton and Beard, this observation was a point of curious pride. Because Americans were so inventive, energetic, and sensitive, they suffered more magnificently than others. "Beard's was an ambivalence characteristically American," observed medical historian Charles Rosenberg, noting that Beard was torn between an "arrogant nationalism and a chronic national insecurity." Nor was Beard alone. Since the late 1700s, Rosenberg continued, physicians such as Benjamin Rush had concluded that "the unique pace of American life, its competitiveness, its lack of stability in religion and government, was somehow related to an incidence of mental illness higher than that of other Western countries."

Alexis de Tocqueville, who mused over the American character in the early 19th century, commented on the national obsession with self. The citizens were "apt to imagine that their whole destiny is in their hands." For the Frenchman, who was accustomed to philosophical acceptance of adversity, it was "strange to see with what feverish ardor the Americans pursue their own welfare, and to watch the vague dread that constantly torments them lest they should not have chosen the shortest path which may lead to it." As an ironic consequence, the impatient individualistic American, straining after an instant cure, has traditionally

---

[*] People appear to undergo psychological stress near the end of *every* century, perhaps because of awareness of a major transition point. As the year 1000 approached, Western Europeans went into a frenzy, believing the world would come to an end at the "millennium." The Witch Craze commenced at the end of the 15th century, but it became most intense a hundred years later during the 1590s. One century later, the Salem witch trials occurred in 1692. Mesmerism surfaced along with the French Revolution in the late 18th century.

placed a dependent faith in the latest theories and self-help books produced by self-proclaimed experts.

George Beard exemplified both the sufferer's search for certainty and the expert's assertion of authority. His father and two brothers were ministers, but Beard could not bring himself to accept that vocation, largely because of his belief in Darwin's theories of evolution. Until the age of 23, when he graduated from Yale, Beard experienced his own brand of neurasthenia, with ringing in the ears, acute dyspepsia, pains in the side, nervousness, morbid fears, and chronic exhaustion. As medical historian Barbara Sicherman observed, intellectuals such as Beard "suffered acutely from the loss of faith that accompanied Darwinism ... and the growing authority of Science. In a society of changing and often conflicting values, the decline of spiritual certitude intensified feelings of isolation."

Beard and his fellow nerve doctors, the forerunners of therapists, made a religion out of their supposedly scientific approach to emotional and spiritual problems. Beard declared that the physician must not only heal, but enlighten the public and become "a *power in society.*" Although Beard died in 1883, his colleague S. Weir Mitchell did indeed become a powerful figure, pulling down $70,000 a year while treating neurasthenics with his "rest cure," which he first tried out on Civil War soldiers. Most of his subsequent patients, however, were upper-class women. According to an 1899 survey of neurasthenic patients, two-thirds were between the ages of 20 and 40, with an average age of 33.3.

In a typical rest cure, Mitchell ordered an afflicted woman to take to her bed, where she was fed and washed by attendants and forbidden to read, use her hands, or even speak. "Mitchell subsequently systematized the treatment to include total isolation of the patient from the family," Barbara Sicherman noted. Such isolation enhanced the doctor's control over the patient, which Mitchell considered all-important, writing: "The man who can insure belief in his opinions and obedience to his decrees secures very often most brilliant and sometimes easy success." He sought a "trustful belief" and was at first surprised "that we ever get from any human being such childlike obedience. Yet we do get it, even from men." Mitchell implicitly recognized that he was usurping the role formerly occupied by a minister. "The priest hears the crime or folly of the hour," he wrote, "but to the physician are oftener told the long, sad tales of a whole life."*

In *The Autobiography of a Neurasthene* (1910), Margaret Cleaves provided, as Sicherman puts it, "a classic study of unresolved dependency needs that were at least partly met by her long-term relationship with her physician," who visited her

---

* In 1873, feminist writer Abba Goold Woolson protested "Invalidism as a Pursuit" in her book, *Woman in American Society.* "Society," she wrote, was "ever doing its best to crush out of them every trace of healthy instincts and vigorous life, and to reduce them to the condition of the enfeebled young ladies that meet us on every side, who are all modelled after one wretched pattern, and as much alike as so many peas."

daily during her worst attacks. Cleaves blamed her rearing for all of her troubles, noting that the arrival of a younger sister deprived her of milk. Also, her father died when she was 14, and she had a recurrent dream of being a child cradled in his arms. Her doctor provided a fine substitute, however. "It seemed worthwhile," she wrote, "to have suffered for the sake of all this comfort."

I have taken us back over a century in some detail for obvious reasons. The similarities between the two eras are striking.* The late 19th century spawned the psychoanalytical enterprise, the shift from priest to therapist, and the abnegation of personal responsibility in the face of social turmoil. By medicalizing neurosis, the early psychologists and physicians initiated a disturbing trend that reached crisis proportions in the late 20th century. As Barbara Sicherman noted, "They were interpreting behavioral symptoms that some found morally reprehensible (an inability to work for no apparent cause, compulsive or phobic behavior, bizarre thoughts) as signs of illness rather than willfulness. They thus legitimized the right of individuals with such difficulties to be considered, and to consider themselves, victims of disease." Beard, she wrote, urged that "kleptomania, inebriety, and pyromania—all safely medical—replace the traditional moralistic designations of stealing, drunkenness, and arson."

Victims All

In the late 20th century, many people took such excuses to new and extraordinary heights. As numerous commentators lamented, virtually everyone claimed to be a victim of *something*. In his 1992 book, *A Nation of Victims,* Charles Sykes provided numerous examples. "An FBI agent embezzles two thousand dollars from the government and then loses all of it in an afternoon of gambling in Atlantic City," Sykes wrote. "He is fired but wins reinstatement after a court rules that his affinity for gambling with other people's money is a 'handicap' and thus protected under federal law." Similarly, overweight people sued McDonald's because the chairs were too small, and those who were chronically late protested being fired, because they suffered from a psychological affliction. With such precedents, it is little wonder that sex abuse allegations—far more serious than habitual tardiness—provided a ready excuse for murdering or maiming a parent, spouse, or other accused molester. One Kentucky woman even managed to avoid responsibility for her admitted adultery by claiming that it was not she, but her *alter,* who had illicit sex. The courts bought her MPD excuse.

As the authors of *The Courage to Heal* explained, "When you first remember your abuse or acknowledge its effects, you may feel tremendous relief. Finally

---

* In 1900, H. G. Wells predicted: "Life is already most wonderfully arbitrary and experimental, and for the coming century this must be its essential social history, a great drifting and unrest of people, a shifting and regrouping and breaking up again of groups, great multitudes seeking to find themselves."

there is a reason for your problems. There is someone, and something, to blame."
In other words, even though it meant believing that your father raped you
throughout your childhood and losing your family, it was worth it because now
you were a victim. None of your problems were your fault.

Since its third edition appeared in 1980 (the fifth was published in 2013), the
Diagnostic and Statistical Manual of Mental Disorders, the psychiatric bible, has
encouraged this trend by codifying almost any human behavior as a potential
mental illness.* Some of the diagnostic categories are truly ludicrous. In a 1994
review of the fourth edition of the *DSM, Scientific American* asked, "Do you use
grammar and punctuation poorly? Is your spelling horrendous, and penmanship
bad, too? You may be mentally ill." Why? You may suffer from the "Disorder of
Written Expression." The *DSM-IV* further described someone with an "Identity
Problem" as suffering from "uncertainty about multiple issues ... such as long-
term goals, career choice, friendship patterns, sexual orientation and behavior,
moral values, and group loyalties." Certainly, these are difficult issues, but hardly
unique. As Charles Sykes put it, "Is this a psychological disorder or a description
of existential angst? Is this illness or man faced with the disorder of modern life?"

In his book, *The Diseasing of America,* social psychologist Stanton Peele objected to the creation of ever more specialized grievance categories, each of which
could blame its difficulties upon some kind of "addiction," each with its own 12-
step recovery group. Sex addicts could not help being promiscuous. Gamblers,
shoppers, gluttons, thieves, procrastinators, and television viewers could all qualify for medical treatment. "We see," Peele wrote, "the ultimate definition of the
ordinary discomforts and challenges in life as diseased events."

The modern prototype for this flood of maladies was alcoholism, a very real,
devastating problem to millions of people. Alcoholics Anonymous published its
"Big Book" in 1939, and since that time, AA has helped many people to achieve
and maintain sobriety. As a result, it has saved lives and reunited families that had
become dysfunctional because of alcohol.

In the early 1980s, other movements attempted to emulate the success of AA,
using the same 12-step methodology, allocating disease and victimhood to
other people. The alcoholic's wife, who remained with him despite his habits,
was labeled "codependent," locked into a sick relationship. His children, raised

---

* Among the various "personality disorders" enumerated by the *DSM-V* are Narcissistic Personality Disorder
(selfishness, grandiosity, and a sense of entitlement), Avoidant Personality Disorder (socially inhibited, feeling
inadequate, hypersensitive), Dependent Personality Disorder (inability to make decisions, needs reassurance
from others), or Oppositional Defiant Disorder (angry, resentful, deliberately annoys people). In other words,
we appear to have turned character traits into certifiable ailments. As sociologist Carol Tavris pointed out in a
scathing 1994 article on the *DSM, the* majority of these "diseases" are aimed at women: "When men have problems, it's because of their upbringing, personality or environment; when women have problems, it's because of
something in their very psyche."

in a dysfunctional household, were irrevocably damaged, according to the book *Adult Children of Alcoholics* (1983). ACOA groups sprang up throughout the country, probably providing a therapeutic outlet for adults who had suffered childhood abuse from alcoholic parents, but also providing a new scapegoat for those wishing to escape responsibility for their own problems. Now it became a badge of honor to have an alcoholic parent. If Dad had a beer after work or a glass of wine with dinner, that meant he was an alcoholic, thus allowing his adult offspring to blame everything on him.

Charles Whitfield, an internist-turned-psychotherapist, masterfully tapped into this new market with *Healing the Child Within* (1987), written not only for alcoholics' offspring, but *any* adult who grew up in a dysfunctional family, which he estimated to be as high as 95 percent of the population. Whitfield stressed that such adults should go to therapy and contact a suppressed inner child, the "True Self." To do so, they must abandon false beliefs such as "Oh, my childhood was fine," and get suitably angry at their parents. "When working in recovery," Whitfield wrote, "most adult children *are* able to work through the denial and to gradually uncover their ungrieved losses or traumas."

In *Codependent No More,* published the same year, Melody Beattie declared that codependency was rampant in American relationships, independent of alcohol. We were all stuck in debilitating marriages, coercive friendships, maladjusted work situations. CODA groups (Codependents Anonymous) sprang up to take their place next to the ACOA meetings. Soon, drug counselors jumped on the bandwagon as well, explaining that substance abuse often stemmed from traumatic childhoods.

The following year, in *Bradshaw On: The Family (1988),* John Bradshaw reiterated what he had already said in his popular television series: 96 percent of American families are dysfunctional, even without the presence of Budweiser or Jack Daniel's, and we must all search out our impoverished inner children. By the 1990s, parents had become pariahs, the monsters who had nearly destroyed their now-adult children, who rushed to buy the latest self-help books, entered therapy, and declared themselves "in recovery" from numerous abuses.

The point here is not to downplay the horrible damage that can be caused by truly dysfunctional families, whether the dysfunctions involve drunkenness, spousal abuse, neglect, sexual or other physical abuse of children, or any combination thereof. But if 96 percent of families were really that sick, then just about everybody needed self-help "recovery" books and years of therapy.

The phrase "adult children" was particularly disturbing. It went well beyond describing grown offspring. Instead, the term apparently meant that these were *literally* children stumbling around in adult bodies, turning themselves into irresponsible spoiled brats, constantly pointing the finger at someone else—usually their parents, but their mates would do. "The National Anthem has become The Whine," as Charles Sykes put it. Or, as commentator Joseph Epstein noted, "We have become connoisseurs of grievance—one nation problematical, with anxiety and aggravation for all."

Similarly, was it necessarily *bad* to be "codependent," to depend on one another? Isn't that in part what mates are for? Of course, there was a grain of truth in all of this psychobabble. But by naming a disease, we often create it. Sure, all families have problems and could easily be called dysfunctional. Yes, all relationships have their strains, and those in them could be called codependent. Unfortunately, these easy labels prevented people from seeing themselves as unique people with the power to make their own decisions.

By constantly defending themselves against imperfect relationships, refusing to be sucked into the codependent role of caregiver, and severing ties with newly perceived abusive families, people ran the risk of narrowing their world to only themselves—a process that, as Tocqueville warned long ago, "throws [every man] back forever upon himself alone and threatens to confine him entirely within the solitude of his own heart."*

By the end of the 1970s, Americans were clearly fulfilling Tocqueville's prophecy, as Christopher Lasch pointed out in his 1978 book, *The Culture of Narcissism*. Lasch noted that Americans had "carried the logic of individualism to the extreme," constituting "the pursuit of happiness to the dead end of a narcissistic preoccupation with the self. Strategies of narcissistic survival now present themselves as emancipation from the repressive conditions of the past."

By the 1990s, that trend had become yet more extreme. U. S. attorney general Janet Reno, who had helped put Francisco Fuster into prison in the Country Walk Day Care case, gave a 1997 speech at the Victims' Rights Conference in which she said: "I draw the most strength from the victims, for they represent America to me.... You are my heroes and heroines." In *Manufacturing Victims* (2000), psychologist Tana Dineen complained that the psychological establishment had become a "voracious, self-serving industry" that profited by turning virtually everyone into victims "who are psychologically needy in one way or

---

* One indication of how personal worlds were rapidly shrinking was the trendy emphasis on *boundaries*. "Picture a bubble surrounding you, separating you from all that is not you," read the directions for "Boundary Formation Exercises" handed out in a 1990s psychiatric ward. "The bubble is your boundary. Make it a color that is pleasing to you." The Bubble Boy, tragically born without an immune system, had to live in a protective sheath all of his life. Yet many adopted a kind of psychic Bubble Boy as an emblem of the age – safe, insulated by well-defined, healthy boundaries. He would not suffer from the indefinable plagues of the era, which physicians actually named *twentieth-century disease*. According to a 1992 article in the *Journal of the American Medical Association*, patients suffering from this illness complained of "difficulty in breathing, depression, headache, fatigue, irritability, insomnia, palpitations, and other cardiovascular symptoms"—in other words, all the classic psychosomatic symptoms.

another." Repressed memory therapy was, Dineen noted, "just one example of a much larger, generalized business of manufacturing victims."

"The self is now the sacred cow of American culture," essayist Robert Hughes observed in *Culture of Complaint* (1993), culminating with the enshrinement of the victim-as-hero. "Hence the rise of cult therapies which teach that we are all the victims of our parents: that whatever our folly, venality, or outright thuggishness, we are not to be blamed for it." Rather, our rearing caused all our current problems. "We have been given imperfect role models, or starved of affection, or beaten, or perhaps subjected to the goatish lusts of Papa; and if we don't think we have, it is only because we have repressed the memory and are therefore in even more urgent need of the quack's latest book."

While intellectuals such as Hughes might sneer derisively at the recovery movement, it was not a joke. As we have seen, the *I've-been-abused* mindset ultimately led to splintered families and shattered lives, suicide attempts and psychiatric wards. Even when it did not reach such drastic proportions, the vogue for self-absorption produced people such as this young woman who wrote in 1994 to a *Psychology Today* advice columnist:

> I've had a lot of therapy and read a lot of self-help books. I've learned to really love myself. I always pamper my inner child. I have overcome any tendency to feel guilt for anything I do. I'm real good at asserting myself and expressing my anger, and I don't let anyone abuse me in any way. I've worked particularly hard on my codependency. I've cut off all my dysfunctional relationships. I'm now ready for a perfect relationship but no one I meet matches my level of mental health. What can I do to get the love I deserve?

She received some old-fashioned common-sense advice from psychiatrist Frank Pittman:

> You are suffering from a deficiency of appropriate guilt. Forget about your mental health, forget about your own feelings, spend some time studying other people's feelings and practicing your manners in dealing with them. See if you can go a whole day talking about everything except your complicated state of mind and the manifold ways in which other people have failed to pamper you sufficiently.

Pop Therapy

We have seen that another incandescent thread leading to the repressed memory sex abuse hunt was the American reliance on experts, self-help books, and therapists. Residents of the United States have always jumped into the latest craze faster than any other nationality. In the 1830s, Tocqueville observed that Americans "frequently allow themselves to be borne away, far beyond the bounds of reason, by a sudden passion or a hasty opinion, and sometimes gravely commit strange absurdities." Speaking of religion, the Frenchman noted that "from time to time strange sects arise which endeavor to strike out extraordinary paths to eternal happiness." In modern times, that "fanatical and almost wild spiritualism" largely turned from organized religion to psychology. The therapist replaced the evangelist.

As veteran psychologist Henry Gleitman put it, "the only time American psychology could be said to have been moderate is when the pendulum happened to be swinging through that mid-point." In the early 19th century, Americans embraced phrenology, spiritualism, and magnetism. A few decades later, they were all neurasthenics with irritated spines trying out rest cures or reflexology.

During the late 19th century, many experts espoused "New Thought" or "mind cure," asserting that people could profitably tap into their subconscious. "In just the degree in which you realize your oneness with the Infinite Spirit," wrote one enthusiast, "you will exchange disease for ease." Another urged readers to "substitute self-realization for self-sacrifice, and development for self-effacement." A third stated that the key to happiness was to "affirm and persistently maintain as *true now* that which you desire." Those who could not solve their problems with such mental gymnastics could purchase patent medicines containing cocaine, morphine, alcohol or cannabis, or buy electric belts to rejuvenate their sex lives.

When Sigmund Freud delivered his 1909 Clark University lectures, Americans avidly took his dogma to their bosoms, and psychoanalysis became popular in the urban United States. Members of the upper crust sought the true meaning of their dreams, ferreted out repressed "primal scenes," and increasingly relied on their therapists to tell them how to live, sometimes with disastrous results. In 1921, for instance, American psychiatrist Horace Frink journeyed to Vienna for a personal analysis with Freud himself. Freud advised Frink and his mistress/patient to divorce their respective spouses. As a consequence, the guilt-ridden Frink became profoundly depressed and suicidal.

Until World War II, only psychiatrists (trained as physicians) served as licensed therapists, and most Depression-era Americans were too absorbed in the daily survival struggle to worry about their psyches. After the war, however, returning soldiers with psychological problems overburdened Veterans Administration hospital psychiatrists. As a "temporary" solution, psychologists were recruited to treat them, and the field of clinical psychology was born.

The 1950s could easily be termed the Freudian decade. Because of the Nazi menace, many prominent European analysts had fled to the United States. German émigré Ernest Dichter told advertisers how to manipulate consumers through subtle use of phallic symbols and "motivational research," while Benjamin Spock advised mothers on the best ways to avoid traumatizing their children. In 1950, Theodor Adorno and fellow researchers published *The Authoritarian Personality*, which essentially equated the stern *pater familias* with Hitler. The family and, by extension, society, were sick, according to Adorno. As Charles Sykes pointed out, "everyday life—especially family life—was demonized, while attacks on the social structure were redefined as therapeutic." As early as 1953, one social commentator could write about "the staggering number of clinics, conferences, lectures, pamphlets and books on the subject of relations between parents and child, between husband and wife." During the '50s, almost every psychological problem—from schizophrenia to anorexia—was blamed on "iceberg" mothers who hadn't provided proper childhood nurturing.

In 1954 science fiction writer L. Ron Hubbard created Scientology, a religion that professes to despise psychiatry but that relies on a pseudo-Freudian theory of repressed memories. Expert "auditors" help people recall "engrams" (traumatic memories), and once all these memories are recalled and left behind a person can supposedly "go Clear" and be enlightened. Hubbard gave his newly-invented religion its name to give it a scientific patina, which it most certainly does not deserve. Hubbard claimed memories going back 76 trillion years, which is longer than the age of the known universe. He called the hypothetically repressed memories "implants," some of which were installed by superior beings called thetans who went bad. "Implants result in all varieties of illness, apathy, degradation, neurosis and insanity and are the principal cause of these in man," Hubbard wrote. Most auditing requires an E-meter to measure tiny changes in electrical resistance through the body when a person holds electrodes (metal "cans"), and a small current is passed through them, lending an additional bogus air of science.

There were various levels of memory retrieval and treatment, all of which cost money. The "church" of Scientology grew wealthy through such counseling/audit methods and sales of books, tapes, and other product. Scientology has a "disconnection" policy, in which some members are required to shun friends or family members who are "antagonistic" to the Church, which may sound familiar to those families torn asunder by repressed memory accusations.

During the 1960s, psychology went pop, with encounter groups and the like, and by the '70s, we were poised for an onslaught of diverse therapies. Social workers joined clinical psychologists as licensed therapists.* As their governmental agency jobs disappeared along with the '60s War on Poverty, social workers increasingly turned to private practice, especially after California led the way in

---

* California was the first state to license social workers in 1945, but the vast majority of the licensing took place in the 1970s and 1980s.

1977 by mandating insurance benefits for therapy provided by social workers and other licensed therapists. "Psychiatrists became the experts on medication," recalled one veteran social worker. "It left the 'walking wounded' to social workers." In most states, everyone could call themselves psychotherapists, regardless of training. As investigative journalists Debbie Nathan and Michael Snedeker observed, "The mental health field during this period was undergoing profound changes, producing increasing numbers of therapists who were less trained than their predecessors and more apt to accept at face value patients' accounts of their pasts."

During the '70s, which critic Tom Wolfe declared the "Me" decade, people sought all manner of therapy, including Synanon, est, Silva Mind Control, transcendental meditation, primal scream, co-counseling, rebirthing, direct analysis, gestalt, and transactional analysis. As Wolfe wrote in 1976, "The new alchemical dream is: changing one's personality—remaking it, remodeling it, elevating, and polishing one's very self ... and observing, studying, and doting on it." The following year, journalist R. D. Rosen published *Psychobabble,* exploring the "bewildering proliferation of self-improvement manuals and popular psychotherapies." As a result, he wrote, "a manic, self-regarding, relentlessly psychological atmosphere had developed." What all of these approaches had in common was the notion that technologically repressed people had to get in touch with their *feelings* in order to feel better.

At the same time, a distinctly anti-family slant had crept into popular psychological literature. In 1969, R. D. Laing published *The Politics of the Family,* in which he proclaimed the nuclear family to be the heart of all problems that only he, the therapist, noticed. "The most common situation I encounter in families," he wrote, "is when what I think is going on bears almost no resemblance to what anyone in the family experiences or thinks is happening." Laing also popularized the notion of repression in his typically convoluted logic: "This is repression. It is not a simple operation. We forget something. And forget that we have forgotten it."

The relationship between client and therapist can be fraught with danger. Far too many therapists have abused their powerful positions; in an effort to "heal" clients, they have actually harmed them. For instance, John Rosen championed "direct analysis," which he practiced from the late 1940s until finally forced to give up his license in 1983. Rosen believed that his patients did not receive adequate love as children. "The therapist, like a good parent, must identify with the unhappy child," he wrote. "He must make up for the tremendous deficit of love experienced in the patient's life."

However, Rosen's notions of love and concern often took the form of emotional and physical torture.* Several patients died under his "care," and he forced fellatio, intercourse, and group sex on other clients. For our purposes, his treatment of Sally Zinman is most informative, because it resembles the hunt for repressed memories in many respects. In 1970, the 33-year-old Zinman, an English professor, woke up one day and felt that she was not herself. She remembered her past, but felt it was not *hers*. At Rosen's private inpatient facilities, no one asked her about her real problems. Rather, Rosen informed her that her mother's milk had been sour and that she had incestuous fantasies about her father. After a month-long stay, she asked to leave. Rosen and an ex-Marine aide stripped and beat her.

Rosen's therapy was similar to "re-parenting," an approach developed in the late 1960s by Jacqui Lee Schiff, a psychiatric social worker, as an off-shoot of transactional analysis. Like Rosen, Schiff got away with it for a while because she specialized in chronic schizophrenics whom other professionals had given up on. She would regress patients *literally* to an infantile status, diapering and spanking them, allowing them to suck on her thumb. To discipline her charges, she would stand them in corners or strap them into heavy wooden "restraining chairs," all methods detailed in her 1970 book, *All My Children*. Eventually chased out of the United States, she restarted her practice in India and landed in England in the mid 1980s. In 1992, she received a thunderous ovation when she addressed the European Transactional Analysis Association.

By the mid-1990s, there were only a few hundred therapists in America who still admitted to "re-parenting," but the practice of regression in which the therapist acted as a surrogate parent was widespread. The most widely publicized case was that of Paul Lozano, a medical student who sought therapy with Margaret Bean-Bayog, a Harvard psychiatrist who encouraged Lozano to regress to a three-year-old state and to call her "Mom," while she composed sado-masochistic fantasies about him. Bean-Bayog also convinced Lozano that he was recovering repressed memories of incest. When she terminated his therapy, he committed suicide. *(See Chapter 9 for a more detailed account of this case.)*

But it was psychologist Arthur Janov who provided the prototype for the trauma therapist with his wildly popular 1970 book, *The Primal Scream*. Janov's patients were told that they must recall repressed memories of trauma at the hands of their parents, and that only in reliving them—and screaming bloody murder—would they be healed. "It is possible that a major Primal Scene can occur in the earliest months of life," he wrote, an event "so intrinsically shattering that the

---

*   Rosen also went out of his way to alienate patients from their parents. "As I continued my pressure toward reality," he wrote about one case, "I called Mary's attention to the fact that in the three weeks that she was in the hospital her mother had not come to see her once. The patient fainted dead away. I should say, in all fairness, that the mother had been acting on my orders.... My purpose was to focus the patient's attention on the pathogenic lack of love rather than to allow her to be confused by the mother's loving attitudes."

young child cannot defend himself and must split away from the experience." The therapist didn't have to worry about a particular symptom list because "*all* neuroses stem from the same specific cause." Once cured by the Primal Scream(s), a patient would lead "a tensionless, defense-free life in which one is completely his own self and experiences deep feeling and internal unity."

The process by which Janov elicited his screams would be familiar to any brainwashing expert. For three weeks, patients must not work or attend school. During the first week, they must stay in a hotel room without TV, radio, or any other distraction. The night before their first session, they should not sleep. "The isolation and sleeplessness are important techniques which often bring patients close to a Primal," Janov noted. "Lack of sleep helps crumble defenses." Noting with satisfaction that patients arrived already suffering, the therapist instructed them to lie spread-eagle on a couch "in as defenseless a physical position as possible." Patients were then encouraged to "sink into the feeling" of childhood. After a "chipping away process" of several hours—during which Janov urged "Feel that! Stay with it!"—they finally arrived at their Primal Scene and screamed something like, "Daddy, be nicer," "Mommy, help!" or "I hate you, I hate you!"

Janov stressed repeatedly that this was an anti-intellectual therapy. "In no case are ideas discussed," he noted firmly. Of course, the *therapist's* ideas were quite clearly conveyed. "Letting down and being that little child who needs a 'mommy' helps release all the stored-up feeling." At the end of the day, the patient returned to his hotel room. "He still may not watch television or go to the movies. He really does not want to because he is consumed with himself."

Virtually any trauma, no matter how trivial, could provoke a Primal Scream from the Primal Pain Pool. Nonetheless, the parents were always to blame, as with a father who forced his child to ride a horse. After the patient finished venting his rage at his father, he switched to the "enabling" mother: "Why didn't she stop him? She was so weak. She never protected me from him." Of course, Janov savored any incest he managed to uncover, even if it wasn't altogether necessary. He recounted one man's memory of a mother's kiss: "She stuck her tongue in my mouth. Can you imagine? My own mother. My God! She always wanted me instead of Father. Mother! Leave me alone! Leave me alone!" This approach to unearthing repressed memories is now called Primal Therapy. The first sentence of its website explains: "Painful things happen to nearly all of us early in life that get imprinted in all our systems which carry the memory forward making our lives miserable."

Joe Hart and Richard "Riggs" Corriere founded the Center for Feelings Therapy, an off-shoot of primal screaming. During the 1970s, their Center turned into a psychotherapeutic cult, as documented by Carol Lynn Mithers in her disturbing 1994 book, *Therapy Gone Mad*. The indoctrination/therapy process she described involved rewriting the patients' past and fostering a complete dependence on therapists. "Men and women with different histories and personalities all emerged similarly furious at their parents, denouncing their past lives and speaking the same loud phrases.... And when patients started feeling confused or lost, they didn't turn to old friends or ways of coping. They turned to the only people who really knew how to feel.... They turned to their therapists."

The Center eventually self-destructed in 1980, spasmodically dying off in numerous lawsuits. Mithers' tragic conclusion sounds eerily similar to the aftermath of recovered memory therapy: "There was no way to undo years of family estrangement, no way to bring back missed Thanksgivings and Christmases or to reconcile with parents who'd died before the Center's end. There was no way to bring back marriages destroyed a decade before."

I have only scratched the surface of this subject here, but it should be clear that the repressed memory craze was part of a continuum of therapeutic approaches that blamed parents for all problems. In the 1950s, it was the refrigerator mother, but by the 1990s, it was the deviant father who was to blame.

One more tragic result of misguided therapy took place in April 2000, when Jeane Newmaker, a North Carolina nurse practitioner, took her ten-year-old adopted daughter Candace to Connell Wakins Associates in Evergreen, Colorado, for "attachment therapy," a form of confrontational, abusive treatment that stemmed from the work of Colorado therapist Robert Zaslow in the 1970s. This theory blamed children rather than their parents, positing that the troubled kids needed to be mistreated and held tightly until they vented their rage and despair, which was considered cathartic. The Association for Treatment and Training in the Attachment of Children (ATTACh) promoted the therapy, which is still practiced in many states and in the United Kingdom.*

Young Candace Newmaker had already seen numerous therapists and been given Ritalin, Dexedrine, Zoloft, Tenex, Effexor, and Risperdal for her diagnoses of Attention Deficit Disorder and Oppositional Defiant Disorder. To this was added Reactive Attachment Disorder, defined by the Diagnostic and Statistical Manual as "markedly disturbed and developmentally inappropriate social relatedness" from a young age.

In fact, according to her school records, Candace had a learning disability but was an average student who helped to protect smaller children or those who had handicaps. She apparently seemed normal to her teachers. But her mother wasn't happy that her daughter didn't express sufficient affection toward her. So she subjected her to attachment therapy at the Guilford Attachment Center in High Point, North Carolina, where therapists would hold the ten-year-old immobile

---

* ATTACh now stands for Association for Training on Trauma and Attachment in Children and held its 29th annual conference in 2017.

and scream at her. She hated it and acted worse. When her mother attended an attachment therapy conference in Virginia, a visiting guru suggested taking Candace to Colorado for an intensive two-week treatment. There, the child endured daily sessions in which she was restrained and yelled at for hours.

Then, on April 18, 2000, Connell Watkins, a social worker, and her staff subjected Candace to a more drastic procedure in which her mother took part. The authors of *Attachment Therapy on Trial: The Torture and Death of Candace Newmaker* (2003) described what happened next:

> Candace was put through a rebirthing session, a crude and inaccurate reenactment of the birth process, from which she was supposed to emerge as her adoptive mother's true daughter, emotionally attached and psychologically committed to the relationship. She was wrapped in a flannel sheet to simulate the tight fit of the womb, and Watkins and the staff, with Jeane Newmaker, placed sofa pillows on top of the child. The adults pressed rhythmically against the pillows in imitation of the contractions of labor. Candace was supposed to wiggle her way out through an opening at the top of the sheet, but as she repeatedly told the adults, she could not do so. Eventually, she could not breathe, either.

As a videotape recorded the entire session, her mother and the therapists suffocated Candace Newmaker. *

The Frantic Pursuit of Happiness and the Boomers

The American Declaration of Independence proclaims every citizen's right to "life, liberty, and the pursuit of happiness." Americans have specialized in the sprint after fulfillment as a national pastime, though they sometimes drive themselves crazy in the process. In the 1830s, Alexis de Tocqueville noted the American "fear of missing the shortest cut to happiness" that ironically rendered the citizenry "more stricken and perturbed." All of his life, the typical American chased "that complete felicity which forever escapes him." A century later, F. Scott Fitzgerald created Jay Gatsby, whose relentless pursuit of the ever-receding "orgastic future" cost him his life. "It eluded us then," Fitzgerald wrote, "but that's no matter—tomorrow we will run faster, stretch out our arms farther...."

That national tendency reached an extreme in the materialistic era following World War II, known as the Baby Boom. Coming out of the Great Depression and war rationing, Americans renewed their pursuit of individual happiness with a vengeance. Mothers, carrying the hope of the future in their wombs, were determined that *their* children should be raised correctly. This new generation

---

* Psychologist-lawyer Christopher Barden testified as an expert witness in the trial, explaining the lack of informed consent and the history of quack therapies. In the widely reported outcome, the two therapists were sentenced to 16 years in prison. In 2005, due to Barden's continuing efforts, a coercive Utah "holding therapy" clinic, which had hundreds of patients a year, was shut down.

would be reared with all the benefits of modernity, including Cheerios, television, Barbie dolls, and G.I. Joes. To help the anxious mother, Benjamin Spock provided avuncular advice in his record-setting best seller, *Baby and Child Care.*

The Boomers were the first generation to be raised permissively. Their parents worried about whether they would become anally fixated or whether they would feel deprived of affection. The underlying message was: "Life is good. You are important, the center of the Universe, and you have every right to expect that when you grow up, you will be happy and fulfilled." Obviously, this is a generalization. There were plenty of '50s children who were not spoiled, but deprived or abused. Despite these exceptions, however, the overall *feeling* of the age was one of entitlement. The family, which had in the past been viewed largely as a necessary economic unit, became a life-long source of true and perfect love. Boomers grew up expecting to find a perfect love-mate who would work with them, in harmony, to raise their own perfect children. Not surprisingly, few of them actually achieved this ideal, which may account for the extremely high divorce rate among Boomers, and the popular view that almost all families are dysfunctional.

The Baby Boomers came of age during a decade when future prosperity seemed assured. Yet at the same time, it was also the "Age of Anxiety," with the constant threat of the mushroom cloud. They were born in the dark shadows of Hiroshima and the Holocaust. "Since 1945," psychologist Bernie Zilbergeld observed, "we have suffered one setback after another, and even our successes were somehow never good enough. The result was the replacement of optimism and faith with cynicism and pessimism." The Korean War proved that we were not invincible, while Sputnik patrolled the very air over our heads, spying on us.

As a result, some curious cultural phenomena emerged. The late 1940s saw the birth of UFO sightings, with the first "abductions" in 1961. The 1950s produced *The Search for Bridey Murphy* and *The Three Faces of Eve.* Invisible, threatening psychic forces boiled within us, while Joe McCarthy's communists lurked under beds. Horror movies featuring threatening "blobs" and aliens became popular. Evil creatures lurked in black lagoons.

In 1959, Robert Heilbroner wrote of "our contemporary feeling of unease and confusion. We feel ourselves beleaguered by happenings which seem not only malign and intransigent, but unpredictable." Despite this underlying *angst,* however, we pretended as a society that we were blessed, that we represented true democracy and freedom for all. We added the phrase "under God" to the pledge of allegiance. Meanwhile, all of the unsolved problems—racism, sexism, poverty, child abuse, environmental pollution—continued to fester. As parents took their children to Disneyland, they were, as Tocqueville had put it so many years before, "serious and almost sad, even in their pleasures."

The Vietnam War shattered any illusions Boomers may have had about living in the best of all possible societies. It pitted their generation against that of their parents and irrevocably changed the nation. As a college student at Harvard in the late '60s, I protested against the war, and I felt some kinship with those who spoke of the inevitable Revolution that would forever change our repressive society. In retrospect, of course, some of the "revolutionaries" were not particularly altruistic. Although I am proud that my generation helped to force this country out of an immoral war and to face many societal injustices, I am not proud that some of my preppie classmates talked about all policemen as pigs, and that some even threw bricks at Cambridge firefighters as they responded to a call.

Perhaps the "us-versus-them" mentality is inevitable within major social movements that involve life and death or basic human dignity. Those on "our" side are beyond reproach, even if their statements sometimes become extreme and hurtful. "We" have to stick together. Those on "their" side are the enemy, and don't deserve to be heard. In the post-Vietnam era, this pattern appeared to infect, to some extent, most important social struggles, including factions of the feminist and other "politically correct" movements.

At any rate, Boomers found it difficult to grow up and take responsibility for their lives. They kept thinking that life was supposed to be fair, that they would find the perfect relationship, that they would find the happiness that was promised to them. In 1980, journalist Landon Jones, in his book *Great Expectations,* wrote: "Unlike previous generations, which found happiness only as a by-product of doing something well, the Baby Boomers [have] pursued it as an end in itself." Consequently, as they entered their 30s, they felt "alienated, fragmented, shattered and disenchanted," according to Jones. The promise of the '60s never arrived. There was no Revolution. They were left with their own problems and mortality, just like every other generation.

Horror writer Stephen King, born in 1947, observed of the Boomers: "We went on playing for a long time, almost feverishly. I write for that buried child in us." King cleverly tapped into that generational discomfort. "He knows that we have been set down in a frightening universe," one critic has noted, "full of real demons like death and disease, and perhaps the most frightening thing in it is the human mind." King said that he pressed "phobic pressure points" in order to exorcise fears. Trauma therapists also knew how to find those points, and how to *fan* the paranoid mental flames. As a consequence, many Boomers accepted the notion that they were irretrievably wounded as children.

Some felt that they must become infants again, nurturing their damaged inner children, clutching teddy bears along with John Bradshaw, finding a way not to grow up. It was the Boomers who began to discover to their horror that they were victims of secret incest. Ironically, the pampered generation turned on its parents, blaming them for the very love they tried so hard to give, twisting it into memories of sexual abuse. The example then filtered downward to those in their 30s and 20s, with even teenagers recalling repressed memories.

In other words, the Baby Boom legacy was passed along to the future generations, often raised by single parents who were too busy trying to "find themselves" to pay enough attention to their children. As William Straus and Neil Howe pointed out in their 1991 book, *Generations,* these children grew up in a "nightmare of self-immersed parents, disintegrating homes, schools with conflicting missions, confused leaders." Consequently, they, too, could find plenty of symptoms that could be interpreted as evidence of buried sex abuse. Not only that, but because of their upbringing, they could choose from a number of possible perpetrators—not only their mothers and fathers, but multiple parental lovers, stepparents, step-siblings, several sets of grandparents, or housemates. Often raised in homes where nudity and discussions of sex were relatively open, they could blame their parents for creating or allowing a sexualized environment.

Psychics, Exorcists, and Truthiness

Another thread contributing to the hunt for recovered memories probably stemmed from the apparent failure of traditional religion to provide answers to life's problems. As a result, at least since the 1960s, interest in the "New Age" and in evangelical, charismatic churches burgeoned.

In part, the growing popularity of psychic phenomena, channeling, angels, near-death experiences, UFO abductions, past lives, demonic possession, and trance states reflected disenchantment with science and logic. Clearly, humans need transcendence. We want meaning in life, and we will sometimes seek it in irrational or destructive ways.

America was a nation in search of spirituality and meaning. In the aftermath of the Vietnam War, the country suffered a massive loss of confidence, with sporadic attempts to recapture a mythic past in which father knew best, God could be trusted to watch over us, and life was good. Instead, people found themselves heading toward the third millennium in a state of upheaval unprecedented in American history.

Consequently, more and more Americans were turning toward miraculous, sometimes fringe belief systems and radical solutions. Human beings have always hungered for spirituality, for transcendence beyond the dimensions of their daily lives. In times of stress, when traditional values and belief systems lie in ruins, they tend to search desperately for alternative ways to fill this spiritual void.

It is no surprise, then, that so many were looking for a miracle, for a benevolent, all-wise guardian angel to see them through, or for a secret message of divine guidance. That's why books such as *The Celestine Prophecy,* by James Redfield, had such appeal. Redfield assured readers that, in mysterious ways, they were moving toward a breakthrough into a wonderful new transcendental awareness. "Perhaps more than any other people in any other time, we intuit higher meaning in mysterious happenings," he wrote. It was clear that this magical transformation was near precisely because of the overwhelming *angst* of the times. "This insight always surfaces unconsciously at first, as a profound sense of restlessness."

The degree to which modern American society embraced the New Age is quite remarkable. For most of the 1970s and 1980s, for instance, the CIA and the Pentagon spent millions of dollars on psychic consultations. We may shake our heads over trusting military intelligence operations to crystal gazers, but what's so bad about looking for answers in this fashion? Going to see a psychic would at first glance appear to be relatively harmless. Why not? Perhaps there was something to it after all, and if what the psychic said resonated, maybe it would help with major decisions about jobs, moves, or relationships.

Unfortunately, when people begin to rely on others to make their decisions, they are usually in trouble. Even more unfortunately, all too many psychics informed clients that they were sexually abused as children and had repressed the memories. The same was true for past-life hypnotists, UFO specialists, channelers, automatic writers, or those who simply read auras. Nurses who espoused "therapeutic touch" (which involved no touch, just hovering hands) sometimes thought they could identify hidden sex abuse victims, just as massage therapists diagnosed "body memories."

In the meantime, traditional churches—Catholic, Protestant, or Jewish—failed to address the raging spiritual hunger of many Americans. Pentecostal and Charismatic non-denominational churches sprang up to fill that need. Here, there was no dry ritual. A lively soft-rock band backed up a choir that sang almost constantly. Everyone in the congregation hugged and praised the Lord throughout the service. Everyone seemed happy, transported. Hands were raised on high in a semi-trance. Sermons were brief and punchy. In many churches, the Devil was a major topic of conversation. Troubled parishioners could be exorcised of their various demons.

Those demons were all too often associated with a belief in repressed memories of sexual abuse, mythical Satanic ritual abuse cults, and presumed multiple personality disorder. In a disastrous melding of New Age influence, secular psychology, and fundamentalism, many pastoral counselors were destroying families in the name of Christ, uncovering illusory incest memories and holding down terrified parishioners to cast out nonexistent demons. Not only that, but the traditional churches were, in turn, heavily influenced by the charismatic movement and psychology, so that the same recovered memories and exorcisms were taking place there as well.

In parallel, the concept of objective truth eroded. What was true for you was your truth, and what was true for me was my truth, and what actually happened or what the facts showed was irrelevant. For repressed memory therapists, that translated into a dismissal of attempts to find out whether the new memories were of real events or not. It was the *feeling*, the *emotion*, that was important.

These cultural movements, originating in the late 20th century, helped to define the beginning of the 21st. On his satirical faux-news program, Stephen Colbert coined the term "truthiness" to describe gut feelings that disdained the need for logic, evidence, or critical examination of the facts. Whatever felt right to you was right in the realm of truthiness.

In a summary paragraph in his 2011 book, *The Believing Brain*, Michael Shermer observed:

> The postmodernist belief in the relativism of truth, coupled with the clicker culture of mass media,…leaves us with a bewildering array of truth claims packaged in infotainment units. It must be true—I saw it on television, the movies, the Internet…. Mysteries, magic, myths, and monsters. The occult and the supernatural. Conspiracies and cabals. The face on Mars and aliens on Earth…. Altered states and hypnotic regression. Remote viewing and astroprojection. Ouija boards and tarot cards. Astrology and palm reading…. Repressed memories and false memories. Talking to the dead and listening to your inner child. It's all an obfuscating amalgam of theory and conjecture, reality and fantasy, nonfiction and science fiction. Cue dramatic music. Darken the backdrop.

The Women's Movement

In the late 1960s and early '70s, the protest movements diversified, splintering from concern primarily with civil rights and Vietnam. Americans had always prided themselves on their compassionate respect for individual rights, but in many ways this attitude had not applied to women, children, homosexuals, or the handicapped. Most conspicuously, an angry women's movement came into being.

The movement's core demands—equal pay and opportunities, relief from sexual harassment, and general recognition of the degradation caused by male sexism—were basic and overdue. And it isn't surprising that the Women's Liberation Movement split off from the anti-war and civil rights protests of the '60s, as many female activists realized that the men who most loudly proclaimed the Revolution still expected them to wash the dishes, raise the kids, be subservient at meetings, and put up with their sexual promiscuity.* Taking their cue from "black

---

* Even in 1969, sexism was thriving enough so that Frank Gray could publish *Scoremanship*, in which he

power," books such as *Sisterhood Is Powerful* (1970), featuring a raised fist on the cover, announced a new, militant feminism. "This book is an action," wrote editor Robin Morgan. "It was conceived, written, edited, copy-edited, proofread, designed, and illustrated by women."

Morgan tapped into a well-spring of seemingly infinite rage. "I couldn't believe—still can't—how angry I could become, from deep down and way back, something like a five-thousand-year-buried anger." Once she realized how endemic sexism was, *everything* triggered her—her unequal pay, her husband's jokes, television commercials, rock-song lyrics, pink blankets for girl babies. "It makes you very sensitive—raw, even," she wrote. She became angry at men as a class with their "linear, tight, dry, boring, male super-consistency." Moreover, she announced, "the nuclear family unit is oppressive to women," forcing them into a "totally dependent position."

But what were the alternatives? "No one," she admitted, "has any answers yet, although a host of possibilities present themselves to confuse us all even further. Living alone? Living in mixed communes with men and women? Living in all-women communes? Having children? Not having children? Raising them collectively, or in the old family structure?" Perhaps men were entirely superfluous. "Test-tube births? Masturbation? Womb transplants?" Or, finally, "Parthenogenesis [reproduction from an unfertilized egg]? Why? Why not?"

Later in the book, Martha Shelly's "Notes of a Radical Lesbian" announced, "Lesbianism is one road to freedom—freedom from oppression by men." By choosing this alternative sexual lifestyle, women could free themselves from dependence upon males for love, sex, money, or the "drudgery of child raising." Most men were included in her sweeping indictment, since "hostility toward your oppressor is healthy." After all, "isn't love between equals healthier than sucking up to an oppressor?" Besides, women could be far more patient, nuanced lovers, freeing women from "hasty and inept [hetero]sexual encounters."

The basic beliefs of the feminist cause—equal rights, equal pay, equal opportunity, freedom from harassment—were adopted in principle by mainstream America. Turning principle into reality has been painfully slow, but most people throughout the political spectrum joined the struggle. The shrill condemnations of the entire male gender by some of the early activists might be compared to the self-righteous rages expressed by those of us in the anti-war movement. And sexism did permeate almost every aspect of American culture, so it is not surprising that some of the early expressions of long-festering rage may have lacked focus.

Yet as many feminist authors noted, some subsets of the feminist movement—

---

explained how *"you too will be able to score with any woman you choose"* by applying the "basic principles of salesmanship." Before he realized that "women like to be mastered," Gray said he had "attempted to *force* a sale too fast" or had not "applied the *right pressure* when it was time to close."

including the Survivor faction—advocated extreme positions that hindered, rather than furthered, social progress. That kind of misguided "feminist" approach led Bonnie Burstow to write *Radical Feminist Therapy* in 1992. "Faced with any female client," she wrote, "we can assume some degree of childhood abuse.... Whenever we encounter a woman who has such large gaps in her memory of childhood, we can usually conclude that she experienced ongoing and severe trauma as a child."

It is little wonder, then, that one commentator wrote in 1991 that "a sort of reverse sexism seems to be creeping into the training of therapists.... I've heard [case consultants] make numerous sexist, sarcastic, and derogatory comments about male clients that would have been vehemently challenged if they had been made about women. Gender prejudices in psychology can lead to a man's disadvantage, even to his harm."

Feminist historian Alice Echols complained in 1984 that what she terms "cultural feminism" embraced the old negative stereotypes, simply trying to turn them into positive stereotypes. According to cultural feminists, women were by nature gentle pacifists, nurturers, intuitive, poetic. Gynecology professor William H. Walling, for instance, embraced similar stereotypes in describing the generic woman in his 1904 book, *Sexology:* "She is in more intimate relation with Nature. Her instincts are stronger, while her personal intelligence is less. She readily achieves many things by instinct at which man arrives less surely by reflection. Man is guided by calculation and personal interest, woman by passion and feeling. Man *sees* truth, woman *feels* it." In 1976, feminist Betty Friedan warned against adopting "the assumption that women have any moral or spiritual superiority *as a class,* or that men share some brute insensitivity *as a class.* This is male chauvinism in reverse; it is female sexism."

Men were labeled aggressive, brutish, compulsively logical. On a 1994 cover, *Time* portrayed a pig dressed in coat and tic, along with the caption, "Are Men Really That Bad?" In the article, commentator Lance Morrow observed that "the overt man bashing of recent years has now refined itself into a certain atmospheric snideness—has settled down to a vague male aversion, as if masculinity were a bad smell in a room.... We have reached the point where the best a man can say for himself is that he is harmless."*

"Cultural feminists are so convinced that male sexuality is, at its core, lethal, that they reduce it to its most alienated and violent expressions," Alice Echols complained. "Sexual intercourse becomes a mere euphemism for rape." She urged

---

* Morrow had a point, but only a few months earlier, the same magazine ran a story about a group of Los Angeles teenage boys who competed with one another to see who could have sex with the most girls. They remained unrepentant about their sexual exploits, which included rape. "Nothing my boy did was anything any red-blooded American boy wouldn't do at his age," one father said. With such attitudes still prevalent, it was more understandable that men should be vilified.

fellow feminists to fight anyone who wanted to "make our sexuality conform to our political ideology.... We must abandon the belief so deeply entrenched in the feminist community that particular sexual expressions are intrinsically liberated or intrinsically degraded."

Other feminists challenged the politically correct stance of woman-as-victim. "Let's not chase the same stereotypes our mothers have spent so much energy running away from," Katie Roiphe wrote. "Let's not reinforce the images that oppress us, that label us victims, and deny our own agency and intelligence, as strong and sensual, as autonomous, pleasure-seeking, sexual beings." Harvard feminist Wendy Kaminer also dared to question the dogma of what she terms "feminist victimology," which underscored women's helplessness

"Today discussions about date rape and sexual harassment also reflect some belief in women's emotional as well as physical fragility," she wrote in *I'm Dysfunctional, You're Dysfunctional.* She lamented "the growth of the memory-retrieval industry during a period of hysteria about child abuse, ritual abuse, Satanism, and pornography." Because of her criticism, Kaminer was labeled "in deep denial," or "part of the backlash." Similarly, social psychologist Carol Tavris was bitterly disparaged for her perceptive 1993 article, "Beware the Incest-Survivor Machine." "To want to throw a small wrench into the abuse-survivor machine," Tavris wrote, "is like opposing censorship of pornography: nowadays, you feel you have to apologize for any support you might be providing to molesters, rapists, pedophiles and other misogynists."

Debbie Nathan begged critics to note that "feminist theory and practice are not monolithic, and that many women's advocates abhor that part of the movement that demonizes masculinity, forges alliances with the antifeminist right, and communicates such a profound fear and loathing of sexuality that—as the ritual-abuse cases demonstrate—it is even willing to cast women as demons." In return for her pleas for reason, Nathan herself was demonized by some who called themselves feminists. Wendy Kaminer observed plaintively, "I wish we were less threatened by debate. It is possible to criticize the recovery movement without condoning child abuse."

Women have been and continue to be subjected to ill treatment at the hands of too many men, ranging from rape to subtle sexism. This does not mean that all women are automatically victims or that all men are automatically aggressors, however. Nor does it mean that "recovered memories" of abuse are true. *Whenever a cause classifies an entire group as the Enemy, it is dangerous, regardless of how just the cause may appear.* It is dangerous for all concerned. The Survivor Movement victimized, in horrendous fashion, not only fathers, but women—in the name of feminism.

Politically Correct Excesses

In this "Revolution of Rising Sensitivities," as Charles Sykes put it, politically correct (PC) college students and their equally PC professors led the charge.

For perspective, it's important to note that the PC movement took on some very important causes. Certainly, America needs better understanding and communication among racial and ethnic groups and among people of different genders and sexual orientations.

But tragically, some who were in conspicuous positions in the movement took their rhetoric to destructive extremes. And many otherwise sensible people who identified with the movement were reluctant to distance themselves from those excesses.

In the climate of the 1990s, "lookism" (looking at a woman with a facial expression that might be interpreted as lustful) was interpreted as sexual harassment. A new puritanism arose in which justice for all didn't seem to matter. "If a woman did falsely accuse a man of rape," one female student opined, "she may have had reasons to. Maybe she wasn't raped, but he clearly violated her in some way." Similarly, an assistant Vassar dean thought a false accusation could actually be *good* for a male: "I think it ideally initiates a process of self-exploration. 'How do I see women? If I didn't violate her, could I have?'"

In women's studies classrooms around the country, male students were often treated as pariahs, hardly daring to open their mouths. "For women, participation [in class] means making verbal contributions," one first-day handout advised in the 1990s. "For men, participation means seriously listening more than contributing to discussions." In one remarkable 1990 *Harvard Educational Review* article, Professor Magda Lewis triumphantly revealed how she routinely squelched any male attempts to question her classroom dogma. Even if they remained mute, the men were not safe, since "the subtleties of body language" gave away their inherently abusive attitudes.

Lewis approvingly quoted a letter from one of her female students, praising the course for creating feminist "anger and a pervading sense of injustice" that was "self-perpetuating." The student was, however, "frustrated and impatient with people who can't see the problems." Consequently, she cut off most social contact and spent most of her time writing furiously—in both senses of the word—in her journal.

Liberal parents sending a daughter to college were likely to nod approvingly when told that she planned to take a course in women's studies. After all, the historical treatment of women was lamentable, and female accomplishments were traditionally minimized. There was, however, a difference between academic exploration and antimale rhetoric. Naive parents had no idea that the women's studies curriculum in many colleges had been hijacked by those whom Christina Hoff Sommers described as "gender feminists" in her disturbing 1994 book, *Who Stole Feminism? How Women Have Betrayed Women.* Teachers in these classes were not interested in encouraging open debate, but in indoctrinating students into a particular belief system with its own jargon. "If the classroom situation is very heteropatriarchal," one St. Louis professor wrote in 1988, "I am likely to define my task as largely one of recruitment... of persuading students that women are oppressed." Sommers not-so-facetiously suggested that these "feminist" bastions should print the following announcement on the first page of their bulletins to parents:

> We will help your daughter discover the extent to which she has been in complicity with the patriarchy. We will encourage her to reconstruct herself through dialogue with us. She may become enraged and chronically offended. She will very likely reject the religious and moral codes you raised her with. She may well distance herself from family and friends. She may change her appearance, and even her sexual orientation. She may end up hating you (her father) and pitying you (her mother). After she has completed her reeducation with us, you will certainly be out tens of thousands of dollars and very possibly be out one daughter as well.

Reinder Van Til wrote in a 1994 *Chicago Tribune* article, and later in the book *Lost Daughters (1997),* about how his 20-year-old daughter turned away from him during her college years, eventually accusing him of ritual sexual abuse. He described his family's 1990 holiday season:

> Kristin announces during Christmas break that she has changed her college major from English to "gender studies," and she is toting around a book entitled *Intercourse* by Andrea Dworkin the way students at fundamentalist colleges carry around the Bible. I've always considered myself a card-carrying feminist, but I know that Dworkin is a radical-fringe lesbian feminist and that *Intercourse* is a man-hating tract the relentless message of which is that any heterosexual intimacy is innately violative of the woman, essentially a euphemism for rape. I sense trouble.

Three months later, Kristin was hospitalized for suicidal tendencies as a result of recovered memories that first involved her Uncle Jack, then her father, and finally her mother as well. Her younger brother, a college freshman, soon entered therapy and discovered similar memories. Both children refused to have anything to do with their parents.

In a similar case, lawyer-psychologist Christopher Barden sued an academic psychotherapist at a prominent university's counseling clinic for convincing three mildly depressed students that they had been abused in a Satanic cult, which made them suicidal. When he deposed the therapist, Barden was shocked to learn that she had a Ph.D. in experimental psychology. "I asked how she could reconcile her professional training in science with the very unscientific nature of her memory recovery treatments." She then explained how she had learned through her feminist studies that "logic and science were simply tools of the white European male patriarchy to dominate and control other races and cultures." Barden won the case and ended her practice. "But I've never forgotten the almost delusional ferocity with which she used her political views to damage the lives of others."

One of the major efforts of the PC movement was to alter the English language, with some beneficial results. People became more conscious than in the past that some commonly-used words and expressions may, unintentionally, imply bigoted, sexist, hurtful sentiments. But the effort sometimes crossed the line between raising of consciousness and stifling of free speech. Such appears to have been the case for University of New Hampshire German professor Roger Brown, who in 1995 had to sue to clear his record after a student complained that he had used "offensive and intimidating language" in class. His sin? He had quoted a German saying which translates: "A pretty back can be charming." In 1992, the University of Missouri School of Journalism's handbook of forbidden phrases and words concluded that the word *glamorous* was sexist; the exclamation *Ugh!* was offensive to Native Americans; *Mafia* obviously bothered Italians; the word *community* "implies a monolithic culture in which people act, think, and vote in the same way."

I should note that the 21st century brought heightened political correctness to college campuses that led to many cases of assumed guilt and punishment without any recourse to due process. Professor Laura Kipnis, a self-proclaimed feminist, wrote about the problem in a 2017 article in *The Chronicle of Higher Education* and in her book, *Unwanted Advances: Sexual Paranoia Comes to Campus*:

> I soon learned that rampant accusation is the new norm on American campuses; the place is a secret cornucopia of accusation, especially when it comes to sex. Including merely speaking about sex. My inbox became a clearinghouse for depressing and infuriating tales of overblown charges, capricious verdicts, and frightening bureaucratic excess. I was introduced to an astonishing netherworld of sexual finger-pointing, rigged investigations, closed-door hearings, and Title IX officers run amok. This was a world I'd previously known nothing about, because no one on campus knows anything about it. Why? Because campus bureaucrats have shrouded the process in demands for confidentiality and threats that speaking about it can lead to job loss or expulsion.

The Fragmentation of the Family

Whatever sense of community Americans once had appeared to be shattered by the 1990s. Up until World War II, the extended family of grandparents, aunts, uncles, and cousins at least provided some sense of grounding, especially in small-town communities.* "Time was," observed historian Peter Laslett in 1992, "when the whole of life went forward in the family, in a circle of loved, familiar faces, known and fondled objects, all to human size. That time is gone forever."

This is not to idealize the family of the past, which was often a constrained, un-happy institution. In *The Way We Never Were* (1992), historian Stephanie Coontz observed that "families have always been in flux and often in crisis." Similarly, in *Embattled Paradise* (1991), family studies professor Arlene Skolnick noted that "the image of a warm, secure, stable family life in past times" was an illusion.

Compared to past generations, however, there were fewer support systems in place, and far fewer parents stayed together to raise their children. "Even if things were not always right in families of the past," Stephanie Coontz admitted, "it seems clear that some things have newly gone wrong." She pointed out that the divorce rate tripled between 1960 and 1982, then leveled off with 50 percent of first marriages and 60 percent of second ones failing. Between 1960 and 1986, the number of children growing up in single-parent homes doubled.

Some observers speculated that unease over having to send children to day-care centers or leave them with babysitters was an underlying cause for the day-care sex-abuse hysteria cases. "It seems it had something to do with this fear that we'd turned our kids over to total strangers," sociologist Catherine Beckett said. "It's as if there was guilt that people we didn't know were raising them for us."

In her 1994 book, *Reviving Ophelia: Saving the Selves of Adolescent Girls,* psy-chologist Mary Pipher suggested that overburdened families were having a dif-ficult time coping with the increasing pressures daughters experienced in the 1990s. These teenagers "know that something is very wrong, but they tend to look for the source within themselves or their families rather than in broader cultural problems." Pipher observed that girls were "coming of age in a more dangerous, sexualized and media-saturated culture." Little wonder, then, that so many young women were searching for answers to their generalized *angst.*

In a sense, the search for repressed memories of incest was a logical exten-sion of the fragmentation of the family. People found themselves more and more alone, afraid. They feared being overly dependent on anyone, yet they yearned for love. They wanted to be innocent children again, but they couldn't be. They felt betrayed somehow, brought into the world and abandoned without much

---

* On the other hnd, Americans have always been mobile, restless people, and American families have always been more unstable than their European counterparts, as Tocqueville lamented in the 1830s: "New families are constantly springing up, others are constantly falling away, and all that remain change their condition; the woof of time is every instant broken and the track of generations effaced." Under such conditions, people "acquire the habit of always considering themselves as standing alone."

explanation. Recovered incest memories provided a rationale—however misdirected—for some of these feelings.

Righting Wrongs

One of the most positive aspects of the women's rights and PC movements was a receptive environment for confronting hurtful and abusive sexual behavior. Ugly family secrets were brought out of the closet. Laws *required* doctors, teachers, and anyone else who had knowledge—or even suspicions—of child abuse to report to social service agencies.

As more people came forward to report the terrible indignities they had suffered in silence for so many years, it became clearer what a poor job we'd done, as a society, in protecting our children. People learned horrible things to which they had turned a blind eye because they didn't *want* to believe they could happen. Children in schools for the blind were being molested by older students and adult supervisors. Altar boys were being sodomized by priests. Teenage girls were forced into sex with their own fathers. For generations, Americans had wanted to believe that in their great country such things couldn't happen.

When they learned that such things did happen, and with some frequency, their instinct was to "get the bastards." Americans moved from an assumption that anybody accused of such atrocities was innocent to an assumption that anybody who was accused was guilty. They wanted to right the past wrongs and felt that if some people were unfairly accused, perhaps that would be a small price to pay—unless, of course, they were among those who were unfairly accused.

This vilification of sex offenders led to the public registration and humiliation of anyone accused of molestation, including young children who played doctor with one another. As Roger Lancaster documented in *Sex Panic and the Punitive State*, the sex abuse witch hunt fit into a broader cultural movement in which the media, politicians, police, lawyers, judges, psychotherapists, and businesses (private prisons) participated. We declared war on our own citizens.

The so-called "war on drugs" led to the demonization of nonviolent people who took proscribed substances and helped produce a "carceral state" that locks up more people than any other country in the world. We now hold over 80,000 people in long-term solitary confinement, a form of slow torture. And because no politician ever got elected for being "soft on crime," the state became ever more punitive. Fear of immigrants in the age of terror led in 2003 to the launching of Operation Predator, in which Immigration and Customs Enforcement (ICE) agents deported an immigrant who urinated in an alley and was convicted of indecent exposure.

In such an atmosphere, false convictions occurred with appalling frequency, we now know, especially in highly emotional cases involving rape or murder. Flawed evidence in such cases involved bad forensics (involving hair, bite marks, supposed arson, shoe prints, blood, gun ballistics, fingerprints, handwriting analysis, and other methods), mistaken eyewitness testimony, jailhouse snitches who received favorable treatment for lying, false/coerced confessions, vindictive police and prosecutors who hid exculpatory evidence, and incompetent defense attorneys, as Barry Scheck and his co-authors wrote in *Actual Innocence*, their extraordinary 2000 book, and further documented by Brandon Garrett in *Convicting the Innocent* in 2011.

DNA evidence exonerated hundreds of innocent men, mostly African Americans put in prison by a racist system.* But for most of the cases covered in this book, there is no DNA evidence to provide proof of innocence, because there was no crime in the first place.

Media Madness and Sexual Schizophrenia

Whatever the trends, they were only exacerbated by sensation-hungry media. In the world of infotainment, sex abuse sold. So did Satanic ritual stories, murder, high-profile trials, multiple personalities, and female victims of all kinds. It seemed that every other movie-of-the-week featured a wronged woman of one sort or another. It would be nice to believe that all TV executives really cared about women's issues, but that wasn't the case. Victimized women were the "in" topic.

In their 1995 book, *Tuning in Trouble: Talk TV's Destructive Impact on Mental Health,* psychologists Jeanne Heaton and Nona Wilson made an observation about multiple-personality disorder coverage, but it could apply to a vast array of talk-show topics. Such shows, they wrote, "work to create interest in a disorder, present it as an exciting eccentricity, and then tell viewers that anyone could have it…. Perhaps if MPD is indeed the syndrome of the '90s we can all thank Talk TV for helping to make it so."

Public radio helped spread the word as well. In 1994, Daniel Zwerdling introduced a credulous segment on Beth Haling, a woman who "discovered" her MPD status with a therapist who "wanted to be another Cornelia Wilbur." Zwerdling solemnly announced: "She has dozens of personalities, an unusually severe case

---

* All too many prosecutors refused to accept DNA evidence, claiming that falsely convicted inmates were *still* somehow guilty. "We don't fold our tents and run," said famed Illinois prosecutor Mike Mermel. "We don't quaver because somebody holds up three letters: DNA." Even when they were proven innocent, as Supreme Court justice Anthony Scalia observed in 2009, "There is no basis…in the Constitution [for] the right to demand judicial consideration of newly discovered evidence of innocence brought forward after a conviction." He concluded, "With any luck, we shall avoid ever having to face this embarrassing question again." In other words, Scalia, emphasized, the Supreme Court had never ruled "that the Constitution forbids the execution of a convicted defendant" merely because he was later found to be innocent.

of a mental illness nicknamed MPD. Researchers believe the disease can be triggered in childhood by repeated physical and sexual abuse." Indeed, Hafling recovered memories of torture and rape by family members and others.

Even in cases where *real* sex abuse survivors were presented on talk shows, the implicit message was negative and misleading. "Watching Talk TV can lead [incest] survivors to believe that they will go on to abuse their own children," Heaton and Wilson wrote, "that good relationships are out of the question, and that at best they can hope for years of therapy with little hope of adequate coping."

This raises a chicken-or-egg-type question. Were people hyper-aware of incest because they saw it constantly in our movies, soap operas, talk shows, news broadcasts, read about it in books, newspapers and magazines, and heard about it on the radio? Or was it simply that the media reflected the reality of public concerns? It was probably a mutually reinforcing vicious cycle.

Roseanne Barr Arnold became an unfortunate symbol of how the media worked, creating and then destroying their own. The more bizarre her statements, the more attention she got. First she was an Incest Survivor who had recovered memories. Then she became a battered wife with twenty multiple personalities. Her sister Geraldine, who was there for their nonabused childhoods, wrote: "Rosey, the Drama Queen, had found her new cause, Victim Chic, a perfect way to avoid taking responsibility in her own life. In fact, over time she would claim that her obesity was partial proof of what she had endured." In other words, she got fat because she was sexually abused.

The media always seemed to feel a need to supply a collective Enemy. With the end of the Cold War, the communists no longer served. The "international conspiracy" of Satanic cults came along at the right time to serve that function, and the secretly incestuous family seemed to be close behind.

In 1995, a public service spot showed a man telling a female office mate that he dreaded a forthcoming family reunion because his father would be there. "Yeah, but why so blue?" she asked. "I've never told anyone," he answered, "but I think my Dad molested me." He explained that "whenever I'm around him, I feel so anxious and uncomfortable. Sounds crazy?" She reassured him that it did not, since *she* had remembered being molested by her brother and a female babysitter. She told him to call Survivors of Incest Anonymous, as the phone number and address flashed onto the screen.

Fortunately, the media were also capable of providing forums for legitimate public discussion. In the case of Cardinal Joseph Bernardin, in which Steven Cook retracted his hypnosis-based allegations in 1995, some newspapers had the grace to apologize for their earlier knee-jerk condemnations of the cardinal.

It's worth noting that the schizophrenic attitude toward sex predates the modern media. In colonial times, when adultery was often a capital crime, it was considered a civic duty to spy on miscreants. In 1643 Maryland, for instance, one couple, hearing suspicious snores, stood on a hogshead of tobacco to peer over a wall, where "Richard Jones Laye snoring in her plackett [a slit in a skirt] and Mary West put her hand in his Codpis." Prying a loose board away, the spies then witnessed Mary West "with her Coates upp above her middle and Richard Jones with his Breeches down Lying upon her." This puritanical disapproval, along with a prurient interest in the proceedings, represent two sides of the same coin—an obsession over an act that is, at once, both disgusting and titillating.

In their 1988 book, *Intimate Matters: A History of Sexuality in America,* John D'Emilio and Estelle Freedman observed that "sexuality has been associated with a range of human activities and values: the procreation of children, the attainment of physical pleasure (eroticism), recreation or sport, personal intimacy, spiritual transcendence, or power over others." They added that "certain associations prevail at different times, depending on the larger social forces that shape an era."

In the 1990s and in the decades to follow, those forces pulled in opposite directions. On the one hand, the media (and now the Internet) was saturated with images of overt, erotic sexuality, celebrating women as sexual objects and men as hunk-studs. The same media told us that men were evil rapists, and that women were perpetual victims. Again, this is the flip side of the same ambivalent coin. We were giving our children confusing, mixed messages. "Sex is easily attached to other social concerns," D'Emilio and Freedman observed, "and it often evokes highly irrational responses."

A Concluding Note

As I stated at the beginning of this chapter, the question of why the repressed memory epidemic occurred in the late 20th century has no simple answer. To summarize briefly, a great many social, historical, and attitudinal factors seem to have conflated into a receptive climate for a flurry of bizarre sex abuse accusations. In the tension-filled '90s, Americans were eager for a new scapegoat for their personal and societal problems. Meanwhile, the horrors and extent of *real* incest emerged from the national closet, so after imagination had run its course about iceberg mothers and communists under the beds, the snake oil of repressed memories may have come along at just the right time.

8   Survivorship as Religion

No one can understand mankind without understanding the faiths of human-
ity. Sometimes naïve, sometimes penetratingly noble, sometimes crude, sometimes
subtle, sometimes cruel, sometimes suffused by an overpowering gentleness and
love, sometimes world-affirming, sometimes negating the world, sometimes in-
ward-looking, sometimes universalistic and missionary-minded, sometimes shal-
low, and often profound—religion has permeated human life since obscure and
early times.

—Ninian Smart, *The Religious Experience of Mankind (1969)*

We see the bloodshed; terror and destruction born of such generous enthusiasms
as the love of God, love of Christ, love of a nation, compassion for the oppressed
and so on.

—Eric Hoffer, *The True Believer (1951)*

HUMAN BEINGS ARE RELIGIOUS ANIMALS. We cannot exist, it seems, without
finding a higher meaning for our lives. We sense that there is more to life than
our five senses convey. Every society or tribe ever discovered has its own brand of
religion, complete with creation myth, ethical imperatives, rituals, and shamans.
Many of our most sublime insights have come from inspired religious leaders,
and their messages have often echoed one another. *We are all one. All life is holy.*
Every major religion has taught its own version of the Golden Rule, urging us to
treat others as we wish to be treated. Similarly, devotees have described the utmost
bliss during ecstatic mystical moments in which they have been consumed by the
Holy Spirit.

Yet religions also have their dark side. More people have been slaughtered in
the name of ideological holiness than any other cause. As Blaise Pascal observed
in 1670, "Men never do evil so completely and cheerfully as when they do it
from religious conviction." All too often, our faiths make us intolerant rather
than compassionate, holier-than-thou rather than humble, filled with righteous
anger instead of understanding, forgiveness, and love. If you're not saved, you're
damned. The Manichean division of the world between God and Satan, pitting
the forces of light and goodness against those of darkness and evil, has led far too

many people to demonize one another, to search out the witch or the warlock.*

It is this darker aspect of the religious impulse that I will explore in this chapter in regard to the Survivor movement. Survivorship became a pseudo-religion that provided intensity and meaning to people's lives in a destructive manner. In making that statement, I do not wish to disparage any religious faith. In fact, belief in God sustained many of the accused parents as well as the retractors who have tried to put their lives back together.

The Substitute Faith

"In a period of religious crisis," historian of religion Mircea Eliade wrote in 1969, "one cannot anticipate the *creative*, and, as such, probably unrecognizable, answers given to such a crisis." Indeed, no one could have predicted the particularly bizarre answer that would arise some twenty years after Eliade made that observation. As I pointed out in the last chapter, one of the primary appeals of the repressed memory Survivor movement was that it served as a substitute religion in an era of shifting values, uncertainty, and confusion. Being a Survivor provided many of the advantages of a born-again sect, including self-righteous indignation or pity for those not yet saved, a warm feeling of communion with those who shared similar beliefs, a strong spiritual/mystical component, and the opportunity to become a martyr for the cause. For therapists, the movement was a crusade against the forces of evil. They were the valued priests who could unlock the secrets of the mind.

To identify the Survivor movement as a religion, you had only to listen for the telltale words and phrases. It is astonishing how often the words "belief" and "faith" came up. "Letting go takes faith," Bass and Davis wrote in *The Courage to Heal.* "You have to trust your capacity to heal yourself." Therapists had to *believe* their patients, or they would retraumatize them. Social workers and judges must *believe* the day-care children. It required a *leap of faith* to *believe the unbelievable.* To doubt any of these stories or to ask for some sort of evidence was tantamount to heresy.

There was also a mystical, non-rational component to this religion. On a computer bulletin board for Survivors, for instance, Randy Emon, a California policeman who once appeared in videos warning about Satanic cults, began to question his beliefs. He asked for some sort of proof and cited an FBI study that failed to find any evidence of such cults or the murders supposedly perpetrated in

---

* The Manichean movement was founded by a Persian named Mani, who lived from 216 to 277 A.D. and taught that the forces of light (good) were continually imprisoned by those of darkness (evil). The evil forces dominated this material world. Consequently, the best way to release the light was to practice severe asceticism and refrain from all sexual intercourse. The Manichean mindset—with its dualistic approach and horror of sex—has had an enormous influence on our culture.

them. In response, another bulletin board subscriber took the skeptic to task for attempting to apply logic to ritual-abuse stories. "When you wish to speak of feelings instead of data and studies, I and many others will welcome your comments," he wrote. "LIFE IS FEELINGS. STRUCTURE IS DEATH OF THE CHILD WITHIN."

Over and over again, I heard Survivors speak passionately of their spiritual journeys. The search for memories, for the precious child within, clearly resembled religious meditation in some respects. "I sense that you are quite spiritual," one woman wrote in 1992 to another on the same computer network, "just in the way you talked about sitting in the meditation (hypnosis) mode and burning your incense while trying to reach your inner child. I have done that many times, and the memories do get clearer and clearer as you continue." She urged her correspondent to find a wise, understanding therapist, then continued: "I guess when one goes in search of their true self and faces the demons that appear along the way, then nothing can get much more spiritual than that, huh? It involves so very much TRUST that we will survive and make it through. I want to share with you that my spiritual growth through this journey has made everything I have experienced—TERROR, nightmares, panic, depression, phobias—the WHOLE 9 yards, well worth it. I would do it all again just to be able to discover my true spirituality."

It is clear, then, that this was a pseudo-religious phenomenon, which begins to explain why so many Christian therapists and pastoral counselors were among the most zealous memory retrieval advocates. In an era when the ministerial role had become more secularized and less influential, the Survivor ideology provided a renewed sense of mission and urgency. As in the past, good Christians could do battle against demons, exposing evil Satanic cults while delving into the mysteries of the mind.

Defining Religion

Perhaps because the religious impulse is so universal, defining it is no simple matter. Philosopher Ninian Smart wrote that religion is "a six-dimensional organism, typically containing doctrines, myths, ethical teachings, rituals, and social institutions, and animated by religious experiences of various kinds." Let us examine each of those six dimensions in turn.

By now, we are well acquainted with the Survivor *doctrine*, which held that all life's difficulties could be explained by forgotten sexual abuse. Recalling the suffering was necessary and redemptive, though only after a "dark night of the soul."

By *myths*, Smart didn't mean to imply truth or falsehood, but oft-repeated stories that demonstrate the essential truth of the doctrine. For the Survivor, these stories were retold and dramatized endlessly in therapy and group sessions—how the perpetrator entered the room, seduced the child, and terrorized her into silence; how the victim repressed or dissociated, watching from a disembodied vantage point on the ceiling; how the perpetrator always denied; how memories surfaced but seemed doubtful at first.

Ellen Bass and her co-disciples offered plenty of *ethical teachings.* Getting in touch with anger was good. Forgiveness was unnecessary, or even, as some survivors asserted, a sin. Sharing abuse stories was a necessary part of healing. Separating from the dysfunctional family of origin and bonding with fellow Survivors was part of the process.

Rituals? "It is worth remarking," Smart wrote, "that even the simplest form of religious service involves ritual, in the sense of some form of outer behavior (such as closing one's eyes in prayer) coordinated to an inner intention to make contact with, or to participate in, the invisible world." What better description could there be of a guided imagery session? In most traditional religions, this "invisible world" was sought somewhere outside the body. In the psychological inner-directed era, Survivors sought it in their own mindscapes. In *The Courage to Heal,* Bass and Davis recommended what they termed "anger rituals," such as burning a perpetrator's photo or writing a divorce decree from one's parents.

As for *social institutions,* Survivors of Incest Anonymous as well as innumerable other associations, 12-step groups, and publications provided as recognizable and widespread a network as any organized religion. A Survivor could move anywhere in the United States and quickly hook up with fellow believers.

That leaves only the sixth dimension of the *organism—religious experiences of various kinds.* What gives a religion its exceptional power is its *personal* significance, its ability to transform the individual it touches. In its most elemental form, religion involves a dramatic conversion experience, defined by a recent sociologist as *"a radical transformation of identity or orientation."** *

Conversion

In 1902, philosopher and psychologist William James delivered a series of lectures entitled *The Varieties of Religious Experience* in which he explored, among many other topics, the commonalities of sudden religious conversion. "Were we writing the story of the mind from the purely natural-history point of view," he said, "with no religious interest whatever, we should still have to write down man's liability to sudden and complete conversion as one of his most curious peculiari-

---

*   "In some ways therapy is similar to prayer," clinical psychologist Bernie Zilbergeld noted. "Both can be comforting and useful even when one does not get what one asks for. Both can keep hope alive; combat boredom and demoralization; decrease loneliness and alienation; help us get things off our chests and clear our minds."

**   Many people of faith have never gone through a dramatic conversion experience. I explore this aspect of sudden belief change because it is clearly relevant to the recovered memory phenomenon.

ties." James offered several first-hand accounts, including one man's wrenching experience:

> I fell on my face by a bench, and tried to pray, and every time I would call on God, something like a man's hand would strangle me by choking.... I thought I should surely die if I did not get help, but just as often as I would pray, that unseen hand was felt on my throat and my breath squeezed off. Finally something said, "Venture on the atonement, for you will die anyway if you don't." So I made one final struggle.... The last I remember that time was falling back on the ground with the same unseen hand on my throat.... When I came to myself, there were a crowd around me praising God.

James hypothesized that those who were most susceptible to conversion were easily hypnotized and highly suggestible. "On the whole," he said, "unconsciousness, convulsions, visions, involuntary vocal utterances, and suffocation, must be simply ascribed to the subject's ... nervous instability." Nonetheless, he was careful to admit that this condition might actually predispose special people to receive "higher spiritual agencies," adding a significant caveat: "The mere fact of [these forces'] transcendency would of itself establish no presumption that they were more divine than diabolical."

The philosopher actually mentioned a possible connection between repressed memories—a new concept that fascinated him—and the conversion experience. In the "wonderful explorations" of Sigmund Freud, Pierre Janet, Morton Prince, and others, James believed that "we have revealed to us whole systems of underground life, in the shape of memories of a painful sort which lead a parasitic existence, buried outside of the primary fields of consciousness, and making irruptions thereinto with hallucinations, pains, convulsions...." He admitted that "these clinical records sound like fairy-tales when one first reads them, yet it is impossible to doubt their accuracy." He wondered whether all "unaccountable invasive alterations of consciousness"—such as dramatic religious conversion—might not stem from "subliminal memories reaching the bursting-point."

Fifty-five years later, psychiatrist William Sargant also noted the similarity between religious conversion experiences and the psycho-therapeutic process, though he attributed both to a physiological process of heightened arousal that promotes changes in belief systems. In fact, in 1957 he dared to equate coercive communist brainwashing—very much on people's minds after the Korean War—with religious conversion and experiences in psychotherapy. Sargant disagreed with James's hypothesis that those prone to conversion were somehow abnormal and exhibited "nervous instability." On the contrary, Sargant asserted, "The ordinary person, in general, is much more easily indoctrinated than the abnormal," because the everyday member of society is more susceptible to social influence.

Sargant pointed out that while the dramatic moment of conversion seems an instantaneous watershed, it is usually preceded by a period of intense anxiety and self-doubt, often generated by the "priest" or therapist. Sargant quoted a personal patient of Sigmund Freud: "For the first few months I was able to feel nothing but increasing anxiety, humiliation and guilt. Nothing about my past life seemed satisfactory any more, and all my old ideas about myself seemed to be contradicted." Only after this patient's former identity was stripped away could Freud "piece everything together in a new setting."

Sargant also referred specifically to the dramatic moment of "abreaction," the emotional catharsis of supposedly recovered trauma memories, as a crucial component in the conversion process. "Many patients who have been subjected to repeated abreactions, during a period of months and even years, on the psychotherapist's couch, are known to become increasingly sensitive to the therapist's suggestions.... They respond more willingly when he attempts to implant new ideas in them ... which they would have rejected without hesitation before."

The psychiatrist hypothesized that some kind of literal biological alteration occurs somewhere in the brain cells to precipitate this shift in belief systems. "Before being able to change behaviour patterns of thought and action in the human brain with speed and efficiency," Sargant wrote, "it is apparently in many cases necessary to induce some form of physiological brain disturbance. The subject may have to be frightened, angered, frustrated, or emotionally disturbed in some way or another."

The dramatic, emotional moment of conversion helps to convince skeptics. Clearly, *something* extraordinary is going on. Thus, in 1739, evangelist John Wesley reported with satisfaction how a local doctor had become a believer:

> We understand that many were offended at the cries of those on whom the power of God came; among whom was a physician, who was much afraid there might be fraud or imposture in the case. Today one whom he had known many years was the first who broke out "into strong cries and tears." He could hardly believe his own eyes and ears. He went and stood close to her, and observed every symptom, till great drops of sweat ran down her face and all her bones shook. He then knew not what to think.... But when both her soul and body were healed in a moment, he acknowledged the finger of God.

Perhaps this woman really was touched by "the finger of God." On the other hand, her experience sounds disconcertingly similar to that of the modern Survivor, whose "strong cries and tears" convinced her therapist that the recovered memories were real and that the patient was re-experiencing the true horror of the past.

In 1964, seven years after Sargant wrote his book, Abraham Maslow published

Religions, Values, and Peak Experiences. Maslow stated that true religious experiences were based on magical "peak experiences," which all humans could naturally experience. In other words, he stripped religion down to only one of the components identified by Ninian Smart: the intense personal experience. In fact, a "non-peaker" is someone "who suppresses them, who denies them, who turns away from them, or who 'forgets' them"—a statement that sounds alarmingly similar to attitudes toward "repressed memories." Maslow's book helped promote the intense search for individualistic, ecstatic fulfillment during the hippie era of the late 1960s, including experiments with LSD.

In the introduction to his second edition in 1970, Maslow sounded a note of caution to those intent on finding peak moments. "Instead of being temporarily self-absorbed and inwardly searching, he may become simply a selfish person.... This trend can sometimes wind up in meanness, nastiness, loss of compassion, or even in the extreme of sadism." He warned that the hunt for peaks could move into "the occult, the dramatic and effortful, the dangerous, the cultish. Healthy openness to the mysterious, the realistically humble recognition that we don't know much ... all these can shade over into the anti-rational, the anti-empirical, the anti-scientific." Finally, he noted "the possibility that the inner voices, the 'revelations,' may be mistaken, a lesson from history that should come through loud and clear."

As William James observed back in 1902, "emotional occasions, especially violent ones, are extremely potent in precipitating mental rearrangements." More recently, psychiatrist Jerome Frank observed that "a sense of isolation and estrangement from others characterizes the pre-conversion state. The dominant affects include despair, hatred, resentment, and helpless fury, often directed toward a parent or parent-substitute." Those previously admired or emulated are either shunned or become targets for conversion to the new faith. Like James, Frank noted that adolescents are particularly susceptible to sudden conversion, perhaps in an effort to establish an independent identity.

Frank referred to the moment of *kairos,* which the Greeks identified as an auspicious moment of intense emotional involvement—either positive or negative—precipitating profound personality change. "A great variety of psychological states in combination with certain external circumstances may be followed by abrupt, large, enduring changes in a person's outlook, values, and behavior." Or, as one Survivor put it in *The Courage to Heal:* "It's a quantum shift in my perception of the universe." Frank concluded that "psychotherapy is always an emotionally charged experience, and the emotions are more often unpleasant than pleasant. To be sure, there are interludes of hope, optimism, even elation; but episodes of unpleasant feelings such as fear, anger, despair, and guilt are apt to be more frequent and more prolonged." Why would anyone continue such treatment, then? For the same reason that a parishioner endures the hell-fire sermon: "expectation of benefit."

Ecstatic Religion and the Possessed Shaman

In his 1971 book, *Ecstatic Religion,* anthropologist I. M. Lewis studied tribes in which spirit possession and shamanism were common. (A tribal shaman acts as a medium to communicate with the invisible spirit world and practices magic or sorcery.) Lewis's comments on this type of dramatic "conversion" reinforce what James, Sargant, and Frank observed. "The initial experience of possession," Lewis wrote, "is often a disturbing, even traumatic experience, and not uncommonly a response to personal affliction and adversity." Even so, many "victims" actually desire to become possessed, because it confers a special status and otherwise unattainable insights.* Also like Survivors, most shamans do not *consciously* seek their vocation. As one anthropologist observed of a typical Vietnamese shaman: 'The more he ostensibly refuses this destiny, the more he resists, the more striking will be the signs, the more gripping and dramatic his vocation." Those seeking visions attempt to induce them through some form of trance. Lewis reviewed "time-honoured techniques" such as hypnotic suggestion, hyperventilation, ingestion of mind-altering drugs, self-inflicted wounds, meditation, or fasting—all of which are characteristic of many modern Survivors as they searched for their memories.

Lewis noted that *women* in many different cultures appeared to be particularly susceptible to dramatic possessions, but he did not attribute this fact to any inherent biological gender difference. Rather, "such women's possession cults are," he observed, "thinly disguised protest movements directed against the dominant sex ... in cultures where women lack more obvious and direct means for forwarding their aims." In other words, the extent to which women acted out these roles was evidence of the near-universal oppression of their gender. Though the anthropologist did not accuse the possessed women of consciously enacting a role to gain their ends, he believed that their form of "illness" did, in fact, offer benefits. "Women who succumb to these afflictions cannot help themselves and at the same time bear no responsibility for all the annoyance and cost which their subsequent treatment involves. They are thus totally blameless."

For many women, Lewis noted, possession becomes a chronic condition. "The patient learns, in effect, to live with her spirit," which is considered "tamed" for the moment, but only at the cost of numerous ceremonies in a group with other

---

*   Lewis also pointed out that men sometimes belonged to peripheral possession cults as well—usually when they, too, found themselves in a subordinate, oppressed condition.

women, under the direction of a female shaman. These activities are essentially cures, Lewis wrote, "and in psychiatric terms, the cult meetings assume much of the character of group therapy sessions." As with Survivors, those initially afflicted often went on to become therapists in their own right: "In the course of time, she may then graduate to the position of female shaman, diagnosing the same condition in other women."

Lewis also observed that these "peripheral possession cults" appeared to thrive during times of social upheaval.* "New faiths may announce their advent with a flourish of ecstatic revelations," he wrote, "but once they become securely established they have little time or tolerance for enthusiasm." So what factors keep radical possession experiences "on the boil"? Lewis asserted that "the answer lies in acute and constantly recurring social and environmental pressures which militate against the formation of large, secure social groups."

Finally, Lewis acknowledged the similarity between psychotherapy and possession experiences in primitive tribes. "The psychoanalyst's mythology both evokes and moulds the putative experiences of his patient," he observed. Similarly, in a peripheral possession cult, "everything takes on the tone and character of modern psychodrama or group therapy. Abreaction is the order of the day. Repressed urges and desires, the idiosyncratic as well as the socially conditioned, are given full public rein."**

Minirth-Meier and the Christian Hunt for Memories

Many of the "peripheral possession cult" characteristics described by I. M. Lewis appeared in mainstream Christian counseling, as in the national chain of Minirth-Meier New Life Clinics (formerly Minirth-Meier Clinics) founded by psychiatrists Frank Minirth and Paul Meier in 1976. Until the '70s, "Christian counseling" generally meant going to confession or talking with a pastor about marital difficulties. But in the late 1970s and 1980s, pop psychology invaded the field, and Christian psychologists such as Larry Crabb, James Dobson, Frank Minirth, and Paul Meier began their lucrative psychological ministries through counseling centers, radio programs, newsletters, and organizations. The Minirth-Meier Hour, nationally syndicated on many Christian radio stations in the 1990s,

---

* Often, peripheral possession cults involved some form of what could be called sexual abuse or deviance. In Italian "tarantism," for instance, the onset of the possession was incorrectly believed to stem from the bite of the tarantula spider. Those seeking a cure summoned the appropriate saint by calling out, "My St. Paul of the Tarantists who pricks the girls in their vaginas: My St. Paul of the Serpents who pricks the boys in their testicles."

** No cross-cultural anthropological study of "recovered memory" has ever been conducted, but there is at least one case in which early traumatic events are presumed to cause distress in later life. Members of some Latin American tribes sometimes suffer from *susto,* stemming from a long-ago "fright," which may have occurred as far back as the womb. Diagnosed by divination, *susto* results in "soul loss," as evidenced by lethargy, vague physical complaints, and depression. The cure involves inducing the soul to return by means of complex rituals.

reached two million people daily on 400 stations and offered advice on everything from tobacco addiction to bipolar disorder and repressed memories.

In 1982, psychiatrist Richard Flournoy joined the Minirth-Meier Clinic in Richardson, Texas. He co-authored several books with Frank Minirth and other therapists. In 1985, Gloria Grady, the 27-year-old daughter of a Baptist minister, sought counseling with Flournoy. She was overweight, depressed, and overly dependent on her parents, with whom she still lived. Flournoy asked Gloria to write down everything bad that had ever happened to her. She had a hard time with the assignment, finally coming up with the fact that her parents wouldn't let her square dance in the first grade. Concerned about Gloria's new attitude toward them, her parents asked for a meeting with Flournoy, but it went poorly. "He wouldn't address us at all," Gloria's mother recalled. "He would say, 'Gloria, how does that make you feel?' She would look to him for answers."

By 1986, Gloria was seeing Flournoy four times a week—twice for individual therapy and twice with a group. With his encouragement, she bought a teddy bear and carried it with her everywhere. She transferred her dependency from her parents to her therapist. In 1987, she cut off contact with her parents. Eventually, with Flournoy's help, Gloria Grady came to believe that from the age of ten until she entered college, her father had repeatedly raped her and inserted a rifle barrel, pistol, and a knife into her vagina. Her parents had been in a Satanic cult along with her brother, grandfather, and other family members. She recalled that they had forced her to undergo five ritual abortions and eat parts of the fetuses.

Richard Flournoy left the clinic late in 1986, and Frank Minirth made a belated effort to get Gloria out of his therapy.* But Minirth and Meier continued to espouse recovered-memory therapy, and their clinic was involved in another disturbing example of therapeutic abuse. On March 15, 1994, a young Georgia father named John Scott Rogers was listening to a Minirth-Meier radio program while driving his car. The program stated that people who were abused as children are likely to abuse their own children in turn.

Rogers, whose father beat him severely as a child, was concerned enough to stop the car and call the 800 number from a pay phone, looking for information and prayer. He spoke with a woman named Melody, who quickly secured his name, address, and insurance carrier. Emotionally overwrought by the radio broadcast, Rogers explained that although he had not yet abused his children, he was afraid that he might at some point, if the radio show was correct. Melody told Rogers, "If you feel you may become an abuser, maybe you're actually doing it now and subconsciously you're shielding it from yourself." He told her that

---
* In 1986 Richard Flournoy went into private practice with Michael Moore, who had worked at Minirth-Meier for six years. Between the two of them, they counseled numerous patients who came to believe that they had been sexually abused in Satanic cults but had repressed the memories. Moore was sued by a former client.

anything was possible, but he didn't think so. By the end of the conversation, Melody told him that he needed to be hospitalized at the Minirth-Meier clinic in Atlanta for a minimum stay of fourteen days. He must go home, pack, and leave immediately, or she would turn him in to the Georgia Department of Family and Children's Services (DFCS). Rogers begged her to let see his wife first; she was driving up from Florida with their son and daughter, ages three and two. Finally, Melody agreed.

Terrified and distraught, Scott Rogers went home and packed. Then he called his pastor, who rushed over. When the pastor heard the full story, he told Rogers not to go to the hospital, that he had done nothing wrong and had nothing to worry about. A relieved Rogers called Minirth-Meier and told Melody that he wasn't coming in. She told him she had no choice but to turn him into DFCS.

The next day, Rogers' wife arrived with two exhausted children. Right behind her in their driveway, a county sheriff pulled in, along with a local DFCS worker, who informed Rogers that he was accused of molesting his son, even though there had been no talk of sexual abuse in his conversation with Melody. In the ensuing two months, Scott Rogers' marriage was nearly destroyed. He was not allowed to be with his children alone. His children were stripped naked, their private parts examined. In addition, the children were subjected to sexualized interviews using anatomically correct dolls. Finally, the case was dropped.

What is particularly disturbing about the Scott Rogers fiasco is that no one at Minirth-Meier ever apologized or acknowledged any wrong-doing. Frank Minirth was sent a videotape, "A Family Betrayed," in which Scott Rogers poignantly told his story. Minirth chose not to respond.

Given Minirth's published beliefs about repressed memories in his 1995 book, *The Power of Memories,* his lack of response to Scott Rogers was ominous. In the book, he told the story of Hannah, who entered therapy at the Minirth-Meier New Life Clinic suffering from postpartum depression and was soon having nightmares of Satanic ritual abuse. "A lot of horrible memories came pouring in like a flood," she recalled. Minirth recounted her memories without a hint of skepticism. "The unspeakable acts she witnessed during the few years of her involvement culminated in the murder-sacrifice of an infant," he concluded. "Traumatized, she recalled none of this until her own son was born."

Minirth also recounted the story of Martha, who couldn't remember fourth grade. "The blank spot at ages ten and eleven was significant," he asserted. "A dark spot in otherwise retrievable memories is a warning flag. Here is something the memory has deliberately blocked out." Eventually, Minirth helped her recall being sexually abused in a shed. "And the torrents came, floods of tears and floods of memories."

Not only did Minirth espouse a belief in repressed memories, he implicated Jesus and God in the process of their retrieval. "Memories are so powerful you must lead them forth from the depths carefully, or they will crush you. As you do it with Christ's spiritual help, He will protect you from receiving too much too fast." Minirth suggested asking God directly for help in a prayer journal. "Tell God you are now ready and willing to go to work on bad memories. Ask Him to accompany you down the pathway to those memories, opening up what He wants to show you. Remind Him that you realize the two of you can face it together."

Equally disturbing were the comments of Dr. Paul Meier on a nationally aired "Focus on the Family" show in February of 1995. True, Meier recognized that some false allegations might arise from hypnotic age regression, which he did not recommend. But he also revealed that the 300 therapists in Minirth-Meier clinics routinely searched for repressed memories through "conscious" processes. Meier himself had helped "literally hundreds" of clients to unrepress "memories" of abuse. Not only that, Paul Meier, like his colleague Frank Minirth, believed in the myth of widespread Satanic ritual abuse cults. "I saw a real case of it just this past week," he said, explaining that his client "didn't even remember how she got pregnant, but she does remember when she delivered the baby, and the baby was sacrificed at a Satanic cult."

Meier told listeners that Minirth-Meier had a "Chicago clinic that specializes in Satanic ritual abuse" and that "there are Satan-worshiping cults all around the country." Of all the people who recovered SRA memories in the Minirth-Meier clinics, he said that he believed two-thirds of them. That was terrifying, considering that between 15,000 and 20,000 people sought Christian counseling at Minirth-Meier clinics *every week.*

Minirth-Meier New Life's literature boasted that the clinic chain was the "nation's largest and most trusted provider of Christian mental health services," offering a "sound integration of medical and psychological principles with Christian beliefs of love, hope, and restoration." Yet this "trusted provider" of services clearly helped to destroy families. Among their listed specialties wee sexual abuse and multiple personality disorders.

Frank Minirth and Paul Meier split in 1996, in part because of publicity over the case of Scott Rogers, and their radio and clinical empire shrank. But the renamed Meier Clinics continue to operate in nine states, offering purportedly Christian counseling for anxiety, depression, family issues, stress, sexual addiction, and trauma—though there is now no mention of repressed memories on their website. In 2016 they were celebrating "Forty Years of Giving Hope and a Future.

James Dobson, the enormously popular director of Focus on the Family, based in Colorado, was clearly concerned about false allegations of sexual abuse at the height of the repressed memory epidemic. "The memory is an imperfect function of the brain," he said on the first day of his February 1995 broadcast on this issue. "Imagine how much more imperfect it is when you're going all the way back and trying to resurrect what happened when you were two or three or four. I simply don't believe it in most cases."

Yet by the time he introduced the second day's broadcast, he had apparently changed his mind. "There are circumstances where a child is sexually abused either by a parent or an uncle or a brother or a sister," he intoned, "and they repress that because it's so painful they can't deal with it emotionally." Later on in life, he explained, "they suddenly remember those experiences that were so horrible during childhood. It does happen, it does happen."

The Christian hunt for repressed memories had been encouraged by Fred and Florence Littauer in their 1988 book, *Freeing the Mind From Memories That Bind,* by Dan Allender in his 1990 book, *The Wounded Heart,* and by James Friesen in 1991's *Uncovering the Mystery of MPD.* Allender's book was the more subtle and less obviously leading, but for that very reason, its message was perhaps more persuasive. He did not recommend strong measures such as sodium Amytal interviews. The memories would come back "slowly, progressively," he wrote. "Choosing to open oneself to memories will, over time, draw them to the surface, where they can begin to be dealt with constructively." This process would be painful, he warned. "Marriages will need to be reshaped; sexual relations may be postponed while the partners devote themselves to prayer and fasting. The fabric of life will need to be unraveled piece by piece as the Master reweaves the cloth to His design."

Throughout, Allender simply *assumed* that his readers harbored repressed memories. "At times, I wonder if every person in the world ... has been sexually abused," he mused. If all the world's population were to read his book, everyone might indeed think so. "The denial [of repressed memories] is an affront to God. It assumes that God is neither good nor strong enough to help during the recall process. Ultimately, the choice to face past memories is the choice not to live a lie."

All too many Christian counselors took such books to heart, and it was usually good Christian families that were blown apart as a result. In 1995, I met Tom Rutherford, an Assemblies of God minister in Springfield, Missouri. His three daughters all believed at one point that one of them was abused. They were counseled by the wife of a fellow Assembly of God minister. One daughter accused her father of multiple rapes and came to believe that she had been impregnated twice. No one bothered to ascertain that Rutherford had a vasectomy when his daughter was four, making it impossible for him to have impregnated anyone. A subsequent medical exam revealed the daughter to be a virgin. All of his daughters eventually came to realize that their "memories" were illusory, and they returned to their family.

Fortunately, concerned Christian counselors such as Colorado pastor Ed Bulkley began to warn against the hazards of recovered-memory therapy. Bulkley's 1995 book, *Only God Can Heal the Wounded Heart,* was an explicit rebuttal to Dan Allender. Bulkley also reviewed Frank Minirth's book, worrying that Minirth's readers "will be convinced that they can find peace of mind by reworking their memories. What a disaster! Instead of finding the peace that God offers through His divine power, Christians are being offered counterfeit solutions that lead them back into pain, sin, bitterness, and defeat." And while many psychologists were questioning the recovered-memory dogma, all too many Christian counselors continued to unearth illusory memories. "Just when secular authorities are dismissing the reliability of recovered memories," Bulkley wrote, "Christian therapists are buying into it like it's a revelation from God!"

Paul Simpson was another Christian therapist sounding the alarm, even though he himself once helped clients unearth "memories." Simpson went on to write a book, *Second Thoughts* (1996), and to counsel those whose lives were upended by this form of misguided therapy. In 1995, he recounted a disturbing story one Christian retractor told him. "The Holy Spirit took her back in time. She could see her father molesting her as an infant. Then the Holy Spirit took her back to her mother's womb, and she could hear hateful things being said at that time. Finally, the Holy Spirit took her right back in time to the presence of God, where she was talking with God before she was born." With such belief systems being advanced in the name of religion, it is little wonder that so much damage was inflicted.

It would be interesting if every minister in the United States were to act on Paul Simpson's suggestion. "Pastors," he advised, "I encourage you next Sunday to ask any families that have been impacted through these kinds of false accusations, whether in the immediate or extended family, come to you privately and share that with you. I think that you will be shocked to see how prevalent this phenomenon is within your own congregations."

The British Evangelical Search for Memories

British ministers who took Simpson's advice might have been surprised— though others might not, since they themselves were helping to unearth recovered memories. "The Satanism panic originated in the United States," observed Philip Jenkins in his book, *Intimate Enemies,* "but such stories could not have attained the power they did unless there was already in existence a domestic audience willing and eager to hear them; and this was found among the swelling ranks of fundamentalist and Charismatic Christians within Britain itself." As far back as 1934, popular British author Dennis Wheatley had published *The Devil Rides Out,* in which the Devil himself leads an orgy involving every imaginable perversion.

"A little cannibalism, my friend," one character in the book observed. "It may be a still-born baby or perhaps some unfortunate child they have stolen and murdered." The book was re-issued in 1966 and made into a film two years later.

Concepts such as spiritual warfare and exorcism had been popular among British evangelicals for many years, along with speaking in tongues. Between 1979 and 1989, membership in independent fundamentalist churches swelled from 44,000 to 128,000 in England and Wales—and that ignores evangelical branches sprouting within the Anglican ranks.

An interdenominational Christian Exorcism Study Circle was formed in 1972, and by 1985, it was counseling some two hundred people who claimed to be fleeing from Satanic or occult groups. The group's secretary warned that "Satanists can be found at the highest levels in our society, in political life and on the boards of multinational companies." Several prominent British clergymen wrote books warning against Satan's influence. The Reverend Russ Parker, who had worked with the Manchester Deliverance Advisory Group, went on to minister to two Leicestershire parishes within the established church and to write *Battling the Occult* in 1990. Anglican vicar Kevin Logan wrote *Paganism and the Occult* in 1988, describing in it a London occult group composed of "high ranking civil servants, top industrialists and prominent City figures." It was in Logan's Lancashire home that "Hannah," a self-professed ritual abuse survivor, committed suicide.

In 1988, the Evangelical Alliance, which claimed to represent a million adherents, formed a committee to look into ritual abuse claims, particularly those of adult survivors. Among the prime movers were Maureen Davies, who claimed to have identified the first British ritual abuse case in 1985, and Diane Core, the organizer of Childwatch on Humberside. Core told a reporter, "About four thousand babies a year are born into covens to be used for sacrifices and cannibalism. This is only the tip of the iceberg." Davies described the job of "brood mares," teenage girls or older women who are intentionally impregnated. "When they are five and a half months pregnant the birth is induced. At this stage, the foetus is alive and can be sacrificed. The blood of the infant is then drunk, then the body is eaten."

In 1990, in his popular book *The Hot Line*, Anglican cleric Peter Lawrence described an exorcism that had apparently become a commonplace event for him: "When I asked the Spirit to come, horrific demons manifested, growling and snarling and throwing her to the floor. Like so many Christians we find with resident demons, she had been an incest victim."

"Deliverance ministries" became quite popular in Great Britain. Some cases were bizarre almost beyond belief. In 1995, British readers were shocked to discover that a former Anglican vicar, 70-year-old Andy Arbuthnot, had induced illusory memories of Satanic ritual abuse in Mary Llewellyn, 50, one of his parishioners at his London Healing Mission. That explained many of her problems, he said, including her bad back. "When I started talking about my childhood, so much was blank," Llewellyn recalled. "He said God wanted me to find out." Arbuthnot treated Llewellyn as a seven-year-old, giving her teddy bears and writing pornographic love letters to her. Eventually, he sought to exorcize her demons through "internal ministry," which involved inserting his fingers, soaked with consecrated wine, into her anus and vagina. Finally, Llewellyn, who had become completely dependent on Arbuthnot, rebelled and went public with her story. "I do have real memories of being abused as a child," she said. "They are very few, and those are the ones that I am keeping."

Rage and the Worship of Self

Anthropologist Clifford Geertz defined religion as a system of thought and belief "which acts to establish powerful, pervasive, and long-lasting moods and motivations ... by formulating conceptions of a general order of existence and clothing these conceptions with such an aura of factuality that the moods and motivations seem uniquely realistic." Note that an "aura of factuality" is sufficient to establish a religion, which requires no objective evidence. That certainly describes the belief in repressed memories.

It is striking that Geertz should single out *moods* as such an important component. The heart of an evangelical religious movement isn't the particular philosophy, then, but the emotional content that it promulgates. There's no question that the Survivor movement fostered one mood above all others: *rage.* Love, tenderness, turning the other cheek, and the Golden Rule may have worked well enough for Jesus, but not for Survivors. The movement's bible, *The Courage to Heal,* called anger "the backbone of healing" and encouraged, sanctioned, and fomented blinding, furious rage. "You may dream of murder or castration," wrote Bass and Davis. "It can be pleasurable to fantasize such scenes in vivid detail. Wanting revenge is a natural impulse, a sane response." With approval, the authors quoted a woman named Vicki who convinced her mother, on the basis of recovered memories, that Vicki's father had violently abused her. "She got fiercely angry at my father. She wanted to go over to his house and shoot his brains out. She wanted to kill him. I loved it."

Anger is a powerful motivator, which most religions understand. If you can demonize your enemies, making them Evil incarnate, denizens of Satan's empire, it is much easier to maintain community. As Eric Hoffer noted in his 1951 classic, *The True Believer,* "Hatred is most accessible and comprehensive of all unifying agents," allowing its members to become selfless workers for a righteous cause.

"Mass movements can rise and spread without belief in a God," Hoffer observed, "but never without belief in a devil."

That is why so many religions, in their formative years, remain remarkably cohesive. Like the early Christian martyrs, they are combating a common enemy, ready to die for the cause. With time, if the religion thrives and puts down roots, it inevitably loses that early fire. It develops an organization, a fixed creed, a hierarchy. It becomes part of the status quo, and in doing so, it begins to miss its early enemies. Without Satanic forces to fight against, without an underdog status, the adherents revert to normal human bickering and in-fighting. Some seek to rekindle the old-time religion through breaking off a new sect or identifying a new Enemy.

In the 1990s, Survivorship was still in its infancy as a new religion, so the original fire in the belly still burned brightly. As we have seen, the allegations expanded into a *literal* fight against Satan, who supposedly sponsored ritual abuse cults throughout the land. These monstrous perpetrators specialized in murdering and consuming babies and skewering every available orifice not only with tumescent penises, but with red-hot pokers, knives, and other implements of destruction. They were Evil, pure and simple.

The "moral crusader" was described by sociologist Howard Becker in 1963 as identifying "some evil which profoundly disturbs." Such a zealot "operates with an absolute ethic; what he sees is truly and totally evil with no qualification. Any means is justified to do away with it. The crusader is fervent and righteous, often self-righteous." Becker pointed out that such reformers tend to up the ante, searching for ever-greater evils to correct, or they would be out of business. "First, they say that by reason of their efforts the problem they deal with is approaching solution. But, in the same breath, they say the problem is perhaps worse than ever (though through no fault of their own) and requires renewed and increased effort to keep it under control." Becker's observations certainly seemed to be borne out by the Survivor Movement.

One of the advantages of a religion based on accusing innocent parents or other caretakers of horrible crimes is that they are bound to fight back eventually. Hence, the creation of the False Memory Syndrome Foundation, or some such organization, was inevitable. It was equally inevitable that the Survivors would fiercely attack the Foundation as part of the "backlash" effort to deny the reality of sexual abuse. It didn't matter how often members of the Foundation wearily explained that they were well aware that incest exists, and they deplored it. No Survivor wanted to hear that. Instead, they had found a new enemy, and they spread the word that the Foundation was a group of perpetrators in denial, well funded and dangerous.

But a religion cannot function solely on rage. Survivorship did promote love, tenderness and devotion for those within its bosom. Survivors supported one another in 12-step groups, seminars, computer bulletin boards, and numerous organizations such as Survivors of Incest Anonymous. Mostly, however, the natural need for love was turned inward in self-absorption.

In 1976, journalist and social critic Tom Wolfe identified what he called the Third Great Awakening of American religious evangelism.* Its mantra, he said, was "the holiest roll of all, the beat that goes … *Me … Me … Me … Me.*" Wolfe wrote that this new psychological religious wave—epitomized by *est* and primal screaming—was on an "upward roll," predicting that the wave would crest some time in the future.

He was right. That wave crested in the 1990s, with the cult of the wounded inner child. Its message: Be kind to yourself, for you have been so terribly wounded in life. Surround yourself with stuffed animals. Allow yourself to feel enormous self-pity. One of the Survivors I interviewed in the 1990s told me, with awe and tenderness, how she had literally fallen in love with herself in a mirror. Her story is worth quoting at length:

> I was real upset one day because of a love affair that wasn't working out, and I was so tired of having this happen to me. I was 46 years old and just utterly tired of having it not work out, you know, and I was crying really hard, and finally I started thinking, "It's just not worth it, I don't ever want to go through this again. I'll do without love affairs, or I'll find a way to be in love by myself. That's it! I'll find a way to be in love all by myself." And I was pounding the bed, angry.
>
> Then the crying stopped, and all of a sudden, I looked at myself in the mirror, like trying to check out my reality. And for the first time in my life, the eyes were real. Always before it was like looking at a photograph in a magazine when I looked in the mirror, or just looking at my eyes, never into my eyes. This I knew was me, because that was what I was demanding, a way to be in love all by myself. And here was this real person looking back at me from the mirror, and I really did love. I know this sounds really ridiculous, but I acted like a little tiny kid, like a two-year-old with a baby, touching the face and the mouth, coming closer and going farther away, just love, an exploration with myself in the mirror. And I was giggly and it was wonderful, just wonderful! So for about 48 hours I was constantly running to the mirror to be sure I was still there. Constantly. And for weeks, this was the most exciting thing that ever happened to me. It was like your average person falling in love.

By quoting this passage, I do not intend to mock the very real grief Frieda obviously felt. Like many of us, she had suffered isolation, loneliness, depression,

---

* The Great Awakening came about in the 1740s with Jonathan Edwards and other evangelical preachers. The Second Great Awakening occurred from 1825 to 1860, out of which many modern-day religions, such as Mormonism, arose.

unrequited love, disappointment, feelings of abandonment and loss. She had wondered if she would ever feel happy or whole. And it is probably true that you must accept and love yourself before you can love others. Yet there is something very sad about her solution. A year after this experience of falling in love with her image in the mirror, Frieda began to seek out her repressed memories of abuse, ultimately graduating to visualizations of Satanic cults. She had found her niche in life, her new religion. She was a Survivor.

Like many such women of that era, Frieda's home had numerous New Age accoutrements: hanging crystals, stuffed unicorns, books on meditation. She talked earnestly about spiritual growth, and she believed in guardian angels. There is nothing inherently wrong with such New Age beliefs, but it was disturbing that the belief in parapsychology and spiritualism—in invisible powers—seemed so closely allied to the Survivor movement and *its* invisible memories.* There was a chapter entitled "Spirituality" in *The Courage to Heal*, a book whose title itself sounded soothing and positive, even though the book was full of bile. Bass and Davis waxed quite lyrical: "There's a part of everything that wants to become itself—the tadpole into the frog, the chrysalis into the butterfly, a damaged human being into a whole one. And that's spirituality: staying in touch with the part of you that is choosing to heal, that wants to be healthy, integrated, fully alive."

It sounds so peaceful, so seductive. Yet the mental state that the Survivor Movement really produced was the precise opposite. Rather than becoming healthy, integrated, and fully alive, its members routinely became ill, fragmented, and suicidal. They didn't eat or sleep. They experienced repeated panic attacks. They became convinced that they were not even themselves, but a conglomeration of other wounded beings, multiple personalities. They were led to wound themselves not only psychically but literally, cutting or burning their own flesh. But why would anyone willingly undergo such horrors, winding up in a locked ward in a psychiatric unit? The creed of the Movement explained it all as part of the slow healing process. "You have to get worse before you get better." The panic attacks, the sleepless nights, the self-hurt—all allegedly stemmed from the terrible sexual abuse experiences of your stolen childhood. Everything could be blamed on the evil Perpetrator. It wasn't a surprise that you were feeling so awful, that you wanted to hurt yourself. You were systematically taught to blame yourself for the incest. The wonder is that you remained alive at all!

---

* A 1993 *Time* poll indicated that 69 percent of Americans believed in angels, and 46 percent believed they had their own guardian angel. This widespread faith might have been harmless and comforting, but its flip side was not. A 1990 survey indicated that 60 percent of Americans believed in the existence of the Devil, up from 37 percent in 1964. Also, the surge of interest in angels might not be quite so harmless as it appeared. A California minister, for instance, called on angel power to help his clients work out "unresolved traumas." This sounds alarmingly familiar.

Bradshaw: The Evangelist of Dysfunction

If Ellen Bass wrote the scriptural text that fomented the Survivor movement, John Bradshaw served as her John the Baptist, a voice crying in the wilderness, preparing the way, telling us that we were all abused children from dysfunctional families, whether we were literally victims of incest or not—but if we could come up with incest memories, all the better. Bradshaw informed *Lear's* readers in 1992 that 60 percent of all incest memories were repressed. "Victims have often cited the smell of chlorine bleach and the sight of toothpaste as provoking memories of childhood exposure to ejaculate," he explained. "Accept the *theory* that you were sexually abused," he advised, "live consciously with that idea for six months ... and see whether any memories come to you."

Although his books were enormously influential, you had to attend a Bradshaw lecture to appreciate the power of this Recovery Movement guru. As journalist Emily Mitchell wrote, "Bradshaw has a high-octane style that is too big for the TV screen. On stage, he is commanding and works a room like a pro. Cordless mike in hand, he is a stand-up psychologist, slinging one-liners or deepening his voice to repeat self-pitying monologues."

She hardly did him justice. Bradshaw, in his early 60s in the 1990s, lived in a monastery for years, quitting the day before his ordination. Even after that, he went back to school for degrees in psychology and religion. Despite evident bitterness at organized religion, Bradshaw, a reformed alcoholic, still called himself a theologian. He also collected wizard figurines with which he clearly identified.

You didn't need to know any of this background, however, to identify his approach as psychological evangelism. You simply needed to listen, swept up by his earnest Houston twang. He spoke in staccato cadences, with the urgent intensity of Billy Graham in his glory years. The words spilled forth, the italics and exclamation points practically visible in the air. He repeated the same key buzzwords, the same phrases—*shame, dysfunctional family, abandonment, abuse*—hammering them hypnotically home. Nearly every sentence ended with an upward keen, bringing audiences to the edges of their seats with tense anticipation. Everything Bradshaw said seemed to be *terribly* important. He was conveying a message of salvation. He had discovered the Truth. Every now and then, he threw in some self-deprecatory humor, but mostly, he whipped up emotions—notably grief and rage.

Bradshaw didn't want you to think. Indeed, there was a decidedly anti-intellectual slant to the Survivor Movement. Feelings were superior to rationality. "Staying in your head's a way to cut off your heart," he intoned. "We've gotta feel as bad as we really feel. Because feelings *move* you. I am *moved* to *tears* by my sadness. I am moved to do something about it by my anger. My anger is my *power*. The Incredible Hulk phenomenon. When I'm angry, I have my power. When I'm sad,

I cry and I ventilate and I heal. Grieving is a healing feeling. When I'm afraid, I'm wise and discerning. If I don't ever feel as bad as I feel, I won't change. I'll go to my death never having known who I was. So you've gotta feel as bad as you feel."

No one in the audience stopped to analyze the words. Like any effective evangelist, Bradshaw knew how to build emotion. Now, like the old-time tent preacher, he practically invited people to come down the aisle and be saved. "Hey! A night like this can do it. You can be confronted enough tonight in your delusion and denial. You see, as children are abused and abandoned, they do something really strange. They idealize their parents." Consequently, people could begin to heal when they recognized the Truth and gave up the "mirage in the desert of their family," the myth that Mom and Dad really loved them. Unless they could do this, they would continue with their "spiritual bankruptcy," he asserted. "There's no kingdom within. Codependency is a conflict of gods."

If you weren't sure you had enough dysfunction to warrant attention and salvation, not to worry. "It's so widespread, this cultural dysfunctionality," Bradshaw assured his audience, "that *everybody* is able to identify and say, hey, we're all—kind of like the old church—we're *all* sinners. We're *all* sinners and we *all* need help. We *all* need salvation. See, and then we can come together as a family. And it does my heart good to look around and to know I'm not alone." In a moment of utter honesty, Bradshaw reveled in the powerful religious ecstasy. "It's *wonderful* to get this kind of energy. It's almost like I feel the energy of a movement in this room. It's exhilarating to be here. So you see some of my self-worth is coming from your faces."

"The first step in recovery," Bradshaw continued, "is to break down these denials and go find what I call a family of choice. Find a new family of choice, some place where you can go and you won't feel shamed." Here it came, the appeal to community, as the real parents and siblings were jettisoned. "So the process of healing will probably mean *leaving* that family of origin, that closed system, that relationship that's destructive to you, going into a group where you can be accepted just for the very one you are. You know, where you share your crud and they *love* on you! I mean, in these groups, you go and tell them all this *crud* and they tell you they love you! And they accept you and listen to you."

Bradshaw's message was seductive. In the unnatural world of the support group, you could whine about your troubles and everyone would not only listen, they would *encourage* you. The more feeling, the more anger, the more tears, the better. "You see, it's like a new family, with new rules. Everybody's equal here, everybody's a sinner here, there's nobody better than anybody else. We're all equally screwed up. We all have a common problem. And there's something that's so *healing* in that." Exactly what was so healing about feeling so screwed up he didn't bother to explain, but rushed onward. "You know, we need some Adult Children of Dysfunctional Families groups," Bradshaw said. "Start one, start a movement!"

In the hierarchy of abuse, Bradshaw made it quite clear that sexual abuse qualified the victim for the most pity, the most love, the most rage. He didn't spend much time on it, just enough to point listeners in the right direction. "An incest victim will depersonalize. She'll dissociate, she'll be up on the ceiling somewhere, or she'll see monsters in the hall instead of Daddy coming in the room. That's the way that nature allows us to survive this. But what happens 35 years later? You see, we've got to know what happened to us. You can't change what's real. So you have to make the abandonment real."

At the end of his lecture, Bradshaw became more overtly religious as he rhapsodized about the child within. "You've got to embrace yourself and love yourself. You're the only one that you'll never lose or leave." Does this sound familiar? Shades of Frieda, who probably got the idea from Bradshaw. "So it's crucial work. You know, as the Bible says, unless you become as children, you cannot enter the Kingdom." He went on to suggest that "you accept your powerlessness, you embrace your shame, and you turn to something greater than yourself. And you pray and you meditate and do what all those spiritual masters said." Then he wandered off into a pseudoscientific New Age sideline, expressing his belief in "morphic resonance" and "remote viewing ESP experiences" in which "people can know what they're gonna see two hours later." Finally, he ascended to his platitudinous peak: "So at some level of higher consciousness, we are all one. When we get out of limited socioculturally conditioned ego, narrowed consciousness, the flashlight self as opposed to the spotlight self."

Before sending people—agitated, angry, and uplifted—into the night, Bradshaw brought it all back to his main theme. "We're on a journey, a beautiful journey, an exciting journey. And thank God there's some brothers and sisters on the journey, because I wouldn't want to be on the journey alone. So go ahead and love that little kid in you. Cause they've been hiding in that closet for years. And they really want to come out And if you stay in your idealization and your delusion and your denial and your-family-was-really-okay-and-nothing-really-happened-to-you, then nothing's really going to happen to you. Go read the Psalms or the Scriptures or any of the religious literature. The call is always that I love you, I think about you every day. I will always be faithful to you no matter what. May God bless you all."

Saving the World

As disturbing as Bradshaw was, he was merely a popular synthesizer for the Recovery Movement. "Bradshaw is a Geiger counter, a loudspeaker for what a million people are doing and saying," Andrew Meacham told me in 1995. Meacham, a former editor of *Changes Magazine*, a Health Communications publication, was intimately acquainted with the self-help movement and knew Bradshaw personally. "He's not even the primary messenger, just the person who has honed the presentation to a fine art." Nonetheless, it was disconcerting that Bradshaw had become the darling of Hollywood liberals. His specials were aired prominently on public television as part of fund-raising efforts. What other televangelist could have attained such mainstream acceptance?

Bradshaw's brand of evangelism helped to promote the more virulent religion of the repressed memory Survivor movement. It is no accident that the "Christian counselors" tended to be the worst kind of suggestive therapists, encouraging memories of Satanic ritual abuse. There was a crusading aspect to the trauma therapists who unearthed these memories. They called themselves "witnesses" and repeatedly talked about the need to "believe." Many who choose the helping professions do so because they genuinely want to save the world. Given the complexity of real mental troubles, which are often intractable, it must be very frustrating for a minister or therapist to listen to problems without being able to offer a simple solution. The uncovering of previously unknown memories provided an exciting way to really help. In addition, it had a mysterious spiritual component, delving within the psyche to heal the ravaged soul.

Similarly, there was a religious aspect for the Survivors as well. The therapists may have been the priests, but the Survivors were the movement's acolytes, its martyrs, its devotees, and often its prophets. For many of the women I interviewed, the hunt for memories had become an exciting spiritual adventure. Those who hadn't "gotten their memories yet" felt left out. They hadn't passed through the required initiation rite. True, they may have had a vague feeling that they were abused, but they hadn't experienced the Pentecostal moment, the flashback, the abreaction, the screaming, the delicious horror. When they achieved this *kairos* moment, they were finally true inductees into Survivorship. Not only that, but if they managed to graduate to the status of multiple personalities, they could commune with their godlike "inner self-helpers" and develop extraordinary clairvoyant powers.

Survivorship as Sect

Some called the Survivor Movement not only a religion, but a cult. I am uncomfortable with that word and all that it implies. It is all too easy to label any fervent group a "cult," with all of its negative connotations. I prefer the word "sect" for most cases. There is no question, however, that some self-contained psychotherapy groups qualified for the term "cult." Take, for instance, the counseling center run by Daronda Blevins in Chesterfield, Missouri, in the

1990s. Blevins isolated her young female wards from their families and friends, controlled what they read and heard, exorcised their demons, helped them recover repressed memories of incest, and screamed at them for hours in confrontation sessions. Her center was guarded by a pit bull.

Similarly, Genesis Associates, a Philadelphia therapy center run by Pat Mansmann and Pat Neuhausel, espoused "detachment" from family as its primary therapeutic modality. Most clients were diagnosed as "people addicts" who also had to uncover hidden memories of sexual abuse. Husbands and wives were told to "detach" from one another as well. Control rested completely with the therapists.

Daronda Blevins and Genesis Associates were extreme examples, but even run-of-the-mill recovered memory therapy, conducted one-on-one in a private therapy setting, shared certain characteristics with a cult. I found a great deal of insight in *Combatting Cult Mind Control (1990),* by Steven Hassan, an ex-Moonie, licensed therapist, and exit counselor who helped people to leave what he termed destructive cults. As I read Hassan's book, I was struck by the remarkable similarities between Survivors and many of the general characteristics he ticked off.*

This form of cult-like thinking is "a *system* of influences that disrupts an individual's identity (beliefs, behavior, thinking, and emotions) and replaces it with a new identity," wrote Hassan. Certainly, that is what has happened to many who had recovered "memories." They were no longer someone's daughters; they were Survivors. Hassan pointed out that in many such religions, new inductees are literally renamed and given new identities. Patty Hearst, for instance, became Tania the Revolutionary. Similarly, books such as *The Courage to Heal* and *Secret Survivors* encouraged those who had recovered memories of abuse to change their names, assuming a new label completely separate from the perpetrating father.

Hassan believed that hypnotism could be used to rewrite the past, creating a "fantasy world that can be used to enslave us." He noted that many sects tell their members to "become like little children"—just as the sex abuse Survivor movement encouraged its members to become psychological infants, identifying with their "inner child."

Self-enclosed sects encourage complete dependence on an authority figure. For the Survivor movement, that figure was usually the therapist, or a book. Many Survivors were totally dependent on their therapists, unable to make the smallest decision without consulting them. Most of the therapists appeared to be convinced that they were on an important, nigh-holy mission. Recovered memory

---

* Hassan's observations were not original. He synthesized and popularized the theories of many sociologists such as Robert Jay Lifton, Margaret Singer, J. Gordon Melton, and Thomas Robbins. Hassan's use of the phrase "mind control," which implied some Zvengali-like power over people, was unfortunate. I prefer Lifton's concept of "thought reform," Lowell Streiker's nomenclature of "mind bending" in his book of the same name, or Robbins' description of "ideological totalism."

guru E. Sue Blume, for instance, wrote earnestly of those who were "driven by conscience and courage to relinquish the safety of their silence," and likened herself to the lone protester facing the tanks in Tiananmen Square. That fit Hassan's general observations: "They believe that what they are doing is truly beneficial for you. However, they want something more valuable than your money. They want your mind! Of course, they'll take your money, too, eventually." Similarly, trauma therapy guaranteed a protracted period of recovery and, hence, a steady income.

People are most often recruited into such belief systems at a *"vulnerable time of stress in their lives,"* Hassan emphasized. "The stress is often due to some kind of major transition: moving to a new town, starting a new job, breaking off a relationship, experiencing financial instability, or losing a loved one." For quite a few of my interview subjects, that generalization appears to have been true. For some, the triggering stress involved the transition from adolescence to adulthood—moving far away, going to college, finding an independent adult persona. For others, it might be marital stress, job difficulties, postpartum depression, the death of a parent, or even the onset of menopause.

The process of induction into a sect involves learning as much as possible about the potential recruit—"his hopes, dreams, fears, relationships, job, interests. The more information the recruiter can elicit, the greater his chance of manipulating the person. The recruiter strategically plans how to bring him step by step into the group," Hassan wrote. The "recruiter," in the Survivor movement, was the therapist—and what better person to elicit all of this information! That's the whole point of therapy. Then the therapist brought the client "step by step" into the sect by telling the potential recruit that these memories would come slowly, that this was a gradual process. Whenever she expressed doubts, the therapist assured her that this was a normal process of denial, and it would pass as she became more convinced of her memories.

Another universal characteristic of such groups is black-and-white thinking. Everyone is either good or bad, a victim or a perpetrator. You either believe, or you're in denial. All communication outside the religion's belief system is cut off. Members are programmed automatically to plug any breaches in that fortress, the self-contained world view.

Typically, a specialized vocabulary, usually with religious overtones, helps solidify member participation. Thus, many therapists called themselves "witnesses" and repeatedly spoke of the need to "believe your memories." They "validated" the feelings. All family members were either "perpetrators," "enablers," or "victims." Like most jargon, these words and phrases became an ingrained way of looking at the world. By labeling something, you often make it reality. Insidiously, the Survivor movement's pet buzzwords also entered the vocabulary of accused parents. They often found themselves talking about denial or validation,

Survivorship as Religion   331

perpetrators and victims. *("The therapists are in denial about what they are doing. The parents are victims of a witchhunt. It is so validating to hear other parents' stories.")* They sometimes became mirror images of their accusing children.

Many groups, according to Hassan, resort to pseudoscientific claims. The entire psychoanalytic movement was founded, as we have seen in Chapter 6, on pseudoscience. Freud and his followers established a mythology of the mind that strove to imitate the medical advances of the time. The concepts of repression and dissociation have never been scientifically demonstrated, however, and tossing around words such as "abreaction" or "endogenous opiates" does not make manufactured memories any more factual.

Most groups create a mechanism to keep members from straying. "Fear is used to bind the group members," Hassan wrote. For one thing, there is usually an outside "enemy" who is persecuting you. In addition, however, the group keeps members off balance, "foster[ing] a feeling of dependency and helplessness.... People are made to have a panic reaction at the thought of leaving [the sect]. They are told that if they leave they will be lost and defenseless in the face of dark horrors: they'll go insane, be killed, become drug addicts, or commit suicide." Does this sound familiar? Survivors were convinced that if they didn't remain in therapy and deal with these memories, their lives would be ruined, they would go insane. The ritual abuse therapists assured their clients that they had been "programmed" by the Satanic cult to return to it. Only by staying in therapy would they be safe.

Most destructive sects bombard their inductees, Hassan asserted, with the notion that "they are badly flawed—incompetent, mentally ill, or spiritually fallen. Any problems that are important to the person, such as doing poorly in school or on the job, being overweight, or having trouble in a relationship, are blown out of proportion to prove how completely messed up the person is." How much more "badly flawed" could you get than to be the victim of repeated sexual abuse in your childhood? The Survivor movement zeroed in on repressed memories of childhood sexual abuse as *the* central issue in people's lives that "explained" why they were unhappy, had troubled relationships, or ate too much.

Finally, Hassan came to the crux of the matter. When I read this passage, I was astonished by its applicability to those who had recovered "memories":

> An individual's memory becomes distorted, minimizing the good things in the past and maximizing the sins, the failings, the hurts, the guilt. Special talents, interests, hobbies, friends, and family must be abandoned.... The group now forms the member's "true" family; any other is just his outmoded "physical family." Some cults insist on a very literal transfer of family loyalty.... The member's past is rewritten. He tends to look back at his previous life with a distorted memory that colors everything dark. Even very positive memories are skewed toward the bad.

First, they stripped you of your real family, your real past. Then, in the midst of the confusion, hurt, and pain, they gave you a new family— your 12-step group, your fellow Survivors, those who shared your anguish. "One of the most attractive qualities of cult life is the sense of community that it fosters," Hassan observed. Indeed, the sisterhood of victimhood was powerful, and there was a real sense of bonding and community.

So close could this bond become, and so paranoid the threat of contact by grieving parents, that some "incest survivors" were deliberately spirited away and hidden by cult-like support groups. In a state of total panic, others with recovered memories literally abandoned their normal lives—complete with house, possessions, and automobiles—and fled, who knows where.

Seeing Cults Everywhere

As insightful and compelling as Hassan's book was, however, I came to have doubts about cult exit counseling, particularly since it is a descendant of "deprogramming," which sometimes referred to an illegal use of force. Hassan disavowed the kidnapping and deprogramming that once freed him from the Moonies, however, and said that he had not participated in such activities since 1977. His *modus operandi*, as described in his book, was simply to get the group member to listen to an alternative point of view, usually for several days. To gain entree, he used a neutral friend or acquaintance, and he also brought an ex-member of the particular group, someone who knew all the feelings and the jargon. Hassan claimed a high success rate with cult members who agreed to listen to him for several days, though that did not count cases in which they ran at the first sign of an "intervention."

Yet Hassan believed in "massive repression." I discovered his attitude the hard way, when I arranged for him to give a one-day seminar to a group of accused parents in the early 1990s. It became clear over the course of the day that he had severely conflicted feelings about this issue. Yes, he thought that some therapists overstepped their bounds and led their clients into false memories. His consciousness was raised when his own sister went to a therapist and was told at her first session that she probably harbored repressed memories. On the other hand, he informed the group that people often repressed memories of years of abuse. He presented this not as an opinion, but as scientific fact.

Later, I asked Hassan for any specific cases that would prove the reality of massive repression. He referred me to Colin Ross, the notorious "expert" on multiple personality and ritual abuse who believed the CIA is programming Manchurian candidate MPDs *(see Chapter 4)*.

Thus cued, I asked Hassan if he believed in Satanic ritual abuse cults. He did.

And when Survivors came up to him after a speech to tell him about their recovered memories, in which their parents killed their little siblings and roasted them in Satanic rituals, he didn't dispute them. He just shrugged.*

Consequently, when one of the ritual abuse Survivors I interviewed began telling me all about "mind control" and the strobe lights that were used to "program" her as an infant, I was disturbed. The pseudonymous Elizabeth Rose quoted from Hassan's book in her 1993 *Ms.* magazine article in which she claimed to be a ritual abuse survivor. Hassan's *Combatting Cult Mind Control* was, in fact, listed as a recommended resource in the second edition of *The Courage to Heal,* under the heading "Ritual and Cult Abuse." On the other hand, Hassan's book was also been praised in retractor newsletters—surely one of the few works to appeal to those on both sides of this debate.

My reservations about Hassan's belief in repression are symptomatic of a problem that threatened to discredit the entire anti-cult movement. The "academic arm" of this movement was the American Family Foundation (AFF), which published *Cultic Studies Journal.* On its editorial advisory board in the 1990s sat Susan J. Kelley, the pediatric nurse (who was hired as a professor at Georgia State University) who interviewed the Fells Acres Day Care children and who maintained a firm belief in ritual abuse cults.**

In 1993, Michael Langone, the editor of *Cultic Studies Journal,* edited a book entitled *Recovery From Cults.* In it—you guessed it—was an article by Susan Kelley called "Ritualistic Abuse of Children in Day-Care Centers." In late 1995, I wrote to Michael Langone, begging him to disavow a belief in mythical ritual abuse cults and to remove Susan Kelley from his board. "Save your organization further embarrassment," I wrote, "by coming out *strongly and clearly* with a statement about so-called Satanic ritual abuse cults." He wrote back, declining to "denounce colleagues simply because some people think they have made grievous errors." Apparently Langone, too, bought much of the ritual abuse scenario. In a 1992 article, he stated, "ritualistic abuse clearly exists." He co-authored a 1990 book with Linda Blood entitled *Satanism and Occult-Related Violence.* Blood, the former lover of flamboyant "Temple of Set" leader Michael Aquino, went on to write *The New Satanists* in 1994, explicitly avowing belief in violent multigenerational Satanic cults.

---

* Hassan later wrote to me: "I also often ask them if they have cut off from their families, and if they have, I tell them that I believe in using professionals to build bridges to family members and not cut them off in a wholesale fashion. I tell them that unless they are making noticeable improvement in the course of therapy to get another opinion. What is most important is the present and the future, not the past. And if they are open to it, I tell them about false memory syndrome."

** Social psychologist and recovered-memory critic Richard Ofshe served on the AFF board briefly. He quit in 1993, upset by the Kelley article in *Recovery From Cults* as well as what he terms a "classic lawyer blackmail letter" sent by AFF president and lawyer Herb Rosedale to a parent accused on the basis of recovered memories.

Constant Rage Can't Last

Despite my reservations about the anti-cult groups, however, I was grateful to Hassan and other experts for their insights into closed-minded religious sects. Whether you called the Survivor movement a cult or not, it most certainly did foster complete dependence on a figure of authority, rewrote the past, demonized the family of origin, encouraged black-and-white thinking, and created a new identity. Ultimately, I was consoled by another Hassan observation:

> It is extremely important to always keep in mind that he [the sect member] has *two* identities…. One moment the person is speaking cultic jargon with a hostile or elitist know-it-all attitude. Then, without warning, he seems to become his old self, with his old attitudes and mannerisms. Just as suddenly, he flips back to being a stranger…. When John-cultist is talking, his speech is "robot-like" or like a tape recording of a cult lecture. He will speak with inappropriate intensity and volume. His posture will typically be more rigid, his facial muscles tighter…. On the other hand, when John-John is talking, he will speak with a greater range of emotion. He will be more expressive and will share his feelings more willingly. He will be more spontaneous and may even show a sense of humor. His posture and musculature will appear to be looser and warmer. Eye contact will be more natural…. Good experiences and positive memories rarely disappear entirely…. Over time, the old self exerts itself and seeks out ways to regain its freedom. This process is speeded up by positive exposure to non-members and the accumulation of bad experiences he has while in the group…. The "real" self holds the keys to what it will take to undo the mind control process!

Perhaps this insight about the difference between the normal and cultic personality accounts for the startling disparity between pre-therapy and post-therapy letters from many children, such as the "before" and "after" letters quoted in this book's introduction.

Many parents commented that their children's accusatory letters didn't sound like them at all, but appeared impersonal and robotic. The parents wondered whether the therapists actually wrote them. I don't think that was necessarily the case. As Survivors, the children were writing out of their new personae. In one such letter, the accusing daughter typed the Survivor part, sounding just like a prosecuting attorney barely controlling her rage. Then, in a handwritten postscript, she reverted to her real self, almost a still, small inner voice trying to come out, saying that she loved her father and to have patience, that this was a necessary process. Accused parents—many of whom remain estranged from their children two decades later—have to hold on to the conviction that somewhere deep inside, buried underneath all the rage and hurt of Survivors, their real children may remember the good times, the love, the laughter and the joy.

Ultimately, I don't think that keeping people in a constant state of upheaval and anger works. Geertz, the anthropologist of religion, talked about *long-lasting* moods and motivations. Ultimately, love is stronger than hatred, truth more durable than fiction. Tenderness can eventually replace rage. Staying angry all the time is self-destructive. It isn't the natural human state.

Conclusions and Recommendations

All hatred driven hence
The soul recovers radical innocence
And learns at last that it is self-delighting,
Self-appeasing, self-affrighting.

—William Butler Yeats, *"A Prayer for My Daughter"*

THE REPRESSED-MEMORY CRAZE CRESTED IN the early 1990s and had waned by the turn of the century. But it has not disappeared and may be experiencing a resurgence. And the family destruction left in its wake remains all too real.

Late in 1993, *Time* and *U.S. News & World Report* ran simultaneous cover stories on the debate over repressed memories, allowing skeptics their say. Various retractors, flanked by professional critics Elizabeth Loftus, Michael Yapko, or Richard Ofshe, appeared on talk-show programs. Skeptical British stories on recovered memory appeared in the early 1990s in the *Observer,* the *Sunday Times,* the *Daily Telegraph,* the *Independent,* and the *Mail on Sunday.* BBC television and radio programs highlighted the issue.

Until then, few people in the media or the public questioned the horrifying stories that self-proclaimed repressed memory or MPD survivors told, nor did they differentiate memories that had *always* been there from those that were newly "discovered." By the late 1990s, most people realized that the validity of repressed memory was at least a hotly debated topic.

Several high-profile cases contributed to public awareness. In November of 1993, Steven Cook accused Cardinal Joseph Bernardin of having sexually abused him when he was a teenager. He recalled the abuse through hypnosis. Months later, Cook dropped his lawsuit, explaining that he realized how questionable hypnotically induced memories could be. (His unlicensed hypnotist, Michele Moul, had earned her master's in psychology from an unaccredited weekend institution and had previously been employed in a print shop and delicatessen.)

Also emblematic of the changing public attitude was the decision in the Holly Ramona case, in which 12 jurors found two therapists guilty of misleading a young woman through the use of sodium Amytal and other suggestive techniques and assumptions.* In other lawsuits, angry retractors sued their former therapists for encouraging them to believe in repressed memories, multiple personalities, and/or Satanic cult involvement. These court proceedings, in which some therapists face as many as six separate suits from as many clients, brought into public scrutiny the outrageous paranoid delusions that passed for therapy. Among those being sued were Houston's Judith Peterson, Chicago's Bennett Braun, and Minneapolis' Diane Humenansky. In the first of these suits to go to trial in 1995, in which Vynnette Hamanne sued Humenansky, the therapist was found guilty of inducing memories of Satanic ritual abuse and fined $2.6 million.

Christopher Barden, the lawyer/psychologist who represented Hamanne and many others harmed by repressed memory therapy and the creation of multiple personalities, observed that the judgment was "a stunning warning to therapists…and to insurance companies that they had better start obeying the informed consent laws and stop using experimental treatments like recovered memory treatments on patients." Barden went on to win another $2.4 million dollar case in 1996, then a record-breaking $10.6 million settlement against MPD guru Bennett Braun in the Pat Burgus case (see Chapter 4). Citing "business reasons," North Shore Medical Center shut down Braun's dissociative disorders unit in January 1998, and Braun had to surrender his license to practice psychiatry. Following a "tsunami of legal victories," as Barden put it, hundreds of similar, less-publicized cases were settled confidentially across the country. "This is the end of the controversy regarding recovered memories," Barden said in a front page New York Times article. "This is its death knell."

Unfortunately, that wasn't true, but there is no question that Barden's cases had a huge impact, terrifying the psychological establishment and finally capturing the attention of insurance companies, which stopped covering repressed memory therapy. Indeed, it bankrupted the malpractice insurance company begun by the American Psychiatric Association in the 1980s, which was sold to a private insurer and liquidated in 2003. In the following years, Barden represented clients who settled out of court in scores of other cases. "I am the only person who knows about all of the hundreds of litigation cases settled quietly," Barden wrote to me in 2017.

Meanwhile, several appeals courts got the message from researchers such as Stephen Ceci and Maggie Bruck that little children can be led into stating and believing the most outrageous falsehoods. Robert Kelly was freed from jail in the North Carolina Little Rascals Day Care case, Violet Amirault and Cheryl LeFave were released in the Massachusetts Fells Acres case, but Gerald "Tooky" Amirault

---

* Despite the absurdity of Holly Ramona's recovered memories, such as her father forcing her to have sex with the family dog, she did not retract but went on to become a therapist herself, helping other to unearth repressed memories.

outrageously remained in prison until 2004 and Bernard Baran until 2009. In Canada most of the Martensville defendants were exonerated.

An important ruling came in 1995 from Judge William J. Groff in New Hampshire. Groff insisted on a pretrial hearing before allowing cases based solely on recovered memories to go forward. One case involved a woman who believed her father had raped her throughout her childhood, right up until two days before her wedding at the age of 23. The other featured a woman who believed her eighth grade teacher had impregnated her when she was 12—even though she did not begin menstruating until she was 14. After hearing scientific testimony, Groff ruled: "The phenomenon of memory repression, and the process of therapy used in these cases to recover the memories, have not gained general acceptance in the field of psychology and are not scientifically reliable." The judge was even more outspoken later in his opinion:

> The very concept of a "repressed" memory, that is, that a person can experience a traumatic event, and have no memory of it whatsoever for several years, transcends human experience. There is nothing in our development as human beings which enables us to empirically accept the phenomenon.... It is inappropriately suggestive for a therapist to communicate to a client his or her belief that a dream or a flashback is a representation of a real life event, that a physical pain is a "body memory" of sexual abuse, or even that a particular memory recovered by a client is in fact a real event.... [Such therapy] thoroughly and schematically violates the guidelines and standards of practice of psychotherapy.

Despite such unequivocal legal judgments, however, repressed memory therapy has not disappeared, as I pointed out in this book's introduction. Most people—including the majority of psychotherapists—still believe that repeated traumatic childhood events can be completely forgotten and then recalled years later.

Sex Panic

Sex abuse hysteria in general, which led to both the day care and recovered memory false allegations, continues unabated, two decades into the 21st century. A sex abuse accusation is still the "nuclear bomb" that can be dropped effectively in the midst of an ugly divorce, family spat, or dispute with a teacher.

Originating in Huntsville, Alabama, in 1985, a network of nearly a thousand Children's Advocacy Centers (CACs) has blanketed the United States. The idea behind the CACs is laudable—avoid repeated, leading child interviews and make sure they are conducted in an open-ended fashion. Yet if the child has been brought to a CAC, she or he will already have been questioned repeatedly by parents, pediatricians, teachers, or social workers, so the seeds for false allegations may have been planted. Thus, when the CAC interviewers follows protocol, eventually asking pointed questions, the children may repeat what they know they are supposed to say—or, of course, in cases of real abuse, they may reveal what actually occurred. A typical CAC protocol suggests asking: "Did somebody [briefly summarize allegations or suspicions without specifying names of alleged perpetrator or providing too many details]." (For example, "Did somebody hit you?" or "Did somebody touch your wee pee [private parts of your body]?")

It is unclear how many CACs videotape their interviews, with published data ranging from 52 percent to 89.5 percent. Without videotapes, there is no available evidence of leading questions or non-verbal cues. Operating under an assumption of guilt and focusing on multidisciplinary "teamwork" between the police and child protective services can result in an endorsement of false allegations. With a focus on "advocating" for child victims, most CACs do not even talk to the accused caregivers—that is left to the police. There has been all too little research conducted on Children's Advocacy Centers or their methodologies.

As a volunteer for the National Center of Reason and Justice (NCRJ), which calls attention to false allegations of child abuse, I have read hundreds of pleas for help. These cases are not merely the tip of the iceberg. They are a snowflake perched on the tip of the iceberg. I secured permission to print the following from all who sent these emails, but I have deleted names and places to maintain anonymity. Unfortunately, this is a representative sampling. I should note that no one has had time to investigate any of these cases, so I cannot vouch for anyone's innocence, but these anguished cries from the heart offer compelling evidence of a system out of control, and most of the desperate people who wrote have limited resources and don't know what to do:

> I've been wrongly accused and charged with assaulting two young boys. We were trying to help a family out because they did not have a place to live. We finally had to kick the family out because the older boy kept hurting our children, hitting us, and hurting our animals, and the mother would not do anything to control. The day we kicked them out she filed a sexual assault claim against me. The biggest problem with the story they gave is that I was at work when they said I assaulted the older boy. The younger boy said I assaulted him while both my wife and his mother were present. It's just complete craziness.

> My son is on his 8th month in federal prison. He accidentally downloaded child pornography, thinking it was adult sex. When my son saw them he deleted them, but there were 2 child porns he never saw among the 2,319 mostly music videos. Eleven ICE agents stormed his small home, tore it apart. They tell me he will be out in less than 2 years and he'll be fine. How can you be fine when you're one of the hated vile sex offenders on the registry, for the rest of your life?

> I took a plea bargain to a registrable offense in 1999 associated w/bathing w/ my 3 year old daughter. My wife at the time (in the process of divorcing) charac-

terized it as molesting, only years later acknowledging that she deceived police to gain custody. I took the plea before Megan's List was passed so now I am listed on a sex offender registry. Daughter now 21 is trying to heal estrangement from her mom, knows she wasn't abused, and is closer to me. We all need support/ counsel re possibilities. I am listed as a sex offender, and it shames me and my daughter.

My boyfriend was wrongly sentenced to 14 years after his ex-partner accused him of being a sex offender. His pitiful lawyer was no help. He was offered a plea bargain of 4–6 months or possible 30 years in prison, and all rested on his 12 year old daughter's word. She had been living with the mother for last 10 months and he was afraid of what she might have been brainwashed into, so considering the alternative he took the plea bargain. The Judge threw it out and sentenced him to 14 years. HE IS INNOCENT. Where do I go, who do I talk to, how do I get my boyfriend out!

It's been 3 weeks since I've seen or spoken to my daughter. The judge agreed with Child Protective Services that I would only be allowed "therapeutic visits," which have not occurred. She is not even allowed to speak with her father or aunt. They took her cell phone away to ensure she is not contacted by anyone. She is 17 and she continues to state that I did nothing to her to cause these few bruises that they have multiplied x's 11. I have a lawyer, but she (my daughter) needs to be heard, as she is a bright and articulate young lady who can and will speak for herself. They claim she is still being evaluated and another lawyer informed me they are trying to say she has Stockholm Syndrome in order to prevent her from speaking in her own defense. I need help immediately, as I do not know what these wicked people's intentions are. Please Help me!!! What they (child protective services) are doing is an injustice of our human rights. Please help me!!! –A desperate mother

I NEED HELP! Please Please Please. Im involved in a situation and now taken away from my family. My fiance is still in the middle of her custody battle with her ex-husband and now he and his girlfriend have led our amazing 4 year old into saying I touched her private parts. This is so hard. I dont know what to do. I know her father and his girlfriend are doing this to try and get custody, and me and my fiance are a wreck over this and my soon to be step-daughter is being traumatized. No child should be put through this as well as our family. Im just so lost and don't know what to do. can anyone help us?

My fiancé was accused by an ex-girlfriend's daughter of molestation. A case of a woman scorned. We have documentation/text messages contradicting the police report and accusations. We even had witnesses that were his ex's employees who came to him with information of her plotting and were willing to testify against her. His attorney flaked on him at the last minute after reassuring we had a great case. Judge threatened him w/ 2 life sentences if found guilty. Attorney pretty much coerced him into take a plea for 15 years, parole after 8 years. He's innocent, and we've got all proof, just not the funds to fight this. He's sitting in prison while his two year old daughter still cries for her daddy. We need help, guidance, anything. This is not right for an innocent man to sit in prison because of a vengeful woman!

My friend was arrested and charged with aggravated sexual assault of a child (a 13 year old girl). There was no physical evidence. There was no investigation. He did not agree to any of the numerous plea deals offered to him. Probation would have been nothing, no jail time, except that he would have to plead guilty. He turned down this slap on the wrist and chose to go to trial, knowing that if he lost, he could get life in prison. He had nothing to gain by going to trial, other than his integrity, and everything to lose, but he went. He would not submit to the lynch mob who said he raped a child, even if it meant spending the rest of his life in prison. The jury returned a guilty verdict where the charge was that a 27-year-old man violently and forcefully raped a 13-year-old girl. Following the verdict, a friend of the accuser said she (the accuser) had admitted to having lied about being raped. Recently, a juror at trial revealed that some jurors believed him to be innocent, but that the few jurors who believed he was guilty would not budge and there was pressure to not spend the weekend sequestered. So the conviction was a bargain of sorts.

My boyfriend was falsely accused of child molestation—long story but it was a family feud, and he was tried and convicted with no evidence, the man that accused him wasn't even there to tell "his story." Now fast forward 8 years later and doing 5 of that in jail, he's out today and living through hell with probation and the threat of going back to jail. We been together for almost 2 years and we now have a son together, and we can't even live together! We just want a normal family but we can't all because of a false accusation that costed him his life. We would really like your help in overturning his sentence because I don't know how much longer he can take going through this, he's breaking apart.

My son has been falsely accused by younger brother of continued sexual molestation over a 10+ year timeframe. I have never witnessed anything that would remotely indicate any evidence of sexual abuse. I believe that accusing son is lying —inconsistencies in story, no signs of emotional/physical harm, and attempt to blackmail me or else accusing son threatened to make up more lies about brother. I believe accusing son has severe personality disorder. Advocacy center police attribute all of accusing son's behavior to consequences of abuse. I don't buy it. Accusing son lies to me on a daily basis but he admitted to me that he wanted to recant his story—but that the DA scared the life out of him with threats of legal repercussions against him! I think these advocacy centers are a joke! Scummy police officers setting people up to meet their quota.

I was a high school basketball coach who was falsely accused of molesting my male basketball players. A disgruntled parent coerced 6 boys to make false allegations against me simultaneously. The parent held a meeting at his home and coached the teenagers on what to say. The very next day the group went to the police to make false allegations. There was no other evidence, no confession, no recordings, no text messages, nothing. When my attorney took depositions, we found evidence that the police detectives also coerced and coached alleged victims on what to say. [Update: The case for the prosecution fell apart because 3 of the 6 boys who were coerced stopped cooperating with the prosecution and actually reached out to me for forgiveness and were in contact with me. One boy sued the school district, which settled for about $100,000. I feel like you can make a movie out of what's happened to me.]

My son has been sitting in jail for a year now on a second-degree sexual assault on a child. Why is his public defender trying to make him sign a plea if he is innocent? We had proof on two telephones that the girl lied because she was jealous. My son has been never in trouble and would never do anything like this. Me and his father are disabled I have multiple sclerosis my husband has Parkinson's disease plus other breathing issues.

My nephew had consensual sex with a girl who lied about her age, he was 17 at the time. Less than one week after he turned 18, he was arrested and picked up on two charges of rape. The alleged victim will not come down to the station, she has not cooperated, not returning phone calls, etc. We are not a wealthy family, he was appointed a public defender who is not working in his favor, offering 15 year plea deal! Please we need all the help he can get, can you please contact me ASAP.

My son has been falsely accused of sexual activity with a minor. He has been held in jail since April. We need help to defend him correctly. He currently has a public defender. We believe he is innocent, as well as others who know him, and legal people who have interviewed him. But the public defender feels it's a win if he can 'settle' instead of going to a risky trial. My son has a wife and 2 children. Any settlement is unacceptable to all of us. What can we do?

I am a 31 year old who has a life of helping others and close friends and family. I went to school and got a license to work in the medical field. I was accused of molesting my best friend's two boys because my friend's stepmother just decided for no reason that I must have abused them when I babysat them. I was charged and arrested, even though the boys didn't say I did anything to them. I had a $50,000 bail even though the only thing on my record was one speeding ticket. I was charged and arrested. I recently had the charges dropped by the prosecutors because there was no case there. But I have lost my ability to work in the medical field, lost my home, and now struggle to get work. My name was posted publicly through all sorts of social media. I am hoping to get help to get this record sealed and possibly sue the lady for falsely filing this. Also, going after the city for twisting the facts and having me arrested and charged.

Last fall, my boyfriend (now, husband), a middle school teacher, was falsely accused, arrested and charged with 24 counts of sex offenses related to 4 students. We've spent the last 9 months worrying, fretting, fearing, and desperately doing everything we could to save him from this horrific, harrowing ordeal.

Fortunately, he had an excellent lawyer with the teacher's union who was experienced and skilled in this type of situation. Nonetheless, it has been a terrible ordeal for our family. The conditions of his bond release prevented him from having contact with his 4 children (ages 15, 13-year-old twins, and 11) for 9 months. During that time, his ex-wife filed for and obtained full custody of those children. We are working now to regain contact, partial custody, and re-establish relationships with his children.

[Update: My husband was found not guilty on all counts. But we are still fighting to have all charges removed from his file, and he has been unable to return to teaching. There was such a media storm surrounding this story that his story made news around the country as well as locally. There was such a presumption of guilt within the community that parents threatened to pull their kids out of school if he returned to teach. He lost his heart for it, and we both feared that even if he did teach, it would only take one rumor to further destroy his career and our lives. I wish I could believe that this sort of thing didn't happen very often and that these results were rare, but we've discovered otherwise. Often, even after the charges are dropped or cleared, the fallout and devastation cannot be undone. We just try to heal as best we can, one day at a time.]

My 14-year-old grandson was convicted as a sex offender for attempted sexual assault that happened at a co-ed rec center. He is now 23 and still required to register. So many restrictions that he is basically homeless except for me trying to help him.

my son iis being falsely accused of sexual assault. hes 11. he was 9 at the time of alleged incident. i have no help.. no advocate. a public defender who refused to look at all of the evidence i have that prove their words wrong. not only that, he wanted my innocent son to plead guilty. please, i dont know what else to do. im literally on the brink of suicide, but that will not help my son. if i cannot obtain some type of advocacy or legal representation, he will be on a registry deigned for horrid acting people. hes innocent!!! what do i do as a poor single mom???

In October 2012, I and the other inmates in this facility that is supposed to rehabilitate and foster pro-social behavior in those with sex offense histories were subjected to a barrage of physical and verbal abuse, intimidation, humiliation, and degradation. Add to that the fact that I am innocent, but nothing justifies this behavior to anyone. On that day over 150 corrections officers descended at 7 a.m. and subjected the inmate population to a reign of terror for the next 16 hours. They destroyed thousands of dollars of inmate property, beat and physically abused more than a dozen. They began cursing and screaming at us, telling us that "We hate you, you're a bunch of mother-fucking faggots and tree jumpers, you're nothing but pieces of shit, just give us a reason to beat you down." With dogs barking and straining at the leash, they made us bunch up against each other, telling us to get into each other's asses ("balls to butts, just the way you fucking faggots like it.")

This is just a small sampling, but you get the idea. These cases are overwhelming. Here is one more plea, evidence that repressed memory therapy continues to contribute to such cases:

> In 2001, my 12 year old daughter was in therapy, at my suggestion, to deal with her mother having abandoned her at age two. I didn't realize that her therapist believed in repressed memories and must have explained them to her. She told her therapist that while she had no memory of any actual incident, she dreamed that I had sex with her when she was four years old. The therapist told her that if she dreamed it, then it really happened, because that's how our minds deal with painful memories (I have this in a supplemental police report I was never supposed to see). The therapist proceeded to report the dream to child protective services and the local police as an actual crime. They investigated and could not substantiate the allegation, yet I was arrested and tried for the crime anyway. I lost the trial and was sentenced to 35 years in prison. I won an ineffective assistance of counsel habeas action and the conviction was overturned but the judge only ordered a "sentence modification." Since then I have passed five polygraphs ordered as part of my "treatment" yet I can't get a soul to look at them. I am desperate as this has completely destroyed my life. I have no contact with my children (adults now) and I cannot find work and finding decent housing has been a challenge as well.

These cases, in addition to those featured on NCRJ.org, indicate that, while the high-profile day care hysteria cases and repressed memory claims are no longer making headlines, unpublicized cases of false allegations of sexual abuse ruin lives every day.* In his 2011 book, *Sex Panic and the Punitive State*, anthropologist Roger Lancaster documented this on-going disaster and linked it to other social trends, such as mass incarceration for non-violent crimes, and the "war on terror." Sex panics have become "a fixture in and fixation of American culture," Lancaster observed. "The never-ending parade of sex panics provides an important model—part metaphor and part blueprint—for the pervasive politics of fear."

Lancaster documented the proliferation of sex offender legislation in the early 21st century that created "a permanent pariah class of uprooted criminal outcasts" who end up living under bridges because they cannot find jobs and may not live within a certain distance of parks or schools. In 20 states and the District of Columbia, even after serving long sentences, sex offenders can still be kept in prison via "civil commitment" statutes because they are deemed "likely" to commit further offenses.

---

* A growing number of false allegations stem from misidentification of "shaken baby syndrome," when grieving parents have been accused of killing their infants. As legal and medical authors Keith Findley, Patrick Barnes, David Moran, and Waney Squier observed in 2012, there is a mistaken hypothesis "that one can reliably diagnose shaking or abuse from three internal findings (subdural hemorrhage, retinal hemorrhage and encephalopathy) and that one can identify the perpetrator based on the onset of symptoms. Over the past decade, we have learned that this hypothesis fits poorly with the anatomy and physiology of the infant brain, that there are many natural and accidental causes for these findings, and that the onset of symptoms does not reliably indicate timing."

A popular television show, "To Catch a Predator," premiered in 2004, setting up sting operations to entrap men who sought sex with minors, generally represented as being young teenagers, and filming their arrest. In 2006, a Texas district attorney named Louis Conradt was accused of making online advances to a decoy pretending to be a 13-year-old boy. When Conradt failed to show up for the assignation, the police and television crew stormed his house. Conradt shot and killed himself. "That'll make good TV," one of the policemen observed. The show was canceled in 2008 because it had become too popular for its own good—it was difficult to find new unwary men to entrap. Nonetheless, the show's host, Chris Hansen, tried to reboot the program, and new segments appeared on "Crime Watch Daily," a syndicated TV show Hansen launched in 2016.

Television host Oprah Winfrey helped fan the flames of paranoid hysteria in 2006, announcing: "The children of this nation…are being stolen, raped, tortured, and killed by sexual predators…. How many times does this have to happen? How many children have to be sacrificed?" This kind of alarmist rhetoric led to a sign Roger Lancaster saw at a YMCA: "If you have any reason whatsoever to believe that any child is being sexually abused here, remember—You don't have to 'prove' anything. Just report your suspicions to us and we'll take over from there."

As Lancaster observed: "We twenty-first-century Americans seem to be exhilarated by fear; we relish the magical power of the accusation, which, like a psychic atom bomb, flattens all that stands in its way; we savor the heady rush of panic as one might thrill to an amusement park ride."

Part of that panic has stigmatized children as sex offenders. In the rush to "protect" children, we have caused them irreparable damage, as Judith Levine documented in *Harmful to Minors* (2002):

> A ten-year-old "touched [two girls] in a sexual manner" (he grabbed at them on the school playground) and was charged with two counts of rape. In New Jersey, a neurologically impaired twelve-year-old who groped his eight-year-old stepbrother in the bath was compelled to register as a sex offender… In 1999, the newspapers briefly bristled with reports of a "child sex ring" in York Haven, Pennsylvania, in which "children as young as 7…taught each other to have sex." An eleven-year-old girl was convicted of rape.

Levine recounted her conversation with a tearful grandmother who told her how her grandson, 11, was kept in a sex-offender institution because he wouldn't confess to something he didn't do. "They kept saying he was 'in denial' and the therapy wasn't taking. So they just kept keeping him locked up." After four years of incarceration, he killed himself.

This new category of "children who molest" has turned kids into criminals. "As young as two, they are diagnosed and treated, and sometimes prosecuted, for 'inappropriate' behaviors like fondling," Levine noted. "Sex play between siblings is considered the gravest [offense], though ironically the commonest."

Not Just a Ten-Year Cycle

In 1992, Johns Hopkins psychiatrist Paul McHugh published an interesting article called "Psychiatric Misadventures" in *The American Scholar*. "During the thirty years of my professional experience," he wrote, "I have witnessed the power of cultural fashion to lead psychiatric thought and practice off in false, even disastrous, directions." He noted that three fads—the notion that schizophrenia was culturally induced, the popularity of sex-change operations, and the proliferation of multiple personalities—seemed to last about ten years.* In some ways, he appears to have been correct, at least about the recovered memory craze. The mass popularity of the hunt for repressed memories faded by 1998, having begun in earnest in 1988 with the publication of *The Courage to Heal*.

But once an idea enters the cultural mainstream, it has a way of resurfacing every few years. No matter how many times you drive a stake through its heart, it comes back. Ever since Freud applied his "pressure procedure" to extract repressed memories of incest, psychologists have periodically imitated the Viennese master. Soon after the turn of the century, Morton Prince hypnotized Christine Beauchamp to "uncover" her multiple personalities, while Boris Sidis and J. E. Donley also used hypnotism to promote "abreactions." In the wake of World War I, there was another spate of traumatic reliving in trance. In the 1920s, "hypnoidalization" was proposed to unearth memories, while Otto Rank convinced his followers that only by reliving the birth trauma could they be healed. Sandor Ferenczi unearthed hidden memories of abuse in the 1930s, while American and British therapists were simultaneously inventing "narco-analysis," using barbiturates to facilitate the recovery of supposedly repressed memories.

During the 1940s, psychiatrists encouraged World War II veterans to "abreact" traumatic memories while under sodium Pentothal or hypnosis. As a result, one soldier acted out the entire battle of Iwo Jima, even though he had never left the United States. In 1944, prison psychologist Robert Lindner published *Rebel Without a Cause* (made into a film in 1955), his account of how he regressed a "criminal psychopath" to six months old, when he "remembered" being trauma-

---

* McHugh was wrong about sex change operations going away. The current "transgender" movement is another example of a cultural fad that is politically incorrect to question—similar to sex abuse claims based on repressed memories in 1992. How *dare* anyone dispute that someone feels they were born in the wrong-gendered body? I guess if adults want to mutilate their own bodies, it is their business, but medical ethics should prevent psychiatrists from prescribing hormone treatments for children, when the long-term effects are unknown. There are shades of the multiple personality fad, too, with some "genderfluid" teens preferring to call themselves "we."

tized by watching his parents engage in sexual intercourse.* And we have seen in Chapter 7 how Arthur Janov and others kept the idea alive in the United States throughout the 1960s and 1970s. Consequently, I will be surprised if the search for repressed memories ever completely disappears.

Psychiatrist Gary Almy and his physician wife Carol wrote a scathing indictment of psychological trends—including recovered-memory therapy—in their 1994 book, *Addicted to Recovery.* As Christians, they were particularly concerned about the extensive involvement of so-called Christian therapists. The Almys concluded their book with this shrewd appraisal:

> Do not expect this psycho-fad to go quietly into the night. This searching of the "subconscious" and probing the past is … at the heart of the false memory phenomenon and the multiple personality fad…. This is the heart and soul of the psychotherapy industry, its major theoretical underpinning and resultant practice pattern. This has come to be economically vital. Entire livelihoods, reputations, and businesses depend on the survival of the recovery industry, and sadly, all too many of these are within the Christian community.

The Almys continued by quoting 2 Timothy 4:3-4: "For the time will come when men will not put up with sound doctrine. Instead, to suit their own desires, they will gather around them a great number of teachers to say what their itching ears want to hear. They will turn their ears away from the truth and turn aside to myths."

Who Became a "Survivor"?

It's worth examining who recovered memories of sexual abuse during the height of the epidemic. Did those who eventually recalled memories have anything in common? Yes. They were all experiencing stress and uncertainty in their lives, or they wouldn't have sought therapy. Many women were feeling trapped by motherhood or marriage. Some sought therapy in the wake of postpartum depression or miscarriages. Others struggled with the transition from adolescence to adulthood. Aside from approaching a vulnerable point in their lives, however, they did not necessarily have much in common, other than a therapist with a particular mindset, or simply being a self-doubting woman at a particular time in history.

The median age of women recovering "memories" appeared to be around the age of 30, though the age range widened as recovered-memory therapy and books espousing it became more popular. Girls as young as 12 were recovering memories. Even preschoolers were told by therapists that they must have repressed memories of sexual abuse. At the same time, therapists began to recruit

---

* In their introduction to *Rebel Without a Cause,* psychologists Sheldon and Eleanor Glueck dismissed "such outworn notions as `guilt; `criminal intent,' [or] `knowledge of right and wrong,' thereby paving the way for the wave of victimology and abnegation of responsibility.

in nursing homes. One 1994 article advised that "psychologically fragile" elderly women, particularly widows, should be helped to recall the incest of their youth.

Most were white women with the time and money to seek psychotherapy, but as the repressed memory rage progressed, it began to spread to minority groups and lower socio-economic levels. Also, about 10 percent of those who recovered memories were men.

While there is no necessary common thread among Survivors, there are several interesting subsets. A number of accusers were very suggestible and hypnotizable, as I mentioned in Chapter 4. Many such Survivors were also quite dramatic, creative, and imaginative. "I can work myself into a state of sobbing over something in a fantasy," one Survivor acknowledged in *The Courage to Heal*. They played roles well, consciously or otherwise. A surprising number were either professional or amateur actors. Many Survivors had always read mystery, fantasy, or horror stories. They enjoyed solving puzzles or envisioning other worlds and possibilities. Often, they sang professionally or exhibited artistic talent.

Many Survivors also seemed to be among the helpers of the world, easily empathizing with those who suffer. They often entered the helping professions, becoming teachers, nurses, or counselors.

A majority who came to believe in their "recovered memories" were high achievers who did quite well in school and may have advanced degrees. Just as they were good students in school, they made excellent therapy clients, dutifully reading recovery books, filling out workbooks, and performing other homework assignments.

Other Survivors were probably *too close* to their parents. While their friends rebelled as teenagers, they continued to consider their parents to be best friends. These overly dependent adult children, who had difficulty individuating from their parents, often had a love/hate relationship with them. They longed to break away but couldn't seem to do it. The incest memories allowed them to do so, but they did not really stand on their own. Instead, they transferred their dependence to their therapists.

Another subset consists of "lifers" who had bounced from one diagnosis, therapist, or movement to another for most of their lives. "I've been mentally disturbed all my life," one such woman told Ellen Bass. Many of them had always suffered from assorted mysterious bodily ailments. Adopting the Survivor persona was simply the latest in a series of explanations for these maladies.

Finally, and perhaps most tragic, there were undoubtedly those who had real disorders such as manic-depression (bipolar disorder), anxiety disorders, obsessive-compulsive disorder, clinical depression, or epilepsy that went undiagnosed. Indeed, the conditions were exacerbated by the acting out that was demanded by the Survivor role.

I cannot overemphasize the strong motivation that impelled people to discover hidden memories, once the idea was planted. They yearned for an explanation for their current despair, and they became dogged in their pursuit of the mystery. "My therapist told me to read *The Courage to Heal*," one woman told me. "I opened the book to the first page, and three hours later, I looked up, sobbing. I was totally consumed by this book. I couldn't read enough, find out enough, couldn't let it go. Everything was leading me down this road. My therapists weren't necessarily saying 'Confront your parents,' but society and books and my need to be healthy were driving me. I was absolutely driven."

Once someone was sucked into the recovered memory vortex, it was clearly difficult to get out. "There is an identity in being a committed survivor of sexual abuse," Bass and Davis accurately observed in *The Courage to Heal*. "It can be hard to give up." More and more memories surfaced, along with diverse perpetrators. Once a confrontation took place, it was hard to back away. Besides, admitting you were wrong would involve losing all your new friends and your all-important therapist. The shame and guilt from admitting false accusations would be overwhelming. Also, people have an innate resistance to cutting their losses, once they've made a major investment. "The memories might not be totally accurate," one Survivor told me, "but what purpose would it serve me to spend so much time, energy, and money to blame my father for something he didn't do?" Therefore, according to this circular logic, he must have committed incest on her.

It seemed painfully obvious in some cases that these "memories" did not seem real, even to those who remembered them. One woman I interviewed never managed to retrieve any memories, though she was still sure she was a Survivor. Another strove in vain to recall incest, but settled for memories of *emotional* incest. "I've concluded that you never overtly molested me," she told her father recently, "but you did violate some very important boundaries. You hugged me too long, looked at me too fondly." I suspect that this nagging uncertainty may be what prevented some children from directly accusing their parents or telling them precisely what they were supposed to have done.

The saddest feature of the "therapeutic" process was the frightful amount of pain it unnecessarily inflicted upon unwary clients. They often went through awful depressions, suicide attempts, and hospitalizations. They lost their families, their jobs, their relationships. Yet somehow, they convinced themselves that they were getting better. Relatively speaking, over the short term, they eventually *did* get better. Few people can keep themselves in such a state of turmoil indefinitely, and when Survivors adjusted to their new status and began to feel relatively calm, they often perceived that they had made great strides. Compared to how they functioned when *entering* therapy, however, most were worse off.

The theory of cognitive dissonance helps to explain why a therapeutic approach that inflicted so much pain could be so persuasive and attract devoted adherents. Studies have demonstrated that initiative rites such as the kind of severe hazing inflicted on new fraternity brothers actually increased loyalty and liking for the group. "If a person voluntarily goes through a difficult or a painful experience in order to attain some goal or object, that goal or object becomes more attractive," observed the authors of *Mistakes Were Made (But Not By Me)*. In other words, to admit that they went through such horrors for no reason would be unacceptable. So the repressed memories must be true, and their new role as Survivors must be worthwhile.

Because they felt better having an explanation for all their previous troubles, they were sure that their memories must be accurate. Why else would they have improved? The answer is that *any* explanation for life's troubles can have a placebo effect. Unfortunately, their newfound purpose came at the expense of grieving families, devastated by false accusations. And, however fulfilling their lives might be, they had been deprived of the support and comfort of their families.

To demonstrate what this process could do to a marriage, let me recount the story of Fred Orr (not his real name). For three years, Orr believed that his wife Shauna really harbored multiple personalities because of sexual assaults by her father, brother, and grandfather. He read the section for supportive spouses in *The Courage to Heal* and tried his best. Orr listened to Shauna's dramatic recounting of therapy sessions, helped her save pickle jars to smash on the garage floor to get out her anger, and even made her a tee-shirt featuring her eight alters (Goodie, Spock, Commando, Ivory, and It, among others). He hated his in-laws, ripping up their Christmas check in self-righteous fury, even though he had heard that Shauna's father was so distraught by the allegations that he often curled up in a fetal position in the corner of a room and wouldn't move. "I figured he was just feeling guilty."

Nevertheless, Shauna began to turn against her husband as well. "She did these boundary exercises," he told me. "It started with no sex. Then, it was don't touch, with an invisible line down the middle of the bed. Then it was off to separate bedrooms. Finally, her therapist, a Ph.D. psychologist who ruled her life, told her to get divorced." In a way, Orr was relieved. "She'd been chopping up wieners with a butcher knife, fantasizing they were her father's penis. You should see the look on her face when she does that. I was glad to get out of that house."

Who Was Falsely Accused?

The majority of those who were falsely accused through repressed memory therapy were parents, though uncles, aunts, grandparents, and siblings were also thrown into the mix, as well as gambling buddies or fellow Rotarians or local policemen in the case of ritual abuse allegations. Repressed memories as well as leading interviews with children also targeted teachers, priests, coaches, and day care providers.

As with those who recovered memories, there is no readily identifiable commonality among those who were accused, other than being in the wrong time and place. The impact on all of them was horrendous, wrecking careers, marriages, and friendships, subjecting them to expensive civil lawsuits, and sometimes landing them in prison.

Many also went through tortured self-doubt. As Franz Kafka's character Joseph K. discovered in *The Trial,* condemned but innocent people begin to believe they must have done something wrong, especially if the particulars are never specified. Almost all of the falsely accused parents questioned their own innocence at one time or another. After all, it was their own beloved children who were arrayed against them. Like Paul Ingram, the policeman whose tragic story is recounted in Lawrence Wright's book, *Remembering Satan* (1994), they thought, "My girls know me. They wouldn't lie about something like this." Some, like Ingram, fell under the sway of zealous therapists/interrogators and confessed to crimes that they never committed.

The words of the beleaguered Job, whose friends told him that he must have done something to deserve his fate on the dungheap, echo from the Old Testament: "I know thou wilt not hold me innocent. I shall be condemned; why then do I labor in vain? If I wash myself with snow, and cleanse my hands with lye, Yet thou wilt plunge me into a pit, and my own clothes will abhor me."

People don't want to believe that a completely innocent person could be accused of such an awful crime by his or her children. If that were true, it could happen to anyone—it could happen to *them.* Thus, we observe a variation of the familiar blame-the-victim scenario. Job's friends, his supposed "comforters," enacted this drama long ago. Eliphaz asked Job, "Think now, who that was innocent ever perished? Or where were the upright cut off?" Job understood what he really meant. "You see my calamity," he told Eliphaz, "and are afraid."

Yet *anyone could be accused of incest without any foundation in fact,* given the proper circumstances. The one characteristic shared by the majority of accused parents was that they were mostly middle to upper-class educated Caucasians with the initial ability and willingness to pay for their children's therapy. Aside from that, they did not appear to have a great deal in common. At the FMS Foundation meetings, octogenarians who never spoke about sex with their children sat next to accused parents in their 40s or 50s whose parenting philosophies were completely different. Some were exceptionally close to their children; others were emotionally or physically distant. Some were strict with their children, others permissive. Many remained in intact, secure marriages; others were either long-divorced or tolerated poor relationships. The only common denominator appeared to be a troubled child who sought therapy.

A third of the parents who contacted the FMS Foundation never learned exactly what their children thought they did. Others found out the precise allegations by cut-off letter or word-of-mouth. Not knowing what they were supposed to have done was maddening. They were left guessing, wondering whether it was something really awful or only a hug or a look misinterpreted as "emotional incest." It could actually be a relief to know the worst, to be accused of Satanic ritual abuse. At least then they knew they didn't do it—unless, of course, they came to believe that they, too, repressed the memory.

In many cases, there was a sibling domino effect. Many families lost first one, then several children to recovered-memory therapy. One father I interviewed had lost four of his five daughters, one of whom accused him of "incestuous" behavior because, when she was 22, he told her about his job dissatisfaction—a conversation more appropriate with a wife, she asserted. Another couple told me they had lost seven of their eight children. These cases were particularly devastating because so many people assumed that if multiple children made the accusations, they must be true. They did not stop to consider the improbability of *several* children completely forgetting abuse for years, let alone one.

In these families, repressed memory accusations were like a contagious virus. One daughter retrieved incest memories and told her sisters. Some of them not only believed her but sought therapy to find their own memories. After all, if the father did this to one daughter, isn't it likely he would have done it to the rest? Indeed, if he was such a pedophile, perhaps he also assaulted his son. The cases in which multiple siblings cut off all contact were particularly difficult. Not only did the parents lose more, but observers often concluded that the allegations must be true. Otherwise, why would several children be saying the same thing?

I interviewed one retired Tennessee doctor whose two daughters in their 40s recovered hypnotic "memories" of how he sexually abused them at his summer home, along with 12 prostitutes, whom he then allegedly murdered and buried. The police led one of the daughters around the property and dug for the bodies, but they never found them. The daughters then sued their father for $4 million each. At least he was not in prison, as was Rhode Island attorney John Quattrocchi. In 1994, Quattrocchi was convicted of molesting his former girlfriend's daughter. Her "recovered memories," which she discovered after months of psychotherapy, went back to when she was three, just prior to the time she first met Quattrocchi. He was sentenced to 40 years but his conviction was overturned two years later, and after a thorough hearing, in which Christopher Barden argued the case for Quattrocchi, in 1999 a judge determined that repressed memories were not admissible as scientific evidence.

The Scope of the Repressed Memory Epidemic

Just how widespread was the recovered-memory epidemic at its height? How many therapists were actively searching for repressed memories, and how many people "recovered" them, cut off contact with their families, and became Survivors? Over 25,000 families contacted the False Memory Syndrome Foundation, but that number is almost certainly a tiny fraction of the actual cases that occurred. Most accused parents were probably too frightened and embarrassed to tell anyone about their situations. Back in the 1990s, to obtain a realistic estimate, I approached the problem via the therapists.

It should be clear to readers by now that a substantial subset of American therapists specialized in helping clients to recall what they believed were repressed memories of sexual abuse. It wasn't difficult to spot them, even through ads in the yellow pages. Many specifically solicited "sexual abuse survivors." Other tell-tale phrases included *inner child work, dream work, adult child of dysfunctional families, hypnosis,* or *guided imagery.* One of the more notorious therapists, involved in several cases that came to my attention, placed an aggressive Yellow Pages ad, featuring a black telephone receiver and a red headline: *"Immediate Help."* The highlighted problems and solutions offered included: "Anxiety and Stress, Sexual Issues, Drugs and Alcohol, Isolation, Survivors of Incest and Abuse, Relaxation Training, Depression, Troubled Relationships, Adult Struggles." Of course, people *do* sometimes need therapy for depression or "adult struggles," but this therapist was likely to explain all such difficulties by uncovering repressed memories.

How many such therapists were there, and how many clients did they infect? Several surveys offered disturbing figures. Michael Yapko, a clinical psychologist whose 1994 book, *Suggestions of Abuse,* questioned the hunt for repressed memories, gathered data in 1992 from more than 860 psychotherapists, most of whom were attending national conventions. The average respondent was 44 years old, with education beyond the master's degree level, and had been in clinical practice for more than 11 years. Of these, 40 percent agreed with the statement: "I believe that early memories, even from the first years of life, are accurately stored and retrievable," and about the same percentage thought that if people don't remember much about their childhoods, it is because of traumatic events. Almost 60 percent thought that any events someone couldn't remember must have been repressed. And 36 percent agreed that "if a client believes a memory is true, I must also believe it to be true if I am to help him or her."

An overwhelming majority (84 percent) of Yapko's respondents thought that hypnotic age regression was a useful technique. Three-quarters believed that hypnosis enables people to accurately remember forgotten events. Nearly half (47 percent) believed that "psychotherapists can have greater faith in details of a traumatic event when obtained hypnotically than otherwise," while 31 percent agreed that "when someone has a memory of a trauma while in hypnosis, it objectively must actually have occurred." Incredibly, 28 percent of Yapko's respondents believed that hypnosis could be used to recover accurate memories of *past lives!* Finally, 16 percent thought that it was *impossible* to implant false memories in a client.

Social psychologist Richard Ofshe called the belief in Satanic ritual abuse the "Achilles' heel" of the recovered memory movement, since the grotesque memories of murder, cannibalism, and aborted fetuses were so unbelievable and never presented any confirming evidence. His point was well-taken. Yet in a huge survey published in 1994, conducted by Gail Goodman and her colleagues, 13 percent of the nearly 7,000 therapists surveyed had elicited recovered memories of ritual abuse, and these respondents "overwhelmingly believed" the memories.

A 1993 survey yielded equally disturbing results. Debra A. Poole and D. Stephen Lindsay conducted a random national survey of Ph.D.-level American psychologists with a substantial female client base. Of their 86 respondents, 76 percent reported that they sometimes used one or more memory recovery techniques, including hypnosis, age regression, dream interpretation, guided imagery, use of family photographs as memory cues, or interpretation of physical symptoms as body memories; 60 percent reported using two or more of these techniques. Most of those surveyed (85 percent) said that at least some clients who initially denied any memory of sexual abuse subsequently recalled it during therapy. Some therapists reported that *all* of their clients recovered memories. Over half (52 percent) claimed that they were sometimes "fairly certain" after the first session that they were dealing with a repressed-memory case.* A disturbing 43 percent of their respondents sometimes recommended *The Courage to Heal* to their clients. Only 8 percent never made quick judgments about sex abuse, used no suggestive techniques, and did not regard memory recovery as an important therapeutic goal.

This survey made it abundantly clear that the *majority* of American therapists sometimes hunted for repressed memories of sexual abuse in 1993, at the height of the epidemic, using suggestive techniques to do so. (Results from another national American survey, published in 1995, indicated that 73 percent of 378 psychologists surveyed had at least one recovered memory patient.) On the other hand, only a minority appeared to *specialize* in recovered-memory work. As an

---

* Some therapists prided themselves on being able to identify repressed memory cases quickly. "I can tell within ten minutes, I can spot it as a person walks in the door," one therapist told a TV talk show host in 1992. Others believed they could pick abuse survivors out of a crowd just by the way they walked or talked.

extreme example of such "memory focused" therapists, Poole and Lindsay described a clinician who routinely told her clients that they were probably abused, then led them in an initial two-hour hypnotic age regression. *All* of her female clients eventually came to recall abuse while in her care. Yet she wrote on her survey sheet that "it is very important not to lead the hypnotized subject."

Poole and Lindsay found that 25 percent of their sample were "memory focused." All of these therapists used two or more memory recovery techniques, thought that they could often spot hidden abuse victims after an initial session, and believed it was important for clients to recall the abuse if therapy was to be effective. On average, these therapists saw approximately 50 adult female clients per year and reported that 60 percent of those whom they suspected had repressed memories eventually came to remember abuse.

From this first survey, it was not clear what percentage of *all* female clients recalled memories, so Poole and Lindsay conducted a second survey of 59 therapists early in 1994, rephrasing the question. The results confirmed that 25 percent of the therapists were memory focused, and that 34 percent of their clients initially denied any memory of abuse but eventually recalled it while in therapy.* Although Poole and Lindsay emphasized that their limited survey could not be considered definitive, it provided at least a rough approximation of the extent of recovered memory work in the therapeutic community at that time.**

In their second survey, Poole and Lindsay were joined by British colleagues Amima Memon and Ray Bull, who gave the questionnaire to 57 psychologists in the United Kingdom, with similar results—about 25 percent appeared to be memory focused. Even more alarming were the results of a 1994 British Psychological Society survey of 810 member therapists. The overwhelming majority, 97 percent, believed in the essential accuracy not only of run-of-the-mill recovered memories, but of Satanic ritual abuse reports! (Fifty-three percent believed such memories "sometimes," 38 percent "usually," and 6 percent "always.") Twenty-three percent of the respondents had clients who had recalled memories from total amnesia while in therapy with them during the previous year.***

---

*   In her compelling 1993 series on repressed memory therapy in the *San Francisco Examiner*, reporter Stephanie Salter interviewed Laguna Beach therapist Douglas Sawin, who provided a template for therapists who sought memories. Of his 50 weekly clients—virtually all of whom recovered memories of sexual abuse—Sawin said, "Not one walked in my office and said, 'I'm an incest survivor.'" This did not stop him from convincing a young client that her parents had ritually abused her, applying carrots, chicken parts, hoses, and broomsticks to her vagina and anus.

**   One Florida retractor told me in 1996 that she had attempted to locate a good counselor for a friend in Daytona Beach. She called over 100 therapists before finding one who did not recommend *The Courage to Heal* or espouse a belief in recovered memories. Thus, Poole and Lindsay's estimate that only 25 percent were "memory focused" may be quite conservative.

***   Unfortunately, the British Psychological Society chose to interpret these disturbing results as evidence that recovered memories were probably accurate: "Memory recovery is reported by highly experienced and well

It is surprisingly difficult to arrive at a firm figure for the total number of practicing American psychotherapists at any given time, because they encompass psychiatrists, clinical psychologists, social workers, psychiatric nurses, masters-level counselors, and pastoral counselors. Nonetheless, in a 1994 article in *Common Boundary,* journalist Beth Baker arrived at an estimate of 254,600 practicing licensed U.S. therapists. Her figure was unquestionably low, for a variety of reasons. For example, Baker got her figure of 80,000 practicing social workers from membership figures of the National Association of Social Workers (NASW). But, as an NASW official told me, there were probably an equal number of practicing social workers who had not joined the organization. The same holds true for figures from the American Psychological Association and others. Because of high dues, many therapists simply didn't belong.

There are other reasons to suspect that Baker's figure was an underestimate. The country's 13,000 school counselors were not included, for instance, although a number of them were involved in repressed-memory cases. Moreover, in most states, *anyone* could (and can) legally hang up a shingle declaring him- or herself to be a psychotherapist—like Lucy in the *Peanuts* cartoon strip—and unlicensed therapists did not show up in these figures. Nor did the body worker/massage therapists, channelers, psychics, or other non-traditional memory-retrieval practitioners.

Nonetheless, let us take Baker's figure and round it *down* to 250,000 therapists. Poole and Lindsay's survey indicated that 25 percent of doctoral-level therapists were "memory-focused." That percentage was likely to be *higher* for social workers or masters-level counselors, who tended to accept the repressed-memory dogma more eagerly than did their Ph.D. colleagues. Taking that 25 percent figure as accurate, however—and ignoring the substantial number of "recovered memories" that arose outside that core group—*we arrive at 62,500 memory-focused therapists.* Poole and Lindsay found that each therapist saw approximately 50 female clients per year, of whom 34 percent recovered memories.

Using simple math (62,500 memory-focused therapists × 50 clients × 34 percent who recover memories), we arrive at *over one million cases of "recovered memories" each year during the height of the repressed memory epidemic.* Even assuming overlap—some clients returned to the same therapist year after year, while others changed therapists frequently—it is reasonable to assume that, since the hunt for repressed memories came to full flower in 1988, several million came to believe they were "Survivors" who had no memory of being sexually abused before going for therapy.

---

qualified therapists who are well aware of the dangers of inappropriate suggestion and interpretation." This assertion was made despite the fact that 33 percent of the respondents did not believe it was even *possible* to create false memories!

And that is only an estimate of women who recovered memories at the hands of hard-core, memory-focused, licensed therapists. It doesn't account for *men* who recovered memories, or for those who worked with clergy or unlicensed therapists, or those who were influenced outside of therapy by books such as *The Courage to Heal.*

In short, by any conservative analysis of the information available, there were millions of cases of "recovered memories," most of which represented shattered lives and destroyed families. If two-and-a-half million women (well over one percent of the U.S. population) identified themselves as "Survivors," then at least one out of every 25 American families was affected.

That astonishing conclusion is also confirmed by anecdotal evidence. I challenge readers of this book to consider how many people they personally know who were affected, either by retrieving memories themselves, being accused on their basis, or belonging to a family system that was shaken by such allegations. If you don't know of any, ask your friends and neighbors about this phenomenon. You might be surprised.

Until 2017, to my knowledge, no one had ever conducted a survey of the general public to determine how many people had recovered abuse memories in psychotherapy. Lawrence Patihis, a psychology professor at the University of Southern Mississippi, had come closest in his 2014 survey about belief in repressed memories, showing that 84 percent of the general public thought that traumatic memories are often repressed. When I mentioned my frustration over the lack of a survey of the extent of actual recovered memory cases, he suggested that we collaborate on such an effort. We created a detailed questionnaire and, modeling the age distribution of the 2010 U. S. census, we launched it on Amazon Mechanical Turk, an online survey instrument.

Shortly before this book went to press, we completed the survey and began to study the results, some of which I summarized in this book's introduction. We will write up a complete summary of the data, with appropriate caveats and acknowledgment of possible limitations, for publication in a psychological journal, and I hope that this first survey will inspire additional research. But I can provide a summary of the preliminary findings here.

We surveyed over 2,000 people, ranging in age from 20 to 98, with a median age of 47. Among those who took the survey, nearly half had sought psychotherapy at some point in their lives. Of those who had therapy, 20 percent reported that their therapist had discussed "the possibility that you might have been abused as a child but had repressed the memories." Of those in the sample who had received therapy, over 11 percent answered "Yes" to this question: "During the course of therapy, did you come to remember being abused as a child, when you had no previous memory of such abuse?"

That means that about 5 percent of the total survey participants came to believe that they were abused, when they had no previous awareness before entering therapy. Adjusting that figure for race, ethnicity, and gender reduces the figure to 4 percent. Multiplying that percentage by the adult U. S. population of 225.5 million, that would mean that more than 9 million people had come to believe that they had repressed memories of abuse.

The data also indicated how influential the authority of the therapist could be. Of those respondents whose therapists suggested they might have repressed memories, 46 percent also reported recovering memories of abuse in the therapy. In contrast, only 2 percent of the sample recovered memories of abuse if their therapist did not suggest repressed memories. As I expected, the worst types of therapy were psychodynamic approaches such as attachment, emotion-focused, or internal family systems therapy, often using hypnosis. I was shocked, however, that even some cognitive-behavioral therapists encouraged recovered memories. Rather than being confined to therapies that transparently declare that they believe in repression of traumatic memories, the practice apparently occurs within most psychotherapy types, at least according to this survey's patient reports.

The biggest surprise for me was the extent of recovered memory cases in the 21st century, long after repressed memory therapy had been thoroughly debunked (or so I thought). Yes, the epidemic of repressed memories had peaked in the early 1990s, with a rate of 18 percent of those entering therapy retrieving abuse memories. But in our sample that rate declined only to 8 percent in the ongoing second decade of the 21st century.

The vast majority of our respondents (93 percent) who recovered abuse memories in therapy still believe that their repressed memories are accurate. Nearly half of them had cut off all contact with their families, with less than 10 percent of them having resumed full contact.

We also asked survey participants if other family members had recovered abuse memories, and nearly 20 percent of them said Yes. Many involved multiple family members, indicating that a belief in repressed memories may be contagious, like a virus, within families, particularly between siblings. One respondent wrote: "Myself and my other 9 siblings have suffered to different levels of degree with suppressed memories." Finally, we inquired about acquaintances, and again, nearly 20 percent knew of one or more people who had recovered abuse memories.

The hundreds of anonymous comments we received along with the surveys range from skeptical disbelief in repressed memories to unquestioning, fervent belief. We also heard from people who had been abused as children and couldn't imagine how anyone could forget it. Some respondents said they thought they must have repressed memories but couldn't yet recall them. Another didn't doubt her friend's memory but lamented its impact: "I saw what she went through when she saw her psychologist. Some things are better left alone." Another wrote: "My friend's memories impacted her greatly. She lost her custody of her children, lost contact with her family and almost lost her mind." One woman with recovered memories wrote simply and poignantly, "I cannot get past the memories; they haunt me," while another revealed "I still have the feeling that maybe I'm making this all up. It is very disturbing, and has impacted my life in very negative ways." Two cases in our survey involved alleged recovered memories of murders. One resulted in a conviction.

Finally, there was this searing revelation: "My sister committed suicide three years after repressed memories were brought to her attention in 2011 through hypnotherapy. I am 100% certain that these 'memories' were false. I was very close to my sister our whole lives and we never experienced sexual abuse or molestations of any kind, but this therapist somehow convinced her that she was raped/molested and sexually abused by multitudes of people including our doctor and dentist as well as multiple family members."

The Backlash: Whose Back? Whose Lash?

There were many disturbing responses to the raging debate over repressed memories. Instead of taking a hard look at what *The Courage to Heal* did and trying to make amends, Ellen Bass and Laura Davis published a third edition in 1994, adding a chapter called "Honoring the Truth." In it, they gave grudging, minimal acknowledgment to the problem of induced memories, but they stressed that therapists *rarely* pushed clients into making false allegations. Further, they asserted that "there is no such thing as false memory syndrome" and that "moving into and out of denial is a natural part of the healing process." If material about false memories was disturbing, Bass and Davis advised: "Give yourself a break and avoid it." They reaffirmed their belief in ritual abuse, dredged up the McMartin tunnel story again, recycled the Frank Fuster Country Walk case, and urged Survivors to "honor your own truth"—as long, of course, as they continued to believe they were abused.

Instead of moderating their tone, Bass and Davis retained all the vitriolic quotations from Survivors, encouraging rage and violent fantasies: "I have such venomous hatred. I pray to God that [my father] comes down with some terrible disease. I'd like him to get AIDS. That or Alzheimer's. I can't wait for his funeral." Or this: "I imagine walking into my parents' house with a shotgun aimed right at my father's balls. 'Okay, Dad. Don't move an inch. Not one step, you sucker. I'm gonna take 'em off one at a time. And I'm gonna take my sweet time about it, too!'"

Despite the mounting criticism aimed at *The Courage to Heal,* many counselors were still assigning it as mandatory reading. In the 1994 book, *The Authoritative Guide to Self-Help Books,* 500 prominent therapists across the country were polled for their recommendations of 350 books. The number one choice? *The Courage to Heal.*

Recovered-memory therapists such as Judith Herman proclaimed that the False Memory Syndrome Foundation was spearheading a despicable "backlash" against those who heroically exposed the extent of sexual abuse. "For the past twenty years," Herman wrote in 1993, "women have been speaking out about sexual violence, and men have been coming up with denials, evasions, and excuses. We have been told that women lie, exaggerate, and fantasize." Then she reviewed "the basic facts," asserting that sexual abuse of children was common and still underreported. "Most victims do not disclose their abuse until long after the fact, if ever."

Much of what Herman said thus far was true, but it was irrelevant to the repressed memory debate. By getting up on her ideological soap box, she diverted the debate away from whether massive repression and recovery actually occurred—and the highly suggestive methods that therapists used—to a diatribe against societal ills. "Violence against women and children is deeply embedded in our society. It is a privilege that men do not relinquish easily. So it's not surprising that we would see serious resistance to change. Historically, every time a subordinate group begins to make serious progress, a backlash occurs."

Having stacked the deck against anything a *man* might say, Herman then reviewed all of the familiar dogma about recovered memories—how the memories come back as sensations or memory fragments, how Survivors don't want to believe these memories themselves and frequently cling to doubts, how support groups are important in the healing process. Finally, Herman admitted that "occasionally" overzealous therapists "try to play detective, leaping to conclusions about their patients' histories without waiting for the memories to emerge." Even in these cases, however, she asserted that "it is most unusual for patients to accept every suggestion their therapists make. Psychotherapy is a collaborative effort, not a form of totalitarian indoctrination."*

Critics such as Herman, who believe that only the most coercive methods of memory extraction are dangerous, ignored the well-documented history of *inadvertent cuing* that can occur in therapy sessions. There is a classic study, for instance, in which research assistants showed subjects the same ten photographs of people's faces, asking them to rate the degree of "success" or "failure" that the

---

* In 1995, Judith Herman found other things to worry about besides the "backlash." She was fined $30,000 in a U.S. District Court for illegally dispensing psychoactive drugs to non-patients. In addition, an audit revealed that over 4,000 pills, including Halcion, Valium, and Fiorinal with codeine, were missing from her clinic. She was subsequently fined another $5,000 by the Massachusetts Board of Registration and ordered to undergo 50 hours of training in prescribing practices.

faces showed. The assistants were informed that the purpose of the experiment was to corroborate previous findings. Half of the research assistants were told that the photos depicted successful people, while the other half believed that previous viewers had rated them as failures. As a result, the experimenters given the "success" expectation obtained uniformly higher ratings than the other group—yet *the experimenters had no idea that they were signaling the subjects* through slight voice inflections or body language. This experiment is also evidence of what researchers call *confirmation bias,* in which clinicians are likely to find confirmation for their own presuppositions.

In such experiments, as psychiatrist Jerome Frank pointed out in 1973, "the greater the power, prestige, or status of the experimenter, the greater his biasing effect," a finding that clearly applies to the "expert" therapist. Not only that, but as the experiments progressed, it became apparent that the subjects and experimenters reinforced one another, so that the experimenter produced increasingly blatant but unconscious cues. "These findings would support the assumption that the longer a person receives treatment, the more he may be influenced by his therapist," Frank commented. "This would be analogous to the *folie à deux* between hypnotist and subject."

The repressed memory process provides an outstanding example of a *folie à deux,* a warped kind of tango in which therapist and client danced through a fractured hall of mental mirrors. During most of the dance, the therapist led, but at other times, the client took over. Between them, they clasped childhood photos and *The Courage to Heal or* other self-help recovery books.

The term *folie a deux,* which literally means "folly involving two," was replaced in the fourth edition of the *Diagnostic and Statistical Manual of Mental Disorders (DSM-IV, 1994)* by the more formal diagnosis of "Shared Psychotic Disorder," defined as:

> ... a delusion that develops in an individual who is involved in a close relationship with another person (sometimes termed the "inducer" or "the primary case") who already has a Psychotic Disorder with prominent delusions. The individual comes to share the delusional beliefs of the primary case in whole or in part.... Usually the primary case in Shared Psychotic Disorder is dominant in the relationship and gradually imposes the delusional system on the more passive and initially healthy second person.... If the relationship with the primary case is interrupted, the delusional beliefs of the other individual usually diminish or disappear.*

---

* In the *DSM-IV Casebook,* there is a fascinating case study of Shared Psychotic Delusion relevant to the repressed-memory controversy. In it, a 43-year-old housewife entered the hospital in 1968, asking to be hypnotized to recall her many infidelities and be cured of them. It turned out that she was not, in fact, having numerous affairs. Her dominant, jealous husband was convinced that she was massively unfaithful, and his wife accepted his version of reality, explaining to the doctors that she "blocked" the memories out.

As Judith Herman observed, therapy sessions *are* a "collaborative effort." It is ironic, to say the least, that a substantial number of well-educated American psychotherapists in the 1990s appeared to suffer from a mental illness that was defined in their own diagnostic manual. Indeed, *they were the transmitters of the disease in millions of cases, and the best cure was to get patients away from such therapists.*

In a further irony, the fifth revision of the *Diagnostic and Statistical Manual (DSM-V, 2013)* demoted Shared Psychotic Disorder to a subsection of "other specified schizophrenic spectrum and other psychotic disorders" and removed the detailed description. A 2014 article in the *Journal of the American Academy of Psychiatry and the Law* observed mildly: "The presence of shared psychotic disorder in DSM-5 will allow continued recognition of this disorder, which, although rare, is occasionally seen in forensic cases, both criminal and civil."

This article did not acknowledge that a major incidence of the disorder had been caused by psychotherapists. Rather than demote and de-emphasize "Shared Psychotic Disorder," the sixth edition of the *DSM* should restore it to an honored place in which a belief in repressed memories and multiple personalities (now called "Dissociative Identity Disorder") should be subsumed as subsets.

Who's in Denial Now?

After the extent of damage done in recovered-memory therapy became obvious, it was remarkable to witness the variety of rationalizations and reactions from the psychology establishment. Instead of welcoming open debate, therapists such as Charles Whitfield, author of *Healing the Child Within,* denied that there is any such thing as false memory syndrome or even recovered-memory therapy.

Although Whitfield admitted that delusive memories could sometimes occur, he asserted—without recourse to any study—that only *2 percent* of parents accused on the basis of recovered memories were innocent. Most of them didn't *know* that they are guilty, however, because 90 percent of them were "unconscious" as they abused their children.

Whitfield also joined therapist E. Sue Blume in dismissing the horrifying, compelling testimony of retractors. They really *were* abused. Their incest memories *were* accurate. It's just that they had slipped back into denial. "Why are we so … willing to accept the validity of the reported withdrawal of an incest memory—by *persons seen as so suggestible that they allegedly have been persuaded to accept a 'false' experience in the first place?*" asked Blume in an aptly-titled 1995 article, "The Ownership of Truth." Who, one wonders, is actually in denial here?

At a 1994 Seattle workshop ironically titled "The False Memory Debate," Whitfield made participants sign a "Statement of Safety" which read, in part: "This is to certify that I am not a False Memory Syndrome Foundation member. I also do not side with them or seriously advocate their point of view that most delayed memories of trauma are false." The following year, Whitfield, following MPD guru Richard Kluft, began to refer to critics of recovered memory as "falsies" or "psycho-terrorists."

In 1995, Whitfield published *Memory and Abuse*, a book filled with all the old misconceptions about memory, intent on "piecing together signs, symptoms and clues," which included chronic headaches, neck and back pain, tight jaws, stuttering, eczema, and accident proneness. And if you didn't have any of the signs? No problem: "One of these symptoms is not being aware of having any of these manifestations." Whitfield flatly denied the reality of infantile amnesia. He espoused the value of what he called "internal corroboration," a kind of circular logic in which abuse memories and "symptoms" provide their own proof. Despite all the publicity about the dangers of leading questions, Whitfield blithely encouraged therapists to ask, "Have you ever wondered if you might have been abused?"

Colin Ross, the former president of the International Society for the Study of Multiple Personality and Dissociation, attempted to distance himself from the sins of his past—without admitting that he ever did anything wrong. In 1994, he began his remarkable metamorphosis. He admitted that "it is a fact that suggestible individuals can have memories elaborated within their minds because of poor therapeutic technique." He also stated that "normal human memory is highly error-prone." His conclusion? *"False memories are biologically normal and, therefore, not necessarily the therapist's fault* [italics added]." Clients were responsible for their own memories, because therapists were merely "consultants."

Ross then engaged in tortuous psychological logic in which he reversed himself, asserting that the incest memories were really accurate. "The therapist has been identified with the incest perpetrator, who implanted semen in his daughter." By a process of "projective identification," the therapist was now accused of "implanting" false memories. "Logically," Ross concluded illogically, "the therapist should be able to sue the parents for false memories of therapy, as much as the parents should be able to sue the therapist, because both parties are pawns of projective identification." But that's not all. Because the clients with recovered memories are "suggestible, vulnerable, easily persuaded," they must have been manipulated by media coverage, the FMS Foundation, and their parents into retracting their allegations. "Therefore, therapists should be able to launch false memory suits against the parents, lawyers, and background organizations suing them. I am considering doing so."

After this flight into absurdity, Ross concluded with a reasonable statement. "Juries need to be instructed in the difficulty of differentiating true from false memories." True. But if juries should be so instructed, did not Ross not see that the poor *patients* should have been told the same thing? Was it not the therapist's professional obligation to inform clients that hypnosis has been demonstrated to enhance confabulations, that human memory is malleable and error-prone, that expectation effects can severely distort perception? Instead, Ross, along with many other therapists, actively encouraged clients to believe in spurious memories, lending the weight of his considerable authority to the process.

This is the same man who espoused a belief that the CIA was clandestinely creating multiple personalities and who allegedly prescribed massive amounts of inappropriate medication to Roma Hart, a patient who sued him. Hart claimed that Ross saw his female patients as "nothing more than white rats for use in experiments," and that he displayed a "weird pseudoscientific interest in manipulating women's minds for profit."

Ross continues to promote the idea of massive dissociation and multiple personality disorder, making his living from this supposed malady. In 1994, he published *The Osiris Complex: Case Studies in Multiple Personality Disorder*. Here, he included the case of Charlene, who recovered hideous memories of sexual abuse which he clearly believed, though he doubted her MPD status. This is the "only case" he ever doubted, however, and he still believed her recovered memories of torture, rape by a minister, and childhood prostitution.

Elsewhere in the book, Ross recounted the story of Margaret, who "had a clear memory of aliens coming into her apartment, impregnating her, coming back later to remove the foetus, then returning years later to show her the half-human, half-alien child they were raising among the stars." When he raised the possibility that the aliens might not be literally real, Margaret cried and accused him of undermining the therapy. He quickly backed down. "Expressing doubt damages the treatment alliance," he concluded, adding that Margaret taught him that "there is a connection of some kind between UFO abductions and the use of women as breeders for Satanic cults." Ross also observed, "I have met many demons, devils, evil characters, representatives of Satan, and Satan himself in the course of my MPD work." Not to worry, however. "All of these entities turned out to be alter personalities, and none was actually a discarnate spirit."

In 1995, Ross published *Satanic Ritual Abuse,* in which he conceded that many of the SRA "memories" were probably bogus. Yet he clearly believed in such cults and spent considerable space trying to convince his readers of their reality. He believes that SRA cults could be "operating in secrecy through a combination of bribery, financial power, political connections, and intelligence expertise."

Colin Ross has survived multiple lawsuits, including one brought by former patient Martha Hurt, who was Ross's patient for several years in the 1990s at Charter Hospital in Plano, Texas, where she became convinced that her parents had abused her in a Satanic cult, in which she had given birth to several babies, whom she stabbed. Hurt's appalling (but typical) story illustrates how several professionals mistreated her. In 1990, the 31-year-old mother sought help for depression from psychiatrist Kathleen Stanley, who used age regression and inner child work to convince her that she had repressed memories of sexual abuse. In 1991, Hurt spent a month at Millwood Hospital, where Dr. Stanley headed the women's treatment program. There she read *The Courage to Heal* and recalled 32 different people abusing her, beginning with her father raping her at age two.

Then Stanley referred Hurt to psychologist Stephen Ash, who specialized in Satanic ritual abuse memories. Ash promptly concluded that she had multiple personality disorder and quoted Scripture to bring out demon alters so that he could exorcise them. Ash had her admitted to Charter Hospital, where Colin Ross was head psychiatrist. There Ash continued to treat her and the 200 alters they eventually identified. When Hurt complained about Ash casting out her demons, Colin Ross began seeing her himself as well as assigning her to counselor Mary Ellen Grundman.

After her discharge, Hurt continued to see both Ross and Grundman. In time, when Ross told her about his theory that the CIA had programmed patients, she complied and recalled CIA abuse as well. During a subsequent stay at Charter Hospital, Grundman told Hurt that the cult had programmed her to kill herself for revealing her family's involvement. Over the next four years, Martha Hurt lost her husband and children and all contact with her parents and siblings. She attempted suicide multiple times.

Finally, in 1998, Hurt gradually realized that none of her abuse memories were true, that she had not been in a Satanic cult, and that Stanley, Ash, Ross, and Grundman had all misdiagnosed and mistreated her, leading her into a destructive belief system. Lawyer-psychologist Chris Barden took her case, calling it one of the worst he had seen. "This is not just junk science—it's evil," he said. The case was settled out of court for a hefty undisclosed amount.

In a sense, justice was done, but as of press time, Stephen Ash was still practicing as a self-described Christian psychologist in Little Rock, Arkansas, treating trauma, PTSD, and personality disorders. He was still a proud member of the International Society for the Study of Trauma and Dissociation. Kathleen Stanley specialized in "Addiction Psychiatry" in Lubbock, Texas, while Mary Ellen Grundman had become a real estate broker.

In 2017, Ross continued to head the Colin A. Ross Institute in Richardson, Texas (www.rossinst.com) "to further the understanding of psychological trauma and its consequences by providing educational services, research, and clinical treatment of trauma based disorders." He consulted in three trauma programs at hospitals in Texas, Michigan and California, as well as offering, through Ross Energy Systems, "devices for scanning the electromagnetic field of the body."

Avoiding the Truth Trap

Of course, we might expect that someone such as Colin Ross would evade admitting culpability. But many other clinicians continued to blame everyone except the responsible professional. In my interviews with therapists, I was particularly disturbed by their tendency to absolve themselves of any responsibility. Almost all of them asserted that it didn't matter whether the memories were literally true or not. The memories represented the "internal truth" for the client, and it wasn't the therapist's job to search out the facts. It apparently didn't disturb them that their clients nearly went crazy thinking such awful things, or that the "memories" often resulted in shattered families and lawsuits.

A case study presented in the *Family Therapy Networker* early in 1994 made this point, even with its headline: "Avoiding the Truth Trap." I thought that this title must surely be ironically intended. No. It meant just what it said. The truth doesn't matter. "Clinicians *are not* judges, police officers or legal experts," explained therapist Bill O'Hanlon, one of the respondents to the case. "We cannot make informed judgments about the reliability of our clients' reports." This equivocation came from a man whose ad for a "Solution-Oriented Hypnosis" workshop was featured in the same magazine a few months earlier, promoting a methodology intended for "survivors of trauma and sexual abuse."

But let us review the case, introduced by Connecticut therapist Henry Schissler, whose presentation was then critiqued by O'Hanlon and two other therapists. "I have seen enough clients who were sexually abused to understand the reality of incest," Schissler began, but he believed that this was a case in which "another therapist jumped to the conclusion that there had been childhood sexual abuse, isolated the client from her family, and provided some very bad therapy." Schissler described a familiar situation in which Jane, the accusing daughter, sought therapy following the birth of her first child, became a Survivor, and accused her father of incest. Jane's therapist refused to talk to Schissler or the parents. Jane also attended a support group at the local YWCA, where the group leader told her that if she felt that she had been abused, then she had been, and encouraged her to sever all ties with her biological family.

Schissler's description of his efforts to help this family prove that there were some decent therapists in practice. He interviewed both the mother and father alone, determining that the father had spent little time with his children, drinking to kill the pain of chronic colitis. The father claimed that because of his physical condition, he could not have carried Jane upstairs to molest her, as she asserted. Schissler also discovered that both of Jane's grandmothers had undergone psychiatric hospitalization with severe post-partum depression. He even reviewed the grandmothers' hospital records and "was struck by the similarities between their behavior and Jane's."

The first respondents to the case, Mary Jo Barrett and Wayne Scott, immediately proclaimed that whether the alleged abuse took place or not was irrelevant. "Mired in a preoccupation with The Truth, family members avoid directly confronting the toxicity that has permeated all their relationships." They asserted that "both actual sexual abuse and false allegations grow out of the same psychological environment—one in which children grow up feeling disempowered, violated and angry." Finally, they concluded that "the goal of family therapy in cases of alleged abuse is not to magically reconcile the survivor and her family. It is to validate the perspective of the adult child by having other family members hear what her experience has been without anyone needing to deny or redefine it."

This case and the responses to it are appalling. It was published in 1994, *after* the magazine in which it appeared ran a long cover story about the repressed-memory debate. Still, everything was blamed on the parents, nothing on the recovered-memory therapist. Even if this were a case of false memory, the respondents maintained, it was *still* somehow the parents' fault. "If parents insist that their child has been brainwashed by irresponsible therapists," Barrett and Scott wrote, "they should consider what in that child's family experience has made her vulnerable to being brainwashed."

We have here an Orwellian world where truth doesn't matter, where the therapist can redefine reality and hide behind the sanctity of his "concern" for the patient. This kind of thinking was, unfortunately, widespread among recovered-memory therapists. "I don't care if it's true," one such therapist told a journalist in 1995. "What's important to me is that I hear the child's truth, the patient's truth. That's what's important. What actually happened is irrelevant to me. It doesn't matter."

The same kind of wagon-circling rationalizations were documented by journalist Eileen McNamara in *Breakdown* (1994), the story of how Harvard psychiatrist Margaret Bean-Bayog convinced medical student Paul Lozano that he had repressed memories of sexual abuse by his mother. As is the norm with such cases, the psychiatrist refused to meet with her patient's family. The situation was worse than most, however. Bean-Bayog not only encouraged Lozano to contact his inner child, but to become a regressed three-year-old. She gave him children's books and wrote him love notes calling him "the boy," signing them "Mom." At the same time, she penned sadomasochistic pornography about him. "You kneel between my legs and begin to lick and nibble my inner thighs," one of the milder fantasies commenced. "You begin to lick my clitoris. I am ecstatic with the pleasure of it, and adore you. You keep licking and sucking me, taking pleasure and aroused, but watching me."

Even before Lozano committed suicide in 1991, all of this material had come to light. Not only did Bean-Bayog deny any inappropriate behavior, she claimed that *she* had been a victim of this manipulative patient. Her sexual fantasies (it is unclear whether they were ever acted out) were explained away as "countertransference." During a deposition, a lawyer asked Bean-Bayog if she ever had sexual fantasies about Paul Lozano? "Not as me, myself, no," she answered. "It was in a countertransference sense."

Perhaps this kind of incredible sophistry could be expected from a psychiatrist caught in such flagrant malpractice, but her peers, well-respected Boston-area psychiatrists and psychoanalysts, sprang to Bean-Bayog's defense, as did feminists, other recovered-memory therapists, the Survivor community, and the *Boston Globe*. Clinical psychologist Kathryn Kogan called her colleague Margaret Bean-Bayog "kind, moral, responsible … a shining light." She defended the reams of pornographic fantasies as a necessary catharsis so that Bean-Bayog could keep her feelings "in a scientific framework." Psychoanalyst John Maltsberger lamented that Bean-Bayog had been "brutalized" by the press. "She had already taken an emotional beating from Paul Lozano and suffered the expectable pain of losing a patient to suicide."

Talking about the case on a national television show, psychiatrist Thomas Gutheil repeated the familiar truth-trap dogma. "If a patient brings up alleged memories or even false memories…, you have to take them as true; otherwise you can't treat a patient. If a patient says, 'I was butchered and beaten with chains and branded with hot irons,' you don't say, 'That doesn't sound plausible.' You say, 'That must have been terrible.' "Gutheil did not mention situations in which therapists actively promoted the notion that sexual abuse occurred and was repressed. It didn't really matter to him whether Lozano's incest "memories" were true or false. "Either [Lozano] really had this experience, in which case she [Bean-Bayog] is right and everything is cool, or he is a liar, in which case she is right and everything is cool."

The rationalization that truth is a trivial nonconcern for psychotherapists continues, as evidenced by Bessel van der Kolk in his 2014 book, *The Body Keeps the Score*: "As a therapist treating people with a legacy of trauma, my primary concern is not to determine exactly what happened to them but to help them tolerate the sensations, emotions, and reactions they experience."

"Moderates" and Other Therapists

Even therapists who recognized the widespread havoc that the hunt for repressed memories caused were often reluctant to address the central problem. For example, psychologist Michael Yapko, the author of *Suggestions of Abuse*, bent over backward to take a "moderate" position. When Yapko appeared with Lenore Terr on *Geraldo*, he hardly mounted an argument against Terr's pseudoscientific pet theories. And on another TV program, while warning that hypnosis could promote illusory memories, Yapko also stated: "I can tell you, as an expert in hypnosis, and working with these kinds of memory recovery techniques, you can use [them] to recover accurate memories that have been repressed." He offered no evidence for this major caveat.

Psychology professor Kevin Byrd acknowledged in a 1994 article in *American Psychologist* that recall could be "shaped by the implicit expectations of the therapist [through] subtle means." Nonetheless, Byrd went on to say that "when hidden trauma is strongly suspected on the basis of objective criteria and the patient's suffering is severe, methods aimed at 'derepression' are justifiable." He recommended asking patients to study old family photographs. "Memory reconstruction should be a gradual process in which the degree of certainty is based on a continuing record of data collected without therapist bias." Yet Byrd offered no insights on how to distinguish between "objective criteria" and "therapist bias."

Similarly, in their otherwise-excellent 1994 review assessing the problems with recovered-memory therapy, psychologists Stephen Lindsay and Don Read *assumed* the reality of repression. "It is very likely," they stated, "that some adult victims of childhood abuse have no available memories of the abuse." Unlike other statements in this meticulously documented paper, Lindsay and Read simply offered this opinion as an unverified assertion. Bending over backward to be fair, they wrote that unearthing repressed memories may be "psychologically beneficial," so that "it makes sense that memory recovery techniques would be used by competent practitioners." In their conclusion, Lindsay and Read suggested that "when childhood sexual abuse … is explored in a non-suggestive, open-minded way, without the use of special memory recovery techniques, there is little ground for concern about the creation of illusory memories."*

Yet therapists, as we have seen, *never* think their methods are suggestive. They *all* consider themselves open-minded. Those therapists who do not use hypnosis or other intrusive methods are the most likely to convince themselves and their clients that the repressed memories have arisen "spontaneously." In fact, if therapists believe in the possibility of massive repression, they will probably convey this belief to clients, even without being aware of it. Elsewhere in this same paper, Lindsay and Read acknowledged that "there are sometimes substantial discrepancies between what therapists apparently believe they do in therapy … and what they actually do."

For perspective, it should be understood that recovered-memory therapists regarded Yapko, Lindsay, and Read as extremists on the other side of the debate. These scholars undoubtedly faced intense professional pressure to moderate their

---

* Fortunately, Stephen Lindsay subsequently made much stronger statements: "The vast majority of victims of traumatic child sexual abuse that occurred after the age of 3 or 4 years are aware of their histories…. There is not a single controlled study demonstrating any beneficial effect of therapeutic efforts to recovered hidden memories of child sexual abuse in clients who report no abuse history."

positions, to avoid giving the appearance of extremism.

In similar fashion, experimental psychologist Julia Shaw, who has extended the work of Elizabeth Loftus in demonstrating how false memories can be created, went out of her way to discredit the term "false memory syndrome" by writing in 2016: "This term is simply inaccurate, false memory syndrome does not exist." She went on to quote another psychologist (who has not studied memory): "Although the term implied scientific endorsement, false memory syndrome is not currently an accepted diagnostic label.... . This syndrome is a non-psychological term originated by a private foundation whose stated purpose is to support accused parents."

This is an extraordinarily unfair characterization of the False Memory Syndrome Foundation, which provided a crucial forum for the study of repressed memory therapy and its impact. The FMS Foundation did indeed support accused parents, but Shaw left out the crucial fact that they were accused on the basis of massively repressed memories. It is unfair to heap more innuendo and abuse upon these falsely accused people.

And the fact that the *Diagnostic and Statistical Manual of Mental Disorders* does not include the term "false memory syndrome" is not surprising. The *DSM* is a political as much as a psychiatric document. As we have seen, it includes Dissociative Identity Disorder, even though it is probably a fictitious, iatrogenic condition. Until 1973, the DSM labeled homosexuality a mental illness.

In medical terminology, a disease with no known cause is called a "syndrome," defined as "a combination of symptoms and signs that together represent a disease process." In the DSM, the term is defined as "a constellation of symptoms that occur together or co-vary over time. The term carries no direct implications in terms of underlying pathology." It has been applied to a wide range of alleged mental illnesses, such as Diogenes Syndrome, characterized by "extreme self-neglect, domestic squalor, social withdrawal, compulsive hoarding of garbage or animals, and lack of shame," or Ekbom's Syndrome, in which people incorrectly think they are infested with parasites or bugs.

It is clear that there really is a syndrome of mental problems and behavior associated with a belief in recovered memories of abuse. But it would be more accurate to call it "repressed memory syndrome" rather than false memory syndrome, since we all have false memories of one sort or another. Because so many psychologists believe in repressed memories, however, it is unlikely that we will see such a syndrome voted into the next DSM revision. Nor will we see "parental alienation syndrome," a term originated by the late Richard Gardner to designate an all-too-real phenomenon in which one parent indoctrinates children into demonizing the other parent.

If the "moderate" position prevails in this debate, recovered-memory advocates are even more likely to continue to promote their discredited theory. Many have moderated their approach, telling patients, "You have all the symptoms of someone who was sexually abused as a child, so it wouldn't surprise me if you recovered memories as you are feeling safer in therapy. But we won't dig for them. If the memories arise, they will do so on their own, in their own good time." Then, the suggestive seed having been planted, it can indeed sprout into a hideous mental vine.

Another popular argument in favor of repressed memories runs like this: "I recovered my memories outside of therapy. I didn't read any of those suggestive books. I just spontaneously started having these flashbacks, and that's why I went to therapy." Indeed, many women recovered their "memories" without the help of a therapist at all. Even if they had never read a book on the subject or gone to therapy, by the early 1990s, virtually every woman in our society with a problem had at least briefly pondered, "I wonder whether this problem stems from repressed memories of sexual abuse?" All too many then sought out *The Courage to Heal* or another similar book. Only then did they enter therapy, having already "remembered" abuse, or *demanding* to retrieve memories. Such Survivors were then convinced that they were never led into such beliefs, and that their memories must therefore be accurate.

In addition, retrospective accounts can be extraordinarily slanted. "No therapist can be accused of misleading me," Sylvia Fraser wrote in a 1994 article, "since none was involved in the initial recovery. I had read no books on incest … and had no conscious interest in this subject." But Fraser's 1988 book, *My Father's House,* offered evidence to the contrary. "Through Freudian and Jungian analysis, I learned how to interpret dreams as messages from my unconscious," she wrote in her book. "Through primal and massage therapy, rolfing, bioenergetics, yoga, meditation, I grew more in touch with my body and my emotions…. Why had I been such an angry child? Why did I hate my father? … I was approaching a time when I would remember. The obsession of a lifetime was drawing to a close." Then Fraser described how her repressed abuse memories came back under hypnosis.

I heard the same argument regarding UFO abduction memories. "I knew nothing about UFO literature." While there is no doubt that these testimonies are sincere, it is quite likely that the *idea* of repressed sexual abuse memories (or UFO abductions) had indeed been implanted, whether consciously or subconsciously, resulting in the "spontaneous" flashbacks. Then, once entered into therapy that accepted the reality of repression, the seeker would find plentiful validation and amplification.

Because illusory sex abuse allegations seem so strange, there is a natural tendency for commentators to search for underlying disturbances to explain them. Common explanations are: (1) Those who have recovered these memories are pathologically disturbed. (2) The memories reflect unconscious sexual desire for the accused parent. (3) The accusations do not reflect actual events, but they are evidence of severe dysfunction within the family system. Overt sexual boundaries may not have been breached, but the accuser must have been emotionally violated throughout childhood, or the child was raised in an overly sexualized atmosphere.

But such memories can be encouraged in almost *anyone* entering therapy in a vulnerable, depressed state, seeking answers to life's problems. When the therapist—the expert, the figure of authority—systematically led the client into believing that buried sex abuse memories provided those answers, and when an entire culture validated the memory-retrieval process, the client developed a new belief system, a new identity as an Survivor. This process occurred over and over again. It does not take a rocket scientist to figure it out, much less a Ph.D. in psychology. *Yet within the psychological community, there is still extreme resistance to admitting any responsibility on the part of members of that community.*

Psychoanalyst Lawrence Hedges provides a final chilling example of how therapists can simultaneously realize that delusive memories have arisen in therapy and, like Freud, deny their own responsibility in having encouraged their creation. Hedges explained in his 1994 book, *Remembering, Repeating, and Working Through Childhood Trauma,* that "no seasoned psychoanalyst ever assumes any memory, no matter how vivid or seemingly true it appears, [is] an indisputable historical fact." But then he went on to search for the "narrative" or "emotional" truth which the memory must, he believed, reveal.

After a good deal of Freudian jargon about "counter cathexis" and "selfobject needs," Hedges got to his own pet theory: recovered memories of abuse are *really* screen memories of trauma suffered "in utero and in the earliest months of life." In other words, the fetus or infant who didn't feel loved or safe maintains an unconscious traumatic memory, which will then surface as a false incest accusation.

Hedges then detailed how one of his female colleagues found herself in a dreadful situation. During six months of therapy with a client, the therapist told Hedges, "all of these abusive memories began coming out during sessions." Her client "became quite fragmented and was having a hard time functioning," so her therapist put her on Prozac and sent her to a Survivor support group, where even more terrible memories emerged. Now, at the urging of her group, the client was about to confront her family. "I don't question whether she has been somehow badly abused," the therapist explained. "I know some horrible things must have happened to her." The therapist was afraid, however, that when the parents denied the abuse, her client would suffer a psychotic break. "What's got me scared is that I have somehow colluded in all of this without really meaning to," the therapist concluded. "I don't know how I got into this jam." She was worried about the parents being upset and wanting information, but she couldn't reveal it because of confidentiality issues. "The bottom line is, I'm fucked!"

In response, did Hedges tell her that she had gotten herself into this mess by believing in repressed memories, by helping her client to "remember" them, by referring her to a Survivor support group, by validating her memories at every step of the process? Did he tell her to stop worrying about herself and start being concerned for a client she had made nearly psychotic rather than better? No! "Your client has succeeded in molesting you," Hedges informed this therapist, "violating your personal and professional boundaries in much the same intrusive or forceful way she may once have experienced herself as a very young child." He explained that the memories might not be completely accurate (because they presumably stemmed from the womb or the first few months of life), but "all this time you have been held emotional hostage in a similar helpless and vulnerable position to the one she felt in as a child—without having the slightest idea of how to protect yourself from this violence."

"Oh, God!" answered the therapist, "I'm sick in the pit of my stomach just realizing how true what you are saying is. I'm feeling the abuse in the symbiotic role reversal of the countertransference." Readers may be excused if, at this point, they, too, feel sick in the pits of their stomachs as a result of Hedges' arrogance in not only exonerating his colleague, but bragging about it in print.

The Professional Associations Respond

I don't think that most recovered memory therapists intentionally promoted illusory memories. And, yes, as the notion of repressed memories became widely accepted in popular culture, starting in the late 1980s, some people "found" their own repressed memories completely outside of therapy, either in support groups, through books ("bibliotherapy"), or triggered by TV talk shows. Nonetheless, *it was the repressed-memory dogma, promulgated primarily by recovered memory therapists, that created the disastrous situation described in this book.* These therapists ignored the most fundamental injunction of the Hippocratic Oath, which exhorts healers: *Primum non nocere—First, do no harm.* As Pamela Freyd, the director of the False Memory Syndrome Foundation, observed, "If any other medical product had more than 13,000 [later many more] complaints and had never been shown to be safe or effective, it would be taken off the market." A 1995 British editorial in *The Mail on Sunday* made a similar point, as it became clear by mid-decade that they, too, faced a major catastrophe as recovered memory therapy spread throughout England. "It seems that there are more safeguards on cold remedies sold over the counter of Britain's High Street shops than there are on some controversial mind-tinkering therapies." It would seem reasonable, in fact, for a watchdog agency similar to the U.S. Food and Drug Administration to be created to test psychotherapeutic approaches to make sure they are safe and effective before being unleashed on an unwary public. That has yet to occur.

Instead, with only one exception, the appropriate professional associations failed to respond in any meaningful way to this very obvious problem. The American Medical Association did issue a 1993 statement about memory retrieval techniques, recognizing that they are "fraught with problems of potential misapplication." The American Psychiatric Association followed late in 1993 with a less satisfactory response to the crisis. It noted that "human memory is a complex process" and that it was impossible to distinguish accurately between true and false memories. Unfortunately, aside from such pro-forma acknowledgments, the rest of the statement embraced Survivor dogma. "Expression of disbelief is likely to cause the patient further pain.... The issues of breaking off relationships with important attachment figures [parents], of pursuing legal actions, and of making public disclosures may need to be addressed."

Most distressing, the American Psychiatric Association statement asserted: "Many individuals who recover memories of abuse have been able to find corroborating information about their memories." I wrote to the association, explaining that I was writing a book on repressed memories and asking for specific cases that had been confirmed. In response, I received a bibliography including citations from Judith Herman, John Briere, and Lenore Terr, among others.

The American Psychological Association created a six-person committee to study the repressed-memory issue. Three of the members were experimental researchers skeptical of massive repression, including Elizabeth Loftus. The other three were recovered-memory clinicians, including Christine Courtois. The committee did battle for two years and was unable to agree on a final joint statement. Instead, each side presented separate conclusions and rebuttals.

The February 1994 edition of *Practitioner Focus,* an American Psychological Association newsletter, contained an article about the repressed-memory controversy, concluding that "nothing less than the integrity of the mental health professions and the trust inherent in the client-therapist relationship is at stake." I could not agree more. Yet the entire concern of the article was how to respond to "biased media attention" to therapy-induced memories. Also, "the directorate's legal and regulatory affairs department would like to know about any instances where psychologists are denied reimbursement in cases involving ... recovered memories." In other words, many professional psychologists appeared to be worried primarily about their images and their pocketbooks—not about creating illusory sex abuse memories. Rather than cleaning house, the APA created a $1.5 million war chest to boost the image of therapists.

One hopeful sign was a position paper issued by the American Psychological Association in the fall of 1995, admitting that *"most* people who were sexually abused as children remember all or part of what happened to them although they may not fully understand or disclose it," adding that "it is impossible, without other corroborative evidence, to distinguish a true memory from a false one."

On the other hand, two months *after* that position paper was issued, in his presidential address to the American Psychological Association, Ron Fox castigated scientists and therapists who "harm the profession" by publicly criticizing repressed-memory clinicians. He even called for "revising the ethical code" of the APA to censure psychologists "who undermine the public's trust in the discipline" by criticizing their peers. The wagon-circling at the American Psychological Association was frantic, drawing in ever tighter spirals to deny any wrong-doing.

In the meantime, the International Society for the Study of Multiple Personality & Dissociation renamed itself, dropping the tarnished MPD moniker in 1994 and becoming the International Society for the Study of Trauma and Dissociation in 2006. In the "President's Message" of 1995, psychiatrist Nancy Hornstein admitted, "We are 'in it,' so to speak, deep. If you don't believe me, check recent adjudications, not to mention multi-million dollar settlements, against therapists." The MPD gurus were running scared, but they never admitted to their gigantic errors.

The National Association of Social Workers took longer to challenge its members to change their ways. At the annual NASW conference held in October of 1995, one therapist detailed her clinical experiences with Satanic ritual abuse and multiple personalities, and another speaker apparently claimed to have 10,000 personalities! The NASW finally issued a cautionary statement in 1996, asserting that "the clinical social worker's decisions should be clinically sound, ethically based, and legally sanctioned." Yet the NASW took no position on the validity of repressed memories: "We will not enter the debate on whether traumatic events are forgotten or how accurately people report their memories."

Why did it take national professional associations so long to take any kind of stand—no matter how vague or ineffective—on this issue? One obvious answer is that they would look bad. Another is that the concept of repression had been accepted for such a long time that it was not seriously questioned. There was, however, a more compelling reason....

Where the Money Is

Recovered-memory therapy, in all its variations, was a *lucrative pursuit*. The repressed-memory craze was a bonanza, not only for private therapists and inpatient psychiatric units, but for retreat centers, continuing-education instructors, and lawyers. As long as insurance companies continued to pay for questionable diagnoses of "post-traumatic stress disorder" or "dissociative identity disorder," therapists could continue to milk the system. One father reported that his daughter's therapy had cost $300,000 over the last five years. That was nothing compared to the three-quarters of a million dollars another woman spent on MPD therapy and hospitalization in just four years. Others spent well over a million dollars for "treatment" that rendered them depressed, suicidal, and utterly dependent.

Some advertisements followed in the grand American tradition of hucksterism. "Are You Ready to Remember Your Childhood?" one such 1994 ad asked in its headline. "If you have 'blank spots' in your childhood memories," it continued, "if you're puzzled by your 'strange' responses to certain situations, if you're continually frustrated in achieving certain goals, if you remember some abuse but suspect there's more, you may hold buried memories that need to surface and be healed." If so, come see the hypnotherapist and lay down your money—and your mind.

A psychiatric hospital placed an even more outrageous ad in *Changes* magazine in December of 1993. "Remembering incest and childhood abuse is the first step to healing," the ad began. "We can help you remember and heal." There followed a laundry list of symptoms indicative of abuse: "Mood swings, panic disorder, substance abuse, rage, flashbacks, depression, hopelessness, anxiety, paranoia, low self-esteem, relationship problems,"—on and on, right down to premenstrual syndrome and irritable bowels. "What we do best is help bring up forgotten memories through our powerful combination of massage, body work, hypnosis, psychodrama, and sodium brevitol interviewing."

In her article about MPD therapist Judith Peterson *(see Chapter 4)*, psychiatric nurse Sally McDonald complained about the abusive treatment patients in the Houston dissociative disorders unit received. Despite repeated protests from the nursing staff, the hospital administrators refused to censure the doctor who ran the unit. The reason? "The dissociative disorders unit housed 10 patients billed at an intensive care unit rate of $1,200 per day—plus billable rates of $80 to $100 each for art therapy, expressive therapy, journal therapy, and abreactive sessions," the nurse wrote. "One patient's average fee per day was $1,560; multiply this by 10 patients, and the hospital received $15,600 per day from this unit alone."

One would think that such whopping bills would have alerted parsimonious insurance companies, who would then send their investigators, but that was not the case. Some insurance companies actually owned stock in private psychiatric hospitals, a clear conflict of interest. In addition, according to one angry psychiatrist, insurance companies *like* large bills. "Big bills mean big premiums and bonuses," a doctor working for a major insurer told him. Finally, insurance officials were often afraid to crack down on mental health fraud. "Insurance companies are petrified [of mental illness]," one expert testified before a congressional committee in 1992. "They don't want to touch it. They don't understand it. All you have to do is threaten to sue them or push them and they back down." Besides, why should they worry about it when they could pass on the bill to corporations and taxpayers?

Those providing services to therapists also cashed in on recovered memories. Continuing-education credits were routinely dispensed to those who wished to learn the latest therapeutic techniques to unleash repressed memories. One course at a 1993 conference offered American Psychological Association credits for learning about "body memories." The course description: "Neuroscientists have recently surmised that the mind is no longer in the head but is in every cell. To understand the concept of cellular memory we will look to genograms, eidetic imagery, past lives, holograms, recent research, the triune brain and unified field theory. We will also discuss various healing techniques." At the same conference, a course taught people how to spot forgotten early childhood trauma through handwriting analysis.

Crash courses in "hypnotherapy" were advertised as a quick way to make money—for everyone concerned. A 1995 flier for a "Hypnotherapy Certification Weekend" in Boston or Philadelphia, offered by the Hypnodyne Foundation in Clearwater, Florida, read: *In Two Powerful Days You Will Develop Techniques and Skills That Will Enable You to Become a Hypnotherapist Certified by the International Association of Counselors and Therapists.* The training would tell you "how you can make $3,000 to $10,000 in one evening by conducting group sessions" and "how to use speed hypnosis and disguised hypnosis." All of this cost a mere $395 for the weekend. It was touted for psychotherapists, chiropractors, massage therapists, clergymen, and police officers.

Another 1995 ad in the *Family Therapy Networker* promised a course in hypnotherapy that took three times as long—"*Certification in 6 days!*" It featured a photo of trainer Diane Zimberoff of the Wellness Institute. Like many other Recovery gurus, Zimberoff glowed with movie-star quality. Her smile was beatific, radiant, warm. Her course, which offered continuing education credits, promised help with "unlocking the inner child, codependency, incest issues."

Typical of many therapists of that era, Zimberoff survived the repressed memory epidemic unscathed and is still in practice in 2017, though she no longer talks openly about incest. Her website identifies her as "a Licensed Marriage & Family Therapist, specializing in trauma resolution and the use of altered states of consciousness for healing and spiritual growth. For over twenty five years she has trained mental health professionals in Heart-Centered Hypnotherapy, a highly effective and unique clinical model."

There was also a lucrative market for material aimed directly at children, such as *I Can't Talk About It: A Child's Book about Sexual Abuse* (1986), *Don't Make Me Go Back, Mommy: A Child's Book about Satanic Ritual Abuse* (1990), or *I Said No! A Kid-to-Kid Guide to Keeping Private Parts Private* (2016). For a mere $19.95, in 1996 psychologists could purchase a computer disk called "No Secrets Anymore," with more than 50 images "selected specifically for children who may have been sexually abused," the ad specifies, including "partially clothed adults and children; children looking concerned, worried, and angry; a dark closet; beds, etc."

Money also flowed freely into the coffers of recovered-memory therapists directly from the government spigot. In a biographical sketch, MPD specialist Colin Ross bragged that he had received "several hundred thousand dollars in research funding." Despite the clear evidence that facilitated communication does not work, the state of Georgia awarded grants for study of this "promising" technique, while my own state of Vermont allows taxes to be used to support facilitated communication in public schools.

In 1996, I witnessed a disturbing example of how greed, media influence, and pseudoscience could combine. While waiting to appear on a Midwestern talk show, I watched while another guest, a self-professed psychic, touted her skills. "My findings are 96% accurate," she boasted, encouraging people to pony up for a dinner at which she would offer psychic counseling. When she came off the set, I asked her whether she could tell if someone had been sexually abused, even if they had repressed the memories. "Oh, yes," she said, "I can read their auras." Later, I complained to the station manager, who informed me that this psychic *paid* for her periodic spot on the show. In other words, her appearance was a well-disguised infomercial.

Law firms specializing in repressed memories were not content to sit back and wait for clients. In a new version of ambulance chasing, one lawyer began distributing a packet of information to women's centers, including a boilerplate letter intended for accused parents. "Dear Mr. and Mrs. Blank," the letter began. "Your child has retained me to represent her for the sexual and physical assaults perpetrated on her by Mr. Blank when she was a minor." It went on to threaten legal action, but stated that "we are prepared to settle the case to $250,000." Another lawyer sent letters to mental health professionals explaining that the statute of limitations for recovered memories had been extended. "Restitution would provide empowerment and closure"—as well as hefty legal fees, of course. Because parents would have to spend substantial amounts to defend themselves, with the attendant negative publicity and risk of losing, many chose to settle out of court when faced with such threats, even while maintaining their innocence.

In 2017, Gretchen Hammond, a former fundraiser for Survivors Network of those Abused by Priests (SNAP), sued the organization for firing her after she exposed a kickback scheme between SNAP and lawyers representing alleged victims. Her suit said that the organization focused on "what will generate the most publicity and fundraising opportunities for SNAP." Lawyers would routinely collude with the nonprofit organization and share settlement payouts. "In reality, SNAP is a commercial operation motivated by its directors' and officers' personal and ideological animus against the Catholic Church," Hammond asserted.

Therapists Facing the Future: "Flocks of Edgy Birds"

In "Endangered Species," a long and remarkably frank cover article in the March/April 1994 issue of *Family Therapy Networker,* senior editor Mary Wylie described therapists "who now fly from one meeting to another like flocks of edgy birds [and] feel they have about as much job security right now as the engineers on the Super Collider project that Congress recently abolished."

Wylie acknowledged that "the therapeutic community has brought its current woes upon itself by its amazing failure … to provide decent explanations, let alone measures of cost and outcome accountability, for its treatment methods." Therapists were "held to almost no objectively measurable, external standards for deciding what is wrong with the client, what to do about it, how long it should take to do it, when it can be considered done and how anybody knows if it is done." Wylie reported that managed care case reviewers she interviewed told her about a rich array of questionable therapies they had been asked to approve—including exorcisms, past-life regressions, and a request for 500 sessions in advance. "In another case, a therapist, who had been seeing a client four days a week for eight years at $200 a pop, wanted more."

The time when "vastly rich corporate patrons" unquestioningly paid for long-term therapy was coming to an end, however, according to Wylie. "The Golden Age of private practice, when the term 'rich therapist' was not an oxymoron," was nearly over. A recovered-memory therapist who saw her practice cut in half by managed care adjusted by offering a special after-work program, featuring a catered dinner and evening sessions. Managed care companies helped fund this program, which supposedly kept people out of the hospital.

Most therapists adjusted by abandoning the overt search for repressed memories of sexual abuse, and the devastation gradually receded, even though millions of families remained splintered by false memories and allegations. As we have seen, those therapists nonetheless continued to believe in repressed memories, and the movement simply went underground rather than disappearing.

Self-justification is part of human nature, as Carol Tavris and Elliot Aronson observed in their important 2015 book, *Mistakes Were Made (But Not By Me).* And the worse people's behavior has been, the more overwhelming the cognitive dissonance would be if they acknowledged it. If their core self-concept is, "I am a caring, compassionate therapist who seeks to help my clients," it would be very difficult to acknowledge simultaneously: "I have caused huge harm to my clients by encouraging a belief in mythical repressed memories of sexual abuse."

Clinical psychologist John Briere, one of the earliest supporters of repressed memory therapy, finally admitted that a few "over-enthusiastic" therapists had tried to "liposuction memories out of [clients'] brains," but that most recovered memories were true—certainly those he elicited. "Evidence suggests that false memories of abuse are quite uncommon," he asserted, offering absolutely no evidence to back up his opinion.

Therapists' memories for how they themselves behaved can be revised. "Memories are often pruned and shaped by an ego-enhancing bias that blurs the edges of past events, softens culpability, and distorts what really happened," Tavris and Aronson observed. Such self-justification "keeps many professionals from changing outdated attitudes and procedures that can be harmful to the public."

Thus, when psychologist Richard Noll called for an examination of how the MPD Satanic ritual abuse epidemic could have taken place in the late 20th century without protest from the psychological establishment, he received only indignant responses from three of the psychiatrists who fomented the epidemic, including Bennett Braun, who lost a $10.6 million lawsuit and had his license revoked because of convincing a client that she was a high priestess in a Satanic cult while hospitalizing her four- and five-year-old sons and getting them to remember fictional atrocities. "I have become accustomed to such slander and misrepresentation, and have been misquoted extensively over the years," Braun wrote in 2014. "The lead plaintiff testified in her deposition that she had originated all the memories herself. I did not implant any memories, she said." Braun took no responsibility for anything he had done.

As of 2017, Renee Fredrickson, whose book, *Repressed Memories*, provided a template for how to get people to believe that they had been sexually abused and forgot all about it, continues her psychotherapy practice in St. Paul, Minnesota. Nonetheless, actions against her, led by lawyer/psychologist Chris Barden, publicized the appalling things she did to her clients, as well as her own paranoia (she thought her phones were bugged and told the police she wanted to hire a sniper to protect her from Satanic cult members). As a result, the Minnesota Board of Psychology banned Fredrickson from conducting repressed memory therapy, from training others, and from publishing about the misguided theory. She settled a lawsuit against her out of court.

Here is an excerpt from the 1999 complaint to the state's licensing board about one of seven patients who complained. Fredrickson's patient "developed memories of ritual cult abuse, including torture, dismemberment, cannibalism, and murder, which she later believed were false. In some of these memories, client #1 developed the following images: (1) she cut off a penis; (2) a knife was inserted into her vagina: (3) she had sex with dogs in a 'ritual abuse ceremony'; (4) she tortured her younger sister; (5) she had knives thrown at her 'William Tell style'; (6) she was raped by her grandfather on the edge of a haymow; (7) she watched her uncle cut up people; and (8) she was programmed to commit suicide if she ever told anyone about the abuse."

In 2016, retired prosecutor Paul Stern finally offered a role model that I hope others will emulate. A long-time board member of the American Professional Society on the Abuse of Children (APSAC), he gave an astonishing speech at the APSAC annual convention, asking, "What in the world were we thinking?" He reviewed the firm beliefs in Satanic ritual abuse and the day care abuse scandals. "Child abuse is both an advocacy field and a political field," he said. "Easy answers manage anxiety, and they get attention. 'Kids never lie!' 'Believe the children!' Great slogans, great bumper stickers, but it's a little more complicated than that...."

Laura Davis and Ellen Bass Keep on Keeping On

In 2003, Laura Davis, co-author of *The Courage to Heal*, published *I Thought We'd Never Speak Again: The Road from Estrangement to Reconciliation*. At first, I was thrilled when I thought she might have seen the error of her ways. She had retrieved memories of her maternal grandfather abusing her in classic repressed memory style. "For ten years of my life," she recalled in her new book, "the fact that I had been sexually abused was the principle around which I organized my existence," and anyone who doubted her abuse memories—such as her mother—was jettisoned. In this book, Davis celebrated her reconciliation with her mother. But she didn't take back her abuse allegations—they just didn't talk about this volatile issue.

Davis was similar to many who came to believe in "recovered memories" of abuse but who still missed their families. A minority retracted their allegations, asked for forgiveness and understanding from accused parents, and fully reunited. Others resumed contact without taking anything back. And most parents, with patience, love, and forbearance, joyfully accepted their returning children and tried to rebuild shattered relationships, without demanding a discussion of the past.

I Never Thought We'd Speak Again is in many ways a wise, hopeful book. "Identifying with past injuries can be limiting," Davis advised. Through case studies stressing the need for nonjudgmental listening, she wrote of reconciliation between parents and children, estranged siblings, victims/offenders, Jews/Palestinians, children of Nazis and Holocaust survivors. "When we grow large enough to embrace our own faults and to honor the flawed humanity of another human being, we open the door to connection, integration, and love," Davis wrote. "We seek to understand the mistakes we made—and that the other person made." But she herself could not admit that her repressed memory allegations were mistaken, and she did not acknowledge the tremendous harm *The Courage to Heal* did by encouraging illusory memories of abuse.

In 2008, Davis and Ellen Bass published a 20th anniversary fourth edition of *The Courage to Heal*, which proved that Davis had not changed. The book was still crammed full of repressed memory theory and examples of "survivors who don't remember anything about their abuse until the memories come crashing in." It's like putting together a jigsaw puzzle, they advised. And if it's not all true, don't worry. "Even though everything you remember may not be a literal representation of what happened, there is always an essential emotional truth to memory." The book contains Laura Davis's account of how she first remembered being abused "by the grandfather I had revered and loved." The book still has the illustrative passage of the woman who acted *as if* she were abused, even though she couldn't remember anything, as well as the remarkable quote from the woman who said, "The more I worked on the abuse, the more I remembered"—first her brother, then, in order, her grandfather, father, and finally her mother. They quoted another Survivor: "The hardest part was accepting and believing that it really happened. Being in the group really helped."

Remarkably, a new-to-this-edition interview with "Sheila O'Connell" ends the book, with Bass and Davis endorsing it as an example of how a therapist should keep "an open mind until your true history becomes clear." O'Connell recounted how she remembered more and more sexual abuse with the aid of three different therapists, starting with her molesting uncles but culminating with her experience at age six in a ritual abuse cult, where the police chief murdered his daughter and placed O'Connell's hand on the bloody knife. "This is impossible; people can't do this," she told Al, her therapist, but he reassured her: "As hard as it is to believe, people do these things." She praised Al for not pushing her, though. "He gave me a framework within which I could believe, not believe, believe, not believe." Al would say, "I have no reason to disbelieve it," but then he added that maybe the blood and feces stemmed from her birth memory instead. But hey, it didn't really matter if all the details were accurate. O'Connell ended her story by explaining how she now practices "mindfulness meditation" as a Buddhist.

Today Laura Davis makes her living by teaching writing, including trips abroad with the writing coach. In 2017 she offered a workshop at Kripalu, a New Age center in western Massachusetts. "If you want to free your writing voice, explore your wild mind, and discover your true stories," the Kripalu website noted, "join master teacher Laura Davis and a vibrant, supportive writing community at a beautiful healing center in the Berkshire Mountains." Davis herself emailed to encourage attendees: "Through creative exercises, guided meditations, and evocative writing prompts, you will learn to transform scraps of memory into a rich written legacy. It will give you a chance to write out your heartbreak and your grief—and your hopes."

In the meantime, Ellen Bass writes poetry. In the 2008 edition of *The Courage to Heal*, she included "Bearing Witness," her poem that concludes: "God is / the kicked child, the child / who rocks alone in the basement, / the one fucked so many times / she does not know her name, her mind / burning like a star."

A 2016 profile of Ellen Bass by Ellen Brown summarized her career. "In the late 1980s, Bass decided to partner with Laura Davis, a former creative writing student, to produce a book about what she had learned in the workshops. Again, there was a ready audience. *The Courage to Heal: A Guide for Women Survivors of Child Sexual Abuse*, published in 1988, sold over a million copies and was translated into a dozen languages. Victims held Bass up as a beacon of hope—finally, someone was lending them a helping hand." The article failed to mention repressed memory therapy but explained:

> Matters were further complicated when the False Memory Syndrome Foundation launched an attack on the credibility of sexual abuse survivors who were speaking out against their alleged abusers. A barrage of newspaper articles, magazine stories, and radio and television talk shows stirred up a public debate about the accuracy of survivor memories and their accusations. Bass felt compelled to speak out in defense of her work and the survivors who were being depicted as liars, hysterics, and troublemakers.

The Unkillable Myths Live On

This kind of misrepresentation and vilification of those who critique repressed memory therapy and its disastrous results continues, as do the careers of others who fomented the false memory epidemic. As I noted in this book's introduction, about 84 percent of the general public still believe that traumatic memories are often repressed, and over 60 percent of psychotherapists agree.

"I think the recovered memory phenomenon is still alive and well," wrote Dorothy, a California retractor, in 2017, "and it is definitely still taboo in most circles to speak up around this issue. I know of a woman who strongly believes she suffered Satanic abuse, and she's been asserting this for decades."

Dorothy believes that most therapists today "would say they try not to plant memories, but that they are very supportive of recovered memory. It would also be very interesting to know what the press understands about the issue. Cable news staffers, for example, may have been too young to remember what happened in the 1990s."

There are ten copies of *The Courage to Heal* in her county's library system. Dorothy's current therapist isn't worried about the possibility of false allegations, since "women were harmed for so many years and had no voice with regard to sexual abuse and molestation for so long." So what if there are a few innocent people accused?

"Yesterday I heard a horrific history of abuse that had been recovered in the last two years by an acquaintance," Dorothy emailed. "It reminded me a little of the Satanic ritual abuse stories. It appears that at least two therapists have fully supported her memory recovery process without question."

The myths of massive repression/dissociation simply will not die. There is a mountain of evidence for this assertion, so that it's hard to know what to include here—it could fill another book.

In 2006, for instance, Gerald Robinson, a Catholic priest in Toledo, Ohio, was convicted of the murder of a nun committed 26 years earlier. The case hinged on a woman's recovered memories of Robinson and other priests abusing her in a Satanic cult. Robinson's DNA did not match the DNA recovered from the victim's underwear and fingernails. He died in prison in 2014 at age 76.

In an eerily similar narrative, *The Keepers*, a popular seven-part documentary series aired by Netflix in 2017, relied heavily on recovered memories of abuse to convince viewers that a now-deceased Catholic priest, Joseph Maskell, or another priest known only as "Brother Bob," murdered a young nun named Cathy Cesnik in 1969, in order to prevent the nun, an English teacher, from reporting sexual abuse of high school students at Keough High School in Baltimore, Maryland. The series is dramatic, artfully constructed, and based on real events, but it is extremely misleading, especially in accepting without question the validity of re-pressed memories.

The star of the series is Jean Hargadon Wehner, known as "Jane Doe" in the dismissed lawsuit, who was a student at Keough from 1967 to 1971. She had no abuse memories until she reached adulthood, but beginning in 1981, the year af-ter the publication of *Michelle Remembers*, she began to see a series of counselors and therapists, including massage and movement therapists. She also learned to put herself into a prayerful trance, which she called "dialoguing with the inner child," a kind of pseudo-MPD in which she identified various internal child per-sonalities named Jeannie, Beth, Gloria, Ethel, and Martha, each of whom appar-ently held different abuse memories. During the 1980s, she recovered memories of how her uncle and an array of strangers abused her from age three to twelve—typical of false "massive repression" memories with a ritual abuse flavor. She also recalled that the uncle abused her ten siblings, though none of them remember it.

During the 1990s, Wehner read an array of popular books about repressed memories, no doubt including *The Courage to Heal*. In 1992, Wehner began therapy with Ph.D. psychologist Norman Bradford (currently in practice and a professor at Goucher College in Baltimore), who had her keep a dream journal. Shortly afterwards, she began to retrieve her first memories of priest abuse, start-ing with Father Nejl Magnus, whom she envisioned masturbating while he took her confession. When she discovered that Magnus was dead, Wehner switched to retrieving memories of abuse by another priest, Joseph Maskell, who had been her high school counselor. She eventually recalled vaginal and anal rape (sometimes with a vibrator), oral sex, enemas, him putting a gun in her mouth, and forced prostitution.

But Wehner's sex abuse memories expanded dramatically beyond Maskell to include two policemen, three high school teachers, a local politician who practiced a political speech while she performed oral sex on him, three more priests (Father Schmidt, Father John, and Father Daniels), four religious brothers (Brother Tim, Brother Bob, Brother Frank, and Brother Ed), two religious sisters (Nancy and Russell), and another religious brother known only as Mr. Teeth, who read from the Book of Psalms as he had sex with her. Wehner also remembered that she herself killed an unidentified nun at her school.

But the millions of people who have viewed *The Keepers* did not learn many of these background facts.* What viewers saw was that Jean Hargadon Wehner seemed to be an attractive, sensitive, self-assured woman with a supportive, wholesome family, and that she claimed to have recovered memories of abuse by Father Maskell and a few others. And director Ryan White—whose aunt was Wehner's high school classmate—went out of his way to portray her memories as real. After listening to her tell her story for hours, White told his producer, "This woman is telling the truth and we need to be part of this."

It is true that Sister Cathy Cesnik, 26, an attractive, popular English teacher, was murdered and probably raped on November 7, 1969. Only three days later, another young woman, 20, was killed two miles away in a very similar fashion. It is quite likely that the same unknown person killed both of them, but the murderer probably didn't know that Cesnik was a nun, because she had just begun working at a public high school and had permission not to wear her habit.

As part of her prayerful memory process, Wehner visualized how Father Maskell had taken her to see Cathy Cesnik's body, and that her face had been crawling with maggots. Maskell must have known that she would immediately repress the memory, just as she allegedly forgot her rapes every time the door clicked shut as she was leaving his office. When Maskell's body was exhumed in 2017 (he died in 2001), his DNA did not match the DNA at the murder scene.

The second star of *The Keepers* is Teresa Lancaster, "Jane Roe" in the 1994 lawsuit, who was a year behind Wehner at Keough High School. She claimed to have always remembered that Father Maskell forced her to disrobe, sit on his lap, endure his fondling, and forced her to take enemas and douches while he watched, and that he was present during a gynecological exam. But it was only after she learned about "Jane Doe's" claims and met repeatedly with Wehner's lawyer (who

---

*   Netflix is notorious for keeping viewer numbers secret, but *Newsweek* revealed that it had the top two streaming shows in 2016, both with over 20 million viewers.

also represented her) that she recovered memories of rape by Maskell, the gynecologist, and a policeman. Those recovered memories were confused and inconsistent.

In 1993, Wehner and her siblings sent letters to other former Keough High School students, asking about possible abuse, and they received many responses. *The Keepers* makes it appear that a hundred or more people claimed that Maskell sexually abused them, but since none of them appeared as plaintiffs in the lawsuit, it is unlikely that any recalled severe abuse. It is more likely that Maskell was indeed inappropriate in many ways, and he may indeed have hugged and fondled girls and watched as they took douches. Others may have recovered memories or tried to. One classmate thought Maskell must have drugged her Coca-Cola. "I've never been certain of what happened. There's so many gaps in my memory of being with him, and I only have fragments." And some may have reinterpreted always-remembered incidents to make them more sinister in retrospect. As one of them said in the series, "Something that may have seemed insignificant at the time has relevance now."

Unforgivably, *The Keepers* put two true believers in repressed memories on screen as "experts." Psychologist L. M. Lothstein asserted: "Some things we experience are so unbearable and so painful that we shut them out. The major systems for protection of the self, the hypothalamic pituitary adrenal, fight-flight response, the vagal response to play dead, to dissociate, to be unaware of something, they'll come right into play in order to protect the self from harm." This is pseudoscientific claptrap. He went on to say, "We now know so much more about memory. It's scientifically accepted that memories can be compartmentalized and not known to the conscious ego." This is absolutely untrue. As we have seen, every reputable memory scientist knows that repeated traumatic events tend to be recalled all too well. As Lothstein pontificates, the filmmakers flashed sensational headlines about a 2004 study, claiming: "Psychologists Offer Proof of Brain's Ability to Suppress Memories," and "A Freudian Theory Proven," even though this was a study of word pairs that demonstrated nothing whatsoever about repressed trauma memories.[*]

The documentary also features psychiatrist Richard Sipe of Johns Hopkins, who served as a witness for Wehner and believed her recovered memories. "There are things that have the ring of truth, even if they are hard to believe," he explains in *The Keepers*. Sipe diagnosed Wehner with post-traumatic stress disorder (PTSD), which he compared to that of war veterans. "Naturally we know so much more about this because of men and women coming home from war and being traumatized. We have all sorts of knowledge now about how the brain handles those."

---

[*]   See Chapter 2 for a critique of this 2004 study by Michael Anderson and colleagues.

But the brain does not handle war experiences by repressing them, but by being unable to forget them. That is what causes PTSD. Sipe criticizes his colleague Paul McHugh, the head of the Department of Psychiatry at Johns Hopkins, as having a "blind spot" about repressed memories because McHugh testified that they had no scientific validity. McHugh apparently convinced the Baltimore judge in the case, who dismissed it before trial, a decision upheld on appeal.

In *The Keepers*, Jean Wehner tells viewers, "There's an awful lot I still don't remember," so stay tuned for more horrific abuse memories yet to come. She demonstrates how she recalls her memories, lighting a candle and lying down to go into her prayerful state. As she does so, the camera zooms in on an angel figure beside her, which says "Believe Believe Believe Believe Believe."

Critical response to *The Keepers* has been overwhelmingly positive and credulous. In a review, a *Baltimore Sun* reporter asked rhetorically why Wehner had not come forward earlier. "Because that's how ritualized long-term abuse works in children," she wrote. "The abuser is able to control the victim through threats and intimidation.... Jean says that to survive the horror, she in effect dissociated herself—severed herself from the experience, put the entire ordeal into a box, sealed it up, and buried it. It would stay buried for over 20 years."

New York Times reviewer Mike Hale called *The Keepers* "a fascinating and devastating experience" and identified Jean Wehner as "a steely heroine." He wrote that "trying to obtain justice based on recovered memories has the outlines of a classic tragedy," without expressing any skepticism about the validity of such memories. *The Guardian* called the series "a breathtakingly brave true crime documentary."

Prompted by *The Keepers* series, *Vice* magazine's Kaleigh Rogers published an article reviewing the alleged scientific validity of repressed memories, asserting that since the 1990s "we've built a much stronger understanding of how and why childhood trauma could lead to repressed memories." As we have seen, that is precisely the opposite of what reputable memory scientists have found. Rogers erroneously concluded: "The science is firm that traumatic events can cause memory loss, and that these memories may resurface years or decades later." I am sure that she sincerely meant well, but from her photo, Rogers is a young Millennial who was swayed by the series and accepted the myth of repressed memory hook, line, and sinker. I fear that she is representative of a new generation who will be vulnerable to these dangerous theories.

Advice Columns, MPD, and More Satanic Abuse

In 2009, someone wrote to "Ask Marilyn," the advice columnist for the widely-read *Parade* magazine: "Recovering lost memories from childhood was a hot form of psychotherapy about 20 years ago. It fell out of favor when some patients exhibited 'false-memory syndrome.' But what about the others? Do many people truly block certain childhood memories, then remember them as adults?" Marilyn assured her, "Some people surely do, but there's no way to know their number because evidence of the memories seldom exists." Although she said that false memories were more common than most people realized, Marilyn's expert assertion that some people "surely do" repress sex abuse memories was horrendous.

Shortly before this book went to press in 2017, Carolyn Steber, a young advice columnist for *Bustle,* an online woman's magazine with 10 million monthly visitors, published an article, "11 Signs You Might Be Repressing Negative Childhood Memories." Steber's opening paragraph: "If something traumatic happened to you as a kid—like some form of abuse—it's possible your brain may have repressed the negative memories, leading to all sorts of issues as an adult. You might experience anxiety, have a fear of abandonment, or feel really strange in certain situations. It can be frustrating, especially if you don't know why you're feeling this way." Steber quoted Texas psychotherapist Bruce W. Cameron, who advised, "It is very important to go to therapy to unlock the memories and likely trauma."

The eleven alleged signs of abuse are vague and common, including strong reactions to certain people, situations that freak you out, having a hard time controlling your emotions, losing jobs, acting childishly, being impulsive, or feeling anxious. Steber quoted four different therapists, including Mark Derian, a graduate student studying psychology who offers advice on his website such as "7 Reasons to Never Date a Girl Who Attends a Protest." Carolyn Steber is a regular Bustle contributor who grinds out other articles such as "Signs You Might Need to Take Better Care of Your Vagina," or "The Most Common Sex Injuries and How to Avoid Them."

Or take the myth of multiple personalities, which keeps selling books, movies, and television shows. In 2007, psychiatrist Richard Baer published *Switching Time,* his account of how his patient, Karen Overhill, came for treatment of post-partum depression in 1989. But by 1993 she engaged his fascinated attention with eleven alters, soon to expand to seventeen. They included Karen Boo, a baby, The Angry One, a male who hated everyone, Karen I, a shy ten-year-old, Holdon, a male protector, and a predictable stereotypical panoply of others. Baer had concluded that Overhill had MPD long before she presented her alters and undoubtedly cued her, but it appears that she mostly came up with them on her own.

In 2008, former football star Herschel Walker published *Breaking Free: My Life with Dissociative Identity Disorder.* After retiring from football in 1998, he felt "this big old hole in my life." In search of a new identity, he found multiple inner alters called Hero, Consoler, Judge, Enforcer, Sentry, Watch Dog, Daredevil, and Warrior—a total of eight, although he noted elsewhere in the book that he had identified "as many as twelve distinct alters." Growing up in Wrightsville, Georgia, Walker was taunted by classmates because he stuttered and was fat. After seeking therapy with Jerry Mungadze, he concluded that he had developed these alters to cope, although of course he didn't know it as he grew up. His trauma was mild compared to the standard MPD fare. Still, "one of the things my alters did for me," Walker wrote, "was to make me forget most of the awful things that had happened to me."

Jerry Mungadze, a native of Zimbabwe, ran a Christian counseling center that specialized in "dissociative disorders, childhood trauma and abuse, post-traumatic stress disorder, and ritual abuse." Walker was fortunate, then, not to recall that his alters took part in Satanic tortures. Mungadze now promotes pseudoscientific "Right-Brain Therapy," in which he interprets mental illness by how people color drawings of the brain, as he demonstrates on YouTube. He can tell, for instance, that if a person uses green crayon for the cerebellum, it means "a lot of family trauma. This is a person who was abused in their family." But they haven't been able to process it, so "their body is storing the trauma."

Also published in 2008, Anne Davis's *Hell Minus One: My Story of Deliverance from Satanic Ritual Abuse and My Journey to Freedom*, regurgitated the stereotypical ritual abuse stories full of blood, vomit, and semen. "The black-robed cultists then knelt around the fire and me on the inverted cross." Her mother stripped her naked and forced her into a robe. "I saw everyone naked on the floor in a frenzied sadomasochistic orgy." Davis did not recall any of this until seeking therapy with Sterling Ellsworth, who "taught me to give myself permission to remember whatever needed to be remembered." But the wise Dr. Ellsworth also explained "that it was vital he not influence my recall process."

When Davis revealed her new-found abuse memories, her siblings apparently sought therapy and retrieved their own memories. When confronted by the allegations, her devout Mormon parents initially said that their children were "hallucinating and possessed." But under pressure from church authorities, her parents wrote gruesome confession letters, *a la* Paul Ingram.

Dr. Ellsworth's website reveals a kindly, smiling man who loves sailing and spending time with his grandchildren, when he is not counseling fellow Mormons. His books and CDs "help us overcome the negative character traits that have accumulated from the challenges of earth life," according to the website. "Dr. Ellsworth incorporates his counseling techniques with gospel teachings and illustrates exactly how you can reach out to love that little child inside of you, who still needs love and caring. When the inner child heals, you heal!"

The books on multiple personality, ritual abuse, and repressed memories just keep coming. *Ritual Abuse and Mind Control: The Manipulation of Attachment* (2011) stemmed from a British conference at which "experts" offered scientific-sounding rationales for their allegations about "amygdala-mediated emotional and sensimotor memories of terror," along with a self-proclaimed Survivor and her lurid stories. Orit Badouk Epstein, the primary editor, identified herself as an "attachment-based psychoanalytic psychotherapist."*

In 2016, Frances Waters, a Michigan licensed clinical social worker who has served as an expert witness in sex abuse trials for two decades, published *Healing the Fractured Child: Diagnosis and Treatment of Youth with Dissociation,* in which she fosters a belief that children can forget trauma by allegedly "dissociating." She has diagnosed children as young as five with internal alternate personalities, whom she helps them name and has conversations with. The former president of the International Society for the Study of Trauma and Dissociation, Waters testified in one case (in which the conviction was reversed because of her inappropriate testimony) that children never lie about sexual abuse and that it is normal for molested children to deny any abuse initially. Nonetheless, Waters continues to promote the pseudoscience of multiple personalities and repressed memories in court and in print.

Also in 2016, Sarah Hemli published *Remember to Forget: A Journey Out of Denial, and Defilement.* "This book invites you to journey with Sarah [the author] as she walks through the most challenging time of her adult life," Hemli wrote. "She spent half a lifetime trying to forget what happened to her just to be able to survive. Now she embarks on a journey to face what was hidden and acknowledge the pain that was too strong to feel. It brings her close to letting go of life. With her, you will go to places of disbelief, despair, hopelessness, and grief as Sarah reclaims the lost memories of her childhood and gains herself in the process."

That book was published by WestBow Press, a "Christian self-publishing house"—not exactly mainstream. But in 2013, Routledge, a reputable academic press, published *The Child Survivor: Healing Developmental Trauma and Dissociation,* featuring "case examples to illustrate hard-to-manage clinical dilemmas such as children presenting with rage reactions, amnesia, and dissociative shutdown," by clinical psychologist Joyanna Silberg, one of the pillars of the MPD movement and long-time consultant to the infamous Sheppard Pratt Hospital in Baltimore *(see Chapter 4).* Not only that, but in 2014 Silberg, who had testified

---

* The United Kingdom remains prone to Satanic panic. In 2014, a child custody dispute veered into allegations of a Satanic cult that allegedly imported babies from around the world, then slit their throats, drank their blood, and danced around wearing the babies' skulls. All of these tales were virtually tortured out of two children who really *were* clearly abused in the process. They eventually retracted their stories, but not before a video of the allegations were viewed by more than four million people on-line.

in favor of the outrageous MPD therapist Judith Peterson, convinced a Maryland judge to allow a trial in which three sisters claimed that their mother's boyfriend sexually abused them in the 1970s but that they had all repressed the memories. The judge ruled that the concept of "dissociative amnesia" was generally accepted within the scientific community. Fortunately, the charges were ultimately dismissed.

Richard Kluft, one of the most infamous MPD guru psychiatrists, provided "expert" guidance to the television show, *The United States of Tara*, which ran from 2009 to 2011. Kluft assured CBS News that there were "easily" hundreds of thousands, probably millions, of people who suffering from MPD but didn't know it. The show featured a suburban housewife and mother with alternate personalities, including a wild, flirty teenager, a wholesome 1950s-style housewife, a loud, male, beer-drinking Vietnam veteran, a five-year-old child, and others. The show made light of MPD/DID, failing to show the devastating impact such a belief system often has on lives and families. Actress Toni Collette won the 2010 Golden Globe Award for Best Actress in a Comedy Series. This show promoted the MPD mythology, with over 2.5 million viewers per show.

In a 2010 movie, *Frankie and Alice,* actress Halle Berry played an allegedly "true" story about a go-go dancer with at least two multiple personalities: Genius, a seven-year-old child, and Alice, a Southern white racist woman. Through regular psychiatric sessions, she begins to recall the traumatic events that led to her split personality.

Talk shows have continued to fan the flames as well. In 2013, for instance, Jenny Hill, a self-proclaimed multiple personality and ritual abuse survivor, appeared on *Dr. Phil*, along with her therapist Judy Byington, who wrote a 2012 book about her called *Twenty-Two Faces*.

In 2017 yet another movie, *Split*, was released, featuring a villain named Dennis with 23 internal personalities, the familiar stereotypes of male and female, with one child and one gay alter. For unclear reasons, Dennis and his alters kidnap three teenage girls, strip them to their underwear, and abuse them. Dennis's female therapist, Dr. Fletcher, is a sympathetic character who spouts pseudoscientific theories about multiple personalities and adds "a dimension of warmth and wit," according to a *New York Times* reviewer, who concluded that *Split* is "sometimes more than a little icky in its prurient, maudlin interest in the abuse of children. It's also absorbing and sometimes slyly funny." He failed to mention that the film is one more dangerous portrayal of a mythical condition fomented by the warm, witty Dr. Fletcher.

Nor did Anthony Lane object in his review of the film in the *New Yorker*. Lane thought it amusing that the Beast, one alternate personality, "has preternatural powers, limited social skills, and a taste for human meat." How droll. "One girl has memories of being abused in childhood," Lane observed, but he didn't point out that this hackneyed plot device validated the myth of repressed memory. He loved the lead actor's MPD role, though. "I felt vaguely cheated that he has time for only a handful of the twenty-three [alters], though I guess he can fill in the gaps when *Split* becomes a Broadway musical. A song for every personality! Bring it on."

The movie review in *Time* magazine did note that MPD/DID is a "controversial diagnosis," but otherwise quoted filmmaker M. Night Shyamalan without skepticism, including his assertion that MPD patients "have been said to flawlessly play Beethoven after merely hearing a piece of music." This is a new one on me—was he thinking of autistic savants? "They can do things we can't," Shyamalan said, "but we call that a disorder?" That might be just our bias, he said, "our lens that we look through." The article did not comment on the biased lens through which the filmmaker depicted this mythical disorder.

Real People's Lives

If it were just in the movies that people with supposed multiple personalities acted out lunatic fantasies, one could argue that it was merely part of the public's fascination with the bizarre. It's just fiction, right? But in reality, the belief in recovered memories and internal alters continues to harm and even kill people. Take the case of Brittney Bennetts, a Montana social worker who cared for terminally ill patients in hospice. Troubled by family issues, she consulted a local therapist who diagnosed her with dissociative identity disorder—i.e., multiple personalities—and set her on the road to self-destruction. In March 2012, Bennetts first entered Timberlawn Behavioral Health System, a psychiatric hospital in Dallas, Texas, where Colin Ross presided as the head consulting psychiatrist. But it was psychiatrist Richard Roskos, who had worked with Ross for 25 years, who supervised Bennetts's care during the 14 in-patient hospitalizations she endured at Timberlawn over the next three years.

Abreaction work with her various induced alters failed to make her better. In fact, she got much worse, which was typical of MPD patients. As Colin Ross acknowledged, one of his surveys found that 72 percent of such patients had attempted suicide, and some had succeeded.

At 1:29 a.m. on Tuesday, December 2, 2014, Brittney Bennetts, then 37 years old, entered Timberlawn again, after a staff counselor wrote in her chart: "Positive suicidal ideation, plan to hang self, overdose on medications.... Depression, anxiety, decreased appetite, decreased sleep...Decreased showering, decreased self-care." At 10 a.m. Richard Roskos saw her, noting that she was "admitted with severe depression with Suicidal Ideation... last week had rope around neck."

Instead of recommending "Continuous Visual Observation," he authorized checking on her every 15 minutes. The next morning at 6:36 a.m., a nurse found her dead in her room. She had torn a strip from her bedsheet, tied it around her neck, attached it to the closet doorknob, and sat down.

In the wake of the suicide, Timberlawn was essentially shut down after the state of Texas and Medicare deemed it an "unsafe environment." The Colin Ross website states: "After 17 years at Timberlawn Hospital, the Ross Institute Trauma Program has transferred to UBH Denton. The core psychiatrists and therapists from Timberlawn have moved with the Program."

With representation by Texas lawyer Skip Simpson, Bennetts's father, representing his daughter's estate, sued Roskos for negligence. In a February 2017 deposition, Roskos asserted that he was an expert on dissociative disorders. "For 25 years, I've met different [internal] personalities." He said that Bennetts may have had one or more "persecutor alters." Lawyer Simpson quoted Colin Ross's book on MPD: "Persecutors carry out their hostile attacks on the other personalities by psychic and physical means. They may burn the personality with cigarettes, cut her wrists, force her to take pills, or jump in front of a truck, and then go back inside just before impact, leaving the host to experience the pain." Roskos agreed.

Reading this deposition, as well as the briefer one with Ross himself, is somewhat surreal. Simpson was focused on the fact that Roskos didn't call for a continual suicide watch on the patient. But the bigger picture is that the diagnosis and creation of DID/MPD destroyed Brittney Bennetts. She was taught to believe in her "persecutor alters" and was practically tutored in how she would self-destruct. Her therapy itself destroyed her. As Roskos said in defending himself, "Well, she talked about when she came in that she was having the voices and sometimes they tell her to kill herself I mean, that was routine for her....I've heard that many times from her." In other words, this was no big deal to him.

Simpson asked if Bennett's MPD might be iatrogenic—i.e., created by her therapists. That sometimes did occur, Roskos admitted, but "I'd say that's highly unlikely with all the people that were involved with her treatment that are skilled in this…. Look, we specialize in this." But that was precisely the problem. It is the "trauma specialists" who are so sure of themselves, the "experts" who create and sustain the belief in self-destructive alternate personalities.

Although many secular psychologists and psychiatrists still promote a belief in massive repression/dissociation, it appears that so-called Christian counselors are among the worst. In 1996, Baptist minister Ed Smith created Theophostic counseling, in which people would go into a trance state, recall childhood abuse, and then Jesus would tell them they needn't be ashamed and that all was well. About half of Smith's female clients recalled childhood sexual molestation. "Focus on that man laying on top of you forcing his penis into your little vagina,"

Smith would say. "Remember the pain and shame." Then he would encourage clients to visualize Jesus. "Look over at Jesus and see if He leads you to another memory." Eventually, Jesus would assure them that it wasn't their fault and that there was no need for shame.

Smith has now changed the name from Theophostic to Transformation Prayer Ministry. The message apparently remains the same, though he never uses the term "repressed memory." On his website, he writes that "when they visited the abuse memory they [his clients] still 'felt' trapped, dirty, out of control, shameful, small and helpless….In Transformation Prayer Ministry we often say the phrase, 'We feel whatever we believe.'" Smith means that people need to reframe their cognitive thought process to stop feeling ashamed, but he is certainly correct that beliefs shape feelings. As poet William Blake observed, "What seems to Be, Is, To those to whom / It seems to Be, & is productive of the most dreadful / Consequences…even of / What seems to Be Torments, Despair, Eternal Death."

In January 2009, Leslie Roberts, then 28 and suffering from depression, entered Theophostic counseling with Christian counselor Wanda Day at Focus on Relationships Inc, a counseling center owned by Hope Spring Counseling in Lexington, Kentucky. She was a high school math teacher and basketball coach with three small children. Over the next four years, in hypnotic "prayer" sessions, Roberts came to believe that she had repressed memories of severe sexual abuse in a Satanic ritual abuse cult and that she had multiple personalities. Wanda Day would "start off with a little prayer asking Jesus to show me something," Roberts wrote in her complaint to the Kentucky licensing board. "If I didn't see whatever she wanted me to see, she would make me do it over and over. Sometimes she would tell me I wasn't working hard enough at my 'memory work' and tell me that until I uncovered all of the abusive memories I would never get better."

Roberts complied. "I had horrific memories and flashbacks of my parents and their cult group sacrificing children. Sometimes they burned them on altars. Sometimes they slaughtered them…. I would have flashbacks of my body hanging from a tree burning, and masses of people raping me."

Not surprisingly, the young mother became paranoid. "I believed everything in life was a trigger: communion at church, certain words (sex, mom, Jesus, and many others). She [Wanda Day] believed, and made me believe, my parents' intent was to make me kill myself so that everything they had done to me would be safe from discovery."

The therapy nearly succeeded in driving her to suicide. "I got to the point where I couldn't do anything. I quit talking to my husband. I barely survived myself, much less take care of my kids…. I thought about suicide almost every minute of every day."

In 2013, Leslie Roberts finally realized that she had been living a delusion and that her therapy had nearly destroyed her. With representation by lawyer Skip Simpson, she sued Wanda Day, Focus on Relationships Inc., and Hope Springs Counseling. Before trial, the suit was settled for an undisclosed amount.

Roberts wrote to me in 2017: "To this day, I still cannot conceive how people use the name of Jesus to torment the minds of clients, human beings who come seeking help, to get better, not seeking magnified misery, resulting in even greater pain. It is sick, really sick!" She thinks now that the goal of such therapy is suicide. "They get what they want from you, then you take your own life. Win-win for them. They get what they want, and no one is left to know what they did."

Two residential programs for women with mental health problems—Mercy Ministries and Castlewood Treatment Center—have apparently specialized in recent years in inducing a belief in repressed memories of abuse. Mercy Ministries (now rebranded as Mercy Multiplied), begun by Nancy Alcorn in 1983, offers six-month residential treatment for troubled young women between 13 and 28 who suffer with eating disorders, depression, self-harm, abuse issues, and drug and alcohol addictions. There are Mercy programs in Tennessee, Missouri, California, as well as New Zealand, the United Kingdom, and Canada, with plans for more facilities. Echoing Theophostic counseling, Mercy counselors have helped residents remember traumatic memories and then seek Jesus to absolve them of guilt, as investigative journalist Jennifer Miller revealed in a 2016 *Slate* article, though Mercy personnel deny practicing recovered memory therapy. Nonetheless, "parents have watched their daughters vanish from their lives after exiting the program, in some cases without any explanation."

Ellen, one such daughter, did provide an explanation in an accusatory letter in which she described "multiple ways in which her parents had abused her, including rape at her father's hands and sex trafficking," according to Miller. "It's nearly impossible to verify or disprove Ellen's accusations, but the events described by her parents fit into a larger pattern that at least nine families of Mercy attendees have experienced: A young woman enters Mercy for issues unrelated to abuse and comes out accusing her family of horrific sexual violations. Of the nine families, seven have lost contact with their daughters."

Meanwhile, Castlewood Treatment Center, outside St. Louis, Missouri, specialized in eating disorders and espoused the Internal Family Systems model, in which people's inner "parts" were sub-personalities—in other words, another version of multiple personalities. Early in 2011, a young woman called Anna (to maintain her anonymity) entered Castlewood, where she came to believe that her father, tutors, coaches, babysitters, and policemen had all abused her, as revealed by her alternate personalities. A judge threw out the case, but Anna remained estranged from her accused father.

Investigative journalist Ed Cara interviewed several Castlewood veterans who no longer believed in their abuse memories, including Leslie Thompson, who once thought she had witnessed sacrificial murders in a cult, and Lisa Nasseff, who identified 20 internal personalities. Both sought help for their eating disorders at the facility between 2007 and 2010. A Castlewood employee who quit in 2013 estimated that half of the patients wound up with recovered memories of abuse. "Most got profoundly more disturbed by being there."

The civil lawsuits filed against Castlewood were settled out of court in 2013, with no real repercussions for the therapists who caused such harm. As Ed Cara observed, "Most therapists who were involved in the recovery of traumatic memories simply moved on, able to choose from a hundred other modalities or methods, many equally unsubstantiated by empirical research."

The Trauma and Dissociation Conference, held in October 2017 in Seattle, featured "internationally renowned clinicians, researchers, authors, and lecturers in the field of trauma-related disorders," according to its website, including Colin Ross, David Calof, Laura Brown, and others notorious for helping to create a belief in forgotten sexual abuse and multiple personalities.* It also featured Lynn Crook, a therapist who recovered her own alleged abuse memories. Speaker Mary Knight is making a documentary "about her recovered memories of extreme childhood abuse, including child pornography, torture, and family controlled human trafficking." Younger practitioners were also speaking, including Kim Lincoln, a "somatic practitioner" of Cranial Sacral therapy. "A survivor of trauma, her passion is to assist others to feel safe in their body, trust their mind, and know their soul." Similarly, the International Society for the Study of Trauma and Dissociation holds conferences and promotes its agenda to true believers.

Stop Mind Control and Ritual Abuse Today (S.M.A.R.T.) continues to offer an annual conference and "disseminate information on the connections between secretive organizations, ritual abuse, and mind control." Other websites for "Survivorship" and "Ritual Abuse, Ritual Crime, and Healing" provide similar misinformation.

In 2016 pop singer Lady Gaga decided that she suffered from PTSD: "I also experience something called dissociation which means that my mind doesn't want to relive the pain so 'I look off and I stare' in a glazed over state. As my doctors have taught me, I cannot express my feelings because my pre-frontal cortex (the part of the brain that controls logical, orderly thought) is overridden by the amygdala (which stores emotional memory) and sends me into a fight or flight response. My body is in one place and my mind in another."

---

* Psychiatrist George Greaves, one of the early MPD experts, was notably absent from the lineup. He was stripped of his Georgia license to practice for "sexual and other misconduct." According to the complaint file, he "hypnotized the patient on numerous occasions during therapy sessions, and while the patient was under hypnosis, would masturbate himself or engage in acts of sexual intercourse and fellatio with her."

Even the *Harvard Review of Psychiatry* published a 2016 article by Bethany Brand and co-authors espousing a belief that Dissociative Identity Disorder is a bona fide condition, not created iatrogenically through misguided therapy, and that DID affects over one percent of the world's population. That would mean that 75 million people are walking around unaware of their horrendous childhood abuse or their multiple internal alters. Not surprisingly, Bethany Brand is a Maryland psychologist whose website says that she "specializes in the assessment and treatment of trauma related disorders including posttraumatic stress disorder and dissociative disorders."

In December 2013, "GoodTherapy.org" published an article by Elise Curtin, which began: "Many people believe that when experiences are too painful or difficult to face, they end up tucked into the unseen corners of the unconscious in the form of repressed memories. The presence of hidden truths in the psyche may then manifest in myriad ways in waking life: panic attacks, nightmares, anxiety, depression, sexual dysfunction, and issues with self-esteem, to name a few." Although Curtin acknowledged that there was a controversy over the issue, she clearly believed in repression, citing the discredited (and overturned) recovered memories of murder in the George Franklin case *(see Chapter 2)*. She concluded that "researchers should defer to the practicing psychologists and therapists who have witnessed countless cases of repressed recall in action, as well as the people who attest to their validity firsthand and experience intuitive healing as a result."

In 2015, Carla Clark, a Ph.D. psychologist identified as "BrainBlogger's Psychology and Psychiatry Section Editor and a scientific consultant, writer and researcher in fields including psychology and neuropsychology, as well as biotechnology, molecular biology and biophysical chemistry," weighed in with an article entitled "Repressed Memories—Fact or Fiction?" She began, "Repressed memories are one of those things that we don't have solid proof of existing, yet typically believe to be real without question," pointing out that movies such as *The Hulk* (2003) and *Shutter Island* (2010) used repressed memories "with hardly a media outcry." Clark noted that scientists and clinicians "with greater critical-thinking abilities are associated with more skeptical beliefs about repressed memories," that there is no proof for repression, and that humans are prone to self-deception.

Then, remarkably, Clark observed that "perhaps a proneness to form false memories is a skill that trauma survivors mentally entrained over the years in order to cope better with the traumatic event….It is reasonable to assume that part of traumatic memory repression involves reinforcing false memories that aid adaptive forgetting of the traumatic event." So…false memories may be an indication that real abuse occurred. This is strange, even strangled, logic. "My personal opinion, for what it is worth," she concluded, "is that unconsciously repressed memories may feel real to the people experiencing them, and may possibly be essential to our existence as socially sensitive and emotional beings living in a world filled with largely unpredictable traumatic events. But don't get hung up on the details." Argh! After all that, she assumed that people really do repress traumatic memories but that it doesn't really matter if they are completely true, an all-too-familiar attitude.

As this book was about to go to press, a new legal case hit the news, with "John Doe 6" suing the Chicago Presbyterian Church for sexual abuse at the hands of a priest. He "further alleges that he repressed memories of the abuse until a news report brought them to the surface in January 2015."

The same month that lawsuit was filed, Jerome Groopman, a physician with training in internal medicine, published a positive book review of *The Voices Within,* by psychologist and fiction writer Charles Fernyhough, in the January 9, 2017, issue of the *New Yorker.* "In the case of people who hear alien [internal] voices," wrote Groopman, "Fernyhough links the phenomenon to past trauma; people who live through horrific events often describe themselves 'dissociating' during the episodes." Groopman then quoted Fernyhough's book: "Splitting itself into separate parts is one of the most powerful of the mind's defense mechanisms." I sometimes feel that I am fighting the tide.

In *The Voices Within,* Fernyhough gave sympathetic attention to the Hearing Voices Network, a British-based group of people who are proud to proclaim that they hear voices. "Many people begin to hear voices as a result of extreme stress or trauma," the website explains. Eleanor Longden, its most famous proponent, gave a 2013 TED talk that has been viewed over 3.7 million times. In the talk, she revealed that each of her internal voices "carried overwhelming emotions that I'd never had an opportunity to process or resolve, memories of sexual trauma and abuse, of anger, shame, guilt, low self-worth."

In her companion book, *Learning from the Voices in My Head,* Longden explained that as a child of unspecified age she suffered from "sustained and sadistic sexual abuse from a group of individuals who preyed on successive groups of children, one of whom was me." Then she quoted Judith Herman about violations "too terrible to speak aloud." Longden's alleged abuse "left behind a tiny child whose mind broke and shattered into a million tiny pieces.... What does a child's brain do to process such an unbearable, overwhelming event?"

Longden had an outwardly normal childhood and excelled in school until she began hearing voices as a young adult. In her book, she never overtly stated that she only remembered her claimed abuse as an adult, but that is clearly what happened. She wrote of "violent threats and cunning manipulations from the abusers not to report what they were doing to me. The legacy of this fear was so powerful and ingrained that I never spoke about it to anyone until I was in my mid-20s, by which time it had been buried so deeply that it would take many more years to piece the story back together. I even went through a phase of insisting that I'd had an idyllically happy childhood."

It appears that Longden came to believe she had been abused in a kind of Satanic ritual abuse cult. She not only heard voices but envisioned some of her abusers: "The most horrifying was a tall man in dark robes with a meat hook where his hand should be and malevolent, glinting eyes."

Her childhood abuse "had literally shattered me into fragments, and each of these pieces had become so disowned I no longer recognized them as part of myself. The voices took the place of the pain, and gave words to it, and their complexity reflected this: They were different ages, harboured different memories, contained diverse repertoires of intellect and emotion." In other words, the Hearing Voices movement, which has now spread to 35 countries, has elements that are virtually identical to the belief in multiple personalities. In her book, Longden went on to write that "dissociation" was the mode she used to forget her abuse, citing Bessel van der Kolk and Colin Ross. "So, if normal memory is like a filing cabinet, then traumatic memory (mediated by dissociation) has files that are missing, scattered, and which come tumbling out at unexpected times." Of course, normal memory is *not* like a filing cabinet, and repressed or dissociated memories do *not* come "tumbling out."

Yet Charles Fernyhough, who questioned the reality of repressed memories in his 2012 book, *Pieces of Light*, accepted Longden's account of her recovered memories of abuse without question, calling it a "gripping and heartrending book." It is alarming that a respected psychologist such as Fernyhough would endorse the tired, stereotypical tropes about dissociation. "People who live through horrific events often describe themselves as dissociating during the trauma," he assured readers in 2016. "It is as though there is some drastic attempt by the psyche to remove itself from the horror that is unfolding." He described approvingly how a therapist asked clients "whether she can speak directly to the [internal] voice"— exactly like speaking to various MPD alters.

I found several online threads from 2016 that made me despair but also gave me some small measure of hope. Someone asked about memories recovered in therapy on "AskReddit." A woman calling herself Mrs. CuckooClock explained how she had recovered memories of being sodomized and forced into oral copulation at the age of three. "I had weird triggers, like the certain way some wash rags would smell. Turns out, he would bathe me after the abuse, so if another wash rag happened to smell like the ones at his house, it would frighten me... I absolutely hate vomiting and figured out it is due to some of the things he forced me to do accidentally would make me vomit."

Most people responded with sympathy and outrage, but another woman said she feared that she had made up her abuse memories, to which Mrs. CuckooClock answered: "Even though I'm super educated in the field and understand why I wouldn't remember, part of me still thinks I must be crazy and made the whole thing up. He was such a great guy to everyone and I have a lot of positive memories associated with him as well. The whole thing feels incongruent to who he was in my other memories, but why on earth would I have these memories now if it didn't happen?"

This exchange provoked another person to write: "Man, this whole thing was incredible to read. I'm not even sure what to say but the way you described the connections you have with what you thought were irrational fears to the actual terrible memories that created them was intense. I am just absolutely fascinated with this subject and you have such a grasp on it. Therapy really must have been tremendously helpful and you seem to really be a lot healthier in your mind."

Finally, someone with some actual knowledge of how memory works and the damage done by the repressed memory epidemic weighed in: "Repressed memory therapy is a dangerous and unethical psychiatric practice which is not endorsed by the mainstream medical community. It is one of the most infamous examples of psychiatric iatrogenesis. Most people don't realize this, but the human memory is an imperfect tool. Our memories are not nearly as accurate as our confidence in them would imply, and they are surprisingly easy to manipulate through outside influences….If you're in this thread and you've 'recovered' memories of abuse that you previously never had, then I'm sorry. You're still a victim, but more likely the victim of a quack psychiatrist than of a child molester."

The Hazards and Uses of Therapy

As psychiatrist Jerome Frank first pointed out in 1961 in *Persuasion and Healing,* the therapist/client relationship—whether it involves repressed memories or not—is fraught with inherent danger. "The patient enters into emotionally charged interactions with someone on whom he feels dependent." Anyone who seeks counseling automatically does so in a distressed, vulnerable frame of mind, searching for answers to life's dilemmas. The therapist has an opportunity to exert enormous influence—particularly when *appearing* to be neutral. "The very subtlety and unobtrusiveness of the therapist's influencing maneuvers," Frank noted, "coupled with his explicit disclaimer that he is exerting an influence, may increase his influencing power. For how can a person fight influences that he does not know exist?" Furthermore, "the patient's tendency to scrutinize the therapist for clues of what is expected of him may be heightened by his belief that relief... from his suffering depends on his doing or saying the right thing."

Mental health writer Mary Wylie recognized how powerful and seductive the therapeutic relationship can be. "Who does not yearn atavistically, when in pain of body and mind, to enter into a mysterious and deeply personal healing communion with a compassionate and skillful magician?" she wrote. True, and what therapist can resist playing the magic guru? As *Family Therapy Networker* editor Richard Simon observed, "Nothing fills the seats in a hotel ballroom like a workshop that promises therapists a new clinical method, some secret knowledge that can produce sudden, dramatic changes in troubled lives." This search for a "quick fix" has led to one dangerous fad therapy after another, usually searching for some secret key in the recesses of childhood.

"Exploration of the patient's past is much more than a fact-finding expedition," Jerome Frank observed. Rather, it is a reinterpretation in which patients actively participate. "Evaluation apprehension, as experienced by most patients, makes them highly sensitive to the therapist's influence, which can be transmitted through cues so subtle that the therapist may not notice them." In conclusion, Frank urged "caution in evaluating patients' productions. If the therapist has an hypothesis in mind ... he may unwittingly convey it to the patient, who may oblige by producing supportive material."

The history of therapist/client interactions is rife with examples that support Jerome Frank's cautions—and more. Because they are placed in such a powerful position, therapists have ample opportunity to abuse their power. In the privacy of their offices, with no supervision, they can—if they choose—play God with their clients' psyches. Ever since Freud's era, when many prominent psychoanalysts, including Carl Jung, had sexual intercourse with their clients, therapists have shown an alarming tendency to sexualize this intensely personal relationship. In several surveys, from 6 percent to 17 percent of the respondents admitted having sex with clients, and I suspect the percentage of actual instances is considerably higher. In one study, 65 percent of those surveyed had treated patients who had been sexually involved with *previous* therapists.

Almost all of the therapists who had sex with their clients rationalized their action, asserting that it caused no harm. Yet 11 percent of their clients were hospitalized as a result, and a substantial minority attempted suicide. Therapists who encouraged clients to visualize fantasies of sexual abuse were, in an analogous manner, abusing their clients in a "therapeutic" context. As a result, their traumatized clients also often required hospitalization and sometimes took their own lives.

A number of critics have argued, fairly convincingly, that the only real benefit of most therapy is a placebo effect. Although many clients report that they feel better as a result, some studies indicate that simple *attention* and *support* combined with the *passage of time* account for the improvement. In addition, the client who has invested substantial effort and money is motivated to believe that therapy was successful. "Despite decades of effort," Jerome Frank wrote in 1973, "it has been impossible to show convincingly that one therapeutic method is more effective than any other," with the possible exception of behavior modification for problems such as obsessive-compulsive disorder.

Consequently, it should come as no surprise that, in one study, professional therapists provided no better results than well-intended, empathetic college professors (with no training in psychology).*

Moreover, *therapy can actually cause considerable harm* because of the biases that therapists convey. Since the 1960s, studies have consistently confirmed that some 10 percent of clients *get worse* in therapy. "Mental health researchers and clinicians see problems and not strengths," Bernie Zilbergeld has noted, "because that is what they are trained to see and because it is in their interest to do so. The more pathology, the greater the need for more studies, more therapists, and more therapy." In schools and textbooks, psychologists learn to concentrate on dysfunctional families, "the ways they harm, oppress, and limit. They do not learn what a healthy or typical family looks like, the ways in which a family provides security, comfort, love, and direction."

A retractor wrote to me, providing great insight into many counselors' predisposition to find dysfunctional families:

> When I was in graduate school for a masters in counseling psychology, I did a two semester practicum at the college counseling center. I had one case of an eighteen-year-old with major body image issues, which isn't particularly unusual. In the intake, she told me that she had a good relationship with her parents. My supervisor insisted that *no one* likes their parents that much. There had to be something else there. Later, my own therapist said the same things, that I had to be hiding something about my parents. And since I had already been trained in that school of thought, it was easy for me to go the next step and apply it to my own life.

In his book, *Beware the Talking Cure*, psychologist Terence Campbell included a list of questions, some of which are reproduced below, to help identify ineffective, dangerous therapeutic approaches.

- Do you feel more worried and discouraged since you began therapy?
- Is your therapist intensely interested in the minutiae of your fantasies, feelings, and/or thoughts?
- Does your therapist focus primarily on the events of your childhood and overlook the present-day issues of your life?
- Does your therapist overemphasize your deficits and short-comings while ignoring your strengths and resources?
- Does your therapist frequently tell you things about yourself which seem wildly speculative?

---

* The conclusion that well-intentioned, compassionate lay therapists can be just as helpful as those with advanced training may appear to contradict another concern I have repeatedly expressed—that poorly trained therapists were enthusiastically misapplying recovered memory therapy on the basis of faulty notions. There is, however, no real contradiction. It was the hunt for repressed memories that was the problem, not the particular training. After all, psychiatrists were the primary culprits in encouraging patients to recall mythical Satanic ritual abuse and MPD.

- Does your therapist seem to regard himself [or herself] as intellectually superior?

- Does your therapist appear to distrust you; is he quick to assume that you are merely victimizing yourself and sabotaging your therapy?

- Does your therapist frequently talk about other people in your life, but refuse to include them in your therapy despite their availability?

- Does your therapist attribute malevolent motivations to other people in your life and indict them as a result?

- Does your therapist act as if he [or she] provides you with a uniquely important relationship that is unavailable to you in other sectors of your life?

- Does your therapist seek to determine where some feeling or emotion is located in your body?

- Does your therapist rely on sympathetic platitudes advising you to "trust yourself' and/or "be kind to yourself"?

If you answer "yes" to many of these questions, it is probably time to switch therapists. It is inappropriate for your therapist to encourage overdependence. The goal should be for you to become independent. Therefore, if you find yourself unable to make any decisions without approval from your therapist, or if your therapist becomes the most important person in your life, something is wrong.

Even if all of the recovered memories were true—which they are not—it is painfully obvious that the obsessive search for them did not usually make clients better. They almost invariably got worse, except for the few who appeared to get a positive placebo effect from their new belief system. It is not healthy to live in a tortured past, nor is it healthy to encourage a client to sever all contact with family members.

Should people *ever* seek therapy, then? Of course, the answer is "Yes." There are times when it makes sense to pay for a professional listener. Sometimes friends and family members offer too much unwanted advice because they are too close to a situation. Or maybe they don't have the time to sit down and pay sufficient attention. Psychologist Peter Gray described the virtues of a good therapist:

> By devoting time to the client, listening warmly and respectfully, and not being shocked at the client's statements or actions, any good psychotherapist communicates the attitude that the client is a worthwhile human being.... In addition, most therapists make at least some common-sense suggestions that have little to do with their theories, of the sort that anyone's wise friend or relative might make, but carrying more weight because they come from a recognized authority.

Also, a professional counselor can sometimes help open clogged communication channels, facilitating understanding and dialogue. Research has shown true family therapy—often involving biological family members, friends, coaches, or others concerned with the client—to be quite effective, especially when therapy helps families identify their resources and strengths to support a troubled family member. While therapy is, indeed, an art form of sorts, it should be based on logic and common sense. Truth does matter. Proven effectiveness matters.

There are hundreds of supposedly different forms of psychotherapy, with the practitioners of each asserting that *their* approach offers the key to mental health. Consequently, it can be confusing when you're shopping around. The particular therapist and his/her personality may make more difference than any orientation, but controlled research has clearly demonstrated that *cognitive and behavioral therapies* are more effective than other approaches. Psychodynamically oriented therapies (including psychoanalysis) have proven less useful, though usually slightly better than a placebo. The most effective therapeutic approaches are short-term (under 20 sessions).

Cognitive therapy concentrates on current problems. Rather than rehashing and reinterpreting the past, cognitive therapists stress how people's belief systems—the ways they think about themselves and others—interfere with their lives. By reframing and modifying self-defeating attitudes, people can better cope with their lives, without years of lying on an analyst's couch.

Behavior modification methods can be a component of the cognitive approach, particularly for anxiety disorders. Such methods as systematic desensitization or counter-conditioning can sometimes help people cope with panic attacks or obsessive-compulsive behavior. I should note, however, that some behavioral approaches, such as "flooding," were used by recovered-memory therapists in destructive ways. Any method that deliberately manipulates strong human emotions has great potential for harm.

Thus, at first the practice of "critical incident stress debriefing," introduced in 1983 and widely adapted in the wake of a tragedy such as terrorist attacks, might seem reasonable. Gather survivors to talk about and process their memories and feelings. Yet, as psychologist Julia Shaw observed in 2016, "by setting up the expectation that everyone who experienced a particular event probably has—or should have—a severe adverse response, critical incidence stress debriefing has the potential to adversely homogenise people's reactions, pushing their memories and responses to be more negative than they naturally would have been." Instead, she suggested that counseling be voluntary rather than mandatory. "Let them bring the event up if and when they need to, and certainly don't force them to talk about things."

Appropriate use of medication can also provide much-needed relief in some cases. I am concerned about an over-reliance on drugs, but there appears to be no question that antidepressants and other medications have made an enormous difference to many suffering from depression or other difficulties, when no form of talk therapy did much good. Also, as I observed in Chapter 2, there is promising research on the use of the beta blocker propranolol to treat anxiety and post-traumatic stress disorder.

If you decide to seek therapy, you should ask what orientation your therapist has and how long the process will probably take. Never forget that *you* are paying for a service and you deserve straight answers. There should be no mystery involved in this interaction between two people.

By and large, Americans place entirely too much faith in therapists. Life isn't fair, and every person's time on earth includes challenges, disappointments, and even tragedies. But most people are basically resilient and resourceful, quite capable of surviving and thriving with a little help from their friends, as the Beatles once sang. It's not clear that long discussions of childhood are necessary or useful. Nor do we need constant monitoring or psychic repair by experts.

How to Tell True from Illusory Memories

One of the few things that adversaries on both sides of the repressed-memory debate agree on is that, without firm external corroborative evidence, it is impossible to distinguish definitively between true and false memories. Given what we now know, however, I think it is possible to hazard a reasonable guess in many cases. First, if a sex-abuse memory stems from massive repression—memories of long-term abuse retrieved after lengthy amnesia—the memory is probably untrue. There may be always-remembered elements that are correct, but the superstructure built upon those elements is probably confabulated.

Beyond that simple criterion built around the concept of massive repression, there are other indicators. In general, I distrust "checklists," since people tend to regard them as iron-clad criteria in an ambiguous world. Nonetheless, I think a positive answer to several of the following questions may legitimate appropriate skepticism for the "memories" involved.

- Did the memories come back during memory-focused psychotherapy, incest group work, or after reading a book such as *The Courage to Heal*?
- Does the claimed abuse go back to the crib, during the period of infantile amnesia?
- Do the recovered memories extend into the teenage years or beyond?
- Do the recovered memories involve actual rape or bizarre ritual abuse elements?
- Do the memories have a "horror movie" quality to them?
- Has the accuser been diagnosed with multiple personalities?
- Did the accusations begin with one person, then spread to multiple perpetrators?

- Were hypnosis, guided imagery, massage, dream analysis, or other such techniques employed to gather memories?

- Does the accuser feel that the memories explain most life problems, such as physical illness, depression, troubled relationships, or work-related issues?

- Does the accuser cut off all contact with anyone who expresses even the mildest doubts?

- Does the accuser seem motivated by monetary compensation?

- Does the accuser appear to be enraged much of the time?

- Has the accuser made being a "Survivor" a main source of identity?

- Did the memories come back during the height of media attention and societal belief in recovered memories, in the late 1980s to early 1990s?

Positive answers to several of these questions provide an indication that the accusations may be based on illusory memories, though negative answers do not necessarily indicate that the memories are accurate. Indeed, now that recovered memories have been widely discredited, many of those who recovered memories may hide or distort that fact. Some convince themselves that the memories arose outside of therapy. Similarly, some who initially stated that their memories sprang back full-blown after a long period of amnesia have revised their stories. "I always sort of remembered. I just pushed the memories to the back of my mind."*

This kind of vagueness makes for a gray area in trying to distinguish true from false memories. It need not be a matter of conscious duplicity. One of the lessons we have learned from recovered memory therapy is how readily human beings can manipulate their pasts. It is quite possible for those who have recovered illusory "memories" to convince themselves that they had *always* remembered. According to several studies, a sizable minority (up to a third) of "UFO alien abductees" claimed continuous memory for their experiences, which usually includes sexual abuse aboard a spaceship.

Thus, each case must be examined carefully. We should certainly not go back to an automatic denial of sex abuse accusations. In general, always-remembered sexual abuse accusations may be true, while those involving massive repression are false.

---

* Cases involving older children or teenagers are particularly difficult. An adolescent daughter may feel trapped by a personal dilemma and want to "get back" at her parents. She knows that accusing her father of sexual abuse will give her automatic power and attention. Once the allegations are made, they take on a life of their own, with social workers and the police involved. Often, the teen wants to take back the accusations once she sees their effect, but is deterred by fear of prosecution. These cases are particularly disturbing because they often arise outside of therapy and do not involve recovered memories. And, of course, in some cases the daughters really were sexually abused by their fathers.

A Hug Is Not Sex Abuse

One of the unfortunate consequences of the paranoia in this country over possible child sex abuse is that many are afraid to express physical affection for children any more. One of my friends, a teacher, told me that she was instructed only to use a "tent hug" to console a student. She demonstrated it, leaning stiffly forward from the waist so that only her head touched mine as she patted me on the back. Day-care providers may be afraid to hold children on their laps during story hour. Parents and grandparents may not help preschoolers wash their genitals.

In 1971, Ashley Montagu wrote *Touching: The Human Significance of the Skin.* "Fondling of the infant can scarcely be overdone," he concluded. "Any abrupt cessation of fondling should be avoided, and it is recommended that in cultures of the Western world, and in the United States in particular, parents express their affection for each other and for their children more demonstratively than they have in the past. It is not words so much as acts communicating affection that children, and, indeed, adults, require." No one would dare say such a thing now. The word *fondling* has been demonized and now refers only to invasive sexual acts.

That's too bad, because Montagu was right. Many Americans have always been uncomfortable about expressing physical affection. The new puritanism, with its emphasis on "boundaries," may deprive new generations of natural, affectionate touch. In a 1992 poll of Virginia mental health and legal professionals, 20 percent of the respondents felt that frequent hugging of a 10-year-old child justified intervention by state authorities. Over half thought that a parent giving a child a brief good-night kiss on the lips was sexually abusive. And 75 percent thought that intervention was required in families where parents appeared nude in front of their five-year-olds.

Ugandan native Joshua Rubongoya, a Virginia political science professor, wrote an article in 1994 complaining about how difficult it was to be a good father in the United States. He mused about "why raising children is so burdensome in America and not so much so in Africa." Part of the answer was that in Uganda, "children were brought up by the community, the neighborhood, the extended family, the school and church." He also recognized that in America "if a dad frequently changes diapers and gives evening baths to the kids, this could become grounds for child molestation charges." He wondered whether fathers would all be "stripped of the joys of parenting, or can fatherhood be retrieved from the heap of social history?"*

---

* A 1994 newspaper article provided chilling evidence that Rubongoya's concerns were realistic. In the article, Tennessee Circuit Judge Muriel Robinson said that she had heard so many false allegations of child sexual abuse in her divorce court that she advised divorced fathers to limit physical contact with their children. "It's very dangerous nowadays for a loving father to be around his children, especially little girls," the judge stated.

It is a good question. Yale child psychiatrist Kyle Pruett wrote *The Nurturing Father* in 1987, the year before *The Courage to Heal* appeared. Pruett called for fathers to be much more involved in the daily care of their children. His ideal father "would be loving and nurturing without embarrassment or fear, open and vulnerable without being a victim. He could foster in his children the freedom to be strongly feminine or tenderly masculine but, above all, abidingly human." These were wonderful sentiments, but increasingly difficult to fulfill in these troubled times.

Humans are Resilient

Another unfortunate result of the modern climate is the assumption that people who really *were* sexually abused are always irretrievably damaged by it, and that all unwanted sexual incidents—ranging from comments on breast size to rape—have an equally harmful effect. Certainly, violent sexual abuse of children is very traumatic and its effects should not be minimized. Nonetheless, humans are far more resilient than such common attitudes would have us believe.

Psychologist Terence Campbell drew an analogy between victims of automobile accidents and sexual abuse. Some people involved in a car wreck suffer severe injury or whiplash. Others walk away with minor injuries, and some appear completely unscathed. Similarly, some victims of sexual abuse appear to suffer severe sequelae, while others do not. The diagnosis on medical charts does not say, "victim of auto accident," but "neck injury." Similarly, Campbell observed, it is wrong to diagnose someone for treatment as a "sex abuse victim." Instead, specific problems such as panic attacks or low self-esteem should be treated.

Maya Angelou's terrible childhood experience with sexual abuse is instructive. At the age of seven, she was raped by Mr. Freeman, her mother's boyfriend. "He called me into the living room. Then he was holding me too tight to move and his pants were open and his 'thing' was standing out and he grabbed down my bloomers. And then there was the pain and I passed out." She was not going to say anything about it, but her mother discovered her bloodied underwear, and the story came out. After the trial, Angelou's uncles murdered Freeman. Irrationally, the little girl felt terrible guilt, and she simply stopped speaking for four years.

Clearly, if anyone could complain of life-long problems resulting from childhood sexual abuse, it is Maya Angelou. Yet she went on to become an inspirational example through her poetry and speeches. "I tell you there's not one thing I would undo, not one," she told an interviewer. "Because look at who I am. I am so grateful to be who I am…. I laugh a lot. I am greatly loved and love greatly, and I cry and I'm pleased with human beings. So I wouldn't undo it, not one thing, not even the rape."

In his classic 1959 book, *Man's Search for Meaning*, Holocaust survivor and psy-

chotherapist Viktor Frankel concluded that "man [or woman] is *not* fully conditioned and determined; he determines himself whether to give in to conditions or
stand up to them. In other words, man is ultimately self-determining." As an example of how psychological theory can promote the very symptoms it supposedly
cures, Frankl discussed a client who had been sexually abused by her father and
sought therapy for her unsatisfactory sex life. "Through reading popular psychoanalytic literature," he observed, "the patient had lived all the time in the fearful
expectation of the toll that her traumatic experience would some day take. This
anticipatory anxiety resulted in … excessive attention centered upon herself."

I edited *The Aftermath*, a moving Holocaust memoir. It tells the story of a
husband and wife who were separated when their ghetto was liquidated, then
survived years of starvation, torture, and abuse in many different concentration
camps. They watched their friends slowly die. They saw children arbitrarily shot.
Nothing could compare to the horror they experienced. Yet they picked up the
pieces of their lives after the war. They moved to America and started anew. They
had children, raised them in a loving manner, and contributed to their community. Like other Holocaust survivors, they experienced profound grief over the
loss of their families. The wounds of the Holocaust would never fully heal for
them or other survivors. But the experience did not ruin their lives. Nor did they
ever forget what happened to them.*

Wendy Kaminer drew the same conclusion in her book, *I'm Dysfunctional,
You're Dysfunctional.* Having listened to the stereotypical stories of self-identified
Survivors in 12-step groups, Kaminer attended several meetings of Cambodian
refugees, *true* survivors of Khmer Rouge atrocities. "These Cambodian survivors don't glibly proffer their stories to strangers," she found. Instead, she heard
about their agony secondhand from social workers and doctors. One woman had
watched soldiers split her husband's head with an axe and was then unaccount-
ably spared after being forced to dig her own grave. "There is more laughter and
lightness in these meetings of vulnerable, impoverished survivors of genocide
than in any twelve-step group I've attended," Kaminer observed, "where people
pursue recovery with deadening earnestness."

Similarly, true incest victims often prefer not to speak of their experiences,
which are too private, too painful. When Melody Gavigan (who later retracted
her repressed memory allegations) formed the first Survivors of Incest Anonymous group in Reno, Nevada, she attracted those who had always remembered
their abuse along with those who had recovered "memories" in therapy. Soon, the

---

* Repressed memory advocates such as Judith Herman and Ellen Bass equated the unequivocal horror of the
Holocaust with supposedly recovered abuse memories. In 1994, Holocaust survivor and historian Elie Wiesel
addressed a national convention of therapists, who clearly wished to co-opt his real suffering in the name
of repressed memory Survivors. Fortunately, Wiesel instead warned his audience of the potential hazards of
recovered-memory therapy.

group split in two. The real incest victims couldn't stand to listen to the gory details of retrieved-memory incest Survivors. It wasn't that the real survivors necessarily doubted the recovered memories. They just felt no need to rehearse and relive the pain continually. They wanted to get on with their lives.

In 1980, Charlotte Vale Allen wrote *Daddy's Girl,* one of the first autobiographical incest accounts. She had, of course, always remembered it. In 1996, during the repressed memory epidemic, she spoke out: "The very notion of assisted 'recovered memories' drives me wild.... Until fairly recently I'd never encountered anyone—man, woman, or child—who'd forgotten being abused. We remembered every bit of it, and had the attendant fears and psychological tics that go along with having lost our right to privacy and to our own bodies."

Allen recounted hearing from an old acquaintance, who boasted, "Guess what? Me, too!" She announced it in a tone of "tremendous self-importance. This woman who'd never been able to find something to do in life that would bring her any satisfaction was now positively brimming with it. With the help of her therapist, she'd at last found her calling—as a victim! She had ludicrous, unbelievable tales to tell of Satanic abuse—in the heart of one of Toronto's oldest, wealthiest areas."

Allen concluded with a query. "What is going on? It's as if some sort of collective lunacy has taken hold of people—the patients and therapists, both lockstepped in a march toward finding a past history of abuse at all costs."

Several studies indicate how resilient humans can be. In a 1993 review of numerous surveys on the impact of child sexual abuse, Linda Williams and David Finkelhor—two sociologists who leaned toward belief in repressed memories—noted that one-third of the victims displayed no apparent symptoms, while two-thirds seemed to have recovered within a year and a half. "The findings suggest the absence of any specific syndrome in children who have been sexually abused and no single traumatizing process," they stated. Not only that, but a comparison between sex abuse victims and other children in therapy revealed that the former were actually *less* symptomatic.

In a 1996 review of the literature on sexual abuse sequelae, Bruce Rind and Evan Harrington concluded that brutal sexual abuse was indeed likely to cause negative repercussions later in life. They warned, however, that "focusing on early sexual experiences when they have little or no influence on later adjustment, while ignoring other factors that have greater influence, represents misplaced attention and is also likely to be counterproductive." Rind and Harrington concluded "that permanent harm [from sexual abuse] is rare and that effects are small on average."*

---

* Rind and Harrington's scholarly conclusions caused an uproar because they were unacceptable to those who believed that child abuse always ruined lives. The U. S. Congress subsequently issued a formal condemnation of the article, illustrating that the scientific study of the results of sex abuse was politically taboo.

Similarly, a 1992 follow-up study of people who were severely battered as children more than 20 years before revealed surprising adult adjustment. As a group, they *did* display relatively high levels of resentment and suspiciousness, which is certainly understandable. Still, "many subjects maintained ties with their troubled parents.... Several had developed long-term stable marriages, and social supports appeared adequate for most subjects in the group. Overall, study findings indicate that early abusive trauma and adult functioning have no simple relationship."

Elizabeth Loftus published a 1990 study of college students in which she asked them to "think of the most traumatic event you have experienced in your life." Of the reports, only 6 percent listed "shootings, sexual assault, dead bodies, and so forth." Over 60 percent reported that their worst memories went back no further than the previous three years.

Two other long-term studies, following children born in the 1930s, indicate that people have an astonishing capacity for regeneration and change throughout their lives. Harvard psychiatrist George Vaillant, who oversaw the studies, described the key factors that allowed his subjects to overcome trauma and adversity: a *sense of humor, empathy for others (including parents), creative resourcefulness, and a supportive mate.* Those less likely to rebound from childhood or adult trauma tended to remain bitter, blaming their problems on others.

In his book, *What You Can Change and What You Can't,* psychologist Martin Seligman, having reviewed all the studies on childhood trauma's effects, came to similar conclusions. "The major traumas of childhood," he wrote, "may have some influence on adult personality, but the influence is barely detectable. ... . There is no justification, according to these studies, for blaming your adult depression, anxiety, bad marriage, drug use, sexual problems, unemployment, beating up your children, alcoholism, or anger on what happened to you as a child."

Seligman was particularly concerned about our culture's obsession with sexual abuse as the supposed root of all adult problems. He related his own experience as a nine-year-old with Myron, an unkempt mentally challenged man who sold newspapers on a street corner by which young Martin walked every day on the way to school. "He and I had a special friendship. He kissed me and we hugged for a few minutes." Then, one day, Myron disappeared. Seligman later surmised that his parents discovered the behavior and had the police quietly scare Myron off. Yet Seligman was never bothered by the abuse. In fact, he retained warm memories of Myron.

"[My parents] did not interrogate me about the intimate details," he writes. "No emergency-room doctor probed my anal sphincter. I did not go to court. I was not sent to therapy to undo my 'denial.' I was not, years later, encouraged to rediscover what I had 'repressed' and then to relive the trauma to cure my current troubles." Seligman was concerned that "well-meaning parents, therapists, and courts of law can slow healing. Sometimes they even repeatedly rip the protective scar tissue off the wound."

It seems clear, then, that the Survivor dogma promoted unhealthy attitudes, even if the repressed memories *had* been accurate. Therapists do not help their clients by encouraging them to obsess over the wounds of the past, assuring them that they are badly flawed for life because of them, and urging them to rage at those who abused them.

Do Not Minimize the Impact of Profound Childhood Abuse

I want to emphasize that child abuse, including child sexual abuse, is abhorrent and really *can have a profound impact on adult life*. It is unfortunate that so many people have come to regard sexual abuse as a *special* category of trauma that inherently causes more damage than anything else. In a way, this is similar to the Victorian view that saw "fallen" women as irretrievably soiled. By concentrating almost exclusively on sexual abuse, we have minimized and neglected the far more prevalent *physical* abuse of children, which was the focus of concern in the 1960s. As feminist therapist Janice Haaken bluntly asked, "Is fondling a child worse than beating her with a belt?" Simple *neglect* is, by far, the most prevalent form of child abuse. "Many more children die from neglect than from physical abuse or sexual abuse," sex researcher Allie Kilpatrick pointed out, but neglect is "less dramatic than physical abuse and certainly less titillating than sexual abuse."

Consequently, "child abuse" is automatically taken to mean child *sexual* abuse by many people. According to recovered memory therapists, the only way to "save" sexually abused children was to destroy their families, even if the children were already adults. Some studies have suggested that helping families work through their problems and stop abusive behavior is preferable to splitting them.

Those who experienced difficult childhoods often have difficult lives as adults, and the worse the abuse was, the worse the outcome may be. The Adverse Childhood Experiences (ACE) Study has demonstrated an association of childhood trauma with health and social problems as adults in what appears to be a dose-dependent relationship. The ACE study, undertaken in conjunction with the Centers for Disease Control and Prevention, looked retrospectively at the childhood experiences of more than 17,000 adults interviewed in the mid-1990s, asking about physical, emotional, and sexual abuse, witnessing domestic violence, and serious household dysfunction, with further follow-up studies in the years thereafter.

The ACE Study findings were alarming, with 28 percent reporting physical abuse and 21 percent some form of sexual abuse. Almost 40 percent of the sample reported two or more of the eight adverse experiences in the survey. Moreover, researchers found that a person's cumulative ACE score had a strong, graded relationship to numerous health, social, and behavioral problems throughout their lifespan, including drug addiction, sexually transmitted diseases, obesity, and cancer.[*]

As with any epidemiological study, it is important to distinguish between cause and correlation. There is no clear scientific proof, in other words, that being severely beaten, left alone for hours in a locked apartment, and raped as a child causes adult dysfunction such as addiction, promiscuity, and criminal behavior. But the data certainly point in that direction, as does common sense. And as traditional, stable family life further deteriorates, our culture fragments, and the gap between rich and poor widens, the result will probably be even more unstable, abusive childhoods.

I have a good friend who, with his wife, has served as a foster parent to troubled children for several decades. His experience is worth quoting at length:

> We've had 17 therapeutic foster kids over the years, and we've gotten to know others in the system as well, all of whom have survived some forms of early abuse or other severe trauma. In a majority of cases, sexual abuse was on the list of bad things that had happened, but usually not remembered as a big deal— the beatings and restraints and the days with no food seemed far worse. (In two cases the sexual abuse did seem to have caused serious problems—both had to be isolated from peers because of aggressive sexual tendencies, which of course inhibited their social life.) But in every case, the kids had suffered terrible trauma during years of their young childhoods, and therefore lagged far behind peers in development of social skills, the ability to regulate themselves and get along with others.
>
> Without a lot of extra attention, these kids have a very high probability of being institutionalized or jailed when they become adults. Fortunately, the dominant therapeutic approach nowadays is to help kids get past their problems, to move forward and overcome their difficulties. Re-living the past would not help. But if you know, or can guess, what the kid missed out on, you can try to replace it—to the extent possible, even though that's hard at an older age. If a kid is terrified of the dark because of earlier night-time attacks, the answer is to help the kid feel safe now, doing whatever it takes to fill in the gaps, with night lights, extra hugs (or in some cases extra personal space), bedtime stories, or whatever works. The last thing we want to do is to encourage them to re-live the attacks!

---

[*] It should be noted, however, that the participants in the study were recruited between 1995 and 1997, so it is likely that some of those who identified themselves as sex abuse survivors had recovered illusory memories rather than those of real childhood abuse.

Recommendations

Finally, I have recommendations that, if implemented, would help to resolve some of the problems I have described in this book.

Advice for Legislators, Regulators, Child Protective Agencies, and Lawyers

Some of the provisions of the Child Abuse Prevention and Treatment Act should be reviewed and carefully revised, so that it will continue to protect children without inadvertently encouraging persecution of innocent adults. Anonymous tips that a neighbor or family member suspects child abuse can be important, but they can also allow personal vendettas to turn into false accusations. There should therefore be no absolute immunity for someone reporting suspected abuse. If it proves to be without any substance or likelihood, those who make false reports should be subject to prosecution.

Once the accused are cleared of official charges, their names should be removed from all lists kept by officials.

All too often, employees hired by child protective services organizations are undertrained, overworked, or incompetent, resulting in a disturbing track record. On the one hand, unabused children can be ripped from their parents without warning and no physical evidence. In some cases the parents are never even interviewed. On the other hand, truly abused children with all the evidence of broken bones and awful bruises have been returned to their abusers, whether parents or foster homes. Children can die as a result. Clearly, screening and training of child protective workers need to be drastically improved, and the workload must be reasonable.

In particular, all interactions with children in response to suspicions that they have been abused should be videotaped, and the children should not be subjected to repeated, coercive interviews. The questioning of children should be open-ended. For instance, if it is suspected that a four-year-old has been molested by his grandfather, the interviewer should ask questions such as, "What do you do with your grandfather? Do you like him? Do you like spending time with him?" The interviewer should *not* ask, "Does your grandfather ever touch you in your private parts? Show us on this doll where he touched you." Of course, if the child makes such an allegation, it should be followed up, but the child must take the lead in describing what happened.

Those recorded interactions should most emphatically include audio or videotaping therapy sessions with children. I know of too many cases in which child protective interviews who failed to get children to "disclose" abuse sent them for repeated counseling sessions in which leading and suggestive methods were used, then sent back for officially recorded interviews after the children's memories and testimony were tainted.

Similarly, all police interrogations, especially for those accused of felonies, should be videotaped. Under current law, police can legally lie to suspects ("Your fingerprints were on the gun. Your DNA was in her underwear") and can interview them for many hours, only turning on the tape recorder when the false confession begins. It should be illegal for police to lie or to interview people without a lawyer present.

Rape shield laws and related legislation and media conventions should be modified to cover the accused as well. Current laws lead to the identity of the victim being hidden, while the alleged perpetrator's name and face are smeared all over the media. People's lives and reputations are ruined long before any trial commences.

In courtrooms, the qualifications for "expert psychological witnesses" should be strengthened so that testimony is allowed only on the basis of scientifically controlled, replicated studies. That would automatically disallow any "expert" testimony espousing the concept of repressed memories. For years, courts relied solely on the "Frye test," a 1923 ruling that allowed scientific evidence if it had "gained general acceptance in the particular field in which it belongs." But just because a notion has gained general acceptance is no guarantee that it is scientifically valid. In 1692, for instance, the search for "witches' teats" would have passed the Frye test with flying colors.

In 1993, the Supreme Court replaced Frye with the "Daubert" ruling, at least for federal trials. The Daubert precedent made the judge a "gatekeeper" who should assure that expert testimony represents the best current scientific knowledge, based on research employing the scientific method that has been peer reviewed, subject to testing and replication, and demonstrating a sufficiently low error rate.

In 1999, the U. S. Supreme Court ruled in the Kumho Tire case that the judge's gatekeeping function identified in Daubert applies to all expert testimony, whether scientific or not.

Lawyer-psychologist Christopher Barden and his multi-disciplinary team used Frye-Daubert-Kumho hearings very effectively to disallow the pseudoscience of repressed memories in many trials, from 1995 to 2009.* Unfortunately,

---

*   See Hamanne, et al. v. Humenansky, Ramsey County Minnesota File No. C4-94-203, Judge Betrand Poritsky, June 30, 1995; Carlson v. Humenansky (Minnesota Trial Ct), Judge Betrand Poritsky (January, 1996); Engstrom v. Engstrom California App., 2nd App. Dist., Div 2, (CA 1997); State of New Hampshire v. Hungerford and State of New Hampshire v. Morahan 698 A.2d 1244 (N.H. 1997); State of New Hampshire v. Walters 697 A.2d 916 (N.H. 1997); Franklin v. Stevenson, 987 P.2d 22 (1999); State of Rhode Island v. Quattrocchi, C.A. No. P92-3759 (R.I. 1999) [on remand from the Rhode Island Supreme Court 681 A.2d 879 (R.I. 1999)]; of New Hampshire vs. Bourgelais, Docket No. 02-S-2834, Judge T. Nadeau, April 4, 2005; Rivers v. Father Flanagan's Boys Town,

some judges are better informed than others, and all legal teams do not work so effectively. In all too many cases, local defense lawyers with only a passing acquaintance with memory science and human suggestibility lose cases. They need to seek help from lawyers and psychologists with extensive experience in this area.

As Barden and his co-author, psychologist William Grove, observed in a 1999 summary article, "Very few attorneys conduct rigorous Daubert (or even Frye) hearings to exclude unreliable, junk science testimony." Unfortunately, that observation still applies in the second decade of the 21st century. Consequently, testimony based on repressed memories (or "dissociated" memories related to so-called dissociative identity disorder) should be banned universally from all courtrooms, without the need for any preliminary hearings. Most hearsay evidence should be disallowed, with no exceptions made for cases involving preschoolers. If interviews that elicit "memories" of sexual abuse are taped, whether conducted by therapists, social workers, lawyers, parents, or police, juries and judges can witness the circumstances soon after the allegations were first made. Unfortunately, the very first conversations with children, with parents, teachers, or others, are rarely recorded, so leading questions may already have contaminated what they say later. That may be unavoidable, but all subsequent discussions with the child about alleged abuse should be taped. If the child has been removed from the home of the accused, it is important to caution the foster parents not to discuss the allegations with the child.

In court, if young children are to testify, they should certainly be treated gently, but they should testify in court just like any other witness They should not be allowed to testify via remote video. When the court allows children to be kept away from defendants, or the defendants are situated so that the children cannot see them, the clear, prejudicial message to the jury is that the defendants are guilty perpetrators who are a threat to the children by their very presence.

State laws that extend the statute of limitations for "decades-delayed discovery" of sexual abuse should be repealed. If the abuse was always remembered, but not reported because of fear, coercion, or other factors, the perpetrator should not be protected by the statute of limitations, as long as the abuse can be corroborated by external evidence. But that's different from bringing charges against an elderly adult based on dreams or hypnosis.

All cases in which adults have been jailed or heavily fined because of children's

---

Doc 1024, Case No. 743, Nebraska State Court Judge Sandra L. Dougherty, November 25, 2005; Duffy v. Father Flanagan's Boys Town, Case No. 8:03CV31, United States District Court for the District of Nebraska, Memorandum and Order of January 26, 2006 by Hon. Laurie Smith Camp, U.S. District Judge; John Doe (Keenan) v. Archdiocese of St. Paul, Case No. 62-C9-06-003962, December 8, 2009, 2nd Judicial District, Judge Gregg E. Johnson.

allegations of abuse or adult children's recovered memories should be systematically reviewed by a specially appointed judicial panel, federal commission, or some other official body. This review panel should be carefully chosen to include those in the fields of law and psychology who are familiar with the salient research on memory and suggestibility. In light of current scientific knowledge, the cases should be re-evaluated and new trials ordered—based on this new evidence for those where a miscarriage of justice may well have occurred.

In an ideal world, the legal system would put an end to all plea bargain deals, which make a mockery of justice in far too many cases, as U. S. District Judge Jed Rakoff observed in a 2014 article aptly headlined, "Why Innocent People Plead Guilty." He pointed out that the vast majority of criminal allegations are settled out of court with plea bargains, with no judicial input, which gives prosecutors enormous power. Because of draconian mandatory sentencing laws, "a significant number of defendants plead guilty to crimes they never actually committed," Rakoff noted. This is particularly true in emotionally charged cases such as those involving sexual abuse allegations. But if plea bargains were abruptly abolished, the entire legal system would turn into a massive log-jam. Surely there is a way to begin to address this injustice.

"If there were the political will to do so," Rakoff observed, "we could eliminate mandatory minimums, eliminate sentencing guidelines, and dramatically reduce the severity of our sentencing regimes in general," all of which makes sense. The judge recommended a system in which magistrates or "special masters" would act as mediators between prosecution and defense before any plea bargain was reached. Such a system should be implemented, along with a reduction in the outrageous length of prison sentences for offenses for which there is no physical evidence. In many cases of false allegations, the accused are frightened and coerced into taking plea bargains that result in false convictions and prison time. Our legal system generally provides some type of protection to those accused of offenses until all appeals have been exhausted. Once found guilty, however, the convicted rarely receive new trials. Appeals are usually won only on technicalities, not on fundamental issues of injustice. Incredibly "actual innocence" can be irrelevant at this stage in a case, and many prosecutors have fought against allowing new trials that could prove innocence in the name of "finality" in cases. Common sense laws should allow reconsideration of such cases.

If the original defense lawyer did not object sufficiently, under current law there may be few grounds for appeal, even if it is clear that the case was based on inappropriate, repeated, coercive questioning of small children or repressed memory therapy. It is now clear, from exonerating DNA evidence, that many people have been falsely convicted in our legal system, especially those involving highly emotional charges of rape and murder. Unfortunately, in most cases of alleged child sexual abuse, there is no DNA evidence that can clear anyone.

When the original accusers retract their allegations and explain why they made them originally (often under pressure), cases should be reviewed, and if these accusations were the only basis for the conviction, the conviction should be overturned. All too often, guilt-ridden people who try to tell police and prosecutors that they falsely accused someone are ignored or told that their original accusations were true and that their retraction cannot be trusted.*

The practice of "civil commitment" of people who have already served their sentences should be abolished.

People who maintain their innocence should not be punished for refusing to take sex offender "treatment" in which they must admit to a crime they did not commit. Nor should their refusal to confess to a mythical crime mean that they will never be paroled.

Whether through legislation or through actions by the professional associations, the standards should be strengthened for those who call themselves psychotherapists or hypnotists. On the federal or state level, a single law should be enacted to cover all psychotherapists. Currently, each state hosts a hodgepodge of regulatory peer review boards for psychiatrists, psychologists, social workers, marriage and family counselors, and the like. Most do a poor job of monitoring or punishing their peers. Usually, the fringe therapists using past life regression or channeling are completely unregulated. Standards should require a specified level of education from accredited institutions, periodic continuing education in approved subjects, and ongoing observation and review. Such education should specifically include research on human suggestibility and the dangers of repressed memory therapy. Review boards should include members of the public, elected officials, and psychologists. To avoid a rubber-stamp peer review, the number of psychologists should not constitute a majority.

Most therapists are never observed as they conduct sessions. Instead, they periodically report their own versions of what happened to a supervisor. Supervisors should implement the use of one-way mirrors so that they can observe sessions directly and randomly (always maintaining strict confidentiality, of course).

The issue of confidentiality is a delicate one. Clearly, clients should feel secure that, under normal circumstances, their unguarded, frank comments during a therapy session will not go beyond the session. On the other hand, in cases of sex abuse accusations based on recovered memory, therapists should be legally bound to turn on a tape recorder, and there should be an obligation to include parents in the subsequent therapy.

---

* In an exceptional case, in 2017 Bernard Young of Detroit was finally freed after 28 years in prison for allegedly abusing two young boys, now grown men who came forward to say that Young was innocent.

In cases where people have been falsely accused because of repressed memory therapy, they should be able to successfully sue the therapists in so-called "third party suits." Only a few such suits have succeeded, because the accused were not patients of the therapist. In such cases, therapists should be forced to turn over their therapy notes.

A 2014 ruling held that aggrieved parents can indeed sue repressed memory therapists, in the case of Joan and Lale Roberts versus Kathryn Salmi. The Michigan Court of Appeals decision stated: "Michigan's common law recognizes a duty of care to third parties who might foreseeably be harmed by the mental health professional's use of techniques that cause his or her patient to have false memories of sexual abuse….. The parent-child relationship is so fundamental to human relations that a parent cannot be equated with a third party in the ordinary sense…. And when a therapist's inept use of therapeutic techniques causes his or her patient to have false memories and make false allegations of sexual abuse, the harm is foreseeable and strikes 'at the core of a parent's basic emotional security.'" Let us hope other states and federal courts endorse this common-sense opinion.*

Continuing education programs should be subjected to systematic review. Therapists should not receive credit for learning how to dig for memories, spot UFO abductees, create multiple personalities, or hunt for past lives.

The *Diagnostic and Statistical Manual for Mental Disorders* should remove "Dissociative Identity Disorder" (formerly Multiple Personality Disorder) as a bona fide mental illness. It is an iatrogenic ailment created by misguided psychiatrists or people who have read misguided books about MPD or who seek an excuse for their behavior.

As part of their training, all future psychotherapists should receive education in current memory research, the hazards of hypnotic confabulations, human suggestibility, inadvertent cuing, panic attacks, and related topics. Educational institutions and professional associations should put this requirement in writing. Therapists should inform clients that the concept of repression is a hotly contested issue within their own field and, despite anecdotal clinical reports, that it has not been proven to exist at all. Pamphlets with that information should be required in all psychotherapists' waiting rooms as a form of informed consent. As psychiatrist Harrison Pope has suggested, clients who have already recovered "memories" should not be told abruptly that they have created imaginary events but, once the therapist suspects that such is the case, clients should be "gently confronted" with that idea.

Skip Simpson, a Texas lawyer who continues to represent clients harmed by

---

* The Michigan Supreme Court upheld this decision in 2016. It is well worth viewing the YouTube of that hearing, in which one of the justices compared repressed memory therapy to treating people with leeches. See https://www.youtube.com/watch?v=TOABe3fLi2g.

repressed memory therapy, makes common sense suggestions: "If something bad has happened to patients anywhere, anytime, or anyplace, then it creates a duty for the mental health industry to investigate it and fix it. The medical schools and graduate mental health programs must: 1) Investigate to determine why clinicians got so much so wrong, and 2) take the steps necessary to prevent it in the future. Licensing boards are also culprits for not testing clinicians on the subject, and when clinicians harm patients, they often fail to suspend or revoke licenses."

Insurance coverage should specifically ban coverage for recovered-memory therapy or any hint of it. Insurance companies should look more closely at claims for post-traumatic stress disorder (PTSD) or dissociative disorders—the two most likely diagnoses based on repressed memories, though PTSD is certainly a real problem, especially for war veterans and real victims of prolonged abuse. Major corporations and the military, both of which pay whopping insurance-premiums for mental health care, should demand investigation of claims based on memory-focused therapy.

A number of organizations already exist that should be addressing this issue. The Protection and Advocacy for Individuals with Mental Illness Act (PAIMI) has set up an advisory council in every state that must include those diagnosed with mental illness and/or their family members. PAIMI should be active in monitoring any use of repressed memory therapy, but that does not appear to be the case.

Back in the 1990s, PAIMI published a "Mental Health Bill of Rights," but it applied only to patients in hospitals, and I can no longer find it via a Google search. If legislation were passed to apply it to all who seek therapy, it would go a long way toward providing protection for unwary clients. Here, in part, are the rights that were covered by that statute:

- The right to an individualized, written treatment plan, providing for periodic reassessment and revision.
- The right to know the objectives of a treatment, the possible adverse effects of treatment, and any available alternative treatments, services and providers.
- The right not to receive a mode or course of treatment in the absence of informed, voluntary and written consent.
- The right to appropriate protection in connection with one's participation in an experimental treatment.
- The right and opportunity to revoke one's consent to an experimental treatment.

Many of the above recommendations and points were included in the "Truth and Responsibility in Mental Health Practices Act," written by lawyer/psychologist Christopher Barden in 1996. His bill mandated (a) informed consent for clients entering therapy, (b) a ban on harmful treatments, (c) a ban on pseudoscience in court, (d) criminalization of fraudulent practice, and (e) a model licensing act, to be enacted by individual state legislatures.

But the law was never passed. "It generated lots of controversy," Barden recalled in 2017, "and the American Psychological and American Psychiatric Association spent a fortune (some say $1 million) lobbying to block hearings on this bill and stopping my earlier letter requiring *proof* of safety and effectiveness before any taxpayer funds could be used for psychotherapy."

Therefore, my most important recommendation is to truly enforce federal law passed in 1974 that requires informed consent from human experimental subjects, including "any individual who may be exposed to the possibility of injury, including physical, psychological, or social injury, as a consequence of participation of a subject." There is no question that a person who goes to a psychotherapist becomes an experimental subject if that therapist espouses a belief in repressed memories. This is an extension of the basic human rights guaranteed by the Nuremberg Code following World War II. As Chris Barden wrote in 2001, "The psychotherapy professions should enthusiastically and voluntarily participate in the process of formulating, implementing, and enforcing informed consent standards."

In its code of conduct, published in 1992, the American Psychological Association called for informed consent that would provide "significant information concerning the procedure" to clients who then "freely and without undue influence express consent." But as the repressed memory epidemic has demonstrated, that code has never been enforced. In 1996, the American Psychiatric Association failed to demand informed consent of psychiatric patients, observing, "There has always been uncertainty as the extent to which the doctrine of informed consent is applicable to psychotherapy." On the contrary, there is no uncertainty, nor should there be.

In this book, I have focused on repressed memory allegations, along with the day care hysteria involving preschoolers. But it is clear that such false allegations of sexual abuse are part of a larger phenomenon in which anyone accused of sexual abuse is demonized and treated as a pariah. Therefore, I have included broader suggestions to address this issue.

Sex offender registrations should be abolished. Crimes of sexual abuse should not be treated as a special category, worse than murder. As Human Rights Watch has suggested, if sex offender registries still continue, at least do not make them public, which stigmatizes and brands people, leaving them subject to ostracism, unemployment, housing discrimination, abuse, death threats, and in some cases actual death. No offender under 18 at the time of the alleged offense should be required to register. No laws should restrict residences (i.e., within a certain distance of elementary schools or parks) for entire classes of former offenders. A long-standing myth holds that sex offenders are compulsive re-offenders. In fact, the recidivism rate for child molesters (3.3 percent) is lower than most other types of crimes.

In short, a sex crime should be treated like other serious crimes. Protect society with appropriate prison sentences and probation requirements, rather than publicly stigmatizing the person for life.

Advice for Parents, Children, and Therapists

In the aftermath of the repressed-memory disaster, all involved—accusers, accused, friends, and therapists—must acknowledge what happened and prevent it from continuing to occur.

ADVICE FOR PARENTS (or others falsely accused on the basis of repressed memories): There is no magic wand anyone can wave to bring your children back. Your best bet is to find someone who can legitimately maintain contact with your accusing child—a sibling, friend, former teacher, minister, lawyer, or fellow worker. If you can gently educate these potential allies about repressed-memory issues, they may eventually be able to introduce education material such as this book in a non-threatening way. (See advice to friends and siblings, below.)

You should seek appropriate support while you prepare yourself for the hoped-for reunion with your children. To understand what has happened to them, you should read extensively on the subject. Let other relatives know what has happened so that they, too, understand. That is one of the reasons I wrote this book.

If your children accept letters or phone calls, try to be as positive and brief as possible. Don't try to argue with them: you will lose. Simply repeat the truth, that you love them, that you miss them, that you'd be happy to see them. Tell them that you did not sexually abuse them, but that you were certainly not a perfect parent, and you would be glad to talk about what they have come to believe. Those of you who are allowed no contact whatsoever cannot do much except wait and try sending a brief letter or postcard every now and then, hoping it will be read.

In the meantime, get on with your lives. Don't allow anyone to guilt-trip you for being depressed sometimes. That's a natural consequence of your situation. But try to overcome the depression by staying active, enjoying friends and your remaining family.

If possible, try to get beyond your inevitable anger at recovered-memory therapists, accusing children, or the general unfairness of it all. Such anger is normal and understandable, but rage is not a healthy emotion. It hurts you, and, unfortunately, it prevents many people from hearing you. Do not demonize the "other side" as they have demonized you. Try to rise above the situation and look at it somewhat philosophically. You can still try to change the situation without living with constant anger. Let peace of mind and compassion be your best revenge—otherwise, those who hate you win, and you become their bitter mirror image.

Volunteering for worthy causes can help. That could include working in schools, with businesses, the homeless, or any organization that interests you. Instead of obsessing over your own troubles, you will be helping others.

If your marriage was shaken by the allegations, try to provide much-needed support for one another during this difficult period. One accused parent, who also happened to be a therapist, offered the following sound advice:

> Don't let the horror of this subject take you away from the precious moments of loving your partner, or you will be eaten alive yourself. Family is first. It's so easy to become haunted by the compelling nature of this material, so much so that one can become as cynical and feverish and negative as the True Believers. I was a True Believer at one time myself. I had no idea the damage I could potentially be doing until it was done to me. But on the other side of things, I see that there is an equal potential for blindness, fervor, and self-righteousness.

It helps to talk about your situation. If you've been too ashamed to talk to your friends and acquaintances, I urge you to do so. If you have done nothing wrong, you have nothing to be ashamed of. You were been caught being a parent at the wrong time, in the wrong place, and your children were swept up in a malignant social movement. If you feel the need, seek counseling for yourself, but vet the therapist carefully.

When or if your children return, they may do so in gradual stages. Many such "returnees" simply re-enter their parents' lives, pretending that nothing happened and refusing to discuss it. Your initial reaction may be to force the issue, but it is probably wise to let the matter be for quite some time. By promoting contact, you are at least reminding your children of old times, that you are not demons or ogres, and that you love them. In time, they may be able to process and discuss what happened to them. As one parent writes, "I think it's important to think positively and not demand apologies, explanations and a pound of flesh as the price of family unity."

On the other hand, some of the falsely accused are uncomfortable just ignoring the hurtful allegations. "We are troubled by the idea that by making it too easy for her to just come back, we are doing precisely what we did that contributed heavily to her susceptibility to this awful syndrome: protecting her from reality, bailing her out, not insisting she take responsibility for her own life," one accused father writes. "She is a college educated mother and professional. But she needs to grow up."

One accused mother's son returned and said, "It's OK, Mom. I love you and want a relationship ... but I still think you did something to me." She asked plaintively, "Do my feelings count in all this? For what it's worth, I still feel violated. I know I did not sexually abuse any of my children. So what am I to do with my feelings?" I would advise this mother to allow renewed contact but say, "I know you think I did those awful things to you, but I also know I didn't. Now let's drop the subject and get on with our visit." In other words, for the time being, agree to disagree.

It is natural, of course, that parents would want a full retraction. Some parents insist on a retraction before allowing contact, assuming that by ignoring the matter, they would only be allowing their children to continue to impose absurd rules. Every family situation is unique, but the "agree-to-disagree" approach is probably the best to promote tentative reunion that can grow in time. I hope that you now understand the tremendous pain that this process has put your children through, and that you can sympathize with them.

Regardless, be prepared for a difficult period of readjustment. Your children were indoctrinated into hating you, and their "memories" of abuse were so well-rehearsed that it may be difficult for them to forget them. On the other hand, if they made a clean break with their therapists, they may rush back to you with total conviction that you are innocent and that they missed you terribly.

If possible, discuss what happened with your children. If you can find a decent counselor who is not imbued with Recovery Movement attitudes and jargon, and who understands the consequences of illusory memories, you might consider going with your children, because talking about this confusing, emotion-laden topic can be too difficult to handle on your own. Of course, rather than spending money on a counselor, you and your children may sit down to talk with a mutually trusted family friend. Regardless of whether you seek professional counseling, remember that healing the breach will take time. Love has never departed, but rebuilding trust will take patience—not just for you, but for your children.

ADVICE FOR ADULT CHILDREN (or others who falsely accused on the basis of repressed memories): Once you realize that your parents did not sexually abuse you, you will feel enormous confusion and guilt, along with relief. For many of you, your therapist and support group became your new family, and breaking ties with them may be difficult and painful. Still, you must get away from their destructive influence in order to see your situation more clearly. If you are on massive doses of medication, try to find a reputable psychiatrist—not an MPD specialist—who can supervise your withdrawal, or who will help you adjust to a proper dosage.

Some of you may have really been molested as children, as one retractor wrote to me: "I had been abused by a neighbor, but of course the real abuse was never dealt with, and the therapy was a million times worse than any actual abuse could be, since it destroys your sanity and at times your will to live." Yet for her to admit she was wrong was equally difficult. "When I realized my beliefs were false, it was almost like a physical sensation of something being pulled out of my brain, like a vacuum sucking something out." Cognitive dissonance guarantees that facing the reality of what happened will be extremely difficult for you.

Once you do face that reality, do not be afraid to call your parents and ask for reconciliation. With very few exceptions, they will welcome you back with joy, love, tears, and celebrations similar to the Biblical story of the Prodigal Son. One good thing that can come out of this mess is a renewed awareness of how much family really means, and of how limited our time on earth really is.

Remember that what happened to you was not unprecedented. "I did it not out of any anger, malice or ill-will to any person, for I had no such thing against one of them, but what I did was [done] ignorantly," wrote Ann Putnam in 1706, fourteen years after she was one of the accusers during the Salem witch trials. "I desire to lie in the dust, and to be humbled for it, in that I was a cause, with others, of so sad a calamity to them and their families."

One positive outcome can be a new openness. Once you've renewed contact comfortably, take advantage of this time to talk about *real* problems that concern you. All families have their problems, and some are quite severe. Without relying on abstract jargon, discuss specific issues. Don't expect your parents to change all that much, though. They've lived a long time, and they're probably not going to alter in any fundamental way. Enjoy them for who they are.

You will need to rebuild relationships not only with your parents, but with your long-suffering spouse (if you have one) and your friends and relatives. Many mates of self-identified Survivors watched their marriages deteriorate and their children suffer, but they tried to be supportive, thinking that the repressed memories of abuse were all true, and that the process was necessary. Once it is clear that it was all a terrible delusion, many spouses can release pent-up frustration and fury, misdirected at you. You will have to weather this understandable reaction.

Similarly, your children may need a great deal of attention and might feel bitterness over your former self-obsession. While you may feel guilty about what you did to your spouse and children—and it is important to apologize sincerely—you should not grovel. Re-establish yourself as a viable, independent member of the family who deserves respect and love.

If your therapist will not admit what he or she did and continues to practice recovered-memory therapy with others, you face the difficult decision of whether to lodge formal complaints with state licensing boards or to sue the therapist. Many retractors simply wanted to walk away and never see their therapists again. Others could not live with themselves unless they tried to prevent the same thing from happening to others. This is a decision each of you must make for yourselves.

You may feel the need to seek a counselor, too, to cope with all your residual feelings of confusion and guilt. If so, use the same criteria I described for your parents.

ADVICE FOR SIBLINGS AND FRIENDS: If you are still coping with a sister, brother, or friend who is accusing your parents of incest, you have been placed in a very uncomfortable position. Many of you believed in the reality of the abuse, went to therapy, found your own "memories," and cut off from your parents or others who were newly accused. If so, the advice to returning children applies to you as well. Other siblings sided with their parents, which means they were cut off, too. In this case, they tended to become extremely angry at their accusing siblings and wanted nothing to do with them or the issue. Still others tried to maintain a "neutral" stance, neither affirming nor denying their parents' guilt.

I don't think there really *can* be a truly neutral stance, but for those of you who do not believe the allegations or don't know what to think, it is imperative that you understand this issue. Educate yourselves about what has happened. Stop being angry at your accusing siblings and begin to worry about them. They are in deep trouble, sucked into a cult-like mindset. You are one of the few people who might be able to help them.

Therefore, if you care enough, it is a good idea for you to maintain a relationship with your accusing sibling or friend, even as you educate yourself about what has happened to her (or him) by reading books such as this. Don't ever agree that your parents were molesters, but remain sympathetic toward your accusing sibling. Say things like, "I hate to see you suffering like this. Is there anything I can do to help you? Would you like to come over for dinner? I'm always here for you. I'm going to call you once a week just to check in with you." At least that way, you will maintain contact, and you can also tell your poor parents how their lost child is doing.

If you can maintain rapport with your accusing siblings, you might ask them for reading material to help you understand what they are going through and how they got back their "memories." They may give you *The Courage to Heal* or other similar material to read, and in reading it, you will, indeed, gain insight into what they have been through. Then, at an appropriate time, you might say, "Gee, I've been reading this other book, and it's got me really confused, because it criticizes some of what *The Courage to Heal* says. I don't quite know what to make of it. Would you mind reading it and telling me what you think?" (Or read this article or watch this video.) If the approach is gentle enough, accusing siblings may actually read the material with an open mind.

When your accusing sibling finally takes back the accusations, you may feel like the always-faithful child at the feast for the Prodigal Son—resentful that the one who caused all the problems is now getting all the attention. Try to understand that your parents' relief and joy are natural. They also love you, the one who was always there for them.

ADVICE FOR THERAPISTS: It will take enormous courage for you to admit what you have done to dozens, perhaps hundreds, of clients, validating their belief in horrible events that never took place.

I first realized how difficult it would be when I interviewed Heather, a speech therapist who formerly used "facilitated communication" and was responsible for one child typing sexual abuse allegations against her parents. After a controlled test with her and the child unequivocally showed that the messages were coming from the facilitator and not the child, she denied the truth for a month. "When I found out the test results, I was crushed," she told me. "I thought, 'No way!' I thought that the person validating FC had a stake in making it fail. I felt I was the only one who cared about this kid at all. I had no reason to believe it was coming from me. I did not intentionally type those allegations."

What finally got to Heather was a journalist who asked her point-blank, "How long do you have to use FC, how many people have to get hurt, before you stop it?" And he sent her a great deal of documentation showing how FC failed to work in test after test. That shook her confidence, but within an hour, she was rationalizing it again. Finally, that weekend, she suddenly came to the realization that she had indeed been responsible for the allegations. She halted all use of FC in her school and publicly declared her position.

As a result, Heather spent over a year in mental agony. She lost all of her old friends in the FC network, who said she was simply a bad facilitator. People in the community were disgusted with her for having created false allegations. Her therapist insinuated that Heather herself must have been sexually abused as a child to have unconsciously typed such things. People at her school didn't want to talk about it for fear of a lawsuit. It took her a long time to come to grips with her guilt and to figure out how this could have happened.

"The trainers tell you that if you don't believe in FC enough, if you don't believe in the integrity of your client enough, it won't work for you," she explained to me. "So they set you up. To be the one that this works for is a real thrill. At this time in my life, I wanted a cause, something to strive for. I would say that FC was like a religion for me." Heather still wasn't sure where the allegations came from, but she did tell me she'd read "a ton of self-help books," and she was aware that many FC clients had allegedly been sexually abused.

After hearing Heather's story, I realized what a personal challenge it would be for therapists to examine what they did, either at the height of the hunt for repressed memories or in more recent times. Unlike for facilitated communication, there is no ironclad test for repressed memories, and you had a much larger professional community to lend you support in your continued rationalizations and denials. When you can admit the truth to yourselves, however, I hope that you have the integrity that Heather displayed and try to reverse the harm. Heather's healing really began, she told me, when she went to apologize to the parents she had accused through facilitated communication. "They were more compassionate than I could have hoped for. I had hoped for the moment when I could just apologize. The father said, 'We want you to know that we have no hard feelings for you. You got caught up in this, just like we did.' The mother later said she thought we could be friends. It blew me away."

Similarly, I hope that you—like retractor therapists Linda Ross and Paul Simpson—will go beyond merely admitting the mistakes you have made and will become an active force for good. Rather than losing your practice or career, you can redirect it to a much-needed specialization in helping families to reunite and process what happened to them. After all, who better understands the Survivor syndrome than you? You can facilitate the healing process, reversing the terrible delusion that you helped to foster.

As former recovered-memory therapists, you have a moral obligation to contact every former client and attempt, as gently as possible, to tell them that you were wrong, that you no longer believe in the concept of massive repression, and that they should consider reuniting with their families. It will be difficult for you to do this, but consider the following analogies. If you were an automobile manufacturer and discovered that one model had a fatally flawed part, would you simply stop manufacturing the car, or would you recall the faulty vehicles? If you were a doctor and prescribed medicine that you now discovered was a slow poison, would you just stop dispensing it, or would you warn patients who might still be taking it?

Please, clear your conscience. You have a precedent from over three centuries ago. On Jan. 14, 1697, Massachusetts declared a "Day of Repentances" for the Salem Witch Trials, which had taken place only five years earlier. In a public statement, the jurors wrote: "We do therefore hereby signify to all in general (and to the surviving sufferers in especial) our deep sense of and sorrow for our errors in acting on such evidence to the condemning of any person, and do hereby declare that we justly fear we were sadly deluded and mistaken."

In the wake of this national tragedy, it is clear that therapists were largely responsible for fomenting it. Yet few human beings set out to do evil. It is, ironically, almost always accomplished with the goal of doing good. With very few exceptions, I believe that therapists urged clients to unearth what they thought were real incest memories, convinced that they were performing a real mental health service.*

It does little good to demonize recovered-memory therapists in the same way many of them encouraged the demonization of parents. There can be no doubt that the therapeutic community must be held *primarily responsible* for promoting this disastrous and misguided form of "therapy." Ultimately, however, no one *intended* harm—not the therapists, not the children, and certainly not the accused parents. You were all caught up in a very unfortunate, destructive phenomenon, and you need to acknowledge it, talk about it, and then get on with your lives, leaving judgmental hatred behind.

And most important—make sure it does not happen again. There are signs, two decades into the twenty-first century, that repressed-memory therapy is coming back into vogue (although it never actually went away), only more quietly this time. If we do not learn from the past, we are doomed to repeat it, in one form or another.

Meanwhile, life continues to be an arduous odyssey for all of us human beings, adrift on this lovely planet, sometimes clinging together to a life raft with family and friends, sometimes falling off to swim or drown alone. Let us learn, over and over again, to be kind to one another in our inevitable imperfections and insecurities. As William Blake, my favorite poet and philosopher, put it in 1793:

> *Mutual Forgiveness of each Vice,*
> *Such are the Gates of Paradise.*

---

* Some therapists cannot be let off so easily, however. A minority appeared to be paranoid sociopaths who enjoyed wielding power over their patients' lives and who never acknowledged the harm they had done, even when directly confronted with it.

Note on Sources

To SAVE SPACE, I HAVE left out the endnotes and full bibliography for *Memory Warp*, but they can be found on my website, www.markpendergrast.com. Here I include essential books and a brief summary of periodicals consulted. Because I left out many subtitles, it is not always clear what the book is about, but it's easy to look them up or to consult the full bibliography.

Books critical of repressed memories and multiple personalities:

Acocella, Joan. *Creating Hysteria: Women and Multiple Personality Disorder* (**1999**)

Aldridge-Morris, Ray. *Multiple Personality: An Exercise in Deception* (1989)

Brainerd, Charles J. and Valerie F. Reyna. *The Science of False Memory* (2005).

Campbell, Terence W. *Smoke and Mirrors* (1998);

Clancy, Susan. *Abducted* (2007)

Crews, Frederick. *The Memory Wars* (1995)

De Rivera, Joseph and Theodore Sabin, ed. *Believed-In Imaginings* (1998)

Dineen, Tana. *Manufacturing Victims* (2000)

Eskin, Blake. *A Life in Pieces: The Making and Unmaking of Binjamin Wilkomirski* (2002)

Freyd, Pamela and Eleanor Goldstein. *Smiling Through Tears* (1998)

Goldstein, Eleanor and Kevin Farmer. *True Stories of False Memories* (1993)

Johnston, Moira. *Spectral Evidence* (1997)

Kenny, Michael G. *The Passion of Ansel Bourne: Multiple Personality* (1986)

Loftus, Elizabeth and Katherine Ketcham. *The Myth of Repressed Memory* (1994)

Lyon, Kathryn. *Witch Hunt: A True Story of Social Hysteria and Abused Justice* (1998)

Macdonald, Gail. *Making of an Illness* (1999)

Maran, Meredith. *My Lie: A True Story of False Memory* (2010)

McHugh, Paul R. *Try to Remember* (2008)

McNally, Richard J. *Remembering Trauma* (2003)

McNamara, Eileen. *Breakdown: Sex, Suicide and the Harvard Psychiatrist*. NY: Pocket Books, 1994.

Mercer, Jean et al. *Attachment Therapy on Trial* (2003)

Merskey, Harold. *The Analysis of Hysteria* (1995)

Mithers, Carol Lynn. *Therapy Gone Mad* (1994)

Nathan, Debbie. *Sybil Exposed* (2012)

Ofshe, Richard and Ethan Watters. *Making Monsters* (1994)

Piper, August, Jr. *Hoax and Reality* (1997)

Pope, Harrison G. *Psychology Astray* (1997)

Science and Pseudoscience in Contemporary Clinical Psychology, ed. Scott O. Lilienfeld (2003)

Showalter, Elaine. *Hystories* (1997)

Simpson, Paul. *Second Thoughts* (1996)

Singer, Margaret Thaler and Janja Lalich. *"Crazy" Therapies* (1996)

Spanos, Nicholas P. *Multiple Identities and False Memories* (1996)

Tavris, Carol and Elliot Aronson. *Mistakes Were Made (But Not by Me)* (2015)

Van Til, Reinder. *Lost Daughters* (1997)

Victor, Jeffrey S. *Satanic Panic* (1993)

Wassil-Grimm, Claudette. *Diagnosis for Disaster* (1995)

Watters, Ethan and Richard Ofshe. *Therapy's Delusions* (1999)

Witness Testimony in Sexual Cases, ed. Pamela Radcliffe (2016)

Wright, Lawrence. *Remembering Satan* (1994)

Yapko, Michael D. *Suggestions of Abuse* (1994)

Books espousing a belief in repressed memories, multiple personalities, and other pseudoscientific therapies:

Adams, Kenneth. *Silently Seduced* (1991)

Allender, Dan B. *The Wounded Heart* (1990)

Allison, Ralph, with Ted Schwarz. *Minds in Many Pieces* (1980)

Baer, Richard. *Switching Time* (2007)

Bass, Ellen and Laura Davis. *The Courage to Heal* (1988, 1992, 1994, 2008)

Bliss, Eugene L. *Multiple Personality, Allied Disorders, and Hypnosis* (1986)

Blume, E. Sue. *Secret Survivors* (1990)

Bradshaw, John. *Bradshaw on: The Family* (1988)

Bradshaw, John. *Family Secrets* (1995)

Braun, Bennett G. *The Treatment of Multiple Personality Disorder* (1986)

Cheit, Ross E. *The Witch-Hunt Narrative* (2014)

Forward, Susan with Craig Buck. *Toxic Parents* (1989)

Fraser, Sylvia. *My Father's House: A Memoir of Incest and Healing* (1988)

Fredrickson, Renee. *Repressed Memories* (1992)

Freyd, Jennifer J. *Betrayal Trauma* (1998)

Friesen, James G. *Uncovering the Mystery of MPD* (1991)

Hall, Liz and Siobhan Lloyd. *Surviving Child Sexual Abuse* (1989)

Hemli, Sarah. *Remember to Forget* (2016)

Herman, Judith Lewis. *Trauma and Recovery* (1992)

Hunter, Mic. *Abused Boys* (1990)

Jacobs, David M. *Secret Life: Firsthand Documented Accounts of UFO Abductions* (1992)

Janov, Arthur. *The Primal Scream* (1970)

Karle, Helmut. *The Filthy Lie* (1992)

Lew, Mike. *Victims No Longer* (1990)

Littauer, Fred & Florence. *Freeing Your Mind From Memories That Bind* (1988)

Lockwood, Craig. *Other Altars* (1993)

Longden, Eleanor. *Learning from the Voices in My Head* (2013)

Love, Patricia, with Robinson, Jo. *The Emotional Incest Syndrome* (1990)

Mack, John E. *Abduction: Human Encounters with Aliens* (1994)

Maltz, Wendy. *The Sexual Healing Journey* (1991)

Miller, Alice. *Banished Knowledge* (1990)

Mollon, Phil. *Multiple Selves, Multiple Voices* (1996)

Peck M. Scott. *People of the Lie* (1983)

Petersen, Betsy. *Dancing With Daddy* (1991)

Pope, Kenneth S. and Laura S. Brown. *Recovered Memories of Abuse* (1996)

Prince, Morton. *The Dissociation of a Personality* ([1905, 1908], 1957)

Prozan, Charlotte Krause. *The Technique of Feminist Psychoanalytic Psychotherapy* (1993)

Putnam, Frank W. *Diagnosis and Treatment of Multiple Personality Disorder* (1989)

Richardson, Anna. *Double Vision* (1997)

Ritual Abuse and Mind Control, ed. Orit Badouk Epstein (2011)

Ross, Colin A. *Multiple Personality Disorder* (1989)

Ross, Colin A. *Satanic Ritual Abuse* (1995)

Sachs, Roberta G. and Peterson, Judith A. *Processing Memories Retrieved by Trauma Victims and Survivors* (1994)

Schreiber, Flora Rheta. *Sybil* (1973)

Silberg, Joyanna L. *The Child Survivor* (2013)

Sinason, Valerie, Editor. *Treating Survivors of Satanist Abuse* (1994)

Sizemore, Chris Costner, with Pittillo, E.S. *I'm Eve!* (1977)

Smith, Michelle and Lawrence Pazder. *Michelle Remembers* (1980)

Stratford, Lauren. *Satan's Underground* (1988)

Tate, Tim. *Children for the Devil* (1991)

Terr, Lenore. *Unchained Memories* (1994)

Thigpen, Corbett H. and Hervey M. Cleckley. *The Three Faces of Eve* (1957)

Timms, Robert and Patrick Connors. *Embodying Healing* (1992)

The Troops for Trudi Chase. *When Rabbit Howls* (1987)

Van der Kolk, Bessel A. *The Body Keeps the Score* (2014)

Walker, Herschel. *Breaking Free* (2008)

Waters, Frances S. *Healing the Fractured Child* (2016)

Whitfield, Charles. *Healing the Child Within* (1987)

Whitfield, Charles L., ed. *Memory and Abuse* (1995)

Wilkomirski, Binjamin. *Fragments* (1996)

Woolger, Roger J. *Other Lives, Other Selves* (1987)

Books about false convictions and sex panic:

Garrett, Brandon L. *Convicting the Innocent* (2011)

Gudjonsson, Gisli H. *The Psychology of Interrogation* (1992)

Hagan, Margaret A. *Whores of the Court* (1997)

Huber, Peter W. *Galileo's Revenge: Junk Science in the Courtroom* (1991)

Kipnis, Laura. *Unwanted Advances: Sexual Paranoia Comes to Campus* (2017)

Lancaster, Roger. *Sex Panic and the Punitive State* (2011)

No Easy Answers: Sex Offender Laws in the U. S. Human Rights Watch (2007)

Scheck, Barry et al. *Actual Innocence* (2000)

Smith, Clive Stafford. *The Injustice System* (2014)

Strengthening Forensic Science in the United States (2009)

Surviving Justice: America's Wrongfully Convicted and Exonerated (2008)

Turvey, Brent E. and Craig M. Cooley. *Miscarriages of Justice* (2014)

Books about day care sex abuse panics and leading interviews of children:

Beck, Richard. *We Believe the Children* (2015)

Ceci, Stephen J. and Maggie Bruck. *Jeopardy in the Courtroom* (1995)

Gardner, Richard A. *True and False Accusations of Child Sex Abuse* (1992)

Goodyear-Smith, Felicity. *First, Do No Harm* (1993)

Horowitz, Emily. *Protecting Our Kids?* (2015)

Levine, Judith. *Harmful to Minors* (2002)

Nathan, Debbie and Michael Snedeker. *Satan's Silence* (1995, 2001)

Rabinowitz, Dorothy. *No Crueler Tyrannies* (2003)

The Suggestibility of Children's Recollections, Ed. by John Doris (1991)

Tong, Dean. *Elusive Innocence* (2002)

Webster, Richard. *The Great Children's Home Panic* (1998)

Webster, Richard. *The Secret of Bryn Estyn: The Making of a Modern Witch Hunt* (2009)

Wexler, Richard. *Wounded Innocents* (1995)

Books about memory, the brain, and suggestibility:

Allman, William F. *Apprentices of Wonder* (1989)

The Anatomy of Memory: An Anthology, ed. James McConkey (1996)

Baddeley, Alan D. et al. *Memory* (2009)

Bartlett, Frederic C. *Remembering* (1932, 1977)

Borbely, Alexander. *Secrets of Sleep* (1986)

Broadbent, Donald Eric. *Biology of Memory* (1970)

Campbell, Jeremy. *The Improbable Machine* (1989)

Cialdini, Robert B. *Influence* (1984)

Fernyhough, Charles. *Pieces of Light* (2012)

Festinger, Leon. *A Theory of Cognitive Dissonance* (1957)

Gazzaniga, Michael S. *The Mind's Past* (1998)

Greenfield, Susan. *The Human Brain* (1997)

Hilts, Philip J. *Memory's Ghost* (1995)

Hypnosis and Memory, Ed. by Helen M. Pettinati (1988)

Johnson, George. *In the Palaces of Memory* (1991)

Kandel, Eric R. *In Search of Memory* (2006)

Laurence, Jean-Roch and Campbell Perry. *Hypnosis, Will, and Memory* (1988)

LeDoux, Joseph. *Anxious* (2015)

Loftus, Elizabeth. *Memory* (1988)

Loftus, Geoffrey R. and Elizabeth F. Loftus. *Human Memory* (1976)

McGaugh, James L. *Memory and Emotion* (2003)

Memory Distortion ed. Daniel Schacter (1995)

Memory Observed: Remembering in Natural Contexts, Ed. by Ulric Neisser (1982)

Milgram, Stanley. *Obedience to Authority* (1974)

Neisser, Ulric. *Cognitive Psychology.* (1967)

Oxford Guide to the Mind, ed. Geoffrey Underwood (2001)

Penfield, Wilder. *The Mystery of the Mind* (1975)

Reed, Graham. *The Psychology of Anomalous Experience* (1988)

Reisberg, Daniel. *The Science of Perception and Memory* (2014)

Rose, Steven. *The Making of Memory* (1992)

Rosenfield, Israel. *The Invention of Memory* (1988)

Rupp, Rebecca. *Committed to Memory* (1998)

Sargant, William. *Battle for the Mind* (1957)

Satel, Sally and Scott O. Lilienfeld. *Brainwashed* (2015)

Schacter, Daniel. *Searching for Memory* (1996)

Schacter, Daniel L. *The Seven Sins of Memory* (2002)

Shaw, Julia, *The Memory Illusion* (2016)

Spence, Jonathan D. *The Memory Palace of Matteo Ricci* (1984)

Squire, Larry R. *Memory and Brain* (1987)

Tulving, Endel. *Elements of Episodic Memory* (1983)

Books related to Sigmund Freud:

Crews, Frederick. *Freud: The Making of an Illusion* (2017).

Crews, Frederick. *Unauthorized Freud* (1999)

Esterson, Allen. *Seductive Mirage* (1993)

Freud, Sigmund. *Standard Edition of the Complete Psychological Works of Sigmund Freud,* 24 volumes (1953–1974)

Hale, Nathan G., Jr. *Freud and the Americans* (1971)

Macmillan, Malcolm. *Freud Evaluated* (1991)

Masson, Jeffrey Moussaieff. *The Assault on Truth* (1984, 1992)

Schultz, Duane. *Intimate Friends, Dangerous Rivals* (1990)

Sulloway, Frank J. *Freud, Biologist of the Mind* (1979)

Thornton, E.M. *The Freudian Fallacy* (1984)

Torrey, E. Fuller. *Freudian Fraud* (1992)

Webster, Richard. *Why Freud Was Wrong* (1995)

Books about incest and other abuse:

Allen, Charlotte Vale. *Daddy's Girl* (1980, 1996)

Armstrong, Louise. *Kiss Daddy Goodnight* (1978)

Butler, Sandra. *The Conspiracy of Silence* (1978)

Finkelhor, David, et al. *A Sourcebook on Child Sexual Abuse* (1986)

Kilpatrick, Allie C. *Long-Range Effects of Child and Adolescent Sexual Experiences* (1992)

Maisch, Herbert. *Incest* (1968, 1973)

Pedophilia, ed. by J.R. Feierman (1990)

Rush, Florence. *The Best Kept Secret* (1980)

Russell, Diana E. H. *The Secret Trauma* (1986)

Rymer, Russ. *Genie* (1993)

Twitchell, James B. *Forbidden Partners* (1987)

Books about religion, cults, history and culture:

Anthropological Approaches to the Study of Religion, ed. Michael Banton (1966)

Bourguignon, Erika. *Possession* (1976)

Briggs, Robin. *Witches and Neighbors* (1996)

Chester, Phyllis. *Women and Madness* (1972)

Cohen, Stanley. *Folk Devils and Moral Panics* (1972, 1980)

Cohn, Norman. *Europe's Inner Demons* (1975)

Coontz, Stephanie. *The Way We Never Were* (1992)

Cowan, Dougles E. and David G. Bromey. *Cults and New Religions* (2007)

D'Emilio, John and Estelle B. Freedman. *Intimate Matters* (1988)

Denfield, Rene. *The New Victorians* (1995)

Ehrenreich, Barbara. *Bright-Sided* (2009)

Eliade, Mircea. *The Quest* (1969)

Festinger, Leon, et al. *When Prophecy Fails* (1956)

Franzini, Louis R. and John M. Grossberg. *Eccentric & Bizarre Behaviors* (1994)

Goffman, Erving. *Asylums* (1961)

Goodman, Felicitas D. *How About Demons?* (1988)

Gould, Stephen Jay. *The Mismeasure of Man* (1991)

Hassan, Steven. *Combatting Cult Mind Control* (1988, 1990)

Hill, Frances. *A Delusion of Satan* (1995)

Hoffer, Eric. *The True Believer* (1951)

Hsia, R. P-Chia. *The Myth of Ritual Murder* (1988)

Hufford, David J. *The Terror That Comes in the Night* (1982)

Hughes, Robert. *Culture of Complaint* (1993)

James, William. *The Varieties of Religious Experience* (1902, 1961)

Jastrow, Joseph. *Wish and Wisdom* (1935)

Jenkins, Philip. *Intimate Enemies* (1992)

Jenkins, Philip. *Pedophiles and Priests* (1996)

Jones, Landon Y . *Great Expectations* (1980)

Lasch, Christopher. *The Culture of Narcissism* (1978)

Lewis, I. M. *Ecstatic Religion* (1971)

Lifton, Robert J. *Thought Reform and the Psychology of Totalism* (1961)

Lutz, Tom. *American Nervousness, 1903* (1991)

Mackay, Charles. *Extraordinary Popular Delusions and the Madness of Crowds* (1841, 1932)

Masson, Jeffrey Moussaieff. *Against Therapy* (1988)

Masson, Jeffrey Moussaieff. *A Dark Science* (1986)

McGrath, Melanie. *Motel Nirvana* (1995)

Meacham, Andrew. *Selling Serenity* (1999)

Melton, J. Gordon. *Encyclopedic Handbook of Cults in America* (1986)

Meyer, Donald. *The Positive Thinkers* (1980)

Michelet, Jules. *Satanism and Witchcraft* (1992)

Moore, R.I. *The Formation of a Persecuting Society* (1987)

Netzer, Carol. *Cutoffs* (1996)

Nickell, Joe. *Looking for a Miracle* (1993)

Norton, Mary Beth. *In the Devil's Snare* (2002)

Oakley, J. Ronald. *God's Country* (1986)

Patai, Daphne and Noretta Koertge. *Professing Feminism* (1994)

Pipher, Mary. *The Shelter of Each Other* (1996)

Pruett, Kyle D. *The Nurturing Father* (1987)

Robbins, Russell Hope. *Encyclopedia of Witchcraft and Demonology* (1959)

Robbins, Thomas. *Cults, Converts & Charisma* (1988)

Roiphe, Katie. *The Morning After* (1993)

Rosen, R.D. *Psychobabble* (1977)

Russett, Cynthia Eagle. *Sexual Science* (1989)

Sagan, Carl. *The Demon-Haunted World* (1996)

Shermer, Michael. *The Believing Brain* (2012)

Shermer, Michael. *Why People Believe Weird Things* (1997)

Shorter, Edward. *From Paralysis to Fatigue* (1993)

Sisterhood is Powerful, ed. Robin Morgan (1970)

Skolnick, Arlene. *Embattled Paradise* (1991)

Smart, Ninian. *The Religious Experience of Mankind* (1969)

Sommers, Christina Hoff and Sally Satel. *One Nation Under Therapy* (2006)

Sommers, Christina Hoff. *Who Stole Feminism?* (1994)

Strauss, William and Neil Howe. *Generations* (1991)

Streiker, Lowell D. *Mind Bending* (1984)

Sykes, Charles J. *A Nation of Victims* (1992)

Thomas, Gordon. *Journey Into Madness* (1989)

Trevor-Roper, H.R. *The European Witch-Craze of The Sixteenth and Seventeenth Centuries and Other Essays* (1969)

Veith, Ilza. *Hysteria* (1965)

Wallerstein, Judith S. and Sandra Blakeslee. *Second Chances* (1989)

Young, Cathy. *Ceasefire!* (1999)

Youngson, Robert. *Scientific Blunders* (1998)

Books about psychology and mental illness:

Barlow, David H. *Anxiety and Its Disorders* (1988)

Beck, Aaron et al. *Anxiety Disorders and Phobias* (1985)

Coleman, Lee. *The Reign of Error* (1984)

Diagnostic and Statistical Manual of Mental Disorders, DSM, (4th ed, 1994, 5th ed, 2013)

Ellenberger, Henri F. *The Discovery of the Unconscious* (1970)

Foxman, Paul. *Dancing with Fear* (2006)

Frank, Jerome D. *Persuasion and Healing* (1961, 1993)

Frankl, Viktor E. *Man's Search for Meaning* (1959, 1963)

Gray, Peter. *Psychology* (1991)

Hall, Calvin S. *The Meaning of Dreams* (1953, 1966)

Hobson, J. Allan. *The Dreaming Brain* (1988)

Hobson, J. Allan. *The Chemistry of Conscious States* (1994)

Horwitz, Allan V. *Creating Mental Illness* (2002)

Jaspers, Karl. *General Psychopathology* (1923, 1963)

Kirk, Stuart A. and Herb Kutchins. *The Selling of DSM* (1992)

Luhrmann, Tanya M. *Of Two Minds* (2001)

MacCurdy, John T. *War Neuroses* (1918)

Milton, Joyce. *The Road to Malpsychia* (2002)

Montagu, Ashley. *Touching* (1972)

Moskowitz, Eva S. *In Therapy We Trust* (2001)

Peele, Stanton. *Diseasing of America* (1989)

Philipson, Ilene J. *On the Shoulders of Women* (1993)

Porter, Roy. *Madness: A Brief History* (2002)

Seagrave, Ann and Faison Covington. *Free from Fears* (1987)

Seligman, Martin E. P. *What You Can Change and What You Can't* (1994)

Sharkey, Joe. *Bedlam* (1994)

Tavris, Carol. *Anger: The Misunderstood Emotion* (1982)

Tavris, Carol. *The Mismeasure of Woman* (1992)

Temple, Robert. *Open to Suggestion* (1989)

Theories of Hypnosis, ed. Steven Jay Lynn (1991)

Vaillant, George E. *The Wisdom of the Ego.* (1993)

Watkins, John G. *Hypnotherapy of War Neuroses* (1949)

Whitaker, Robert. *Anatomy of an Epidemic* (2010)

Whitaker, Robert. *Mad in America* (2002)

Wilson, Ian. *All in the Mind* (1982)

Wood, Garth. *The Myth of Neurosis* (1986)

Zilbergeld, Bernie. *The Shrinking of America* (1983)

Documentaries cited:

Capturing the Friedmans, dir. Andrew Jarecki (2003)

Freeing Bernie Baran, prod. Daniel Alexander (2010)

"From the Mouths of Babes," *ABC News 20/20* (Oct. 22, 1993)

"From the Mouths of Children," *Fifth Estate,* CBC (Feb. 15, 1994)

Indictment: The McMartin Trial, prod. Oliver Stone. HBO (1995)

Innocence Lost—The Verdict, Part I and II, by Ofra Bikel. *Frontline* (July 20 & 21, 1993)

The Keepers, Netflix 7-part series (2017)

The Memory Hackers. Nova TV (May 5, 2016)

Prisoners of Silence, Frontline TV (Oct. 19, 1993)

Witch Hunt, prod. Sean Penn. KTF (2008)

Index

A

abreaction 122, 148, 250, 311, 346
  and body memories, 142
  and MPD 31, 166-167, 174, 176, 189, 197-198, 376, 392
  and religion, 314, 328, 331
  definition of 31
  in groups, 151, 331
Abused Boys (Hunter) 51, 88
accusations 17-66, 115, 148, 298-305, 338-352, 395, 406-418, 427
  and witch trials 239-242
  based on facilitated communication 17, 136-137, 378, 427, 428
  by children, 202-235
  in religious context, 319
  of sexual abuse 26, 26–64 *passim*
accused parents 17, 26, 152, 207, 331-335, 351-353, 429
  See also parents
  called "in denial" 89
  extortion letters to 378
  in False Memory Syndrome Foundation 23, 353, 370
  religious faith 307
  reunion with 381
accusing children 227, 266, 331, 422
actors or actresses as Survivors 71, 201, 348, 392
addictions as symptoms 36, 49, 52, 279, 365, 413
adult children, 22, 280, 327, 348
  advice for 424–429
Adult Children of Alcoholics (ACOA) 119, 280

Adverse Childhood Experiences (ACE) 412
advice to readers 442-429
Against Our Will (Brownmiller) 27
age regression 30, 57, 130-136, 317, 354-355, 365
  and MPD 157, 166, 168
  surveys of therapists regarding 355
aggression, 237
  and gender stereotypes 294–305
Alcoholics Anonymous 51, 279
Allison, Ralph 58, 158-161, 164, 168
alternate personalities (alters) 59, 156-201, 350, 365, 388-399
American Association for Marriage and Family Therapy 116
American Family Foundation (AFF) 333
American Journal of Psychiatry 147
American Medical Association 14, 281, 374
American Nervousness (Beard) 275
American Psychiatric Association 33, 116, 164, 337, 374, 421
American Psychological Association 116, 356, 374-377, 421
American Society for Clinical Hypnosis 195
amines 137

Amirault, Gerald (Tooky) and family 222–227, 234, 337
amnesia 78-81, 134, 168, 237, 251-253, 406 *See also* source amnesia
  belief in, encouraged by therapists 46, 52, 77, 134, 156, 161, 196, 199-200, 355, 390-391
  infantile 79, 112-117, 363, 405
  organic 99, 123
  post-hypnotic, 127-128
  psychogenic 100, 122-123, 185
  source 132
amygdala (brain) 99-103, 112, 390, 397
anal rape *See* sodomy
anal wink test 216, 231
anatomically correct dolls 34, 219-220, 227, 230, 316
anecdotal evidence 86, 122, 357
Angelou, Maya 408
angels 167, 292, 324
anger 41, 42, 325, 423
  righteous 295
animal magnetism 249, 251, 253
animals 137-138, 211, 370
  as alternate personalities 59
  in children's fantasies 213, 222
  murdered in Satanic cults 194-195, 204-205 222, 225
  used in experiments 73
anonymity, issue of vii, 20, 174, 177, 202, 339, 358, 395, 414
anorexia nervosa 37, 146, 253, 284
anti-intellectualism 287, 325

anus 142, 211, 231, 321
  objects inserted in 134, 183, 210-212, 252, 355
anxiety attacks 29, 63, 246
  See also panic attacks
Aplysia (sea slug) 104
Arnold, Roseanne Barr 61, 115, 304
Aronson, Elliot 13, 18, 379-380
Artemidorus 138
artificial intelligence 109
art therapy 53, 54, 376
AskReddit 399
Assault on Truth, The (Masson) 31, 266
Atler, Marilyn Van Derbur 86-87
attachment therapy 288-289
attention-seeking 13, 89, 93, 167, 204, 237, 244, 246, 272-273, 304, 326, 406, 409
  and MPDs 155, 158, 167, 172, 187-189, 194, 270, 388
aunts (as abusers) 350
Australian cases 17, 31, 33-34, 46, 60, 135-136, 216, 220, 222
authority, figures of, influence 24, 95, 109
  hypnotist 128
  in history 238, 246, 257, 277
  in MPD cases 190, 364
  in sects 329
  therapist 334, 358, 372, 403
autistic children 111, 135-136
automatic writing 138, 268, 269. See also journaling

B

babies (murder of) 21, 32, 59, 320, 322, 364, 390
  in MPD 59
backlash (against Recovery Movement) 95, 104, 297, 322, 360
Baby Boomers 49, 289-292
Baddeley, Allen 91
Baez, Joan 61
Baker, Robert 126, 128, 130, 140

barbiturates 148, 346
Barden, R. Christopher 15, 106, 200-201, 289, 299-300, 337, 352, 365, 380, 415-421
Barlow, David 143-145
Bartlett, Frederic 68-73, 91, 98, 103, 110, 151, 218, 274
Bass, Ellen 12, 25-51, 71, 118, 141-149, 166, 241, 262, 309, 325, 348-349
  and Holocaust 409
  third edition Courage to Heal 359
  fourth edition Courage to Heal 381-383, 409
battered women 103
Battle for the Mind (Sargant) 139
Bean-Bayog, Margaret 286, 367-368
Beck, Aaron 144
bedwetting 210, 223
belief systems 147, 150-151, 243, 292, 299, 404
  and children 219, 232
  and hypnosis 200
  and MPD 391
  and repressed memories 16, 40, 77, 119, 130, 154, 365, 372, 403
  and ritual abuse and sects 151, 292, 310-311, 319, 330
  and UFOs 131–133
"Believe the Children" 24, 203, 205, 216, 232-235, 380
Bernardin, Cardinal Joseph 304, 336
Bernheim, Hippolyte 128-129, 258
Betrayal Trauma (Freyd) 85-86
Beware the Talking Cure (Campbell) 402-403
Bianchi, Kenneth 168
Bible 35, 245, 299, 327
biological studies 84
bipolar disorder 315, 348
blackouts 122, 142, 187

body memories 54, 115, 141-145, 152, 273, 293
  and Bessel van der Kolk 21, 104-107
  belief in survey 354
  credit for course on 377
  in judicial opinion 338
  in MPD 178, 182
  in UK 171
body workers, 142, 356
Bradshaw, John 41, 280, 291, 325-328
brain 18, 67-73, 96-99, 110-123, 189, 245, 248, 311, 344, 387
  and dreams, 137
  and hypnosis 127
  and MPD, 156, 161, 172, 191-200
  and neuroscience 101-109
  and pseudoscience 81, 104-107, 211, 254, 377, 386-389, 396, 398
  split-brain 98
brainwashing 26, 43, 141, 181, 191-196, 287, 310, 340, 367
Brainwashed (Satel and Lilienfeld) 108
Bravos, Zachary 179
Braun, Bennett 58, 164, 175-181, 195, 199, 248-249, 337, 380
Briere, John 55, 77-78, 374, 379
British False Memory Society 14, 16
British repressed memory cases 14-17, 34, 45-47, 61, 197-198, 336, 355, 373, 390, 398
  Christian counselors 319-321
  MPD cases 169-171
British child care cases 215-222
Bruck, Maggie 205-206, 230, 337
Buckey family 203-204, 224, 235
bulimia nervosa 37, 146, 147, 174
buried alive 84-85, 177

Burgess, Ann 30, 215
Burgus, Pat 175, 337

C

Calof, David 197, 199, 396
Canadian cases 16, 31, 188-189, 204, 213, 274, 338, 395
Castlewood Treatment Center 20, 395
castration 248-249, 321
  as cure 248
  fantasies of 321
catalepsy 251, 253
Ceci, Stephen 205-206, 210, 337
Center for Feelings Therapy 287
Changes Magazine 328
channelers 293, 356
Charcot, Jean-Martin 254-258, 267
Cheit, Ross 86-88, 116, 121-122
Chesler, Phyllis 236, 273
Child Abuse Prevention and Treatment Act 202, 414
child accusations 202-235
  See also day care hysteria cases
child prostitution 26, 132
Child Protective Services (CPS) 183, 207, 208, 340
children, sexual behavior of 210
Children's Advocacy Centers (CACs) 338-339
choking, as psychosomatic symptom 143-144, 147
  evidence for repressed memories 17, 51, 143, 260
  in history 241-242, 245-246, 310
Christian counselors 22, 46, 120, 161-164, 171, 193-198, 217-218, 308-328, 347, 365, 389-394
Church of Satan 192
CIA 196, 293, 333, 364-365
Clever Hans (horse) 136
clinical psychologists 19, 130, 195, 284, 356

clinicians 73-76, 173, 211, 361, 366, 374-375, 396-397, 402, 420
clitorectomies, as cure 248
co-counseling 285
codependency 93, 274, 280, 282, 377
cognitive dissonance 149-151, 349, 379
cognitive-behavioral therapy 358, 404
colposcope 231
Combatting Cult Mind Control (Hassan) 329-334
computer (as brain analogue) 67, 109-111
confabulations 126, 130-131, 137, 148, 152, 166, 364, 419 See also false memory syndrome; memory
confessions, false 215, 239-241, 263-264, 272, 303, 389, 415
confirmation bias 75, 119, 361
confrontation of accused 42, 50, 51, 329, 349
Conspiracy of Silence (Butler) 28
contagion, social 148–154
continuing education 375
conversion, religious 309–335
convulsions 248-254, 310
coping mechanisms 36-37, 44, 105, 170
corroboration of memories 116-122, 130, 374
  circumstantial 64-65, 76-77, 118, 363
  from false confession 121
  external 166, 375, 405, 416
  in children's cases 210, 223
  in Freud's cases 258, 263
  in Witch Craze 242
  no evidence for massive repression 121
cost of therapy 284, 330, 375–429
counselors 19, 105, 179, 355-356, 359, 402, 418 See

also Christian counselors; Exit counselors; therapists
  accused father offers to see 40
  as "True Believers" 423
Christian 293, 308, 318-319, 328, 393-395
  drug 280
  in children's cases 93, 229, 233
  looking for repressed memories 43-46, 51, 63, 93, 365, 384
  Survivors become counselors 348
  uses of 404, 426
countertransference 368, 373
Country Walk Day Care case 213-215, 281, 359
Courage to Heal, The (Bass & Davis) 12-14, 21, 25-26, 118, 120, 278-279, 333, 405
  and ritual abuse memories 191, 365
  critique of 34-44, 66, 71, 74, 141, 149, 278-279, 307, 309, 312, 321, 324, 348-350
  fourth edition of 381-383
  on bookshelves 18
  passing reference to 78, 94, 100, 133, 202, 238-239, 261, 329, 333, 346, 357, 371, 384
  recommended 25, 228-229, 354-355, 360, 426
  third edition of 359-360
court cases 14-19, 74, 83, 91-96, 106, 278, 303, 336-337, 365, 378, 390, 396, 408
  advice regarding 415-422
  in day care cases 207-235
  in witch trials 238-242
Courtois, Christine 28, 55, 374
Cranial Sacral therapy 396
crib, abuse in 13, 28, 64, 72, 78, 115, 183, 245, 405
  memories from 113
crucifix, rape with 60, 228-229
cucumber as penis substitute 53, 139
Culture of Narcissism (Lasch) 281

D

Dancing with Daddy (Peterson) 71-72

Daubert ruling 415-416

day care hysteria cases 18, 23-24, 34, 202-235, 281, 307, 337-339
  passing reference to 120, 333, 344, 351, 381, 407, 421

Davis, Laura 12, 25-35, 49, 51, 55, 71, 141, 145, 149, 241, 359, 381-383

defense mechanisms 73, 79, 85, 398

demonic possession 292-293
  See also exorcism
  historic 187, 240-245, 251-253, 268
  modern MPD 58, 160-169, 320-321, 329, 364-365
  passing reference to 128, 140, 186, 308

denial, in 14, 21, 74, 188, 208, 280, 297, 322, 330-331, 359
  and Freud 261-262
  and John Bradshaw 326-327
  in children's cases 23, 34, 206, 221, 234, 345
  in repressed memory books 37, 44, 52-54. 56, 161
  in witch cases 238, 244
  of harm by therapists 362-365, 428
  real cases 89-91

De Tocqueville, Alexis 276, 281-282, 289-290, 301

depersonalization 144, 327

depression 247, 406. 411, 422
  and children
  and MPD 15, 159, 169-170, 177, 183, 190-191, 392-393
  as result of therapy 82, 212, 283, 308, 349, 376
  as symptom of repressed memories 12, 22, 30, 36, 45, 52
  as woman's role 236
  effect on memory
  postpartum 330, 347, 366, 388
  reason for entering therapy 32, 51, 62, 93, 153-154, 208, 299, 315-316, 349, 353, 365, 372, 392-397

Descartes, René 241, 244-245

detective, playing 39, 57, 130, 360

"direct analysis" (Rosen) 285-286

Diseasing of America (Peele) 279

dissociation 36, 57, 331, 396
  and MPD 157, 161, 165, 173-174, 267-269
  definition of 184-186, 267-268
  in repressed memory books 51, 53, 56, 189, 390, 399
  myth of massive 21, 83, 105-107, 116, 121, 364, 384, 393

dissociative identity disorder 21, 58, 155, 189, 362, 370, 375, 389, 392, 397, 416, 419 *See also* multiple personality disorder

Divided Memories (Bikel) 115, 117

divorce 24, 39, 48-49, 290, 301
  involving sex abuse allegations 207, 338
  result of therapy 176-177, 229, 283, 350

Divorcing a Parent (Engel) 44

Dobson, James 314, 317-318

Dolan, Judge Elizabeth 225-232

drama in repressed memory Survivors 71, 167, 187, 189, 244, 304, 348 *See also* psychodrama

dream interpretation 125, 137-140, 237, 272, 406
  Freudian 12, 138, 283
  in children 219, 344
  in court decision 338, 417
  in MPD cases 182
  in repressed memory cases 24, 29, 30, 49, 62-63, 86, 93, 118, 137-140, 228, 353-354, 384
  in repressed memory books 53-57, 156, 371

drugs 19, 302, 313
  and ritual abuse 191, 193, 196
  as recovered memory aid 100, 148, 157
  as memory suppressant 104
  drug abuse as sex abuse symptom 36, 48, 352

in day care cases 213-214, 225
overprescribed to Survivors 178, 188, 360
useful 147, 405

dysfunctional families 110, 191, 279-282, 290, 297, 309, 353, 402
  Bradshaw on 325-327

E

eating disorders 12, 20, 37, 45, 52, 145-147, 152, 395-396

Eckstein, Emma 256-258, 264, 266

emotional incest 47-50, 110, 191, 349, 352, 372

emotions 65, 76, 123, 151, 237, 250, 325-326, 404 *See also* anger
  and religion 311-312, 321
  and MPD 196, 200
  as proof of recovered memories 19, 39, 63, 92, 133, 266, 371, 388, 390, 398
  for Freud 261-262
  in recovered memory books 39, 44, 55-56, 133, 142
  focus on 294, 358
  real memory enhanced by 101, 185
  past colored by 69
  stored-in-body theory 106-107, 144
  with false memories 94-96, 151-152

epilepsy 45, 95-99, 189-191, 241, 254-255, 348

Erickson, Milton 89-90

evidence
  anecdotal 73, 84, 86
  Charcot's 254
  denial as 34, 45, 52, 54, 89, 161, 208, 221, 238, 244, 261, 318, 326, 330
  experimental 74, 123
  Freud's 255–273
  legal 13, 79, 207, 210, 214, 229-232, 303, 339-344, 353-354, 416-418
  of illusory memories 70, 103, 189, 369, 405

exit counselor 329

exorcism 58, 128, 160-164, 192, 243-244, 251, 320

expectancy effect 91, 97, 100-
101, 122, 129, 138-143,
152-154, 361, 364, 400, 404
in day care cases 210-211
in facilitated communication
136
in history 236, 243-254, 409
in MPD 82, 172-173
in past lives and UFO abductions 133-135

F

facilitated communication
(FC) 17, 135-137, 378,
427-428
false memory syndrome 333,
359-362, 370, 388
False Memory Syndrome
Foundation 13-14, 22-23,
94, 322, 353, 360-363, 370,
373, 383
families, destruction of 184,
336\
fathers, allegations against 12,
26-64 *passim*, 240, 260, 297
incest actually committed by
33, 302, 406
role of 407-409
Fells Acre Day Care Center
222-227, 229, 233-234, 337
fondling 346, 407
as molestation 26, 29, 45, 121,
385, 407, 412
in day care cases 203, 213
foster parents 82, 220, 413,
416
*Freeing the Mind from Memo-
ries that Bind* (Littauer)
318

Freud, Sigmund 31, 67, 71,
165, 255-267, 372
and Charcot 255
and hypnosis 29, 31, 174, 249,
253
critique of 73-74, 104, 255-
268, 311, 331, 386
dream analysis 138
in America 283
infantile amnesia 113-116
nose operation 248, 257
Oedipus complex 26, 256, 265
pressure procedure 165, 259,
266, 346

repressed memory theory 122,
265-267
seduction theory 11-12, 31,
260-266
Freyd, Jennifer 85-86
Freyd, Pamela and Peter 14,
22-23, 373
Fuster, Frank and Ileana 213-
215, 235, 281, 359

G

gestalt therapy 285
grandparents (as abusers) 39,
41, 54, 59, 119, 208, 229-
230, 315, 350, 381-382
in Satanic cult 180, 380
guided imagery 50, 52, 103,
111, 128-129, 145, 154,
309, 353-354, 406 *See also*
hypnosis
in day care cases 214
in MPD 162, 189, 194
Gutheil, Thomas 368

H

Hacking, Ian 167, 267
hallucinations 127, 140-141,
190, 253, 255, 257, 310
Hammond, Corydon 178,
195-199
happiness, pursuit of 281,
283, 289-292
unhappiness 20, 125, 128, 142,
146, 166, 276
Harrington, Evan 410-411
Hart, Roma 188, 364
Hassan, Stephen 329-334
Healing the Child Within
(Whitfield) 280, 362
hearsay evidence 118, 416
helplessness, fostered by
therapy 13, 144, 297, 331
Herman, Judith 29-34, 55-58,
94, 362, 398, 409
on "backlash," 104, 360
"proof" of repression, 76-77,
106, 119, 263
hippocampus 67, 99, 101-
103, 112, 114
Hippocratic Oath 17, 373
Hoffer, Eric 306, 321-322
Holmes, David 74-76

Holocaust memories 56, 102,
409
homosexuality 294, 370
homophobia 227-228
Hoult, Jennifer 103
hugs as abuse 349, 352, 386,
407-408, 411
human subjects in experi-
ments 73, 94
hypnosis 38, 125-138, 143,
249-273, 294, 346, 361 *See
also* mesmerism
and MPD 59, 155-159, 165-
178, 182, 187, 189, 193-196,
346
and panic attacks 145
and religious states 310, 313,
317, 329
and repressed memories 12-
13, 30-32, 50-54, 57, 87, 125-
135, 147-148, 304, 308, 336,
352-355, 358-359, 368-377,
394-396
critique of 100, 125-135, 152-
154, 364, 406, 418-419
Freud and 29, 31, 174, 249, 253
in court cases 93, 106
in the UK 216
hypnotherapy 19, 359, 376-
377, 418
hysteria 247-248, 253-261,
272
mass 199
over sex abuse 16-18, 23, 88,
198, 296, 338
in day cares 23-24, 34, 202, 212-
213, 218, 222, 233, 301, 344

I

iatrogenic illness (doctor-
induced) 100, 170, 172,
254, 370, 393, 397, 419
imagination 128, 133, 136,
240, 245
in children 210
in MPD 269-270
to create sex abuse memories
52-55, 71, 111, 138, 154

in denial *See* denial

inadvertent cuing 128, 137,
193, 218, 242, 360, 419

incest, recovered memory claims 12-14, 31-64 *passim entire book. See also* sexual abuse
reality of 27-29
Incest Survivors (via recovered memory) 31-37, 43-46, 52, 59, 87, 297, 304, 332, 410
incubus 140, 162, 237
infantile amnesia 79, 112-117, 363, 405
Ingram, Paul case 121, 240, 351, 389
inner child 41, 44, 46, 59, 61, 87, 139, 166, 280, 282, 291, 294, 308, 323, 329, 353, 365, 367, 377, 384, 390
International Society for the Study of Multiple Personality & Dissociation 61, 164, 171, 363, 365
renamed 375
intergenerational abuse 52, 60, 192
intuition of abuse 35, 40, 55, 72, 120
clinical 210

J

James, William 101, 109, 270, 309, 312
Janet, Pierre 105, 184, 267, 310
Janov, Arthur 122, 286-287, 347
Jeopardy in the Courtroom (Ceci & Bruck) 205-206
Journal of Abnormal and Social Psychology 156, 199, 268
journaling and automatic writing 138, 182, 268-269

K

Kaminer, Wendy 297, 409
Kandel, Eric and Minouche 103-104
Keepers, The (TV documentary) 18, 384-387

Kelley, Susan 224-225, 333
Kenny, Michael 163, 172, 186, 267, 270
Kihlstrom, John 15, 100
Kiss Daddy Goodnight (Armstrong) 28
Kluft, Richard 58, 164-166, 187, 363, 391
Kraepelin, Emil 270-274

L

Laing, R. D. 285
lawsuits *See* court cases
leading questions 126, 193, 264, 339, 363, 416
in day care cases 203, 217, 225
Ledoux, Joseph 68, 101-102
lesbian identity 28-29 *See also* homosexuals
as ideological statement 29, 43-44, 295, 299
letters, accusatory 12, 42-43, 51, 152, 334, 352, 378, 395
licensing boards 184, 380, 394, 420, 425
Lindsay, Stephen 83, 354-356, 369
Littauer, Fred and Florence 318
Loewenstein, Richard 173, 181
Loftus, Elizabeth F. 73-83, 91-97, 132, 138, 336, 370, 374, 411
as FMFS advisor 14
car crash memory 110
on Holocaust memories 102
on hypnosis 127
on infantile amnesia, 113
Los Angeles Ritual Abuse Task Force 199
Love, Patricia 47-49
Ludwig, Arnold 159

M

MacFarlane, Kee 203-206, 224, 234
Mack, John 133-135
MacLean, Harry 92-94

Malleus Maleficarum (Sprenger) 14, 238-239, 261
Manchurian candidates 196, 333
Maslow, Abraham 311-312
massage therapists 19, 50, 87, 142, 272, 293, 356, 371, 376-377, 384, 406
Masson, Jeffrey 31, 248, 266-267
Matamoros murderers 192
McDonald, Sally 176-177, 180-182, 376
McGaugh, James 101-107, 111-112
McHugh, Paul 14, 122-123, 167, 172, 346, 387
McMartin Preschool case 23, 34, 203-206, 211, 215, 221-224, 234-235, 359
McNally, Richard vii, 14-15, 81, 105, 117, 122, 199-201
media, role of 14-15, 18, 22-23, 301-305, 336, 397
bad science reporting 81, 378
critical of repressed memories 104, 336, 374
credulous of repressed memories 12, 38, 60, 89, 192
promoting moral panics 22, 192-193, 293, 302, 342-343, 406, 415
in day care cases 205, 208, 216-217, 219, 226, 232
in MPD 172, 180, 186-187
memory, human 12, 15, 65-124 *passim entire book*
declarative 99, 101
highly superior autobiographical 111-112
implicit 99-105
malleability of 18, 24, 69, 90-91, 112, 364
neuroscience 101-108
reconstructive nature of 66-72, 91, 98, 109-112
"Memory Wars" 18, 23
Mercy Ministries (Mercy Multiplied) 395
Mersky, Harold 127, 171-173

mesmerism (Franz Anton Mesmer) 249-252, 276
See also hypnosis
Michaels, Kelly 120, 206, 212, 235
Michelle Remembers (Pazder) 32, 58, 143, 160, 205, 384
Miller, Alice 17, 28
"mind control" 59, 196-197, 329, 333-334, 390, 396
Minds in Many Pieces (Allison) 58, 159-160
Minirth-Meier New Life Clinics 314-317
Molaison, Henry (H. M.) 99
moral panics 11, 193, 203, 215
mothers
  accused of abuse 13, 28-51 *passim*, 60, 81-85, 118-119, 138, 157, 292, 299, 367, 382, 389, 424, 428
  blamed for other problems 50, 146, 284-288
  in day care cases 203, 223, 227-229
  in divorce/custody cases 207, 220-221
  in ritual abuse 162, 170, 174, 177-178, 180, 183, 194, 198
  who side with accusing children 64, 77, 321, 340
Multiple Personality Disorder (MPD) 14-21, 41, 58-61, 100, 155-201, 293, 324, 346, 362-365, 375, 392-399, 406, 419
  in Christian counseling 317, 347, 392-394
  compared to cataleptics 252
  history of 267-270, 346
  in books 43, 47, 58, 156-171, 364, 388-392, 399
  in cases 82, 100, 176-186, 337, 350
  media promotion of 60, 303-304, 388-392
  special powers of 59-60, 328
Munchausen's syndrome by proxy 204

My Secret Life (anonymous) 26

N
National Association of Social Workers (NASW) 356, 375
neglect of children 280, 412-414
Neisser, Ulric 73, 91, 97, 113
New Age 150, 292-293, 324, 327, 382
New Thought 283
New Zealand cases 10-11, 31, 61, 220-222, 395
nightmares as symptoms 35, 37-38, 45, 275, 308, 316, 397
  in day care cases 210, 212, 214-215, 223
  in MPD 188-190
  In Witch Craze 237

O
obsessive-compulsive disorder 112, 147, 348, 402, 404
Obsidian Mirror, The 25
Oedipus complex 26, 256, 265
Ofshe, Richard 14, 96, 175, 240, 333, 336, 354

P
panic attacks 12, 25, 125, 142–145, 324, 397, 404, 408, 419 *See also* anxiety attacks
  in MPD cases 189-190
parents 13-14, 21-22, 292, 348, 414, 419 *See also* accused parents
  abusive 89
  advice for 335, 422–426
  embarrassment of 13, 353
  of day care children 203-207, 210, 221-227
  religious faith 307
  self-doubts 240, 351, 389
  therapist blame of 40-54, 86, 189, 280, 286-288, 299, 315, 326, 366-367, 402
Pazder, Lawrence 32, 205
Peck, M. Scott 160-165
Perkins, Bruce and Carol 208-209, 228
Peterson, Judith 177-184, 337, 376, 391

physical abuse 58-59, 157, 281, 412-413
pickles, fear of 145-146
placebo effect 350, 401-404
Pomeroy, Wardell 27
Poole, Deborah 354-356
Pope, Harrison Jr 14, 81, 121, 147-148, 419
post-partum depression *See* depression
post-traumatic stress disorder (PTSD) 56, 101-105, 235, 396
  as diagnosed for recovered memories 63, 133, 145, 200, 365, 375, 386-389, 420
  in children, 211, 229
  priests 18, 86
  in repressed memory cases 17-18, 86, 105-107, 119, 351, 384-385, 398
Primal Scream, The (Janov) 286-287
primal therapy 122, 284, 286-287, 323
Prince, Morton 156, 173, 268-270, 310, 346
psychiatrists *See* counselors, therapists
psychoanalysts *See* counselors, therapists
psychodrama 43, 50, 57, 179, 314, 376 *See also* drama
psychologists, clinical. *See* counselors, therapists
psychologists, experimental 68, 73-76, 83, 94-98, 103-104, 113, 129-130, 154, 189, 300, 370, 374,
psychotherapists, psychotherapy *See* counselors, therapists
psychics 270, 276, 292-293, 356, 378
Putnam, Frank 58, 164-167, 172, 190

R
Ramona, Holly case 146, 336-337
recovered memories 11-64, *passim entire book*
  massive repression highly unlikely 122-124
  possibly true examples 116-123

Remembering Satan (Wright) 121, 240, 351

Remembering Trauma (McNally) 81, 122, 201

Reno, Janet 214-215, 281

reconciliation 49, 381, 425

rebirthing ritual 194, 285, 289

reparenting 250, 286

retractors 13, 15, 149-150, 163, 307, 319, 333, 336-337, 355, 362, 383, 402, 426

ritual abuse *See* Satanic ritual abuse

Rosen, John 285-286

Ross, Linda 21-22, 428

S

Salem witch trials *See* witch trials

Satanic ritual abuse 11, 14, 16, 19, *passim entire book*. *See* particularly 58-61, 191-199

Scandanavian cases 16, 222

Schacter, Daniel 11, 99-102, 123

sea slug Aplysia 104, 107

Seligman, Martin 411-412

sexual abuse *See also* incest, Incest Survivors
  and Comet Ping Pong fake news 18
  reality of 17-18, 26-29, 32-33
  recovered memories of 11-64, *passim entire book*

Sexual Behavior in the Human Female (Kinsey) 27

Shorter, Edward 245-248, 255

sleep paralysis 139-141

social workers 188, 209, 284-289, 356, 392, 409, 418
  as child interviewers 23, 202, 205, 223, 229, 307, 338, 406
  in UK 216-220
  in NZ and Australia 220-222
  as repressed memory therapists 19, 21, 356, 375, 390, 416
  in UK 34-35, 46

sodomy 60, 191, 198, 260, 302, 385, 399

in day care cases 201, 203-204, 213-216, 224, 226, 231

source amnesia 68, 132 *See also* amnesia

Spanos, Nicholas 73, 129-130, 163, 167-169, 186, 243-244, 251-254

Split (movie) 391-392

Steinem, Gloria 61

Stop Mind Control and Ritual Abuse Today (S.M.A.R.T.) 396

Strange Case of Dr. Jekyll and Mr. Hyde, The (Stevenson) 267

Suicidality 142-143, 236, 282, 286, 320, 331, 343, 349, 359, 365, 367-368, 401
  in MPD cases 159-161, 174-175, 178, 181, 188, 381, 392-395

Summit, Roland 55, 233-234

Survivors, self-identified with recovered memories 15, 17, 25, 35-65, *passim entire book*

symptoms checklists for sexual abuse 12, 40, 36, 45, 92, 110, 145-146, 154, 281, 292, 363, 371, 376
  historical 236, 238, 245-248, 251-258, 263-275, 278
  in day care cases 210-211, 223
  in MPD/ritual abuse 193
  lack of 410
  of panic attacks 143-145
  results of therapy taken as symptom 52, 63, 184, 212, 409
  temporal lobe epilepsy 190

T

Tavris, Carol 13-14, 18, 42, 279, 297, 379-380

Terr, Lenore 55, 74, 84-93, 100, 124, 146, 263, 368, 374

Toxic Parents (Forward) 44

Theophostic counseling 393-395 *See also* Transformation Prayer Ministry

Therapists 12-25, 29-64 *passim entire book. See also* counselors, Christian counselors
  advice to 427–429
  belief in repressed memories 19-20, 353-356
  British 17, 61
  feminist 12-13, 29-31, 55, 189, 193, 215, 273, 296-300, 412
  hazards and uses of 400-405
  interviews with 15
  lawsuits against 14-19.91-96, 299-300, 336-337, 365-408 *passim*
  MPD 58, 155-201, 303, 390-399
  other countries 16-17, 31
  overdependence on 13, 32, 170, 188, 269, 288, 315, 321, 329-334, 348, 400, 403
  past life & UFO 132-135
  retractor 21-22
  work with young children 23, 204-234

Transformation Prayer Ministry *See* Theophostic counseling

triggers (memory) 34, 38-39, 50, 53, 65, 83, 89, 93, 99, 107, 110, 122, 141-142, 373, 399
  in MPD cases 175, 177, 196-197, 394

Try to Remember (McHugh) 123

tunnels 167, 205, 220-224
  and McMartin Preschool 205, 224

Type I/Type II trauma (Terr) 84-85, 92, 124

U

UFO abductions 131-135, 292, 364, 371

uncles (as abusers) 65, 77, 119, 138, 299, 318, 350, 381-384

urine, drinking of 59, 194, 204, 212-213, 221, 225

V

van Der Kolk, Bessel 21, 71, 104-107, 368, 399

W

Walker, Herschel   388-389

We Believe the Children (Beck)
    203

Webster, Richard   109, 220,
    246, 254

Wilbur, Cornelia 58, 156-158,
    164, 167, 303

Wilkomirski, Binjamin   102

Witch Craze 14, 77, 193, 195,
    237–245, 276

witch hunt, modern 19, 24,
    88, 241, 263-264, 274, 302,
    331
    in day care cases , 202-205,
        208, 217-220

witch trials 14, 202, 241-243,
    276, 415, 425, 428

womb, memory back to 113,
    131, 314, 319, 373

Wright, Lawrence 121, 240,
    351